HISTORICAL DICTIONARIES OF EUROPE
Jon Woronoff, Series Editor

1. *Portugal*, by Douglas L. Wheeler. 1993. *Out of print. See no. 40.*
2. *Turkey*, by Metin Heper. 1994. *Out of print. See no. 38.*
3. *Poland*, by George Sanford and Adriana Gozdecka-Sanford. 1994. *Out of print. See no. 41.*
4. *Germany*, by Wayne C. Thompson, Susan L. Thompson, and Juliet S. Thompson. 1994.
5. *Greece*, by Thanos M. Veremis and Mark Dragoumis. 1995.
6. *Cyprus*, by Stavros Panteli. 1995. *Out of print. See no. 69.*
7. *Sweden*, by Irene Scobbie. 1995. *Out of print. See no. 48.*
8. *Finland*, by George Maude. 1995. *Out of print. See no. 49.*
9. *Croatia*, by Robert Stallaerts and Jeannine Laurens. 1995. *Out of print. See no. 39.*
10. *Malta*, by Warren G. Berg. 1995.
11. *Spain*, by Angel Smith. 1996. *Out of print. See no. 65.*
12. *Albania*, by Raymond Hutchings. 1996. *Out of print. See no. 42.*
13. *Slovenia*, by Leopoldina Plut-Pregelj and Carole Rogel. 1996. *Out of print. See no. 56.*
14. *Luxembourg*, by Harry C. Barteau. 1996.
15. *Romania*, by Kurt W. Treptow and Marcel Popa. 1996.
16. *Bulgaria*, by Raymond Detrez. 1997. *Out of print. See no. 46.*
17. *United Kingdom: Volume 1, England and the United Kingdom; Volume 2, Scotland, Wales, and Northern Ireland*, by Kenneth J. Panton and Keith A. Cowlard. 1997, 1998.
18. *Hungary*, by Steven Béla Várdy. 1997.
19. *Latvia*, by Andrejs Plakans. 1997.
20. *Ireland*, by Colin Thomas and Avril Thomas. 1997.
21. *Lithuania*, by Saulius Suziedelis. 1997.
22. *Macedonia*, by Valentina Georgieva and Sasha Konechni. 1998. *Out of print. See no. 68.*
23. *The Czech State*, by Jiri Hochman. 1998.
24. *Iceland*, by Guðmunder Hálfdanarson. 1997. *Out of print. See no. 66.*
25. *Bosnia and Herzegovina*, by Ante Cuvalo. 1997. *Out of print. See no. 57.*

26. *Russia*, by Boris Raymond and Paul Duffy. 1998.
27. *Gypsies (Romanies)*, by Donald Kenrick. 1998. *Out of print.*
28. *Belarus*, by Jan Zaprudnik. 1998.
29. *Federal Republic of Yugoslavia*, by Zeljan Suster. 1999.
30. *France*, by Gino Raymond. 1998. *Out of print. See no. 64.*
31. *Slovakia*, by Stanislav J. Kirschbaum. 1998. *Out of print. See no. 47.*
32. *Netherlands*, by Arend H. Huussen Jr. 1998. *Out of print. See no. 55.*
33. *Denmark*, by Alastair H. Thomas and Stewart P. Oakley. 1998. *Out of print. See no. 63.*
34. *Modern Italy*, by Mark F. Gilbert and K. Robert Nilsson. 1998. *Out of print. See no. 58.*
35. *Belgium*, by Robert Stallaerts. 1999.
36. *Austria*, by Paula Sutter Fichtner. 1999. *Out of print. See no. 70.*
37. *Republic of Moldova*, by Andrei Brezianu. 2000. *Out of print. See no. 52.*
38. *Turkey, 2nd edition*, by Metin Heper. 2002. *Out of print. See no. 67.*
39. *Republic of Croatia, 2nd edition*, by Robert Stallaerts. 2003.
40. *Portugal, 2nd edition*, by Douglas L. Wheeler. 2002.
41. *Poland, 2nd edition*, by George Sanford. 2003.
42. *Albania, New edition*, by Robert Elsie. 2004.
43. *Estonia*, by Toivo Miljan. 2004.
44. *Kosova*, by Robert Elsie. 2004.
45. *Ukraine*, by Zenon E. Kohut, Bohdan Y. Nebesio, and Myroslav Yurkevich. 2005.
46. *Bulgaria, 2nd edition*, by Raymond Detrez. 2006.
47. *Slovakia, 2nd edition*, by Stanislav J. Kirschbaum. 2006.
48. *Sweden, 2nd edition*, by Irene Scobbie. 2006.
49. *Finland, 2nd edition*, by George Maude. 2007.
50. *Georgia*, by Alexander Mikaberidze. 2007.
51. *Belgium, 2nd edition*, by Robert Stallaerts. 2007.
52. *Moldova, 2nd edition*, by Andrei Brezianu and Vlad Spânu. 2007.
53. *Switzerland*, by Leo Schelbert. 2007.
54. *Contemporary Germany*, by Derek Lewis with Ulrike Zitzlsperger. 2007.

55. *Netherlands, 2nd edition*, by Joop W. Koopmans and Arend H. Huussen Jr. 2007.
56. *Slovenia, 2nd edition*, by Leopoldina Plut-Pregelj and Carole Rogel. 2007.
57. *Bosnia and Herzegovina, 2nd edition*, by Ante Čuvalo. 2007.
58. *Modern Italy, 2nd edition*, by Mark F. Gilbert and K. Robert Nilsson. 2007.
59. *Belarus, 2nd edition*, by Vitali Silitski and Jan Zaprudnik. 2007.
60. *Latvia, 2nd edition*, by Andrejs Plakans. 2008.
61. *Contemporary United Kingdom*, by Kenneth J. Panton and Keith A. Cowlard. 2008.
62. *Norway*, by Jan Sjåvik. 2008.
63. *Denmark, 2nd edition*, by Alastair H. Thomas. 2009.
64. *France, 2nd edition*, by Gino Raymond. 2008.
65. *Spain, 2nd edition*, by Angel Smith. 2008.
66. *Iceland, 2nd edition*, by Guđmunder Hálfdanarson. 2009.
67. *Turkey, 3rd edition*, by Metin Heper and Nur Bilge Criss. 2009.
68. *Republic of Macedonia*, by Dimitar Bechev. 2009.
69. *Cyprus*, by Farid Mirbagheri. 2009.
70. *Austria, 2nd edition*, by Paula Sutter Fichtner, 2009.

Historical Dictionary of Austria

Second Edition

Paula Sutter Fichtner

Historical Dictionaries of Europe, No. 70

The Scarecrow Press, Inc.
Lanham, Maryland • Toronto • Plymouth, UK
2009

SCARECROW PRESS, INC.

Published in the United States of America
by Scarecrow Press, Inc.
A wholly owned subsidiary of
The Rowman & Littlefield Publishing Group, Inc.
4501 Forbes Boulevard, Suite 200, Lanham, Maryland 20706
www.scarecrowpress.com

Estover Road
Plymouth PL6 7PY
United Kingdom

Copyright © 2009 by Paula Sutter Fichtner

All rights reserved. No part of this publication may be reproduced, stored in a retrieval system, or transmitted in any form or by any means, electronic, mechanical, photocopying, recording, or otherwise, without the prior permission of the publisher.

British Library Cataloguing in Publication Information Available

Library of Congress Cataloging-in-Publication Data
Fichtner, Paula S.
  Historical dictionary of Austria / Paula Sutter Fichtner. – 2nd ed.
    p. cm. — (Historical dictionaries of Europe ; no. 70)
  Includes bibliographical references.
  ISBN 978-0-8108-5592-2 (cloth : alk. paper) – ISBN 978-0-8108-6310-1 (ebook)
  1. Austria–History–Dictionaries. I. Title.
  DB35.F53 2009
  943.6003–dc22   2009000242

∞ ™ The paper used in this publication meets the minimum requirements of American National Standard for Information Sciences—Permanence of Paper for Printed Library Materials, ANSI/NISO Z39.48-1992.
Manufactured in the United States of America.

For EGF, gratefully

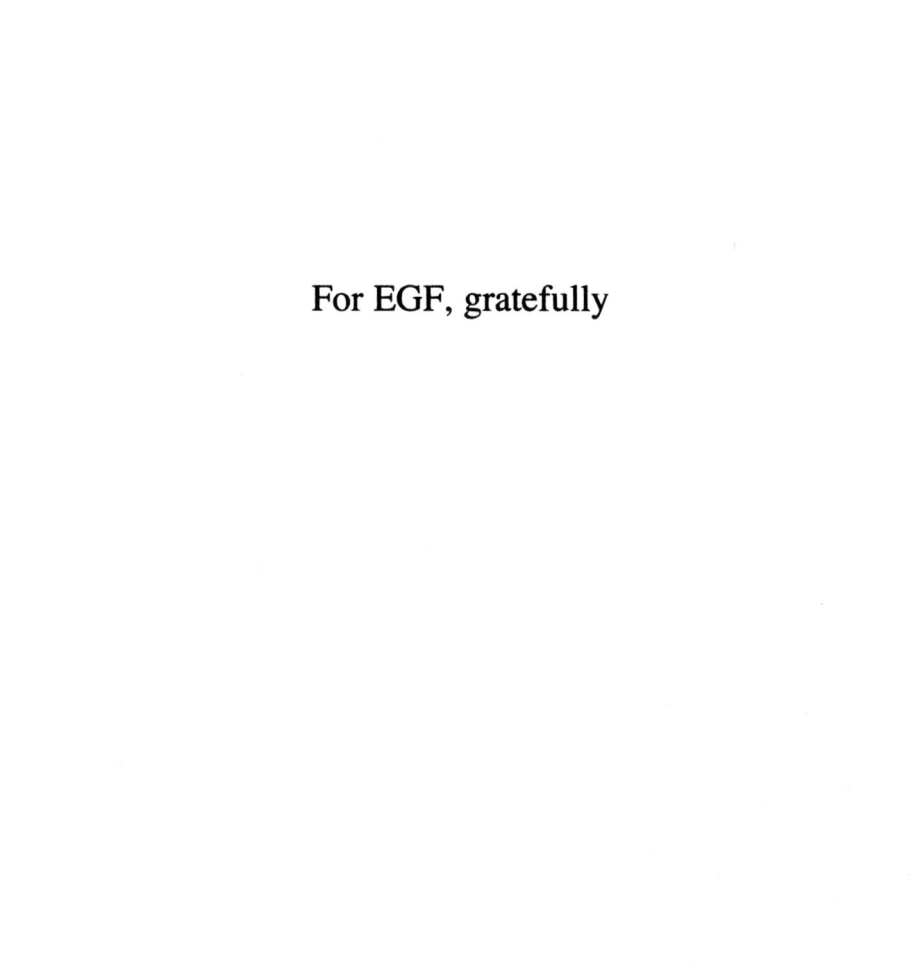

Contents

Editor's Foreword *Jon Woronoff*	xi
Preface	xiii
Acknowledgments	xvii
Acronyms and Abbreviations	xix
Maps	xxi
Chronology	xxv
Introduction	xlv
THE DICTIONARY	1
Appendix: Heads of State	353
Bibliography	357
About the Author	409

Editor's Foreword

Even in the often-confusing patchwork of European states, few are as difficult to define as Austria. It began as a loose cluster of lands dominated by petty territorial overlords, then expanded into a massive empire whose rulers were among Europe's most powerful. Its contraction in the 20th century was no less dramatic. Deprived of even some of its core lands, Austria ended up as a minor state. Its political personality has also varied considerably. Once ruled by emperors, it had to make do with prime ministers, until it was forcibly "connected" with the Third Reich under the Nazi dictatorship. Finally independent again, it has grown into a more mature democracy with a reasonably strong economy. Today it is an active part of the European Union. Despite this, Austria remains in some ways special, with a cultural impact that spreads far beyond its borders.

It is obviously not easy to capture such an entity in a historical dictionary. But the attempt here has been very successful. This book includes the many faces of Austria: the vast empire and the tiny state, imperial rule, dictatorship and democracy, a struggling and then more viable economy, and its impressive culture. These all have entries in the dictionary section, which naturally includes numerous persons, many of whom left an impact not only on Austria but also on Europe and sometimes the world. The chronology traces this long and often complicated history; the introduction helps readers follow the many twists and turns. Because this is one of the more fascinating countries, readers who wish to learn more should consult the bibliography.

This is the second edition of the *Historical Dictionary of Austria*. It was written by Paula Sutter Fichtner, who has updated and expanded her first edition as well as adding many new entries on a broader range of topics. Dr. Fichtner spent more than three decades as professor of history at Brooklyn College, where her lectures covered early modern and modern Europe, with an emphasis on central Europe. Along with many articles, she has also written several books, most recently *The Habsburg Monarchy, 1490–1848: Attributes of Empire* and *Terror to Toleration: The Habsburg Empire Confronts Islam, 1526–1850.* This book, which focuses more on the contemporary period, could, however, not be as strong without a solid foundation in an older Austria, and it is only by studying a centuries-long evolution that one can begin to understand present-day Austria. It is certainly a worthwhile study because, despite its small size, Austria remains a very intriguing country, and certainly one we should know more about.

Jon Woronoff
Series Editor

Preface

Austrians today often seem to believe that they have two histories. One is their republican present. The other is what they call the *Kaiserzeit*, by which they mean the centuries that their forebears spent as part of the multiethnic Habsburg Empire. Though no one shakes loose the past quite so easily, there is some political reason for citizens of the small Alpine republic to think as they do. Although Vienna was the seat of the sprawling Habsburg Empire, the Austrian lands as a whole were not its most significant component. Unlike the kingdoms of Hungary or Bohemia, which fell under Habsburg control in the 16th century, "Austria" had no collective official identity under Habsburg rule. The dynasty did call itself the House of Austria from the 15th until the 18th centuries, when it became the House of Habsburg–Lorraine. However, they knew the Austrian part of their patrimony only as provinces with historic names such as Styria, Carinthia, the Tyrol, and so on. Austria as a single political unit did not exist, at least for those who governed it before 1918.

Only occasionally were the Austrian territories at the heart of political and economic life in the Habsburg Empire. The dynasty acquired Bohemia as a late medieval industrial and commercial hub, and the kingdom would resume that role in modern times. When the Habsburg Empire collapsed after World War I, the greatest share of its industrial stock was within the new republic of Czechoslovakia, of which Bohemia was a part. As for Hungary, it was in many ways the political and military epicenter of the Habsburg Empire from beginning to end. During the 16th and 17th centuries, Habsburg rulers were preoccupied with either defending the kingdom from the Ottoman Empire or driving the Turks from the territories the latter held in the realm. In modern times, the problem became one of accommodating the distinctive Hungarian constitution and the Hungarian reading of it to the structure of the empire as a whole. The Habsburgs generally spoke the German of their Austrian subjects and raised what taxes they could from them. They enthusiastically vacationed on Austrian lakes and in the surrounding mountains. But the dynasty, which ruled these lands for so long, normally had more than Austria on its mind.

Contemporary Austria is a fixture among Europe's democracies. It is part of the European Union. Its government, culture, and egalitarian economy are a far cry from the monarchical and highly stratified society of the old empire. Almost all Austrians are content with these arrangements. Indeed, there are many signs that as a people Austrians are secure enough in their present to connect more comfortably with some features of their past. Their enduring affection for Biedermeier decor, their preoccupation at the end of the 20th century with fin de siècle Vienna a hundred years earlier, and the popularity of massive historical exhibitions from the imperial period generally all indicate that Austrians want to be part of their history more than they once did.

They have not, however, reached that conclusion easily. Austria since 1918 has been as tortured a polity as any in central Europe, in part because of its Habsburg legacy. To begin with, Austrians had no clear national identity when World War I came to an end. Unlike the Czechs, Hungarians, and Poles of the Habsburg Empire, who lost control of their political affairs but never the sense of who they were, Austrians defined themselves primarily as members of a larger structure and not by their relationship to one another. Developing a state that commanded the loyalty of the population at large was a slow and uncertain process. In part, this was because of intractable economic difficulties during the years between 1918 and 1938 that bedeviled many more places than Austria. But in part it was because Austrian governments remained largely faithful to political, social, and economic agendas set before World War I that were the product of a variety of influential factions, not national consensus. Understanding those problems and working through them afresh was perhaps the central accomplishment of Austrian governments that followed the dual catastrophes of the German Anschluss and World War II.

If history has a central axiom, it is that there is a developmental relationship between past and present. Its practical corollary is that this link can be demonstrated selectively. The entries in this dictionary have been chosen to close the gap between Austria's two histories a little bit more—politically, socially, culturally, and economically. Experts will certainly question my particular choices. However, few would deny that the duality of the Austrian historical record make it resistant to probes for shape and meaning. Some polarity will never be overcome. In creating their history, Austrians and those who have ruled them have given European civilization some of the worst of times. They have also left some stunning accomplishments that have enriched many of the world's cultures immeasurably.

Acknowledgments

The author is deeply grateful to the New York Public Library for providing her with the resources and the quiet writing space for the completion of this project. She also wishes to thank Trude Desmond of the Austrian Cultural Forum in New York City for providing access to, and use of, the Forum's archive of photographs.

Acronyms and Abbreviations

ABGB	Allgemeines Bürgerliches Gesetzbuch (General Code of Civil Law)
BAWAG	Bank für Arbeit und Wirtschaft (Bank for Labor and Economic Development)
BZÖ	Alliance for the Future of Austria (Bund für die Zukunft Österreichs)
CP	Christlichsoziale Partei (Christian Social Party)
Czech.	Czech
DNSAP	German National Socialist Workers' Party; Austrian Nazi Party (Deutsche Nationalsozialistische Arbeiter Partei)
EC	European Community
ECSC	European Coal and Steel Community
EEC	European Economic Community
EFTA	European Free Trade Association
Eng.	English
EU	European Union
Gestapo	Geheimestaatspolizei (State Secret Police)
FPÖ	Freiheitliche Partei Österreichs (Freedom Party of Austria)
Hung.	Hungarian
KPÖ	Kommunistische Partei Österreichs (Communist Party of Austria)
Lat.	Latin
LiF	Liberales Forum (Liberal Forum)
MHG	Middle High German
NATO	North Atlantic Treaty Organization
Nazi	National Socialist Workers' Party of Germany
ÖIAG	Österreichische Industrieverwaltung Aktien Gesellschaft (Austrian Industrial Management Corporation

ÖVP	Österreichische Volkspartei (Austrian People's Party)
ÖRF	Österreichische Rundfunk (Austrian Broadcasting System)
RAVAG	Radio-Verkehrs-AG (Radio Broadcasting Corporation
SA	Sturmabteilung (Storm Troops)
SDAP	Sozialdemokratische Arbeiter Partei (Social Democratic Party)
SPÖ	Sozialistische Partei Österreichs (Socialist Party of Austria)
SS	Schutzstaffel (Defence Squadron)
Ukr.	Ukrainian
UN	United Nations
U.S.	United States of America

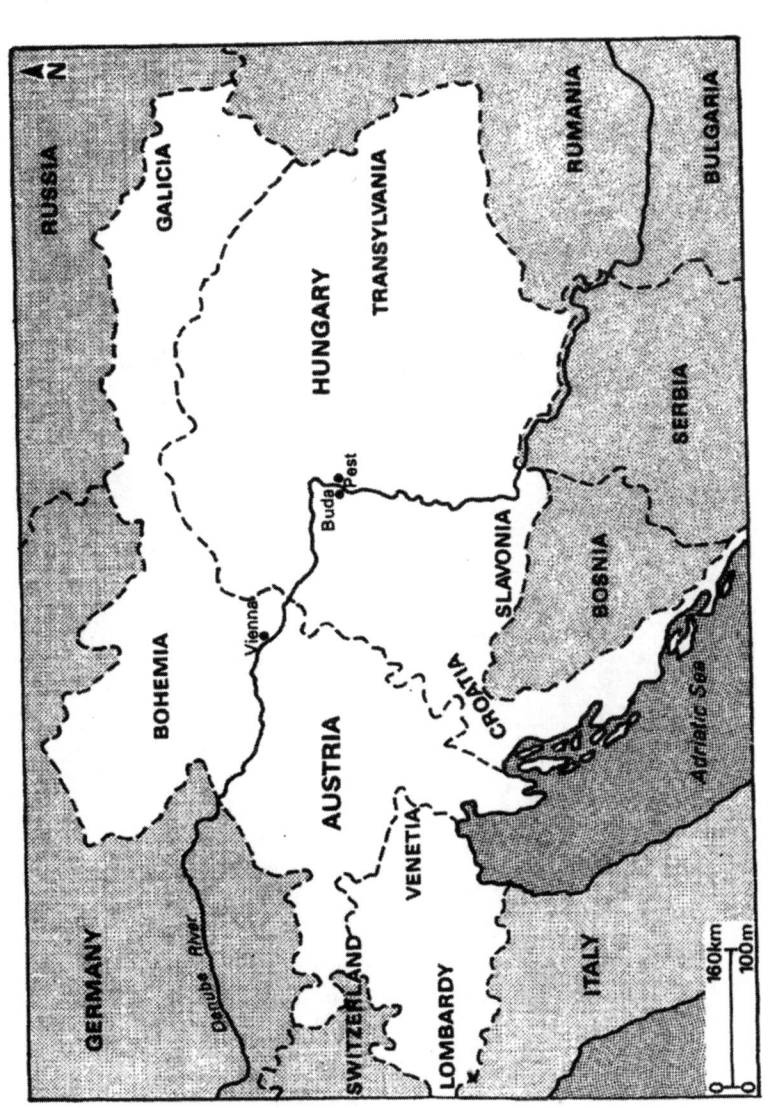

Austrian Empire, 1848

Boundary of Austro-Hungarian Empire after the 1867 *Ausgleich* (Great Compromise) replaced the Austrian Hapsburg Empire (1282-1867) with the Austro-Hungarian Dual Monarchy.

∙∙∙∙∙∙ Extent of area annexed by Austro-Hungarian Empire in 1908

Nations or Eastern Europe and the former Soviet Union (June 1993)

Current national boundaries

Austro-Hungarian Empire, 1867

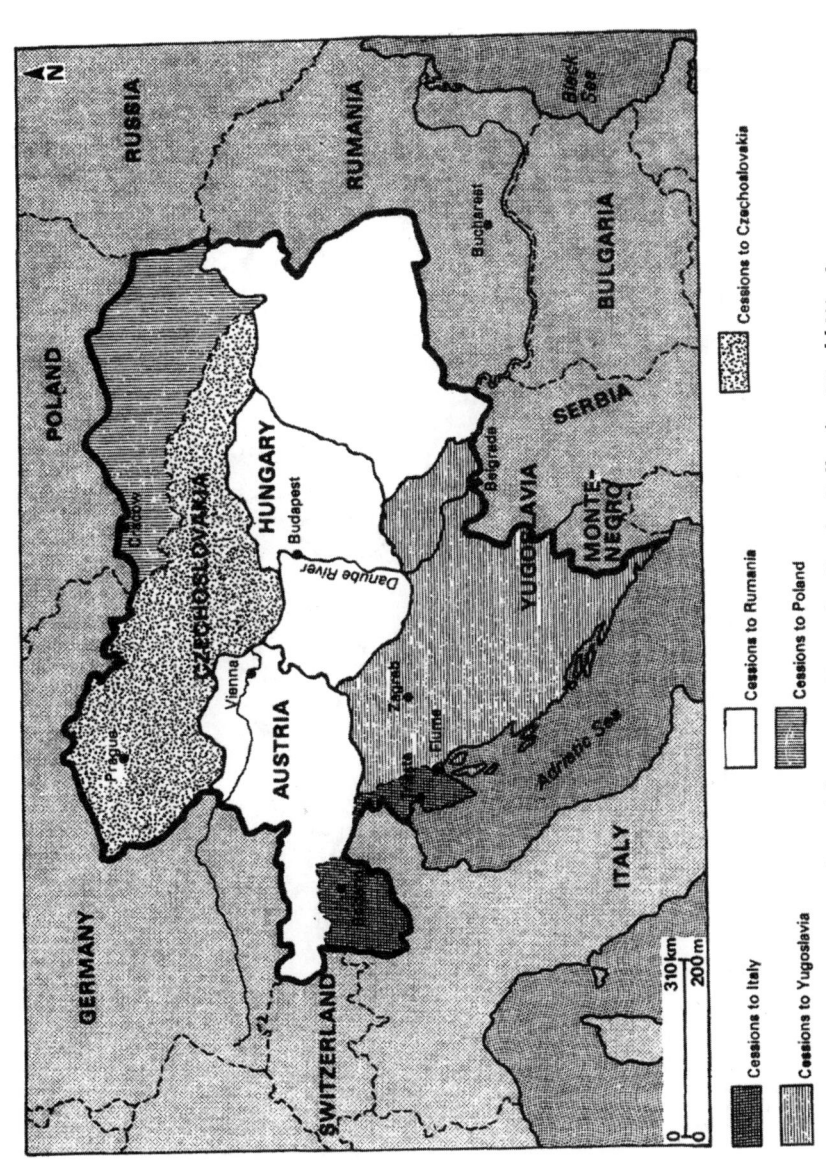

Breakup of the Austro-Hungarian Empire Following World War I

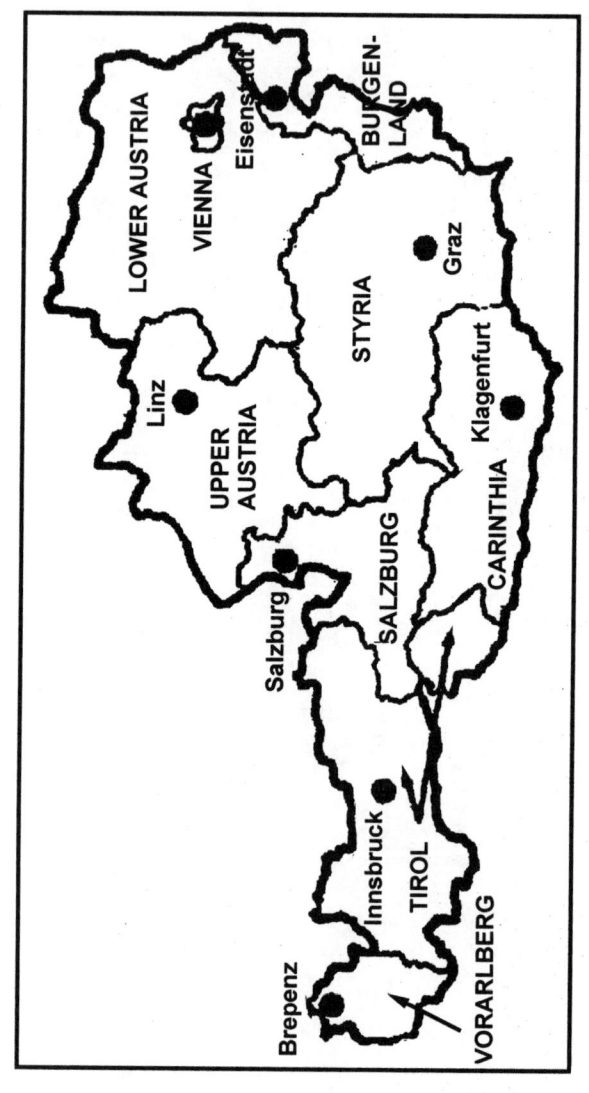

Map # 4 Modern Austria: Provinces and Capitals

Chronology

5000 BCE Late Stone Age culture.

2000 Indo-Germanic settlements northwest of Vienna.

800 Bronze Age settlements on the Vienna Hoher Markt.

750 Hallstatt culture.

400 Celtic culture.

15 Roman occupation of province of Noricum.

180 CE Death of Roman Emperor Marcus Aurelius in Vindobona.

280 Emperor Probus authorizes viticulture in Danubian region.

405 Roman withdrawal from Vindobona.

433 Vindobona destroyed by Huns.

500–700 Invasion and sporadic occupation by Lombards, Goths, Avars, and Slavic tribes. Increased settlement by Bavarian tribes.

After 782 Establishment of Carolingian Eastern March or Ostmark.

909 Invasion of Eastern March by Hungarians.

955 German Emperor Otto I defeats Hungarians and reestablishes the Eastern March.

975 Otto I names Leopold of Babenberg margrave in the Eastern March.

1156 *Privilegium minus*. The Babenberg Henry II Jasomirgott is given extensive legal privileges in his Austrian lands by Emperor Frederick I (Barbarossa). These effectively exempted the Babenberg holdings from feudal obligations to the emperor and marked the beginning of ducal territorial sovereignty in Austria.

1246 Death of the last Babenberg, Frederick II the Quarrelsome. Subsequent invasion of Austrian lands by Ottakar II, the king of Bohemia.

1273 Count Rudolph of Habsburg crowned German king. He was never officially crowned as emperor by a pope.

1278–1282 Rudolph I becomes ruler of Austria after defeating Ottakar II of Bohemia. He enfeoffs himself and his family with the former Babenberg possessions. The city of Vienna given its charter in 1278.

1358–1359 *Privilegium maius.* Although a forgery, this document, issued by Archduke Rudolph IV, was eventually confirmed by a later Habsburg, Emperor Frederick III, in 1443 and 1452. It conferred the title of archduke or archduchess on the Habsburg dynasty and laid the groundwork for other important privileges of the house.

1365 Foundation of the University of Vienna by Archduke Rudolph IV.

1442 Frederick V of Austria becomes German king. In 1452, he was crowned Emperor Frederick III by Pope Nicholas V in Rome, the last time that the imperial coronation would take place in that city. From that time until Napoleon I's dissolution of the Holy Roman Empire in 1806, control of the imperial office would be in Habsburg hands. The lone exception was the period 1742–1745.

1477 Marriage of Archduke Maximilian, son of Emperor Frederick III, to Mary of Burgundy.

1495 Marriage of Archduke Philip (Philip the Handsome) to Infanta Juana, daughter of Ferdinand of Aragon and Isabella of Castile.

1515 Vienna Double Betrothal Agreement engaging Maximilian I's granddaughter, Archduchess Mary, to Prince Louis of Hungary and Bohemia, and Louis's sister, Princess Anna, to one of Mary's two brothers, Archduke Charles or Archduke Ferdinand.

1516 Archduke Charles (Emperor Charles V) becomes king of Spain.

1521/1522 Austrian Habsburg lands turned over to Archduke Ferdinand I for governance. Marriage in 1521 of Ferdinand and Princess Anna of Hungary.

1526 Battle of Mohács between the Ottoman army of Suleyman the Magnificent and Hungarians. King Louis of Hungary and Bohemia killed. Archduke Ferdinand elected as King Ferdinand I in Bohemia, Hungary, and Croatia.

1529 Ottoman army forced to break off its siege of Vienna.

1551 Ferdinand I brings Jesuit order to Vienna in effort to stem Protestantism, which was spreading quickly in the Austrian lands.

1618 Defenestration of Prague signals rejection of Habsburg rule in Bohemia by estates. Opening stage of Thirty Years' War.

1620 Habsburg victory over Bohemian estates at Battle of the White Mountain. Beginning of major Habsburg efforts to consolidate the powers of the dynasty in their various territories.

1648 Treaty of Westphalia ends Thirty Years' War. Habsburg efforts to recatholicize Germany come to a halt.

1683 Ottoman forces driven back from their last siege of Vienna. Beginning of Habsburg reconquest of Hungary and areas in southeastern Europe from Ottoman control.

1701–1714 War of the Spanish Succession. Austrian Habsburgs abandon claims to Spanish throne.

1713 Pragmatic Sanction of Emperor Charles VI, which declares the unity of the Habsburg lands in preparation for the succession of his daughter, Maria Theresa.

1716–1750 Period of construction of major Baroque architectural features of Vienna. Lower Belvedere Palace of Eugene of Savoy completed in 1716, Karlskirche (Church of St. Charles Borromeo) begun in 1719, Imperial Hall of State (Prunksaal) of the Hofburg and the Upper Belvedere Palace finished 1724–1726. Schönbrunn Palace completed in 1730, then adapted for Maria Theresa, 1744–1749.

1740–1748 War of the Austrian Succession/First and Second Silesian Wars. Maria Theresa's succession to Austrian lands challenged. Attack by Frederick II (the Great) of Prussia on Silesia. In the Treaty of Aix-la-Chapelle of October 1748, Maria Theresa cedes Silesia to Frederick the Great. Pragmatic Sanction recognized by signatories. Period of major restructuring of Habsburg financial and military administration follows.

1756–1763 Seven Years' War/Third War of the Austrian Succession. Failed Austrian attempt to regain Silesia from Prussia. Treaty of Hubertusburg reconfirms Prussian seizure of Silesia. Frederick the Great promises to support Maria Theresa's son, Archduke Joseph, in imperial German election.

1772 First Partition of Poland. Habsburg Empire acquires Galicia, part of Cracow and part of modern Ukraine (L'viv).

1778–1779 War of the Bavarian Succession.

1780–1790 Reign of Emperor Joseph II. Influenced by progressive notions of enlightened absolutism, Joseph issues edicts (1781) granting religious toleration and emancipation of serfs throughout the empire. There is intense local resistance to many administrative reforms, especially in Austrian Netherlands and Hungary.

1795 Third Partition of Poland. Habsburg Empire acquires rest of Cracow.

1801 Peace of Lunéville. Territorial breakup of Holy Roman Empire.

1806 Title of Holy Roman Emperor abolished. Francis I becomes Emperor Francis I of Austria.

1809 Uprising in the Tyrol against Franco–Bavarian occupation. Count Klemens Wenzel von Metternich appointed minister of foreign affairs by Francis I.

1814–1815 Congress of Vienna.

1815–1848 *Vormärz* (Pre-March). Under direction of Francis I and his chancellor, Metternich, political activity is strictly regulated. Period of rich musical and theatrical life. Biedermeier style emerges.

1848 Revolutions throughout Habsburg Empire. **December:** Francis Joseph I becomes Austrian emperor.

1849 Hungary declares independence. Revolutions generally suppressed by Habsburg army.

1851 New Year's Eve Patent declares supremacy of Austrian emperor. Empire largely administered directly from Vienna.

1852 Beginning of construction of Semmering mountain rail line between Lower Austria and Styria.

1855 Concordat between Austria and the Holy See.

1859 Austro–Piedmontese War.

1860 October Diploma proposes a measure of decentralization in Austrian Empire.

1861 February Patent creates Imperial Assembly for all lands of Austrian Empire. Hungarian boycott.

1862 Treaty of Villa Franca. Habsburg Empire cedes Lombardy to Napoleon III of France, who turns the territory over to King Victor Emmanuel II of Sardinia–Piedmont.

1864 Austro–Prussian–Danish War.

1866 Seven Weeks' War.

1867 Compromise of 1867 (*Ausgleich*). Habsburg Empire becomes Dual Monarchy of Austria–Hungary. Hungary becomes internally autonomous. Ruler, foreign policy, army, and some financial matters declared to be in common.

1867–1873 Intense industrial and commercial development in Austrian half of Dual Monarchy (*Gründerzeit*).

1873 Vienna World's Fair. Financial crisis.

1878 Congress of Berlin. Austria–Hungary allowed to administer Bosnia–Herzegovina and the Sanjak of Novi Bazaar. Occupation of Novi Bazaar begins in 1879.

1879 Celebration of silver wedding anniversary of Emperor Franz Joseph and Empress Elisabeth ("Sissy") in April with massive historical pageant. Count Edward Taaffe becomes minister-president of antiliberal coalition government. **October:** Dual Alliance of Austria–Hungary and Germany.

1882 Triple Alliance of Austria–Hungary, Germany, and Italy. Electoral reform in Austrian half of monarchy lowers to five gulden the amount of income tax required to exercise franchise. German National Association founded.

1883 Establishment of Austrian–Hungarian postal savings bank.

1887 Founding of Christian Social Union in Vienna.

1888 Development in Vienna of a four-cylinder, gasoline-powered automobile by Siegfried Marcus.

1888–1889 **31 December–1 January:** Hainfeld Program unites factions of Austrian Social Democratic movement. **30 January:** Deaths of heir apparent Archduke Rudolph and Mary Vetsera. **April 4:** Introduction of obligatory accident insurance for workers. **20 April:** Birth of Adolf Hitler in Braunau in Upper Austria.

1890 First socialist May Day celebration. **8 November:** Founding of Christian Social Party.

1897 **14 April:** Emperor Franz Joseph confirms Karl Lueger as mayor of Vienna. **22 May:** First Vienna Secession founded, with Gustav Klimt as president. **26–28 November:** Parliamentary crisis in Austrian half of the Habsburg Empire over Badeni Language Ordinances.

1898 **10 September:** Assassination of Empress Elisabeth in Geneva by Italian anarchist.

1899 Founding of the Federation of Austrian Women's Organizations. **October.** Opening of Vienna Municipal Gas Works.

1902 Completion of Vienna Municipal Electric Works.

1903 **12 May:** Founding of Wiener Werkstätte.

1907 **26 January:** Introduction of general male suffrage in Austrian half of Habsburg Empire. **September:** Adolf Hitler makes his failed attempt to enter the Vienna Academy of Fine Arts.

1908 **5 July:** Annexation of Bosnia–Herzegovina.

1910 **10 March:** Death of Vienna Mayor Karl Lueger. Founding of the Vienna and International Psychoanalytic Society.

1912 **30 September:** Outbreak of First Balkan War.

1913 **30 May:** End of First Balkan War. **30 July–10 August:** Second Balkan War. First productive oil well east of Vienna opened.

1914 **28 June:** Assassination of heir apparent to Habsburg Empire, Archduke Francis Ferdinand, in Sarajevo. **28 July:** Emperor Francis Joseph declares war on Serbia.

1915 **4 May:** Italy declares War on Austria–Hungary.

1916 **21 October:** Assassination of Austrian minister-president Count Karl von Stürgkh by Friedrich Adler, son of Austrian Social Democratic leader Viktor Adler. **21 November:** Death of Emperor Franz Joseph. Emperor Charles I (King Charles IV of Hungary) succeeds to crowns of Austria–Hungary.

1917 **30 May:** Emperor Charles reconvenes suspended parliament of Austrian half of monarchy. **4 December:** United States declares war on Austria–Hungary.

1918 **8 January:** President Woodrow Wilson offers Fourteen Points for peace in World War I. **16 October:** Emperor Charles I issues manifesto turning Habsburg Empire into a federal state, recognizing national autonomy. **11 November:** Emperor Charles withdraws from all participation in the business of state. **12 November:** Announcement of the founding of the Republic of German Austria.

1919 **12 March:** National Assembly declares that Austria is a part of the Republic of Germany. **15 March:** Territorial Commission of the Paris Peace Conference confirms the integrity of existing boundaries between Austria and Germany. **3 April:** Expropriation of Habsburgs and expulsion from Austria. **September:** Austria and the victorious allies sign Peace of St. Germain. **October:** Name of Austria officially changed from "German Austria" to "Austria."

1920 **4 June:** Hungary signs Treaty of Trianon, which calls for the incorporation of the Burgenland into Austria. **16 December:** Austria joins League of Nations.

1921 26 March–4 April and 20–24 October: Former Emperor (King) Charles fails to restore himself to throne in Hungary.

1922 31 May: Ignaz Seipel, of the Christian Social Party, forms his first government, with himself as federal chancellor. **4 October:** With the Austrian currency, the crown, at all-time low, Seipel arranges for state loan from the League of Nations.

1923 12 April: Founding of the Republican Guard, paramilitary arm of the Social Democratic Party of Austria. **20 November:** Karl Seitz, a Social Democrat, becomes mayor of Vienna.

1924 12 June: Attempted assassination of Chancellor Seipel. **December:** Schilling becomes Austrian currency.

1925 10 March: Assassination of Jewish author Hugo Bettenauer by a National Socialist. **30 July:** Constitutional reform centralizes Austrian financial administration.

1926 9 June: League of Nations lifts supervision of Austrian government finances.

1927 9 July: Workers' demonstration in Vienna ends in burning of the Ministry of Justice building. Police action leaves 90 dead and approximately 600 wounded. **26 November:** Unsuccessful attempt of a monarchist to assassinate Vienna mayor Karl Seitz.

1929 4 October: The Creditanstalt Bank takes over assets of failed Agricultural Credit Bank (Bodenkreditanstalt).

1930 6 February: Signing of Italian–Austrian Friendship pact. **18 May:** Proclamation of the Korneuburg Program by *Heimwehr*.

1931 6–10 May: Creditanstalt Bank crisis. **20 May:** Engelbert Dollfuss becomes Austrian chancellor. **6 September:** International Court in the Hague disallows tariff union of Austria and Germany.

1933 30 January: Adolf Hitler becomes German chancellor. **4 March:** Austrian Parliament collapses on procedural question. Dollfuss government declares state of emergency and resorts to wartime provision that permits rule by decree. **31 March:** Socialist paramilitary Republican Guard disbanded by government. **20 May:** Founding of Fatherland Front.

1934 12–16 February: Heavy fighting throughout Austria between *Heimwehr* organizations and Social Democrats. Social Democratic party outlawed. **1 May:** Proclamation of authoritarian May Constitution. **25 July:** Murder of Chancellor Engelbert Dollfuss in failed Nazi putsch. Kurt von Schuschnigg becomes Austrian chancellor.

1935 11–14 April: Stresa Conference of France, Great Britain, and Italy affirms independence of Austria. **13 July:** Ban on entrance of Habsburg family into Austria lifted.

1936 14 May: Schuschnigg becomes leader of Fatherland Front. **11 July:** Agreement between Austria and Nazi Germany recognizing independence of Austria. Amnesty granted to Nazis in Austria. **7–11 October:** All paramilitary groups in Austria disbanded.

1938 12 February: Schuschnigg signs Berchtesgaden Agreement with Hitler, permitting Nazi party activity in Austria to resume. **9 March:** Schuschnigg announces referendum on Austrian independence, then cancels it under pressure from Hitler. **11 March:** Germans march into Austria, which is quickly put under a Nazi regime (Anschluss). **10 April:** 99.97 percent of Austrians voting in a plebiscite approve of Nazi government.

1939 1 September: World War II begins.

1942 April: Formation of communist-backed Austrian Freedom Front in Carinthian and Styrian mountains. **27 July:** United States declares that it never recognized German annexation of Austria.

1943 30 October: Moscow Declaration of Allies that Austria should be "liberated" from German occupation.

1944 18 December: Prewar Austrian political parties begin discussing provisional government. 05 Group begins organizing armed resistance to Nazis.

1945 April: Surrender of Nazis in Austria to Allied armies. Bitter fighting in Vienna. **23 April:** Establishment of multiparty provisional government. **May:** World War II in Europe ends. **25 November:** First free elections since 1930 held in Austria, with Austrian People's Party (ÖVP) and Social Democrats (SPÖ) receiving largest number of votes.

1946 **7 January:** Occupation powers recognize new federal Austrian government. **26 July:** Nationalization of heavy industry, transportation facilities, and utilities by Austrian National Assembly.

1947 **14 January–25 February:** Negotiations on an Austrian state treaty begin in London. **20 November:** Austrian Communist Party withdraws from coalition government.

1948 **20 July:** Marshall Plan agreement signed between Austria and the United States; aid begins to arrive in Austria.

1949 **19 June:** Soviet Union announces that it will no longer support Yugoslav territorial claims in Austria.

1950 **7 March:** Austrian government asks Allied powers to alter conditions and financing of occupation. **September–October:** Soviet-supported general strike in key Austrian industries.

1951 **19 January:** State of war between Austria and Yugoslavia ends. **6 May:** First popular election of a president of the Austrian republic.

1952 **2 April:** Austrian governments protests continuation of Allied occupation. **20 December:** General Assembly of the United Nations adopts resolution asking Allied powers to agree on an Austrian state treaty.

1953 **5 March:** Death of Soviet leader Joseph Stalin. **1 July:** Marshall Plan aid for Austria runs out. **31 August:** Soviet Union, following France, Great Britain, and United States, stops billing Austria for occupation costs.

1955 **11–14 April:** Austrian delegation to Moscow assures Soviet Union of willingness to remain neutral. **15 May:** Signing of Austrian State Treaty. **25 October:** Evacuation of all Allied troops from Austria completed. **15 December:** Austria allowed to enter United Nations.

1956 **2 March:** Austria the 15th state to join Council of Europe. **28 May:** First muster of Austrian army. **15 October:** Vienna chosen as permanent site for International Organization for the Peaceful Uses of Nuclear Energy. **23 October:** Hungarian uprising against Soviet occupation. Austria will eventually host 152, 218 Hungarian refugees.

1957 1 January: Television broadcasting starts in Austria. **9 February:** Beginning of Austrian–Italian disagreement over status of German-speaking minority in South Tyrol. **25 July:** Soviet Union agrees to accept goods rather than oil as part of Austria's war reparations payments. **1 October:** First conference of Nuclear Energy Organization held in Vienna. **15 December:** Austria signs European Human Rights Convention.

1958 6 May: Opening of Austrian pavilion at Brussels International World's Fair. **17 July:** Austria declares U.S. use of Austrian air space in military transportation to Lebanon a violation of Austrian neutrality. **22 July:** United States apologizes for violation of Austrian neutrality.

1959 20 February–6 March: Tensions between Austria and Italy over South Tyrol grow sharper. Austrian consulate in Rome attacked with Molotov cocktail on 6 March. **21 September:** Austrian Foreign Minister Bruno Kreisky addresses United Nations General Assembly on South Tyrol problem.

1960 1 January: Austria joins European Free Trade Association.

1961 New levels of violence reached in South Tyrol problem. **5 June:** Otto Habsburg, son of Charles I of Habsburg–Lorraine, declares his loyalty to the Austrian republic. **15 November:** Beginning of debate over South Tyrol question at the United Nations. Austrian television begins broadcasting *Herr Karl* series with Helmut Qualtinger.

1962 27 March: European Human Rights Commission rejects Slovenian complaint of discrimination in Austria. **4 April:** Austrian parliament accepts agreement between Austria and Germany on fiscal and property claims that arose after World War II. **August:** Austria stands in first place in United Nations (UN) survey of traffic accidents per 100,000 people.

1963 9 March: Foreign Minister Bruno Kreisky rejects Soviet objections to Austrian economic integration into European Economic Community. **2 April:** Ministers of European Economic Organization begin discussion of association with Austria. **30 December:** Austria makes final delivery of oil as required reparations to Soviet Union.

1964 January–June: Foreign tourism reaches record high in Austria. **20 February:** All Austrian reparations to Soviet Union at an end.

1965 Income from foreign tourism sets another record high. **2 March:** Ministers of European Economic Community resolve to begin discussions with Austria about a tariff union. **29, 31 March:** Clash in Vienna between supporters and opponents from Austrian resistance movement of anti-Semitic professor Taras Boradaikewycz. **9–15 May:** Celebration of 500-year anniversary of founding of University of Vienna. **20 July:** Province of Lower Austria issues citizenship papers to Otto von Habsburg and his wife. **26 October:** Austrian national holiday celebrated for first time.

1966 **19 April:** First single-party government in Austria since World War II, under ÖVP with Joseph Klaus as chancellor. **14 May:** Taras Boradaikewycz. compelled to retire from Academy for World Trade. **1 June:** Otto von Habsburg granted an Austrian passport. **16 December:** Establishment of Austrian Industrial Management Corporation to oversee state interests in nationalized industry.

1967 **20 March:** Soviet Union warns Austria against association with European Economic Community. **5 July:** Otto von Habsburg makes first visit to Vienna since end of World War II.

1968 Major student and leftist demonstrations throughout the year. **12 November:** National Assembly lowers voting age to 19.

1969 **25 July:** Austria and Italy sign agreement on the status of the South Tyrol. **3 November:** Subway construction begins in Vienna. At the end of the year, Austria registers highest growth in exports of any European country.

1970 **21 April:** First SPÖ single-party government in Second Austrian Republic, with Bruno Kreisky as federal chancellor.

1971 **15 July:** Required active military service in Austria reduced to six months, with 60 days of supplementary training to be fulfilled at 15 days per calendar year. **1 September:** State assumes cost of Catholic schools in Austria. **1 October:** Chancellor Bruno Kreisky declares that state has no further plans for nationalizing industry. **22 December:** Kurt Waldheim becomes Secretary General of the United Nations.

1972 **1 January:** Austrian workweek now 42 hours. **22 July:** Austria, along with other European Free Trade Association (EFTA) members, signs agreement with European Economic Community on trade relations.

1973 Austria has highest growth rate of any industrialized state in Europe. **1 January:** Value-added tax in effect in Austria. **16 January:** Austria a member of the United Nations Security Council for the first time. **28 September:** First act of Palestinian terrorism in Austria. Jewish hostages freed after government agrees to close Jewish transit center in Lower Austria.

1974 **14 January:** Trade Ministry orders an "automobile free day" to meet gasoline crisis. **23 June:** Rudolph Kirchschläger elected president in an election in which 94.6 percent of all Austrians eligible to vote did so, a record rate of participation.

1975 **11 April:** National Assembly passes Reorganization of University Law. All higher schools (Hochschulen) become universities. **21 December:** Terrorists attack meeting of Organization of Petroleum Exporting Countries (OPEC) in Vienna. Perpetrators allowed to leave Austria safely.

1976 **7 July:** Ethnic Groups Act regulating language use in schooling and public life for Croats and Slovenes in Austria. **3 December:** 400,000 rounds of ammunition sequestered from army supplies and destined for Syria discovered at Vienna airport in Schwechat.

1977 **19 January:** National Assembly begins inquiry into munitions affair and its implications for Austrian neutrality. **1 May:** Austrian unemployment at a low of 1 percent.

1978 **5 November:** In a plebiscite, 50.47 percent of Austrians voting reject activation of atomic energy plant at Zwentendorf in Lower Austria.

1979 **23 August:** Opening of UN-City in Vienna. **20 November:** Consecration of first mosque in Vienna.

1980 **12 March:** Kreisky government extends de facto recognition to Palestine Liberation Organization of Yasser Arafat. **8 September:** Judicial investigation of massive corruption surrounding construction of new Vienna General Hospital begins. **11 December:** Finance

Minister Hannes Androsch announces resignation in wake of financial scandals.

1981 1 July: Hannes Androsch becomes director of Creditanstalt Bank. **29 August:** Three Arabs attack Vienna synagogue, leaving 2 dead and 20 wounded.

1982 16 May: Former Empress Zita visits Austria for first time in 63 years.

1983 24 April: Bruno Kreisky steps down as chancellor, to be replaced by Fred Sinowatz. **10 September:** Pope John Paul II visits Austria for 300th anniversary of defeat of Ottoman army before Vienna. **29 October:** Sinowatz elected SPÖ chairperson.

1984 30 March: Vienna City Council authorizes expenditure of 400 million schillings for renovation of historical residential housing. **31 March:** Study by Austrian Agricultural University shows that about 18 percent of Austrian forests have been damaged by air and ground pollution. **21 October:** Green Party wins its first seat ever in a regional parliament in the Vorarlberg.

1985 28 March: Opening of exhibition "Traum und Wirklichkeit on Vienna 1870–1930." **30 May:** Nationalized tire firm Semperit sold to German company because of financial problems. **29 August:** Austrian National Assembly proposes law to protect quality of Austrian wines after adulteration scandal.

1986 1 January: Austrians have right to minimum of five weeks vacation. **8 June:** Controversial election of Kurt Waldheim as Austrian federal president. Franz Vranitzky replaces Fred Sinowatz as federal chancellor. Small coalition government of SPÖ and Freedom Party of Austria (FPÖ). **15 September:** Jörg Haider elected head of FPÖ; resignation of Sinowatz as federal chancellor in favor of Vranitzky.

1987 21 January: Reconstitution of Grand Coalition between SPÖ and ÖVP. **27 April:** United States refuses to allow Kurt Waldheim to enter country. **1 September:** Austrian historical commission to investigate Waldheim's role in World War II begins work.

1988 24 January: Hannes Androsch resigns as director of Creditanstalt Bank. **2 February:** Austrian historical commission investigating Waldheim concludes that he did not participate in war crimes, but may have known about them. **25 April:** Government coalition partners agree on modest extension of shopping hours in Austria.

1989 **14 March:** Former Empress Zita dies in Switzerland. **7 July:** Foreign Minister Alois Mock submits Austrian application for membership in European Community. **10 August:** Soviet ambassador to Austria presents Russian reservations about status of Austrian neutrality should Austria join EC. **10 September:** Hungary opens border with Austria for citizens of German Democratic Republic to cross freely. **17 December:** Alois Mock and Jiri Dienstbier, Czechoslovak foreign minister symbolically split the "Iron Curtain" at Czechoslovak–Austrian border.

1990 **19 July:** Death of Bruno Kreisky. **13 August:** Austria joins United Nations in sanctions against Iraq. **25 August:** President Kurt Waldheim wins release of Austrian hostages from Iraq. **7 October:** Federal elections reconfirm Grand Coalition of SPÖ and ÖVP. **6 November:** World War II Allies accept Austrian modifications of 1955 State Treaty. **13 December:** Austrian investigators declare Slovak atomic power plant in Bohumice unsafe.

1991 **21 June:** Jörg Haider forced to resign as governor of Carinthia. Kurt Waldheim announces that he will not run for a second term as federal president.

1992 **24 May:** Thomas Klestil elected federal president. **26 June:** More restrictive new law on asylum made operative.

1993 **8 July:** Franz Vranitzky pays first official visit of an Austrian federal chancellor to Israel. **1 February:** Austria begins formal negotiations for entry into European Community. **4 February:** Founding of Liberal Forum (LiF) in split with the FPÖ. Initiative to restrict immigration receives 417, 278 signatures. **1 July:** New law on foreign residence in effect.

1994 **1 March:** Agreement between Austria and the European Union (EU) on conditions of Austrian membership. **12 June:** 66.6 percent of voters participating in referendum approve Austria's entry into European Union. **11 November:** National Assembly ratifies EU agreement on Austria.

1995 **1 January:** Austria becomes member of EU and removes customs controls at borders for EU member states. **5 January:** Austria begins participation in currency exchange and intervention mechanisms of EU. Konsum, a large national grocery chain founded by socialists in 19th century, declares bankruptcy.

1996 **13 October:** In elections to European Parliament, SPÖ fails to win more than the narrowest possible plurality. Austria records negative balance of trade for 14th consecutive year.

1997 **12 January:** Creditanstalt Bank sold to Bank Austria after extensive negotiations. **18 January:** Franz Vranitzky steps down as federal chancellor in favor of Viktor Klima, who is sworn in on 28 January. **27 February:** First female instrumentalist joins Vienna Philharmonic. **13 March:** SPÖ and ÖVP agree on changes to immigration law that stress integration of foreigners into Austrian society rather than simply setting terms of entry. **17 April:** National Assembly eases restrictions on Austrian participation in international peacekeeping forces

1998 **13 January:** Minister of Culture and Education Elisabeth Gehrer announces program to inventory materials acquired by Austrian museums during and after World War II. **1 April:** First female recruits enter Austrian military. **19 April:** Thomas Klestil elected to second term as Austrian president. **5 May:** Both chambers of Austrian parliament memorialize victims of National Socialism for the first time. **1 July:** Austria is first new member of EU to hold office of president. **28 July:** Julius Meinl, tradition-laden Austrian grocery chain, acquired by German Rewe conglomerate. **5 November:** National Assembly agrees unanimously to return artworks illegally acquired during and after World War II to rightful owners. **28 November:** National Assembly agrees upon a program to establish "secure third countries" to which asylum seekers can be sent.

1999 **25 January:** Intense discussion of economic cooperation among Austria, Hungary, and Slovakia at annual meeting. **11 February:** Austria returns several artworks to full possession of the Rothschild family. **14 February:** Austria wins 14 medals and first place at international ski competition in Vail, Colorado. **8 April:** Jörg Haider reelected by provincial legislature to governorship of Carinthia. **13 May:** Despite massive Austrian protests, the Czech Republic resolves to complete construction of nuclear energy facility at Temelin. **27 May:**

Federal government forbids cultivation of genetically engineered corn. **4 June:** Chancellor Viktor Klima declares that Austria will refuse taking military action not covered by the UN Charter. **14 July:** Austria introduces bachelor's degree that requires six to eight semesters of study at a university. **4 October:** FPÖ makes substantial gains in elections to National Assembly. **12 November:** Massive demonstration of around 25,000 people in Vienna against racism and National Socialism.

2000   **6 January:** U.S. Court in New York agrees to collective settlement for victims of Nazi regime in Austria and Bank Austria. **4 February:** Coalition government of ÖVP and FPÖ sworn in. European Union threatens, then implements, sanctions against Austria. **19 February:** Demonstration on Vienna's Heldenplatz against new government. **24 February:** Regular Thursday demonstrations in Vienna against new government begin. **28 February:** Jörg Haider withdraws from coalition government, to be replaced by Susanne Riess-Passer. **12 April:** Federal President Thomas Klestil pleads before the European Parliament for end of sanctions. **1 May:** Riess-Passer becomes chair of FPÖ. **17 August:** Bank for Labor and Economic Developments (BAWAG) takes over Austrian Postal Savings Bank. **12 September:** European Union announces that sanctions have been lifted. **20 November:** Shares of Telekom Austria offered on the New York Stock Exchange for the first time.

2001   **17 January:** Austria and the United States agree on amount of compensation for Jewish victims of Austrian Nazi regime. **23 January:** Chancellor Wolfgang Schüssel declares that Austria is not neutral but "alliance free." **29 January:** Foreign Minister Benita Ferrero-Waldner declares that Austria's neutrality is its affair alone. **31 January:** National Assembly unanimously approves a law compensating victims of Nazi "Arianization" policy. **8 February–11 February:** Russian president Vladimir Putin visits Austria to express his reservations about Austrian membership in NATO. **20 May:** Austrian director Michael Haneke wins Cannes Film Festival prize for *The Piano Player*, based on the novel by Elfriede Jelinek. **28 June:** Opening of the new Museum Quartier. **1 October:** Electricity supply network privatized. **12 December:** National Assembly and political parties declare Austria an "alliance free" state. **13 December:** United Nations Educational, Scientific and Cultural Organization (UNESCO) designates the historical center of Vienna as part of the world's cultural heritage.

2002 1 January: The euro replaces the schilling as Austria's official currency. **8 January**: The federal council of ministers authorizes deployment of 60 Austrian military personnel for Afghanistan peacekeeping force. **28 February:** As part of program to make higher education more efficient, Education Minister Elisabeth Gehrer proposes separating medical faculties from universities and making baccalaureate a terminal degree at Austrian vocational colleges. **18 April:** Opening of the controversial Austrian Cultural Forum building in New York, designed by Austrian architect Rainer Abraham. **24 June:** Constitutional Court declares prohibitions against homosexual relations illegal. **6 August:** Massive flooding after unprecedented rainfall in Lower and Upper Austria and Salzburg. Cost of damage roughly 8 billion euros. **3 September:** Half of delegates at FPÖ convention express dissatisfaction with government leadership. **8 September:** Three ministers from FPÖ, including Vice-Chancellor Riess-Passer, resign from government. **27 September:** Hundreds of asylum seekers in Austria sent out of country because their petitions had no chance for success. **26 November:** Chancellor Schüssel asked to form another government.

2003 21 January: Statistics indicate that Austrian birth rate is climbing. **24 January:** Chancellor Schüssel declares that Austria will not participate in any coalition to invade Iraq. **24 February:** Commission of Historians finds that Austria was dilatory in addressing issue of victims of National Socialism. **28 February:** New coalition government of ÖVP and FPÖ sworn in. Wolfgang Schüssel once more chancellor. **20 March:** Austria declares its neutrality in the case of Iraq and closes its air space to combatants. **23 June:** Venerable Viennese baking firm Ankerbrot sold to German company. **20 July:** Israel announces that it will send its first ambassador to Austria. **29 August:** Private television broadcasting begins in Austria. **1 August:** Extended evening and Saturday shopping hours start in Austria. **5 November:** Federal government announces national scientific research initiative.

2004 14 February: Architects from firm Coop Himmelb(l)au win international competition to design the European Central Bank in Frankfurt. **16 February:** Index of Vienna Stock Exchange (ATX) closes at a record high of 1,803.42 points. **18 February:** Ministry of the Interior announces that applications for asylum in Austria have dropped by almost 39 percent. **2 March:** Council of Ministers resolves to increase Austrian military presence in Bosnia–Herzegovina. **28 March:** Austrian swimmer Markus Rogan sets European record for 200-meter backstroke (1:51.37). **30 March:** Provincial elections show a decline of support for Austrian Freedom Party. **31 March:** Jörg Haider once again chosen governor by Carinthian provincial legislature. **24 April:** Heinz Fischer elected Austrian president, the first Socialist candidate to win the office since 1980. **3 October:** Former Emperor Charles I beatified by Pope John Paul II.

2005 Year of Remembrance of Defeat of National Socialism (1945); the signing of the Austrian State Treaty (1955) and accession to the European Union (1995). **April:** Founding of the Alliance for the Future of Austria (BZÖ) by Jörg Haider and other disgruntled members of Freedom Party. **9 July:** Vienna Police Commissioner Roland Horgacher suspended from office based on allegations of receiving improper gifts and passing confidential information to journalists. **11 November:** British Holocaust denier David Irving arrested in Vienna for expressing doubts about existence of Auschwitz gas chambers in 1989.

2006 **20 February:** David Irving convicted and sentenced to three years in prison. On 20 December, Irving's sentence was commuted. He was quickly deported to the United Kingdom. **April:** Effort begins to sell the financially unsound Bank for Labor and Economic Development (BAWAG) to investment houses around the world. **19 June:** Former American ambassador to Austria Ronald Lauder purchases Gustav Klimt's portrait of Adele Bloch-Bauer for a record $135 million. The picture belonged to an Austrian emigré, Maria Altmann. **August:** Ongoing scandal over use of illegal home care worker by relative of Chancellor Schüssel. **23 August:** Of 45 planned research initiative centers, only 15 remain operative. **1 September:** Heavily publicized debut of daily newspaper, *Österreich*, which openly challenges established Austrian press both economically and stylistically. **1 October:** State elections lead to an extremely tight race between the ÖVP and the SPÖ, neither of which receives achieve a majority. Close to 25 percent of vote goes to small parties.

2007 **9 January:** Socialist Alfred Gusenbauer forms coalition government with the ÖVP. **19 August:** Six Austrians on the long list of 20 for the prestigious German Book Prize. **24 August:** Government announces that as part of its reform of bureaucracy, in 2008–2009, only one-half of personnel vacancies will be filled. **25 August:** Head of Islamic community in Austria announces need for new mosques.

2008 **8 July:** Vice-Chancellor Wilhelm Molterer withdraws ÖVP from coalition. Chancellor Gusenbauer announces new elections for September 28. **2 September:** Voting age in Austria lowered to 16. **28 September:** Far-right Austrian Freedom Party (FPÖ) and Alliance for the Future of Austria (BZÖ) take 29 percent of vote in parliamentary elections. SPÖ receives around 30 percent, and the ÖVP 26 percent. **10 October:** World financial crisis hits Austria. Short selling forbidden on Vienna Stock Exchange; trading securities forbidden when price fluctuates by more than 10 percent. **11 October:** BZÖ leader Jörg Haider killed in car crash. **2 December:** Werner Faymann sworn in as chancellor.

Introduction

To those following European affairs in the first decade of the 21st century, Austria seems to reach the headlines only with shocking accounts of long-term kidnapping and incestuous father–daughter relations. An older generation gleaned its first impressions of the country from one or both of two films that would eventually achieve cult status. The first, *The Third Man* (1949), was a riveting insight into the political, psychological, and moral tensions that gripped Vienna in the early years of the Cold War. The city was oppressively grey and shabby and its residents emotionally drained; the climactic scene on a huge Ferris wheel in a run-down amusement park a chilling reminder of the dangers that lurked in even the most innocent pleasures. The second, *The Sound of Music* (1959), adapted from a stage musical that has seen countless revivals, was a cloying but nevertheless upbeat celebration of human goodness in the face of public and private adversity, filled with fresh-faced children, tuneful music, improbably handsome adults, and eye-popping mountain scenery.

The two pieces could not be more unlike in spirit. Even factoring in the 10 years that separated them and included the rebirth of Austria economically and as an independent national state, audiences beyond central Europe could understandably ask which image of the country is more in touch with the reality of the place. The historian's answer, of course, is both. Discounting the embellishments that screenwriters and directors always bring to their work, the country has long identified itself with its musical culture, both high and popular. It has also been among the sites of Europe's calamitous, social, political, and economic upheavals in the 20th century, a theme not wholly absent from the otherwise sunny *Sound of Music*. Indeed, the sharp contrasts in Austria's historical record have defined its past and are far from forgotten.

LAND AND PEOPLE

Though covered by mountains over 62 percent of its land, modern Austria is geographically diverse. The entire area of the country amounts to 83,855 square kilometers in the heart of central Europe. Only western Austria—the Vorarlberg, Tyrol and South Tyrol, parts of Styria, and Salzburg—is distinctively alpine, both climactically and topographically. In the east, northeast, and southeast, where the provinces of Lower Austria, the Burgenland, Upper Austria, and parts of Carinthia lie, the terrain flattens out dramatically. Hills taper down to the Vienna Basin, which is one of the major breaks between the Alps and the Carpathian Mountains farther to the east. From here, one enters the Pannonian Plain, which extends through Hungary; Lake Neusiedl, which lies on the border between Austria and Hungary, is so shallow that great parts of it disappear temporarily during extended droughts. Conversely, the water table lies very near to the surface of the land. Flooding can be a serious problem during protracted rains and violent thunderstorms, which deluge the region in July and August.

If its mountains are the predominant feature of Austria's terrain, the Danube River runs a close second. Only the Vorarlberg, which the Rhine touches, is completely disconnected from Danubian influence. Flowing generally from the north to the southeast, the Danube crosses the country for 351 kilometers, from the German border at Passau to its exit into Hungary in Lower Austria. Its tributaries—the Alpine Inn, Enns, Salzach, and Drau—are considerably shorter, but play a very important role in the Austrian landscape and economy. Although the Danube has long challenged navigators—in some places it is very shallow, in others exceedingly narrow—the river and its feeders are central to Austria's highly developed hydroelectric infrastructure. Austria also contains several large lakes, some of alpine origin, which along with its skiing facilities, are the basis of an elaborate tourist and recreation infrastructure. Indeed, it is through foreign vacationers and sightseers that the country has managed to maintain a favorable balance of trade.

Austria's complex geography shapes its climate as well. At the center of Europe, it is open to influences from the North Atlantic; the Mediterranean; and somewhat less regularly, a hot and dry—in winter, cold and dry—drift of air that comes from the south of Russia. The alpine regions are most affected by the Mediterranean and North Atlantic flows, both of which contribute to frequent rainfall, or snow, especially at higher elevations. Salzburg and environs are locally notorious for so-called *Schnürlregen*, steady precipitation that falls not in drops, but in ribbonlike streams or *Schnürl*. Weather on the southern side of the Alps is more heavily steered by Mediterranean conditions, particularly one called *Föhn*, a warm, moist air mass from the south that can arrive at any time, but is particularly common in the fall. Austrians and south Germans generally attribute behavior from simple lethargy to thoughts of suicide to such episodes.

The eastern part of Austria, particularly Lower Austria and the Burgenland, can be searingly hot, with temperatures regularly topping 30°C in July and the first half of August. However, the winters in this part of the country are by no means as snowy as in the west. Generally abundant rainfall in western and central Austria has created its dense forest cover, one of Europe's largest. More than 39 percent of the terrain of the entire country is wooded. Forestry and refining of forest products remains one of Austria's major industries. It is for this reason that there has been great concern since the late 1970s about acid rain (moisture combined with highly polluted drifts of air that are produced by industries and domestic consumers throughout Europe). The trees of Upper Austria, particularly the conifers, have been especially hard hit.

By the beginning of 2006, the total population of Austria was 8,265,900: 7,451,900 Austrians and 814,100 foreign residents, about half of whom came from the former Yugoslavia or Turkey. The overwhelming number of Austrians are native speakers of German. Small, largely bilingual minorities of Hungarians, Slovenians, and Croatians live in the eastern and southeastern parts of the country. The most thickly settled, thought not necessarily most prosperous, areas of the country lie in the east. The largest city, and the capital, is Vienna, with around 1.5 million inhabitants. Graz, the capital of Styria to the southeast, is the second largest municipality, with around 240,000 residents.

HISTORY

Prehistory and Antiquity

The terrain covered by modern Austria has had some form of human habitation since the Early Stone Age. The first evidence for humans into the alpine valleys comes from around 150,000 years BCE. During the

Early Iron Age, that is between about 1000 and 400 BCE, an amalgamation of Indo–European Illyrians and Celts established the so-called Hallstatt civilization. Toward the end of that period, the Celts cobbled together a kingdom called Noricum. When the Romans began to appear in the region, shortly before the beginning of the Christian era, they turned Noricum into an administrative province, which encompassed much of what today is Austria. Modern Vorarlberg and parts of the Tyrol belonged to the province of Raetia, while the easternmost reaches of today's Austria, including the Vienna Basin, were in Roman Pannonia. Carnuntum, near modern-day Hainburg in Lower Austria, and Vindobona, on the site of present-day Vienna, were both significant military and administrative centers.

During the Roman occupation, both the economy and the culture of the alpine and Danubian regions changed swiftly. The Romans laid down major thoroughfares to move their armies through the region. They also introduced viticulture where the climate and soil would support it. Roman law found its way into some aspects of local custom. Aside from Vienna, both Salzburg and Linz, today leading cities in Austria, trace their origins to Roman settlement. Christianity began to drift into the Alps and the Danube valley around 300 CE.

Approximately 100 years later, Germanic tribes, who had been infiltrating for some time, overran the region. The Romans withdrew from Vindobona in 405. Between 500 and 700, the German Bavarians settled throughout much of what is modern Austria, bringing with them the dialect that has shaped the structure, pronunciation, and vocabulary of modern Austrian speech. However, their presence was contested by Huns, Avars, and the Franks. Under Emperor Charlemagne (r. 771–814), the Austrian lands above and below the Enns River, today Upper and Lower Austria, were converted to a margravate in 788. This served as the launching point for the reconquest of the area from the Avars, which took place between 791 and 796. In 880, the Austrian lands were once again conquered by the Magyars, whose origins were in central Asia. They, in turn, were driven back to what is today Hungary by German Emperor Otto I (r. 936–973) at the Battle of the Lechfeld (955). The Austrian lands were once more a part of the medieval Holy Roman Empire.

Austria in the Middle Ages

In 976, Emperor Otto II (r. 973–983) enfeoffed the Babenberg dynasty with the Austrian lands, which they would rule and expand until they died out in 1246. They gradually moved their center of power eastward, until one member of the house, Heinrich II Jasomirgott (r. 1141–1177), settled upon Vienna as a seat and erected the beginning of what would become the Imperial Palace or *Hofburg*. Heinrich also received from Emperor Frederick I Barbarossa (r. 1151–1190) the *Privilegium minus*, in 1156. This charter granted the Babenbergs the title of duke in the area now covered by Lower Austria; it also largely freed its rulers from imperial jurisdiction and other feudal obligations. Heinrich's successor, Leopold V (r. 1177–1194), acquired the duchy of Styria in 1192.

The Austrian lands generally prospered under Babenberg rule. Gold, silver, and salt mines were opened and exploited, and major religious orders, chief among them the Benedictines and Cistercians, settled throughout the Austrian lands and played important roles in clearing land and developing regional agriculture. Their monasteries sponsored important intellectual, scholarly, and educational programs as well. The Babenberg courts themselves were significant cultural centers. The famous German verse epic of the Nibelungs in all likelihood received its final form at the hands of an Austrian who was at the court of Leopold VI (r. 1198–1230) and also active in a circle around the bishop of Passau.

The death of the last Babenberg duke, Frederick the Quarrelsome (r. 1230–1246), in battle against the Magyars in 1246 brought unsettled times to the Austrian lands. For a time, Styria fell to King Béla IV of Hungary (r. 1235–1270). King Otakar Premysl II (r. 1253–1278) controlled the duchy of Austria itself, as well as Styria, Carinthia, and Carniola, the latter in modern-day Slovenia.

Habsburg Austria from 1273 to 1490

Otakar of Bohemia's expansionist drive ended violently in 1278. Instrumental in organizing his defeat was the German emperor, Rudolph

I, count of Habsburg (1218–1291), who was elected to his new dignity in 1273. Of Alsatian origins, Rudolph had substantial holdings in southwestern Germany and in Switzerland, but was not a leading figure in the empire by contemporary standards. Nevertheless, he was shrewd and aggressive, qualities that stood him and his family in good stead both in his lifetime and in the centuries to come. As emperor, he asked the king of Bohemia to declare an oath of allegiance in return for the latter's rights in Austria, Styria, Carinthia, and Carniola. Otakar's refusal led to a temporary standoff between the two men. By 1278 they were in open conflict, which ended with Rudolph's victory in the Battle of the Marchfeld; Otakar was not only vanquished but killed. Four years later, Rudolph enfeoffed two of his sons, Albrecht and Rudolph, with the duchy of Austria and Styria. Carinthia and Carniola remained beyond his reach, but by the 14th century these had been incorporated into the Habsburg domains as well, along with land as far south as Istria, at the head of the Adriatic Sea, along with Trieste, now in Italy.

Although from a purely geopolitical standpoint the Habsburgs had assembled a sizeable and strategically crucial territorial complex, they were not always able to fully exploit the advantages that these acquisitions conferred. Following contemporary practice among German princes, after 1379 the rulers of Austria divided their lands among their sons. Although the number of partitions varied with the number of available heirs, they often followed three basic configurations: Lower Austria, which comprised today's Upper and Lower Austria; Inner Austria, made up of Styria, Carinthia, Carniola, the Istrian coast, and Trieste; and Outer and Upper Austria, which took in the Tyrol, acquired in the 14th century, the Vorarlberg, and the Habsburg possessions that remained in the German southwest and in Switzerland.

The fortunes of the Habsburgs waned noticeably throughout the 14th and much of the 15th centuries. The German crown was held by other houses from 1308 until 1438. Switzerland spun out of the Habsburg orbit during this period. Although the dynasty gave lip service to the fiction that its lands were a single entity, the reality was quite otherwise. Patrimonial divisions and redivisions almost always provoked conflicts that sapped the resources of the Austrian provinces. They also opened the way for local noble families to play an important part in the governance and defense of their regions. Nevertheless, the Habsburgs continued to think of themselves in big terms, territorially and otherwise.

In his spurious *Privilegium maius*, Duke Rudolph IV (1339–1365) conferred the title of archduke on male members of his line, giving their house equivalent status to the electors of the Holy Roman Empire. The dynasty tried to arrange for itself a succession in the kingdom of Bohemia through a compact with the ruling house of Luxemburg there. Indeed, the Habsburg German Emperor Albrecht II (1397–1439) was king of both Bohemia and Hungary for the years 1437–1438.

It was not, however, until the latter half of the 15th century that the house of Austria's pan-European ambitions were realized. Archduke Frederick V (1415–1493), who became Emperor Frederick III in 1440, was something of a joke among his contemporaries for his phlegmatic ways and military ineptitude. He emerged the winner in a protracted struggle over division of the Habsburg Austrian patrimony with his brother Archduke Albrecht VI (1418–1463) only by outliving the challenger. Nevertheless, he began the almost unbroken line of Habsburgs that would hold the imperial title until the empire came to an end in 1806. The dignity also gave Frederick marital bargaining power. In 1477 his only son, the future Emperor Maximilian I (1459–1519), wed Duchess Mary of Burgundy (1457–1482), the lone direct claimant to the rich complex of lands in the Netherlands held by a cadet line of the French ruling house of Valois.

The Burgundian marriage produced offspring who married into the Spanish royal house. With these two unions, the Habsburgs became European, rather than Austrian, princes. Though both the Iberian and central European lines of the house continued to call themselves the house of Austria, their responsibilities and interests extended far beyond their central European homeland. Maximilian I continued to be very mindful of Austria. The Tyrolean capital of Innsbruck was his favorite residence, and he endowed it with some of its most notable landmarks and monuments. But he was intensely preoccupied with the Netherlands, where the kings of France challenged his rule, and with German imperial affairs. The latter ran the gamut from territorial wars to restructuring the constitution in ways that would strengthen the hand of the emperor. Persist though he did, Maximilian was only partially successful.

Similar efforts in Austria met the same fate. To free himself from having to appear personally in his individual lands to do business with the local estates, Maximilian made a start on creating administrative bodies to act in his name. Such offices were deeply resented by the estates, who insisted on personal contact with their ruler. This was especially the case when Maximilian was requesting taxes for special purposes such as military campaigns. The estates of the Tyrol wrested an agreement from him that very carefully specified the conditions under which they would contribute to his armies.

Maximilian created other social and economic difficulties for himself and for his successors in the Tyrol. The province was well known for its productive silver mines, especially in Hall and Schwaz. These were considered the property of the territorial ruler, and the incomes were therefore sequestered for his treasuries. However, to raise quick cash, Maximilian was forced to mortgage these revenues to the German merchant house of Fugger, an arrangement that eventually sparked armed uprisings by a resentful local population.

Thus, from the outset, Habsburg greatness and Austrian interests, defined by the Austrians themselves, were not altogether coextensive. The Austrian lands were not among Europe's most prosperous; the decades of intermittent warfare between Albrecht VI and Frederick III had taken a severe toll on the economy. And although Maximilian was the first of his line since 1379 to control the entirety of the Habsburg patrimony, the fiscal demands that he placed upon it strained available resources badly. What he asked of his Austrian patrimony, however, was modest compared to what was to come. More distressing yet, there would be every reason for the Austrian lands to pay.

The Ottoman Empire in Central Europe

Maximilian left the Habsburg holdings in Austria to his two grandsons, Archdukes Charles (1500–1558) and Charles's younger brother, Ferdinand (1503–1564). Neither had grown up in central Europe — Charles had spent his youth in the Netherlands, and Ferdinand had been raised in Spain. Following the wishes of their grandfather, they negotiated a division that, in a short time, left the Austrian lands under Ferdinand's control. Both men would be German emperors, Charles as Charles V from 1519 to 1556 and Ferdinand from then until his death. Charles, however, as king of Spain, grew increasingly preoccupied with Spanish affairs. Ferdinand became the manager of his family's interests in central Europe.

Ferdinand faced three serious problems when he arrived to govern Austria in 1521. One was the outright sedition in several provincial estates that Maximilian I's administrative arrangements had prompted. These the young archduke put down; in Vienna, he executed several leading dissidents, including the mayor of the city, Martin Siebenbürger (1475?), in 1522. The government of the city was put under the tight supervision of the territorial ruler, a power that the Habsburgs would retain over their capital until well into the 19th century.

The remaining two issues proved far more intractable, in part because they were interrelated. Perhaps the most urgent was a military challenge that had hung over eastern Europe for some time—the gradual conquest of the entire Danube Valley from southeast to northwest by the Ottoman Empire. The first European military victories of the Turks, as contemporaries called them, had come in the latter decades of the 14th century. Although they had suffered setbacks since then, often through the efforts of the armies of Hungary, the sultans had always resumed their expansionary policies. In 1526, the king of Hungary, Louis II (r. 1516–1526), was killed in the southwest of his realm at Mohács as he fled from a powerful Turkish offensive. Louis was also king of Bohemia, so two thrones were now vacant. Married to Louis's sister, Princess Anna, Ferdinand of Habsburg claimed both crowns for himself. These he soon got, though by election, the traditional practice in the two kingdoms, and not by inheritance as he wished. Nor did he ever control all of Hungary, part of which was held by the Ottoman Empire. A third region, the principality of Transylvania, preserved some semblance of autonomy although becoming a vassal principality of the sultan in Constantinople.

Ferdinand scrambled mightily to defend his new Austrian lands from the Turks, along with Bohemia and what he controlled of Hungary. The danger was genuine. Sultan Suleyman the Magnificent besieged Vienna in 1529 and threatened to repeat the performance several times during his career. Much of Ferdinand's time was taken up with raising money for armies, which he always hoped would drive the Turks from Hungary, but they never retreated in his lifetime. He begged virtually all of Europe for support, but mostly his Austrian lands—which, though they begrudged him every coin, had little choice other than to meet his requests.

Although the Ottomans did not conquer the Austrian provinces, they nibbled away at them with intermittent skirmishing. Carinthia and Styria were especially vulnerable. The Turkish Wars, as contemporaries called them, had other effects on Austria as well. Vienna, a prosperous trading center in the Middle Ages, became far less vital economically as businesses sought more secure environments. The city's most prominent architectural feature became its fortifications, which were enlarged considerably during the 16th and 17th centuries. Ferdinand's fiscal policies made themselves felt in rural Austria, too. By the end of the 16th century, a major peasant uprising broke out in what today is Upper Austria. The ire of rural labor was directed against oppressive landlords, who recovered from their tenants and agricultural workers the costs of increased taxation imposed by their territorial princes.

The Ottoman Empire remained a central worry for the Habsburgs and for Austria until the end of the 17th century. In 1683, the sultan and his advisers decided to mount another assault on central Europe, which once again reached the walls of Vienna. Emperor Leopold I (1640–1705) fled the city, leaving its defenses in the hands of a local militia aided by a pan-European army, which successfully resisted the Ottoman forces and began the process of driving them from the Habsburg lands altogether. This task, largely centered in Hungary, was virtually completed by 1699. The Habsburg armies then moved into southeastern Europe, where they added some pieces of the Ottoman realm to their own, but eventually had to evacuate Belgrade. There would be future confrontations with the sultans' forces, but not in the Austrian lands themselves.

Reformation, Counter-Reformation, and Catholic Reformation

The Ottoman threat vexed Ferdinand I's career in another way. His arrival in Austria coincided with the gathering together of a major religious upheaval. In 1517, an Augustinian monk named Martin Luther had challenged papal control of Christian doctrine. A new confession, identified with Luther and eventually given his name, spread rapidly in Austria. By the end of the 16th century, most of its provinces, with the exception of the Tyrol, were heavily Lutheran. Ferdinand himself was a devout Catholic, but he also acknowledged his church's serious flaws. He worked tirelessly to rectify these and was one of the chief supporters of reform of Catholic education and moral standards among the clergy.

Nevertheless, Ferdinand's financial dependence on the estates of the Austrian lands helped to alter the confessional makeup of his domains. He was willing to compromise with the Protestant nobility in these bodies to get the funding for his military enterprises against the Ottomans. In this way, the Muslim Turks made it easier for Protestantism to establish a foothold in Austria and to strengthen the influence of regional governments and administrations at the expense of Habsburg rule.

The Protestant ascendancy in the Austrian lands proved, however, to be short-lived. At his death, Ferdinand divided his lands among his three sons. Even the most broad-minded among them, Emperor Maximilian II (1527–1576), although not wholly unsympathetic to Luther and his followers, was deeply disturbed about ruling subjects of differing religions. His brothers, Archduke Ferdinand (1529–1595), who received Upper Austria, which included the Tyrol, and Archduke Charles (1540–1590), who was given Inner Austria with Graz as its seat, were vigorous Catholic partisans. Protestantism never did take very deep root in the Tyrol, so Archduke Ferdinand was not faced with the challenge of recatholicizing large numbers of his subjects. The Styria and Carinthia of Archduke Charles were quite another matter. With the enthusiastic support of his Bavarian wife, Archduchess Maria (1551–1608), Charles began reversing the concessions that his Lutheran subjects had received. His work was continued by his son, Emperor Ferdinand II (1578–1637), who was strongly under the influence of his mother.

It was Ferdinand II who served as the political spearhead of the Counter-Reformation in central Europe, which ended with Catholicism being preeminent throughout all of the Habsburg lands. Becoming German emperor in 1619, he encountered rebellion in the kingdom of Bohemia, which refused to accept him as its ruler and chose instead the German Elector Palatine Frederick V. Ferdinand's decision to militarize the dispute set off the Thirty Years' War, which, when it closed in 1648, had engulfed much of Europe. Ferdinand himself did not live to see the conflict through to its conclusion. He had, however, realized two of its main objectives—the restoration of himself to the throne in Bohemia and the return of most people in his lands to the church of Rome. However, neither he nor his successors were able to recapture Protestant Germany for their faith.

Thus, by the end of the 17th century the Habsburgs had realized decade-long objectives in all of their holdings. They had pushed back the Ottoman forces to their Balkan confines and unified their realms confessionally. From the last third of the 17th century to 1740, the Habsburg Empire experienced an outpouring of cultural and religious activity that would stamp it until the very end of its existence in 1918. Monies long given over to costly defense measures went into the monumental secular and ecclesiastical construction projects of the Baroque era. From the expansion of the Vienna *Hofburg* during the residency of Emperor Leopold I to the triumphant spread of the monastery of Melk along the Danube in Lower Austria, the victory of Christendom over the Muslim challenge was visually proclaimed.

Within the Austrian lands themselves, the suppression of Protestantism also reduced the influence of regional estates, whose nobles had once spearheaded the advance of the new faith. The Bohemian estates had lost many of their powers and privileges as well, though they had retained residual rights to negotiate financial arrangements with their Habsburg rulers. The house of Austria had been least successful politically in Hungary, where the nobility had held tenaciously to many features of their medieval constitution, including the right of armed resistance to any ruler who violated their privileges. Nevertheless, by the beginning of the 18th century, even the Hungarians had recognized hereditary Habsburg rule in their kingdom.

In no case had the house of Austria ever intended to wipe out the traditional political and social customs of their lands. What the Habsburgs wanted were estates that were more cooperative. Indeed, nobility throughout the Habsburg lands retained significant administrative rights. These included judicial authority over a helpless peasantry, which was still largely bound to the land. Modern scholars call this combination of princely and local authority "functional dualism." Like the architecture of the Baroque, it continued to shape the Austrian experience well into the modern era.

From Reform to Revolution

Even as the Habsburg dynasty triumphed over enemies both domestic and foreign, new and demanding problems confronted it. During the 18th century there was barely a year or so during which all of Europe was at peace. Several of those conflicts were of crucial importance to the house of Austria, including the War of the Spanish Succession, which ended in 1713. The death of the last male Habsburg of the Spanish line, the sickly Charles II (1661–1700), opened the way for his central European cousins to claim the Iberian kingdom for themselves. Though this bid fell short—the Spanish throne fell to a Bourbon, Philip V—it did bring Austria new holdings in northern Italy. The one-time Spanish Netherlands became the Austrian Netherlands as well.

Worried that he would not be able to father a male heir, Emperor Charles VI (1685–1740) set about ensuring that the estates of his various lands as well as foreign powers would allow the Habsburg patrimony to pass intact to his eldest daughter, Archduchess Maria Theresa (1717–1780). The matter, at least in his mind, dwarfed all other affairs of state. Concerned that his empire was not enjoying the financial rewards of overseas expansion that had increased prosperity in other European kingdoms, Charles chartered trading companies to undertake similar enterprises. But his concerns over the fate of his successor dampened his interest in the venture quickly, especially when potential allies in his territorial plans discouraged it. Charles's Ostend Company in the Austrian Netherlands prospered, but as a private firm, not as a state undertaking.

When Maria Theresa did indeed succeed her father in 1740, she needed all the extra financial help she could get. The ambitious king of Prussia, Frederick II (1712–1786), launched an attack on Silesia, one of the Bohemian crown lands, that same year. With a lively manufacturing and commercial culture based on the production of linen, the area was highly desirable for economic reasons. At first hoping to regain Silesia, Maria Theresa and her advisors undertook a series of administrative and political reforms in the Habsburg lands that they hoped would move them toward this goal.

Although Maria Theresa never regained more than a very small piece of what she had lost—an issue finally settled at the end of the Seven Years' War in 1763—the changes that the Theresan reforms brought to the entirety of the Habsburg Empire significantly rearranged its political and economic structure. The Habsburg army was given a far more stable financial basis when estates, for whom the idea of Prussian expansion was an altogether repellent prospect, agreed to fund military budgets for as much as 10 years at a time. Furthermore, these monies went directly to a treasury in Vienna, not to regional depositories, then to be forwarded to the capital.

But administrative reforms were only part of a larger program to modernize the Habsburg domains while at the same time retaining the dynasty's control over them. The empress and her councilors were eager to make all of their lands more economically productive and were willing to protect their industries to make them competitive. For the first time in its history, the Habsburg Empire became a customs union. The lone exception was Hungary, which Maria Theresa wanted to punish for not paying what she thought was a fair share of its military taxes. Though Hungarians took exception to this way of acknowledging their distinctiveness, this arrangement had its benefits in the other Habsburg holdings. Lower Austrian vintners, for example, were sheltered from their competitors to the east. Factories, especially in Bohemia, but also in the eastern Austrian lands, were also encouraged. Partly out of conscience, partly hoping to improve productivity, the empress also took some cautious steps toward lightening the legal burdens of serfs. Devout Catholic though she was, Maria Theresa was also persuaded that education had to meet the needs of the state. Although primary instruction was still left largely in the hands of the Catholic clergy, she abolished their direct control over university curricula. The University of Vienna developed into a center of medical study by the end of the century.

Maria Theresa's reforms sprang from her genetically pragmatic intellect and character; they focused single-mindedly on ways to keep her dynasty's empire intact. Her son and successor, Emperor Joseph II (1741–1790), was a reformer too and certainly concerned with the fortunes of his house. His measures, however, were often the inspiration of reason coupled with raw willfulness, rather than political common sense. They touched on every aspect of life in the Habsburg domains, some of which were changed forever. Persuaded that only firm state direction would make his lands more productive, Joseph sought to put them under the close supervision of his government at the expense of traditional authorities. A particular target was the church. In 1781, he lifted most restrictions on worship for the major Protestant denominations as well as for the Greek Orthodox Church. Jews were also free to live throughout the city and to engage in more occupations. Although Joseph believed that active parish programs were essential to the moral well-being of his people, he harbored no such thoughts about cloistered orders. He regarded their members as economic parasites and shut down large numbers of monasteries and nunneries in 1782. Their often otherworldly residents were to find employment in education or hospitals. The assets of erstwhile clerical properties were to be devoted to founding new dioceses and supporting new pastors. Even theological education was to be turned over to a state seminary. In 1781, Joseph abolished serfdom throughout the empire. Eight years later, he imposed a new land tax throughout the empire, which both landlord and peasant resisted strenuously.

When Joseph died, an exhausted and bitter man, his lands were in serious disarray. Hungary was in outright rebellion. It fell to his younger brother, Emperor Leopold II (1747–1792), to preserve the most useful and viable of his brother's measures, through a series of wily compromises. Serfdom was never formally reinstituted, though the status of servility itself was allowed to continue through landlord–peasant contracts. Leopold's most serious concessions were probably in Hungary, where Joseph had eradicated traditional administrative counties and even tried to introduce German as an administrative language.

Leopold was faced with possible war abroad, and he had to bring domestic peace to his lands. He had no alternative other than to scale back his elder brother's program. Nevertheless, it would be difficult to overestimate the significance of Joseph's reign both for Austria and for the Habsburg lands as a whole. At the very least, his generous support of industry through tariffs had set the stage for the beginning of the Industrial Revolution in Bohemia and Lower Austria. In general, Joseph's policies set the tone for future agendas of reform, though none of these would ever be as comprehensive as he envisioned. He brought a spirit of thoroughgoing secularism to Austrian affairs, still known as Josephinism. Perhaps most important of all, Joseph was the true founder of the modern Habsburg bureaucracy, an institution whose procedures and values have influenced the culture of republican Austria profoundly.

The Revolutionary Era, 1789–1848

Like every other state in Europe, the Habsburg Empire was affected heavily by the French Revolution and the Napoleonic Wars that followed. The French replaced the monarchy with the revolutionary nation as the sovereign element of their new political system. Although this notion led to seismic upheavals in all aspects of French life, it did not necessarily threaten the territorial integrity of France itself. Should this idea spread to the individual Habsburg lands, the very structure of the empire would collapse. Napoleon I (1769–1821) and his armies brought the ideals of the French Revolution to much of central Europe. Their flag read "Liberty, Equality, Fraternity," with the last term justifying their conquests. Concern for their brothers in humanity allegedly moved the French to spread the new politics of the revolution elsewhere.

The Habsburg Empire fought in coalition and alone against Napoleon. Although it was occasionally successful, these episodes were few and far between. The French emperor occupied Vienna briefly in 1809 and married one of the daughters of Francis I (1768–1835). With the collapse of the venerable Holy Roman Empire and the title that went with it, the emperor now officially ruled only the house of Austria's holdings, to be known until 1867 as the Austrian Empire. Napoleon's decline began with his ill-conceived invasion of Russia in 1812; by 1814, he had been decisively checked by an alliance of European powers, the Habsburg Empire among them. That same year, a great diplomatic conclave gathered in Vienna to reset the political boundaries of Europe, which Napoleon had often reworked to suit his administrative and strategic convenience.

The guiding hand at the Congress of Vienna was Francis I's foreign minister and eventual chancellor, Prince Klemens von Metternich (1773–1859). Though not opposed to the study of national cultures and languages, he was deeply hostile to political nationalism and did what he could to discourage it, both during the Congress of Vienna and afterward. His particular worries were movements supporting the unification of Germany and Italy. The first he feared because it might command the loyalty of the German-speaking Austrian lands. Italy was dangerous because its nationalists would take the Habsburg Italian lands out of the empire altogether to join a new state. Should such dismemberment of the Habsburg Empire begin, it would be very difficult to stop.

To counter these possibilities as well as the general challenge to monarchy of political liberalism, Francis I and Metternich put in place a system of censorship and close policing of their population that smothered some sides of intellectual life throughout the empire. Higher education was especially affected. Within the Austrian lands themselves, a number of important writers—the playwrights Franz Grillparzer (1791–1872), Ferdinand Raimund (1790–1836), and Johann Nestroy (1801–1862) have achieved classic status in the Austrian literary canon—made their accommodations with the system. Indeed, they produced brilliant work in doing so. But the overall legacy of the Metternich era in Austria was to validate quiet private pleasure as an end in itself. The domestic coziness of the Biedermeier style, which flourished during this time, underscored decoratively a larger attitudinal norm.

From an economic standpoint, the Metternich era was far more dynamic. The Napoleonic Wars played havoc with the Habsburg Empire's finances. By the end of the conflict, its currency had inflated ludicrously. Metternich realized that if the monarchy were to survive at all, this situation would have to be remedied. Excess money was blotted up through bonds. A national bank supervised by representatives both of the government and the public had the sole right to issue new tender and to extend credit to the state.

Metternich also supported entrepreneurial activity as a way of growing the Habsburg Empire's economy. In 1836, Austria's first steam railway opened for traffic between Vienna and Polish Galicia, which had become part of the empire at the end of the 18th century. Lower Austria and Bohemia grew as centers for textile manufacturing. However, the industrial development of these two areas far outstripped others throughout the empire, an imbalance that would never be rectified.

However modest these developments were compared to England, for example, they did enrich a growing bourgeoisie, especially in the eastern Austrian lands, in Bohemia, and in Moravia, one of the kingdom's associated crown lands. Vienna itself prospered, and its population, as well as that in neighboring areas, grew. New wealth also encouraged a measure of public self-confidence in the middle class as well as among more humble folk. This was particularly important because the relationship between economic self-interest and political change became increasingly clear in the minds of many. In rural areas as well, particularly in the Austrian lands, the vestiges of serfdom seemed more onerous. Private ownership of land became more attractive to peasants; some wanted to be free of their situation altogether and simply leave for new opportunities elsewhere.

For their part, entrepreneurs believed that greater economic productivity from the land would enable them to feed their new labor force more cheaply. Government protection of such archaic institutions as artisan guilds through limitations on trade and commerce was another general complaint. Taxation, though it had done much to relieve the post-Napoleonic financial crisis, remained oppressively high. The factory laborers in the city and on its outskirts were decidedly marginal to the potential alliance of industrial capital and agriculture. Nevertheless, they were developing some sense of economic injustice, epitomized by the squalid housing conditions that would be their lot for the entirety of the century.

Restlessness in Vienna had its parallel throughout other regions of the Habsburg Empire. Taxation was resented by everyone, including people who had every reason to support the monarchy on social grounds alone. The nobility in the Bohemian estates were a notable case. Czech intellectuals, personified by the historian Francis Palacký (1798–1876), began to argue for the primacy of their national culture in educational and artistic life. However, it was in Hungary, where Count Stephen Széchenyi (1791–1860) had promoted a reform movement centered on improving education, transportation, and industry in the kingdom, that dissatisfaction with Habsburg absolutism was most complex.

A revolution in Vienna, which exploded on 3 March 1848, was quickly followed by similar outbursts throughout the Habsburg monarchy, particularly in Prague, Budapest, and northern Italy. By the end of the year, the dynasty's army had put an end to all of these upheavals, except in Hungary, which in 1849 declared itself to be independent. The Habsburgs quenched this movement, but only with the aid of Russia in 1849.

From Neoabsolutism to the Ausgleich of 1867

Viewed politically, the Revolutions of 1848 temporarily gave absolutism a new lease on life. A new, young, and altogether inexperienced emperor, Franz Joseph (1830–1916) wanted above all to preserve his empire and the place of his house in it. He was therefore willing to take the quickest and most authoritarian steps required to meet these goals. Advised by the sympathetic Prince Felix of Schwarzenberg (1800–1852), he turned his back on any form of serious popular and national input into Habsburg government. The administration of the empire was tightly centralized in Vienna. This policy included Hungary, which lost its historic counties once again. Transylvania and Croatia, both part of the Hungarian crown, were cut from the kingdom and governed directly from the Habsburg Austrian capital.

Nevertheless, the Revolutions of 1848 had some positive outcomes as well, particularly for the commercial middle classes. Equality before the law was recognized in the New Year's Patent of 1851. Densely bureaucratized though the post-1848 Habsburg government was, it was largely honest, efficient, and predictable—all preconditions of a positive economic climate. The police force grew, a constraint on political activity, to be sure, but an aid to personal security. Serfdom was finally abolished, thus creating a far freer labor market. Guilds and their restrictions came to an end as well, a positive step for industrial entrepreneurs, though a distressing one for small artisans, particularly in large urban centers such as Vienna. Their competitive disadvantages in the face of industrial-scale production would become a thorny social problem in the Habsburg lands and for the modern countries they became. Municipal franchises were considerably broadened, opening the way for wider middle-class participation in the management of local affairs.

Perhaps the most important of the middle-class-oriented changes to take place during the era of neoabsolutism, as it is called, were in the educational system at all levels of society. Although Franz Joseph and his advisors were unsympathetic to democracy in any form, he had begun his reign by proclaiming that the languages and cultures of his peoples were all equal. The Roman Catholic Church continued to exercise heavy control over primary education, but instruction itself was now conducted in the language spoken by the majority of people in each district. Both in secondary schools and at the universities, new standards for curriculum and scholarship brought these institutions up to international norms, most notably those found in Germany, which set the pace for Europe until World War I.

Franz Joseph and his government hoped that these measures and many others would created a stronger Habsburg Empire, immune to the onslaughts of nationalism and liberalism, which temporarily derailed the dynasty's government in 1848. They were sadly disappointed. Scholars studying the Habsburg Empire today question the centrality of national issues to the collapse of the Habsburg monarchy in 1918. They have not, however, discounted them altogether, and neither did the emperor and his councilors. The unification of Italy and Germany proceeded apace, with Franz Joseph's armies suffering bad defeats. The new kingdom of Italy received the bulk of the Habsburg holdings in Lombardy in the Treaty of Villafranca (1862). Only the South Tyrol and parts of Venetia remained in Austrian hands. The unification of Germany, masterminded by the Prussian minister-president Otto von Bismarck, brought with it a humiliating loss to the kingdom's armies in the Seven Weeks' War of 1866. Worse yet, there was now an avowedly German national state, which from an ethnic standpoint was far closer to Franz Joseph's German-speaking subjects than were the Slavs, Magyars, Romanians, and other non-German peoples who were also his subjects.

Both military setbacks and the political consequences that accompanied them forced Franz Joseph and his government to rethink their style of governing. A variety of constitutional experiments took place. One, the October Diploma of 1860, never went into effect. Its concessions to pressures for decentralization angered liberals, Austrian Germans prominent among them, who called the arrangement a sellout to conservative arrangements of the pre-1848 era. The second, the February Patent of 1861, actually did create an operative government. A central Imperial Assembly, or Reichsrat, in Vienna could initiate legislation and pass on the crown's budget proposals. Its 300 members were chosen by subsidiary deliberative bodies throughout the empire, so that monied and propertied classes continued to have a great deal of political influence. The emperor, who retained control over the army and foreign affairs, could dismiss and call this body at will.

This constitution had many problematic features, chief among them Hungarian resistance to a central legislature that political leaders in the kingdom boycotted. As war with Prussia loomed in the 1860s, there was even some hint that Hungary would support Bismarck and the Hohenzollerns against Franz Joseph. This possibility led the Habsburgs to open negotiations with Hungarian political leaders, most notably Francis Deák (1803–1876), to find some way of accommodating the aspirations of the Magyars to the interests of the house of Habsburg. The result was the Compromise of 1867 (*Ausgleich*), which would remain technically in effect until the last days of the World War I.

The provisions of the Ausgleich were few and simple. What would come to be known as Austria (on paper it was called Cis-Leithenia, or the lands to the west of the Leitha river that separated Austria and Hungary) and the kingdom of Hungary were to have a common army, a common foreign policy, and a common ruler, though he would carry different titles in each of his realms. In Hungary, he would be called only by the royal title of king. In the Austrian half, he would be emperor, or in German kaiser. This led to the "k.k." or "k.u.k." found on official buildings throughout the empire even today. Every 10 years a joint financial commission came together from both halves of Austria–Hungary, as it was rather quickly called. They hammered out such thorny questions as tariff rates and the financing of the common offices.

Beyond these areas, the kingdom of Hungary, which also encompassed Transylvania and Croatia, operated quite autonomously in its domestic affairs. The same privilege was accorded to the Austrian side. Each half had its own constitution, which varied strikingly in important respects. Though both provided for parliamentary government of a sort, the methods by which these bodies were elected came to be very different. Initially, the franchise in both Austria and Hungary was very restrictive, but Austria moved far more quickly toward electoral democracy. By 1907, males over the age of 24 had the right to vote, with minor residential exclusions. The Hungarian constitution had many liberal features. It assured the more important ethnic groups in the kingdom, the Romanians and Croatians, some place in the parliament, which met in Budapest. Nevertheless, the number of these representatives was fixed. Moreover, the Hungarians were very careful to confine voting rights to the landowning classes and urban bourgeoisie, who often shared aristocratic values.

From 1867 to 1918

The Compromise of 1867 left Franz Joseph with the two powers he jealously guarded: control over the army and foreign affairs. He could also name ministers—who were, however, constitutionally responsible to their individual parliaments in Vienna and Budapest. Nevertheless, he could confer with them at his own choosing and develop policy absent parliamentary input. If the Reichsrat in the Austrian half of the monarchy could not function, he had the right to rule by decree.

Thus the emperor had some reason to keep the Compromise of 1867 in operation. So did the Hungarians, who achieved the preeminent status in their half of the Dual Monarchy that the Germans, by virtue of their economic power, had in Austria. Deprived of anything resembling equivalent political status in either part of the Habsburg Empire, the Slavs resented these arrangements enormously. The Czechs were especially vocal in their protests and were bitterly disappointed when the emperor gave up any attempts to give them some kind of exceptional status as well. The Reichsrat was the scene of many angry clashes between Czech and German representatives over such matters as official administrative languages, often bringing business to a halt.

Despite these difficulties, however, the period between 1867 and the outbreak of World War I was an enormously productive one for most of the Habsburg lands, particularly those in the west. A spectacular economic boom took place between 1867 and 1873 within the Austrian half of the monarchy. This ended in a dramatic stock market crash in 1873, but not before the financial and cultural landscape of the area, particularly around Vienna, had been transformed. Middle-class prosperity produced ambitious residential construction, often modeled on the aristocratic palaces that were still a prominent feature of the city. The financial collapse that followed dampened some of these activities, but by the end of the 1870s they had resumed, albeit at a more modest pace. Similar changes took place in Prague, as it turned into a major banking and industrial center, and in Budapest, where important grain-processing facilities sprang up. By the beginning of the 20th century, all three cities had well-to-do middle classes with sufficient discretionary income not only to afford grand living quarters but to patronize the remarkable flowering of musical, literary, and artistic life that historians have since associated with the period.

These economic currents, both positive and negative, changed not only the lives of the monied class but also those of people of more modest means. As Vienna, Prague, and lesser cities grew, they attracted large numbers of industrial workers. Often housed in the most crowded and unsanitary circumstances imaginable, they became the targets of political movements that addressed their needs directly—or at least professed to do so. One was the Marxist Sozialdemokratische Arbeiter Partei (Social Democratic Workers'Party), free to operate as a political party according to the new Austrian constitution. Under the leadership of Viktor Adler (1852–1918) and Karl Renner (1870–1950), it put together a platform that stressed the improvement of workers' lives by education as well as through redistribution of wealth through the nationalization of private property. Social Democratic campaigning was instrumental in bringing about the electoral reform of 1907 in the Austrian half of the Habsburg state.

Another party that also spoke to those in unpretentious circumstances was the Christlichsoziale Partei (Christian Social Party). The product of Catholic concern over the growth of atheistic Marxism in the working classes, the Christian Social movement promised to better the lives of the urban masses through vast public works programs, which would bring electricity and water into households that could not afford such conveniences individually. Cheap and efficient public transportation was another major priority. This party, closely associated in the late 19th century with the name of Vienna's wildly popular mayor, Karl Lueger (1844–1910), did capture some support from the industrial laborers of the capital. Its core electorate, however, was the lower middle class, in whose ranks were the petty shopkeepers and artisans who had lost their economic protection after 1848. They resented big capital and industry enormously, which they often associated with Jews. Anti-Semitism became an axiom of their rhetoric. The German Austrian peasantry too, many of whom were hard put to farm small plots of land profitably, came to nurture similar grievances and to attribute them to the same sources. By the beginning of the 20th century, rural Austria was shifting its political loyalties to the Christian Social Party.

All of these problems were present to one degree or another throughout 19th-century Europe. Indeed, from economic, cultural, and even political standpoints, the Habsburg Empire seemed to be accommodating itself reasonably well to the rampant liberal values of the age. However, Austria–Hungary had serious difficulties that were all its own. The issue of nationalism continued to fester, and although no one was arguing for the empire's dissolution, many believed that it could happen. The men who governed Austria–Hungary were particularly concerned. The wars over the unification of Germany and Italy had underscored the possibility that foreign countries that claimed to be the true national homes of Franz Joseph's subjects could pick the Habsburg Empire clean of its peoples.

As it turned out, neither Germany nor Italy played that role, at least immediately. The government in Rome decided that more conciliatory behavior toward Franz Joseph and his ministers was to its advantage, so although there was noisy popular discussion of folding the remains of Habsburg Italy into the new national kingdom, nothing came of it. For his part, Otto von Bismarck, now the chancellor of the new German Empire ruled from Berlin, had never intended to wipe the Habsburg state from the map. Worried about his exposed eastern borders with Russia, Bismarck did not exploit pan-German sentiment in the Austrian lands, which was urging closer political, cultural, and economic ties to the new Germany. Rather, he worked to bring Austria–Hungary into an alliance system that would lighten his defensive burdens in the east. The result was the Dual Alliance (1879) between Germany and Austria–Hungary, in which each state pledged mutual military support should one or the other be attacked on its eastern frontiers by Russia.

But it was a Russian client state, and not Russia itself, that both Vienna and Budapest thought far more threatening to the integrity of the Habsburg monarchy at the beginning of the 20th century. This was Serbia, which had gradually freed itself from Ottoman overlordship throughout the 19th century and was eager to expand in the Balkans. Orthodox Christians like the Russians, the Serbs had sympathetic, though inconsistent, support in St. Petersburg. But were Serbia to serve as the national homeland for all Serbs, as many of their politicians were urging, the kingdom would have to include ethnic Serbs, erstwhile refugees from Turkish rule, who had lived in southern Hungary for several centuries. And if Serbia were to spearhead the unification of all south Slavic peoples, as some were also proposing, this would remove Croatia from Hungary and the Slovenes from the Austrian half of the Habsburg state. The prospect became something of an obsession with the government in Vienna. In 1908 Austria–Hungary, following the provisions of an international treaty it had signed in Berlin in 1878 and subsequent agreements, annexed Bosnia–Herzegovina to protect access to its naval installations on the Adriatic. The Serbs were furious and relations with the Habsburg regimes both in Budapest and Vienna became more tense than ever.

This explosive mixture of frustration and fear set off the chain of events that led to World War I. Between 1908 and 1914, the Serbian government encouraged hypernationalist feelings among its own peoples and in the Serb diaspora throughout the Balkans. The Habsburg regime took all of this very seriously and began to talk of war not only as a theoretical possibility, but even as a desirable way of keeping Serbia a minor Balkan kingdom forever. One of the strongest voices in Vienna against such a strike was the heir apparent to the empire, Archduke Franz Ferdinand (1863–1914). The nephew of Franz Joseph, the archduke was no pacifist. He feared, however, that the Habsburg Empire would never survive any generalized conflict should the war spill beyond the Balkans, as official military planning projected. He was also associated with a scheme called Trialism, which would give the Habsburg South Slavs some political identity of their own under the government of his dynasty. It was an idea that was on a direct collision course with Serbian national visions. Indeed, it made Franz Ferdinand a specific target for radical nationalist groups, one of which plotted to assassinate him on a visit to the Bosnian capital of Sarajevo. The archduke and his wife were shot to death on 28 June 1914. A direct link between the Serbian government and the conspiracy, however, has never been established.

Franz Ferdinand was no favorite in the circle around the emperor; Franz Joseph had no great love for his nephew, either. Nevertheless, the Habsburg government believed that a military strike against Serbia was in order and worked a month to concoct a pretext for initiating it. The attack on Serbia came at the end of July; the complicated alliance structures that tied all of the major European powers together were activated when Russia mobilized in Serbia's aid. By August 1, Europe was at war.

Austria–Hungary was put under emergency rule from the very beginning, a policy that turned the empire into a military dictatorship. However, some aspects of this condition were already familiar. The Reichsrat, for example, had been prorogued since March 1914 because it could not do business. Some political leaders opposed this illiberalism mightily and would be jailed for their pains. Many were surprised, however, at the loyalty with which most of the empire's national groups responded to Franz Joseph's call for their services. The Czechs were the only exception, but even among them, only a small minority deserted.

But the conflict went badly for the Habsburg armies; the Germans rescued them, in Serbia and on the eastern front generally. The suggestion that Austria–Hungary was becoming a direct client of Berlin alarmed the monarchy's Slavs, and mounting casualty lists and economic deprivation distressed everyone. On 21 October 1916, Friedrich Adler (1870–1960), a young socialist who wished to see parliamentary government restored in Austria, assassinated Count Karl

Stürgkh (1859–1916), the emperor's minister-president. The latter had steadfastly refused to reconvene the Reichsrat, the lower house of the Austrian parliament, for fear that it would only be a showcase for ethnic conflict. Franz Joseph died the following month.

The new emperor, Charles I (King Charles IV of Hungary) (1887–1922), was eager both to extricate Austria–Hungary from the conflict and to win the confidence of his populations. He succeeded at neither. Hoping to make a peace something along the lines suggested in the Fourteen Points offered in January 1918 by Woodrow Wilson, the president of the United States, Charles issued a manifesto the following October 1918 that would have reconfigured Austria–Hungary as a federation of nations. No one was particularly interested. Even before the war ended, Hungary had detached itself from the Austrian half of the monarchy, and the various Slavic peoples of the monarchy were declaring themselves independent. On 11 November1918, Charles agreed to withdraw from the business of state altogether, though he did not obligate his family to follow his lead. It was left to the First Austrian Republic in 1919 to formally exclude the house of Habsburg–Lorraine from any position in an Austrian state. Charles made two failed attempts in 1921 to regain a crown, but in Hungary, which constitutionally was still a kingdom.

The First Austrian Republic, 1918–1938

The Austrian First Republic was declared to be in existence on 12 November 1918. A provisional National Assembly (Nationalrat), in which the Social Democratic Party played a prominent role, had been working on a constitution since the end of October. On 1 November, a Socialist Party congress had demanded that the future state should be a republic, and it soon became clear that the movement would use its position in the new state to introduce serious social and economic reforms. On 19 December the eight-hour day was introduced, first into factories; it would later be extended to other kinds of enterprises.

Though a large segment of the Austrian population welcomed such changes, there was little reason to be happy with the republican reality that was suddenly theirs. Food shortages, unemployment, and a nearly worthless currency were immediate problems. In some areas, fighting continued, particularly in Carinthia and Styria, where a new South Slavic state—to become the kingdom of the Serbs, Croats, and Slovenes—hoped to expand even more. The Austrian forces were often no more than local militias. Nevertheless, they were the beginning of the *Heimwehr*, right-wing and generally nationalist paramilitary organizations that would heavily influence the politics of the Austrian republic until they were disbanded in 1936. A socialist equivalent, the Republican Guard, was established in 1923.

Among the most unpleasant tasks that confronted the new government was signing a peace treaty. The losses of former Habsburg lands in Bohemia, Hungary, Poland, and what was to become a south Slavic kingdom were more or less accomplished fact. Indeed, the first official name of the new Austria was German Austria (Deutschösterreich), a term implying that many of the Habsburg Empire's former peoples had no cultural home there. After hard bargaining, the Allies accepted Austria's claims to the Burgenland, once a part of the kingdom of Hungary. But the Treaty of St. Germain, signed by the Austrian delegation on 10 September 1919, subtracted from Austria other lands that, from an ethnic perspective, it could still plausibly claim. Among them were areas of mixed German–Slavic settlement in Carinthia and Styria and the South Tyrol, which went to Italy. Becoming part of Germany (Anschluss) was also forbidden, a provision that definitively canceled a declaration of the Austrian National Assembly the previous March that the country was "a part of the German Republic." The National Assembly changed Austria's name from "German Austria" to simply "Austria" on 21 October.

The Socialist ascendancy in the Austrian federal government was brief but effective. Disregarding serious unrest throughout the country and precarious finances, party representatives pushed through basic social reforms that changed conditions of work and life for most citizens. By 17 December 1919, the eight-hour day was the law for anyone who could find a job. Full-pay vacations were available for all workers. All Austrians, however, were not Socialists. The center of the latter's strength was in Vienna itself, which, with its population of a little over two million, was rich in votes—but not rich enough to offset decisively the rest of the country, where Christian Social, agrarian, regional, and national movements were also beginning to take hold. Elections to the National Assembly on 17 October 1921 returned no party with a clear majority, but gave the Christian Socials a plurality. It was a pattern that would haunt Austrian political life throughout the existence of the

First Republic. The Socialists would continue their extensive agenda of social and educational reform, but mostly in Vienna, where their municipal housing projects, their programs for maternal and child care, and their elaborate recreational and other public facilities made them models for urban reformers throughout the world.

Until 1933, Austrian governments were typically fragile coalitions led by the Christian Social Party in frequent conjunction with the nationalist Pan-German (Grossdeutsch) and Agrarian (Landbund) parties. Although they shared some goals, particularly a hostility to Marxism, they often disagreed on others. The most prominent of the chancellors during this period was a clergyman, Ignaz Seipel (1876–1932), whose strong commitment to Catholic belief and values was a bedrock principle among those who followed him. German nationals on the whole were far more secular in outlook, and not as partial to Austrian independence as was Seipel. Although they did not press for complete amalgamation with Germany, they certainly wished to coordinate Austrian political and economic life as closely as possible with their linguistic brethren to the north.

The conservative coalitions that ruled Austria were not eager to dismantle the social programs that their Marxist colleagues had put in place at the end of the war. The common man had always had a prominent place in Christian Social philosophy. Nevertheless, the instability of the currency forced Seipel to seek foreign loans and to introduce fiscal austerity at home. A new monetary unit, the schilling, which had been issued in 1924, held steady, and inflation receded. But all of this came at a price resented by a broad segment of the population. Government employment had to be reduced. A sales tax imposed in 1923 was particularly onerous.

Public disagreement on these matters was not confined to debates in the Austrian parliament. Political parties and factions fought them out on the streets of Vienna, in regional capitals, and in remote villages throughout the country. A large workers' demonstration in July 1927 was brutally suppressed by the Vienna police after the headquarters of the Ministry of Justice was burned down. Clashes continued between branches of the *Heimwehr* and workers of either socialist or communist leanings. A new element on the scene, the Austrian National Socialists, was also becoming a frequent participant.

The worldwide economic crisis of the 1930s affected Austria as badly as any place in Europe. Indeed, it virtually began there, with the collapse of the Creditanstalt Bank in 1931. Unemployment, an intractable problem since the end of the war, grew ever worse. In 1931, the government tried to arrange a customs union with Germany, only to have it rejected by the allies of World War I. In 1932, Engelbert Dollfuss (1892–1934) took over the chancellor's office. A Christian Social politician whose experience was largely in agricultural affairs, he tried to rescue Austria with more financial assistance from abroad, but with little luck. His greatest foreign supporter was the Italian dictator, Benito Mussolini, who was eager to remain Europe's premier fascist and worried that Adolf Hitler, who became German chancellor in 1933, would displace him. Mussolini's asking price would be that Dollfuss would suppress all activity in Austria by the Socialist, Communist, or Nazi parties.

The Austrian chancellor was certainly not unsympathetic to these ideas, and events fell his way. Procedural confusions in the Austrian parliament led to its permanent suspension in 1933, driving political activity even more into the streets and other informal public arenas. The Dollfuss government increased its restraints on left-wing political rallies. In 1934, after a brief burst of fighting among various branches of the *Heimwehr*—the Social Democrats, the Austrian police—and the army, the Social Democratic Party was disbanded and declared illegal. In July of that same year, Dollfuss was murdered in a failed National Socialist putsch, which led to the outlawing of the Austrian Nazi Party as well.

Dollfuss's successor, Kurt Schuschnigg (1897–1977), a young lawyer from the Tyrol with strong Catholic and monarchist sympathies, was committed to maintaining the independence of Austria. Though authoritarian in principle, he was no friend of National Socialism. By 1936, it was becoming known that Hitler intended to bring Austria into the Greater Germany of his dreams and that 1938 was the probable date for this to take place. In conferences with Schuschnigg at the beginning of 1938, Hitler stepped up his pressure. The Austrian chancellor yielded, allowing Nazis to join his cabinet and relegalizing the party in February. But as German invasion became more probable, Schuschnigg called for a referendum to reaffirm Austrian independence on 9 March 1938. Hitler demanded that this be canceled, and Schuschnigg complied. On 13 March, the German armies appeared in Linz, the capital of Upper Austria. Two days later, the German chancellor addressed a wildly enthusiastic crowd at the center of Vienna.

Anschluss had taken place. The Nazis moved swiftly to institutionalize their presence. The German National Bank took over its Austrian counterpart. The Austrian railway system, postal and telegraph service, and financial administration were absorbed into their German equivalents by the end of March. Hermann Göring, Hitler's lieutenant, had declared that Vienna would be "cleansed" of Jews within four years. In 1939, the provinces of Austria, now officially the Eastern March (Ostmark), were reconfigured as Nazi *Gauen*, an archaic German word for administrative district. Those who resisted found themselves in Nazi detention camps—even, for a time, Kurt Schuschnigg himself.

Austria from World War II to 1955

Though initially spared some of the worst effects of World War II, Austria had become an Allied target by 1943. Destructive air raids had begun to take a heavy toll on both residential and industrial buildings in major manufacturing centers such as Linzin Upper Austria, and Graz in Styria. Nevertheless, the United States, Great Britain, China, and even the Soviet Union were persuaded that there were enough significant anti-Nazi elements within Austria to treat it as a German-occupied country. In 1943, they declared the liberation of Austria to be one of their chief military objectives.

This process got underway in earnest in March 1945, as Soviet troops crossed over the eastern boundaries of the country; British and American forces entered from the west. Vienna was the scene of particularly bitter fighting; indeed, the heavy damage done to the center of the city took place largely in the last days of the war. A temporary regime made up of Social Democrats, Communists, and members of the new Austrian People's Party (Österreichische Volkspartei), the successor to the Christian Social movement, was created on 27 April 1945, even as hostilities were still going on. Led by Karl Renner, the Social Democratic elder statesman, it proclaimed the constitution of the First Republic, as amended in 1929, to be once again in effect. Laws dating from the National Socialist period were declared null and void. Delegates from the Austrian provinces confirmed the arrangement in September as its authority was gradually extended to the entirety of the country.

In that same year, France, Great Britain, the Soviet Union, and the United States divided Austria into zones of occupation. Vienna was split among the four powers, with the center of the city, the First District, an international zone. They also created an Allied Council for Austria, to which the provisional government theoretically answered. However, its procedures were so cumbersome that the Austrian regime found that it had a considerable amount of latitude, at least in domestic affairs. In the first election to the restored National Assembly (Nationalrat), the Austrian People's Party came away with a narrow plurality, a position it continued to hold until 1970. The new federal president was Karl Renner; the first chancellor, Leopold Figl (1902–1965) of the Austrian People's party. Until 1966, Austrian politics were notable for a high degree of cooperation among the major parties, a sharp contrast to the ideological antagonisms that had poisoned all political life in the country during the interwar period. The government of the country respected a system that was known as *Proporz*, or proportionality. Each of the parties agreed to distribute everything from high federal ministries to local offices among themselves, more or less according to the size of the vote each had won in general elections. In practice, this arrangement worked out to a grand coalition between the People's Party and the Social Democrats, because the Communists refused to participate after 1947.

The dreadful economic circumstances that prevailed in Austria after 1945 certainly discouraged ideological factionalism. The first year or so after the war found many people on the brink of starvation. Once the Marshall Plan and the European Recovery Plan were in place in 1948, this situation eased considerably, but Austria was hardly a country where big profits were to be made. The Socialists pressed for nationalization of heavy industry and utilities, and given the general impoverishment of the population, it was wise to adopt many of these measures, as the government did. By the late 1950s, however, as some prosperity returned, sentiment for a greater degree of free market activity began to appear, particularly within the younger ranks of the People's Party.

If economic recovery was the highest priority on the agenda of postwar Austrian governments, freeing the country from the Allied presence was a very close second. Indeed, the two goals were functionally related. One of the drags on the Austrian economy was Soviet occupation policy in the eastern part of the country, where resources and productive capacity were ruthlessly exploited for the benefit of Moscow. Of equal concern was the fear that Austria might be permanently divided, as had apparently taken place in conquered Germany. The Austrian government took advantage of every possible opening to rid itself of foreign forces. The expense of their Austrian duties began to bother the Allies; the death of the Soviet dictator Joseph Stalin, in 1953, gave the Austrians yet another window of opportunity to argue for their true independence. When they accepted the condition of permanent neutrality, without which the Soviets might have prolonged their occupation, the stage was set for the Austrian State Treaty of 1955, which effectively made the Federal Republic a sovereign nation once again.

Austria from 1955 to the Present

In sharp contrast to the First Republic, the Austrian People's Party and the Socialist Party of Austria continued to find ways to work toward common goals, so much so that as much government took place in private discussion as in public arenas. Nevertheless, the return of national independence made serious partisanship a realistic possibility once more. By 1966 the People's Party, many of whose members were eager to reduce the public sector of the economy, attempted to govern the country alone. In 1970, however, the Socialists won the relative majority in an election. In 1971, they won an absolute majority and undertook single-party government, led by Chancellor Bruno Kreisky (1911–1990). The party was reconfirmed in that position in elections in 1975 and 1979. However, financial scandals increasingly plagued the Kreisky regime. When his party won only a plurality in elections held in 1983, Kreisky left office altogether. His successor, Fred Sinowatz (1929–2008), was forced into coalition governments with the right-wing Freiheitliche Partei Österreichs (Freedom Party of Austria).

Sinowatz resigned in 1986, plagued by scandals not always of his own making, and nation-wide protest over the election of former United Nations (UN) Secretary General Kurt Waldheim, who was accused of concealing the full, and allegedly Nazi-besmirched, story of his World War II career. The new chancellor was Franz Vranitzky, a man with a strong background in finance and economics. He was faced with leading a country whose president, still Waldheim, had become a pariah on the international scene. Vranitzky found it impossible to cooperate in a so-called Small Coalition with the Freedom Party. The latter had acquired a leader, Jörg Haider (1950–2008), whose strident criticism of the increased number of foreigners, asylum seekers, and those looking for economic opportunities in Austria offended many moderates and many more liberals. Vrantizky returned to a Large Coalition with the People's Party, which endured under his successor, Viktor Klima (1947–), until 2000. The chancellor was a Socialist, the vice-chancellor a member of the People's Party.

The condition of permanent neutrality put strong constraints on Austria's role in foreign affairs after 1955. Unlike neutral Switzerland, however, the Second Austrian Republic took every legally viable opportunity to play some role beyond its borders. Austria became a member of the United Nations in 1955 and joined the Council of Europe a year later. As chancellor, Bruno Kreisky often used Austria's neutral status to inject himself as a broker for peace in the Middle East during his terms of office. With the collapse in 1990 of the Soviet Union, the state that was particularly eager to neutralize Austria, the government in Vienna became somewhat more openly supportive of Western military operations. During the Persian Gulf crisis of 1991, for example, American and British aircraft were allowed fly-space over Austria. Like Russia and China, however, Austria did not support the American military intervention in Iraq in 2003.

Reconciling Austrian neutrality with Austrian economic interests was far more complex. The formation and success of the European Common Market after World War II showed many economic and political leaders in Austria that their country would remain an economic backwater unless it could meaningfully integrate its markets and productive capacities with a larger west European trading zone. In 1960, Austria joined the European Free Trade Association (EFTA). Made up of Great Britain, Denmark, Norway, Sweden, Switzerland, and Portugal, along with Austria, it provided a preferential trading area for members without forcing them to give up some measure of their sovereignty as was foreseen in the Common Market. However, the latter, called the European Economic Community (EEC) after 1957, was clearly the more powerful economic engine; Great Britain itself applied for associate membership in 1961. Over the objections of the Soviet Union that Austrian involvement with the EEC would violate a requirement of the State Treaty—that Austria could not associate itself with Germany—Austria also applied for associate membership. This Italy vetoed, but discussion of joining the EEC continued in Austria. The Socialists were especially opposed to the move, unless both the Eastern and Western blocs agreed to it.

The collapse of the Soviet Union in 1989 eased the way for Austrian entry into the European Union. In 1991, Austria applied for full membership; in 1995 it was admitted. Austria has held the rotating presidency of the European Union Council, once in 1998, again in 2006, and Austrians have held major positions in the union's administration.

Neutrality, however, had become an agreeable arrangement that gave Austrians and their country a distinctive quality in the international community, yet freed them collectively from unwelcome and expensive military responsibilities. The numerous compromises with neutrality that have taken place since the chancellorship of Bruno Kreisky and Austria's entry into the European Union (EU) have somewhat diminished Austria's sense of national identity, a feeling that was never well-defined at any time.

Polls have long revealed that Austrians have far less faith in their police, courts, administration, army, and parliament than do the Germans and the Swiss. Nor do important alternative institutions that have long given shape, meaning, and even financial security to large numbers of Austrians command unquestioned public confidence. Throughout the 1990s, the Austrian Roman Catholic Church, which had been central to the cultural and spiritual lives of almost all Austrians, regardless of social class, was mired in a series of financial and moral scandals. Angry protests with cries of "We are the church" erupted in 1991 when Kurt Krenn, a Catholic clergyman who reputedly abused seminarians and was given to public diatribes about Muslim immigrants, was named bishop of St. Pölten, the capital of Lower Austria. Krenn himself fully resigned his episcopal post only in 2004, still calling his conduct "stupid boyish behavior." The revelation in March 1995 that Vienna's archbishop, Hermann Groer, had also carried on improper relations with a student led to a 32 percent rise in Austrians cutting ties to Catholicism a month later. Traditional youth organizations, often associated with political parties, have also faded away. On the other hand, ad hoc activism among students has increased considerably.

The great rise in their personal wealth has encouraged Austrians to develop individualized private and even public life styles quite apart from norms once drawn from job status or membership in established social classes. Indeed, the state itself is no longer the sole source of personal security. Although the Austrian redistributionist tax structure still significantly curbs gross differentials in wealth—by 2005 Austrians generally had larger discretionary incomes than people in the Federal Republic of Germany—the state has also tried to cut its budgets sharply. From 2000 to 2006, Chancellor Wolfgang Schüssel and the coalitions he headed explicitly set out to deconstruct many features of the Austrian welfare system and public services. Once untouchable state monopolies such as the post office moved toward complete privatization during these years, with branch closings and job losses as the result. Although some of the unemployed found work in the worldwide boom that took place in the first years of the 21st century, Austrians, especially younger ones, came to realize that the social protections that had been routine since 1945 were things of the past. Even as they prospered between 2000 and 2008, they bought private medical and retirement plans, well aware that they could not rely upon the state to support the standard of living to which they had now become accustomed.

Financial pressures have even led some Austrians to question their highly federalized constitution. By 2000, serious arguments had been made for saving money by moving to a more centralized political structure. Provincial legislatures were particularly vulnerable, especially because Austria's membership in the EU had already limited some of their prerogatives. Although economists who had studied the issue had concluded by 2004 that neither model was inherently more advantageous financially, they agreed that reform of the system was desirable.

Austria's political machinery has adapted itself to many of the value adjustments that came with the social protests of the 1960s and 1970s. Women now play a far greater role in political institutions, even on the provincial level, and the voting age is very youth-friendly. It was lowered to 16 in 2008. None of this, however, has stemmed the general loss of confidence in traditional sources of support, both material and spiritual, that has noticeably afflicted political parties. Austrians, who characteristically seemed to transmit membership in the SPÖ or the ÖVP to their children through their germplasm, have decided that political parties that celebrate market economics in one election cycle only to denounce such policies in the next have no comprehensive solutions for modern problems. The politically driven preference for full employment rather than competitiveness that paralyzed nationalized industry by 1985, plus a string of major scandals in the upper echelons of the

SPÖ that continued into the first decade of the 21st century, destroyed the faith held by many in the effectiveness of state-guided management and the moral superiority of social market economies generally. Indeed, the governments of Franz Vranitzky and Victor Klima, both from the SPÖ, began the divestiture of state shares in industry in the late 1980s and the painful job dislocation that followed. It was Schüssel, however, along with several of his neoliberal ministers from his coalition partner, the Freedom Party of Austria (FPÖ), who supported the policy most programmatically between 2000 and 2006. Indeed, his ÖVP received over 40 percent of the vote in an election in 2002, an unusually solid endorsement of a single party.

However, tired of broken promises from both parties to soften these harsh measures with tax reform, irked by paying service fees once covered fully or in part by the government, and generally worried about the impact of immigration on employment and social entitlements, voters began to show their mistrust visibly in the national elections of 2006. Scandal in Schüssel's family over employment of illegal immigrant labor and a growing popular reluctance to make greater financial contributions to such national services as health care and education, particularly higher education, had markedly antagonized the electorate. The election, however, was exceedingly close. Alfred Gusenbauer (1960–) led the SPÖ to its narrow plurality and became chancellor of a coalition with the ÖVP that proved to be unworkable. Plagued by ÖVP obstructionism and by controversial policies developed by ministers who came from his own party—a plan to raise the minimum wage without raising pensions was typical—Gusenbauer's government lasted little more than a year. It was the shortest first-term chancellorship in the history of the Second Austrian Republic.

New elections in September 2008 brought even more bad news for the major political parties. Drawing upon a relatively stable number of voters, who remained deeply fearful of the cultural and economic impact of immigration, and a more volatile number of people who wished to register a general protest against ÖVP–SPÖ political infighting, the FPÖ, led by Heinz-Christian Strache (1969–), and a splinter party established by Jörg Haider in 2005, the Alliance for the Future of Austria, took almost 30 percent of the vote. Just what the results mandated for Austria's political future became even more uncertain when Haider died in a car crash not quite a month after the polls closed.

Modern Austria is among several European countries now resetting their political gyroscopes. It remains to be seen whether material wealth and the social reorientation that has accompanied it will spin off humanistic values that persuade an unprecedentedly well-to-do number of people that personal comfort is only one among several aspects of a full life. No longer an unwanted by-product of two of the 20th century's several horrific conflicts, Austria is among those polities that is positioned to offer serious answers to this question.

ECONOMIC DEVELOPMENT

The topography of Austria has very much determined the way Austrians made their livings, even in the 20th century. The eastern and northeastern region is agricultural, with wheat, barley, maize, potatoes, and sugar beets as its chief crops. Large-scale livestock farming, centered around swine, poultry, and, to a lesser degree, cattle, also goes on here; an extensive dairy industry is found in Upper Austria as well as in the Vorarlberg, to the west. The most productive vineyards are in Lower Austria, especially in the Wachau region, and in the Burgenland. The mountainous regions have for centuries been sources of precious metals, chiefly silver found in the Tyrol and iron in Styria. The latter region has long been a center for mining, processing, and manufacturing heavy metals. The country's domestic petroleum reserves are largely concentrated in Lower Austria, especially around refineries in Schwechat, the site of the Vienna airport. Crude oil that has been extracted in the western part of the country is processed there as well, as is petroleum from the Middle East, which is then conveyed to central Europe along a pipeline that originates in Trieste, in Italy. Austria also possesses significant reserves of natural gas.

After a comparatively slow start in the second half of the 18th century, the industrialization of the Habsburg Austrian lands moved ahead rapidly in certain regions. These were Vienna and neighboring districts of Lower Austria, and somewhat later, Styria. The other provinces remained agricultural, indeed, pastoral. After World War II, however, the western regions of the country proved to be the economically more dynamic ones. Austria manufactured a wide variety of goods, with specialized steel products, textiles, petrochemicals, wood and paper products, foodstuffs, and glass and porcelain products especially well represented.

Today, almost all of the nine provinces of the federal republic are dominated by service industries such as banking, which are coming to play an ever more prominent role in the economy. Employment in major heavy industry has dropped dramatically, though a global market for specialized steel products remains. For many years, the Federal Republic of Germany and the other countries in the Common Market were Austria's chief trading partners. The United States and the former Soviet Union also were at times important customers for Austrian goods.

Membership in the European Community starting in 1995 swiftly intensified Austria's economic relations with member states. By the first half of 1998, overall exports from Austria had risen by 12.5 percent, two-thirds of which were going to EU countries. By 1998, agricultural exports to the EU had grown by 136.7 percent, with Germany and Italy as chief customers. Exports generally had risen to 28.5 percent of the Austrian domestic product. An unfavorable balance of trade had begun to drop markedly. In 1997, it had gone from 100 million schillings to 75 million schillings. After 2002, the Austrian balance of trade became consistently positive, driven largely by exports to quickly developing lands such as China.

But none of these changes has come without causing pain to some segment of Austrian society. Familiar grocery chains have largely been taken over by French, British, and especially German and Italian firms. A new competitive atmosphere has arisen to challenge an economy notorious for its intricate protectionism and manipulation by domestic political interests. Austria's energy infrastructure, for example, was among the least competitively organized on the continent. A law of 1955 required that some government authority hold at least 51 percent of the equities of all energy-producing firms. The European Union, however, requires member states to deregulate their power suppliers. Foreign companies have bought far more than retail grocery stories in Austria. And the takeovers and mergers that have encouraged management to rationalize business and manufacturing practices have made unemployment, once rare in Austria, more common. The opening up of Austrian universities, especially its medical faculties, to students from other EU countries, especially Germany, has been a subject of rancorous debate.

Austria's banking facilities were historically both fragmented and inefficient, in part because of their ties, either open or clandestine, to the major political parties. By 1990, large institutions had one branch for every 1,400 Austrians. Generation of investment capital was slow and weak. Bank consolidation became the rule of the day. In the early 1990s, Bank Austria was created by the merger of the Z-Bank, once owned by the socialist-controlled city of Vienna, and the Austrian Provincial Bank (Länderbank). In 1997, Bank Austria acquired the tradition-ridden Creditanstalt Bank, but under heavy criticism from the Conservative Austrian People's Party, which was close to the Creditanstalt and was reluctant to have it absorbed by the "red" Bank Austria. Though these movements improved Austrian competitiveness in world financial markets, they also exposed the country's fiscal institutions to opaque investment and accounting strategies that could play havoc with domestic savings and investments. The collapse of the Bank for Labor and Economic Development (BAWAG) after 2005 epitomized this problem.

There is still much about Austria's institutional structure generally that will continue to make adaptation to EU membership and the global economy difficult. Although the entrepreneurial ethic has always been present in Austria, it has been compromised by the comforts of government-generated high employment, a general reluctance to forego the pleasures of private life, and deference to long-standing institutional arrangements. The traditional universities resist coordinating advanced academic study with business and industry. There is now, however, an Elite-Universität, dedicated largely to primary research in the natural sciences and experimental adaptation of its findings, even though much of the investment capital for this work must come from abroad.

Nevertheless, with the notable exception of those who have had only basic educational training, Austrians generally agree that EU membership and participation in international markets generally has brought them many advantages. To leave the EU would prompt other countries in the organization to withdraw their industrial research facilities in Austria and close Austrian students off from exchange privileges at universities throughout the EU lands (the Erasmus program). Farmers would no longer receive agricultural subsidies that have allowed

Austria to develop environmentally sensitive agricultural and animal husbandry techniques.

In other words, prosperity in Austria has been closely tied to participation in the EU and to world economic developments generally. The massive financial crisis that spread from the United States to the entire world in the summer and fall of 2008 hit Austria hard. Projections for economic growth dropped sharply, from around 2.1 percent in 2008 to 1.4 percent in 2009. A rise in unemployment, always a troubling political issue in Austria, seemed very likely. With right-wing populism roiling the national political arena, the outcome of a major economic recession could take several forms. But it is difficult to imagine a return of good times to Austria without EU membership and a continued cultivation of foreign markets and capital sources, however loud the nationalist grumbling becomes.

The Dictionary

– A –

ADLER, ALFRED (1870–1937). Among **Sigmund Freud**'s most important students, Adler followed his mentor's early career trajectory as well. He trained as a physician and psychiatrist and worked in the laboratory of the brain specialist Theodore Meynert (1833–1892). Unlike Freud, Adler actually studied with **Richard von Krafft-Ebing**. Sickly as a child and raised in impoverished circumstances, Adler was fascinated by the compensatory adaptations the human body makes to disabilities.

Adler broke with Freud around 1912 because of their differences over the origin of neuroses and the role of human volition in dealing with them. Whereas Freud saw the condition as the result of repressed sexual urges and trauma, Adler described it as a by-product of social maladaptation developed from the child's will to survive. Depending on an individual's experience with this process, he or she could acquire an inferiority complex, a term he coined to describe the exaggerated need for approval. Adler's therapy was to give such persons a more secure sense of self, thus enabling them to conduct their lives in more realistic ways.

A social democrat, Adler welcomed the establishment of the First Austrian Republic in 1918 for the opportunity it presented to promote mental health among a wider public. Encouraged by **Otto Glöckel**, the director of **Vienna**'s schools, he helped to develop guidance clinics for elementary school pupils. In 1929, Adler began lecturing on child psychiatry at the Vienna Pedagogical Institute. He continued to do this semiannually after 1932 as he expanded his career to New York and Great Britain. He was giving a talk in Glasgow when he died.

ADLER, VIKTOR (1852–1918). The practical founder of the **Social Democratic Party** (SDAP) in the 19th-century **Habsburg Empire**, Adler was of Jewish extraction. He was baptized as a Protestant, however, and in his youth supported German nationalist circles in **Vienna**. As a student of medicine, he saw much suffering in the working classes of the Habsburg capital and became a lifetime advocate of the socialist cause, though not necessarily adhering to every doctrine. Only reluctantly did Adler come to grips with Marxism as a science. He preferred to concentrate on improving opportunities for personal development among the working classes through widened educational and cultural programs. He did believe, however, that monopoly ownership of the means of production was the central flaw of liberal society.

Within the SDAP, Adler worked to harmonize its often-fractious national and ideological elements. Convinced that the party could cooperate with both the crown and bourgeoisie, he played a central role in the Hainfeld Program of 1888–1889. This bridged differences between his position and those of his more radical colleagues, who were under the spell of 19th-century anarchism. Adler continued to argue that the individual was the central element in the body politic, and that the most successful party program was one that did not offend any party member. He also believed that the emotional commitment of the SDAP to its cause was as important as the members' rational and volitional engagement. Adler turned the annual May Day event, which began in Vienna in 1890, from a demonstration for specific political and economic reforms such as an eight-hour working day and broadened franchise into an international celebration of worker solidarity. As Austrian foreign minister after **World War I**, Adler supported *Anschluss* with Germany. *See also* AUSTROMARXISM; LINZ PROGRAM.

A.E.I.O.U. *See* FREDERICK III, EMPEROR.

AGRICULTURE. Austria's dramatically differentiated topography has determined the country's varied agriculture. The eastern region of the country, which falls rapidly into the vast Pannonian Plain that extends deeply into Hungary, provides for the broad stretch of flatland dependably warm summers required by many grain crops. Much of the rest of the country is hilly and, nearer to the **Alps**, dauntingly mountainous, more suitable to animal husbandry and forestry. Wood has long been an important Austrian commodity, both domestically and for export. Certain localities produce excellent fruit, most of which is consumed by Austrians themselves: Styrian apples, along with peaches and cherries raised in the region. With the exception of apples, however, these crops satisfy only seasonal tastes and not year-round needs.

Agriculture was the primary occupation of Austrians not only in the Middle Ages but long after. Well into the 1930s, around a third of the population still worked the land either full or part time. Several of Austria's traditional staple crops were cultivated from medieval times on. Eastern Austria was an early granary for the entire region and a center of the grain trade as well. Wood and forest products were very important long before the modern era, especially as peasants often sold them as a source of income when other crops, grains especially, dropped in price. These commodities became even more important in the 18th century as a rising population required more of them for heating, even as developing industries were calling upon them for energy and building. The first tree nursery was opened in Austria in 1720, marking the beginning of a policy of planned reforestation. (The modern-day Agricultural University [Universität für Bodenkultur] was not established until 1872.) Viticulture, again in the eastern and southeastern parts of the country, created a market of scale; the sale of **wine** in the late Middle Ages was an especially lucrative source of revenue for towns, monasteries, and noble houses.

Between 1550 and 1570, the cultivation of certain specialty crops reached a high point: flax, especially in **Upper Austria**; hops; saffron; poppy seeds; mustard and one of its varieties, rape, which produces seeds that are processed for cooking oil; and woad and madder, the source of red and blue dyers' extracts. Sheep husbandry was also important; by the 18th century the Austrian lands were self-sufficient in wool. *See* AUSTRIA, UPPER.

Wine virtually disappeared as an Austrian export at the end of the 17th century. Viticulture fell into the hands of small peasants and farmers, who often prized quantity over quality. Nevertheless, abandoned vineyards had their uses. By the 17th century, they had been seeded with corn, which was initially cultivated in the Ottoman lands. Other new and important crops were **tobacco**, introduced in 1648 in Upper Austria, then a year later in **Lower Austria**. Fruits became a significant crop in southern and eastern **Styria** at the same time. Mulberry trees were brought into Austria in the 18th century to supply raw silk to manufacturers in northern Italy.

Until Austrian **industrialization** of the late 18th and early 19th centuries took them over for factories, the outlying areas of such cities as Vienna were the sites of vineyards, vegetable truck gardens, and dairies. Agricultural production in the **Habsburg Empire**, however, continued to underperform until the middle of the 19th century, largely because of the persistence of serfdom and the constraints on land use associated with it. Empress **Maria Theresa** and her son and successor, **Joseph II**, had made a start on reforming these arrangements to enlarge crop yields. The government also introduced model farms in the 1760s. But it was not until the complete abolition of serfdom after the **Revolutions of 1848** that it was possible for people generally to profit from agriculture. The introduction of sugar beet cultivation into Austria in the second half of the 19th century proved to be lucrative for farmers and manufacturers alike as the sweetener, once a comparative luxury, became affordable for even modest households. Wheat and barley, along with clover (a cattle fodder), were also grown on a far larger scale.

Food production dropped precipitously in the early years of the First Austrian Republic. Only about 18 percent of the country was arable. The population of the new state was small, however, and probably could have met its basic needs had appropriate technology and **transportation** facilities been in place. But the investment capital to finance these changes in agriculture was not available. Countries of the former Habsburg Empire that had exported farm commodities to the Austrian lands were more intent on protecting their domestic consumers than on selling farm commodities abroad. The Austrian provinces often balked at shipping their food products and commodities beyond their internal borders. Vienna, a city that in 1913 received deliveries of 900,000 liters of milk a day, was getting 60,000.

Agrarian production had improved by the outbreak of **World War II**. Nevertheless, only massive amounts of foreign aid in 1946 from the **United Nations** Relief and Rehabilitation Administration (UNRRA) and the Cooperative for American Remittances to Europe

(CARE) saved many Austrians from starvation once again. After 1948, the **Marshall Plan** also added significantly to the country's food supply.

The agricultural recovery of the Second Austria Republic since World War II, however, has been sustained over time. Farm technology improved greatly, to the point where the number of people engaged in agriculture had fallen from 23.7 percent in 1959 to a little under 10 percent in 1977. After the adoption of the **Austrian State Treaty** in 1955, governments continued to protect milk, meat, and grain, the preeminent staples of the Austrian diet. By 1980, however, these commodities were in surplus, and Austria began exporting them. Membership in the **European Union** (EU) has required Austria to cut back heavily government subsidies on basic agriculture that made the country virtually self-sufficient in basic commodities by 1986. But these disadvantages for growers have been offset to some degree by Austria's successful shift to a high-wage industrial and service **economy**. A large number of citizens can now set their tables with foods imported from members of the EU and the rest of the world. Nevertheless, some Austrian agricultural specialties—most notably pumpkin seed oil—remain unique and very expensive both domestically and abroad. The 1985 scandal over adulterated wine has led Austrian vintners to limit production in the interests of quality and to charge higher prices for wine as well.

ALBERTINA. A palace and **museum** in **Vienna** that belonged to Archduchess Maria Christine (1742–1798), the favorite daughter of Empress **Maria Theresa** and her husband, Duke Albert-Kasimir of Saxony-Teschen (1738–1822). The archduchess was a talented painter, and her husband was a man of refined aesthetic sensibilities; the marriage gave him the financial wherewithal to collect high-caliber prints, drawings, and watercolors. They acquired the core of the French, Netherlandic, German, and English holdings of the museum during travels and administrative assignments in **Italy** and the Low Countries.

An Italian connoisseur, Count Giacomo Durazzo, played a key role in the development of the collection. He presented Duke Albert with a huge body of material—over 30, 000 prints and 1,400 drawings alone. More important, the count persuaded Albert to organize his holdings according to region of origin and chronological order, rather than by subject, which was the prevailing custom in princely galleries. Thus the Albertina was, from the beginning, a resource for scholars and aesthetes alike.

The Albertina contains some of Albrecht Dürer's best-known drawings; the graphic output of Michelangelo, Raphael, Leonardo da Vinci, and Rubens is also well represented. Significant modern acquisitions include works by Manet, Modigliani, Cézanne, and the Austrian Expressionist **Egon Schiele**. Duke Albert ordered that the collection, which was expanded during the 19th century through purchases and exchanges, pass intact to his heirs and their successors. After both **World War I** and **World War II**, there were efforts to break it up for commercial sale. None of these, however, was realized.

ALLGEMEINES BÜRGERLICHES GESETZBUCH (ABGB)/ GENERAL CODE OF CIVIL LAW. Completed in 1811 and put in force the following year, the ABGB originally applied to the Austrian and Bohemian lands of the **Habsburg Empire** and to Polish Galicia. Though much amended and expanded through special statutes, it remains the heart of the modern Austrian legal system, particularly in laws covering property and testamentary rights, rights of guardianship, as well as measures that govern commercial exchanges and recovery of damages.

The ABGB had its origins in the legal reforms of Emperor **Joseph II**, issued in 1787. These introduced the idea of equality before the law in criminal cases and limited torture. Although capital punishment continued, it was to be meted out as a deterrent to crime rather than as a form of retribution. The durability of the ABGB has been attributed to its focus on legal principle rather than detail; its flexibility, which allows it to accommodate other laws that new economic and social needs required; and its anticipation of liberal ideals, which became political and societal realities only after the code was published. *See also* JUDICIARY.

ALLGEMEINES SOZIALVERSICHERUNGSGESETZ/GENERAL SOCIAL INSURANCE LAW (ASVG). Enacted in 1955, this measure brought virtually all Austrians into a single **govern-**

ment-managed pension and social insurance network. Many of its provisions had already been part of **welfare** arrangements introduced by the imperial **Habsburg** government and the First Austrian Republic.

The law, which has been repeatedly amended but not substantially altered, provides for unemployment compensation, sick pay and leave, accident insurance, and retirement pensions. It is funded through employer and employee contributions according to income. Where these contributions do not cover service costs, the state makes up the difference.

Medical insurance includes physicians' fees, pharmaceuticals, and hospitalization. In the case of accidental injury and death, the ASVG covers the expenses of physical therapy, disability, and survivors' benefits. Retirement pensions are based not only on age but also on declining ability to work.

ALPBACH FORUM. A major summer gathering place in the Austrian **Tyrol** for discussions of global problems and issues by leading politicians, academics, and intellectuals. These meetings began in 1945 under the aegis of the International Higher Education Week. The forum was strongly supported by the American occupiers of the province. Its founder, Otto Molden (1918–2002), was the brother of Austrian **resistance** leader Fritz Molden (1924–), both of whom were sons of liberal Austrian publisher Ernst Molden (1886–1953). Many participants had been in the resistance at the close of **World War II**.

The initial meetings of the group focused on general European questions. At its fifth conference in 1949, the flag of a common Europe, a green "E" on a white background, was raised for the first time.

ALPS. Although modern Austria has a varied climate and a wide range of vegetation, its mountains have shaped much of its history. The eastern Alps, their foothills, and the Carpathian foothills, near Austria's border with Slovakia, account for almost 75 percent of the territory of the modern Federal Republic. The Grossglockner, rising 3,740 meters (12,270 feet), is the highest peak and lies between the East **Tyrol** and **Carinthia**.

Geologically a very young chain, the Austrian Alps are limestone, granite, and sandstone formations, depending on the region where they arose. Some of their most distinctive features appeared during the Ice Ages; the numerous glaciers, which still cut through their surfaces, are a product of these periods.

Negotiating the Alps on a north–south axis has challenged humankind from prehistoric times. The Romans broke through the Brenner passage during the emperorship of Septimus Severus around the beginning of the third century. A way over the Semmering from **Lower Austria** to **Styria** was found during the Middle Ages, and the passage from Leoben to Hieflau in Styria appears to have been traversed very early. The tunneling of the chain for rail and automotive traffic took place in the 19th and 20th centuries.

From an economic perspective, the Alps have both helped and hindered Austrian development. They have left the country with relatively little arable land—only about 20 percent of its surface. In earlier times, famine was a common occurrence in the mountainous parts of the country. Some regions of the Alps, however, have been the source of rich mineral deposits, particularly silver. These were concentrated in the Tyrol around Schwaz and Hall, though they had substantially run out by the 17th century. Today the greatest value of the Alps, aside from **tourism** and recreation, is their role in the generation of hydroelectric energy both for export and domestic consumption.

ANSCHLUSS. Though the term is especially associated with the Nazi takeover of Austria on 11 March 1938, the notion of Anschluss, from the German *anschliessen* (Eng.: to connect), has a long history in Austrian thinking. For centuries the Austrian lands were part of the German **Holy Roman Empire** and contributed materially to its defense. Austrian territorial rulers sat and voted in the imperial estates. Save for a few years in the 18th century, the **Habsburgs** served as German kings and Holy Roman Emperors from 1440 until they assumed the title of Emperors of Austria in 1806. Linguistically and culturally, the inhabitants of the Austrian lands were largely "German" and called themselves that. The Habsburgs presided over meetings of the **German Confederation**, the loose organization of German states created at the **Congress of Vienna**.

Proponents of **Germany**'s unification in the 19th century could find no place in their schemes for the **Habsburg Empire** and its huge non-German population. With Prussia's defeat of Emperor **Franz Joseph**'s armies in 1866 and the establishment of the Hohenzollern Empire in 1871, there were two central European states with claims to German loyalties. From then until the collapse of Austria–Hungary in 1918, several political movements in the German-speaking regions of the Habsburg lands argued for closer connections with the new Germany.

At the end of **World War I**, this sentiment became a political priority for many Austrians. Doubting the viability of an independent Austria, the national assembly declared its desire to join Germany on 12 November 1918. Both the **Social Democratic Party of Austria** and a new Greater German Party supported the idea. They were opposed by the **Christian Social Party**, which was strongly Catholic in outlook and loathe to cooperate with a state in which 64 percent of the population was Protestant. The discussion became somewhat academic when the **Treaty of St. Germain** stipulated that such a move required approval from the Council of the League of Nations. Nevertheless, support for Anschluss in Austria remained high for a time. Both the **Tyrol** and **Salzburg** voted in 1921 to become part of the Weimar Republic. Though nothing came of these actions, private clubs, political groupings, and even factions within the Christian Social movement continued to promote close coordination with German policy. Few Austrians, however, endorsed outright annexation. In 1931, Germany and Austria agreed on a tariff union, only to have the decision overturned by the International Court of Justice in the Hague.

Once Adolf Hitler became chancellor of Germany in 1933, Austrians advocating union with Germany received greater encouragement from Berlin. The Austrian **Nazi** movement did what it could to destabilize the **government** in **Vienna** through boycotts, terrorism, and the like. **Chancellor Engelbert Dollfuss** and his successor, **Kurt Schuschnigg**, tried to curb these activities. Indeed, following an abortive Nazi putsch in July 1934, which ended with the murder of Dollfuss, the party was declared illegal. Hitler continued his pressures, though he made no outright military preparation for the move until the beginning of 1938. On 11 March, German troops crossed the border of the two countries. Enthusiastic crowds greeted them wherever they appeared. The government resigned, to be replaced by a Nazi-controlled regime headed by Arthur Seyss-Inquart (1892–1946), a lawyer from Vienna. On 13 March, Austria was declared to be a province of Germany. In a plebiscite held on 10 April 1938, almost 100 percent of those who voted endorsed the arrangement, which endured until 1945. Article 4 of the **Austrian State Treaty** (1955) forbids Anschluss once again. *See also* LANGUAGE; SEVEN WEEKS' WAR.

ARBEITERZEITUNG/WORKERS' NEWSPAPER. Founded in 1889 by **Social Democratic Party of Austria** (SDAP) leader **Viktor Adler**, the *Arbeiterzeitung* at first appeared only twice a month. From 1895 to 1934, it came out daily, though from 1933 to 1934 it was heavily censored. Finally forbidden to publish at all by the right-wing regime of **Engelbert Dollfuss**, the journal was transferred to Brno in Czechoslovakia, where it was published as a weekly and smuggled into Austria until 1938.

The *Arbeiterzeitung* was the central organ of the SDAP; it reflected those views both in its editorial columns and in its selection of news. Its intellectual level was characteristically high, reflecting both the sophistication of the party leadership and its serious commitment to educating the Austrian working class. In the years before **World War I** and into the early 1930s, the *Arbeiterzeitung* often took outspoken, militant positions on questions such as interclass warfare. Its reporting sometimes embarrassed the conservative and right-wing governments that controlled Austria in the 1920s and 1930s. In January 1933, the *Arbeiterzeitung* disclosed that Austria was violating the **Treaty of St. Germain** by accepting shipments of weapons from **Italy** supposedly intended for Hungary. *See* ST. GERMAIN, TREATY OF.

From 1945 to 1989, the *Arbeiterzeitung* was restored as a party daily. However, its reportorial tone became much more neutral and its editorial content more tabloidlike. In 1991, after two years of publication without any political identification, it folded for economic reasons. *See also* PRESS.

ARCHITECTURE. As a region on the borderland of many cultures, the Austrian people have made several major architectural styles their own from the early Middle Ages to the present, often with distinction. Least well represented is arguably the Romanesque, a preeminent style in western and central Europe from 950 to 1150. Although monasteries such as **Melk** and **Heiligenkreuz** were originally built in the Romanesque style, they have been drastically remodeled over the centuries. The best example of Austrian Christian Romanesque is the cathedral of Gurk in northern **Carinthia**, built sometime around 1140–1200. Its crypt, supported by 100 columns, is a splendid example of a Romanesque interior.

Medieval architecture in the Gothic style came to the Austrian provinces in the 13th century from both **Italy**, where Gothic churches were built with three-tower facades and made more use of ornamental color on their exteriors, and France, where the designs, especially at the outset, were more austere. Austria's most notable Gothic structure is St. Stephen's Cathedral in **Vienna**. Its builders, who began the work in 1304 on top of an earlier foundation, were in close contact with colleagues in Regensburg and Strasbourg to the west. The interior of St. Stephen's, like most Gothic churches in Austria, is distinguished by a long central church hall, with several naves all of the same height. As in other regions of Europe, Gothic architecture made its way into secular buildings in Austria as well, an excellent example being the 15th-century Golden Roof of **Innsbruck**.

Austrian scholars have long debated the nature of the Renaissance in Austria. During the 16th century, a number of buildings were constructed that took their inspiration from classicizing Italian styles. Especially successful examples are the graceful Porcia palace in Spittal an der Drau in Carinthia and the lovely terra cotta courtyard of Schallaburg castle in **Lower Austria**. This was an age, however, when Austrian financial resources were directed elsewhere, combating both Ottoman invaders from the east and what **Catholics** saw as **Protestant** heresy at home. Renaissance architecture, therefore, left comparatively few traces on Austrian soil.

The Austrian lands more than compensated for this deficit during the age of the **Baroque**, which, running through the 17th century, peaked in its latter decades. Austria's Baroque architects, such as **Johann Bernhard Fischer von Erlach**, **Johann Lukas von Hildebrandt**, and **Jakob Prandtauer**, gave Austrian architecture buildings and monuments of world stature, expressions of the twin triumphs the Catholic Counter-Reformation and the final defeat of the Ottoman Empire, which took place during that period.

The Baroque gave way, after 1750, to the more delicate rococo and neoclassical styles from southern Germany and France. The next truly striking Austrian architectural style, albeit largely confined to interiors, was the **Biedermeier**, which dominated the decorative imagination in the **Habsburg** lands, especially the German-speaking ones, from the end of the Napoleonic Wars in 1815 to the outbreak of the **Revolutions of 1848**.

Growing prosperity that came to the **Habsburg Empire** during the second half of the 19th century, especially in its western reaches, brought significant changes in its built environment, especially in large cities. The decision to create an urban circumferential boulevard, the **Ringstrasse** in **Vienna**, opened the way for massive official and residential structures, largely in the historicizing neo-Renaissance style that was the architectural canon of the day. Instrumental in the Ring's planning after 1836 was Ludwig Förster (1797–1863), who after 1842 taught at the Vienna Academy of Fine Arts. His strong respect for traditional styles influenced such important students as **Theophile Hansen** and **Otto Wagner**, though in very different ways.

Wagner, along with **Josef Hoffmann**, broke sharply with this school at the end of the 19th century as members of the **Secession**. Seeking to combine purpose with beauty, they drastically simplified even the most elegant (and expensive) of structures. Adolf Loos (1870–1933) carried the principle even further, proscribing ornament of any kind unless it played an unequivocally functional role in a building.

Such ideas, however, led to the undistinguished structures built from visibly cheaper materials that abound in Austrian cities today. Tight material circumstances created by the **economic** downturn that followed **World War I** lowered ceilings and scaled back room space for the once-comfortable middle classes. The population shifts and destruction of housing stock that took place during and immediately after **World War II** left architects with few options besides stripped-down functionalism, at least in municipal apartment design. Although perhaps necessary, given the needs of the population and the resources available to satisfy them, these structures have little aesthetic merit.

Contemporary Austrian architecture, however, is quite a different story. In the final decades of the 20th century, the protean Austrian artist and architect **Friedrich Hundertwasser** introduced more fanciful elements into housing design. Currently Austrian architecture, including highly experimental designs by such firms as **Coop Himmelb(l)au**, is in demand throughout the world. *See also* ART.

ART. Though Austria has a long and rich tradition in painting, sculpture, and the decorative arts, the country's enormous collections are, on the whole, more notable than individual Austrian artists. There is a fine gallery dedicated to Austrian art in **Vienna**, but it is not usually what draws art lovers to the city. The **Habsburg** dynasty, which ruled the area from the end of the 13th century to 1918, was among Europe's great patrons of painting, sculpture, and the decorative arts. They happily, and often cannily, bought wherever their tastes led them, often from artists who themselves had no connection with Austria whatsoever. For this reason, the Austrian National Museum of Art (Kunsthistorisches Museum) is among the great galleries of the world. Austrian painters and sculptors, however, do not dominate its holdings.

As was the case in much of Christian medieval Europe, Austrians produced their share of illuminated manuscripts and wall frescoes, more often than not anonymously. Striking examples of Gothic (13th–15th centuries) sculpture are to be seen in St. Stephen's cathedral in Vienna. Unlike the earlier Romanesque work in the same genre, the figures stand in open spaces rather than against walls. The "servants' Madonna" is particularly interesting. However, there is little that distinguishes this work from its contemporary counterparts elsewhere in the south German area. The same may be said of painting, even the highly expressive **Danube School** of the late 15th and 16th centuries.

The Austrian **Baroque** did give rise to an impressive group of painters and sculptors, though they too often came from beyond the confines of Austria itself. The ceiling and wall frescos done for the **Austrian National Library**, once the imperial court library in Vienna, by Daniel Gran (1694–1757), and those done by Paul Troger (1698–1762) in the cloister of **Melk**, have an airy brightness and dynamism that distinguishes the visual arts in Austria during this period. The same may be said of the great sculptor George Raphael Donner (1693–1741), even though his preferred medium was lead.

At the beginning of the 19th century, Austria produced a small, but highly original, school of artists, somewhat scornfully called the Nazarenes, who hoped to breathe new life into painting by giving it new religious content. The **Biedermeier** comforts of the age and the quiet pleasures of the local landscape fill the canvasses of local genre painters, among them Ferdinand Waldmüller (1793–1865). However, the artistic movement most closely associated with Austria is the so-called **Secession** and the artistic handicrafts studio associated with it, the **Wiener Werkstätte**, which gave Austrian art international prominence. A rebellion against the historicizing conventions that dominated the Vienna Academy of Art and against the pedestrian design of mass manufacture, particularly of household goods, both movements drew heavily upon inspiration from similar movements elsewhere in Europe. However, the intense eroticism, coupled with psychic vulnerability, which haunted the subjects of such painters as **Gustav Klimt** and **Egon Schiele**, and the general quality and originality of the Wiener Werkstätte's products, raised esteem for Austria in the world of art. Twentieth-century Expressionism had truly outstanding Austrian representatives as well, such as **Oskar Kokoschka**.

The advent of **Nazi**-dominated government following the **Anschluss** of 1938 devastated Austrian artistic life. Artists such as Kokoschka could not have been more politically unacceptable; their work fell easily into a category the Nazis labeled degenerate. Austrian public interest in its fin de siècle artistic heritage, much less modern art generally, rekindled only gradually after **World War II**.

More recent Austrian art has more than made up for its isolation from international movements in the 1930s and 1940s. The idiosyncratic work of **Friedrich Hundertwasser** is difficult to categorize. Movements such as **Fantastic Realism** and **Vienna Actionism** have won much attention abroad for coloristic quality and, in the case of Actionism, sheer provocativeness. Austrian artists have also worked extensively with multimedia techniques. *See also* ARCHITECTURE; MUSEUMS.

ASYLUM. As a signatory to the Geneva Convention of 28 July 1951, Austria agreed to give refugees the same treatment as other foreigners resident in the country. In some respects, they could enjoy the privileges of Austrian citizens. They had legal standing before Austrian courts and rights to mandatory public **education** and Austrian travel documents. A general law of citizenship passed in 1965 privileged refugee requests for this status over those coming from other foreigners applying for naturalization. Unlike in **Germany** and **Italy**, however, the Austrian constitution did not guarantee the right of asylum in and of itself.

Austria played a key role in the movements of two significant refugee groups. Large numbers of Hungarians crossed their western border following the failed uprising there against Soviet Communism in 1956. Temporary housing for many of them was primitive, to say the least. Nevertheless, the Austrian government, and private refugee organizations that gave significant assistance, successfully relocated these people throughout Europe, the Americas, and Australia. Many Hungarians stayed in Austria itself and found rewarding careers in a broad range of occupations.

A second wave of refugees that made Austria a target were **Jews**, who left the Soviet Union in large numbers during the 1970s and early 1980s. Housed at first in the castle of Scan, and then at a camp in Wöllersdorf in **Lower Austria**, they were generally in transit to Israel and, to a lesser extent, the United States. A number settled in **Vienna**, however, especially in the second district, the Leopoldstadt, the traditional Jewish quarter of the modern city.

The unrest in east central, southeastern, and eastern Europe that accompanied the collapse of the Soviet Union in 1989 brought unusually large and disorganized numbers of political and economic refugees to Austria. Under great popular pressure, especially from the **Freedom Party of Austria** led by **Jörg Haider**, the parliament passed a law regulating the conditions under which asylum was granted on 1 June 1992. Anyone seeking political asylum had to apply for the privilege one week after crossing the Austrian border. Those who came to Austria from a so-called safe country, that is, a politically free one, were to be returned to that country. Failed applicants for asylum were to be deported immediately without appeal. *See also* LAW OF RESIDENCE.

AUSGLEICH/COMPROMISE OF 1867. Following a humiliating loss in 1866 to Prussia in the so-called **Seven Weeks' War**, Austrian Emperor **Franz Joseph** and his advisors were under intense pressure to shore up the position of the **Habsburg Empire** domestically. The loyalty of the Hungarians was especially problematic; discussions of revising their relationship to the monarchy had been underway even before the conflict began.

The Ausgleich raised the status of the Hungarians to that of a ruling nation within the empire, a step much resented by other Habsburg subjects, particularly the Czechs in Bohemia. The Habsburg holdings were formally divided, with two capitals, **Vienna** and Budapest, with the Leitha River the boundary between them. The lands ruled from Vienna were officially named Cis-Leithenia; those under Hungarian control were called Trans-Leithenia. Both terms were so awkward that the entire structure was rather quickly called the Austro–Hungarian empire, and then Austria–Hungary.

The Ausgleich established a few offices common to both halves of the monarchy. The Habsburgs ruled as emperors in the "Austrian" half of their lands and as kings in Hungary. There was a common foreign office and common army, both subject to extensive oversight by the sovereign. There was a joint ministry of finance as well, but its responsibilities were limited to fiscal matters connected with military and diplomatic affairs. Both parts continued to use the same currency and postal service. Every 10 years a commission with membership drawn from both halves of the monarchy met to resolve other financial questions, such as commercial and customs policies and credit obligations, which encumbered both halves of the state. Should this gathering be unable to agree, the resolution of these problems would be turned over to the monarch.

The Reichsrat, or Imperial Assembly, in Vienna legislated on domestic matters for the "Austrian" side of the monarchy, where Germans, Poles, and Czechs were heavily concentrated. The Hungarian Diet did the same for its lands, where ethnic Magyars were a conspicuously small minority among the South Slavic peoples and the Romanians under their control. Both sides used local constitutions and paraconstitutional statutes to govern internal affairs, the Austrian December Laws of 1867 and in Hungary, the March Laws of 1848. At the outset, both regimes were thoroughly undemocratic, with very narrow electorates. By the outbreak of **World War I**, the regime in Vienna, which formally recognized the right of its peoples to cultivate their own **language** and nationality, had extended the right to vote to all male citizens who were 24 years of age and not excluded for other reasons. In Hungary, where the landed nobility was very influential, the franchise was carefully restricted. *See also* BADENI LANGUAGE ORDINANCES.

AUSTRIA, LOWER. The largest in territory of the nine provinces of the Austrian Federal Republic, Lower Austria is also its economically most diverse. It is one of the country's important **agricultural** regions, producing grain and fine white **wines**, such as Gumpoldskirchner, Vöslauer, and Pfaffstätten, as well as many lesser vintages.

Until the beginning of **World War I**, the region was one of the leading industrial centers of the **Habsburg Empire**. The collapse of that structure adversely affected the traditional markets and capital sources of Lower Austria. Heavy bombing during **World War II** undermined it even further. The **Soviet** occupation that followed exploited agricultural and mineral wealth ruthlessly. Close proximity to the Iron Curtain after 1945 made the province less attractive to investors than the western areas of the republic. Today, Lower Austria is a thriving center of the country's service industries.

Administered since the 13th century as Vierteln or quarters, Lower Austria had its capital over the centuries in **Vienna**. After World War I, while the seat of Lower Austria's government remained in the city, Vienna and the region were made two provinces of the First Austrian Republic. In 1986, as the region became more populous and economically complex, Lower Austria's government moved to St. Pölten.

Lower Austria is historically rich. Some of the most famous artifacts of European prehistory were found here. Among them are the Venuses of Galgenberg and Willendorf, which indicate that the area had been settled since the Ice Age. There are numerous sites of Bronze Age settlements (Mannersdorf, Pitten, Franzhausen) as well. Wallburgen, or mound fortifications, testify to a Celtic presence by the New Ice Age.

The Romans occupied Lower Austria south of the **Danube** around 15 BCE and erected fortresses along the river. **Melk**, Klosterneuburg, and Ybbs on the Danube were only a few among many such installations. Major Roman settlements such as **Vindobona** and **Carnuntum** were geographically part of the region as well. Germanic tribes, particularly the Marcomans and the Quadens, began to drift southward in the second century. By 480, another group, the Rugiers, had established regional control centered around Krems. Christianity also penetrated the territory at about the same time. The departure of the Romans from the region at the end of the century left what was to become Lower Austria open to further disorganized wanderings of German and, by the sixth century, Slavic tribes. Avars and Bavarians also entered the area. Charlemagne incorporated Lower Austria into his empire at the end of the eighth century. Parts of the land subsequently fell under the control first of the Slavic Great Moravian Empire, then the Magyars. In 970, 15 years after German Emperor Otto I crushed the latter in the battle of the Lechfeld, he turned the Lower Austrian region into an imperial *Mark* (Eng.: march). His successor, Otto II, enfeoffed the **Babenberg** dynasty with the territory in 976.

From the time the Babenbergs acquired their hold on Lower Austria until their line died out in 1246, the family expanded and consolidated its hold on the region. On 17 September 1156, the mark was raised to a duchy through the so-called *Privilegium minus*; its territorial rulers received wide-ranging legal and political privileges in the same document. The effect of the entire decree was to free Babenberg Austria from imperial jurisdiction.

From 1278 until 1918, the Habsburgs were the territorial rulers of Lower Austria. It was a **Habsburg** prince, Rudolph IV (1339–1365), who raised Lower Austria to the status of archduchy in the spurious *Privilegium maius*, worked out between 1358 and 1359.

Throughout the latter part of the Middle Ages, the high nobility, knights, prelates, and townspeople of Lower Austria developed a strong system of corporate representation in their estates. Even at the end of the 13th century, they were using German in their administrative affairs. By the 15th century, they were able to exercise considerable financial constraints on their territorial rulers. After 1513, they had their own provincial assembly building in Vienna. Their sense of independence became especially troublesome to the Habsburgs in the 16th century, as many members of the estates became Lutherans and often held back from paying contributions to territorial defense against the Ottoman Empire unless further religious freedoms were granted them. Nevertheless, because Lower Austria was directly on the path of invasions from the southeast, the estates generally ended up paying more for their defense than did the other Austrian lands of the Habsburgs. Recatholicized in the 17th century, Lower Austria became the seat of some of the most spectacular building to come out of the Counter-Reformation. The monastery of Melk is an especially good example of this activity.

Lower Austria was one of the first parts of the Habsburg Austrian patrimony to begin the process of industrialization. The 18th century brought the first textile mills to the area. However, it was the region immediately around Vienna that would profit the most from this development, which really only peaked during the second half of the 19th century. *See also* ARCHITECTURE; CATHOLICISM; PROTESTANTISM; RELIGION.

AUSTRIA, NAME. In German, the word for Austria is *Österreich*. It first appears as *Ostarrichi* in charters issued in 996 and 998 by German Emperor Otto III. It may actually have been applied to the Carolingian **Danubian** march even earlier; a ninth-century German–Latin glossary gives *Ostarrichi* as the equivalent of *oriens* (Eng.: east), though no specific territory was associated with the term. Indeed, during this period the word seems to have referred to the entire complex of Carolingian eastern marches. Moreover, during the High Middle Ages, the German *Reich* (MHG: *riche, richi*), or empire, did not have the complex and expansive connotations that it does today. Rather, it merely denoted a general area under a specific ruler's control. In Latin documents, the word *Austria* crops up in a certificate of Emperor Conrad III from 1147. This was probably derived from usages among the Franks and Lombards, for whom the words *Auster*, *Austria*, and *Austrasia* referred generally to lands in east central Europe. *See also* BABENBERG, HOUSE OF.

AUSTRIA, UPPER. Known throughout much of its history as Austria above the Enns, Upper Austria is the most industrialized of all the Federal Republic's provinces. It accounts for about 25 percent of modern Austria's industrial output and exports. It is an **agricultural** center as well, and its numerous and picturesque lakes make it a favorite summer resort. Like **Lower Austria**, it is administered in four historic quarters (Germ.: *Vierteln*), which took shape over several centuries of development and territorial acquisition. The capital is **Linz**, which is both a manufacturing center and a port on the **Danube River**.

There is evidence for the settlement of Upper Austria from the early Stone Age. An elaborate culture developed around **Hallstatt** during the Ice Age. During the Roman era in the history of central Europe, the part of Upper Austria that lies south of the Danube was incorporated into the imperial province of Noricum. The modern city of Wels (Lat.: *Ovilava*) was its capital. Bavarian infiltration began in the latter part of the sixth and beginning of the seventh centuries; Slavs appeared in the east and southeast of the region. As part of the Bavarian duchy of the Agilofinger, Upper Austria was incorporated into the Carolingian Empire under Charlemagne in 788.

The 10th and 11th centuries were especially unsettled times in Upper Austria, as control over parts of it shifted among Magyar invaders, local dynasties such as the Lambachs, the Bavarians, and the Otakar dynasty, which would eventually come to control **Styria**. The **Babenbergs**, based in Lower Austria, who already controlled a great deal of the surrounding area, acquired title to the territory above the Enns in the second half of the 12th century. The move was part of a general expansion of the dynasty's influence throughout the Austrian lands; a separate territorial identity for Upper Austria developed only after this time. It was not until the middle of the 13th century that Upper Austria (Lat.: *Austria superior*) was used to designate noble judicial and communal structures in the terrain roughly between Ybbs and Hausruck.

Once the **Habsburgs** took over the area in the latter third of the century, it became a distinct administrative unit with its own governor. The coat of arms of Upper Austria dates from 1390. By the 15th century, Upper Austria was acquiring greater provincial identity through its local estates. Nevertheless, the precise nature of its legal relationship to Lower Austria was not clarified until well into modern times. In 1861, Austria above the Enns was granted equivalent status to Austria below the Enns within the Habsburg domains. The archbishoprics of **Salzburg** and Passau also had extensive territorial holdings in Upper Austria, some of which endured until the collapse of the **Holy Roman Empire** during the Napoleonic Wars.

Upper Austria was especially troubled by the events of the Reformation and Counter-Reformation. The site of stubborn agrarian unrest at the end of the 16th century, the area was also heavily **Protestant**. Significant elements of the local nobility sympathized with the Bohemian uprising against Habsburg rule that set off the **Thirty Years' War**. The re-catholicization of the area, which began in the 1620s, was especially brutal. The Habsburgs continued to add to the territory; the settlement following the War of the Bavarian Succession brought the Inn Viertel under Habsburg control. The **Anschluss** with Germany in 1938 finally gave Adolf Hitler (1889–1945), born in Braunau on the Inn, a German birthplace.

Following **World War II**, Upper Austria was divided into two zones of **occupation**. The area south of the Danube was under American control; the territory north of the river was largely in Soviet hands. Its industrial facilities and its port infrastructure in Linz were quickly rebuilt. *See also* CATHOLICISM; ECONOMY; HABSBURG EMPIRE; RELIGION.

AUSTRIAN BROADCASTING SYSTEM/ÖSTERREICHISCHE RUNDFUNK (ÖRF).

Reconstituted after **World War II**, the Austrian radio network made political impartiality a central goal. Communists were among its initial editors; one radio program was the *Russian Hour*. On the other hand, the powers that oversaw the **occupation** kept their hand in broadcast media operations—the Americans had their own station in **Linz** and **Salzburg**, Red-White-Red (*Rot-Weiß-Rot*) the color of the Austrian flag, and the British controlled the transmission station in **Graz**.

All of this ended by 1954. The ÖRF, formally established as a **nationalized** service in 1957, was already in operation by 1955. The first Austrian television program, carried through transmitters in **Vienna**, Graz, and Linz, went out in August 1955. Daily TV programming was available by 1959; commercial advertising slots were introduced the same year.

The system often suffered from fiscal shortfalls, and early hopes for nonpartisan operation faded quickly as well. *Proporz*, the custom of giving parties equal treatment in government jobs, impinged upon all nationalized enterprises, television and radio among them. Public criticism of the quality and political slant of programming became routine after March 1963, when the major parties formally agreed to observe *Proporz* when distributing positions in Austrian broadcasting. An influential Vienna daily, the *Neuer Kurier*, began a protest campaign that not only won support from other influential print media, but numerous letters, telegrams, and telephone messages from listeners and viewers. The effort led to the first referendum of the Second Austrian Republic in 1964, asking for reform of the ÖRF.

In 2001, the ÖRF laid down rules for private TV channels. It was also transformed into a foundation under the direction of a council, an arrangement that in no way put an end to political wrangling over control of the system. The choice of general director in 2006 was hotly contested between the **Socialist Party of Austria** and the **Austrian People's Party**. *See also* COMMUNICATIONS; PRESS.

AUSTRIAN FEDERATION OF TRADE UNIONS/ÖSTERREICHISCHE GEWERKSCHAFTSBUND (ÖGB). A supraparty corporative organization of all members of **trade unions**, the federation was established in 1945. It represents the interests of **industrial** labor before the government. Approximately 50 percent of all such workers in Austria belong to the organization.

Like the parallel bodies in other sectors of the Austrian **economy**, the federation must be consulted on laws affecting its membership before such measures are put in force. It also has an important voice in Austrian **educational** policy, particularly in matters concerning vocational training. The various factions within the organization continue to reflect the views of **political parties** whose ideologies are most congenial to them; indeed, party leaders have often been members of the Federation and played key roles in setting its agenda.

The **Socialist Party of Austria** (SPÖ), with the single largest delegation in the organization, has frequently dominated its policies. However, the federation has often rejected extreme leftist political and economic measures. It did not support the call for a general strike that came in 1950 from the Austrian **Communist Party**, backed by the Soviet Union. The failed initiative was the last time the Soviets would try to steer Austrian domestic affairs during the **occupation**.

As government deficits mounted throughout the late 1970s, the federation and Anton Benya (1912–2001), its leader from 1963 to 1987, cooperated with **Bruno Kreisky**, the SPÖ chancellor, who wished to link wage increases with greater labor productivity. The federation has general congresses every four years. During the intervening period, an executive presidium conducts its business. *See also* CHAMBER, AGRICULTURAL; CHAMBER, ECONOMIC; CHAMBER, WORKERS AND SALARIED EMPLOYEES.

AUSTRIAN INDUSTRIAL MANAGEMENT CORPORATION/ ÖSTERREICHISCHE INDUSTRIE AKTIEN GESELLSCHAFT (ÖIAG). As a heavy shareholder in Austrian **nationalized industry** and **banks**, the government in 1970 set up the ÖIAG as a holding company to oversee these complex operations. The conglomerate also paid dividends: in 2002 it distributed 300 million euros to stockowners. Jobholders in ÖIAG firms were ultimately government employees. Numbering at this time around 170,000, they were part of an operation that was Austria's single largest employer in Austria itself. The ÖIAG also supervised the merger and restructuring of some of Austria's heavy **industrial** infrastructure, primarily iron and steel in 1972. Its managerial responsibilities also extended to monitoring Austria's competitive position in the world market. To this end, the ÖIAG initiated rounds of personnel layoffs in the heavy metals sector after 1980. It also arranged the sale of industrial assets. ÖIAG firms have been caught up in the wave of **privatization** that accelerated during the chancellorship of **Wolfgang Schüssel**. The first of these companies to separate itself from government oversight was the steel manufacturer Böhler-Uddeholm, in which the ÖIAG relinquished all of its shares in 2003.

AUSTRIAN NATIONAL BANK. Established in 1816, the bank was modeled on a similar institution in France. Its chief purpose was to bring some order into the chaotic finances and **currency** fluctuations that had plagued the **Habsburg Empire** during the Napoleonic Wars. The bank was exclusively empowered to issue currency in the empire and theoretically independent of state influence. Aided by heavy government taxation, which blotted up large quantities of money, the bank played a major role in restoring fiscal order in the

Habsburg lands. However, it maintained its position as a chief lender to the **government**, and extended credit only to a limited number of wealthy clients. It did set up a mortgage department in 1855.

Refounded by the First Austrian Republic in 1923, the Austrian National Bank was absorbed by the German Reichsbank following the **Nazi Anschluss** in March 1938. Gold and currency reserves held by the Vienna institution were transferred to Berlin. An Austrian National Bank was re-created in 1945 and once again given a monopoly on the issuance of currency. The National Banking Act of 1955 constituted it as a joint stock company, with 50 percent of the shares in the hands of the government. The other half was in the hands of various Austrian **economic** interests such as corporations and businesses. The institution's role is still to ensure the stability of Austrian currency. *See also* BANKING.

AUSTRIAN NATIONAL LIBRARY. One of Europe's major research libraries and manuscript repositories, the library is the former Imperial Court Library and was largely the private property of Austria's **Habsburg** monarchs. Part of it was made accessible for scholars in the first third of the 18th century. A reading room was opened at the beginning of the 20th century in an adjacent Augustinian monastery. Known as the Augustinian Reading Room (Germ: *Augustiner Lesesaal*), it is still in use for those who wish to consult the rare books and materials published before the 20th century. Following **World War I**, the library was **nationalized** and operated as the National Library. It has carried its present title since 1945. In 1966, the main reading room was moved to the newer part of the Imperial Palace (Germ: *Hofburg*) itself. Further renovations that updated its electronic infrastructure were completed in 2004.

The Habsburg collection in all likelihood dates from the 14th century, but it was during the Renaissance that it began to take on library-sized dimensions. Emperor **Frederick III** brought the books and manuscripts in his house's possession to a central location; Emperor **Maximilian I** added significantly to the manuscript collection through acquisitions he made in his marriages to both Duchess Mary of Burgundy (1457–1482) and Bianca Sforza (1472–1510) of Milan. In 1575, Emperor Maximilian II (1527–1576) engaged Hugo Blotius (1534–1608), a humanist from the Netherlands, as the first formal director of the collections; under the latter's supervision the holdings, then numbering around 9,000 items, were first cataloged systematically.

In 1737, the library acquired the 15,000-volume collection of Prince **Eugene of Savoy**. These were housed in the interior architectural centerpiece of the National Library, the so-called *Prunksaal* (Eng: Hall of State), a virtuosic ensemble of **Baroque** design and decoration conceived and built between 1719 and 1726 according to the specifications of the Austrian master of the style, **Johann Bernhard Fischer von Erlach**. His son, Joseph Emmanuel (1693–1742), saw the project through to completion.

Today, the library also serves as a repository for all materials published in Austria and as a training school. Its various collections now number around 7,400,000 items.

AUSTRIAN PEOPLE'S PARTY/ÖSTERREICHISCHE VOLKSPARTEI (ÖVP).

Tainted, indeed sometimes stained by associations with **Austro-Fascism**, and with authoritarian leanings generally, Austrian conservatives decided after **World War II** to establish a party to replace the **Christian Social Party** of the interwar years. Though many still held fast to the strong **Catholic** convictions of the interwar organization, they realized that much of their position had lost its popular appeal. Nor were their connections with authoritarianism kindly received in international circles.

Their new movement, the Austrian People's Party, brought forth in 1945, tried to identify itself with both modern democratic currents and still acceptable elements of its past. Pledging its support for parliamentary democracy, an independent Austria, and a social market **economy**, the ÖVP made the integration of all sectors of Austrian society its overarching mission. While it generally built its programs around a Roman Catholic understanding of man and society, it moved away from any pronounced commitment to a single confession or religious institution. Priests were actually forbidden to run for office. The party stated these views with special force in its Salzburg Program of 30 November 1972. Perhaps its most traditional feature was its quasi-corporate call for peasants, businesspeople, civil servants, and salaried employees to be represented in organized groups rather than individually. The **Women**'s movement, the

Austrian Youth Organization, and the Senior Citizens' Union enjoy some representation in party deliberations as well. The party also strove to act as an ideological umbrella organization for all bourgeois positions: conservative, liberal, and social Catholic.

From November 1947 until March 1970, the ÖVP dominated the Grand Coalition with the **Socialist Party of Austria** (SPÖ) that governed Austria. Members of the ÖVP served as federal **chancellors** from 1947 to 1966 and held the majority of the significant ministries. Indeed, from 1966 to 1970, the party dispensed with a coalition altogether. Leading party functionaries such as **Julius Raab**, **Leopold Figl**, and **Alphons Gorbach** played major roles in the reconstruction of Austria internally and the eventual lifting of the Allied **occupation** in 1955. From 1970 on, however, the electoral fortunes of the ÖVP have dimmed. It was not until 1987 that it reentered a coalition government with the SPÖs and then as a very weak member. Throughout the 1990s, its appeal continued to wane, until scandal in the SPÖ, a general popular acceptance of neoliberal economics, and wariness of foreign immigration increased the ÖVP's appeal. In 2000, led by **Wolfgang Schüssel**, the ÖVP entered into a widely deplored coalition with the **Freedom Party of Austria** to govern the country until 2006. Though at first predicted to perform more strongly in the national elections of 2008, it fell behind the SPÖ in the popular vote once again. *See also* POLITICAL PARTIES.

AUSTRIAN SCHOOL OF ECONOMICS. Classical economic theory based its theory of value on the costs that went into the production of a given item. The Austrian School of Economics, led by Eugen von Böhm-Bawerk (1851–1914), Karl von Menger (1840–1921), and Friedrich von Wieser (1851–1926), all of whom taught at the **University of Vienna** for at least part of their careers, argued that the value of goods and services was not determined by cost, but rather by their utility for a prospective purchaser. The idea had occurred to others as well around 1870, most notably the Englishman William Stanley Jevons and the Swiss Leon Walras. However, it was the economics faculty in **Vienna** who spread the notion to a generation of economists, who had distinguished careers in England and the United States: Josef Schumpeter (1883–1950), Ludwig von Mises (1881–

1973), **Friedrich Hayek**, Fritz Machlup (1902–1983), and Gottfried Haberler (1900–1995), to name some of the most important.

Of the three Viennese scholars, Menger was the least mathematically inclined. Rather, he stressed the role of human psychology in determining ratios of exchange. It was von Wieser (the successor to Menger's chair in economics at the university) who systematized the latter's insights and coined the term *marginal utility*, referring to the diminishing prices of goods and services as the market for them reached the point of satiation. Böhme-Bawerk extended these concepts to capital formation, investment, and savings.

Menger and Böhme-Bawerk were generally hostile to ideology, particularly any that tampered with the free market, such as Marxism. Though no Marxist, Wieser was more inclined toward a so-called mixed **economy** that combined features of both systems. Their students, von Mises, Haberler, and Hayek, have been among the most vigorous defenders of the free market system and exchange rates in the 20th century.

AUSTRIAN STATE TREATY. Signed in **Vienna** on 15 May 1955 by John Foster Dulles for the **United States**, Harold Macmillan for Great Britain, Vyachyslav Molotov for the Soviet Union, Antoine Pinay for France, and **Leopold Figl**, Austrian foreign minister, the treaty ended 10 years of Allied **occupation**. It thus marked the reappearance of an independent Austria. Negotiations concluded some months earlier had established that Austria would also be neutral, though this arrangement was not a formal part of the State Treaty itself. However, without prior accord on **neutrality**, the State Treaty would have been very difficult to conclude. The Soviet Union was anxious that Austria not be a part of any hostile **military** alliance, particularly one that involved **Germany**. The death of the Soviet dictator Joseph Stalin in 1953 temporarily relaxed tensions between the North Atlantic Treaty Organization (NATO) and the Soviet Union, which made Austrian sovereignty possible.

The State Treaty officially described Austria as invaded, then occupied, by Germany from 1938 to 1945. Active Austrian responsibility for the war was thereby ruled out. Nevertheless, the arrangement clearly acknowledged that for many Austrians the **Anschluss** had not been altogether unwelcome. The State Treaty forbids any kind of political and economic union of Austria and Germany and requires that Austria respect human rights, including those of resident minorities. Anyone who served in the German army with the rank of lieutenant or above was forbidden to serve in the army of the Austrian republic. With some minor adjustments, the boundaries of Austria in 1938 were to apply to the new state. Germany, for its part, recognized Austria's independence. Austria was to foster democratic institutions and prohibit all National Socialist and fascist organizations and parties. It was also to renew the **Habsburg Exclusion Act** of 1919.

The Allies promised not to exact any reparations. They also agreed to return to local ownership German assets that the victors had seized in Austria in 1945, as permitted in the Potsdam Treaty. These properties included significant industrial installations and oil fields, banks, insurance companies, and the equipment and capital of the **Danube Steamship Company**. The Soviet Union insisted on some compensation for its lost rights in these enterprises, which it valued at US $150 million. The Austrians agreed to pay this off in kind, rather than cash. This they did with large quantities of manufactured products and petroleum. The obligation was completely fulfilled by 1963. *See also* FOREIGN POLICY; RAAB, JULIUS.

AUSTRO-FASCISM. A disputed term often applied to the authoritarian regime established in the First Austrian Republic between 1933 and 1934 under the chancellorship of **Engelbert Dollfuss**. Heavily influenced by the Italian model, Austro-Fascist ideas were especially prominent in circles connected with the ***Heimwehr*** and some elements of the **Christian Social Party**. Some of the thinking of the social philosopher **Othmar Spann** also figured in the movement. The heart of the program, however, lay in the Korneuburg Oath, presented at an all-Austrian *Heimwehr* festival on 18 June 1930. Its chief author was Richard Steidle (1881–1940), who headed the Tyrolean wing of the movement. The program explicitly rejected Western parliamentary forms of government and the representative functions of political parties in the state. The organization of public opinion was to take place within corporative estates that represented sectors of society rather than individuals. Liberal capitalism and Marxist collectivism were deemed equally destructive to society. *See also* AUSTRO-MARXISM.

AUSTRO-MARXISM. The first stirring of a workers' movement in the Austrian lands of the **Habsburg Empire** began with the Vienna **Revolution of 1848**. Karl Marx himself spent a few days in the city during the latter stages of the turmoil, only to conclude that conditions did not favor a workers' revolution. Local authorities suppressed proletarian protest decisively, executing some of its most vocal representatives.

Until 1867, workers' unions were illegal throughout the empire. The Austrian **constitution** of 1867 guaranteed the right of free assembly, but even after that time, the police had the right to disband meetings if they were deemed hostile to the state.

The movement was split between two influential factions until 1888. A moderate wing, inspired by the ideas of the German Social Democrat Ferdinand Lassalle, sought to realize its program through cooperating with the crown and, on a more qualified basis, the bourgeoisie. A more radical group was oriented toward 19th-century anarchism. But socialism's most significant challenge was to advance an international ideology in the environment of ethnic and national tensions that bedeviled the **Habsburg Empire** from 1867 to 1918. Indeed, it was for this reason that some of social democracy's leaders supported the continuation of the Habsburg monarchy, particularly a more democratized one. The fragmentation of east central Europe into national entities made proletarian solidarity much more difficult to accomplish. By the latter third of the 19th century, workers in Bohemia were already asking for autonomous status within the new **Social Democratic Party of Austria** (SDAP).

These constraints gave socialism in the Habsburg lands its distinctive quality. The movement's leading 19th-century spokesmen, **Viktor Adler** and **Karl Renner**, dedicated themselves to developing an agenda that minimized these frictions. The practical outcome of Adler's efforts was the Hainfeld Program of 1888. By advocating reforms of interest to all workers, such as universal suffrage, the secularization of **education**, the abolition of private property, and the eight-hour working day, the physician-turned-political activist managed to transcend national and ethnic particularism.

Austro-Marxism also reflected these concerns on the theoretical level. Adler refused to use conflict and confrontation, in which majorities triumphed over minorities, as a way of developing SDAP positions. For him and for Renner as well, the purpose of party activity was to encourage all members to express themselves. Participation in the democratic process was central to the development of a fully realized individual, who, because his voice had been heard and taken account of, was able to internalize the ideology that eventually emerged from these discussions. Viewed functionally, politics was a matter of compromise in which no one ever got all that he or she wanted, but their interests were never altogether ignored.

Adler and his followers also believed that a revolution in human consciousness had to parallel the revolution in **economic** relationships, which they regarded as inevitable. They therefore stressed the need to offer educational opportunities and aesthetic experiences to workers. Just as the bourgeoisie had marginalized the humanity of the proletariat with their monopolistic hold on the means of production, they had, according to **Engelbert Pernerstorfer**, a leading Austrian social democrat, robbed the laboring classes of their rightful place in the cultural community. Such programs gave Austro-Marxists the reputation of being the most cultivated socialists in Europe.

Adler supported such SDAP commonplaces as nationalization of the means of production. Renner believed that it was society through conscious action, not the law of nature, that brought about human equality. Nevertheless, the general thrust of their views, and of those who followed them, emphasized political tactics and strategy rather than grand intellectual constructs. Influential socialist thinkers and political leaders in 20th-century Europe, such as the Italian Antonio Gramsci and the future dictator of Yugoslavia, Josip Broz (Tito), spent time with them in **Vienna** during **World War I** and immediately afterward. The generally cautious nature of their activities aroused the contempt of more radical Marxists elsewhere. After several stays in Vienna between 1907 and 1914, Leon Trotsky (1879–1940) dismissively dubbed the Austro-Marxists "the guardian angels of the Vienna **Creditanstalt**," the most influential bank in the city. Joseph Stalin ridiculed them in 1913 as fellow travelers of the bourgeoisie. Renouncing both Bolshevism, in 1917, and terrorism a year later, the Austro-Marxists were repudiated by the Communist International in 1918. *See also* BAUER, OTTO.

– B –

BABENBERG, HOUSE OF. In 976, German Emperor Otto II invested a certain Luitpold, or Leopold, with the Ostmark (Eng.: Eastern March) and the title of margrave associated with it. Part of what is today **Lower Austria**, the territory was one of several such units that Charlemagne had established for defensive purposes along the sprawling boundaries of his empire. Later historians, most notably Bishop Otto of Freising (d. 1158), himself a descendant of Luitpold, attached the name Babenberg to the house.

Much about the early background of Luitpold and his family remains unclear. The term *Ostmark* itself first came into widespread use among 19th- and 20th-century historians. Nevertheless, it was he and his heirs whose acquisitions and policies gave geopolitical shape to modern Austria. South of the **Danube River**, Luitpold enlarged the lands of the Ostmark to the **Vienna** Woods. To roughly the middle of the 12th century, the Babenbergs were very active in expanding their holdings in all directions; they never abandoned this policy altogether. It was only in 1186, for example, that they acquired claims to the duchy of **Styria** from a local and fading dynasty, the Otakars. Often cooperating with the German emperors—who rewarded them accordingly—the Babenbergs built their territorial complex at the expense of the Hungarians and Bohemians on their borders, as well as by purchase and inheritance of lands from local noble families and ecclesiastical foundations. They made good use of dynastic alliances as well. Some married into the families of their regional territorial aristocracies; a few wedded the daughters or widows of both German and Byzantine emperors.

Under Margrave Leopold III (r. 1095–1136), after 1663 the patron saint of Lower Austria, signs of a specific sense of Babenberg, even Austrian, territoriality began to appear. Documents issued by the margrave characteristically refer to him as a prince of the land (*principatus terrae*). One literary source, Bishop Altmann of Passau's chronicle of his life, refers to specific legal custom (*ius illius terrae*) practiced in the Babenberg lands.

The most important step in this development was the *Privilegium minus*, given by the German Emperor Frederick I Barbarossa (ca. 1125–1190) to Leopold III's son, Henry II, in 1156. Called Henry *Jasomirgott* ("Yes, so [help] me God") because of the oath he swore on the occasion, Henry agreed to give up claims that he had recently acquired to the duchy of Bavaria. As compensation, Frederick I granted him wide-ranging privileges in his Austrian lands. The margravate was raised to a duchy, and the Babenbergs received the title "duke." Both the male and the female lines of the house had rights of inheritance in these lands. Should Henry and his wife be childless, they, not the emperor, could name their successor. No foreign legal codes were operative in the territory without the new duke's consent. The imperial military obligations of the dukes were limited to defending the borders of their territory.

The generosity of the *Privilegium minus* has led some historians to question its authenticity, especially because there is no extant original document. What we know of it comes from copies. Contemporaries, such as Otto of Freising (d. 1158), speak of its existence however, and the general opinion is that it is genuine. Although the *Privilegium* certainly was not intended to detach the Austrian lands from the **Holy Roman Empire**, centered in **Germany**, it was nevertheless a milestone on the way to distinctive Austrian territoriality. By the end of the 12th century, the Babenbergs had effectively freed their lands from claims of princes who lived outside of their duchies and from many of the sprawling ecclesiastical jurisdictions interspersed throughout their holdings.

Henry II also shifted his court from Klosterneuburg to **Vienna**. He gave the future Austrian metropolis some of its most distinctive institutions. He was the founder of the Vienna **Benedictine** monastery (*Schottenkloster*) and constructed a Hofburg, literally a court castle, which would be enlarged and reconstructed throughout the centuries to come.

Babenberg rule came to an end in the Austrian lands with the reign of Duke Frederick the Quarrelsome (r. 1230–1246). Few men were ever more accurately described by their epithets. Embroiled in conflicts with the cities and officials in his own lands, he also tangled episodically with the Bohemians, the Hungarians, and the Wittelsbach dukes of Bavaria. Even his own mother, the Byzantine princess Theodora, complained about him to Emperor Frederick II. The latter placed an imperial ban on Frederick's head in 1235 after the duke refused to appear before him. He died in battle against the Hungarians in 1246, with no heirs.

BACHMANN, INGEBORG (1926–1973). Arguably the preeminent lyric poet of post–**World War II** Austria, if not in the German language as a whole, Bachmann was born in **Carinthia**. An extraordinarily conflicted personality, she early became a committed anti-**Nazi**, even though her father was a firm supporter of the movement. Her doctoral thesis, which she completed at the **University of Vienna** in 1951, was on the philosopher Martin Heidegger, himself sympathetic to some aspects of Nazism. She was also deeply offended by the countercultural student upheavals of the 1960s, antifascist though many demonstrators claimed to be.

During her student years in Vienna, Bachmann worked briefly as an intern in a local psychiatric asylum. She was also close to several postwar Austrian intellectuals and writers, who met regularly at the Café Raimund in the neighborhood of **Vienna**'s great **museums** and the Vienna People's Theater (*Volkstheater*). The organizing figure at these gatherings, **Hans Weigel**, supported her work vigorously. He was also one of several men with whom she became emotionally and often self-destructively involved. Another major author among her lovers was the Swiss novelist Max Frisch.

Bachmann offended some prominent cultural figures in Austria when she broke her ties to the Raimund group and associated herself with the German literary circle Gruppe 47. Nevertheless, she won major prizes for her writing from both the Second Austrian Republic and the Federal Republic of Germany. She was versatile as well as gifted. Her literary output included novels, criticism, libretti for musical works such as the German composer Hans Werner Henze's (1926–) *The Prince of Homburg* (1960) and *The Young Lord* (1965), and a series of highly imaginative radio plays.

But poetry was her major calling. With her crushing depressions often lying just beneath her lines, she exploited her uncanny ability to examine her emotions even as she experienced them, then to translate both thought and feeling directly into words. Bachmann burned to death in a fire in her apartment in Rome. *See also* LITERATURE; WOMEN.

BADENI LANGUAGE ORDINANCES. Although the **Ausgleich** of 1867 granted the kingdom of Hungary considerable autonomy in its internal affairs, this privilege did not extend to Slavic national groups in the **Habsburg Empire**. Perhaps the most resentful were the Czechs in the kingdom of Bohemia, who had long asked for similar recognition. Among their most vocal and consistent demands was for permission to use their own tongue in administrative and legal affairs within Bohemia. This brought them into regular conflict with a large German minority, which also had a historic presence in the kingdom. The issue spilled over to the parliament of the Austrian half of the monarchy where, by 1897, there was an assertive Czech representation. Although they could be outvoted by delegates of German-speaking constituencies, the latter were not gathered into a single **political party**.

Needing Czech support for other measures he was promoting, the minister-president, Count Casimir Badeni (1846–1909), a Pole, offered proposals that required all civil servants in the kingdom of Bohemia to be functionally bilingual in written and spoken German and Czech by 1901. Whereas most educated Czechs could use both languages with some fluency, the same thing was not true of the Germans in the kingdom. German rioting over the measures broke out in Prague as well as in smaller urban centers in Bohemia and in the Austrian lands. In the face of this opposition, Badeni resigned his position, and his proposals did not take effect. The antagonism between Germans and Czechs in Bohemia deepened, making local parliamentary life often a bitter affair. This was also true in the Austrian Imperial Assembly where, from the beginning of the 20th century through most of **World War I**, business had to be conducted by emergency decree. *See also* GOVERNMENT; HABSBURG EMPIRE.

BANKING. Before 1848, Austria had few banking institutions worthy of the name. The **Austrian National Bank**, created in 1816, catered to the credit needs of the **government**, the aristocracy, and the wealthiest segment of heavy **industry**. Small businesses, artisans, and rural populations generally had little access to deposit facilities or loans beyond what local moneylenders were prepared to offer. The First Austrian Savings Bank (*Erste Österreichische Sparkasse*) was founded in 1819, but had few immediate counterparts.

Spurred on by the public press, after the **Revolutions of 1848** the **Habsburg** government, along with major Austrian private bankers such as the Rothschilds and a few members of the high aristocracy, set up the Austrian Credit Institution for Trade and Manufacture *(K.K. priv. Österreichische Credit-Anstalt für Handel und Gewerbe)* in 1855. Once again, the **Creditanstalt**, as it was familiarly known, confined itself to serving the monied and creditworthy in Austrian society—the bank was heavily invested in the Austrian **railroad** system, for example—but by this time other facilities were beginning to offer similar financial services to **agricultural** enterprises of scale in the countryside. The Land Credit Bank (*Boden-Credit-Anstalt*), organized in 1863 and backed heavily with French money, was a prominent example; it took savings deposits and extended loans, though still not widely enough to satisfy the fiscal requirements of the general population. The Anglo–Österreichische Bank of 1863 also brought much-needed foreign capital into the Austrian banking market, but again largely for investment and development purposes.

Nevertheless, banks like the Erste Österreichische Sparkasse, which offered people of modest means a way to put aside money relatively safely and draw interest on it, were more numerous after 1840. Seventeen were in place by the end of the decade. Their chief function was to cover local demand for mortgages and cash advances to local governments. They also quite intentionally, from the standpoint of the government, encouraged thrift and industriousness among the lower echelons of society. Upper classes made good use of these services, too. Yet another public banking convenience was the Austrian Postal Savings Bank (*Österreichische Postsparkasse*), established in 1883 as the first savings institution in Europe that coupled mail services with check-writing privileges. Communal savings banks were established in 1855 in part to help municipalities pay for public poor relief.

Connections with French and British capital briefly survived the collapse of Austria–Hungary in 1918, though in neither case were the investors or their governments obligated to shore up their

Vienna operations in any liquidity crisis. The British, however, were no longer positioned to serve as lenders to the world. Indeed, the end of the monarchy in 1918 and the establishment of the First Austrian Republic severely tested the viability of Austrian banks. Catastrophic inflation, the inevitable side effect of trying to pay off the country's outstanding war debts by printing more money, left banks more dependent than ever on an inflow of hard **currency** from abroad. The general lack of fiscal discipline in Austria following the collapse of the Habsburg Empire in 1918 led to the creation of the Austrian Currency Bank (*Österreichische Notenbank*), which controlled the issuance of new legal tender, while the Austrian National Bank oversaw the Austrian foreign debt and the amount of money in circulation at any one time.

Banks both large and small regularly folded during the First Republic from the end of **World War I** to the **Anschluss** with Nazi Germany in 1938. The pervasive economic nationalism of east central Europe made it very difficult for Viennese banks to restore connections in Czechoslovakia and elsewhere. These failures often hit what social protections Austrian society had to offer, such as foundations that supported crippled children and municipal housing projects. Those institutions that remained solvent were increasingly capitalized from Germany even before Hitler's takeover.

Major Austrian banks, such as the Creditanstalt, along with industrial concerns and utilities, were officially **nationalized** in 1946 to prevent their assets from falling into the hands of the occupying forces, particularly those from the Soviet Union. These firms, however, were run as profit-making financial institutions in which the state was a heavy, though not exclusive, stockholder.

Coalition governments led from 2000 to 2006 by **Wolfgang Schüssel** of the **Austrian People's Party** encouraged the **privatization**, already underway for about a decade, of many financial institutions. Austrian banks were merged, consolidated, and taken over by foreign competitors and investment groups with dizzying speed. At the same time, the collapse of the Soviet Union opened the way for major Austrian banks and their affiliates to gain a firm and profitable foothold in the redevelopment plans of countries in eastern and east central Europe. Although Austrian financial conglomerates and the banks that participated continued to profit handsomely from these ventures, there have been notable failures too, chiefly the Bank for Labor and Economic Development (**BAWAG**) investment operation.

BAROQUE. Along with the **Biedermeier** of the post-Napoleonic period and turn-of-the century Jugendstil, the Baroque is clearly among the artistic styles to have made permanent marks on Austria. Indeed, all three terms now characterize entire historical epochs rather than simply **architectural** and artistic forms.

The origins of the term *Baroque* are obscure. Some **art** historians trace it to a Portuguese term for an irregularly shaped pearl. Its hallmarks are grandiose representational buildings and interiors, both secular and spiritual. In the lands of the Habsburg monarchy, the Baroque style was prevalent in the 17th and early 18th centuries. It is especially linked with the success of the Catholic Counter-Reformation and the reconquest of east central Europe from the Ottoman Empire by the house of Habsburg and its allies. Throughout much of the dynasty's eastern lands, new building was as much a necessity as a luxury, since the long wars with the Ottomans had devastated many structures. **Vienna** itself had become a very run-down city. Baroque artists and architects enjoyed generous patronage from Emperors Leopold I (1640–1705), Joseph I (1678–1711), and Charles VI (1685–1740). Noble houses throughout the **Habsburg Empire** employed them as well, as did wealthier cloisters.

The initial stages of Baroque building and decoration in the Austrian territories took place largely in ecclesiastical settings. The work was usually done by Italians, in whose land the style had first appeared. Most important among these monuments are St. Peter's Cathedral in **Salzburg**; the mausoleum of Emperor **Ferdinand II** in **Graz**; and, in Vienna, the facade of the Church am Hof. In the case of the latter, the alterations followed the austerely elegant lines prescribed by the **Jesuits** for their churches in **Italy**. A substantial new wing of the Imperial Palace (*Hofburg*), called the Leopoldine Tract, also dates from this period. Austrian artists worked on the decorative features of these structures, but they were not initially as accomplished as either their Italian or Netherlandic counterparts.

This situation changed following the defeat of the Ottoman army before Vienna in 1683. Austrian builders and architects received lavish support from both the imperial court and its imitators and the upper hierarchy of the church. Architects such as **Johann Bernhard Fischer von Erlach** and **Johann Lukas von Hildebrandt**, who was actually born in Genoa, were inspired and supported not only by the 17th-century victories of their Habsburg rulers but by the challenge to outdo the court style of Louis XIV, the Austrian dynasty's formidable enemy to the west. It was within this context that Fischer von Erlach drew up his first, and never realized, plan for Schönbrunn, the Habsburg summer residence in Vienna, and Lukas von Hildebrandt designed the Belvedere Palace for **Prince Eugene of Savoy**, the great imperial general. Another significant architect from **Lower Austria**, **Jakob Prandtauer**, planned the remodeling of the imposing cloister of **Melk** on the **Danube**. The Baroque building style worked its way in a somewhat more modest vein into municipal architecture as well by the middle of the 18th century.

The painting and sculpture of the Austrian Baroque often served decorative functions within these larger buildings. The rich colors and dynamic lines of such work contrast brilliantly with the weighty lines of the structures that house them. The outcome can be seen in the great ceiling frescoes of Melk and the walls and ceilings of the so-called Prunksaal (Eng.: Hall of State) of the **Austrian National Library**. *See also* MUSIC.

BAUER, OTTO (1881–1938). Among the leading theoreticians of **Austro-Marxism**, Bauer also played an important part in the practical work of the Austrian **Social Democratic Party** (SDAP). Following the death of **Viktor Adler** in November 1918, he served as foreign minister of the new Austrian Republic until 1919. Bauer was also his party's leader. He functioned in the latter role until 1934, when, after the **February Uprising**, which ended in a smashing defeat for Austria's SDAP, he fled Austria for Czechoslovakia. Here Bauer founded and headed the office of his party in exile. Four years later he died in Paris.

Bauer's most important theoretical work took up the question of how nationalism and international socialism were to be reconciled (*The National Question and Social Democracy*, 1907). Like many Austro-Marxists, he argued that socialists should treat their proletarian constituents as individuals. Regardless of their ethnic identity, workers should be given the opportunity to better themselves through **education**. Linguistically and nationally different though they might be, they could all be part of a larger cultural community.

Though Bauer generally hoped to realize the SDAP agenda through parliamentary and peaceful means, he did not rule out the use of violence altogether, especially should the opposition to the party program itself become undemocratic. His opinion, and that of others like him, was expressed in the Declaration of **Linz** in 1926. This statement also justified dictatorship should the counterrevolutionary bourgeoisie refuse to accept socialist measures, however democratically adopted. The middle class and peasant population of the First Austrian Republic remained wary of such rhetoric, which identified Bauer with the left wing of his party.

BAWAG (BANK FOR LABOR AND ECONOMIC DEVELOPMENT/BANK FÜR ARBEIT UND WIRTSCHAFT).

Established in 1922 as the Worker's Bank (*Arbeiterbank*) by the Austrian Social Democrat and political leader **Karl Renner**, the bank was initially capitalized by the **Social Democratic Party** (SDAP). Liquidated for political reasons in 1934, it was refounded in 1947 and named the BAWAG (Bank for Labor and Economic Development) in 1963. It maintained its identification with the workers' movement and with the postwar **Socialist Party of Austria** (SPÖ). In 1995, the Provincial Bank of Bavaria (*Bayerische Landesbank*) acquired 45 percent of its shares; the Socialist-sponsored supermarket conglomerate Konsum and the **Austrian Federation of Trade Unions** holding another 45 percent between them.

By then BAWAG had become a major economic force in Austrian **banking**, following goals and business strategies firmly rooted in the dynamics of late-20th-century global capitalism. Merger and acquisition maneuvers were a central part of its operations. In 2000, BAWAG took over the venerable Austrian Postal Savings Bank (*Österreichische Postsparkasse*) to further enlarge its network of branches throughout the country. By 2006, however, dishonest bookkeeping practices hidden in offshore activities, reckless speculation, and unsavory fiscal relationships with the upper echelons of the SPÖ and organized labor, as well as reckless speculators, had badly damaged BAWAG's fiscal standing and the reputations of its highest management in the international banking community. *See also* TRADE UNIONS.

BEETHOVEN, LUDWIG VAN (1770–1827). The composer was the offspring of a **musi**cal family that had emigrated to **Germany** from the Netherlands. At 13 years of age, Beethoven played viola and harpsichord in the house orchestra of the prince-bishop of Bonn. He studied briefly at the local university, but never took a degree.

Beethoven stayed briefly in **Vienna** in 1787, but he returned to Germany because of family obligations. After 1792, he made the **Habsburg** capital his permanent residence. There he studied counterpoint with **Joseph Haydn**, to whom he dedicated his first three piano sonatas. He also worked with other local teachers, including Anton Salieri, the music director of the imperial chapel and court orchestra. His musical output was not only sizeable, but strikingly original. His nine symphonies, five piano concertos, 32 piano sonatas, 16 string quartets, and many other works owe a great deal to the models of **Mozart** and Haydn, as well as to other 18th-century German composers, but move well beyond them in expressive force. This is particularly true of the Ninth Symphony and the introspective string quartets of his last years. His deafness, which had become total by 1820, clearly influenced the mood of the latter.

Beethoven was well connected to the musical circles of Vienna. His patrons were among the most influential nobles of the city and even the imperial family itself. He gave music lessons in 1803–1804 to Archduke Rudolph (1788–1831), to whom the composer dedicated several works, including the Emperor (Fifth) Piano Concerto. Along with two noblemen, Rudolph set up an endowment to keep Beethoven from taking employment elsewhere, an arrangement that collapsed when the government declared bankruptcy in 1811. The composer's funeral, from the Church of the Holy Trinity, was a major public spectacle.

BENEDICTINES, ORDER OF. Originating in **Italy**, the Benedictines played a central role in the Christianization of Austria. Their first establishments date from the 7th through the 10th centuries. During this time, they were often competing with Irish monastic practice, which also appeared early in the Austrian lands. The Benedictines served more than spiritual functions; they also cleared and cultivated the land that they occupied.

Invasions by the Magyars in the 10th century temporarily brought much of their work to a standstill. However, following the defeat of these raiders from the east by Otto I, the emperor in **Germany**, the Benedictines resumed their work and became the dominant cloistered order of Austria in the period between 1060 and 1230. Thirteen of medieval Austria's 22 Benedictine monasteries still exist. Among these are St. Peter (ca. 700) in **Salzburg**; **Kremsmünster** (777) and Lambach (1056) in **Upper Austria**; Göttweig (1094), **Melk** (1089), and Altenburg (1144) in **Lower Austria**; Admont (1074) and St. Lambrecht (1076) in **Styria**; and the Schotten (Irish) Monastery (1158) in **Vienna**. Of the original nunneries, there is only one left, Nonnberg in Salzburg.

The Benedictines were medieval Austria's teachers and scholars. The larger cloisters, such as Göttweig and Kremsmünster, operated both internal schools for their own clergy, and external academies that trained young boys, largely from the nobility, who would follow secular careers. The Benedictines were also notable scholars and writers, not only in Latin but in the German of the day. Melk was a center of vernacular religious and didactic poetry. The oldest named female author in the German language is in all likelihood Frau Ava, a member of a nunnery associated with Melk. Before her death around 1127, she composed a rhymed history of the life of Jesus and a poem on the last judgment.

The cultural high point of Benedictine monastic life in Austria came during the era of the **Baroque**. In the wake of the triumphant Counter-Reformation of the 17th and early 18th centuries, the cloisters were turned into residential castles and hired the finest architects to design and supervise the transition. While they continued their **educational** and scholarly missions, the Benedictine cloisters became **theatrical** and **musical** centers as well. To this day, many Benedictine abbeys have high schools and continue to house some members who carry on professional scholarly activities. They have always enjoyed a large degree of independence, even though there has been a central office for the order in Austria since 1930. *See also* CATHOLICISM; EDUCATION; MUSIC; RELIGION.

BERG, ALBAN (1885–1935). Along with **Arnold Schoenberg** and Anton Webern (1883–1945), Berg was a central figure in the so-called Second Vienna School of composition, in which **music** was constructed in series of tonal rows made up of the 12 half steps of the chromatic scale. He studied with Schoenberg between 1904 and 1910, and the two men became lifelong friends.

A perfectionist, Berg did not leave behind a large body of work. Nevertheless, much of what he did was important. His opera *Wozzeck* (1925) and his violin concerto (1935) have secure places in the modern musical repertory. Berg never broke quite as sharply with classical harmonic patterns as did his mentor. Twelve-tone technique and surging Romanticism are prominent features of both *Wozzek* and the violin concerto. His other major opera, *Lulu*, a gritty series of tableaux depicting the range of erotic depravity, is more relentlessly atonal. Unfinished at his death, the third act of the work was realized by the modern Austrian composer Friedrich Cerha (1926–). The first performance of this version of the piece was in 1979. Berg also produced some poetry and was a notable essayist on musical topics.

BERNHARD, THOMAS (1931–1989). Along with **Peter Handke**, Bernhard was the most widely known Austrian writer in both in the German-speaking world and elsewhere after **World War II**. Born out of wedlock in the Netherlands to an Austrian mother and father, who killed himself in Berlin in 1940, Bernhard's life was troubled from childhood to death, both psychologically and physically. He spent most of his youth with his maternal grandparents, briefly in **Vienna** and then in **Salzburg** and its immediate environs during **World War II**. Bernhard had many artistic gifts. He received a degree in **music** from the Salzburg Mozarteum in 1957, the same year he published his first volume of poetry.

An attack of pleurisy, then the onset of tuberculosis in his late teens, marked the beginning of his mordant worldview. His first stabs at creative writing took place in a sanatorium where he lived from 1949 to 1951; his entire corpus of drama, fiction, and poetry is full of medical and pathological referents, for example *Ja* (*Yes*, 1978). His lifelong contempt for state-run institutions also began early in his career. Bernhard lived his final 10 years well aware that he would never recover from the variety of respiratory and cardiovascular afflictions that beset him.

Bernhard was seemingly careful to place his stories in specific locations, often in mountainous regions that could readily be taken for areas around the Salzburg of his youth. His first novel, *Frost* (1963), a picture of psychological decomposition set in provincial Austria, established his reputation as a serious and original writer. Nevertheless, the situations he explores could take place anywhere. The impact of his texts on a reader comes from the incongruity between the icy detachment of his descriptive prose and the desperate inner lives of his characters. In his fiction, personal identity is fleeting at best, and conventional situations suddenly turn into major psychological events. Although his characters are not always wholly mad, they are often on the brink of it. With no way to deal with their trouble, they withdraw from human society altogether. Often compared with the late 19th-century cultural critic **Karl Kraus**, Bernhard also laced his texts with caustic commentary on the social and aesthetic conventions of contemporary Austria, including its self-styled avant-garde. His later work took a wittier and more humanitarian turn, but it was hardly generous.

Bernhard claimed that his work had little to do with the society and politics of his time. Nevertheless, his popularity in the 1960s and 1970s clearly stemmed from the widespread disdain for established authority and traditional behavior patterns among the youth of those decades. **Bruno Kreisky**, the dominant political force of Austria from 1973 to 1983, was in Bernhard's unsparing words, "an aging, self-satisfied state clown." The more criticism his work drew from the Austrian cultural and political establishment, the more widely it sold. Bernhard's fiercely provocative play *Heldenplatz* (*Heros' Square*) in 1988, the 50th anniversary year of the **Anschluss** with **Germany**, had a much more explicit agenda than did his earlier work. A critical study of Austrian anti-Semitism in which a **Jewish** academic family, headed by a father who sounds a great deal like Karl Kraus, leaves the Austria of Bernhard's day, it reinforced the writer's reputation as his country's most biting contemporary critic. The emigration of the early 20th-century philosopher **Ludwig Wittgenstein** also lurks in corners of the script. Bernhard's will forbade any future performances, publication, or public readings of his work in Austria after his death. *See also* LITERATURE

BIEDERMEIER. A term with multiple meanings in the cultural history of Austria and **Germany**, Gottlieb Biedermeier was a totally fictional schoolteacher, pious, dutiful, and placid, the satiric invention of a mid-19th-century Swabian humorist, Ludwig Eichrodt. Following the **Revolutions of 1848**, the word applied not only to the personalities of those like Mr. Biedermeier himself, but an entire civic culture between 1815 and 1848 in the Austrian Empire. The period is also called the Vormärz, or pre-March, because the revolutions in the **Habsburg Empire** first erupted in **Vienna** in that month.

The Biedermeier outlook was associated with the middle classes of the time, who allegedly thought far more of personal comfort and private aesthetic satisfactions than of grand schemes for political and intellectual change. The intrusive censorship of the contemporary Habsburg **government** contributed much to this attitude. These ideals, however, also had a higher philosophical resonance, as shown in the writing of **Adalbert Stifter**.

The locus of Biedermeier cultural life was the well-appointed bourgeois home or homelike setting, such as upscale **coffeehouses** or elaborate countryside picnics. For those of more modest means, there were suburban wine gardens (***Heuriger***) and dance locales. Indeed, the better-endowed members of society frequented these places, too. Landscape painters such as Ferdinand Waldmüller (1793–1865) and Rudolph von Alt (1812–1905), whose work drew heavily on the English painter Thomas Lawrence, fashioned exquisitely detailed but idealized pastoral scenes that diverted Vienna's middle classes from changes that modern **industrialization** was already bringing to the landscape around them. Waldmüller and Friedrich von Amerling (1803–1887), among several notable painters, did miniatures for which the subjects as well as the patrons came from the bourgeois families of the day.

The furniture styles of the era juxtaposed classically graceful lines and pronounced lines, which were often reinforced by bentwood components. Highly polished veneers, metal filigree ornamentation, and bright colors further heightened the sharp appearance of these products. The first luxury home furnishing store to be opened in Vienna, run by a designer of the period, Josef Ulrich Danhauser, featured such items, along with table, tea, and coffee services. Subsequent schools of Viennese **art** and design, most notably the **Secession** and the **Wiener Werkstätte**, consciously exploited many of these patterns. Biedermeier styles are still incorporated into contemporary Austrian interior decoration; original Biedermeier artifacts can be very valuable.

Despite all that Habsburg officials did to suppress intellectual originality, the period 1815–1848 was a high point in Austrian **music**, **literature**, and art. The **Society of the Friends of Music**, founded in 1812 as a private organization by a group of music-lovers, continues to sponsor concerts of the **Vienna Philharmonic Orchestra**. The composer **Franz Schubert** and the playwrights **Franz Grillparzer**, **Ferdinand Raimund**, and **Johann Nestroy**, exasperated though they often were with their restrictive environment, worked brilliantly in it. See also ARCHITECTURE; METTERNICH, KLEMENS WENZEL NEPOMUK LOTHAR, PRINCE OF.

BREGENZ. A Roman garrison since 15 BCE, Bregenz, the capital of the **Vorarlberg**, was named a Roman municipality (*Brigantium*) in 50 CE. The Alemanic German invaders who destroyed the settlement in 259–260 reinhabited it by around 450. Saints Gallus and Columban, missionaries from Ireland, proselytized in the area between 610 and 612. The Udalrichs, a local dynasty who called themselves the counts of Bregenz, made the area their residence after 917 until their line died out in 1170. The town was formally founded in 1249 by the Swabian Count of Montfort, Hugo I. The **Habsburgs** acquired Bregenz between 1451 and 1523 through purchase. During the Napoleonic Wars, Bregenz was governed by Bonaparte's Bavarian allies.

From the 18th century on, Bregenz played an increasingly important role in the administration of the Vorarlberg. In 1786, it became a regional administrative center, in 1861, the seat of the provincial parliament. These developments were in part attributable to the city's growth as a **transportation** hub on Lake Constance. In 1884, **railroads** could cross the Arlberg, a mountain, and steamboats could dock in its harbor.

BREUER, JOSEF (1842–1925). An internist and physiologist, Breuer was born in **Vienna**, the son of a **Jewish** religious teacher. A graduate of one of the capital city's most prestigious secondary schools, the Academic Gymnasium, he was the first to locate the autonomic control of breathing in the vagus nerve.

An abidingly modest man, Breuer's place in medical history is largely the result of his relationship, which dated from the late 1870s, with the young **Sigmund Freud**. It was Breuer who encouraged his junior colleague to move from physiology into general practice and from there to psychiatry.

Breuer developed the so-called talking cure for neuroses while treating a Vienna-born Jewish girl, Bertha Pappenheim, later to become famous as Anna O. Though periodically lucid, she frequently suffered from crippling episodes of sleepwalking, paralysis in her limbs, and numerous false pregnancies. Encouraging her to speak while he had her under hypnosis, Breuer discovered that her symptoms and the fantasies associated with them subsided after she talked about them. Working from the hypothesis that his patient's troubles stemmed from long-repressed inner conflicts, he concluded that by bringing these issues to the level of the conscious, he could free the young woman from their worst effects. He himself became so distressed by listening to these outpourings that, after she left his treatment, he turned all similar cases over to Freud. The two men continued to collaborate however, publishing their *Studies on Hysteria* in 1895. *See also* VIENNA SCHOOL OF MEDICINE.

BRUCKNER, ANTON (1824–1896). One of late 19th-century Austria's most noted composers, and a prodigiously gifted organist, Anton Bruckner was born in **Upper Austria**. While teaching school in 1848, Bruckner became the organist at the monastery of St. Florian, where he is buried under the instrument. From 1855 to 1868, he held the same position in the cathedral of **Linz**, the provincial capital. At the same time he studied composition and **music** theory in **Vienna**. In 1868, he became professor of music theory at the Vienna Conservatory and the imperial chapel organist. From 1875 to 1892, he lectured regularly on harmony and counterpoint at the **University of Vienna**, the first person to hold such an appointment.

A deeply devout **Catholic** who interrupted his classes to observe the angelus, Bruckner ranks with Franz Liszt as a composer of important choral works for the church. It is, however, his massive symphonies, nine in all, that are most widely performed today. Several of these he rewrote obsessively. An admirer of the work of Richard Wagner, he worked in dense and repeated blocks of sound, which have a powerful cumulative impact upon a listener. The Fourth is perhaps the best example. Considerable melodic inspiration and richly inventive orchestration, a by-product of long years spent at the organ, enabled Bruckner to avoid the tedium always lurking in his larger musical strategy.

Bruckner and Wagner were targets of relentless criticism from the influential Viennese music critic **Eduard Hanslick**, who championed the classical structure in the music of yet another contemporary in Vienna, Johannes Brahms (1893–1897).

BURGENLAND. As its name, which means Land of Castles, implies, the modern Austrian province of the Burgenland is both historically and geographically a border area. It was called that, however, only after 1919 and referred to the four counties of Hungary of which the region had been part on and off since the 10th century.

The Burgenland was settled in the Mesolithic period (10,000–5000 BCE). By 5000 BCE, peasants were living in large numbers around Lake Neusiedl and the Pullendorf basin. Local copper and antimony deposits encouraged mining throughout the Bronze Age; the rich viticulture of the modern Burgenland can be traced back to around 700 BCE. The Celts had settled the area by 450 BCE, and it eventually was gathered into the Roman province of Pannonia 15 years before the beginning of the Christian era.

The barbarian migrations brought Huns, Goths, Lombards, and Avars to the region. Around 800 Charlemagne defeated the Avars, thus bringing the Burgenland under Frankish–Bavarian control until 907, when the Magyars conquered it. While the Magyars continued to control its fortifications, the Burgenland was heavily settled by German-speaking peasants and artisans. **Benedictine** and Cistercian monasteries played an important role in bringing the terrain under cultivation as well.

During the High Middle Ages, the Burgenland was largely under the control of local magnate families, the Güßing and the Forchtensteins in particular. During the second half of the 15th century, a few locations in the region came into the hands of the **Habsburgs**, who mortgaged them to local noblemen. Heavily damaged during the war with the Ottoman Empire in the early modern period, the Burgenland was fully reincorporated into the kingdom of Hungary as the sultans' armies withdrew during the second half of the 17th century. From this time on, educational, ecclesiastical, and legal norms observed in the kingdom of Hungary prevailed in the Burgenland. The 17th century also brought the Hungarian magnate family, the Esterházy, to the Burgenland and to the town of **Eisenstadt**. Their influence over the politics and economy of the northern and central Burgenland endured even after the collapse of the Austro–Hungarian empire. Their palace in Eisenstadt became a hub of musical and artistic life in the 18th century, employing among others the composer **Franz Josef Haydn**. Adam Liszt, the father of the great Hungarian pianist and composer Franz Liszt, also worked for the Esterházy estates.

As early as the 18th century, some German Burgenlanders asked that their land be joined to the German-speaking areas of Austria, particularly the province of **Lower Austria**. These feelings intensified somewhat after the **Ausgleich** of 1867, which gave the regime in Budapest a freer hand in Magyarizing the populations under its control. More important, however, were the **economic** links that were springing up between western Hungary and the region around Vienna. Heavily **agricultural**, the Burgenland became a crucial purveyor for the kitchens and public eating establishments of Vienna in the 19th century. Surplus farm labor found work in the factories of the capital and in Lower Austria.

It was chiefly for this reason that, when the Habsburg monarchy collapsed in the fall of 1918, the inhabitants of western Hungary, which also had a small, historic Croatian minority, demanded in large numbers that they be incorporated into the Austrian republic then taking shape. Preoccupied with making a state out of the territories acknowledged to belong to what was for a time cautiously known as the Provisional Republic of German Austria and in no condition to defend a takeover of western Hungary, the government in Vienna did not support the step.

The first Hungarian Republic under Michael Károlyi proposed making the area autonomous within Hungary, an idea that attracted favorable attention. However, the Károlyi regime fell to a short-lived Bolshevik regime led by Béla Kun. The increasingly desperate economic situation in the new Austria raised the possibility that it would go the same way. Thus, the victorious powers at the Paris Peace Conference awarded the Burgenland and its capital Ödenburg (Hung.: *Sopron*) to the government in Vienna in the **Treaty of St. Germain**, signed on 10 September 1919, and its Hungarian equivalent, the Treaty of Trianon, completed in 1920.

The arrangement brought armed resistance from the Hungarians, opening a year of skirmishing along the new border that left parts of it under Austrian control. Other areas remained in the hands of Hungary. Italian mediation led to a plebiscite in Sopron in 1921. The reliability of this was questionable, given the circumstances under which the ballots were cast. The Hungarian army continued to occupy the town and surrounding neighborhood even as the vote was taken. Sopron and environs chose to remain with Hungary, but the rest of the Burgenland joined the First Austrian Republic. Its new capital became Eisenstadt.

Today, with a population of around 280,000, the Burgenland is still a provisioner to the Austrian capital, even though only a very small percentage of the population makes its primary living from agriculture. The area sends large numbers of commuters to **Vienna** and Lower Austria for jobs, either on a daily or weekly basis. Around 88 percent of the population is German speaking; Croatian- and Hungarian-speaking minorities have declined to around 7 percent and 3 percent of the population, respectively. The Hungarian-language population is swiftly aging out. In districts with substantial Croatian populations, there are 28 bilingual grammar schools in which German and Croatian are **languages** of instruction, as required by the Austrian School Law for Minorities passed in 1994. There is one bilingual high school, a bilingual technical track, and five high schools where Croatian or Hungarian can be studied. Electronics and agricultural processing remain important local industries. *See also* EDUCATION.

BURGTHEATER. Among the oldest **theaters** with a continued existence in the world, the **Vienna** Burgtheater, or court theater, traces its origins to Empress **Maria Theresa**. In 1741, she commissioned the theatrical impresario Joseph Sellier to reconfigure a ballroom on the northeast corner of the *Hofburg* for theatrical performances.

The initial project was completed in 1748, with further modifications of the stage arrangements taking place in 1756. Known as the Theater Next to the Burg, it was closely connected to the court. The imperial family could enter its box in the auditorium directly from its quarters in the Hofburg. The court, however, did not directly manage the house. Until 1752 the Burg, as it is familiarly known in Vienna, was in the hands of concessionaires, who used it for Italian **opera** and French classical drama, which were very popular at a court that spoke those **languages** daily. Performances in German were relatively rare.

Maria Theresa put the theater under court administration between 1752 and 1756; a period of important activity in **music** drama followed. Calling for opera to be a musical and dramatic entity rather than a showcase for vocal athleticism, the composer Christoph Willibald Gluck (1714–1787) had his leading works performed in the Vienna Court Theater. *Orpheo and Euridice* had its Vienna premier in 1762, *Alcestis* in 1767.

Nevertheless, the Burgtheater's finances remained shaky until 1776, when Emperor **Joseph II** put it under imperial patronage, renaming it in the process as the National Theater Next to the Burg. In a short time, it was known as the German National Theater. As both titles implied, the monarch had an agenda. Eager to wean audiences from what he and his advisor who developed the program, Josef Sonnenfels (1733–1817), deemed trivial and coarse popular comedies, the new theater was to offer the very best works of the world operatic and dramatic stage. The new German-language plays of Gottfried Lessing, Johann Wilhelm Goethe, and Friedrich Schiller, which cultivated Europe was taking seriously, were to be well represented. The performers themselves became state employees, with pension rights upon retirement. Though the theater often had to struggle with the constraints of censorship, it reached its greatest heights in the middle decades of the 19th century. Indeed, Burgtheater companies set performance standards for the entire German-speaking world. Two general directors were especially significant. Joseph Schreyvogel (1768–1832), who served in the position from 1814 to 1832, solidified the role of the German classics as well as the works of the great Austrian dramatic poet **Franz Grillparzer** in the repertory. It was Schreyvogel who fostered the company's use of "Burgtheater German," a pronunciation of the language that became a model not only for actors and actresses but for those who tried to speak a relatively standard form of the tongue in everyday speech. Under Heinrich Laube (1806–1884), who headed the theater from 1849 to 1867, the Burgtheater rose to its commanding position in the German theatrical world, able to mount an enormous repertory of 164 plays.

Until the **World War I**, the Burgtheater continued to offer a broad palette of the classics, as well as some new works from the realist and naturalist theater then emerging in Germany and elsewhere in Europe. Shortly before the outbreak of the war, the once-scorned Viennese popular comedy, as represented by **Ferdinand Raimund** and **Johann Nestroy**, also found its way into the program. Nevertheless, the pace of accommodation to new theatrical forms and subjects was too slow for many, and other theaters, more attuned to modern trends, appeared in Vienna to compete with the Burgtheater. Among the more enduring was the People's Theater (*Volkstheater*), which opened in 1889 under private management.

The Burgtheater, housed since 1888 in a neo-Renaissance building on the **Ringstrasse**, suffered heavy damage toward the end of **World War II**. Rebuilt and reopened in 1955, it continues to offer the classics of the world theater along with newer works. In the season of 1922–1923, it took over the more intimate Akademietheater, where members of the company could perform lighter and more experimental works. However, the debate over the proper balance between the classical and the contemporary has never ended, either among state theater officials or the general public. The Burg has recently turned over some of its interior space to small experimental productions.

– C –

CALVINISM. *See* PROTESTANTISM; RELIGION.

CARINTHIA. Carinthia is the southernmost province of modern Austria, with a current population of around 550,000. Its name apparently is reminiscent of a Slavic tribe, the Karantaner, one among several who inhabited the area during and after the eighth century CE. Generously endowed with four large and beautiful lakes—Wörther, Ossiach, Millstätt, and Weissen—as well as around 2,000 smaller ones; a varied landscape of mountains and long, luxuriant valleys; and a more consistent summer climate than the rest of Austria, Carinthia is a major attraction for vacationers, both domestic as well as those from the rest of Europe. Ninety-seven percent of the population is German speaking; the remaining 3 percent consists of a Slovenian-speaking minority in the south, especially in the Gail, Rose, and Jaun valleys.

The first archaeological artifacts and settlement of Carinthia date from the Paleolithic period. Copper mines in the region appear to have prompted far denser settlement in the fourth and third centuries BCE. The Celts came to the area around 300 BCE and eventually established a kind of tribal federation that would later become the kingdom (*Regnum*) of Noricum. During the Roman occupation, Carinthia became part of a Roman province of the same name, which encompassed a great deal of what is today's Austria. Under attack from the Avars at the beginning of the eighth century, the Karantaner called upon the Bavarians to their north for help. This Germanic tribe quickly dominated the area and promoted its Christianization, which had already taken hold during the Roman occupation.

Arnulf (ca. 850–899), an illegitimate son of the Carolingian ruler of Bavaria, Carloman, was charged with governing Carinthia in 876. Emperor Otto II made the territory, which included parts of **Italy** (until 1173) and modern **Styria**, an independent duchy in 976. Carinthia thus was the earliest of the Austrian provinces to bear this rank. As one ruling family succeeded another in the duchy from the end of the 10th to the middle of the 11th centuries, many of these territories fell away. The political unity of Carinthia was further undermined by ecclesiastical holdings in the territory that belonged to the bishoprics of **Salzburg** and Bamberg. King Ottokar II of Bohemia controlled the area from 1269 to 1276, having inherited it from the last of the noble families to rule Carinthia, the Sponheim. In 1335, Emperor Louis IV (the Bavarian) enfeoffed the Habsburgs with Carinthia.

From that time on until the collapse of the **Habsburg Empire** in 1918, Carinthia was just one among the many of the house of Austria's possessions, with all of the advantages and disadvantages that such status conferred. In 1518, **Klagenfurt** became the capital when Emperor **Maximilian I** gave the local estates the city as a place for their meetings. Carinthia was very exposed to the marauding of the Ottoman armies, especially in the 15th century. It also became heavily **Protestant** during the Reformation; to this day it has the highest number of Protestants of any province in Austria. But the Habsburg-supported Counter-Reformation behaved ruthlessly here in the 17th century, and many of the evangelical faith simply left altogether. Following the Napoleonic Wars, Carinthia was part of a so-called Habsburg Illyrian Kingdom ruled from Laibach, now Ljubljana, the capital of modern Slovenia. In 1849, it was declared a crown land unto itself, which it remained until 1918.

Historically an **agricultural** center, with an especially important timber industry, Carinthia was the site of bitter political and **military** controversies in 1918–1919 and again after 1945. With its Slovenian population, the province became the target of Serb, Croatian, and Slovenian troops to the south, who were anxious to incorporate as many of their ethnic cohorts as possible into the new kingdom that was to emerge from the Paris Peace Conference. A month before **World War I** ended, a Slovenian national council meeting in Ljubljana empowered itself to speak for its ethnic cohorts in Carinthia. The fighting between a Carinthian militia and the troops from the new kingdom to the south lasted from 1918 to 1919. In May 1919, South Slavic troops occupied Klagenfurt.

Both Italy and the **United States** had reasons to contain the territorial reach of what was to become Yugoslavia. They and the other victorious powers meeting at the Paris Peace Conference ruled that a two-stage plebiscite should be held to decide the political future of the Carinthian Slovenes. The disputed area was divided in two: zone A to the south, where the majority of Slovenes lived, and zone B, the region around Klagenfurt, which was heavily German. In October 1920, close to 60 percent of the population in zone A decided to remain with Austria, a gesture that made a vote in zone B superfluous. It was therefore never taken. The **Treaty of St. Germain** did, however, cede two areas, the Miess valley to Yugoslavia and the Kanal valley to Italy.

After **World War II**, Yugoslavia, supported by the Soviet Union, claimed around 259,000 hectares in Carinthia, including Klagenfurt, and $150 million as reparations for the war. However, when Stalin and the Yugoslav Communist leader, Marshall Tito, had their historic falling-out in 1948, the Soviets decided to accept the borders of Austria as they had been in 1938. Yugoslavia entered into direct negotiations on the Carinthian claims with Vienna, and eventually dropped them in return for the right to confiscate Austrian property in Yugoslavia and Austrian promises to protect the rights of the Slovenian minority—at that time between 20,000 and 50,000 people—within its borders. Slovenes were to have the right to organize politically, to operate their own press, and to study in their own **language** in primary and secondary school. Slovene and German would be the two official languages in the province. Where the Slovene population was especially heavy, signs with place-names were to be in German and Slovene.

In 1972, the Austrian National Assembly passed a law calling for dual-language signs wherever the Carinthian population was 20 percent or more Slovene. Because that population had been declining, no one was exactly sure how many of the minority lived in any given area. Speakers of German, some of whom called upon unpleasant memories of Yugoslav demands after both world wars, began tearing these signs down, which led to vigorous protests from Belgrade. In 1977, the Austrian government activated the Ethnic Groups Act, passed the previous year. Dual-language signs were to be erected wherever a quarter of the population was Slovenian-speaking. The Austrian state also subsidized two Slovenian language newspapers and a radio station in Klagenfurt that broadcast in the language.

CARNUNTUM. Perhaps the most striking and important Roman archaeological site in Austria, Carnuntum lies roughly 80 kilometers southeast of **Vienna**. The name may be of Celtic origin. Established by the Romans in 15 CE, it was initially used to quarter a military legion of 6,000 infantry and a cavalry of 120. Lying on both east–west and north–south trade routes of the late Roman Empire, the settlement was raised from *municipium* to *colonia*, the highest rank that the Romans conferred upon provincial cities. It would become the administrative seat for the Roman governor who supervised Upper Pannonia, roughly eastern and southeastern Austria today. At its peak, Carnuntum had about 50,000 inhabitants, who had at their disposal such amenities as paved roads, covered sewers, a hospital, thermal baths, cultic temples, and, uncovered in 1976, a water system from the second or third century that was still functional. Not far away there was an amphitheater that accommodated 13,000 spectators for animal baiting and gladiatorial contests. Also in the neighborhood is the striking Heathen Gate (*Heidentor*), a freestanding, and much-eroded stone arch; its purpose—possibly ceremonial, possibly memorial—has yet to be clarified.

Carnuntum was progressively destroyed by marauding Germanic tribes after 395, but the excavated layout is remarkably well-preserved. The oldest archaeological artifacts, today displayed in a small museum within the compound, date from the first century of the common era. The Emperor Marcus Aurelius (121–180) wrote part of his *Meditations* during a stay in the fortress. See also AUSTRIA, LOWER; HALLSTATT CULTURE.

CATHOLICISM. The history of Austria is closely tied to the history of Roman Catholic Christianity in Europe. The faith took hold in the area over several stages, from its tentative beginning during imperial Roman occupation in the first and second centuries CE. At the end of the seventh and beginning of the eighth centuries, Bavarian, Irish, and Anglo–Saxon missions to the region began the process of popular conversion in earnest. The **Benedictine** missionary St. Boniface (672/673?–754), who was born in Wessex and known as the apostle of the Germans, created a network of bishoprics throughout southern Germany to manage the affairs of the church. Two of these, **Salzburg** and Passau, played key roles in promoting the Christianization of the Austrian lands and those of the neighboring Slavs as well.

By the end of the 10th century, the Catholic church had a durable and articulated organizational structure in Austrian territory. This encompassed parishes—at first associated with castles, then later with urban settlements—along with substantial monasteries that grew in both size and number after the 11th century. As was true throughout medieval Europe, the church in Austria set the intellectual, spiritual, and aesthetic norms of the time. It also was a serious competitor with secular authority throughout the Austrian territories, with the holdings of major abbeys and bishoprics extending to enclaves within the lands of lay territorial rulers as well. Salzburg and Passau had an especially pervasive presence.

The 16th-century Protestant Reformation shook the Austrian Catholic church at its roots. While the **Habsburg** rulers of the Austrian territories remained officially true to the cause of Rome, the nobility of the Austrian provinces, with the exception of the **Tyrol**, became staunch supporters of Lutheranism. They asked for, and won, many concessions from their rulers, including the right to hold Protestant services, at least in the confines of their homes.

The process of re-catholicization, or Counter-Reformation, as it is somewhat inaccurately known, began during the reign of Emperor **Ferdinand I**. It was he who in 1555 called to Vienna the **Jesuit** catechist and educator Peter Canisius (1521–1597), with whose help the restoration of Roman Catholicism to the Habsburg lands got under way.

This initiative, however, was somewhat blunted when Ferdinand ordered that the Habsburg Austrian patrimony be divided after his death in 1564. In 1583 his grandson, Emperor Rudolph II (1552–1612), transferred the imperial government to Prague. The first serious reversals of **Protestantism** in the Austrian lands took place, therefore, not in **Vienna** but in **Styria**, where Ferdinand's youngest son, Archduke Charles (1540–1590), and his Bavarian wife Archduchess Maria (1551–1608) were deeply committed to the re-establishment of Catholicism. By the middle of the 17th century, the Habsburg Austrian lands of the time were almost fully Catholic.

The victory changed the landscape of Austria itself. It was roughly between 1650 and 1750 that some of Austria's most notable religious edifices were either built or, more often, expanded and remodeled in the exuberant **Baroque** style. The cloister of **Melk** on the **Danube** in **Lower Austria** is only one of many spectacular examples. The process took somewhat longer in Salzburg, which was still a prince-bishopric with an altogether separate seat in the German imperial estates. By the mid-18th century, however, it too was fully under Catholic ecclesiastical control.

Influenced by the Enlightenment and the general need to develop a productive population, **Joseph II** renewed the attack on the position of the Roman Catholic church in the Austrian lands from a somewhat different angle. Joseph believed that the church should serve as an arm of the state. If it had a mission at all, it was to minister to the everyday moral needs of his subjects rather than to prepare them for the afterlife. By the emperor's death in 1790, the number of cloisters had dropped by a third, from over 2,000 to 1,324, although the number of dioceses and pastoral positions increased substantially. Both he and his far more religiously conventional mother, **Maria Theresa**, curbed clerical influence in lay affairs generally. Public **education** was an especially important concern. When the papacy temporarily abolished the Jesuit order in 1773, the empress confiscated their property and used the income from it to develop a secular primary school system theoretically open to all her Austrian subjects.

The general conservatism of the post-Napoleonic Habsburg government led to a renewal of Catholic influence in public life. The Jesuits were returned to the Habsburg lands by the Austrian Emperor Francis I (1768–1835). A Concordat with the papacy in 1855 gave the church the power to review educational materials for items that were in conflict with its teachings. However, the idea that the church had a social, as well as an evangelical and contemplative mission, endured. The **Christian Social** movement of the last third of the century had the common man at the center of its concerns and was often quite critical of more traditional members of the Austrian Catholic hierarchy, who were often close to the throne.

All wings of Catholic thought in Austria were deeply hostile to doctrinaire Marxism, so that in the first half of the 20th century the church became more conservative on social issues. Fidelity to Catholicism was a central tenet of the **Austro-Fascist** governments of chancellors **Engelbert Dollfuss** and **Kurt Schuschnigg**. Under the leadership of **Franz** Cardinal **König**, post–**World War II** Austrian Catholicism once again reemphasized its social mission. It also adopted more flexible attitudes toward other religious persuasions. The fate of Roman Catholicism in the Soviet bloc was also one of König's central concerns.

The Austrian **constitution** recognizes the right of all faiths to practice their beliefs, the Catholic church being only one among them. Nevertheless, the church still has a complex and extensive institutional presence in modern Austria. This is supported by lay contributions raised by the state as part of the general tax system. Nevertheless, the general secularization of life in the second half of the 20th century, and a rash of clerical scandals, have tempered the influence of Roman Catholicism in Austria markedly, though a substantial part of the population acknowledges its general moral ideals. Between 1981 and 2007, the proportion of Catholics in the Austrian population had dropped to 74 percent. In 2007, only 15 percent of all Austrian Catholics still attended Sunday services regularly, and only one in five prayed daily. Around 1,180,000 declared themselves to be observant, even though officially they numbered 4,900,000 in 2007. *See also* RELIGION; SCHÖNBORN, CARDINAL CHRISTOPH.

CHAMBER, AGRICULTURAL/LANDWIRTSCHAFTSKAMMER. Popularly known as the Peasants Chambers, the various branches of this decentralized organization represent the interests of small farmers and forestry enterprises in economic and political affairs that affect them. Like the other chambers, which represent employers, labor and salaried workers, and the **trade unions**, the **agricultural** chamber is legally charged to perform this function.

Though demands for such an arrangement date from the late 19th century, it was only after the end of **World War I** that provincial **governments** throughout Austria approved it. Between 1920 and 1932, chambers for farming and small forestry concerns were established throughout all of the provinces of the First Republic. Even today, agricultural affairs are regulated regionally rather than by the central government in Vienna. *See also* AUSTRIAN FEDERATION OF TRADE UNIONS; CHAMBER, ECONOMIC; CHAMBER, WORKERS AND SALARIED EMPLOYEES.

CHAMBER, ECONOMIC/WIRTSCHAFTSKAMMER. The oldest of Austria's four self-governing corporations legally empowered to speak for the major interest groups of its **economy**, this chamber was an outcome of the **Revolutions of 1848**. At first these organizations represented a class of voters designated in a short-lived **constitution** issued that year. Called Chambers of Commerce and existing only as regional groupings, they became spokesmen for business owners in all sectors of economic life and continue to do so today. A federal chamber has existed since 1937, although following the **Anschluss** with **Germany**, it ceased to function. It was reestablished in 1946.

Membership in the organization is obligatory for all employers. The chambers have statutory consultative rights over local and national legislation that bears upon the interests of their constituents. They also run their own training schools and institutes to further **trade** and **industrialization** domestically and abroad. Today each of the Austrian provinces has its own chamber, each with subdivisions representing manufacture and handicrafts, heavy industry, trade, **banking**, credit and insurance organizations, **transportation**, **tourism**, and recreation. In 2007, the chambers had around 370,000 member businesses. *See also* AUSTRIAN FEDERATION OF TRADE UNIONS; CHAMBER, AGRICULTURAL; CHAMBER, WORKERS AND SALARIED EMPLOYEES.

CHAMBER, WORKERS AND SALARIED EMPLOYEES/ ARBEITERKAMMER. Set up in 1920 and reestablished in 1945, these organizations are peculiar to the Austrian sociopolitical structure. They oversee the interests of the generality of wage earners. Only high civil servants, along with agricultural and forestry workers, are exempt. **Vienna** and the **Burgenland** are exceptions to this rule. Should a worker lose his or her position, the regional chamber continues to represent that person for a fixed amount of time. Each of the nine Austrian provinces has such an organization; there is also a countrywide central chamber. Like the other Austrian chambers (for employers, farmers, and **trade unions**), workers' chambers have consultative rights in legislative matters that bear upon their constituency. They can suggest measures to the **government** and are especially active safeguarding working conditions and living standards for their constituents and their dependents. They also establish apprenticeships and have much to say about measures to protect the young who serve in them. Workers' chambers cooperate with the trade unions and employers on these questions. A full congress of these organizations meets every five years. Austrian citizenship is not required to become a delegate to this body. *See also* AUSTRIAN FEDERATION OF TRADE UNIONS; CHAMBER, AGRICULTURAL; CHAMBER, ECONOMIC.

CHANCELLOR, FEDERAL. The title of chancellor (Germ.: *Kanzler*) in the Second Austrian Republic was passed on from the administration of the First Republic. Though some high officials of the former **Habsburg Empire** and the Holy Roman Empire had also been called chancellors, their duties and their relationship to monarchical sovereignty had been very different.

Modern Austrian chancellors were at their most powerful under the constitutional arrangements introduced by the quasi-dictatorial regime of **Engelbert Dollfuss**. They had wide powers to intervene in provincial **governments** and to guide the work of federal ministers closely.

Since 1945, four federal chancellors have been acting **presidents** of Austria when that office was temporarily vacated. The federal chancellor in Austria today, however, is formally a rather weak figure, much like his counterpart in the **Constitution** of 1920. He presides over meetings of government department ministers and presents programs and resolutions that arise from these gatherings to the lower house of the Parliament. Ministers, however, are constitutionally empowered to formulate policy for their specific portfolios quite independent of the chancellor.

Until 1964, Austrian chancellors presided over coalition governments of the **Austrian People's Party** (ÖVP) and the **Socialist Party of Austria** (SPÖ). Each side was heavily committed to a closely regulated **currency** and **banking** system as well as a social market economy to which private and public enterprise contributed significantly. Both parties stressed the need for social harmony in a country that had seen relatively little of that in the 20th century. By the 1960s, however, a wing of the ÖVP began to argue for liberalizing the Austrian economy and integrating it more closely with the fiscal and industrial policies of the West. Leading spokesmen for this move were **Alfons Gorbach**, federal chancellor of the coalition government in power from 1961 to 1964, and, more aggressively, Josef Klaus (1910–2001), who assumed the office in 1964. After two more years of coalition government with the SPÖ, Klaus declared that he and his party were ready to lead Austria alone. His chancellorship, which ran from 1964 to 1970, was the first systematic effort to move Austria from paternalism to a society that offered more leeway for individual decision and initiative. Klaus and his supporters within his party claimed to be developing what they called a new Austrian society, in which modern managerial practices and computer-run data management techniques would continue prosperity for all. Although Austria did begin to make significant changes in manufacturing and commerce, a serious ebb in economic activity, coupled with higher taxes imposed during Klaus's tenure, weakened the appeal of his governments considerably. The appeal of **Bruno Kreisky**'s four chancellorships (1970–1983) rested, in large part, on his commitment to fiscal and social egalitarianism and to keeping unemployment to a minimum.

Kreisky's bypassing of ministerial prerogative, especially in **foreign relations**, was often controversial. A one-time foreign minister of the Second Republic, he was deeply interested in world events throughout most of his tenure; he engaged himself actively in Middle East and North–South affairs and became for many the voice of his country on these matters. As foreign ministers, he had two professional diplomats and one constitutional scholar, none of whom belonged to a **political party** at the time he held office. Kreisky appears, however, not to have intruded in the routine operations of that office.

The SPÖ leaders who succeeded Kreisky as chancellor, Fred Sinowatz (1929–2008), **Franz Vranitzky**, and **Viktor Klima**, brought into their governments—all coalitions with either the ÖVP or the **Freedom Party of Austria** (FPÖ)—inherited one unfortunate side of the Kreisky years. Sinowatz particularly, an unassuming educator who visibly disliked the cut and thrust of Austrian politics, was plagued by scandals that had begun in the governments of his predecessor. The far more worldly Vranitzky enjoyed high public approval, embodiment though he was of a generation of Austrian SPÖ functionaries who were as much at home in world investment banks as they were on picket lines. He had many opportunities to exercise his skills abroad. His first three chancellorships (1986 to 1994) coincided in large part with the presidency of **Kurt Waldheim**, who was persona non grata in the **United States** and virtually throughout the world for failing to disclose his role in Nazi armies in the Balkans during **World War II**. Vranitzky was thrust into performing the representative functions normally exercised by Austrian presidents before foreign states. By 1997, the ongoing impact of old scandals coupled with some of Vranitzky's own making, along with popular fears about the upsurge in immigration from eastern Europe and the

Muslim world, had eroded much popular support for the SPÖ. Vranitzkty resigned, to be replaced as chancellor by Viktor Klima, who was no more effective in reversing the sliding fortunes of the SPÖ in elections. In 2000 the ÖVP, led by **Wolfgang Schüssel** of the ÖVP, received the largest plurality in a national vote.

As chancellor, Schüssel entered into a highly controversial coalition with the FPÖ, whose standard-bearer was the populist **Jörg Haider**. Faced with the sanctions of the **European Union**, Schüssel succeeded in having them canceled in the fall of 2000. An advocate of free markets and a general rollback of state entitlements, Schüssel and his finance minister from the FPÖ, Karl-Heinz Grasser (1969–), labored for almost six years to reduce Austrian state debt and deficits. Finally brought down by a public weary of budget cutting and a regime that often made exceptions for its members where fiscal austerity and skirting the law were concerned, Schüssel's government collapsed in 2006. His successor as chancellor, **Alfred Gusenbauer**, also had little lasting public appeal. His government lasted only for a year. In the summer of 2008, Gusenbauer was replaced as SPÖ chair by Werner Faymann (1960–), who was the party's standard-bearer, in a close election in September 2008. Faymann became federal chancellor that December. *See also* FIGL, LEOPOLD; SCHUSCHNIGG, KURT; SEIPEL, IGNAZ.

CHARLES I, EMPEROR OF AUSTRIA AND KING CHARLES IV OF HUNGARY (1887–1922). A nephew of the Emperor **Franz Joseph**, Charles received a broad but strictly **Catholic** education. Although on friendly terms with his uncle, Archduke **Franz Ferdinand**, and even persuaded that the **Habsburg Empire** required serious reform to survive, Charles remained aloof from the political antagonisms that the heir apparent's policies engendered. He therefore was in far better standing with the emperor than the confrontational heir apparent. Indeed, though Franz Joseph was both shocked and alarmed at the assassination of Franz Ferdinand in Sarajevo, he was not altogether displeased to have Archduke Charles emerge as his successor.

Becoming ruler of the Habsburg lands at the midpoint of **World War I** in 1916, Charles was convinced that his dynasty's empire would not survive the conflict intact. Encouraged by his strong-willed wife, Zita of Bourbon-Parma (1892–1989), whom he had married in 1911, he set about trying to extricate Austria–Hungary from the war. He also worked to reconcile his peoples, whom **economic** privation and wartime curbs on civil liberties were making increasingly restless, to Habsburg rule at home. He and his **government** blundered badly in all respects. In 1917, Charles ordered the release of Austria–Hungary's political prisoners. Because a number of these were Czech nationalists, many Germans of the empire resented concessions to people whose disloyalty had spared them the perils of combat. Secret and unilateral peace initiatives he entered into with France were made public by the French prime minister, George Clemenceau, in 1918. Austria–Hungary's German allies, who had saved the Habsburg armies from complete disaster on the eastern front, reacted sternly, especially because part of the bargain to be cut with France was Austria–Hungary's willingness to see Alsace-Lorraine returned to French control. Charles's subsequent apology, made personally to Emperor William II at the latter's wartime residence in Spa, convinced many Habsburg subjects, especially the Czechs, that the dynasty could no longer stand between them and German expansion.

On 16 October 1918, Charles issued a manifesto promising to turn the Habsburg Empire into a loose confederation in which various nationalities would have a wide degree of autonomy. The document only encouraged the emperor's peoples to move toward complete independence. Indeed, that same day Hungary declared the Compromise of 1867 (*Ausgleich*) to be no longer in effect. On 11 November 1918, Charles signed a manifesto in which he removed himself from participation in the government of Austria, though he did not explicitly renounce claims to any throne. He left Vienna with his large family for an outlying castle, Ekartsau, in **Lower Austria**. The following year, he went into exile altogether in Switzerland. From there, he made two attempts in 1921 to reclaim the crown in Hungary. Both efforts failed, and the Western powers banished him to the Portuguese island of Madeira, where he died within a year. *See also* HABSBURG EXCLUSION ACT.

CHRISTIAN SOCIAL PARTY/CHRISTLICHSOZIALE PARTEI
(CP). From the late 19th century until 1938, the CP was the **political**

party of preference among the Viennese petty bourgeoisie. Though it was established only in 1893 under the leadership of **Karl Lueger**, the charismatic mayor of the Habsburg Austrian capital of **Vienna** from 1897 until his death in 1910, the historical genesis of the movement was long and complex. Its philosophical father, Karl Freiherr von Vogelsang (1818–1890), from Mecklenburg in **Germany**, was a **Catholic** convert who deplored the secularization of both political and material conditions in the modern world. He was a critic of both Marxism and capitalism, with which he identified **Jews** and liberals. Vogelsang aired these views in the conservative publication *Vaterland*, which he edited after 1879. He wished to reestablish what he termed Christian society, by which he meant reviving **economic** protections, once provided by such institutions as guilds, which he believed made life more secure for many classes of people in medieval Europe.

Although utopian, such ideas had considerable support among the classes most affected by the displacement of **industrialization**, particularly those in the traditional handicrafts. Vogelsang's thinking also found a receptive audience among the lower Catholic clergy, who were dismayed at the materialism of the industrial workers in the parishes of Vienna and **Lower Austria** generally. Another significant figure was Prince Alois von Liechtenstein (1846–1920). Influenced by the Catholic Reform movement then underway in France, he was active in the Austrian imperial parliament on behalf of the artisans. He was particularly eager to expand the franchise to the lower middle classes.

It was Lueger, however, who forged a practical social and political program from these ideas. Coupling an appeal to ethnic resentment with massive changes in public amenities in the city of Vienna, he led a party that dominated the city from the last years of the 19th century until the end of **World War I**. The CP also won the support of the substantial Catholic and conservative elements among the Austrian peasantry. The latter became increasingly important to the political survival of the Christian Social movement, when the **Social Democratic Workers Party** (SDAP) began its long domination of Viennese municipal politics soon after Lueger's death. The more prosperous Austrian bourgeoisie, once liberal in their politics, also became more sympathetic to CP positions when Marxism became a major alternative at the polls.

At the end of World War I, the CP supported both the establishment of the First Austrian Republic and **Anschluss** with Germany. A national coalition government between the party and the SDAP lasted from 1918 to 1920. From then until 1938 the party, in one form or another, governed Austria. Though it drew the single largest number of votes, it would never have a majority. Therefore it was faced with the problem of maintaining coalitions with the Greater German People's Party (*Grossdeutsche Volkspartei*) (1920–1932) and the Agrarian League (*Landbund*) (1932–1934), which supported Christian Social positions on many matters. The German national movement could not wholly accept the close connection of the CP with Austrian Catholicism.

With the end of parliamentary government in Austria in 1933–1934, the CP folded itself into the Fatherland Front of **Engelbert Dollfuss**. Following **World War II**, several functionaries of the CP participated in the founding of the **Austrian People's Party** and played leading roles in it.

COFFEEHOUSE/CAFE/CAFEHAUS. Though coffeehouses are perhaps more closely associated with **Vienna** than with any other city in the world, they came to the city relatively late. Outside of Constantinople itself, where **Habsburg** emissaries had drunk the beverage for some time, Venice had such establishments in 1645, London in 1652, Hamburg in 1671, and Paris in 1672.

Vienna's first coffeehouse opened in 1685, two years after the second, and last, unsuccessful Ottoman siege of the Habsburg capital. Consumption of the beverage itself, however, had been going on in Vienna for some time. Once established, coffeehouses caught on quickly. By 1736, there were imperially licensed coffeehouses selling the drink tax free, and 19 ordinary houses that did not have this privilege, but offset their higher prices with a more dignified level of service and atmosphere than the often-raucous inns of the city. By 1703, such coffeehouses were buying periodicals for their customers to read with their refreshment. Billiard tables were also frequently available. For those who had neither the time nor the money to lavish on such comforts, there were numerous street purveyors who sold both coffee and a very popular spiced brandy (*Rosolio*).

Coffee became a special seasonal pleasure in Vienna around 1750 when one proprietor, Gianni Tarroni, whose establishment was on the Graben in the center of the city, was licensed to serve customers out of doors in the summer. Its contemporary name—Gianni Garden—has been crunched through the phonetics of **Wienerisch** as *Schanigarten*, the term for any sidewalk eating facility with umbrella and tables. By 1788, small musical ensembles were playing in cafes, a custom that continues to this day, though in only a few facilities and at specific times, usually weekends.

The inner decor of cafes grew very elaborate following the Napoleonic Wars. Wall mirrors, chandeliers, plush chairs and banquettes, and silver cutlery made their way into the more pretentious establishments. Some became lively centers for artistic and political discussion. Card games and chess were also available as was a wider selection of reading material, including foreign journals. The importance of cafes as centers of intellectual activity endured through **World War I**. The Griensteidl (1847) and the Central (1860) were especially prominent in the artistic and literary life of the city; the Landtmann (1873), which is very close to the Parliament and the City Hall on the **Ringstrasse**, was, and is, a meeting place for political figures.

Following **World War II**, many coffeehouses closed, made obsolete by the fast-paced lifestyle of economic recovery, soaring property values and rents, and finally television, which turned the home into a center of family entertainment. Since 1990, there has been some recovery of coffeehouse culture. Several of the great cafes, including both the Central and the Griensteidl, have been elegantly renovated. Like their more modest counterparts, they now combine restaurant service along with their more traditional beverage offerings and assorted baked goods.

COLD WAR. The competitive standoff between the democracies of the Western world and the Eastern bloc controlled by the Soviet Union between 1945 and 1989 touched upon every country in Europe in some way. The period, however, changed Austria profoundly. Poised after 1955 between the two military alliances that divided the continent, the Soviet Warsaw Pact (1955) and the North Atlantic Treaty Organization (NATO, 1949), Austria began a transformative balancing act after **World War II** that was institutionalized by its pledge of **neutrality** in the **Austrian State Treaty** of 1955.

Austria's initial concerns during Allied **occupation** were to regain state sovereignty and the assets associated with it. Its spokesmen could ill afford to offend any of the victorious powers, even though firsthand experience of Soviet brutality, particularly with women, convinced many Austrians that they wanted to be part of the non-communist West. The Soviets, however, were uniquely positioned to help Austria with a very pressing territorial problem. Yugoslav Communist boss Marshall Tito (1892–1980) sent forces into **Carinthia** in 1945 and was at that point on comparatively good terms with Soviet dictator Joseph Stalin. Fortunately for Austria, the problem more or less took care of itself. In 1948, Tito broke with Stalin, exposing Yugoslavia to potential Soviet retaliation. A year later, the Soviets renounced formal support of Yugoslavia. Tito gave up territorial claims in Carinthia and confiscated Austrian property in his country rather than demanding formal reparations for war damages. Well into the 1950s, Austria feared attack by the combined forces of Czechoslovakia and Hungary or by Hungary alone. Nevertheless, during the especially dangerous moment in 1956 when the Vienna government opened its borders to fleeing Hungarian rebels, the Soviets wanted Austria to seal its borders at the **Burgenland** and did not invade it.

Soviet suppression of rebellions in Hungary in 1956 and Czechoslovakia in 1968 virtually destroyed the **Communist Party of Austria** by splitting it. Before that, however, the Western occupying powers led by the United States (U.S.) did all that they could to turn Austria into a redoubt against the advancement of Soviet communism. The U.S. was ready to withhold **Marshall Plan** funds and credits in 1958 to discourage any Austrian deviation from its pro-Western orientation. The U.S., along with France and Great Britain, supported the clandestine remilitarization of Austria, especially after the Prague Communist coup of 1948. Between 1950 and 1955, Americans promoted rearmament so intensely and secretively that only a select group of top cabinet officials in the **Vienna** government knew about it. By the end of the occupation, a "core army" was in place, staffed by some gendarmerie units and the police, 6,500 of whom were trained between 1952 and 1955. Their central mission was to put down any communist subversion that arose in Austria after the State Treaty was signed. Only in 1996 did the Austrian public learn that the American Central Intelligence Agency (CIA) had maintained 79 weapons arsenals in their country between 1952 and 1955. Informal conversations with NATO defense planners went on as well. Even in the late 1950s, as the Soviets sharpened their watch on Austrian neutrality, the U.S. sent military equipment to Austria. Indeed, the practice continued through 1962. Moscow's transfer of **military** equipment to the Vienna regime was negligible by comparison.

The Berlin Blockade and Allied airlift of 1948–1949 strongly suggested that Soviet communism and its Western opponents could go to war to defend their territorial and ideological interests in Europe. Some loosening of international tensions took place after Stalin's death in 1953, but central Europe remained an unsettled place. The exchange of sovereignty for neutrality in the State Treaty positioned Austria well to play the role of a bridge between the two sides; Vienna, particularly its foreign minister **Bruno Kreisky**, fashioned Austrian **foreign relations** accordingly. During the 1960s, he and others worked to bring the Soviets and the U.S. together to discuss their apparently intractable differences, especially the divided status of **Germany**. Although these contacts were largely unproductive—the sulfurous Soviet–American Vienna Summit in 1961 was exemplary—they did give Austria a distinctive place in world affairs.

Though **trade** with Hungary, Czechoslovakia, and other Eastern bloc countries was renewed soon after the end of World War II, the main focus of Austrian commerce and manufacture shifted from the Vienna Basin westward. Soviet occupation of eastern Austria and confiscation of its assets hastened pastoralization of the area. The closely controlled Soviet trading system made it far more profitable for Austria to redirect its business toward market-driven **economies** in Europe and throughout the world. Moreover, the U.S. blocked Austrian export of strategic materials to the east. The nearer one came to these boundaries in the 1950s and 1960s, the shabbier and more economically backward the surrounding area looked. Many areas still subsisted on farming and forestry. Serious **tourism**, a lucrative source of hard **currency** for Austria after World War II, was virtually absent near its eastern borders. Only in 1991 did these regions join the general shift of the Austrian economy toward service enterprises.

The Cold War revived **immigration** from former lands of the **Habsburg Empire** to Austria. The most dramatic cultural change in the country, however, came from the American occupation and its aftermath. As part of its program to push Austria, along with the world, toward entrepreneurial values and liberal political institutions, governments in Washington sponsored America Houses with programs and libraries open to all who wanted to learn something about life in the United States. Even Austrian farming came in for attention: 577 4-H Clubs, 264 alone in the former Soviet occupation zone, taught local boys and girls how to raise crops and domestic animals efficiently and profitably. Disillusioned with many of the traditional social, political, and even aesthetic preferences of preceding generations, which had brought them **Nazism** and dictatorship, Austria's young took to American popular culture—jazz, Mickey Mouse, Coca-Cola, and all—with heartfelt, and sometimes lasting, enthusiasm. *See also* ASYLUM; MILITARY.

COMMUNICATIONS. Austria's first telegraph line began operation between **Vienna** and what was then the suburb of Floridsdorf in 1845. Two years later, the longest transmission line on the continent linked Vienna to Prague and Brno, now in the Czech Republic. The Vienna Private Telegraph Society laid out Austria's initial telephone network in Austria in 1881. Working under **government** commission, the company had only 154 subscribers at the outset. Financial institutions such as the **Creditanstalt Bankverein**, the major **railroad** stations, several hotels, and the newspapers quickly bought the service. Public officials, the mayor of the city, even the police, took much longer. Overland telephone communication between Vienna and Brno went into operation in 1885.

The first wireless transmission in Austria took place in 1904, but long distance facilities did not develop before **World War I**. By 1924, however, radio broadcasting was underway on a daily basis. **Klagenfurt** in **Carinthia** and **Innsbruck** in the **Tyrol** had their own transmitters by 1927; **Salzburg** and **Linz** in **Upper Austria** had such facilities after 1930. Short wave transmission started in 1929. The major Vienna sender of the Austrian Radio Communication Corporation (RAVAG) opened on the Bisemberg, just outside the city, in 1933.

Austrian broadcasting was at first intellectually ambitious; stations were not only for the latest headlines and government reports, but for cultural and critical themes. Work by the composer Richard Wagner made up the first program sent over the RAVAG. Strict political neutrality was to be the rule in newscasts. The realization of such programming—relentlessly dry narrations of daily events and hour upon hour of light music played by small ensembles—was less than ideal.

For all of its commitment to balance, the RAVAG played a central role in the deadly power struggle between Austria and Germany in the 1930s. The drama of the 1938 **Anschluss** came over Austrian airwaves on 11 March as Chancellor **Kurt Schuschnigg** made his farewell address to his countrymen. The **Nazis** understood the uses of the new technology for spreading their message. On 18 March 1938, Nazi Minister of Propaganda Josef Goebbels made 22,000 radios available to Austrian communities where residents did not have access to them. Content, however, was tightly controlled. On 30 August 1939, Austrians were forbidden to listen to "enemy broadcast stations," a euphemism for foreign programming that the regime could not censor.

Independent Austrian radio went into operation under the management of the **Austrian Broadcasting System** soon after **World War II** ended. The first Austrian television program went out from transmitters around Vienna, Linz, and **Graz** on 1 August 1955. By 1962, satellites were beaming Austrian television around the world. The country's first color telecasts took place in 1965.

COMMUNIST PARTY, AUSTRIA/KOMMUNISTISCHE PARTEI ÖSTERREICHS (KPÖ). Founded in 1918 from the left wing of the **Social Democratic Party of Austria**, the Austrian Communist Party had a precarious beginning. Heavily oriented toward their mother party in the new Soviet Union, the Austrian Communists only had around 21,000 voters by 1930 and had elected none of their members to the various representative bodies in the First Republic. Declared illegal in 1933, they maintained a shadowy underground existence. Nevertheless, communists were prominent in the anti-**Nazi** resistance of the pre–**World War II** era.

In April 1945, the KPÖ was recognized as one of the three legal **political parties** in newly occupied Austria. Until 1947, it was one of the three political organizations represented in the provisional Austrian government. The high point of its appeal at the polls came during 1953, when party candidates received between 5 and 6 percent of the vote. After 1959, the KPÖ had no seat in the federal National Assembly (*Nationalrat*) and also lost votes in the provincial parliaments. The party remained true to the Stalinist line coming from the Soviet Union, even when its efforts during the 1950s to increase its influence in Austria through labor, youth, and **women**'s groups largely fell flat. The party's failure seemed even greater in light of the advantages it had in operating industries and trading companies chartered in the Soviet-occupied areas of Austria, which received special consideration in commerce with the Soviet bloc.

The suppression of the Prague Spring in 1968 and the direct Russian occupation of Czechoslovakia that followed gave rise to an ideological split within the KPÖ. The new directions of the Mikhail Gorbachev regime in the Soviet Union after 1985 had the same effect. The latter spurred efforts from younger members of the party to reconfigure the organization as a more democratic party of the left. However, these changes led to a stark drop in traditional Communist membership, which sank by about one-third.

CONGRESS OF VIENNA. Lasting from September 1814 to June 1815, the Congress of **Vienna** had two chief purposes. One was to reconstruct the boundaries of states that Napoleon I of France had reshuffled with his armies and administrative reforms. The Treaty of Paris, concluded in May 1814, had reduced France to its 1792 territorial limits. Nevertheless, the territorial configurations of Europe's other sovereignties remained unsettled. The second task facing the Congress was coming to some agreement on a code of international relations to ensure that whatever new order came out of the gathering would last.

The momentous nature of the decisions to be taken was well appreciated by European states both large and small. The Congress was called by the **Habsburg** ruler Francis I (1768–1835). Once

Holy Roman emperor, he was now emperor of Austria, thanks to Napoleon's reorganization of **Germany**'s boundaries and governments. Prince **Klemens von Metternich**, of Rhenish origin but since 1809 the foreign minister of Emperor Francis, generally orchestrated the conclave. But states, ranging from large and important ones that were instrumental in Napoleon's defeat—Prussia, **Russia**, and Great Britain as well as Austria—to very small ones, saw it in their interest to attend. Stripped of its Bonapartist pretensions, France was represented by the wily Bishop Charles de Talleyrand, who did much at the gathering to reestablish his country's role in continental affairs.

Both Prussia and Russia came to the Congress hoping to enlarge their boundaries, Prussia by absorbing Saxony, Russia chiefly by taking control of the Duchy of Warsaw, a Napoleonic creation designed to serve as the nucleus of a reunited Poland. Having faced Louis XIV in battle at the beginning of the 18th century and Napoleon a hundred years later, Great Britain wished to maintain a balance of power on the Continent that would discourage hegemonic aspirations of any one state there. The **Habsburgs**, humiliated by Napoleon's victories in central Europe and **Italy** and worried about the nationalist sentiments they often inspired there, were eager to block Prussian and Russian expansion and to prevent any reordering of Europe along national lines.

The work of the Congress, or rather the multilateral negotiations that went on between and among the various states in attendance, was held up for long stretches of time by the conflicts these ambitions provoked. Napoleon's escape from Elba in March 1815, his return to France, and his reassembling of an army were other serious distractions. All of these concerns shaped the so-called Final Act of the Congress, which was signed by eight of the powers present at the meeting on 9 June, more than a week before Napoleon was beaten once and for all at Waterloo. The Austrian Empire gave up territories the Habsburgs had held in southwestern Germany for centuries. Some Habsburg Polish land was turned over to Russia as well. In return, however, Emperor Francis I was allowed to annex Lombardy and Venetia in Italy; King Ferdinand of Sicily agreed to follow Austria's direction in military and foreign affairs. These provisions were generally seen as a way of preventing any further French insurgencies. The German-speaking core of the Habsburg lands was rounded out through the annexation of the archbishopric of **Salzburg**, once an independent prince-bishopric in the **Holy Roman Empire**. In Germany, the Habsburgs, through their sovereignty in their German provinces, joined the **German Confederation**, a loose association of the German territorial states. Reflecting a tradition of long standing, the Austrian emperor was made president of the body.

Some mechanisms were put in place to guarantee that these and corresponding arrangements for the other signatories would endure. Metternich was not terribly enthusiastic about a project of Tsar Alexander I of Russia called the Holy Alliance, signed by Russia, Prussia, and Austria in September 1815. As rewritten by the Austrian foreign minister, it called for monarchs to observe the principles of fraternity among themselves, a sentiment that was read to mean that the participants should come to one another's aid should their thrones be threatened. The Quadruple Alliance, formed by Russia, Great Britain, Austria, and Prussia two months later, called for the sovereigns of all four countries to consult periodically on ways of maintaining peace in Europe.

CONSTITUTION, AUSTRIA. Construed broadly, the constitution of the Federal Republic of Austria has three parts, the **Austrian State Treaty** of 1955, the Law on Permanent **Neutrality**, and the *Bundesverfassung*, or Federal Constitution (which covers such matters as the structure of the federal **government**, the locus of sovereignty and the philosophical and legal principles that govern its exercise, and the relationship of the nine federal provinces to national political and legal institutions). Alteration of the basic principles of the constitution may take place only after an affirmative popular plebiscite.

The Federal Constitution incorporates much of the constitution of the First Republic, issued in 1920 and amended in 1929. It therefore reflects many of the values of the jurist **Hans Kelsen**, who was largely responsible for the 1920 version and who defined democracy as the greatest amount of personal freedom consistent with societal reality. It was suspended in 1934 by the government of **Engelbert Dollfuss**; it was declared operative again in 1945.

Many of the individual rights guaranteed by the Second Austrian Republic were taken from a constitution issued in the Austrian half of the Dual Monarchy that was in place following the Compromise

(*Ausgleich*) with Hungary in 1867. The current provisions have been further reinforced by the European Convention for the Protection of Human Rights and Fundamental Freedoms, to which Austria was a signatory in 1958.

The ultimate source of legal authority in the modern Austrian Republic is the people, directly represented on the federal level in the National Assembly (*Nationalrat*), the lower house of the parliament, and indirectly in the upper house, the Federal Chamber (*Bundeskammer*), which represents the nine provinces and is chosen in local legislatures. The seats in both chambers are allocated based on the number of votes the contending parties receive. The Federal Chamber has the right to register objections to and suggestions for legislation from the lower house. It cannot block measures that the National Assembly adopts. The National Assembly is also charged to consider any popular initiative endorsed by 100,000 eligible voters or minimally one-sixth of franchise holders in each of three provinces. It need not, however, enact such initiatives into law. Upon a vote of a majority, the National Assembly may also ask for a public referendum on legislation it has passed. Should the question be an amendment to the constitution, only one-third of the body's total membership of 183 may call for such a measure.

The **chancellor**, the vice-chancellor, various ministers, and their immediate subordinates direct the work of the government. Each of the provinces also has its own deliberative body, which has important local powers and elects a governor. The latter is responsible for the conduct of federal affairs in his or her state. The **judiciary** is independent.

A federal **president**, elected for a term of six years, may hold only two terms consecutively. Since 1951, the Austrian electorate has chosen its president by direct vote. The president is not so much a representative of an individual party as of the Austrian people as a whole. He or she represents the republic in **foreign policy**, convokes and recesses parliaments, and can dissolve the National Assembly one time during a presidency. The president is also the commander-in-chief of the Austrian **military**; actual deployment of these forces is in the hands of the Ministry of Defense. Military service is obligatory for Austrian males. They must spend six months on active duty and return for two months of training exercise annually for 12 years thereafter. Their deployment, however, has been explicitly restricted by the 1955 Law of Permanent Neutrality.

COOP HIMMELB(L)AU. A cooperative **Vienna**-based architectural firm founded by Wolfgang Prix (1942–) and a Vienna-trained Pole, Helmut Swiczinski (1944–), in 1968. Both men studied and taught in London, and Prix taught in Los Angeles as well. Their work received its first major international acclaim at a show called "Deconstructivist Architecture," put on by the New York Museum of Modern Art in 1988. Coop Himmelb(l)au now has offices in the United States (U.S.) and Mexico.

Prix and Swiczinski declared war on the drab, and cost-conscious, functionalism of much post–**World War II** building design in central and east central Europe. The name of their firm means "sky blue" with the "l" and "building into the sky" without it. Neither man made any serious distinction between **architecture** and **art**.

The hallmark of Himmel(b)lau's products is a daringly dramatic use of undulating lines and improbable angles that, asymmetrical as they appear at first glance, flow seamlessly from buildings and set off the surrounding environment. Crisply finished planes on roofs and building exteriors advertise the cutting edge nature of their designs. Recent, and very successful, examples are the BMW motor vehicle showroom in Munich and an addition to the Akron Museum of Art in the U.S., both of which opened in 2007.

COUDENHOVE-KALERGI, RICHARD (1894–1972). A pacifist and writer, Coudenhove-Kalergi laid the ideological groundwork for the modern **European Union** with his book *Paneuropa* in 1923. A periodical of the same name and with the same purpose appeared for the first time the following year. In 1926, the first meeting of the Paneuropean Movement took place in **Vienna** with Coudenhove-Kalergi as chairperson. The group's periodical, also called *Paneuropa*, came out for the first time that year as well.

Coudenhove-Kalergi immigrated to Switzerland in 1938, then to the United States in 1940, where he taught and lectured in New York. The **University of Vienna** withdrew his degree in 1942. He returned to Europe soon after **World War II**, where as general secretary of the European Parliamentary Union he began working toward the creation of a single Europe once again.

CREDITANSTALT BANKVEREIN. Upon successful petition to the **government** of **Franz Joseph**, the Creditanstalt or the Creditanstalt for **Trade** and Manufacture was founded in 1855. The initial capital was put up by several leading aristocratic houses with ties to the court and by contemporary bankers, the most significant of whom was Anselm Rothschild (1773–1855), whose family had important establishments in Frankfurt, London, and Paris. The Creditanstalt would be the **Habsburg Empire**'s private **bank** until the collapse of the monarchy in 1918.

With far greater backing than any other bank in the Habsburg lands—its initial net value was higher than even the **Austrian National Bank**—the Creditanstalt was a significant source of investment capital and credit for major **industrialization** and infrastructure projects, such as **railroads**, for the rest of the 19th century. It specialized in lending to highly creditworthy clients in heavy industry and the aristocracy. By 1860, it had opened six branches in urban centers throughout the Habsburg territory.

The Creditanstalt continued to play this role, albeit on a more modest level, in the First Austrian Republic, even taking on the debts of weaker financial institutions such as the Anglo–Austrian Bank (1926) and the General Austrian Agricultural Credit Bank (1929). The latter had buckled under the combined pressures of inflation, the restrictions placed on the convertibility of the new Austrian **currency**, the schilling, and the general economic hard times of the era.

It was the Creditanstalt's policy of assuming the financial obligations of sister banking institutions that made it the center of world attention in May 1931. Unable to muster the capital to satisfy creditors, the Creditanstalt declared it could not meet their demands. German banks, which had invested heavily in Austria, began to withdraw their deposits, thus setting off a run on banks throughout Europe. The ensuing international monetary chaos did much to set off the Great Depression of the 20th century. Within the First Austrian Republic itself, the bank was reorganized with the financial assistance of the state and the Austrian National Bank. In 1934, it merged with the Bank of Vienna (*Wiener Bankverein*).

During the period 1938–1945, the bank was under German control; many of its assets, including equities, were transferred to the Deutsche Bank. Some of these were returned as part of the **Austrian**

State Treaty of 1955. In 1946, the Creditanstalt was **nationalized** as part of a general Austrian government program. A policy of attracting both private investors and borrowers was in place by 1957. The mid-point of the 1970s found the Creditanstalt among the hundred largest banks in the world, as **privatization** continued. It opened branches in London, New York, and Hong Kong. By 1987, the state of Austria had only a 51 percent interest in the Creditanstalt. Four years later, the federal minister of finance was authorized to sell the remainder of the nationally held shares. These were taken over in 1997 by Bank Austria. *See also* ANSCHLUSS.

CURRENCY. After rocky fiscal experiments with paper money throughout most of the 19th century, the **Habsburg Empire** moved to the gold standard in 1892. The long-circulating gulden was replaced by crowns and heller, with 100 heller equal to 1 crown. Various names for smaller units of the gulden were used colloquially into the 1930s.

The imperial crown inflated wildly at the end of **World War I**. To bring some order into its desolate **economy**, the First Austrian Republic introduced another monetary unit, the schilling, made up of 100 groschen. Though Austrian material conditions improved very little, the new coinage took hold and solidified very quickly.

The **Anschluss** of 1938 brought the German Reichsmark into Austria at a very unfavorable rate for the schilling. But Austria's fiscal independence was short lived; on 17 March 1938, the **Nazi** regime transferred all the gold and currency reserves in the **Austrian National Bank** to **Germany**'s national bank in Berlin.

With **World War II** over, Austria quickly restored the schilling as its official medium of exchange in 1945. The Reichsmark and the Allied military schilling disappeared very fast. By 1947, in an effort to curb inflation, Austrian authorities sharply reduced the exchange rate for the schilling, a step that annoyed the powers of the **occupation** but had the desired fiscal effect. Nevertheless, even when the currency rose considerably in value, the government kept very tight controls on the amount of money in circulation. By 1959, the schilling was completely backed either in gold or foreign hard currencies. It continued to rise in value in relationship to the dollar and other hard currencies, weathering various waves of inflation from the 1960s to the end of the 20th century.

The nationalist **Freedom Party of Austria** raised great objections to abandoning the schilling for the euro in 1997. By 1999, however, Austria, as a member of the **European Union**, had adopted the euro as its legal tender, though not yet in cash transactions. As of 2002, the euro was the currency to be used in all areas of Austrian economic life.

– D –

DANUBE RIVER. Running generally on an east–southeast course, the Danube is the second-longest river in Europe. It traverses 2,850 kilometers (1,767 miles), around 2,300 of which are navigable. Some 340 kilometers of the river flow through Austria, which has been a member of the international consortium of Eastern European countries that regulates the river's uses since 1960. Within Austria itself, the Danube has several significant tributaries, such as the Enns.

Historically, the Danube has been a mixed blessing for Austria. The Romans well understood the strategic importance of the river and fortified it carefully. The imperial naval headquarters were on the outskirts of what would become **Vienna**. The Ottoman Empire, whose armies seriously threatened the entire **Habsburg** monarchy from the 15th century until the final siege of Vienna in 1683, used the Danube Valley as an avenue of access. The Ottoman occupation of Buda and Pest, which was not challenged in the 16th century after 1542, gave them a major riparian redoubt. Falling back to the west on the Danube, the Habsburgs used Bratislava (Germ: *Pressburg*; Hung.: *Pozsony*) as a Hungarian capital until the 18th century.

From the standpoint of geopolitics, the Danube confers a kind of unity on central and southeastern Europe; the **Habsburg Empire** is often referred to as the Danube empire. To ease the economic strains on the region after **World War I**, several unrealized proposals were put forward to create a **trade** zone among its constituent states. The prospect, minus the imperial form of organization, has been raised again since the dissolution of the Soviet bloc in 1989. Austria has been particularly interested in close economic cooperation with Slovakia.

First and foremost, however, the river has been a significant artery of trade with **Germany** and Hungary. It was particularly important for the economy of **Upper Austria** and its capital of **Linz**, which became, and still is, an important Danubian port. As early as the 17th century, the city was a hub for the transshipment of imported and domestically produced textiles and Hungarian minerals and wines. During the same period, the river also served as one avenue for the export of iron, lead, and mercury from **Styria** and **Carinthia**, though these areas also made use of Italian harbors for such products.

Although Vienna also was a port and trading center for river traffic, it gradually lost this function, becoming instead the administrative center of the Habsburg Empire by the beginning of the 18th century. The city lies in a stretch of the river prone to flooding. During the 1890s, a series of locks and canals were constructed to remedy this problem, which reduced the physical presence of the Danube in the city. In the late 20th century, the river and the complex biology of the life that surrounds it became a matter of intense interest to Austrian environmentalists, especially the **Green Party**. The issue has worked its way into Austria's **foreign policy**, because significant pollution of the river is the result of **industrial** and **agricultural** policies of the former Communist bloc.

DANUBE SCHOOL/DONAUSCHULE. A dramatic pictorial style that arose in Bavaria and the Austrian lands in the late 15th century, the Danube School was not a single movement. Rather, the term applies to a number of widely scattered **art**ists who used much the same subject matter and techniques to portray it. Its hallmarks were the placement of religious and sometimes secular themes in identifiably natural settings and the use of intense color. In the **Vorarlberg**, Wolf Huber (ca. 1485–1553), who was responsible for the St. Anna's altar in Feldkirch (1521), did the first genuine landscapes to appear in the art of central Europe. The figurative outlines of all elements in the work were heavily linear and often wildly contorted, thus heightening the expressive force of the entire piece.

The most notable Austrian representatives of the style were Roland Frueauf the Younger, who created the altar cycles of St. John around 1498–1499, and St. Leopold (1505?) in the **Benedictine** abbey of Klosterneuburg. Well-known painters from all over southern **Germany** left notable artistic monuments in Austria. Lukas Cranach (1472–1553) painted in St. Pölten and Zistersdorf in **Lower Austria** at the beginning of the 16th century. Perhaps the most well-known artist, Albrecht Altdorfer (ca. 1480–1538), who was from Regensburg, came frequently to the Austrian lands and worked on the St. Sebastian altar cycle (1509–1518) for the cloister of St. Florian in **Upper Austria**. Though there is some scholarly debate about the authorship of a cycle depicting the life of Emperor **Frederick III** and the childhood of his son, **Maximilian I**, it is highly likely that it was done either by Altdorfer himself or by someone very closely associated with him. Some of the artists remained anonymous, for example, the Master of the Pulkauer Altar (ca. 1520), also in Lower Austria. This was also true of the "Masters of the Miracle of Mariazell" (1512, 1519) in **Styria**.

DANUBE STEAMSHIP COMPANY. Established as a joint-stock venture in 1830 by two Englishmen, John Andrews and Joseph Pritchard, the Danube Steamship Company started freight and passenger service between **Vienna** and Budapest one year later. Two Austrians had been licensed for a similar undertaking in 1818, but had never exploited the privilege. The company expanded its service to **Linz** in 1837. Ten years later, it had acquired 41 vessels, which were transporting over 850,000 passengers and around 200,000 tons of freight per year. The company used its capital to finance other important projects in the Austrian Empire, such as **railroads**, waterways, and some mining ventures. Until 1914 it was the largest inland shipping company in the world.

As part of its compensation from Austria for damage incurred during **World War II**, the Soviet Union acquired a role in the direction of the company. In an economic side agreement to the **Austrian State Treaty** of 1955, Austria paid the Soviet Union $2 million in return for the latter's share in the company. *See also* ECONOMY; TRANSPORTATION.

DODERER, HEIMITO VON (1896–1966). Acknowledged as one of the masters of Austrian **literature** for his linguistic virtuosity and narrative gifts, Doderer had to wait many years before his reputation was assured. His youth had some of the epic qualities of his greatest novels, *Die Strudelhofstiege* (*The Strudelhof Stairs*, 1951) and *Die Dämonen* (*The Demons*, 1956). A prisoner of war in Russia during **World War I**, he returned to **Vienna** in 1920. He had traveled at least part of the way on foot. During the interwar period, he worked as a journalist and tried painting, neither of which brought him any particular recognition.

In 1933, Doderer joined the outlawed **Nazi** Party, something he came to regret deeply. Burning his party membership card before friends in 1938, he converted to **Catholicism** in 1940. It was an effort, as he put it, to reestablish his humanity. He became a sharp critic of all ideology, in the belief that it warped humankind's conceptual and psychological powers. Doderer also spent much of **World War II** as a captive, this time in England.

Doderer's writing, particularly his mature novels, is conceived on a grand scale. *The Strudelhof Stairs* and *The Demons* are the second and third volumes of a trilogy that he had worked on episodically from 1931. Filled with a rich assortment of characters from the lands of the former **Habsburg Empire**, interwar Austria, and especially Vienna, the works are not so much depictions of social reality as repositories of material in which writers are to find inspiration. Doderer himself took note of these figures and his impressions of them in detailed diaries. Their impact on the reader depends in part on the **language** Doderer used to describe his creations, in part on the great care with which he structured his prose. He was much influenced by the organizing principles of musical composition, and compared his sprawling novels to the symphonies of **Ludwig van Beethoven**. He was also preoccupied with the relationship of modes of sexuality to what he termed the apperception of reality.

DOLLFUSS, ENGELBERT (1892–1934). Chancellor of the First Austrian Republic from 1932 until he was murdered in his office building on 25 July 1934, Dollfuss came from the peasant community of Texing in **Lower Austria**. Born out of wedlock, he was subsequently adopted by his stepfather. His full height as an adult was not quite five feet. Dollfuss was decorated several times for bravery during **World War I**, when he served in **Italy**. After the conflict ended, he became active in the **Christian Social Party** (CP), in which he concentrated on **agricultural** questions. He was secretary of the Lower Austrian branch of the Agrarian League (*Landbund*), which spoke for peasant interests and participated in coalitions with the Christian Socials. In 1927, Dollfuss was made director of the Lower Austrian **Chamber for Agriculture**. He became federal minister for agriculture and forestry in 1931 and served in that capacity under three governments, before he took over the chancellorship. Dollfuss also acted as his own foreign minister.

Dollfuss assumed these offices in 1932 at a chaotic moment in Austrian history. Only the previous year, the failure of the **Creditanstalt Bankverein** had sparked a worldwide **bank** panic that set off the Great Depression of the interwar years. Operating in the Austrian parliament in coalition with the Agrarian League and the Homeland Bloc (*Heimatblock*), the political arm of the right-wing *Heimwehr*, the new chancellor had little room to maneuver. Under pressure from the Austrian **Nazis** and the **Social Democratic Workers' Party** (SDAP) to hold elections, which he feared the CP could lose, Dollfuss used a temporary leadership vacuum in the Austrian parliament to shut it down altogether in March 1933. Freedom of speech, the **press**, and assembly were sharply restricted; the Nazi and **Communist** parties were outlawed, as was the **Republican Guard**, the paramilitary arm of the SDAP.

Dollfuss justified these measures on the basis of the Economic Empowering Act. Issued in World War I, it gave the **government** extraordinary leeway in dealing with emergencies. However, the real instrument of the chancellor's authority in Austria was his control over the police and the army, along with his cooperative relations with the *Heimwehr* and substantial aid from fascist Italy. In May 1933, Dollfuss announced the creation of the **Fatherland Front**, an ideological umbrella for those who supported some or all of his program. Both the Communists and Nazis went underground; important members of the latter movement found their way to Germany, where they continued to work toward a takeover of Austria by their party.

Under continued pressure from Benito Mussolini in Italy and the local *Heimwehr*, Dollfuss continued to narrow the freedom of the SDAP. Police searches for caches of socialist weapons became more frequent. Continued provocation led to armed, but unsuccessful, socialist resistance in February 1934. Once this was put down, Dollfuss outlawed the SDAP as well.

A Concordat Dollfuss reached with the papacy in 1934 tied Austria even more explicitly to the Roman Catholic Church. The Rome Protocols, signed in the same year with Italy and authoritarian Hungary, obligated Austria to consult with both countries on foreign and domestic affairs. In May 1934, Dollfuss put forth a new **constitution**. It was based on **Catholic** and corporative principles, which were to encourage greater cooperation between labor and management. The Catholic church, the *Heimwehr*, and the Austrian peasant organizations supported the arrangement. However, it was never fully implemented.

On 25 July 1934, Austrian National Socialists, many of whom had former ties with the army and had been cashiered for their ideological leanings, staged an uprising in **Vienna**. Their goal was to capture the government for their party. Though their hopes to find Dollfuss and his ministers together were dashed, putschists did locate the chancellor, whom they shot. Denied either medical help or a priest to perform the last rites, Dollfuss died over two hours after he had been mortally wounded. *See also* AUSTRO-FASCISM; FEBRUARY UPRISING; JULY PUTSCH; MAY CONSTITUTION.

DUAL ALLIANCE. Anxious about the possibility of being caught between France and Russia in future military conflicts, Otto von Bismarck, chancellor of the new German Empire after 1871, began cultivating cordial relations with the **Habsburg Empire** soon after defeating its army during the **Seven Weeks' War** in 1866. Signed in 1879, the Dual Alliance committed each participant to defense of the other should Russia attack either party in the east. Should another, unspecified, state attack either **Germany** or Austria–Hungary, neither of the latter would help the aggressor. Were **Russia** to aid whoever opened the offensive, however, Germany and Austria–Hungary would come to one another's aid. The alliance was renewable five years at a time. Should neither signatory request a review of its terms, the agreement would run for an additional 36 months. The terms of the Dual Alliance were not fully disclosed until 1888. *See also* FOREIGN POLICY.

DUAL MONARCHY. *See* AUSGLEICH.

– E –

ECONOMY. The shift from an agrarian to a capital-driven industrial economy has taken longer in Austria than in many other regions of Europe. The **agricultural** base of the Austrian lands has always been in the east, especially **Lower Austria**; its mountains, the **Alps**, although they are heavily forested and once held important veins of precious metals, particularly in the **Tyrol**, have limited both population and economic growth in those regions for centuries.

As part of the **Habsburg Empire**, the Austrian lands were both advantaged and disadvantaged economically. The dynasty's pan-European responsibilities—defense against the expansion of the Ottoman Empire from the 16th through the end of the 17th centuries and the wars associated with the re-catholicization of central and east central Europe during the Counter-Reformation—siphoned off capital from the Austrian lands that otherwise might have gone into economic enterprises. Cities such as **Vienna**, an important trading center in the Middle Ages, were reduced to administrative garrisons, and by the beginning of the 18th century could not compare with Paris, London, or Amsterdam in economic importance. The nobility of the Habsburg lands, including those territories now in modern Austria, retained extensive control over their agricultural workforce, much of which was enserfed, thus discouraging the labor mobility that would be a precondition for economic growth throughout Europe.

The **industrialization** of the Habsburg Empire began seriously in the second half of the 18th century during the reigns of **Maria Theresa** and her son, **Joseph II**. Starting in the textile sector, the growth of manufacturing was immeasurably encouraged by the spread of **railroads**, which began in the first half of the 19th century. However, this development did not take place uniformly throughout Austria. Rather, it was concentrated in **Lower Austria** and, to a lesser extent, in **Styria** and **Carinthia**. Private **banking**, represented by such institutions as the **Creditanstalt Bankverein**, also grew significantly during this period.

The most explosive spurt to the industrialization of Austria came after the **Ausgleich** between Austria and Hungary in 1867. Large numbers of firms were founded, many of which would not survive the financial panics that were a feature of the 19th-century economy or would be absorbed into huge conglomerates organized by leading industrialists such as **Carl Wittgenstein**. Some of these enterprises were in the east and southeast of Austria, but the most important of them lay in the kingdom of Bohemia.

World War I and the **Treaty of St. Germain**, which ended the conflict for Austria, produced an economic catastrophe. Traditional markets in eastern Europe shunned Austria as a partner in international **trade**, and aside from forestry, the instability of Austria's currency discouraged the development of new export markets. The bulk of the Habsburg Empire's heavy industrial infrastructure remained in the new Czechoslovakia. Unemployment was rampant throughout the interwar period, and the country depended heavily on subsistence agriculture. Although German investment in Austrian heavy industry during **World War II** brought about some recovery in that sector, Allied bombing had heavily damaged manufacturing and transportation sites.

It was not until after **World War II** that the Austrian economy returned to pre-1914 productivity levels. Led by textiles and heavy metals, the latter heavily **nationalized**, Austria joined the ranks of industrialized nations. Its primary agricultural population shrank significantly. Challenged by greater global competition, Austria began to privatize its economy systematically in the latter half of the 20th century. Membership in the **European Union** since 1995 has only intensified this development.

In 2005, for the first time the economic performance of Austria outdistanced the Federal Republic of **Germany** in per capita gross domestic production and growth and a favorable ratio of debt to Gross Domestic Product. Austrian labor costs, corporate income taxes, and unemployment figures were lower. Germans, on the other hand, worked about 200 hours less per year than their Austrian counterparts. The rate of corporate relocations from abroad to Austria, German firms among them, was up as well. Although taxes remain relatively high—roughly 42.9 percent of gross pretax earnings—various kinds of income transfer payments and subventions in the country lower that figure to around 16.20 percent. In 2006, close to 68,000 Austrians were worth over 1 million euros.

The international economic downturn that began in the summer of 2007 affected Austria seriously. Financial and government authorities thought that the country would avoid the worst consequences of the mortgage meltdown in the **United States**, but major Austrian banks were as heavily invested in aspects of this market as some of their German and Swiss counterparts. As equity prices fell in the credit crisis of 2008, the Austrian Financial Credit Authority that oversees the Vienna Stock Exchange prohibited short selling on 10 October. It also ordered the suspension of trading should prices of securities fluctuate up or down by 10 percent. In a special session called on 20 October, the Nationalrat adopted a financial package that provided unlimited guarantees for savings and other personal accounts.

EDUCATION. As in most of central Europe in the Middle Ages, schooling in the Austrian lands of the period was a haphazard affair. Churches in larger towns and monasteries such as **Melk** often educated young boys, but primarily for clerical careers. Young nobles often received some instruction in monastery programs. By the 14th century, the need for advanced training for both clerical and administrative careers had spurred the foundation of institutions of higher learning such as the **University of Vienna**. However, the number of people who received such training remained very small.

The **Protestant** Reformation, which stressed biblical literacy among even modest folk, generated a real need for widespread primary education. To counter this, **Catholic** princes, including the Austrian **Habsburgs**, supported the takeover of Lutheran elementary schools by the Catholic church, especially its **Jesuit** order, a crucial player in Austrian educational history from the 17th until well into the 18th centuries. A new university, dedicated to the improvement of Catholic learning, was opened as well in **Graz**. Little effort, however, was devoted to expanding the number of elementary schools themselves, so that the numbers who received such instruction, particularly in more rural areas, were still comparatively meager.

The reversal of the clerical domination of Austrian education began in the 18th century. Both **Maria Theresa** and her son, **Joseph II**, aspired to make their subjects economically productive. The secularization of learning was a key part of their agendas. When in 1773 the papacy itself abolished the Jesuit order, Maria Theresa seized their properties in her lands and used the income to support expanded educational opportunity. In 1774, six years of public schooling became theoretically compulsory for children of both sexes. However, the rule was laxly enforced, especially in the countryside, where the notion and the procedures that accompanied it were often regarded with great suspicion.

The political upheavals of the French Revolution and Napoleonic Wars somewhat dampened Habsburg enthusiasm for an educated populace. The stifling censorship of the regime ordered by Emperor Francis I (1768–1835) and his **chancellor, Klemens Wenzel von Metternich,** did little to further education at any level. Universities suffered especially, in part because they were in themselves mediocre, but also in comparison with new German foundations such as the University of Berlin, which had been expressly founded to promote teaching and research.

After the **Revolutions of 1848**, however, education at all levels improved substantially throughout the **Habsburg Empire**. Especially important were the reforms of **Count Leo Thun-Hohenstein**, which granted universities much more latitude in conducting their intellectual and administrative affairs. Clerical influence remained strong, especially in primary education, but secondary education in so-called Gymnasiums (*Gymnasien*) now offered a thorough grounding in scientific and historical subjects, though classical languages remained the heart of the instructional program. The Realgymnasium, or Modern Gymnasium, stressed technical subjects and modern languages somewhat more than did its more academically oriented counterpart. In 1869, eight years of education became compulsory for all Austrians. When **World War I** broke out in 1914, schools providing vocational training and teacher education existed alongside establishments responsible for general education. Correspondence courses were available as well and had large numbers of students throughout the Habsburg Empire.

The collapse of the empire in 1918, and the brief rise of the Austrian **Social Democratic Workers' Party** to power in the First Republic, opened the door to the systematic democratization of education in Austria. Under the leadership of **Otto Glöckel**, expanded educational opportunity for the entire Austrian public became a key goal. The general thrust of this movement was blunted, first by the appearance of more conservative Austrian governments in the 1920s and 1930s, then by the **Nazis** after the **Anschluss** of 1938.

Since 1962, Austria has put in place an elaborate system of public education that seeks to meet the needs of the spectrum of human talents and inclinations. Nine years of compulsory schooling are now required. Primary education (*Volksschule*) lasts from the ages of 6 through 10. Once this is completed, pupils move in one of several directions. They may continue in a Volksschule, which eventually leads to advanced technical training and apprenticeship. Should they opt for basic secondary education, they will attend a Hauptschule, which lasts until the age of 14. At that point, students can move into vocational training or to a Realgymnasium. The latter can be used as a route to university or university-level work. A third option is to enter an academic Gymnasium, expressly designed to train students for study at one of Austria's 15 universities. Among these universities are former specialized conservatories, such as the Academy of Musical and Theatrical Arts, which began to function as the University for Music and Theatrical Arts in 2002 (*Universität für Musik und Darstellende Kunst*).

Debates about offering secondary education in a more inclusive setting (*Gesammtschule*) are still common in Austrian political and pedagogical circles. So is the question of opening medical and other faculties of Austrian universities to applicants from the **European Union** at large. The globalization of competitive marketplaces has also raised questions in Austria about the quality of its scientific and technical research in traditional universities. In 1999, Austria mandated the establishment of more than 40 industrial study and research centers (*Kompetenzzentren*). Here research, funding, and representatives of **industry** and business are encouraged to work together to help Austria meet the standards of the broader world economy and modern science. An "elite" university for high-level scientific research has been established in **Lower Austria**. *See also* WOMEN.

EISENSTADT. With the incorporation of the **Burgenland** into Austria after the end of **World War I**, Eisenstadt in 1925 became the provincial capital. Before then, the city and the Burgenland itself were part of the kingdom of Hungary. During **World War II**, the **Nazi** regime in Austria revoked the region's provincial status altogether. Eisenstadt resumed its position as a capital after the conflict.

Prehistoric settlement of the site dates from the **Hallstatt** culture of the first millennium BCE. Roman artifacts have been turned up there as well. The first documentary mention of the later Eisenstadt is as "minor Martin" (Hung.: *Kismárton*) in a Magyarized Latin text from 1264. In 1373, it was called "Eisenstat." By 1388 it had become a market.

The Habsburg Archduke Albrecht VI (1418–1463) acquired Eisenstadt in 1445, and for the next 200 years it was in **Habsburg** hands, though the dynasty mortgaged the town in 1622. In 1648, it was acquired as part of a land grant made by the Habsburgs as kings of Hungary to the Hungarian magnate family of Esterházy. A grandiose palace built by the Esterházys dominates the center of the city to this day. Eisenstadt became a royal Hungarian free city. From 1761 to 1790, the composer **Franz Joseph Haydn** was the chapel choir director of the family. In this position, he wrote not only at the command of the house, but privately as well. A substantial portion of his voluminous output dates from his years of employment in the Esterházy Palace.

EUGENE, PRINCE OF SAVOY (1663–1736). Prince Eugene was one in a long line of **military** leaders who came from other lands to lead the **Habsburg** armies in desperate moments. Indeed, he is the most celebrated of all the house of Austria's generals. Born in Paris, he was the son of a member of the Italian house of Savoy and Olympia Mancini, a great-niece of Louis XIII's chief minister, Cardinal Mazarin.

Denied a career befitting his station in the French army, Prince Eugene entered imperial service in 1683. He took part in the defense of **Vienna** against the Turks during that year, then fought to push back the sultan's armies in Hungary. From 1689 to almost the end of his life, he fought against both the forces of Louis XIV on the western front in the War of the Spanish Succession and the ever-retreating Ottoman Empire in the east. In both theaters, he quickly gained a reputation for imaginative strategies and boldness in applying them. The latter quality was especially helpful in winning for him the confidence and cooperation of Habsburg troops, who were often underpaid and underfed.

As commander in chief of the imperial armies in the east, Eugene masterminded several spectacular victories against the Ottoman Empire, the most notable being the battle of Zenta in 1697. Twenty thousand of the sultan's troops were killed in the encounter; another 10,000 drowned in the Tisza River as they fled the imperial onslaught. By 1717, the prince's forces had reached Belgrade, though Habsburg armies were unable to maintain this position for long. Against the French, Eugene joined his army with the British Duke of Marlborough. Although he participated in some notable victories between 1704 and 1709, he was not playing a prominent role by the end of the protracted conflict.

Prince Eugene was unusually versatile, as much at home as a diplomat and administrative official as he was in military affairs. He negotiated the Treaty of Rastatt (1714), which ended the War of the Spanish Succession advantageously for Austria. He was a key advisor to Emperors Leopold I (1640–1705), Joseph I (1678–1711), and Charles VI (1685–1740), acting as president of the imperial military council from 1703 on. He served as Charles VI's governor in Milan from 1716 to 1724, and later he was general overseer of all the Habsburg possessions in Italy. He was governor-general of the Austrian Netherlands, which came under Austrian Habsburg control at the end of the War of the Spanish Succession.

Eugene also contributed some key components to the Austrian cultural legacy. Among them are his garden palace, the Belvedere, and his collection of rare books, which are a central part of the collection of the **Austrian National Library**. *See also* BAROQUE; FISCHER VON ERLACH, JOHANN BERNHARD; HILDEBRANDT, JOHANN LUKAS VON.

EUROPEAN FREE TRADE ASSOCIATION (EFTA). With the national **economy** recovering at a swift pace during the latter half of the 1950s, the Austrian coalition government was eager to establish closer commercial relations with Western Europe. Austria's official status as a neutral country made integration into the European Economic Community (EEC), the predecessor of the **European Union** (EU), problematic, even though Italy and Germany were fast becoming its most important **trading** partners.

At first the Austrian regime pressed to turn all of Europe into a free trade zone. In 1960, at a meeting in Stockholm, Austria joined with Denmark, Great Britain, Norway, Portugal, Sweden, and Switzerland to form the European Free Trade Association. Each promised to give special tariff considerations to the exports of member states. The group agreed to lower quantitative limits on imports from one another's countries. Unlike their counterparts in the EEC, EFTA participants were not required to synchronize the regulatory structures of their internal economies.

The Austrian economy profited from the EFTA relationship. Austrian exports to EFTA countries rose from around 12 percent of its total exports in 1959 to more than 28 percent by 1970. At the same time, while the monetary value of its exports to the EEC rose dramatically—from 12.4 billion schillings to 30.6 billion in 1970—the overall percentage of Austrian imports in the EEC declined. However, the general thrust of Austrian policy was almost always to find a modus vivendi with the EEC, as was true of other EFTA states. In 1961, Great Britain had already made known its interest in joining the European Economic Community. A species of free-trade arrangement was set up between the EFTA and EEC members in 1973. The Soviet Union, which was eager to preserve Austrian **neutrality**, did not oppose the arrangement. Austrian membership in the EEC, which began in 1995, effectively abrogated the EFTA relationship.

EUROPEAN UNION (EU). An economic, and increasingly political, organization of 15 European states. Austria gained admission in 1995. The administrative headquarters of the EU are in Brussels.

The EU has developed as a fusion of international organizations that arose after **World War II**. Their general purpose was to promote the **economic** recovery of Europe and to foster interstate ties that would discourage further wars among them. The first of these ties was the European Coal and Steel Community (ECSC, 1952), which turned into the European Economic Community (EEC) in 1958. In 1967, the European Atomic Community was incorporated into the EEC, which was then called the European Community (EC). In 1987, the EC declared European political unity to be a central goal and set up a mechanism for regular conferences of European heads of government. An agreement signed in Maestricht in 1993 established a timetable for both the political and economic integration of the continent.

In 1994, 66 percent of all Austrians participating in a referendum supported their country's membership in the EU. Behind this vote lay some complex and delicate problems. The Soviet Union had accepted the **Austrian State Treaty** of 1955 only on the condition of Austria's perpetual **neutrality**. What the Russians wanted most to prevent was any kind of formal linkage of Austria and **Germany**. The Russians wanted to keep Austria out of the North Atlantic Treaty Organization (NATO) as well, particularly when by 1954 West Germany had been invited to join that alliance.

Julius Raab, the first **chancellor** of a sovereign Austria following the signing of the State Treaty, argued that military neutrality did not affect Austria's **economic** and cultural relations with foreign countries. In 1956, Austria entered into a customs agreement with the ECSC, and there was some discussion of outright membership. However, the Soviet suppression of the Hungarian Revolution in the fall of that year made Austrian politicians a great deal more cautious. Their reservations seemed even more justifiable when the Soviets moved forces into Czechoslovakia in 1968 to put an end to the liberal Prague Spring. Both **Kurt Waldheim**, as Austrian foreign minister in the late 1960s, and Bruno Kreisky pursued very active foreign policies. However, their focus was largely on regions of the world where Austria was not likely to be called upon to engage itself militarily.

By the late 1970s, the reformist wing of the **Austrian People's Party** (ÖVP) began calling for a stronger Austrian presence in the economic mainstream of Western Europe. Austrian profits from trade with the Soviet bloc and the developing world were now lagging behind the revenues generated by commerce with the West; a rethinking of import–export relationships seemed warranted. Austria had participated in the **European Free Trade Association** (EFTA) since 1960, but the most important member of that organization, Great Britain, had applied for membership in the EC the following year. Although French President Charles de Gaulle vetoed that, the EC and its successors were clearly the more dynamic of the two economic groupings of noncommunist Europe. By 1977, Austrian industrial goods could enter the EC duty-free. The Soviet Union offered no serious objections.

The 1980s seriously altered the political-economic landscape both of the EC and of Austria's relations with it. Faced with global marketing challenges from both the **United States** and Japan, the EC resolved to tie itself together more closely monetarily and politically to remain economically competitive. Its Single Europe Act, in force after 1 July 1987, called for the development of a common **foreign policy** for member states.

Debate on Austria's relationship with the EC had long fallen along political lines, the **Socialist Party of Austria** (SPÖ) taking a generally minimalist approach, the more entrepreneur-friendly ÖVP arguing for far tighter integration. In 1986, however, with another Grand Coalition (SPÖ—ÖVP) governing Austria, the two parties substantially narrowed their differences. **Alois Mock**, a longtime supporter of Austrian participation in the EC, was foreign minister and vice-chancellor, thus giving these views a strong advocate within the regime. At first Austria was inclined toward greater cooperation with the EC. Nor, as Chancellor Franz Vranitzky made clear, did it want to abandon its position in EFTA. After the EC announced early in 1989 that only full members would have decision-making powers in its councils and that real political and military integration was part of their final plan, Austria's prospects for membership looked dim.

However, the stagnation of the Austrian economy in the 1980s and the collapse of the Soviet Union, which began in 1989, encouraged the Vranitzky government to press on for EC membership. Public opinion, however, remained skeptical. At the end of 1988, a poll showed that opposition was growing. The environmentally oriented **Green Party**, the **Communists**, pacifists, farmers frightened by the prospect of regulation from Brussels, and some Socialist politicians spoke out against the arrangement. The letter of application for membership in the EC, which Foreign Minister Mock submitted on 17 July 1989 to Roland Dumas, his French counterpart, listed several items covering domestic environmental and social matters that Austria wanted to set as conditions for its participation. Above all, it wished to have its neutral status recognized.

Once again, the EC was not enthusiastic. The Soviet Union, too, expressed its concern about the possible breach of the **neutrality** agreement. By 1990, with the Soviet Union fast becoming a part of history, Austria was ready to commit itself to the Single European Act, including participation in the formulation of foreign and security policies. In 1993, the EC declared its willingness to receive an Austrian application for membership. Two years later, acceptance came.

– F –

FANTASTIC REALISM. A style of Austrian painting produced by artists who grew up between the two world wars of the 20th century. The term was coined by a **Vienna art** critic in 1956. The style, which became prominent not only in Austria but also in other world art markets after 1951, combined technical virtuosity and faithfulness to traditional forms with the imaginative insights of Surrealism.

The inspiration for Fantastic Realism came from the painter Albert Paris Gütersloh (pseud. Albert Conrad Kiehtreiber) (1887–1973), a one-time professor at the Vienna Academy for Visual Arts (*Akademie der bildenden Künste*). Representative members of the school are Ernst Fuchs (1930–), Erich Brauer (1929–), Anton Lehmden (1929–), Rudolf Hausner (1914–1995), Wolfgang Hutter (1928–), and especially Fritz Janschka (1919–), who spent much of his career in the United States at Bryn Mawr College.

FASCHING. Among Europe's many pre-Lenten festivals, the Austrian Fasching is one of the most elaborate and enduring. Beginning with the Feast of the Three Kings in January, it ends with Ash Wednesday. In **Vienna** itself, Fasching has become the so-called Ball Season. The highlight of this period is the Opera Ball, a very formal evening of dance, drink, and supping that puts some of the Second Republic's most prominent citizens on display. However, the city abounds in such events—greengrocers, firemen, policemen, and various municipal districts all hold their own balls, formal, informal, or in fanciful costume. The celebration comes to a climax in the last week, beginning with *foasten*, or "Crazy Thursday."

Many cultures have left their marks on Fasching—peasant practice, courtly festivals, and the celebrations of premodern guilds and other groups of artisans. There are still some regional variations in Austria, beginning with the name of the custom, which in the western part of the country is Fastnacht. In parts of the **Tyrol** and **Vorarlberg**, the season ends only on the first Sunday in Lent with the burning of a doll called a *Hexe* or witch. Flaming chunks of wood into which rods have been driven are slid down mountainsides.

FATHERLAND FRONT/VATERLÄNDISCHE FRONT. In an effort to rise above the highly partisan discord between the **Christian Social Party** (CP) and **Social Democratic Workers' Party** in the First Austrian Republic, **Engelbert Dollfuss** established the Fatherland Front on 20 May 1933. The following September, speaking before an audience at a local trotting track, he issued a general call for converting Austria into a "social, Christian, German state" to be corporately organized and authoritarianly governed. Political parties were to be disbanded.

This structure, in which the Front would serve as the only avenue for the formation and expression of public opinion, owed much to the thinking of the Austrian economist and social philosopher **Othmar Spann** and the pressure for such changes coming from the contemporary Italian dictator Benito Mussolini. The emblem of the Fatherland Front was a crutched cross; its slogan, reflecting Dollfuss's commitment to an independent Austria, was "Austria Awake." These two words were about the extent of the organization's program. The Front was not a political party in the sense that the Italian Fascists or the German **Nazis** were. Though the Front's followers were often government figures, the movement was not to interfere with state authority in Austria, either local or federal. Dollfuss was the supreme leader of the Front until his assassination in July 1934. He was followed by **Count Ernst Rüdiger Starhemberg**, a leader of the *Heimwehr*, who was replaced in 1936 by **Kurt Schuschnigg**, who had succeeded Dollfuss as **chancellor**. Schuschnigg held the office until the **Anschluss** with Nazi Germany in 1938.

The Fatherland Front made itself felt in Austrian public life during the relatively short time of its existence. It extended throughout the Austrian provinces. Membership was obligatory for civil servants. It sponsored a variety of youth organizations and opened a political bureau to reach out to former socialists, whose party was by this time illegal. Perhaps most important from the standpoint of creating domestic peace, it absorbed the CP-oriented paramilitary *Heimwehr* in favor of a militia open to members from all the former parties.

In general, however, the Fatherland Front fell far short of its objectives. Dedicated to the preservation of Austrian sovereignty, it failed to rally the bulk of the First Republic's population to that cause. The leadership and support came largely from Austria's traditional ruling circles, the **Catholic** clerical hierarchy, the monied bourgeoisie, and segments of the former nobility. Thus, the change of political class, however incomplete, brought about by the Nazis in Germany and the Italian Fascists, eluded Austria's Fatherland Front. Most destructive to the organization was the relentless infighting over leadership of the Front between CP political functionaries and their counterparts. *See also* AUSTRO-FASCISM.

FEBRUARY UPRISING/FEBRUARKÄMPFE. Armed skirmishing among the paramilitary *Heimwehr*, the **Christian Social Party** government, local police, and the illegal Socialist-oriented **Republican Guard** broke out in **Linz**, the capital of **Upper Austria**, on 12 February 1934. Spreading erratically to provincial industrial centers and **Vienna**, the fighting lasted for three days. Under pressure from Benito Mussolini in **Italy** to curb the influence of Marxism in Austria, the government of Chancellor **Engelbert Dollfuss**, local police, and branches of the *Heimwehr* had been raiding Socialist centers to root out caches of weapons allegedly hidden there. It was just such a strike by the *Heimwehr*, uniformed as auxiliary police, against a **Social Democratic Workers' Party** (SDAP) hospice in Linz, that provoked a group of the Republican Guard to respond with gunfire.

The conflict in Vienna was especially intense. Military artillery was deployed against public and communal housing projects inhabited by industrial workers and their families. The most notorious of these attacks was on the cavernous Karl-Marx-Hof, built between 1927 and 1930.

The Socialists were both disorganized and poorly led. Some of their leadership was already imprisoned. A general strike called by the party temporarily shut down electricity and streetcar lines, but the mail, telegraphic and telephone networks, and **railroads** continued to operate. When the resistance ended, the Social Democratic side had suffered around 200 dead and more than 300 wounded. Some of its leaders were captured and executed. Others, most prominently the ideologue **Otto Bauer**, took refuge abroad.

The failure of the uprising cost the SDAP dearly. The Dollfuss government banned the party, its **trade unions**, and the organizations that it sponsored for workers. The bodies that represented the party's constituents in the various provincial and communal administrations were also dissolved. The government side counted 128 fatalities and 409 casualties. The episode pushed Austria ever further along the road toward authoritarian government. *See also* AUSTRO-FASCISM.

FELLNER, WOLFGANG (1954–). One of the major figures in the Austrian **press** in the latter decades of the 20th century, Fellner and his businessman brother, Helmuth (1956–), gained their reputations for hardhitting feature stories, eye-catching visuals, painstaking marketing research, and precise identification of readership with the magazine *NEWS*, which first appeared in 1992. Wolfgang had been a presence in Austrian journalism since the age of 14 with his *Rennbahn-Express,* a young people's magazine first published in 1968 that eventually circulated not only in **Salzburg**, where he lived with his parents, but throughout Austria. His next important creation, *Basta,* packaged gossip, sensationalism, and sexual innuendo deliberately targeted at Austrian twenty-somethings.

His most recent, and most ambitious, venture was the daily *Österreich,* which made use of all the techniques on which he had relied in the past, as well as a flat-price scale that undercut most of Austria's established dailies. Unlike previous Fellner periodicals, *Österreich,* which first came out in September 2006, belongs to Wolfgang alone.

Fellner has been widely criticized in Austria for what some see as his disregard for intellectual seriousness, his heavy reliance on tie-in offers, and pandering to the public fascination with personal scandal to bulk up his readership and subscription list. Even his naysayers, however, admit that he has done much to keep print journalism in Austria alive. *NEWS* alone doubled the circulation of national magazines after it came out.

FERDINAND I, HOLY ROMAN EMPEROR (1503–1564). Born in Spain, Archduke Ferdinand I was the offspring of the Spanish–Austrian marriage arranged in 1495 by his grandfather, Emperor **Maximilian I**. His father was Maximilian's son, Prince Philip (1478–1506), his mother Princess Juana (1479–1555), a daughter of Ferdinand of Aragon and Isabella of Castile. His elder brother, Charles V (1500–1558), who became king of Spain in 1516 and Holy Roman Emperor three years later, effectively ceded him the central European patrimony of their house in agreements concluded in 1521 and 1522.

Married to Princess Anna (1503–1547), a daughter of the king of Hungary and Bohemia, Ferdinand was the founder of the **Habsburg Empire** in central and east central Europe. When his brother-in-law, King Louis, died fleeing the battlefield at Mohács in Hungary against the forces of the Ottoman Empire in 1526, Ferdinand persuaded the estates of both kingdoms to elect him as their ruler, though both the Ottoman sultan and native claimants kept him from gaining complete control of Hungary. A mediocre military leader, he would never recapture that realm from the Turks. He did, however, nudge the kingdom of Bohemia somewhat closer to hereditary, rather than elective, monarchy. Nor, as the **Protestant** Reformation spread from the German territories to his lands, was Ferdinand able to bring them back to **Catholic** orthodoxy, a goal to which he and the majority of his successors would unwaveringly aspire.

But Ferdinand had great strengths as well. Imaginative and energetic, he developed an administrative framework for the new empire that endured well into the 18th century. The core of the structure was made up of a central treasury, court council, privy council, and somewhat later, a corresponding body for military affairs. A common chancellery conducted the written business of all these offices. The system functioned much less effectively in practice than on paper—Bohemia and Hungary both resisted cooperating with it—but it was widely imitated or adapted in many other German territories.

A gifted negotiator who stood in for his brother in Germany ever more frequently over the years, Ferdinand was the architect of the 1555 Peace of Augsburg, which established some measure of confessional peace between Lutherans and Catholics in the second half of the 16th century. Emperor in his own name after 1558, he was also instrumental in keeping the cause of Catholic reform alive during the last session of the Council of Trent, which met from 1562 to 1563. *See also* HABSBURG, HOUSE OF; HOLY ROMAN EMPIRE; RELIGION.

FERDINAND II, HOLY ROMAN EMPEROR (1578–1637). Ferdinand II was born in the Styrian capital of **Graz**, the son of **Ferdinand I**'s youngest son, Archduke Charles (1540–1590), and his wife, Marie of Bavaria (1551–1608). Charles had been given the so-called Inner Austrian lands, roughly corresponding to today's **Styria** and **Carinthia**, in the division of the Habsburg patrimony laid out in Ferdinand I's will. Ferdinand II would do much to establish primogeniture in his house, thereby considerably strengthening the hold of the head of the dynasty on its resources.

Raised in a sternly **Catholic** environment, Ferdinand became the territorial ruler of Inner Austria in 1596. Following a sojourn in Italy, he returned and made it clear that he intended to recatholicize his lands where Protestantism had made heavy inroads. His infirm and heirless uncles, the grandsons of Ferdinand I, agreed that he was the fittest prospect his house had at hand to govern the bulk of the **Habsburg Empire** and to succeed to the imperial throne in 1619. But Ferdinand II's reputation for religious orthodoxy did not sit well with many of his subjects, especially in Bohemia. The decision of the estates of that kingdom to reject him in favor of the German Elector Palatine Frederick V precipitated the **Thirty Years' War** in 1618. It eventually afflicted much of continental Europe.

Although Ferdinand did not succeed in reincorporating Germany into the Catholic fold, he did, through the Renewed Land Ordinances (1627) in Bohemia, succeed in limiting the power of the local estates to the point where Habsburg rule became truly hereditary in all those lands. He also moved forward the work of recatholicizing the kingdom, forcing non-Catholic nobility to abandon their properties, then installing an aristocracy loyal to its **Habsburg** king.

FIGL, LEOPOLD (1902–1965). Trained as an agricultural engineer, Figl was one of the moving forces in the refounding of the **Christian Social Party** (CP) as the **Austrian People's Party** (ÖVP) following **World War II**. A spokesman for Austrian farmers and agrarian interests in the interwar period, Figl was the executive officer of the Lower Austrian Peasants' Union between 1934 and 1938. Deeply opposed to German **Nazism** and the **Anschluss,** Figl spent the war in two concentration camps, Dachau between 1938 and 1943 and Mauthausen from 1944 to 1945. Serving in a variety of political offices as a representative of his party—from 1945 to 1953 he was the Austrian **chancellor** and from 1953 to 1959 the foreign minister—Figl worked to erase the ideological antagonisms that had poisoned relations between the CP and the **Social Democratic Workers' Party of Austria** between the two wars. His personal political agenda stressed goals that a majority of Austrians supported: economic recovery and the restoration of independence.

Figl signed the **Austrian State Treaty** for his country in 1955. His flexibility and willingness to accommodate the Socialists, however, were heavily criticized within his own party, leading to his resignation from the chancellorship in 1953 in favor of **Julius Raab.** *See also* POLITICAL PARTIES.

FILM. Several experiments with continuously flowing pictures took place in Vienna just before and after 1850. Perhaps most notable was the effort in 1846 of Lieutenant Field Marshall Franz von Uchatius to display moving images on a wall. It was, however, French technology that produced the first film shown in Vienna, in 1895. Cinemas quickly sprang up all over the city and the **Habsburg Empire** as a whole, particularly in urban areas. Vienna alone had 150, many of which stood in the **Prater** until the end of **World War II.** Some films even incorporated color effects.

Creative filmmaking flourished in Austria during **World War I** and roughly a decade and a half thereafter. The first Austrian film company, Sascha Films, was founded in 1916 by Alexander von Kolowrat-Kratkowsky (1886–1927), a nobleman who was equally adept in commerce and the visual arts. His company continued to work in the central European states spun off from the Habsburg monarchy after 1918. Nor was Vienna the sole center of the industry. Regional companies such as the Exl-Stage (*Exl-Bühne*) in Tyrol did significant work as well.

From the start, Austrian film benefited greatly from the availability of stage performers, who gave their time and their name-recognition value to the new medium. The great classical comic actors Alexander Girardi (1850–1918) and Hansi Niese (1875–1934), beloved by audiences at Vienna's Peoples' Theater (*Volkstheater*), were among the first, followed by many others. Austrian directors and performers were welcome throughout Europe, both in German-speaking regions and, somewhat later, the New World. Legendary film stars made their initial appearances in Vienna. Georg Wilhelm Pabst's (1885–1967) *The Joyless Little Street (Die freudlose Gasse*, 1925) gave Greta Garbo her first major role. Austrian and German cinema personnel crossed one another's borders to the great benefit of moving picture production in both countries. Filmmakers from areas once ruled by the Habsburg Empire came to Vienna as well. Among the most important was Mihály Kertész (1886–1962), who, as Michael Curtiz, would go on to a major career in Hollywood.

The Austrian silent films of the early 20th century were often serious melodramas. They examined social issues such as the exploitation of **women** and the miseries of urban laborers and rural families. The first Austrian film academy (*Lehrinstitut für Tonfilmkunst*) opened in Vienna in 1933. But the world financial crisis of the early 1930s and the advent of sound, which sharply raised film production costs, hit the Austrian industry very hard. Directors and producers looked to other parts of the world for work. Box-office returns became crucial, and the Austrian cinema concentrated on being entertaining rather than imaginatively challenging. The specifically "Viennese" film, which exploited the city's landscape, vocal and behavioral mannerisms, **music**, and sentimental historical clichés, prevailed, closely associated with one of Austrian film's most acclaimed performers and directors **Willi Forst**. Sumptuous costuming and heavy use of the music of **Johann Strauss** the Younger did their part, too.

Cinema in Austria following the **Anschluss** with **Germany** continued to rework these themes, encouraged by a **Nazi** regime that was initially eager to market films that depicted all branches of German-language culture, provided that they did not glorify the recently removed **Habsburg** dynasty. Only one film company, Vienna Film (*Wien Film*), operated in the country; major actors such as Forst, **Attila** and Paul **Hörbiger**, **Hans Moser**, and Paula Wessely (1907–2000) worked for it, laying themselves open after 1945 to accusations of furthering Nazi programs.

By 1943, however, the Nazi regime in Berlin had realized that these movies had enough of the specifically Austrian about them to make plain the differences between local culture and the standards of imperial Germany. Government demands for conformity to the norms of standard German became much more intense.

After the war, there was some hope that serious filmmaking could revive in Austria, particularly between 1946 and 1959. A step in this direction was *Councilman Geiger* (*Hofrat Geiger* (1947), with Moser and Paul Hörbiger trying to recapture the basic nature of Austrians and their society. But local settings and themes, absent Nazi propaganda, continued to prevail in Austrian cinemas after 1945, in part because government support of the cinema was very thin. "Homeland Films"(*Heimatfilme*) employed some of Austria's most notable directors, chief among them Franz Antel (1913–2007), who had begun his career with the Wien Film company. With light social comedy his specialty, he hired established actors from earlier cinema and stage, such as Moser and Paul Hörbiger, for such enormously popular ventures as *Hey There, Porter* (*Hallo Dienstmann*, 1952). He also capitalized on a latent nostalgia for the former empire, bringing the Habsburg monarchy back to the Austrian screen if not to national politics. Antel's films remained popular through the 1970s. Though critics scorned him for lack of seriousness, Antel continually identified himself with the popular cinema that had made his career. With the **Austrian Broadcasting System** entertaining virtually every corner of Austria by the 1970s, audiences no longer thronged to the latest *Heimatfilm* at neighborhood theaters. Austrian moviemaking dropped from world screens, as the federal government refused to underwrite serious cinema.

The socially radical **New Austrian Film** of the 1980s abruptly reversed this downturn. Morally and aesthetically grounded in the political and social upheavals of the 1960s, it often received financial help from public resources. Nevertheless, the mostly Austrian creative and technical personnel who worked on these productions developed their scenarios independently and with comparatively low budgets. Their work characteristically deals with specifically Austrian themes, but without any sentimentality. Directors focus on the squalid side of human character and behavior, but so unintrusively that audiences could well be watching highly disciplined documentaries. Contemporary settings and real people often take the place of studio scenery and professional performers. Michael Glawogger's (1959–) *Workingman's Death* (2005) exemplifies the genre. With plotlines that are clear antitheses to standard *Heimatfilm* narratives, several of these productions have been acclaimed by juries at cinema festivals and by audiences worldwide. An Austrian film, *The Counterfeiters* (*Die Fälscher*), a riveting exploration of the moral ambiguities of the Nazi concentration camp experience, won the American Academy award as the best foreign film of 2007. *See also* OPERETTA; THEATER.

FINK, JODOK (1853–1929). A farmer from the **Vorarlberg**, Fink was a member of the **Christian Social Party** and served from 1890 through 1920 in the provincial diet. In 1911, he also was the governor of the province. Fink was in the Imperial Assembly in **Vienna** after 1911; there he became close to Mayor **Karl Lueger**, also a parliamentary delegate. Their relationship stemmed from the union in 1907 of the Christian Social movement in Vienna with the German conservatives from the alpine provinces of the monarchy. From this time forward, rural voters would be among the most reliable supporters of the **Christian Social Party** (CP) in Austria.

During **World War I**, Fink headed the office responsible for allocation of food in the Austrian half of the **Habsburg Empire**. He was one of the three presidents of the provisional government that took the monarchy's place in 1918. There he played a crucial role in promoting cooperation between left and right in the turbulent days that followed the end of the war. He would also support a broadened franchise. In 1919, now vice-chancellor of the First Austrian Republic, Fink mediated between the government in Vienna and dissidents in the Vorarlberg, who wanted to break away from Austria altogether and attach the province to Switzerland. From 1920 until his death, Fink was a CP delegate in the National Assembly of the First Republic.

FISCHER, HEINZ (1938–) Growing up in **Graz** in a family of loyal followers of the **Socialist Party of Austria**, Fischer became **president** of the Second Austrian Republic in 2004. He was first elected to the Austrian National Assembly (*Nationalrat*) in 1971; from 1983 to

1987 he was minister of science in the government of Fred Sinowatz (1929–2008). He had also been a professor of political science at the University of **Innsbruck** since 1993.

Known for his even-tempered ways and a conciliatory approach in political negotiations, Fischer has often been compared to one of his predecessors, **Rudolf Kirchschläger**. He has, however, also been charged with lacking political courage, a trait that some found evident in his failure to criticize Chancellor **Bruno Kreisky**'s ill-advised vendetta against Simon Wiesenthal, the highly profiled **Nazi** hunter.

FISCHER VON ERLACH, JOHANN BERNHARD (1656–1723). Of all the master **architects** of the Austrian **Baroque**, Fischer von Erlach's work is the most closely associated with the ascent of Austrian **Habsburg** power during the late 17th and early 18th centuries.

Fischer was born in **Styria**. Von Erlach was the name of his mother's first husband, which her son appropriated for himself. His biological father's name was Fischer; he supervised his son's early efforts as a sculptor. Beginning in 1670, Fischer von Erlach spent many years in Italy, where he developed contacts with such masters as Gian Lorenzo Bernini (1598–1680) and studied the techniques and style of Francesco Borromini (1599–1667). He settled in **Vienna** around 1686, where he worked on one of the city's most famous monuments, the Plague Column (*Pestsäule*) in the First District. He also labored in other provinces of the **Habsburg Empire**, among them his native Styria and the Bohemian lands. Emperor Leopold I (1640–1705) engaged him as a court architect–engineer and as architectural tutor to his son, the future Emperor Joseph I (1678–1711). He returned to the position of inspector of imperial buildings under Joseph I in 1705 and was reconfirmed in the position by Joseph's brother and successor, Emperor Charles VI (1685–1740).

Although Joseph I made Fischer his inspector of imperial buildings in 1705, the architect had long been disappointed with the few and paltry commissions that came his way. Only after 1710 did he become a favorite among the rich and powerful of the Habsburg Empire.

A close student of the buildings and monuments of classical Rome—Fischer's scholarly *Plan of Civil and Historical Architecture*

(1721) included the first general treatment of the subject—his fluent manipulation of imperial themes from antiquity reinforced the public images of the imperial family and the nobility, who often were able to pay Fischer more than the Habsburgs themselves. To all of this he added French and more generally Baroque elements, thereby giving his work a far more eclectic character than that of his equally important contemporary, **Johann Lukas von Hildebrandt**. His exteiors could be boldly fanciful and monumental at the same time; the plans that he drew up in 1714 for the Church of St. Charles Borromeo consciously brought together classical, Near Eastern, and even orientalizing motifs. His best-realized achievements were his interiors, which bring longitudinal and latitudinal spaces into harmony. The design of the State Hall (*Prunksaal*) of the **Austrian National Library** is a conspicuous example. Other buildings Fischer planned in Vienna were the winter palace of **Eugene of Savoy**, the graceful Bohemian Chancellery building, and the Trautson Palace. He also did the initial designs for Schönbrunn Palace, the suburban residence and retreat of the imperial family. His plan, however, was revised heavily before the complex was erected in the 18th century. *See also* ART.

FOREIGN POLICY. If the **Habsburg** monarchy could be said to have had a business, it was war and diplomacy. The dynasty's armies and eventually naval forces expanded and defended its empire; ambassadors, consuls, and special envoys from **Vienna** worked with colleagues from other states to arrange peace and often to prolong it. Until Austria–Hungary fell apart in 1918, its emperor and king had formal and functional control over **military** affairs and foreign policy.

As part of the Habsburg enterprise, Austrians lived with the outcome of their rulers' international agendas abroad for over 600 years. By the last decades of the 15th century, the house of Austria with its enormous holdings was a major factor in the power struggles of continental Europe and would remain so. Until the second half of the 19th century, when some parliamentary oversight of government military expenditures went into effect, the sole check upon the monarch's military prerogatives was the unwillingness of local estates to fund their rulers' adventures. Failing support from these quarters, the Habsburgs, like their reigning counterparts, simply borrowed.

Enemies changed, sometimes into formal allies, depending on their usefulness to the cause of Habsburg self-preservation. The high point of this elaborate balancing act was probably the **Congress of Vienna** (1814–1815), as a result of which the **Habsburg Empire** was reassembled under the leadership of **Prince Klemens von Metternich** following the Napoleonic Wars. France (royal, republican, or Bonapartist); the Ottomans; Great Britain; **Russia**; Prussia, and then, after 1871, the unified **Germany**; the new kingdoms of **Italy**; and Serbia all were allies or enemies of the house of Habsburg from the 15th century to the end of **World War I**. A well-educated, trained foreign policy bureaucracy developed over the centuries in Vienna to handle the practical demands of this work. The roots of the Consular Academy set up in 1898 by Emperor **Franz Joseph** go back to the Oriental Academy, established in 1754 to train a select group of boys as translators and interpreters of Oriental languages for Habsburg emissaries to Constantinople.

The First and Second Austrian Republics inherited the Habsburg concern for self-preservation. The Ministry of the Imperial and Royal House and Foreign Affairs completely closed down only in 1920. Neither state, however, had the military infrastructure of the erstwhile monarchy. They were therefore in no position to continue the general militarization that characterized Habsburg foreign policy immediately before **World War I**, even though the First Republic drew heavily upon men from the old monarchic elite for diplomatic service. Furthermore, the federal **chancellor**, the highest executive official in the government, remained a key player in Austria's international affairs. From 1933 to 1938, foreign policy was run from a subdepartment of the chancellor's office.

Regardless of who administered it, the foreign policy of the First Republic was first and last a holding action. An ongoing focus was stabilizing Austria's **economy** and financial system, so disordered that government expenditures were put under the close supervision of a commissioner from the League of Nations right after the war. Two crucial and massive loans were arranged between the government in Vienna and the League in 1922 and 1932.

The other challenge was maintaining Austrian independence, a status heavily conditioned by the interests and ambitions of Germany to the north and Italy to the south. The **Treaty of St. Germain** proscribed **Anschluss** with Germany, so that as long as the Weimar Republic respected that condition, Austria was protected from German takeover. Once Adolf Hitler violated the provision in 1938 and incorporated Austria into the Third Reich, Austria lost all control over its foreign policy. The Italian fascist dictator Benito Mussolini had for a time cultivated the Austrian state with military and economic assistance that would foster a buffer state between himself and Germany. By 1936, however, he had chosen to make common cause with Hitler and left Austria to fend for itself.

The most pressing task in foreign affairs for the Second Austrian Republic was dealing with the Allied occupation that followed upon military defeat in 1945. The greatest fear of various governments in Vienna between 1945 and the signing of the **Austrian State Treaty** in 1955 that restored independence to Austria was that the occupying powers would follow the German model and divide the country.

With **neutrality** a condition of the State Treaty, Austrian foreign policy after 1955 focused on presenting the country as a bridge between Eastern and Western Europe in the era of the **Cold War**. The flood of asylum seekers into Austria following the Hungarian uprising of 1956 severely strained the fundamentals of that assumption in the eyes of both the Soviet Union and its satellite government in Budapest. When the military and political barriers between both regions fell in 1989, Austria decided to continue in this role, but its efforts to date have been largely commercial. Membership in the **European Union** since 1995 has considerably weakened Austria's claims to neutrality as well.

Austrian foreign policy today is subject to far more democratic scrutiny than at any time in its history. The change, however, has come quite slowly. A separate Ministry of Foreign Affairs was finally established in 1959 and still faces more than normal intrusions from the office of the chancellor, though not on the level that made **Bruno Kreisky** unique. Since 1990, significant aspects of Austrian international relations, such as its neutrality during the Gulf War (1991), the settlement of the **South Tyrol** question (1992), and prospective membership in the European Union (EU) (1994–1995), have been vigorously debated in the national parliament.

EU membership has brought with it foreign policy challenges of its own. Having struggled to revive its sovereignty after 1945, Austria is once again subject to constraints from abroad. Intense negotiations were needed to persuade the EU to lift the sanctions it imposed on Austria in June 2000 in response to the **Austrian People's Party** forming a coalition government with the **Freedom Party of Austria** of radical nationalist **Jörg Haider**. The open borders policy of the EU has forced Austria into talks with member states over rationalizing the impact of large immigrant flows from eastern Europe and Turkey. Negotiations on this question began in 2000, but have made little progress because of Freedom Party resistance. *See also* GERMANY, RELATIONS WITH; IMMIGRATION; ITALY, RELATIONS WITH; RUSSIA, RELATIONS WITH; UNITED STATES OF AMERICA, RELATIONS WITH.

FORST, WILLI (WILHELM) (1903–1980). Boyishly handsome, with a small but intimate voice, Forst was born in **Vienna** and died there. A theatrical virtuoso, he was acclaimed as an actor and a director who could also sing and incorporate **music** into **film** very skillfully. *Maskerade* (*Masquerade in Vienna*, 1934), which he directed, has been called the finest Austrian film ever made. It also made the actress Paula Wessely (1907–2000) a serious movie star, much admired by German Nazi Minister of Propaganda Joseph Goebbels (1897–1945), among others.

Forst's high standing in the Vienna films of the National Socialist era laid him open to charges of collaborating with the regime's agenda. Nevertheless, his distinctively Viennese accent, mastery of ironic repartee, and urbane acceptance of the moral ambiguity that runs through his films was read by many, Forst included, as a put-down of **Nazi** social clumsiness. He could perform in quite standard German if he chose to. Forst's refusal to film *Jud Süß*, a relentlessly anti-Semitic Nazi propaganda tract, incurred the open displeasure of the regime. His life, however, was never in danger, and his movies drew enthusiastic audiences during the war years. Typical of his work were *Operette* (1940), *Viennese Blood* (*Wiener Blut*, 1942), and *Viennese Girls* (*Wiener Mädeln*, 1945–1949), the first Viennese feature film in color.

Forst hoped to revive the independent Austrian film after 1945. Though one of his productions, done in Germany, *Die Sünderin* (*The Sinner*, 1951), provoked enough displeasure from Austria's Roman

Catholic hierarchy to become a *succès de scandale*, Forst failed to regain his earlier artistic luster. The last film that he made in his homeland came out in 1957. *See also* THEATER.

FRANZ FERDINAND OF AUSTRIA-ESTE, ARCHDUKE (1863– 1914). After the death of his cousin, Archduke Rudolph (1858–1889), Franz Ferdinand was generally accepted to be the heir apparent of his uncle, **Franz Joseph**, though his position was not officially confirmed. He and his uncle were never comfortable with one another— the archduke was willful, opinionated, and morose, and quite critical of the aging emperor's management of the **Habsburg Empire**. Their relationship was also complicated by Franz Ferdinand's misalliance with Countess Sophie Chotek in 1900. Though noble, the lineage of the Choteks was not distinguished enough to qualify them for marriage into the ruling house; Franz Joseph permitted the wedding to take place only after his nephew accepted morganatic status for his wife-to-be and their future offspring.

Regardless of the tension between them, Franz Joseph left important responsibilities to his heir apparent. By the end of the 19th century, Franz Ferdinand was representing his uncle in all **military** affairs; he was especially influential in the development of the Habsburg navy and promoted the use of air power in combat. However, he worked to avoid engaging Habsburg forces in major conflict. He was particularly concerned not to provoke Russia and unsuccessfully opposed the Austrian annexation of Bosnia in 1908 on this ground. He was more persuasive in arguing against Austria–Hungary's participation in the Balkan Wars of 1912 and 1913.

Franz Ferdinand was no pacifist, but he believed that the empire was domestically too fractured to survive such a test. To soothe national resentments over the privileged position accorded the Hungarians in the 1867 **Ausgleich**, he and his advisors gave serious consideration to a scheme called Trialism that would have given the South Slavic peoples of the empire a similar status to the Germans and the Hungarians. These views won him few friends, especially among Hungarian politicians, but even among the South Slavs. The recently independent kingdom of Serbia vigorously promoted pan-Serbian nationalism in the Balkans, and opposed any plan that would keep their ethnic cohorts throughout the region from their reach. They also worried that Franz Ferdinand's efforts to improve the Habsburg military infrastructure presaged some future attack from Vienna.

Named inspector general of the army in 1913, the archduke was responsible for all its maneuvers and reported directly to his uncle, the emperor. It was in this capacity that he went to Sarajevo in 1914 where, on 28 June, he and his wife were assassinated by a student, Gavrilo Princip, a nationalist Bosnian Serb. *See also* HABSBURG, HOUSE OF.

FRANZ JOSEPH, EMPEROR OF AUSTRIA, KING OF HUNGARY (1830–1916). A grandson of Emperor Francis I (1768–1835), Franz Joseph grew up in a sober and serious household that placed a high priority on piety, duty, and industriousness. These values took even deeper root in the character of the young prince under the formal spiritual tutelage of Joseph Othmar von Rauscher, later to become the cardinal-archbishop of **Vienna**. Although Franz Joseph had, and continues to have, many critics, few if any have ever questioned his devout **Catholicism** or his commitment to his responsibilities as he saw them.

A succession crisis set off by the **Revolutions of 1848** brought Franz Joseph to power. With the mentally unstable Emperor Ferdinand I (1793–1875) on the throne of the post Napoleonic Austrian Empire, key members of the house of **Habsburg** concluded that the survival of their empire required that he abdicate in favor of someone of sound mind and psyche. After considerable discussion and dispute, in which Franz Joseph's mother, Archduchess Sophia (1805–1872), played a prominent and crucial role, the house called upon the 18-year-old prince to replace his good-natured but erratic uncle. The young man began his lengthy reign on 2 December 1848.

The first few years of Franz Joseph's rule were spent in restoring the domestic position of a monarchy badly shaken by the liberal and national challenges of 1848. Convinced of the divine origins of his mission, and even further encouraged in his views by Prince Felix von Schwarzenberg (1800–1852), his first minister-president, Franz Joseph presided over a brief period of major social and economic change. Beneficial though these developments were, they took place in an environment of heavy censorship and political repression.

The beginning of the Italian struggle for national unification in 1859, in which Franz Joseph personally commanded Habsburg troops for a time, ended this interlude. From that point on, until his death during **World War I**, the emperor's state was challenged again and again by two potent ideological opponents of traditional dynastic rule. One was nationalism, the other, political and economic liberalism. Endowed like most of the Habsburgs with a solid sense of the possible, Franz Joseph allowed several constitutional programs to go forward that he and his advisors hoped would quiet these demands. So long as he retained final power over foreign policy and control of his military, he was not averse to compromise.

The most lasting of these experiments was the **Ausgleich** of 1867. This agreement between what became the Austrian and Hungarian halves of his territories left him, as monarch, the central figure of the personal union that embodied the idea of the **Habsburg Empire** as one. Franz Joseph was also left in control of both the army and foreign policy of the reconfigured polity. But the relentless emergence of national states in central and east central Europe—**Germany** after the **Seven Weeks' War** of 1866 and Serbia, whose long-sought independence from the Ottoman Empire won international recognition in 1878—made the continued existence of his polyglot domain ever more doubtful. Franz Joseph himself was especially troubled by the appearance of a kingdom of Serbia, which could, and eventually did, offer the South Slavic peoples of the Habsburg lands a political alternative to government from alien **Vienna** and Budapest.

As he grew older, Franz Joseph became, if anything, more aloof and austere than he had been as a young man. He did, however, come to enjoy both the respect and even personal affection of his peoples. The travails of his private life humanized him for many. Deeply in love with his striking cousin, Elisabeth of Bavaria (1837–1898), he had married her in 1854. The match rapidly soured, at least for her; in his later years, the emperor, with his wife's approval, turned for companionship to Katharina Schratt (1855–1940), a Viennese actress.

Nevertheless, Elisabeth's death in 1898 at the hands of an anarchist shocked Franz Joseph deeply, as had the suicide of his son and heir, Archduke Rudolf (b. 1858), in 1889, and the execution in Mexico of his brother, Archduke Maximilian (b. 1832), in 1867. But publicly he retained the tight self-control for which he had become legendary. Even when he collapsed at the funeral of Archduke Rudolph, the emperor was back at his desk by the afternoon. Indifferent to most of the technological conveniences that the 19th century made available, he was, into his last years, a commanding presence erect on horseback. *See also* CONGRESS OF VIENNA; FOREIGN POLICY; HABSBURG, HOUSE OF; MAYERLING.

FREDERICK III, EMPEROR, ARCHDUKE OF AUSTRIA (1415–1493). Best known for his doodled acronym A.E.I.O.U (Lat.: *Austriae est imperare orbi universo*; Germ.: *Alles Erdreich ist Österreich Untertan*); Eng: *All the World Is Subject to Austria)* Frederick did not live up to these later readings of his jottings. Indeed, one finds the motto very seldom in **Habsburg** representational settings. A notable exception is the principal domed ceiling of the Stately Hall (*Prunksaal*) in the **Austrian National Library**.

Born when the Habsburg Austrian patrimony was still divided three ways, Frederick himself came into possession of the bulk of these lands after years of war with his brother, Archduke Albrecht VI (b. 1418), who finally died in 1463. A cousin continued to hold the **Tyrol**. The size of Frederick's Austrian holdings, did not, however, increase his influence. The long conflict between the two men had drained their lands of money and other resources, and Frederick would remain forever vulnerable both to noble opposition within his own territories and foreign invaders. Hungary under its ambitious King Matthias Corvinus (1458–1490) was especially problematic.

Effectively German king after 1442, Frederick was crowned emperor in Rome in 1452, the last ruler to receive the dignity in that city itself. The position gave him a certain amount of bargaining power with other European rulers; he used it with the last duke of Burgundy, Charles the Bold, to arrange a marriage between Charles's daughter, Duchess Mary (1457–1482), and his son, the future **Emperor Maximilian I**. The union, which took place in 1477, laid part of the groundwork for the Spanish–Austrian **Habsburg Empire** of the 16th and 17th centuries *See also* HABSBURG, HOUSE OF.

FREEDOM PARTY OF AUSTRIA/FREIHEITLICHE PARTEI ÖSTERREICHS (FPÖ). Organized in 1949 as the League of Independents, the movement drew together disparate constituencies that did not fit conveniently into either the **Austrian People's Party** (ÖVP) or the **Socialist Party of Austria** (SPÖ). These included German national elements still left from **World War II**, monarchists, classical liberals, former Nazis, and anticlerical conservatives. The movement regrouped under the name the Freedom Party in 1956. Anton Reinthaller (1895–1958), its first leader, was an erstwhile **Nazi Party** member who had been minister of agriculture in the first Austrian government following the **Anschluss** in 1938. From 1958 to 1978, the FPÖ was headed by Friedrich Peter (1921–2005), once an officer in the Schutzstaffel (SS). Its program stressed the German character of the new Austrian state, traditional social values, and the rights of private property. Though fusion with Germany was out of the question, the party agenda was very supportive of a European union that would promote close relationships between the two countries.

Somewhat marginalized in Austrian politics by its leadership and its ideology, the FPÖ functioned as a voice of opposition in the Austrian parliament until 1983. In that year, led by Norbert Steger (1944–), it entered a coalition with a minority SPÖ government headed by Fred Sinowatz (1929–), the successor of **Bruno Kreisky**. Their cooperation, however, was short-lived. In September 1986 **Jörg Haider**, the leader of the movement in **Carinthia**, replaced Steger. The former's free market philosophy and strident criticism of Austrian immigration policy was unacceptable to a new SPÖ **chancellor**, **Franz Vranitzky**, and the coalition dissolved. Elections in November raised the size of the Freedom Party delegation in the parliament from 12 to 18. From 2000 to 2006, the party was in formal coalition with the government of Chancellor **Wolfgang Schüssel** of the ÖVP. A split within the party over Haider's negative views on Austrian membership in the **European Union** and **immigration** policy led some FPÖ members to form the **Liberal Forum** in 1993. Haider and his party nevertheless remained a problematic presence in Austrian politics. Basically a contrarian, he indicated in 1998 that he would be willing to continue his political activities apart from the FPÖ, and he did so until his death in 2008. The FPÖ, however, under the leadership of **Heinz-Christian Strache**, has seen a major resurgence of its fortunes. In the national election of 2008, it took close to 20 percent of the vote. *See also* POLITICAL PARTIES.

FREEMASONS. Founded in England in the early years of the 17th century, the Order of Freemasons promoted ideals of the brotherhood of men irrespective of economic and political station (**women** were not admitted to lodges), social welfare, religious toleration, and the primacy of human reason. Members were enjoined, however, to observe the legal norms of the lands in which they lived. The first Masonic Lodge in Vienna was "At the Three Cannons," founded in 1742. Emperor Francis I (1708–1765), the husband of Empress **Maria Theresa**, was among the first members.

Some of the most important progressives of the Austrian Enlightenment were Freemasons. Ignaz von Born (1742–1791), a Bohemian nobleman, who was a published mineralogist and geologist, was the guiding force of the lodge "True Harmony," where he, and others like him, promoted scientific and technical education. Among the most active supporters of these efforts was Josef von Sonnenfels (1733–1813), at times often a close advisor to Emperor **Joseph II**. Leopold Mozart (1719–1787), the father of the great composer, was also associated with "True Harmony."

Though **Wolfgang Amadeus Mozart** himself belonged to another lodge, "Benevolence," he apparently admired Born enough to use him as the model for the noble humanitarian Sarastro in his *The Magic Flute* (1791). A strain from Mozart's masonic music is the basis of the melody of today's Austrian national anthem.

The influence of the Freemasons waned in the **Habsburg** lands during the French Revolution and the conservative reaction that followed. The **Catholic** church especially frowned heavily on programmatic **religious** toleration. Freemasonry was banned, only to be relegalized after the liberal-inspired **Revolutions of 1848**.

After the **Ausgleich** of 1867, Freemasons in the Austrian lands vigorously supported policies that advanced the general welfare, such as classes in household management and more extensive public **education**, construction of student residences, appropriate custodial conditions for prison inmates, Boy Scouting, and the like. Leading political figures in the social politics of the First Austrian Republic, such as **Julius Tandler**, were Freemasons. Masons played an important role in the crisis-ridden years of the First Republic, getting needy children to Holland after the war where they could be fed and housed safely and arranging for endangered youngsters to flee to England after the **Anschluss** of 1938. Banned once again by the **Nazi** regime in Austria, Freemasons also participated actively in the Austrian resistance movements between 1938 and 1945. In July 1945, they regained legal status once again, marking the event with the opening of a new lodge, "Humanity Reborn."

FREUD, SIGMUND (1856–1939). The son of a wool merchant who had migrated from Galicia to Habsburg Bohemia to Leipzig to **Vienna**, Freud showed great intellectual promise even as a young boy. For the last six years of his secondary **education** at the Sperlgymnasium, he ranked first.

Freud's initial medical training was as a physician and clinical neurologist. He worked in the laboratories of some of the **University of Vienna**'s most prominent experimental physiologists, among them Ernst Wilhelm Brücke (1819–1892), who was especially interested in developmental embryology and the forces that drove it, and Theodore Meynert (1833–1892), a noted experimentalist in the physical anatomy of the brain. Much research led Meynert to conclude that human beings had a primary ego, which arose through an infant's awareness of the disconnect between its body and its environment. This process took place in the lower cortex. A secondary ego, the result of socialization, controlled these perceptions. It was housed in the upper cortex. In 1885–1886, Freud was in France with the neurologist and psychiatrist Jean Charcot. Here the young physician first made the link between psychic disorder, in this case hysteria, and physical symptomology.

Back in Vienna, Freud befriended the physician **Josef Breuer**, from whom he learned the techniques of arousing the repressed experiences of patients, who recalled them while under hypnosis. *Studies on Hysteria* (1895) was the work of both men. Freud would abandon hypnosis in his practice rather quickly, but he pursued the study of the role that subconscious data and recollection played in human psychology. *The Analysis of Dreams* (1900) was an extended summary of both his findings and his theories and laid the foundations for modern psychoanalysis. A lecture tour to the United States in 1909, where Freud appeared at Clark University in Massachusetts, marked the beginning of his international reputation.

Although Freud himself was the guiding spirit of the Vienna Psychoanalytic Society and hoped to see his ideas propagated through its auspices, his findings were not well received in the Austrian capital. Notions such as infant sexual experience troubled the moral convictions of many. The essentially psychic rather than physical nature of his "cures" led his empirically oriented colleagues in Vienna to question his work closely and skeptically. Freud's theories and clinical methods found a far greater welcome in Berlin and New York after **World War I**. Nor did his ventures into social psychology, such as *Civilization and Its Discontents* (1929), persuade all readers. His practice in Vienna remained lucrative, however, until he was forced to flee the city in 1938 after the **Anschluss**. He died in London. *See also* VIENNA SCHOOL OF MEDICINE.

FRISCHMUTH, BARBARA (1941–). Known for her novels, translations, radio plays, and even children's literature, Frischmuth is well within the tradition of highly versatile Austrian writers. Unlike many contemporary Austrian novelists in the second half of the 20th century, she has never altogether positioned herself as an outsider in Austrian society and its history. A student of Eastern cultures, particularly their mystic and literary features, she has devoted much attention to the problems of cultural diversity in Austria, particularly as it applies to Turks. *Kai und die Liebe zu den Modellen* (*Kai and the Love of Models*, 1979) shows the problems of approaching the alien "Other" through the fictionalized eyes of a Turkish worker. Frischmuth's 1998 novel *Das Verschwinden des Schattens in der Sonne (The Shadow Disappears in the Sun)* deals with the efforts of an Austrian to approach the Islamic-Turkish "Other" and the somewhat compromised, though not wholly negative, results. *See also* LITERATURE.

– G –

GERMAN CONFEDERATION. Part of the settlement of the **Congress of Vienna**, the Confederation was a loose organization of 39 sovereign German territories (including four free cities) that had once been part of the **Holy Roman Empire**. The **Habsburg Empire**, or, from 1806 to 1867, Austrian Empire, together with the kingdom of Prussia, were the leading states in the organization. Austria was to hold its presidency in perpetuity. One of the Confederation's central charges was to secure the territorial integrity of all participants, a distinct advantage for weaker principalities. States sent delegates to a diet, which met in Frankfurt. The Confederation could also receive and send ambassadors, declare war, and make treaties.

German nationalists gathered at the so-called Frankfurt Parliament during the **Revolutions of 1848** suspended the organization briefly. With the collapse of their demands for a **Germany** unified under the leadership of the king of Prussia, the Confederation was restored and continued to function for another 17 years. During the **Seven Weeks' War** between Austria and Prussia in 1866, significant members of the Confederation—Saxony, Bavaria, Hanover, and Württemberg—supported the monarchy of **Franz Joseph**. Prussian victory in July 1866 and the Treaty of Prague, which closed the war, brought about the dissolution of the Confederation. The disappearance of the body ended whatever formal influence the **Habsburgs** still held over the German lands north of their multiethnic empire. *See also* METTERNICH, KLEMENS WENZEL NEPOMUK LOTHAR, PRINCE OF.

GERMANY, RELATIONS WITH. It is not until its unification in 1871–1872 that Germany became a "foreign" state to the **Habsburg** rulers of Austria. The dynasty supplied the kings and emperors of "Germany" from the middle of the 15th century until 1806. Even though individual German principalities were free to establish their own **foreign policies** after the end of the **Thirty Years' War**, there were restrictions on participating in wars against their emperor.

Habsburg interest in Germany remained strong. By the second half of the 17th century, Habsburg emperors had to keep a close watch on territorial princes, who had ambitions of their own and sometimes looked abroad for help in realizing them. The dynasty's preeminence in the area depended more and more on **military** strength and advantageous alliances, both with foreign powers and with rulers of some German states. In a sharp reversal of traditional antagonisms, the Habsburgs turned to the king of France for an alliance in 1756 to curb the aggressive Frederick II of Prussia. Austro–Prussian relations henceforth were not always hostile. The two states cooperated after 1805 in rolling back the conquests of Napoleon Bonaparte. Habsburgs still presided over the **German Confederation**. Prussia, however, took up the mission of unifying Germany, particularly after its king, William I (1797–1888), made Otto von Bismarck his prime minister in 1862. In 1866, Prussia lured Emperor **Franz Joseph** into the **Seven Weeks' War**, which ended with the creation of a Second German Empire that excluded the Habsburg lands.

With these hostilities behind them, however, the new German state and the Habsburg monarchy quickly discovered that they needed one another. The **Dual Alliance** of 1879 committed them to mutual defense. They were not at the outset worried about the same enemy; **Russia** was Austria's major problem, particularly in the Balkans, whereas Bismarck's great fear was the French revanchism that followed upon the Franco–Prussian War (1870–1871). Heavily dependent on German military support on the eastern front in **World War I**, Austria–Hungary remained tightly committed to the Dual Alliance almost to the end.

Relations between Weimar Germany and the freshly created Austrian republic were not completely under the control of either country. The **Treaty of St. Germain** prohibited **Anschluss** with Germany, a step widely supported in Austria after 1918. German capital was shoring up Austrian **banks** long before 1938; Germans accounted largely for the profits of the Austrian **tourism** industry as well.

Enthusiasm for incorporation into Germany cooled somewhat in Austria after Adolf Hitler became German chancellor in 1933. Governments in the First Republic turned to the League of Nations and other countries for support of Austrian independence. In 1933, Chancellor **Engelbert Dollfuss**, Great Britain, France, and **Italy** declared that Nazi subversion in Austria violated Article 80 of the Treaty of Versailles with Germany and Article 11 of the League's charter. They repeated their statement the following year. As **chancellor**, **Kurt Schuschnigg** continued trying to arrange some kind of collective security pact with Great Britain, France, and Italy from 1934 to 1936, even as he tried to persuade Hitler's regime that Austria was not anti-German. Failing miserably, he turned to working out some modus vivendi with Nazi Germany that would not threaten Austrian sovereignty. The two countries did come to an agreement in 1936 that recognized Austria's independence on the condition that

Vienna grant amnesty to 17, 000 illegal National Socialists then in the country. Austria was allowed to treat its **Nazis** as it saw fit, but Schuschnigg agreed to bring a number of people into his government who were "nationally inclined." The compact also left room for some form of German intervention.

With the end of **World War II** in 1945, Austria set itself to negotiating the most favorable treatment possible from the countries that sponsored the **occupation**. Russia, Great Britain, the United States, and France were inclined to treat the country as just another part of the German question. Perhaps the most serious, if misleading, achievement of Austria's spokesmen was to convince the Allies by 1948 that their country was a victim of Nazi aggression. But almost up to the signing of the **Austrian State Treaty** of 1955, Austrian politicians feared that the Allies would divide their land as they had Germany.

The State Treaty did formally make Austria a sovereign state, but it was the **neutrality** provision of the document that sealed Austria's independence in West Germany's political thinking. For the Austrians, neutral status gave them a unique standing in a Europe divided by an Iron Curtain. West German Chancellor Konrad Adenauer, who was eager to bring the Federal German Republic into the North Atlantic Treaty Organization (NATO), called neutrality "immoral."

Normalization of **trade** relations between the two lands was underway by 1948, and Austria was soon well tied into the West German **economy**. In 1984, German-owned industries in Austria employed over 100,000 Austrians, a figure that approached the number of Austrians who held jobs in **nationalized** Austrian enterprises. But Austria's first **governments** remained bent on differentiating their countrymen from the **Anschluss** regime and Germans as a national group, sometimes quite ruthlessly. Compensation for Austrian expropriation and expulsion of resident German citizens after 1945 was not fully settled upon by Vienna and the German Federal Republic until 1958. As sovereign countries, Germany and Austria resumed full ambassadorial relations in 1955.

Formal relations were thereafter formally correct between Austria and the West German state, though a certain amount of cultural tension existed between them as well. Many in the German Federal Republic complained, not altogether wrongly, that Austrians were never forced, as were the Germans, to acknowledge and study their instrumental role in the Holocaust. In the opinion of Germans, where foreign governments and the public media quickly took note of the slightest incident of anti-Semitism in Germany, the same behavior in Austria escaped notice. Austrian provincialism encouraged a kind of xenophobia and right-wing rhetoric that Germans had learned to deplore. For their part, Austrians from all levels of society were painfully aware that Germany had arisen from the ashes of World War II to outstrip its southern neighbor both in industrial might and living standards. Any signs of German self-congratulatory arrogance were relentlessly parodied and criticized in the Austrian press and among the citizenry at large. Well into the 1980s, the **currency** relations between the German mark and the Austrian schilling favored the former. Germans, among them Helmut Kohl, the West German federal chancellor who presided over the reunification of his country, bought vacation real estate in Austria in great quantities. To some Austrians, it was a sign that their whole country was up for sale. Though former chancellor **Bruno Kreisky** welcomed the fall of the Berlin Wall in 1989, his successor, **Franz Vranitzky**, was by no means as supportive, in part because he resented the sovereign manner in which Kohl conducted his summer household in the Austrian Salzkammergut. A staple of summer journalism in Austria is always a story or two about how German as spoken in the Federal Republic to the north is destroying distinctively Austrian **language** usages.

Nevertheless, Austria actively cooperated in the unification of Germany by assisting East German citizens to get across Hungarian and Czech borders in 1989. Vranitzky's foreign minister, **Alois Mock**, was especially eloquent in his call for German reunification, telling British Prime Minister Margaret Thatcher, who had deep reservations about an enlarged Germany, that she should be grateful that such an event took place so peacefully. Helmut Kohl vigorously supported Austrian membership in the **European Union** (EU).

Partners in the EU after 1995, Germans and Austrians have had contentious moments. German Chancellor Gerhard Schröder and his foreign minister, Joschka Fischer, spearheaded a movement to impose sanctions on Austria's coalition government in 2000 that included **Jörg Haider**'s **Freedom Party of Austria**. But this contretemps subsided quickly. In 2004, Austria joined with Germany and the Czech Republic in a common effort to combat terrorism. In 2007 and 2008, as gasoline prices drove many Germans into once again taking their holidays in the land of their near neighbor, Austrian hoteliers and restaurant personnel welcomed their return as tourists. The two countries, ambiguous feelings and all, remain firmly linked to one another, culturally, economically, and politically. German and Austrian performing artists, theatrical directors, filmmakers, and musicians go back and forth across one another's borders continually. Germany remains for Austria its chief international **trading** partner, both for imports and exports. Germany was buying a little over 30 percent of Austria's exports in 2003; about 40 percent of Austria's imports were coming from the Federal Republic. In 2007, these figures were virtually the same. *See also* FOREIGN POLICY.

GLÖCKEL, OTTO (1874–1935). An educational reformer and teacher, Glöckel was a key member of the Freie Schule (Free School) movement founded in 1905. Among its demands were the total removal of clerical influence in public **education**, free instructional materials such as books to all pupils, and increased schooling opportunities for the educationally disadvantaged.

Serving as undersecretary for education in the brief **Social Democratic Workers' Party** regime that governed the First Austrian Republic in 1919–1920, Glöckel put many of these reforms into practice. Falling back on a decree that had been first issued under the Dual Monarchy in 1869, he ended requirements that all students participate during school hours in such **religious** rituals as the **Catholic** mass and processions.

In federal office for so short a time, Glöckel could not realize proposals for such far-reaching changes as compulsory education for all children between the ages of 6 and 14. The termination of compulsory religious observances was among the measures that endured, though religious instruction did remain obligatory. He was somewhat more successful in implementing his agenda in **Vienna**, where he chaired the municipal council for education from 1922 to 1934. In 1923, he was a major sponsor of the Vienna Pedagogical Academy. The Austrian **Christian Social Party** bitterly opposed his policies, particularly those that curbed the Catholic influence in public education.

GORBACH, ALFONS (1898–1972). A jurist and **Austrian People's Party** (ÖVP) politician after 1945, Gorbach's early career unfolded in **Styria**, where he was the provincial leader of the **Fatherland Front**. He spent the years 1938–1942 and 1944–1945 in **Nazi** concentration camps.

As party leader from 1960 to 1963 and **chancellor** from 1961 to1964, Gorbach found it possible to cooperate closely with many politicians of his own generation. These included members of the **Socialist Party of Austria**, who had shared his experiences with the Nazis. Gorbach's conciliatory approach also extended in a general way to Austria's ex-Nazis, particularly when, in his view, the exploration of his country's National Socialist years might give **Communists** and Marxists ideological ammunition. His methods fell out of favor with a younger cohort of men within his own party, led by Josef Klaus (1910–2001), who were eager to substitute a free market economy for the corporative policies that had come increasingly into favor in the ÖVP since 1945. Klaus replaced Gorbach as party leader in 1963 and as chancellor the following year.

GOVERNMENT. The Second Austrian Republic is governed as a federally organized democratic republic that observes a separation of powers among legislative, executive, and juridical institutions. Both citizens and members of their government are answerable to law that is developed according to procedures outlined in its **constitution**.

Though this political and administrative structure marked a dramatic break with the **Nazi** regime in place between 1938 and 1945, it was not altogether new to the Austrian experience. Indeed, successive Austrian constitutions had been drawing upon their predecessors for almost a century. The general principles of the post-1945 system were adapted from the constitution of the First Austrian Republic, issued in 1920. This, in turn, drew some fundamental features from the constitution granted in 1867 to the Austrian, or Cis-Leithenian, half of the **Dual Monarchy**. That document, in turn, had its roots in an earlier arrangement introduced in **Franz Joseph**'s February *Patent* of 1861.

Following its suppression of the liberal **Revolutions of 1848**, the **Habsburg** government returned to some practices taken from a more absolutistic past. However, challenged by breakaway nationalism and middle-class dissatisfaction with his military expenditures, the emperor adjusted to more conciliatory tactics. His *Patent* turned the **Habsburg Empire** into a constitutional, though hardly democratic, state. The document called for a two-house parliament in which the lower branch could vote on military and budgets. Its representatives were chosen by provincial diets throughout the monarch's lands that were organized in four interest groups or *Curia*. To qualify for membership in these assemblies, one had to pay a certain amount in direct taxes. The propertyless and the impoverished generally had no franchise. An upper house, the House of Notables (*Herrenhaus*), chosen by the emperor, was even less representative.

The constitution granted on 21 December 1867 retained the two-house structure, with the lower branch exercising some fiscal controls over the government and its **military**. The emperor held the power to declare war, command the army, make peace, and conduct **foreign policy**. Laws were promulgated in the name of the emperor, though an independent **judiciary** soon developed. The monarch governed through ministers, who served at his pleasure. Nevertheless, the latter were also responsible to the lower house of the parliament. But the most significant innovation in the arrangement was its explicit guarantee of basic civil liberties: personal property, equality before the law, privacy, freedom of **religion** and speech, and the right of assembly among them. Though not always respected by Franz Joseph's governments, these concessions remained formally intact in the Austrian half of the monarchy until emergency rule became the norm in **World War I**. Voting privileges expanded progressively as well. The emperor granted universal manhood suffrage in 1907, effectively abolishing voting by economic class.

The two-house parliament carried over into the First Austrian Republic after 1918. The fragmentary and semiprovisional Constitution of 1920 designated the lower branch, the National Council (*Nationalrat*), as the highest governing body in the state. With the franchise now extended to **women**, directly elected representatives named ministers and chose the national **president**, who was formally the head of state but practically a ceremonial figurehead. The second house, the Federal Council (*Bundesrat*), spoke for the provinces that selected its members. It could veto legislation, but the National Council could reintroduce it. The 1920 Constitution also prescribed the republic's federal organization. It retained the list of civil rights that were recognized by the former emperor in 1867.

Economic and political pressures led to important changes in the structure of government in the First Republic by 1925. Centralism was stressed at the expense of federalism. Austria's provinces had often acted quite autonomously in the chaos that followed World War I; new constraints were now placed on them. Provincial governorships were folded into a state supervisory office, and national administrators could question provincial expenditures, taxes, and financial policies generally.

Even greater centralization came in 1929. The federal government took on a larger role in provincial security affairs. The powers of the National Council were also significantly limited, and the role of the president redefined. Now directly elected, he or she could call and adjourn the National Council and proclaim states of emergency. The president commanded the army and named the president of the Constitutional Court.

In 1934, the authoritarian regime of **Engelbert Dollfuss** introduced a series of allegedly emergency measures passed by a cooperative rump of the National Council. The Constitutional Court was shut down and popular sovereignty set aside. Austria was no longer a republic but rather the Austrian Federation (*Bundesstaat Österreich*) made up of **Vienna** and eight provinces under the direct control of the state government. "Leadership" was in the hands of the federal **chancellor**. Laws were drawn up by four "Organs": the Council of State, the Economic Council, the Council of Provinces, and the Cultural Council of the Provinces. A federal assembly (*Bundestag*) of 49 members chosen from the four Organs, which prepared legislation, voted on the proposals. The president named provincial governments.

The government of the Second Austrian Republic is far more participatory both in tone and structure. Youth is no barrier to political activity. The minimum age for voting is 16. Candidates must be 18 to run for elective office, with the exception of the **presidency**, for which one must be 35. Legislatively and administratively, Austria in the 21st century is far more regionalized than was the case from the 18th century on. Although nationwide lawmaking is primarily left to the lower house or federal assembly (*Nationalrat*), referenda and popular initiatives are permitted and used. Another form of formal public advisory input, especially on fiscal and **welfare** issues, is various **chambers** that are grouped according to economic interests.

Austria's nine provinces have their own parliaments with substantive powers. Seated, like the Nationalrat, according to proportional representation, they choose their respective provincial governors, who have both federal and local duties. Provincial legislatures can set some tax rates as well as salary and pension scales for territorial civil servants. If the federal government believes that a measure passed at the provincial level threatens the national interest, it can veto the bill. Nevertheless, the provincial parliament can override the move. The Austrian provinces also send spokespersons to their national delegation at the **European Union** in Brussels.

Yet other subdivisions of Austrian local government are the districts (*Bezirke*), the smallest units of federal administration and local communes, which have their own mayors and councils with administrative, but no legislative, responsibilities. A quasi-independent body, the Central Auditing Office, monitors expenditures of both the Nationalrat and the provincial parliaments and issues annual reports on these activities. Such documents can become the basis of both legislative and party programs of the Austrian parliament.

The most independent component of Austrian government is the judiciary, responsible to the law alone. Though some municipalities are authorized to maintain local police forces, the chief law enforcement powers in the country are distributed among several departments accountable to the federal minister of the interior. The chief unit is the Federal Security Guard, an outgrowth of a civilian-organized police guard established during the **Revolutions of 1848**. A federal gendarmerie, organized along more regular military lines, is posted in all of the Austrian provinces except Vienna and is especially active in emergencies, both personal and national. The State Police provide security details for high government officials and conduct counterintelligence and counterterrorist investigations. The Criminal Intelligence Service both works within Austria and cooperates with Interpol. The Administrative Police deal with violations of import and export regulations and immigration law and supervise customs procedures. *See also* POLITICAL PARTIES.

GRAZ. The capital of **Styria**, Graz, with a population of around 240,000, is the second largest city of Austria. Its highly diversified **economy** has become far livelier since the reintroduction of free markets in eastern and southeastern Europe after 1989. The fracturing of the former Yugoslavia in the 1990s brought a stream of refugees into Austria who used Graz both as a transit point for travel to the north and west and as a natural site for relocation.

Archaeological digs in and around the city have turned up artifacts from the New Stone Age. The Romans, who entered the region around 16 BCE, laid down an important thoroughfare that touched upon what are today the western outskirts of the city. Slavic tribes left their mark on the names of places, rivers, and mountains. The name of the city itself is derived from a common Slavic term for a fortification or castle. Bavarian settlement began after the middle of the 10th century. The first documentary mention of the town dates from 1128; a castle from the 12th century also stood on the Graz Castle Hill and served as the seat of a local government. Margrave Otakar III established a market near the center of modern Graz around 1160. In 1172, the market of Graz was mentioned; by 1286, it was called a town.

In 1379, the **Habsburgs** made the city one of their residences and administrative centers, but it was in the 15th century that **Frederick III**, himself the offspring of the Styrian line of his house, made the Graz castle a real city residence. To protect it from the aggressive Ottoman Empire, he also expanded the fortifications around the settlement considerably. Following a three-way territorial division among **Ferdinand I**'s sons, Graz became the administrative capital of Inner Austria. The government of Ferdinand's youngest male heir, Archduke Charles (1540–1590), and his devoutly Catholic Bavarian wife, Archduchess Maria (1551–1608), took the first determined steps during the last decades of the Reformation toward recapturing the heavily Protestantized Austrian lands for Roman **Catholicism**. The University of Graz was founded in 1586 by the **Jesuits** to serve as a center for the educational program that the order brought to the Counter-Reformation. Though Charles and Maria's son, **Ferdinand II**, moved his court to **Vienna**, he is buried in the Styrian capital.

Until 1749, Graz was the capital for the entirety of Inner Austria, which included **Carinthia** and Carniola, today Slovenia, as well as Styria. As the Ottoman threat subsided in the last half of the 17th century, Graz was both built and rebuilt in the **Baroque** style. Remains of the period are still to be seen in the central part of the city, despite the destructiveness of Allied bombing in **World War II**, during which 16 percent of the city's buildings were completely destroyed.

Even after the region's **industrialization**, which began with the development of rail transportation to the city in 1844, Graz was, and is, known as *Pensionopolis*, because its comparatively mild climate and moderate price scale attracted many retirees, especially those from the military and civil service. Its economy received considerable support from the Nazis in the latter years of World War II, as they tried to move German industrial production within the shelter of Austria's mountains. The mines of the so-called Iron Mountain (*Erzberg*) were considerably modernized as a result of these attentions. Prior to the **Anschluss**, the Austrian **Nazi** movement was especially well-organized and entrenched in Graz among civil servants and university students and faculty.

Though Graz and its environs remain important manufacturing centers for iron and steel products, precision instruments generally, paper, chemicals, and some textiles, the economy of the city and region had shifted over to service industries by 1991. But the most notable change in the city has been its growing significance as a cultural and intellectual center. The university itself has long attracted a wide variety of foreign students, especially from southeastern Europe. Austrian participation in the **European Union**, however, has forced the country to open its borders to students from all member states; the medical school at the University of Graz now attracts many young people from the Federal Republic of **Germany**, where there are strict limits on the number of people who can study to become physicians.

In the years between 1950 and 1970, Graz also began the systematic renewal of its historic inner districts. In 1988, led by City Councilman Herbert Strobl, the local government embarked on a drive to stimulate the local economy by promoting cultural tourism. The strategy was to buy art not for installation in museums, but rather for display in conventional urban spaces, both internal and out-of-doors. The emphasis has been on the contemporary; during certain times the streets and courtyards of the city become impromptu galleries for a wide variety of artifacts. Indoor arenas, such as the Graz **Opera**, are turned over to correspondingly experimental **music** and **theater**. The event cooperates with other seasonal musical and cultural festivals such as the Styrian Autumn (*Steirischer Herbst*) and the Styriade. In 1999, United Nations Educaational, Scientific, and Cultural Organization (UNESCO) named Graz one of its World Cultural Heritage Sites, a distinction that was lavishly celebrated in the city's presentations in 2003. *See also* GRAZ GROUP.

GRAZ GROUP/GRAZER GRUPPE. In 1958, several young intellectuals, architects, and artists in the Styrian capital proposed to convert the once elegant, but now shabby, Cafe Stadtpark in the heart of the city into a center for experimental **literature** and **art**. After four years of critical exchange and discussion in their new meeting place, the writers of the movement decided to call themselves the Grazer Gruppe. In this way, they declared their intention to set themselves off from Gruppe 47 (Group 47), the loose but powerful gathering of German writers—Heinrich Böll, Günther Grass, Hans Magnus Enzensberger, and others—who had dominated German-language literature since the end of **World War II**. The Graz Group counted among its numbers the dramatist Wolfgang Bauer (1941–2005) and novelists and poets Alfred Kolleritsch (1931–), Günter Waldorf (1931–), **Barbara Frischmuth**, and Gerhard Roth (1942–).

For **Peter Handke**, arguably the best-known member of the **Graz** movement, the work of the Germans, particularly their prose, was excessively weighted toward a descriptive realism focusing on the representation and examination of social and political fact. Nor did Handke have much use for the then-iconic German Marxist dramatist, Bertolt Brecht. From Handke's standpoint, Brecht's work offered little more than trite situations packaged in left-wing clichés.

It was the dynamics of language itself, argued Handke and his cohorts, that created the comedy and drama of a given text. The group did not stress the content of novels, short stories, and plays, as much as it did innovative intent. Their journal, *manuskripte*, which first appeared as a handout in 1960, developed under the editorship of Kolleritsch and Roth into the chief outlet for experimental writing in German.

The Graz Group's aesthetic had a social, political, and wider cultural agenda. Nevertheless, its thrust was broadly contrarian and not specifically ideological. Like conventional radicals among their countrymen, they wished to purge Austrian literary and artistic life of all longing for the monarchy and the conservative ethos that went along with it. But the group also declared war on the sentimentalism often found in depictions of country life and rural society. In the writing of the Graz Group, the working class could be equally unheroic, especially in domestic circumstances. *See also* VIENNA GROUP.

GREEN PARTY/DIE GRÜNEN. With representatives in and out of the Austrian National Assembly since 1986, the Austrian Green Party has become considerably more professionalized than it was in its formative stages. Its recent leaders have shown a far greater willingness to observe the protocols of Austrian parliamentary life than did their immediate predecessors. A product of environmental concerns common to many European countries since the 1970s, the Green movement in Austria developed during controversies over nuclear power plant construction during the last years of Chancellor **Bruno Kreisky's government**. Environmentalist opposition to such an undertaking helped to swing public opinion against it—a referendum in 1978 rejected the project by the narrowest of margins. The Greens also whipped up public opinion in 1985 against erecting a hydroelectric plant at Hainburg in Lower Austria.

Despite its very small size—in 1990 it had only around 2,000 members—the party has enjoyed a great deal of publicity, which has attracted disaffected voters for reasons well beyond environmental issues. Corruption scandals in both major **political parties** and **Kurt Waldheim**'s controversial **presidency** have contributed to what, until electoral losses in 1995, seemed to be a rising tide of Green support. The initial appeal of the party was among the young, but its leadership has been willing to look beyond that constituency for leadership. In 1992, the Greens ran Robert Jungk, a 78-year-old writer, as a candidate in the presidential elections. University of Innsbruck professor of economics Alexander van der Bellen (1944–) has chaired the party since 1997. He has often cooperated with the **Socialist Party of Austria**, but has carefully avoided bringing the Greens to any federal coalitions.

GRILLPARZER, FRANZ (1791–1872). One of German **literature**'s greatest poetic dramatists, Grillparzer was born in **Vienna**, where he also died. His family was close to influential theatrical and government circles in the Habsburg capital. In 1813, following philological and legal studies at the **University of Vienna** and a brief turn as a private tutor in a noble household, Grillparzer began training to draft documents for the imperial court library. After 1823, he did this on a full-time salaried basis for the court treasury. From 1832 until his retirement in 1856, he served as director of the treasury archives. He was among the founding members of the Austrian Academy of Arts and Science in 1847, and from 1861 until his death a member of the upper house of various legislative bodies established in **Franz Joseph**'s experiments with **constitutionalism**.

His career as an author and dramatist developed even as he toiled somewhat resentfully as a bureaucrat. In 1816, the young man's translation of *Life Is a Dream* by the 17th-century Spanish playwright Calderon*ḍ* de la Barca favorably impressed the dramaturg of the imperial court **theater**, Joseph Schreyvogel (1768–1832). With the latter's encouragement, Grillparzer turned his hand to writing for the stage. His first success came with *Sappho* in 1819; it won him a five-year contract as court theater poet.

Grillparzer quickly abandoned this post, choosing to travel throughout a good part of Europe between 1821 and 1826, years in which he produced much of the dramatic writing that made his reputation. Inspired by classical and historical themes, these plays are intense probes of the inner lives of people torn apart by the conflict between duty and personal, often erotic, inclination. The great trilogy *The Golden Fleece* (*Das Goldene Vließ*) was finished in 1822; the tragedy *King Ottokar's Fortune and End* (*König Ottakars Glück und Ende*), based on the 13th-century conflict between the ruler of Bohemia and Rudolf I of Habsburg over control of the Austrian lands, was completed in 1825.

Other successes followed, but there were failures as well. A crucial disappointment was *Woe unto the Liar* (*Weh dem der Lügt*, 1838), a comedy in which Grillparzer had invested much hope. The negative public reaction persuaded the hypersensitive dramatist to stop writing for the stage altogether. Unpleasant experiences with government censorship and a general ambivalence toward authority also shaped his decision. He was bitingly critical of the **Metternich** regime between 1815 and the **Revolutions of 1848**. Nevertheless, he celebrated the Habsburg suppression of these upheavals in one of his most famous poems "To **Radetzky**," a paean to the field marshal who put down national upheavals in the dynasty's Italian lands. Three plays that Grillparzer wrote between 1847 and 1851, including the political drama *A Conflict among Brothers in the House of Habsburg* (*Ein Bruderzwist in Habsburg*), one of his most complex and important works, were performed only after his death. Indeed, he ordered in his will that they never be produced.

GUSENBAUER, ALFRED (1960–). A native of **Lower Austria**, Gusenbauer earned a doctorate in political science and law from the University of Vienna. Beginning with his election in 1984 as head of the **Socialist Party of Austria**'s (SPÖ) youth organization, he worked his way up the organizational ladder of the movement to become party leader in 2000 and federal **chancellor** in 2007. He had also been a member of the upper house (*Bundesrat*) of the Austrian parliament and served in several Austrian delegations to the **European Union**.

Gusenbauer's short-lived coaltion **government** with the **Austrian People's Party**, which collapsed in 2008, was politically fractious. The cause of his SPÖ was further weakened by its continued association, through the **Austrian Federation of Trade Unions**, with the **BAWAG** banking scandal. Gusenbauer's efforts to discipline the federation brought him under fire from the group. He also found it very difficult to realize any of the fiscal and social reforms that he had promised in the hotly contested federal election campaign of 2006.

– H –

HABSURG, HOUSE OF. Of Alemannic origins, the Habsburgs take their name from the castle of Havisberch, or "Habichtsburg," in the Swiss canton of Aargau. The structure probably dates from 1020, but the dynasty is said to have begun to take shape a half-century earlier. Serving as counts in various regions of southwestern **Germany** and Alsatia, the Habsburgs were close to the Hohenstaufen emperors.

They became a central European political force when Count Rudolph IV (1218–1291) was elected German king in 1273. Though not among the prominent dynasties of the **Holy Roman Empire**, the Habsburgs were by this time well endowed with both feudal and allodial properties and with protective rights over ecclesiastical establishments (*Kirchenvogteien*). It was the hope of those who elected Rudolph, who was never actually crowned Holy Roman Emperor by the pope, that he would check the expansionist ambitions of Ottokar II, the king of Bohemia, without threatening their own independence. Indeed, Rudolph would never be crowned Holy Roman Emperor by the pope. However, when he defeated Ottokar in 1278, the Habsburg took the opportunity to improve the territorial standing of his house considerably in central Europe. He enfeoffed himself with the then-vacant Austrian lands ruled until the middle of the 13th century by the **Babenbergs**. He also conferred titles to **Styria**, **Carinthia**, Carniola, and the Wendish March on his two sons, Albrecht I (1255–1308) and Rudolph II (1270–1290).

Like all German princes of the day, the Habsburgs observed partible inheritance, though their territories were considered as one. The arrangement led to episodic quarreling among the male members of the house, which seriously undermined the advantageous position that Rudolph had created for his family. By 1406, there were actually three lines of the house. It was not until 1493 that all of the Austrian lands were once again held by a single Habsburg, **Maximilian I**. His grandson, **Ferdinand I**, would redivide them among his three sons in the second half of the 16th century.

It was under Maximilian that the Habsburgs rose to pan-European eminence. Married by his father, **Frederick III**, to Mary, the Duchess of Burgundy (1457–1482) and the heiress to the rich agglomeration of territories loosely known by that name, Maximilian was a canny nuptial engineer himself. It was he who arranged the wedding of his son, Philip I (the Handsome 1478–1506), and Princess Juana of Castile (1479–1555), which led to Habsburg control of the Iberian kingdom until that branch of the house died out in 1700.

Though both the Spanish and German lines of the dynasty frequently disagreed on religious, political, and military matters, they supported one another as well. Spanish money and troops went to central Europe to fight both **Protestantism** and the Ottoman Empire, and Habsburg German emperors permitted Spanish recruiting in Germany and access through the southwestern part of the empire to the Netherlands. Parts of the latter were held by Spain until the 18th century. Neither branch of the house ever fully renounced its rights of succession to the holdings of the other, a policy that the repeated intermarriage between them generally reinforced.

A series of dynastic crises at the beginning of the 17th century ended with the recognition of the Styrian branch of the house, founded by Archduke Charles (1540–1590), the youngest son of Ferdinand I, as the leading line of the Austrian Habsburgs. With **Ferdinand II** making primogeniture the rule of the house in 1635, the line continued through unbroken male succession until the death of Emperor Charles VI in 1740. He was the last in the direct male descent of the line. With only two daughters, Charles had assured the succession of the eldest of them, Archduchess **Maria Theresa**, to the Habsburg patrimony in central and east central Europe without challenge. The outcome of his efforts, the Pragmatic Sanction of 1713, would remain one of the basic legal documents defining the relationship of the dynasty to its lands until the end of the **Habsburg Empire** in 1918. The marriage of Maria Theresa to Duke Francis Stephen of Lorraine (1708–1765) forever changed the name of the dynasty as well, as the house of Habsburg became the house of Habsburg–Lorraine.

Though the union was initially unfruitful, the couple eventually generated 12 children, whose offspring and succeeding progeny played the roles accorded to the dynasty in the various governments of the Habsburg Empire until the end of **World War I**. Their heirs also generated cadet lines, which were especially important in Italian affairs. The branch of the house that produced **Franz Ferdinand**, the victim of the assassination at Sarajevo, was descended from Leopold II's (1747–1792) son, Duke Ferdinand III (1769–1824) of the line of Habsburg–Tuscany.

The last Habsburg ruler of Austria–Hungary, **Charles I** (Charles IV of Hungary) (1887–1922), had eight offspring. The eldest, Archduke Otto (1912–), has long been involved in the politics of the European Parliament. Through the Pan-European Union founded in 1923 to promote, among other things, a Habsburg restoration, he has also been very active in conservative and **Catholic** movements. His father was beatified by Pope John Paul II in 2004 for alleged Christian humanitarianism during World War I, a move heavily criticized among progressive and national circles in Austria itself. *See also*

COUDENHOVE-KALERGI, RICHARD; HABSBURG EXCLUSION ACT; HABSBURG, OTTO.

HABSBURG, OTTO (1912–). The eldest son of **Charles I (IV)**, the last Austrian emperor and king of Hungary, Otto is the current pretender to a **Habsburg** throne, in the unlikely event that the office will ever exist again. Legally forbidden any form of Habsburg succession in the First Austrian Republic, which emerged from **World War I**, Otto studied with private tutors and at foreign universities. In 1935, the University of Louvain granted him a doctorate in political science.

During the 1930s sympathy grew in Austria for a Habsburg restoration as a counterweight to the threat of **Nazi** authoritarianism. The **Habsburg Exclusion Act** was repealed in July 1935, and the erstwhile ruling family was allowed to reclaim much of its property in Austria. With the **Anschluss** of 1938, however, the Nazi regime in Austria reconfirmed the exclusion measure.

Otto fled the Nazis from Belgium to New York in 1940. While in the United States, he made influential contacts with American officials in Washington, including Secretary of State Cordell Hull and President Franklin D. Roosevelt. Otto argued for classifying Austria as an occupied country rather than an enemy belligerent, once **World War II** ended. He also suggested some form of a Danubian confederation to block the probable expansion of the Soviet Union. His presence in Austria, however, remained very conditional. He was only allowed to visit the country in 1966.

In 1978, Otto von Habsburg became a German citizen; he officially resided in Pöcking in Bavaria. As a member of the Bavarian Christian Social Union, he has been an activist in the cause of the European Parliament located in Strasbourg. He was elected to that body in 1979 and continues to promote pan-European unity. His arguments for a common defense, foreign, and financial policy are, by his own admission, inspired by the structure of the 1867 **Ausgleich** between Austria and Hungary. He has also vigorously supported the incorporation of the former communist states of eastern and east central Europe into the **European Union**.

Otto and his family scoff at talk about a Habsburg restoration. Two of his sons, however, have also been active in pan-European affairs.

A daughter, Walpurga, tried to enter electoral politics in Sweden in 1998. She is prominent in several charitable and advocacy organizations throughout the world. *See also* HABSBURG EMPIRE.

HABSBURG EMPIRE. Though the term has never had any legal standing, the Habsburg Empire is widely understood in modern times to have consisted of the nine provinces of modern Austria along with a wide variety of lands throughout eastern, southern, and southeastern Europe. These were territories in **Italy** (Lombardy–Venetia), Poland (Galicia), Ukraine (Bukovina), and, after 1908, Bosnia, as well as the crown lands belonging to the kingdoms of Bohemia and Hungary, respectively. The former comprised the province of Bohemia itself, the margravate of Moravia and, until the 18th century, Upper and Lower Silesia and the two Lusatias. The Hungarian Crown of St. Stephen was made up of Hungary along with Transylvania, now in Romania; the Banat, part of today's Serbia; and the kingdom of Croatia–Slavonia.

The **Habsburgs** had acquired these territories from the 16th through the 20th centuries through war, inheritance, treaty, and, in some cases, purchase. The kingdoms of Bohemia and Hungary fell to the dynasty in 1526. However, it was not until the end of the 17th century that the Ottoman Empire evacuated the latter realm to Habsburg control. Portions of Polish Galicia were incorporated into the Habsburg Empire in the last third of the 18th century, though Cracow and environs were not annexed until 1846.

Another branch of the dynasty ruled Spain and its possessions from the beginning of the 16th century until it died out with the sickly King Charles II in 1700. During the War of the Spanish Succession (1702–1713) the Vienna line tried to win the Spanish crown, but they failed. As compensation, the Vienna Habsburgs received the so-called Austrian Netherlands, today Belgium. Austrian Emperor Francis I (1768–1835) subsequently renounced these provinces as part of the post-Napoleonic territorial settlement reached by the **Congress of Vienna** in 1815. Aside from the loss of most of what it ruled in Italy between 1859 and 1866, the Habsburg Empire in east central Europe remained intact until its collapse in 1918.

Until 1804, the Habsburgs governed these territories not through a single title, but with the traditional titles carried by rulers in each of these lands. Thus, they were simultaneously kings of Hungary and Bohemia, counts of the **Tyrol**, dukes of **Styria**, and the like. Little serious political account was taken of the ethnic and linguistic relationships between the peoples of these lands and those who held political authority over them. One was the subject of one's king or duke, regardless of the latter's national background. What conflicts the Habsburgs had with their populations—Germans, Magyars, a variety of Slavs who eventually became the single largest ethnic group in the empire, Romanians, and Italians—arose from religious and political differences, not questions of ethnicity. Especially troublesome were relationships with various local nobilities and the estates, in which they negotiated directly with their rulers. The **Thirty Years' War** and the Counter-Reformation gave the Habsburgs the opportunity to bring their Austrian and Bohemian territories under central control. Nevertheless, it has been argued that the only common feature that the Habsburg Empire had was **Catholicism** and Catholic culture, which became a virtual norm by the end of the 17th century.

Only during the 18th century and the reign of **Maria Theresa** did the balance of authority in the Habsburg Empire tip decisively toward a central government in **Vienna**. It was she and her advisors, particularly Count Friedrich Wilhelm von Haugwitz (1702–1765), who persuaded estates throughout much of the realm to fund the Habsburg **military** establishment for as much as 10 years at a time. However, a strong case could be made that this development really never took place in Hungary, at least on a durable basis.

The Napoleonic Wars, which ended in 1815, made political nationalism a serious challenge to Habsburg rule. Bonaparte had made the liberation of peoples from multinational states part of his agenda; his defeats of the Habsburgs in the first few years of the 19th century made his case all the more plausible. The Habsburgs recovered from this setback, but the issue of national states or at least national autonomy within the empire was a prominent cause of the **Revolutions of 1848**. Once again, the empire survived thanks to socioeconomic divisions among the revolutionaries and superior military force. However, the success of the Italian national movement after 1859 showed that the empire was fracture-prone along ethnic and linguistic lines. Following the Prussian defeat of Austria in the **Seven Weeks' War** of 1866, some elements among Emperor **Franz Joseph**'s subjects fell increasingly under the spell of the new Hohenzollern state arising to the north.

National unrest, as well as social and economic changes that came with the industrialization of the 19th century, made the Habsburg monarchy increasingly problematic to govern. Franz Joseph experimented with constitutional structures that offended as many national leaders among his peoples as they pleased. The so-called **Ausgleich** of 1867, which served as the constitution of Austria–Hungary until the end, gave the Hungarians substantial political powers in the domestic affairs of that kingdom, but angered Slavs throughout the empire.

However, it was not until **World War I** that the Habsburg Empire truly fell apart. Outright military defeat was the immediate cause, but almost as important was the feeling among Habsburg subjects that the dynasty would no longer act in their interests. The dominant German presence in Austrian military affairs convinced important national leaders that the Habsburgs would be little more than agents for Berlin's hegemonic designs on central and east central Europe. The Bolshevik Revolution of 1917 in **Russia** also inspired popular resistance to a war that had brought enormous hardship to the common folk throughout the Habsburg state.

HABSBURG EXCLUSION ACT. As **World War I** came to an end in November 1918, Emperor **Charles I** (King Charles IV of Hungary) issued a declaration in which he removed himself from participation in the **government** of the Austrian republic, which was beginning to take shape. Though he left **Vienna** with his family, he continued to reside in a nearby castle. On 23 March 1919, he departed the country for exile in Switzerland. At the Swiss–Austrian border, however, he produced a second manifesto that seemed to leave open the possibility that he and his heirs would not respect the form of government taking hold in the new state.

Fearing attempts at a **Habsburg** restoration that would further complicate an already chaotic political situation, the National Assembly passed the Habsburg Exclusion Act on 3 April 1919. This stripped sovereign rights in Austria from the house of Habsburg–Lorraine forever. The "former holder of the crown," Charles and his heirs, had to leave the country unless they swore to live as loyal citizens of the republic. This meant that they would have to renounce their membership in the house of Habsburg and their claims to serve as rulers. The First Austrian Republic seized the landed property of the dynasty and its cadet lines as well as other assets. These were to be used to aid those whose health was impaired by the war or who had lost their breadwinners in the conflict.

HAIDER, JÖRG (1950–2008). Born in **Upper Austria**, Haider began his political career as a spokesman for the national wing of the **Freedom Party of Austria** (FPÖ) in **Carinthia**. He led the party between 1986 and 2005. Trained in legal studies, he served as governor of the province from 1989 to 1991. During the latter year, a favorable remark he made during a debate in the regional legislature about **Nazi** employment policies led to demands for his resignation from liberal circles abroad and the Austrian federal government. On 21 June 1991, Haider lost a no-confidence vote in the Carinthian State Diet initiated by the **Socialist Party of Austria** and supported by representatives of the **Austrian People's Party** (ÖVP). In the regional state elections of 1991, however, the FPÖ gained votes. In 2000 he joined with the ÖVP, led by **Wolfgang Schüssel**, in a controversial coalition that drew sanctions from the **European Union**. In 2005, he broke with the FPÖ to launch another party, the Alliance for the Future of Austria (BZÖ). In an election in September 2008, the BZÖ tripled its vote over its last performance, winning 40 percent of the electorate in **Carinthia** and 11 percent nationally. A month later, Haider was killed in a car crash in which he was driving alone. *See also* ASYLUM; POLITICAL PARTIES.

HAINISCH, MARIANNE (1839–1936). The founder of the Austrian Women's Movement, dedicated to the cause of equal rights for **women**, Hainisch called in 1870 for the opening of modern secondary **educational** institutions (*Realgymnasien*) to females. She also asked that they have access to university degrees. Her Federation of Austrian Women's Clubs, established in 1902, had 90 member organizations by 1914. She continued to chair the group until 1918.

Following **World War I**, Hainisch devoted much of her time to the cause of world peace. After **Bertha von Suttner** died in 1914, Hainisch directed the Peace Commission of the Austrian Women's

Federation. She was also responsible for the introduction of Mother's Day to Austria, the first of which was observed in 1924. Hainisch was the mother of Michael Hainisch (1858–1940), a moderate German nationalist, who, though representing no party, was president of the First Austrian Republic (1920–1928).

HALLSTATT CULTURE. In 1846 Johann Georg Ramsauer, a mining inspector from Hallstatt in **Upper Austria**, discovered an Iron Age gravesite. His report of his findings was the first written account of a prehistoric burial ground in central Europe. Ramsauer turned the area into a **tourist** attraction, visited by, among others, **Emperor Franz Joseph** and his wife, Empress Elisabeth (1837–1898), in 1856.

The grave and some 2,000 more like it in the region were part of a wider civilization that stretched between eastern France to the Balkans from approximately 700 BCE to the beginning of the Common Era. Significant finds of artifacts and burial grounds have taken place in all provinces of modern Austria. The peoples were ethnically Illyrian. After about 400 BCE, however, they were joined in Upper Austria and **Salzburg** by significant numbers of Celts. The Romans, who occupied the region shortly before the beginning of the Common Era, called both peoples Taurisci.

The chief occupation of those who lived around Hallstatt was salt mining. Celtic settlers around Vienna began the cultivation of **wine** on the Leopoldsberg, today within the city limits, and the surrounding area. The practice has endured into the 21st century. *See also* CARNUNTUM.

HANDKE, PETER (1942–). Born in **Carinthia**, Handke attended a high school that trained students for admission to **Catholic** seminaries. Even as he studied law from 1961 to 1965 in **Graz**, he had begun a career that would make him one of the most famous writers to emerge from post–**World War II** Austria. Unlike many of his literary countrymen, Handke has been widely translated abroad. He has also had numerous foreign residences that make cameo appearances in his work, giving it a more general European quality than the output of his literary contemporaries in Austria. He is also highly versatile, fluent in all the major genres of **literature**, including **film** scriptwriting. He has directed films as well.

An early participant in the **Graz Group**, Handke initially followed much of its program. *The Hornets* (*Die Hornissen*, 1966) and *Sorrow Beyond Dreams* (*Wunschloses Unglück*, 1972) strip rural life of the idyllic qualities found in the typical Austrian version of the genre, the *Heimatroman* (Eng: homeland romance). Handke specializes in shifting narrative perspectives, random use of language, and fugitive plotlines. Far from the conventions of standard literary realism, these devices deliberately try the patience of a conventional reader. In the play *Insulting the Audience* (*Publikumsbeschimpfung*, 1966), he worked consciously and hard to offend and anger those who came to see his piece. What they find are four jeans-clad men who rail for over an hour against the traditional theater and those who attend it. As the author sees it, the four figures are not even actors.

Kaspar, first performed in 1967, perhaps best reveals the philosophy of language that underlies much of Handke's early writing. A famous near-mute in **Germany** during the first decade of the 19th century, Kaspar is made to show that the constraints of language afflict all of humanity. To learn to speak at all, he must, in Handke's view, be programmed by others, a situation that can be generalized to mean that all of us are in some way the product of external linguistic manipulation.

Didactically constructed though it is, Handke's work often has a deeply personal undertone. Writers' block, the birth of a daughter, his marital difficulties, and especially the miserable life and suicide of his mother, figure recognizably in some of his texts, such as *Sorrow Beyond Dreams*. His work since the middle of the 1970s has been more straightforward, inviting comparison with **Adalbert Stifter**, one of Austria's most original and highly regarded classical authors. Handke's technique of getting to the heart of subjects by persuading readers to contemplate the externals he describes rather than to search below surfaces for deeper meaning parallels the aesthetic philosophy of his earlier countryman, **Hugo von Hofmannsthal**. Handke also has a keen ear for the natural prosodic rhythms of German that enables him to turn his otherwise dry narratives into something close to poetry. His use of extended periodic sentences that are almost stripped of verbs adds to the pictorial quality of some of his prose, such as *Once More for Thucydides* (*Noch einmal für Thucydides*, 1990).

HANSEN, THEOPHILE (1813–1891). Born in Copenhagen, Hansen did his first professional work as an architect in Athens, where he absorbed at first hand the lines and ornamentation of classical antiquity and Byzantium. He went to **Vienna** in 1846, where he worked closely with Ludwig Förster (1797–1863). He also became Förster's son-in-law.

Hansen passed on his deep respect for historical styles of **architecture** to his students at the Vienna Academy of Fine Arts, where he taught after 1868. His mature work often located buildings in a particular culture. The elegantly classical parliament (1874–1883) on Vienna's **Ringstrasse** recalls the Athenian origins of Western democracy and represents his work at its finest and most disciplined. Other buildings were somewhat more eclectic; a new stock exchange that he began in 1874 was typical. Hansen also designed several imposing residential structures along the Ring and in the immediate neighborhood that are good examples of 19th-century neo-Renaissance design and construction in Vienna and elsewhere in the **Habsburg Empire**.

HANSLICK, EDUARD (1825–1904). One of the most feared **music** critics of his or any other age, Hanslick was born in Prague. Both a scholar and aesthetic theorist, he became a lecturer in musicology at the **University of Vienna** in 1856, then professor of music history and aesthetics in 1861. The first person to hold such a position at the institution, he developed what in all likelihood was the first university-level course in music appreciation anywhere in the world.

In his youth, Hanslick was a vigorous advocate of musical Romanticism and the early operas of Richard Wagner. By 1850, however, he had rejected these views in favor of the musical classicism he associated with the work of **Wolfgang Amadeus Mozart**, **Ludwig van Beethoven**, and in his own day, Johannes Brahms (1833–1897). The ideal score, he argued, consisted of tones set in motion. Composers were inspired not by emotion, but by a kind of inward singing, which arises from the structure of sound. Expression of these relationships could come only through musical composition. For Hanslick, the text of a song had little to do with music itself. Performers could use any text they pleased without changing the effect music had on the hearer.

Such views set Hanslick at odds with the explicitly programmatic music of the New German School, represented in his day by the mature Wagner, **Gustav Mahler**, and **Anton Bruckner**. The vehemence of Hanslick's reviews so discouraged the hypersensitive Bruckner that he asked **Franz Joseph** to put an end to such writing. Wagner was a far tougher opponent. The critic argued that the sense of tension that ripples through Wagnerian chromatics comes not from emotional arousal, but merely from auditory experience with disintegrating musical forms. Responding to this and countless other unfavorable evaluations, Wagner based the figure of Veit Beckmesser, the scheming but unimaginative pedant in *Die Meistersinger von Nürnberg*, on his perceptions of Hanslick. Indeed, in the earliest sketches of the opera, Beckmesser is called Veit Hanslick.

HAYDN, FRANZ JOSEPH (1732–1809). The first of the major classical composers of the Viennese tradition, Haydn was born in the rural village of Rohrau in **Lower Austria**. His father was a master blacksmith. Haydn learned the rudiments of composition apparently on his own. However, his **musical** talents were recognized very early, by others as well as, on his own testimony, by himself.

In 1740, Haydn became a choirboy at St. Stephen's Cathedral in **Vienna**. After his voice changed nine years later, he supported himself in a wide variety of musical jobs, as a dance violinist, as a choral accompanist, and as a choir director. He wrote his first symphony around 1761.

By 1766, Haydn was the musical director of the Esterházy household in **Eisenstadt**, then in Hungary, and now the capital of the Austrian **Burgenland**. He remained in the service of these immensely wealthy patrons until 1790, when the choir was disbanded. Haydn then left for Vienna. The 24 years at the Esterházy Palace were among his most productive, spreading his reputation far beyond the provincial confines of his daily life. His works were performed in Paris and London, and he received an honorary degree from Oxford University.

Haydn wrote over 100 symphonies, more than 70 string quartets, and countless other musical works for a wide variety of instruments. Perhaps his most impressive compositions are his oratorios, such as *The Creation* (1798) and *The Seasons* (1801), and masses such as the

Lord Nelson Mass (*Missa in angustiis*, 1798). Though the composer never lost the popular inspiration that lies at the heart of his music, his formal achievements were very important in the development of both the Austrian and the Western musical idiom. He brought the thematic structure, along with the harmonic and expressive content of the sonata, to a new level of complexity, at the same time paying attention to the interrelatedness of all the musical elements of the work.

HAYEK, FRIEDRICH AUGUST (1899–1992). Though an advocate of the classical liberal values of private property and individual initiative, Hayek is firmly enshrined in the pantheons of modern conservatism. A student of the **Austrian School of Economics** at the **University of Vienna**, he was, in 1927, one of the founders of the Austrian Institute for the Study of the Business Cycle, today the Institute for Economic Research.

Hayek had a long and influential career in Europe before becoming a British subject in 1931. His teaching position at the London School of Economics brought him into contact and debate with John Maynard Keynes, whose theories on the role of government intervention in economies differed sharply from Hayek's views. Hayek also taught at the Universities of Chicago, Freiburg im Breisgau, and Salzburg. His most important work was in monetary and business theory, for which he shared the Nobel Prize in Economics in 1974 with the Swedish economist Gunnar Myrdahl.

Hayek was a scathing critic of National Socialism and of Bolshevik communism, which he analyzed in his best-selling *The Road to Serfdom* (1944). Both ideologies, in his view, promoted the collectivism that characterizes totalitarian societies. These, in turn, undermine the "spontaneous social order" that is part of the basic human condition of freedom. Nevertheless, while Hayek deeply respected human reason and its role in advancing human welfare, he believed that it could lead to what he called a false individualism. This, in turn, made people overlook the important role that tradition and experience played in sustaining a truly free society.

HEILIGENKREUZ. Located south of **Vienna**, this Cistercian monastery, founded in 1133 by the **Babenberg** Margrave Leopold III, is the second oldest establishment of the order in Austria. It takes its name from an alleged piece of the true cross, which the deeply pious margrave, today the patron saint of the province of **Lower Austria**, presented to the house. During the Middle Ages, it was one of the major centers for the compiling of written chronicles. Heiligenkreuz served as the mother house for several other Cistercian foundations in **Lower Austria**: Zwettl (1138), Baumgartenberg (1142), Marienberg (1197), and Lilienfeld (1202). The entire complex is a good example of the major **architectural** and decorative styles that have shaped the buildings and interiors of Austria throughout its history. Its core has both Romanesque and Gothic elements; the monastery church, consecrated in 1187, is a Romanesque basilica with a Gothic nave and choir. The facade was renovated in the neo-Gothic fashion of the 19th century. The wellhouse on the grounds has stained glass windows installed around 1290. The **Baroque** altar painting dates from the first half of the 18th century. The guest quarters are also Baroque and date from the second half of the 17th century. *See also* CATHOLICISM; RELIGION.

HEIMWEHR. The term is a collective applied to the voluntary self-defense organizations that sprang up throughout the Austrian provinces immediately after **World War I**. At first they were connected with no specific political party, nor, with the exception of their hostility to Marxism, did they espouse any particular ideological viewpoint. They drew their membership from Austrian society as a whole. **Jews** and Christians participated. They served as local police, and where a region was under attack from foreign troops—in **Carinthia**, for example—they played a significant role in preserving the territorial integrity of the newborn First Austrian Republic.

These organizations were gradually consolidated into a single group throughout the alpine lands. Seeing the militia as a way of offsetting similar organizations within the socialist camp, major industrialists, especially in Upper **Styria**, supported the *Heimwehr* heavily. The organization assembled an impressive arsenal, partially from local sources, partially with the aid of Benito Mussolini in **Italy**, who was much interested in maintaining a significant presence in Austrian affairs. They were uniformed, their colors the white and green of Styria, and kept alive their public presence through parades and other forms of demonstration, which brought them into direct and often violent conflict with their socialist counterparts, the **Republican Guard**.

The authoritarian drift in Austrian politics after 1927, when street clashes in **Vienna** between socialists and the police ended in the burning of the Ministry of Justice building, moved the *Heimwehr* directly into the political arena. As **chancellors**, **Ignaz Seipel** and **Engelbert Dollfuss** supported and made use of the movement. Though a major wing of its membership was more German nationalist than the intensely **Catholic** leadership of the **Christian Social Party**, the vigorous anti-Marxism of both camps promoted cooperation between them. Indeed, neither Seipel nor Dollfuss would have been able to govern without the participation of the German national bloc in their coalitions.

The leaders of the *Heimwehr*, **Count Ernst Rüdiger Starhemberg**, Major Emil Fey (1886–1938), Richard Steidle (1881–1940), and Walter Pfrimer (1881–1968), pledged their support of fascist principles in the Korneuburg Program of 1930. In doing so, they foreswore democracy, parliamentary government, and capitalism. They urged the creation of a corporate state and announced that they intended to take over the government. The display of unity was, however, deceptive; Fey, who spoke for Catholic and monarchist interests, and Starhemberg, who was an advocate of the German-national cause, were on especially bad terms. In September 1931, the Styrian segment of the *Heimwehr* led by Pfrimer swung its support to the Austrian National Socialist movement.

In the first years of the Dollfuss government, members of the *Heimwehr* occupied key ministerial positions, including the vice-chancellorship and the Ministry of the Interior. The continued rivalry in the organization led to its dissolution in 1936 and the incorporation of its fighting forces into the **Fatherland Front**. *See also* AUSTROFASCISM.

HERZL, THEODOR (1860–1904). A journalist and one of the major ideologues of modern Zionism, Herzl was born in Budapest. He drifted to Vienna, where he became the literary editor of the *Neue Freie Presse*. His early views on Jewish–Gentile relations were wholeheartedly assimilationist—he once suggested that Viennese

Jews set an example for their coreligionists and receive baptism en masse.

Increasing experience with anti-Semitism, both within the **Habsburg Empire** and in Paris, where he was a correspondent during the Dreyfus Affair, led Herzl to the idea of establishing a Jewish homeland. Although the notion was not original with him, Herzl was probably its most effective European publicist. Influenced by a Zionist society in **Russia** and friends at home, he brought out a book, *Der Judenstaat* (*The Jewish State*), in 1896, which proposed carving out such a polity of Palestine, then under the control of the Ottoman Empire. Rebuffed by the sultan in Constantinople, Herzl then asked the British government to turn over land in what is today Uganda for the scheme.

The more religiously orthodox Zionists rejected this idea. Though Herzl fell short of his objective, he did lay the groundwork for continued Zionist activism.

HEURIGER. For Austrians, and especially the Viennese, this term has two applications. The first, and more general, refers to the most recent (Germ.: *heur* = this year) available vintage of the local **wine**. This is usually white and comes from the *Grüner Veltliner* grape, which has a slightly sour undertone. It is considered *Heuriger* until 11 November, St. Martin's Day, of the following year. Second, a *Heuriger* is a garden site where such wine is both sold and consumed, particularly in **Vienna**'s outlying districts, where productive vineyards still operate. Vienna has cultivated vineyards in and around the city at least from 1132 to the present. It is the only major city in the world with an extensive viticulture within its city limits. The diversity of its soils also allows for the cultivation of grapes for red wines and white Rieslings.

Heuriger can be exceedingly modest, with only a few picnic tables and benches and a limited choice of bread, cheese, and cold cuts to accompany the beverage. They can also be quite elaborate, offering among other attractions *Schrammel* music. These are popular tunes played by a characteristically Austrian ensemble of guitars, violins, and accordion. The first director of such a group was Joseph Schrammel (1850–1893). Single entertainers who sing **Wiener Lieder** (Vienna songs) often perform in these places, too.

A bundle or wreath of pine twigs hung above the entrance to the property advertises the presence of a true Viennese Heuriger within. The shrubs also announce to the thirsty that the grower is prepared to sell his or her wine. The right to dispense the vintage under this sign goes back to a patent issued by Emperor **Joseph II** in 1784. This has been incorporated into provincial law in **Lower Austria**, the **Burgenland**, and **Styria**. In 2006, there were around 180 Heuriger. While the traditional young wine is still drunk copiously on the spot, *Heuriger* also carry on an increasingly lively trade in a much higher quality bottled product. Real estate development in Vienna's outlying districts, however, has sharply reduced the number of true *Heuriger*. From around 180 in the 1970s, only 12 survived by 2008 in the traditional wine garden area of Grinzing.

HILDEBRANDT, JOHANN LUKAS VON (1668–1745). Among the most celebrated practitioners of Austrian **Baroque architecture**, Hildebrandt was born in Genoa. Beginning his career as a military engineer, he entered imperial service in 1701. His greatest works, such as the Belvedere Palace (1721–1723) in **Vienna**, which he designed for **Prince Eugene of Savoy**, and the cloister of Göttweig in **Lower Austria**, are characterized by highly imaginative central staircases. These buildings were also placed in comparatively rural settings—Belvedere was beyond the city walls of Vienna at the time—allowing Hildebrandt to exploit the massive proportions and dynamic lines of his exteriors to great effect. These he further enhanced with spacious formal gardens. Other significant Hildebrandt structures in Vienna are the Daun-Kinsky (1713–1716) and Schönborn (1706–1711) palaces.

HOFER, ANDREAS (1767–1810). The leader of a Tyrolean uprising against Bavarian rule imposed by Napoleon in the treaties of Pressburg (Bratislava) and Schönbrunn (1805, 1809), he was an innkeeper in his native **South Tyrol**. In 1790, he became a delegate to the Tyrolean estates. Hofer was a militia captain as well, and for a time enjoyed the patronage of **Habsburg** Archduke Johann (1782–1859), who believed that the French emperor could be brought down through popular resistance. Resentment of the Bavarians ran high; the Enlightenment-inspired government in Munich offended the deeply Catholic population to the south, especially in rural areas. Conscription of Tyroleans into the Bavarian army added to local grievances.

The uprising began on 9 April 1809, with Hofer designated as the "chosen commander of the house of Austria." The movement enjoyed some initial successes, but by July, French troops were once again in **Innsbruck**. Hofer rallied his forces, retook the city, and governed the Tyrol from there until October 1809. His resistance finally collapsed in November. Attempting to flee, he was betrayed and captured. He was executed in Mantua the following year on Napoleon's orders.

HOFFMANN, JOSEF (1870–1956). An architect and interior designer, Hoffmann was one of the founders of the **Secession**, with which his name is still closely associated. He studied both in **Italy** and at the Vienna Academy of **Art**. Here he came under the influence of the architect and urban designer **Otto Wagner**. Hoffmann began his professional career in the latter's studio. From 1899 until 1937, he taught at the Vienna School of Applied Arts. After 1920, he served as the building supervisor for the municipality of **Vienna**. He developed plans for the city's massive public housing projects after both **World War I** and **World War II**.

Like almost all of the members of the Secession, Hoffmann was enormously versatile. His most important architectural project was the Palais Stoclet (1905–1911) in Brussels, which encapsulates his **architecture** at its most mature, a blend of linear severity offset by the disciplined curves in the decorative features. Several villas he planned still stand in Vienna's 19th District, in the Hohe Warte and Kaasgraben areas. The depressed economy in Austria after World War I sharply reduced Hoffmann's professional commissions. The work he did during the period was increasingly influenced by Cubism and DeStijl, the latter coming from the Netherlands.

A very private personality, Hoffmann left little in the way of personal papers or theoretical expositions of his work. He was awarded the Austrian State Prize in 1950.

HOFMANNSTHAL, HUGO VON (1874–1929). The son of a bank director, Hofmannsthal was an awesome literary prodigy. His early, and already accomplished, verse appeared under the pseudonym of

Loris because publishing the writing of minors was illegal. Though he studied at the **University of Vienna** for a degree in Romance languages, he abandoned academic pursuits in 1899 to concentrate on a full-time career in **literature**. His early lyric poetry, marked by an extraordinary sensitivity to linguistic nuances, along with verse dramas completed before 1902, established his international reputation as a major poet and exemplary aesthete.

But doubts about the moral and epistemological basis of aestheticism appeared in his work fairly soon. In 1902, he published *From the Letter of Lord Chandos*, in which he raised serious questions about the capacity of language and the human mind to present and comprehend reality in all of its fluid complexity. For a few months after publishing this piece, Hofmannsthal gave up writing altogether. Though he recovered from this particular crisis of uncertainty, four years later he broke off his friendship with Stefan George, the central figure in a famous German circle of aesthetes dedicated to the proposition that society could be redeemed through **art**. These concerns never disappeared from his subsequent work altogether, which took on an increasingly ethical character.

He also became more driven by practical concerns, including the need for financial security. In the same year that Hofmannsthal severed relations with George and his circle, he began his collaboration with the composer Richard Strauss, as his librettist. Though their creative exchanges were marked by sharp disagreements—Strauss had a far surer instinct for the stageworthy than did his Viennese partner—the two were responsible for several of the masterworks of the 20th-century musical theater. Among their major achievements were *Elektra* (1909), *Der Rosenkavalier* (1911), two versions of *Ariadne auf Naxos* (1912, 1916), *Die Frau ohne Schatten* (1919), and *Arabella* (1933), performed four years after Hofmannsthal's death.

Hofmannsthal's growing concern about constructing bridges between the artist and the larger concerns of society led him temporarily into service as a propagandist for the **Habsburg Empire** in the early years of **World War I**. As editor of the occasional pamphlet series Die österreichische Bibliothek (The Austrian Library), he hoped to enlighten the subjects of the monarchy about important aspects of their history as a way of persuading them to remain true to the house of **Habsburg**–Lorraine, as most of them did until the end. Financial problems with the series, plus Hofmannsthal's own distaste for the nitty-gritty of politics, led him to withdraw from this and similar enterprises even before the conflict came to an end.

Hofmannsthal produced a significant body of writing following the collapse of the Habsburg monarchy in 1918. Two masterful comedies, *Der Schwierige* (*The Difficult One*, 1921) and *Der Unbestechliche* (*The Incorruptible One*, 1923), explore on a social level the problems of linguistic misunderstanding and inadequacy that had troubled him from the beginning of the century. His concern with reknitting Austrian society following the political trauma of World War I led him to play a central role in the creation of the **Salzburg Festival**.

Though far too subtle and refined an intellect to be an effective ideologue, Hofmannsthal also became a spokesman for the so-called Conservative Revolution, which attracted many important intellectuals and artists during the 1920s, such as T. S. Eliot in England and Charles Maurras in France. In "Das Schrifttum als geistiger Raum der Nation" ("Literature as the Spiritual Arena of the Nation"), an address delivered in Munich in 1927, Hofmannsthal described the traditionally individualistic German intellectual as now seeking to find bonds with the totality of German society. The outcome of these efforts was to be a fusion of the aesthetic and the political, which would make it possible for all to play a role in national regeneration. Two years later he died on 15 July, preparing to attend the funeral of his son Franz, who had committed suicide two days earlier.

HOLY ROMAN EMPIRE. Created on the basis of the Carolingian state of the eighth-century Franks, the title of Holy Roman Emperor was first held by Charlemagne from 800 until his death in 814. The Frankish ruler received the title, somewhat reluctantly, from Pope Leo III (r. 795–816), thus laying the groundwork for an ambiguity that plagued imperial politics from the empire's inception down to its dissolution at the beginning of the 19th century. Who, ultimately, was Christendom's supreme authority, pope or emperor? At the end of the fifth century, Pope Gelasius I had proclaimed that his own office was responsible for the spiritual welfare of Christendom and the Holy Roman Emperor was charged with securing secular order.

Nevertheless, the relationship between the two officials was never that clear-cut.

The popes and emperors vied with each other throughout medieval and early modern times over theoretical and practical understandings of their competence. By the end of the Middle Ages, the papacy had clearly prevailed. Though the emperor was formally sovereign in the German lands and in certain areas of the Italian peninsula as well, his authority was increasingly more nominal than real.

As late as the beginning of the 15th century, the emperor still spoke for the German territories in matters of foreign policy and defense and was responsible for domestic peace and some higher forms of justice. He also had the right to confer and remove titles, a crucial power as long as the German lands were largely governed by princely territorial authority grounded in the imperial constitution. Nevertheless, the dominant tendency of German imperial politics, from at least the 13th century on, was the strengthening of territorial rule in **Germany** at the expense of imperial control. The **Protestant** Reformation of the 16th century, which territorialized the **Catholic**, Lutheran, and after the end of the **Thirty Years' War**, Calvinist churches, further reinforced these developments.

Habsburg Austria, and even the larger entity of the **Habsburg Empire**, played central roles in the Holy Roman Empire until its collapse. The **Lower Austria** of the Middle Ages was the eastern march (*Ostmark*) of the Carolingian and of the Holy Roman Empires; its **Babenberg**, then **Habsburg** rulers were often central figures in medieval German politics and culture. The **Tyrol**, **Styria**, **Carinthia**, and the **Vorarlberg** were important parts of the Holy Roman Empire, as was **Salzburg**, then governed by a prince-bishop. All were liable for some imperial taxes levied upon their holdings.

Moreover, Habsburg involvement with the Holy Roman Empire went far beyond the Austrian lands. From the latter third of the 13th century down to the middle of the 15th, Habsburgs served off and on as emperors. From 1440 until they formally laid down the emperorship in 1806, the dynasty held the imperial office, except for the years between 1742 and 1745. When they became kings of Bohemia in 1526, the Habsburgs could also participate in choosing the emperor, because the title made its holder an imperial elector along with the archbishops of Cologne, Trier, and Mainz and the territorial rulers of Brandenburg, the Rhenish Palatinate, and Saxony.

The ambitions of the Habsburgs and those of the imperial estates, made up of three chambers representing electors, spiritual and secular princes, and towns, were rarely congruent. The estates always suspected that Habsburg-inspired reforms were more in the interests of the dynasty than of Germany as a whole. They therefore refused to cooperate with efforts on the parts of such rulers as **Maximilian I**, Charles V (1500–1558), and **Ferdinand I** to create some form of an imperial standing army and to centralize the administration of justice.

The German territorial states, for their part, did develop regional and local structures based on territorial divisions called circles (Germ.: *Kreis*), established in 1512. These were often quite effective in resolving some of the conflicts that the religious differences of the Reformation brought to Germany, as well as generally securing domestic peace. Subcommittees of the imperial estates and regular consultations among the imperial electors and their emperor helped develop policy on such matters as the use of mercenary forces abroad as well. But the drift toward the virtual independence of the territorial states continued. The Peace of Westphalia (1648), which closed the **Thirty Years' War**, gave the German princes a free hand in conducting their own foreign policies.

Wars with Louis XIV of France, who was eager to move French boundaries to the eastern banks of the Rhine, and a final, unsuccessful assault by the Ottoman Empire on central Europe, which ended in the second siege of **Vienna** in 1683, temporarily restored the Habsburg role in defending Germany's small and midsized states. The house of Austria itself continued to protect its imperial title, if only to keep some unfriendly power from capturing the office and orienting German policy away from Austrian interests. The Napoleonic Wars, however, put an end to any notion that the Holy Roman Empire served a useful political or military purpose. Following the provisions of the treaty of Lunéville (1801), the German states and Emperor Francis I (1768–1835) began indemnifying themselves at the expense of their weaker brethren to make up for French conquests along the Rhine and in **Italy**. In 1806, the victorious Bonaparte cobbled together the Confederation of the Rhine, abolishing about

300 political units of the old empire in the process. Knowing well what awaited him in Germany, Francis I had provided a new title for himself, Emperor of Austria, in 1804.

HÖRBIGER, ATTILA (1896–1987). One of Austria's greatest actors, Hörbiger belonged to one of **Vienna**'s great thespian dynasties. He was the brother and occasional stage partner of the equally accomplished Paul Hörbiger (1894–1981). The latter, however, specialized more in comic roles and often played with another Viennese master of that art, **Hans Moser**. Attila Hörbiger married the popular actress Paula Wessely (1907–2000) in 1935. He was the father of Elisabeth Orth and Christiane and Maresa Hörbiger, who have followed careers in film, in the **theater**, and in television.

Attila Hörbiger made his debut in 1919 and spent several years in provincial engagements before joining Vienna's **Theater in the Josefstadt** in 1928. He was a member of the company until 1950, when he joined the ensemble of the **Burgtheater**. He also played at the Vienna *Volkstheater* (People's Theater) and in Berlin. As an actor, Hörbiger was enormously versatile, at home in comedy as well as more serious works. He played both leading and minor roles, devoting scrupulous attention to both the vocal and physical inflections that gave his performances a unique intensity. One of his most notable parts was that of Everyman (Germ.: *Jedermann*) in the 1935–1938 **Salzburg Festival** productions of the **Hugo von Hofmannsthal** drama.

HORVATH, ÖDÖN (Edmund) VON (1901–1938). Dramatist, novelist, and essayist, Horvath was born in Fiume (Rijeka), then the seaport for the Hungarian half of the **Habsburg Empire**. His father was in the Habsburg diplomatic service. Moving with his parents from Belgrade to Budapest, he then went to Munich in 1913. By his own testimony, he wrote his first sentence in German at the age of 14. During most of **World War I**, he was in school in Pozsony (Bratislava). Shortly before the end of the conflict, he returned with his family to Budapest.

During the interwar years, Horvath lived in **Germany**, Hungary, and Austria, writing 17 plays between 1926 and 1936. An outspoken opponent of **Nazism**, he left Austria for Paris in 1938. Felled by a branch from a tree that had been struck by lightning, he died the same year.

Horvath has exercised considerable influence on modern Austrian writing, particularly that of the experimental **Graz Group**. Like them, he laid bare the artificiality of language and its communicative deficiencies in works such as *Don Juan Kommt aus dem Krieg* (*Don Juan Comes Home from the War*, 1937). He was a harsh critic of the values prevalent among the German and Austrian petty bourgeoisie, whom he saw driven by cynical egoism and insecurity, and as lacking common decency. This is especially true of his male figures, as seen in his best-known play, *Geschichten aus dem Wiener Wald* (*Tales from the Vienna Woods*). Completed in 1931, it was first performed in **Vienna** before unreceptive audiences in 1948. His women either know too much about men to have a comfortable relationship with them, or are victims of male psychological, often physical, brutality. Because so many of his best works deal with the lesser people of the central European world, he is sometimes said to have put the 19th-century Viennese popular comedy of **Johann Nestroy** on a modern footing. However, although Nestroy's work took on an increasingly bitter tone, it never achieved quite the acerbic pitch that Horvath often reached. Horvath also wrote several works that picked apart Nazism and its followers. Among them were *Godless Youth* (*Jugend ohne Gott*, 1937) and *A Child of Our Times* (*Ein Kind unserer Zeit*, 1938). *See also* LITERATURE; THEATER.

HUNDERTWASSER, FRIEDRICH (1928–2000). Born Friedrich Stowasser, *Sto* meaning *Hundert* or 100 in any number of Slavic languages, Hundertwasser was perhaps the best known artist of late-20th-century Austria. Gifted with a highly fanciful visual and coloristic imagination, he made the spiral the center of his artistic vision. Though the bulk of his career was in **Vienna**, he traveled widely and made such global concerns as ecology, endangered species, world peace, and opposition to Austrian membership in the European Union part of his intellectual agenda.

Hundertwasser, whose first major artistic success was at the Venice Biennale of 1962, worked productively in many genres of **art**, among them painting, graphics, and **architecture**. He has left his imprint on Vienna with his Hundertwasser House (1985), actually a municipal apartment complex that he designed as an alternative to what he regarded as the faceless character of modern architecture. Located in the Third District (*Landstrasse*) of the city, its startlingly brilliant hues, irregular outlines, and seemingly random juxtaposition of style have made it a major tourist attraction. He also took on more conventional commissions, such as postage-stamp design for the government.

– I –

IMMIGRATION. As part of the multinational **Habsburg Empire**, Austria has historically absorbed a wide variety of immigrants and temporary foreign residents. The Habsburg court drew countless "foreigners" into its service, including some very noteworthy ones: **Eugene of Savoy**, the greatest military commander that the dynasty ever had, was one; another was the statesman and diplomat Prince **Klemens von Metternich**, from the Rhineland in **Germany**. Hungarians, Poles, Czechs, Hungarians, Italians, Croatians, Spaniards, Netherlanders, and **Jews** were also, at one time or another, advisors, ministers, and various kinds of aids to Habsburg rulers and their families. Commercial relations in the 17th and 18th centuries with southeastern Europe also brought Turkish and other Levantine merchants to Vienna, some of whom stayed on.

Mass internal immigration to the Austrian lands in the multinational Habsburg state was a by-product of 19th-century **industrialization**. People of many linguistic backgrounds sought factory and construction jobs, small handicraft work, or domestic service in **Vienna** and just beyond the city in **Lower Austria**. The largest number of new arrivals to Vienna as its population grew sharply toward the end of the 19th century came from Bohemia and Moravia. By 1900, there were around 100,000 in the city, along with substantial numbers of Poles, Italians, Hungarians, and Germans from the north. Within two to three generations, these groups were largely German-speaking and assimilated.

A steady immigration flow went on from after **World War I** until about 1935. Between 1919 and 1936, 234,000 foreigners had become Austrian citizens, though not always by the same procedure. Many were from one-time lands of the Habsburg monarchy, though these numbers were somewhat offset by people who chose to leave Austria to become nationals in the new sovereign states of east central and southeastern Europe. Especially striking, in view of their later history in Austria, was the number of Jews, who had begun fleeing pogroms in Galicia in 1914–1915. By 1925, 21,000 Jews had been naturalized.

The tectonic political and demographic shifts in Europe after **World War II** brought masses of economic and political refugees to Austria along with large numbers of formal **asylum** supplicants. Most were from Eastern Europe. Almost 400,000 ethnic Germans came from Czechoslovakia, Poland, Romania, and Yugoslavia. Around 29,000 Hungarians remained after fleeing their failed uprising in 1956. The Soviet suppression of Czechoslovakia's deviant communist regime in 1968 sent a substantial groups of Czechs over their border westward; Poland's introduction of martial rule in 1981–1982 to put down labor unrest resulted in a community of about 24,000 Poles in Austria. The militarized breakup of Yugoslavia in the early 1990s added around 56,000 Yugoslavs to an already large community.

By 1990, Austria had absorbed around 650,000 foreigners into a population of about 7,250,000. Swelling the former figure considerably, though accidentally, were around 260,000 "guest workers." Most of these were from Turkey and Yugoslavia, and their jobs allowed them to remain indefinitely. All in all, 10 percent of the Austrian population in 1993 had been born outside of the country.

The countries of origin for Austria's immigrants were even then changing. In 2001, roughly one-third of Austria's foreigners had come from Muslim communities around the world. The largest number were still from Turkey and Bosnia, but more were coming from the Middle East and North Africa. About 80,000 had become citizens. Nor were these changes domestically tension free. Even in the early 1990s, many Austrians had deep worries about the impact of continued immigration on their extensive social **welfare** programs and on their cultural and political norms. Membership in the **European Union** and the opening of borders to one another's citizens, a condition that Austria accepted in principle in 1997, provoked much concern about an influx of impoverished and cheap labor into the country, particularly from eastern and southeastern Europe. The

Freedom Party of Austria has remained particularly vociferous on the subject. Under such pressures, Austria has continued to require 10 years of continued residence before an alien may apply for citizenship, though there are stated exceptions to this rule. He or she must also have completed state-supported German-**language** instruction and citizenship training courses. Voters, however, had discovered by 2006 that illegal aliens have their uses, particularly for domestic home care. *See also* ISLAM; SCHÜSSEL, WOLFGANG.

INDUSTRIALIZATION. The hallmark of the Industrial Revolution was the mechanization of labor in factory production. The process in the Austrian lands of the **Habsburg Empire** began with textiles: silk weaving facilities opened in **Vienna** in 1619 and in Walpersdorf in **Lower Austria** in 1666. Lower Austria also began manufacturing cotton and paper around the same time. After 1672, wool was manufactured in **Linz**.

Seventeenth-century **Styria** was also a site for ironware manufacture, especially weapons for Habsburg troops fighting the Ottoman Empire. With the ebbing of Turkish military prowess in the 18th century, Austrian-made armaments were redirected to, and sold well in, **trade** abroad. Technological advances in mining iron and salt greatly furthered industrialization throughout the Habsburg domains in the 18th century. The presence of a growing labor force, the result of a population boom, helped too. Most crucial, however, was the Habsburg government's resolve to augment its income. For both Empress **Maria Theresa** and her son **Joseph II**, manufacturing was a means to that end. The latter was quite willing to upend traditional socioeconomic structures to further industry and commerce; though he did not succeed, Joseph tried to end restrictions on production and trade with which artisanal guilds had long sheltered their livelihoods.

The greatest growth in textile production and industry as a whole came in Bohemia, Moravia, and the part of Silesia still under Habsburg rule after the Seven Years' War. Together the three provinces had more manufacturing establishments in 1770 than did all of the other Habsburg lands combined. But important developments also took place in Lower Austria and Vienna. Maria Theresa took over failing producers and nationalized them, often successfully. The

Augarten Porcelain Works, founded in 1718 in an outlying district of Vienna, became a state enterprise in 1744. By 1783, emissaries from such faraway places as Morocco were eager to inspect its production techniques. Sugar manufacture, an industry that grew exponentially in the decades to come, started in Lower Austria around 1780 with cane imported from the West Indies.

Manufacture of iron goods and textiles continued in the early decades of the 19th century and even expanded. Paper production was mechanized. By the 1830s, sugar was being processed from local sugar beets, lowering the retail price markedly. Chemicals, especially for dyes, soaps, matches, and even rubber goods were also available.

Yet for all the reserves of iron ore and coal in the Habsburg domains, Austria included, the state was still economically disadvantaged after the Napoleonic Wars. England's textile manufacture surpassed that of any other European country, but even parts of Germany to the north had a more developed industrial base than the Habsburg Empire. Artisanal workshops were still very much the rule in the monarchy's holdings; factory production, the exception. Investment capital also remained in short supply. Entrepreneurship was socially suspect among aristocrats and would-be aristocrats, of whom there were many, and **transportation** was too fragmented to supply commodities efficiently for manufacture of scale. The overwhelmingly agrarian character of the general population kept discretionary income low and consumption standards modest. The pattern haunted the monarchy until its end in 1918.

Industrialization of scale in the Austrian lands took place only after the **Revolutions of 1848**. With serfdom abolished, **agricultural** labor was free to market itself to the highest bidder. An increasingly elaborate system of **banks** matched investment capital with industrial needs. The expansion of **railroads** gradually made shipment of commodities to factories more reliable. The bulk of Austrian industry, particularly its more specialized branches, was largely housed around **Vienna**, with lesser centers in **Styria** and **Vorarlberg**.

Production of iron and steel flourished, as did manufacture of related metal goods—wire, tools, including farm implements, and even motor cars. Between 1898 and 1912, six automobile companies were in operation around Vienna. Electrical goods; textiles, especially in the west of the Austrian lands; and paper mills were also significant sectors in the **economy**. Abundant new construction throughout the Habsburg Empire relied on brick works in Vienna and cement production in the Tyrol. Nevertheless, Austrian manufacturing in the 19th century developed inconsistently. It took place in three stages: the first two, 1850–1860 and 1867–1873, were aborted by serious recessions. The last upswing, between 1896 and 1913, preceded a catastrophic war.

The collapse of the Habsburg Empire following **World War I** dramatically reversed these advances. A lively interest in American and German mass production techniques and labor force rationalization existed in the new country, but on-the-ground conditions more than offset it. Except for iron ore, primary industry in the Austrian lands of the former monarchy had depended on other Habsburg crown lands for raw materials. The newly independent Austria had only .5 percent of the former empire's coal resources. Government policies were often counterproductive. To keep people working, the Socialist regime governing the country in 1919 took over several key industries such as chemicals, heavy metals, and textiles; wary investors withheld their capital. The First Republic never would put the improvement of Austrian industrial technology high on its list of priorities. By the summer of 1919, major industry was at a standstill.

In 1923, Austrian industry briefly reemerged from its slump; it entered the international market in a small way, and unemployment dropped. Positive though they were, these developments were short-lived. The German economic takeover of major Austrian industries began in 1925 when the German United Steel Corporation (*Vereinigte Stahlwerke AG*) acquired a majority holding in the Austrian–Alpine Mineworks Society (*Österreichisch–Alpinen Montangesellschaft*).

As the world economic crisis began unfolding in 1929, Austrian industry, which was at the mercy of domestic banks for development credits, plunged downward once again. Personnel layoffs in the hundreds and occasionally thousands started immediately: 125,850 people were without work in October 929; two months later, there were 226,567 unemployed. By 1930, 20 percent of Austrians eligible for unemployment compensation were drawing it, some 284,543 men and women.

The **Nazi** regime promoted Austrian industrialization aggressively from the **Anschluss** until about 1943. Eager to hide steel and other war-sensitive manufactures from Allied bombing raids, the Nazis established and expanded existing factories in **Styria** and **Upper Austria**, especially around Adolf Hitler's hometown of **Linz**.

Post–**World War II** Austrian industry quickly resumed its upward growth. **Marshall Plan** investment capital helped in the first few years. A period of close government regulation of major industry in the late 1940s was loosened considerably in the 1950s, because the dominant **political parties**, the **Socialist Party of Austria** and the **People's Party of Austria**, differed sharply on the ways of managing a quasi-**nationalized** economy. Market demand, both domestic and foreign, was high for ferrous metal products and basic construction materials to be used in rebuilding Europe; Austrian manufacturing profited accordingly.

Although energy supplies were initially low, after 1946 steel plants were functioning in Upper and Lower Austria and Styria. Aluminum production resumed that same year in Upper Austria, as did automotive manufacturing in the town of Steyr. Papermaking, especially important as an export, and rayon factories reopened around the Upper Austrian town of Lenzing in 1947. By 1949, the textile industry, concentrated in **Vorarlberg**, was in full swing. Steel production had also reached prewar levels, although rolled steel products were still lagging behind.

Austrian heavy industry in the last three decades of the 20th century faced serious competition from abroad. The steel industry survived, in part by manufacturing for highly specialized niches, and by adopting cost-saving techniques such as the LD-*Verfahren* (LD-Process), first operational in 1953. One traditional manufacturer after another, however, has disappeared, either because of fiscal problems or price-cutting by counterparts abroad, where labor costs are lower. Emblematic of the change was the takeover in 2003 of Grundig, the venerable but bankrupt Austrian electrical goods manufacturer, by a Taiwanese conglomerate.

INNITZER, THEODORE (1875–1955). Archbishop of **Vienna** from 1932 to 1955 and a cardinal from 1933, Innitzer had a long scholarly career behind him when he assumed those offices. In 1911, he became a professor of New Testament exegesis at the **University of Vienna**, where he also functioned as its rector in 1928–1929. He also served as minister for social affairs (1929–1930) in a government that generally favored middle-class interests. Here Innitzer was a spokesman for low-income pensioners.

Innitzer was generally a supporter of the **Austro-Fascist** regimes of **Engelbert Dollfuss** and **Kurt Schuschnigg**. On 18 March 1938, with Adolf Hitler's takeover of Austria an accomplished fact, Innitzer and other Austrian bishops presented a declaration of loyalty to the new regime. They thought that such an action would preserve the position of the church. Meeting with Hitler, Innitzer received assurances from the Nazi dictator that the **Catholic** role in Austrian education would continue.

These hopes faded quickly. On 8 October 1938, bands of the Hitler Youth and Austrian Sturmabteilung (SA) broke into the archbishop's palace in Vienna. Innitzer shifted his approach somewhat, establishing an agency to help "Non-Aryan Catholics" even during the Nazi dictatorship in Austria. Following the end of **World War II**, he reestablished the Austrian Catholic Academy and worked to increase the role of the laity in the church.

INNSBRUCK. The capital of the **Tyrol**, Innsbruck is dominated by the various alpine ranges, which all but surround it. After Grenoble in France, it is the largest city in the **Alps**. The Inn River basin, within which Innsbruck sits, has been settled in some form for 3,000 years. The Roman Via Claudia, laid out in 46–47 CE, ran near the outskirts of the present municipality. The Romans had an administrative and military settlement in Wilten, which lies immediately to the southwest.

The Old Town, which is today the center of Innsbruck, sits south of one of several bridges over the Inn. The original structure was erected in the second half of the 12th century by the Bavarian Counts of Andechs, who had a market settlement in the region. The area had developed into a town by the beginning of the 13th century. The counts of the Tyrol acquired Innsbruck in 1263. It passed from them to the house of **Habsburg** exactly a century later.

In the 15th and 16th centuries, Innsbruck became the economic and political center of the province and a favorite residence of its

Habsburg rulers. **Maximilian I** gave the city some of its most important monuments, such as the Golden Roof, a glittering loggia covered with over 2,000 gilded copper tiles added to the front built by the counts of Tyrol. Though Maximilian himself is not buried at Innsbruck, he left plans suggesting an elaborate cenotaph surrounded with 24 alabaster reliefs and 28 oversized bronze figures. This his successors installed in the Franciscan court church. In the 18th century **Maria Theresa**, who was also partial to Innsbruck, built the Imperial Court Palace from an earlier structure erected by Maximilian and a predecessor, Archduke Siegmund the Rich (1427–1496). Just beyond the city lies Ambras Castle, remodeled by Archduke Ferdinand II (1529–1595) both for his wife, Philippine Welser, the bourgeois daughter of a leading merchant family of Augsburg, and for his curiosity collection, one of Europe's most remarkable.

During the Napoleonic Wars, Innsbruck was under the control of the Bavarians. Reverting to Habsburg government in 1815, it increased in importance as an alpine transit point in the modern era, with the construction of locomotive connections with Munich (1856–1858), through the Brenner Pass to Bolzano (1864–1867) and to the west. With the development of the **railroads** came the establishment of textile and food processing industries in the region. Heavily bombed between 1943 and 1945 in **World War II**, it was rebuilt and much expanded in the latter half of the 20th century. Today it is among Austria's most vigorous economic centers, with a thriving **tourist** industry and a diversified manufacturing base. *See also* HOFER, ANDREAS.

ISLAM. The position of Islam in the Second Austrian Republic is closely tied to the history of the **Habsburg** monarchy's relations with the Muslim Ottoman Empire. From the 15th to the beginning of the 18th centuries, the two polities contested the control of central and southeastern Europe from **Vienna** down the **Danube River** to Belgrade.

It was only after 1683, when a final Ottoman siege was broken by an international coalition of Christian forces, that Ottoman sultans became Habsburg partners in international power politics and accommodation to Islam in Austria began. Though worship at home or in other informal settings remained the norm for Muslim residents and visitors to Vienna for decades, **Joseph II**'s Edict of Toleration (1781) allowed Muslims to exercise their faith throughout the Habsburg lands.

As a way of making both their **military** and diplomatic contacts with the Ottoman Empire more effective, Habsburg governments cultivated serious academic study of their one-time antagonists. Under the leadership of such scholars and writers as Joseph von Hammer-Purgstall (1774–1856), Vienna became one of Europe's main centers for oriental scholarship in the 19th century.

Further institutional and attitudinal adjustments to Islam in Austria followed the Habsburg occupation of Bosnia in 1878 and the outright annexation of the province, which had around 300,000 Muslim residents by 1908. Bosnian Muslims become one of the elite forces in the **Dual Monarchy**'s army. Bosnians served Emperor **Franz Joseph** as bodyguards; imams conducted the troops' devotions. Plans for a large mosque in Vienna were in place by 1916 but fell by the wayside in the economic chaos of **World War I** and its aftermath.

A law of 1912 that certified Islam as an official religious community carried over from the Habsburg Empire to the Second Republic, in which the number of Muslims grew exponentially after 1960. Bosnians accounted for a new wave of **immigration**, followed by Turks in search of economic opportunities. Muslims from a variety of Middle Eastern states have settled in Vienna as well. Altogether, Muslims were roughly 10–15 percent of the city population by 2000.

The 1912 law was expanded in 1979 and again in 1988, when all schools of Islamic religious law were declared operative in the community. Officially charged with representing interests and affairs of Muslims in Austria before the government, the Islamic Religious Community in Austria brings together the many different Islamic communities. It has customarily supported integrationist policies. The first mosque on Austrian soil opened in 1979. The kingdom of Saudi Arabia financed the exterior structure; money for the building interior came from other Muslim governments.

Islamic and non-Islamic relations in Austria have sometimes been strained and even hostile, particularly as some local Muslims have publicly endorsed worldwide terrorism. Nor have intra-Muslim relations been wholly cordial. A Turkish Association, founded in 1990 and directly supervised by the Office of Religious Affairs of the Turkish State, has contributed to intra-Muslim tension. Control over religious **education** has often been contentious, especially after 1983, when Austrian schools started to provide such instruction to Muslim students. See also COFFEEHOUSE; RELIGION.

ITALY, RELATIONS WITH. As Holy Roman emperors until Napoleon put an end to the office in 1806, **Habsburgs** were titular sovereigns in several principalities throughout the Italian peninsula. In the 16th century, the Spanish branch of the house of Austria occupied and administered Milan, Naples, and Sardinia. This arrangement came to an end with the extinction of the Habsburg line that ruled from Madrid; throughout the 18th century these regions and several others in Italy were passed back and forth among France, the Austrian Habsburgs, and Spain, ruled by a line of the French Bourbons following the War of the Spanish Succession (1701–1714). Tuscany came under Habsburg control in 1737; Habsburg cadet lines ruled Parma and Modena as well.

The **Congress of Vienna** restored these areas, along with Lombardy, to the Habsburg Empire at the end of the Napoleonic Wars and added Venetia to Emperor Francis I's lands for good measure. Having such a major territorial position on the Italian peninsula, governments in Vienna put a great deal of military and diplomatic energy into defending it. The architect of the post-Napoleonic settlement, **Klemens von Metternich**, worked at the Congresses of Troppau and Laibach (Ljubljana) in 1821 and 1822 to reinforce alliances with Prussia, **Russia** and, unsuccessfully, Great Britain, to suppress antimonarchical and nationalist sedition in Italy.

The unification of Italy, largely completed in 1870, did not really change thinking about Italy in Habsburg governments. The new kingdom of Italy, ruled by the house of Sardinia–Piedmont, was the first national polity to fall away from the Habsburg Empire in the 19th century. Nationalism had led to a national state, the emblematic worst-case scenario for many of Emperor **Franz Joseph**'s advisors. Having once targeted individuals, movements, and individual principalities, such as the kingdom of Sardinia–Piedmont, as its enemies in Italy, Habsburg ministers now had a whole Italian state to mistrust and dislike. Only a few Italian lands still remained with Austria, but they had to be defended: Venetia, at the head of the Adriatic just north of Trieste and Fiume (Rjeka); Austrian and Hungarian commercial ports; and an increasingly important imperial naval base at Pola. There was also the **South Tyrol**, a region that gave the Habsburgs a strategic foothold in the Italian peninsula itself.

Regardless of the Kingdom of Italy's entrance into the Triple Alliance with Austria–Hungary and **Germany** (1882), Italy was enemy number one in the eyes of Austrian military and diplomatic planning even after the turn of the 20th century; Serbia assumed that role only shortly before **World War I**. Italy's declaration of war on Austria–Hungary in 1915 only confirmed long-held expectations in Vienna.

The loss of the largely German-speaking South Tyrol to Italy after World War I infuriated may Austrians, particularly in the northern part of the province still left to the new Austrian republic. The government in Vienna, however, put territorial pretensions aside to cultivate **trade** and **military** relations with the Italian dictator, Benito Mussolini (1883–1945). These contacts became especially crucial for Austria after Adolf Hitler became the German chancellor in 1933, and Austrian independence seemed even more precarious. The Rome Protocols, signed in 1934 by Italy, Hungary, and Austria, gave the latter two economic preference in the Italian market. Austrians also hoped to get weapons from Italy to compensate for limitations the country had accepted in the **Treaty of St. Germain**. The Franco–Italian Military Accords of 1935, though never formally adopted in either country, promised Austria military assistance in case of German attack.

Mussolini's invasion of Ethiopia in 1936 and his African adventures generally earned him the enmity of the entire League of Nations and made an Austrian alliance with him altogether counterproductive. Neither France nor Great Britain, who had the most to lose from Italian expansion in Africa and the Middle East, were willing to do anything for Austria. Mussolini turned to Hitler for support, thus removing any possibility that Italy would oppose the **Anschluss**, which did go forward in 1938.

Relations between republican Italy and the Second Austrian Republic after 1945 were also contentious, and not only between Vienna and Rome. The problem of the large German-speaking minority in the South Tyrol also stirred up passions in the Austrian Tyrol, which, like all Austrian provinces, was constitutionally entitled to conduct foreign relations up to a certain level with states that impinge on its borders. The Austrian Tyrol, particularly its governors, who were all from the **Austrian People's Party**, devoted much effort to bringing the two lands together again. When the issue of German minority rights came before the **United Nations** in 1960, Austrian Tyroleans were among the negotiators. An agreement signed between Austria and Italy in 1969 called for a number of cross-border initiatives, including joint meetings of the two regional parliaments.

Though the Italian and Austrian constitutions treat the question of provincial participation in foreign affairs very differently, efforts to promote cooperative relationships between both Tyrols continued after 1992, when Rome and Vienna brought their larger quarrels to an end. Both sides have willingly fostered a nonpolitical identification of a common Tyrolean "region" since 1998. Such an arrangement—**Salzburg** also has one with Berchtesgaden and Trauenstein on the boundary with Bavaria—enables localities to address practical cross-border problems quickly and efficiently, though the larger issues of the volume of transit traffic and the noise and pollution that accompany it are still under discussion.

For all the contentiousness and occasional serious violence that the South Tyrol question raised in postwar Italy and Austria, the period since 1945 has been marked by considerable efforts by both countries to overcome nationalist resentment on both sides dating back to World War I and before. The Austrian **Alpbach Forum** opened useful discussions among scholars, students, intellectuals, and politicians on national differences and similarities. Italian and Austrian historians were quick to reestablish cooperative research arrangements that had existed between the two states even before 1914. Both countries have sponsored many serious conferences and publications on relations between them. Austria and Italy have worked together in international organizations, beginning in 1948 in the Organization for Cooperation and Economic Development (OCSE) and, by 1995, in the **European Union** (EU) itself. In 2001, the Italian parliament made it possible for Austrian citizens who were in lands annexed to Italy after World War I to hold Italian citizenship as well. Italy remains a very important trading partner of Austria; occupying second place in Austrian commerce with EU states after Germany. In 1998, all three states formally opened their borders for free trade among themselves, as required of EU member states.

Possible points of trouble still remain. Some Austrians grumbled publicly about the sanctions imposed by the EU in 2000 on the participation of **Jörg Haider**'s right-wing **Freedom Party of Austria** in a coalition with the **Austrian People's Party**, but failing to do the same in 2001 when Italian premier Silvio Berlusconi included neo-fascists in his government. In negotiating a more comprehensive constitution for the EU in 2003, Austria has frequently sided with the newer and smaller members of the EU. Italy, on the other hand, with Berlusconi as its spokesman, stood with the larger and initial member states of the EU, particularly Germany and France. By 2004, 10 percent of the student body at the University of **Innsbruck** came from Italy, most German speakers from the South Tyrol or the Upper Adige, whose fraternities still foster the politics of resentment. But with foreign relations between Austria and Italy now often mediated by the EU, serious friction has been avoided. *See also* FOREIGN POLICY.

– J –

JELINEK, ELFRIEDE (1946–). Born in **Styria**, Jelinek received wide-ranging aesthetic training as a student of fine arts, music, and theater history. Her mercilessly critical fiction and writing for the stage negate all possibility of moral values and altruistic action in human life. Although she has been strongly identified with **women**'s issues in her work—her *The Pianist (Die Klavierspielerin*, 1983) won international acclaim as a **film** in 2001—Jelinek has as much contempt for her own sex as for males. The sexual tensions that often underscore her work lead to little more than humiliation of all her protagonists. Her relentless cynicism is further underscored by prose in which she seemingly trivializes works from the German literary tradition, which she interfaces with strikingly dissonant materials found in popular culture. Tabloids, TV shows, and mass entertainment of all sorts are favorite targets. Jelinek won the Nobel Prize for **literature** in 2004.

JESUITS (SOCIETY OF JESUS). The order was founded in 1534 by a Spanish soldier-turned-cleric, Ignatius Loyola (1491–1556), who vowed to devote his life to bringing those won over to the **Protestant** Reformation back into the **Catholic** fold. Accepted as an order by the papacy in 1540, it was, and is, under direct papal supervision. Throughout much of the 16th and 17th centuries, the Jesuits were eagerly patronized by members of the **Habsburg** dynasty, who saw the new brotherhood as a useful tool for the preservation and reinstitution of Catholicism in their lands.

In 1551, **Ferdinand I** called the Jesuits to **Vienna,** where they established a college. They proceeded to establish schools and colleges in **Innsbruck** (1562), **Graz** (1572), **Linz** (ca. 1600), and eventually **Klagenfurt.** In the first two cases, their colleges developed into universities that still function today.

Until the 18th century, Jesuits served as confessors to many members of the ruling house and as teachers as well as pastors and preachers. Their most important representative in Vienna in the 16th century was the Netherlander Peter Canisius (1521–1597), whose new Catholic catechism Ferdinand I specifically endorsed. Central to their influence were the high educational and moral standards they set for themselves, a sharp contrast to the corruption in Rome and in the traditional Catholic hierarchy that had inspired Martin Luther's protests in 1517.

It was the Jesuits who were largely responsible for modernizing **education** in the Austrian lands in ways prescribed by Renaissance humanism. Sound religious practice could come only through a sound understanding of language; the order's pedagogy laid great stress on scholarship in classical tongues. Nevertheless, by the middle of the 18th century, the religious orientation of the Jesuits and their hold on the organs of government began to run afoul of proponents of the Enlightenment in Austria. Their authority over education and censorship was largely removed as part of the process of centralizing power in the hands of the state. In 1773, the Jesuit order was dissolved in the Habsburg lands and its property confiscated. It was reestablished in 1814. *See also* RELIGION.

JEWS. There is reason to think that Jews may have been living in and around the future city of **Vienna** when the Romans arrived there around 15 BCE. However, the history of the Jews in the Austrian lands replicates the history of the diaspora in many other areas of the world—acceptance in varying degrees, followed by rejection, often violent, followed by acceptance once more. In dealing with the earlier phases of this history, one must be especially careful not to generalize about Jews in "Austria," because the chronology of their experiences differed considerably. Jews were driven out of **Lower Austria** in 1420–1421, but out of **Carinthia** and **Styria** in 1496.

It is the Jews of Vienna, however, who were most tightly linked to the generality of Austrian history. Their original quarter was in the First District of the city. One of its streets is still called the Judengasse (Street of the Jews). In 1622, the community was formally assigned a place to live, the Leopoldstadt, today Vienna's Second District, still a place with a significant Jewish population. The **Habsburg** emperors used Jewish taxes and credit lines to help finance both the dynasty's wars and its construction projects. Such policies, however, did not exempt the community from serious discrimination. Emperor Leopold I (1640–1705) expelled them from the city altogether in 1669–1670, blaming them for the wars and plague then afflicting both Vienna and the **Holy Roman Empire**.

The fortunes of the **Habsburg Empire**'s Jews took a sharp turn for the better under the reign of Emperor **Joseph II**. Interested in exploiting the full productive potential of all his people, Joseph allowed Jews to engage in almost any trade. Restrictions on dress and access to public places were abolished, though the special tax on Jews, to be paid every two weeks, was retained. Jews had new obligations as well; they were now liable for military service and had to purchase hereditary last names. No synagogue was allowed in the city until 1832. Jews were also forbidden from entering the legal profession or civil service. They also could not buy land.

However, allowed to engage in finance, handicrafts, medicine, and private tutoring, Jews came to Vienna in larger numbers, many as household servants, artisans, and laborers. They mingled with the dominant non-Jewish majority, and often converted. For women this step was a way of legitimizing children whose fathers were Christian. By the end of the 19th century, when almost all professions were open to them, including the lower rungs of the civil service, Jews made up about 12 percent of the Viennese population. Although that percentage had dropped by the beginning of **World War I** because of **immigration** of largely Christian populations from other parts of the Habsburg Empire, the numbers rose, from around 99,450 in 1890 to approximately 175,300 by 1910.

Jews or people of Jewish extraction played a major role in the cultural explosion associated with fin de siècle Vienna. **Sigmund Freud** achieved world stature. Composers such as **Gustav Mahler** and **Arnold Schoenberg**; writers such as **Hugo von Hofmannsthal, Arthur Schnitzler**, and **Karl Kraus**; and **theatrical** luminaries such as **Max Reinhardt** made central contributions to these developments. Jews were also prominent in the construction of the Austrian **Social Democratic Party**; **Viktor Adler** was only one among many.

The stunning success of Jews such as the Rothschilds and the **Wittgensteins** in business and finance, and the presence of more recent immigrants to the city from other areas of the empire, who competed with the poorer classes of the city for work, fostered the rise of political anti-Semitism in Vienna at the end of the 19th century. An important spokesman for these sentiments was the city's famous mayor, **Karl Lueger**, who became the leader of the **Christian Social Party**. These views became even more virulent in the 1920s and 1930s, as Austria was in a state of near permanent financial crisis and serious unemployment.

With the **Anschluss** of 1938, the Jewish community of Vienna, which numbered around 170,000, and of the entire First Republic became the target of **Nazi** ethnic cleansing. Anti-Semitic rioting by Austrians was, if anything, more vicious than corresponding activities in Germany. Offices of the Gestapo (*Geheimestaatspolizei*, State Secret Police) were set up throughout Austria shortly after the German occupation began. Emigration was encouraged. Many Jews quickly left Austria. Among them were some who had fled Nazi Germany after Adolf Hitler became chancellor in 1933, in the hope that Austria would be a more hospitable German-speaking environment. Of those who remained in the city, around 65,000 were killed. Of the approximately 33,000 Jewish firms and other businesses in Vienna, 7,000 were broken up, 21,236 were shut down, and 4,36l were "Arayanized," including the famous Ferris wheel of the **Prater** and the tradition-laden Gerngross department store. Austria has relaxed its once carefully circumscribed measures setting the conditions for the **restitution** of property confiscated or otherwise seized by its Nazi government after 1938.

Today there are between 7,000 and 8,000 Jews in Vienna, in part the result of emigration during the 1970s and 1980s from the Soviet bloc. The original first synagogue of the 19th century has been restored and reopened. There is a new Jewish museum in another part of the district that enables visitors to trace the long history of the community in the Austrian capital. Jews have again risen to considerable prominence in several areas of Austrian life, perhaps the most notable being the former federal chancellor, **Bruno Kreisky**. Although the question of how much anti-Semitism exists in Austria remains a lively one, it is also worth noting that significant numbers of the population are vocal critics of such ideas. *See also* CREDITANSTALT BANKVEREIN; HERZL, THEODORE; RELIGION.

JONAS, FRANZ (1899–1974). Mayor of **Vienna** from 1951 to 1965, when he was elected **president** of the Second Austrian Republic, Jonas played a crucial role in both the physical rebuilding of the capital and the political reconstruction of Austria generally. He had solid socialist credentials, having served as the secretary of the district branch of the **Social Democratic Workers' Party** in Floridsdorf, a socialist redoubt in Vienna, from 1932 to 1934. He spent the year 1935–1936 in prison for his political activities. In 1946, Jonas became district leader of the **Socialist Party of Austria** in Floridsdorf; from 1948 to 1951, he supervised the municipal Bureau of Nutrition and Housing.

Jonas was elected Austrian president twice. Running the second time in 1971, he defeated **Kurt Waldheim**. Jonas did not, however, live to complete his second term. While in office, he followed a generally conciliatory policy toward all of Austria's constitutionally recognized **political parties** and contributed significantly to easing ideological tensions on all sides. He followed this path even after the contest in 1971 that left Austria for the first time since the end of **World War II** with a president and federal **chancellor, Bruno Kreisky**, from the same party.

JOSEPH II, HOLY ROMAN EMPEROR, KING OF BOHEMIA AND HUNGARY (1741–1790). Few **Habsburg** rulers had so immediate and direct an impact on their lands as did Joseph II. Few also aroused so much controversy and heated opposition. Though his formal education was relatively conventional, Joseph began to think seriously about improving the situation of Habsburg government and its subjects as a very young man. But as long as his mother, Empress **Maria Theresa**, lived he was constrained by her wishes, which reflected her increasingly cautious, even passive, temperament. Though Joseph was elected German king in 1764 and was named his mother's coregent a year later, he had very little influence on domestic policy. He redirected some of his energies into a series of journeys that he took throughout Europe in the 1760s and 1770s, which further stimulated his thoughts about reform.

Once Maria Theresa had passed from the scene, Joseph pressed for far-reaching changes in the governance and institutions of the monarchy and its culture. His goals—the centralization of sovereign power in **Vienna** and increasing the productivity of his peoples everywhere—were very much the same as those of the late empress. Many segments of society, however, were both offended and threatened by the single-minded way in which he pursued his aims. The landed nobility throughout the Habsburg territories were politically and economically aggrieved by his efforts to curb the powers of local estates and to force them to pay regular taxes on their properties and incomes. The **Catholic** church opposed his measures to turn men and women in cloistered religious vocations into economically active subjects and to make clerical **education** the responsibility of secular authority. In Hungary, always the most resistant to Habsburg efforts to centralize monarchical rule, his requirement that German be the administrative **language** of his realms was hotly contested by the nobility of the Hungarian national estates, for whom Latin remained the language of true rulers. His decision to abolish the traditional counties into which Hungary had been divided and to replace them with newer and more rationally structured administrative districts was also much resented.

By the time of Joseph's death, important areas of the monarchy, Hungary and the Austrian Netherlands among them, were in open rebellion against his rule. However, he left a legacy of programmatic reform that served at least as a partial model for those of his successors who had to confront many of the issues he had. Chief among

Emperor Franz Joseph's bedroom in the Schönbrunn Palace. Courtesy of Austrian Cultural Forum

Gross Glockner Peak in Carinthia. Courtesy of Austrian Cultural Forum

Loge entrance of the Burgtheater in Vienna. Courtesy of Austrian Cultural Forum

Monastery of Melk in Lower Austria. Courtesy of Austrian Cultural Forum

Mozart's residence in Vienna. Courtesy of Austrian Cultural Forum

Secession building in Vienna. Courtesy of Austrian Cultural Forum

Interior of church in Stams in the Tyrol. Courtesy of Austrian Cultural Forum

Traditional wine house in the Burgenland. Courtesy of Austrian Cultural Forum

these was his abolition of serfdom (1781) and his Edict of Religious Toleration (1781), which applied to the Greek Orthodox, **Protestant**, and **Jewish** subjects of his realms. He also took important steps in the modernization and professionalization of the Habsburg bureaucracy. *See also* ECONOMY; HABSBURG EMPIRE; RELIGION.

JUDICIARY. The judicial and legal system of modern Austria is heavily rooted in historical practice. **Joseph II** effectively introduced the principle of equality before the law in 1781. But it was the constitution of the Austrian half of the Dual Monarchy, promulgated in 1867, that laid out the basic structure of a judiciary and legal system that carried over into both the First and Second Austrian Republics. Judges were, and are, nominated by ministers of justice and confirmed by heads of state. Their duty is to interpret the law as it is written, not based on what individuals or **government** authorities claim it says. They are removable from office only after a judicial investigation and can be transferred only for disciplinary reasons or as part of some institutional reorganization.

Today's highest court in Austria is the Constitutional Court (*Verfassungsgerichtshof*), which came into being under the First Republic but was inoperative after 1933. The Second Republic re-created it to protect the **constitutional** rights of citizens, especially from abuse of authority. Administrative courts (*Verwaltungsgerichtshof*), first created in the Austrian lands in 1875, initially hear and often adjudicate such complaints. If the case revolves around basic constitutional issues, it may move on to the constitutional court specifically charged to prevent abuses of power and authority.

Criminal proceedings take place at several levels. The 1867 structure brought back into practice trial by jury, a custom with a long ancestry in the Germanic legal tradition. This arrangement was reintroduced in 1951. In very serious cases, juries pronounce guilt or innocence; the panel of judges presiding over the case determines what punishment is called for. Purely civil suits are usually handled at courts in administrative districts (*Bezirke)* or at the provincial level. A High Court (*Oberster Gerichtshof*), which first came into use in 1850, sits as the final appellate court in both civil and criminal cases.

JULY PUTSCH. Though National Socialism had been outlawed in Austria since 1933, an Austrian National Socialist (DNSAP) overthrow of the **government** of **Engelbert Dollfuss** and the installation of a **Nazi** regime had been discussed since the late winter of 1934. With the leadership of the movement under the Austrian Theo Habicht (1898–1944) operating out of Munich, the planning was known to the German Nazi leadership. Adolf Hitler, however, had reservations about the timing.

In June, conferring with Benito Mussolini in Spa, the German dictator announced that although he did not want to annex Austria, he would welcome the replacement of Dollfuss with an Austrian Nazi regime. But according to one source close to the plot, Rudolf Weydenhammer, Hitler told Habicht that he wanted no "small putsch." Rather, he asked for a large uprising. Accompanying these machinations were discussions among Austrian Nazis about moving ahead with such a strike. Their chief concern was whether what was left of their movement in Austria, particularly the paramilitary Austrian *Sturmabteilung* (SA), could function reliably and effectively.

Rumors of the conspiracy, indeed information about it, reached Austrian official circles, so when the uprising began on 25 July, it was hardly a surprise. Some 154 members of the Vienna SA dressed as soldiers and policemen broke into Dollfuss's apparently ill-guarded office. The conspirators planned to arrest him and his government and install a Nazi regime under the leadership of **Anton Rintelen**, once a **Christian Social** politician and governor of **Styria**. At least this is what they announced from the Austrian broadcasting station, which they also captured. A general uprising was called for on the air.

Dollfuss's ministers had been alerted and left the building, though the **chancellor** himself was still there. Dollfuss was shot; he died from his wounds about two hours later. The chancellorship was passed to the minister of justice, **Kurt Schuschnigg**.

Armed skirmishing between the Austrian army, which along with the *Heimwehr* remained loyal to the government, and Nazi cells took place over the next few days in parts of **Upper Austria**, **Styria**, and **Carinthia**. Minor disturbances broke out in **Salzburg** as well. In the actual fighting, 107 died defending the Austrian government, while 140 Nazi supporters were killed. But local authorities contained the uprisings relatively quickly; 13 of the putschists were executed and around 4,000 of their followers were interned. Around 1,000 fled to Yugoslavia, where they were once again interned; upon release, they went to Germany.

The putsch was a real, though temporary, setback for the Austrian Nazi movement. Hitler himself was sufficiently cautioned by the general show of Austrian loyalty to their government to curb the activity of Habicht and his followers sharply. Habicht was removed from his position, the Austrian party center in Munich was dissolved, and what remained of the party in Austria itself was told to limit its activities.

JUNG WIEN (YOUNG VIENNA). A groups of Austrian writers of the pre–**World War I** era, the most prominent being the playwright **Arthur Schnitzler**, the man-of-all-letters **Hugo von Hofmannsthal**, and the critic Hermann Bahr (1863–1934). Their program called for the updating of **literature** in the city. Hofmannsthal, for example, was much impressed at the time by the French poet Arthur Rimbaud.

– K –

KARAJAN, HERBERT VON (1908–1989). Born in **Salzburg** in a family with a distinguished history in Austrian cultural affairs, in his youth Karajan experienced a meteoric rise as a conductor. By 1941, he was in Berlin and quickly became a competitor of Wilhelm Furtwängler, another bright, and somewhat jealous, star in the contemporary **musical** firmament.

Too close to some elements of the **Nazi** regime for the postwar occupation regime, von Karajan was forbidden to perform in Germany immediately after the conflict ended. In 1947 he returned to Austria, where he conducted at the **Vienna State Opera**, and led performances of the **Vienna Philharmonic** for the **Society of the Friends of Music**. Von Karajan was general director of the opera from 1957 to 1964. His international reputation was established through a large output of recordings, done largely with the Berlin Philharmonic, which he led after 1954, and at the **Salzburg Festival**, where he was director between 1956 and 1960, and again in 1965. A man of enormous personal charisma and self-confidence, he established his own very successful Easter Festival in the city beginning in 1967.

KELSEN, HANS (1881–1973). Kelsen, who came from Prague, was the architect of the constitution of the First Austrian Republic, issued in 1920. Widely known as a professor of constitutional and administrative law, he was also a philosopher and a practicing magistrate. He served on the bench of the Austrian Constitutional Court from 1921 to 1930, when he left Austria for a professorial position in Cologne. He taught there until 1933. Of **Jewish** extraction, he then went to Geneva and Prague and, in 1938, to the United States, where he lectured at Harvard for two years. In 1942, he was called to the University of California at Berkeley, where he taught for 10 years until 1952. He later died in California.

From the standpoint of jurisprudence, Kelsen was a legal positivist, believing that law was essentially a creation of the state, rather than an expression of social or ethical standards found in society at large. Legal codes were therefore the practical realization of norms that governments expected their citizens to follow. He reinforced this view, which he called pure theory of law, with an epistemological dualism that owed something to Immanuel Kant. Human consciousness, he argued, was endowed to think in terms of Being (*Sein*) and What Ought to Be (*Sollen*). Neither category was a logical derivative of the other; it was What Ought to Be and its construction by those who spoke for the state that gave law its form and substance.

Writing during a period of intense ideological and societal polarization in Austria, Kelsen and the successor to his chair at the **University of Vienna**, Adolf Julius Merkl (1890–1970), had a receptive audience among those whom he taught. The students, who were to become the country's judges, lawyers, civil servants, and commercial functionaries, were heavily influenced by his thinking. As finished jurists, they constituted what came to be called the Vienna School of Legal Theory. *See also* JUDICIARY.

KIRCHSCHLÄGER, RUDOLF (1915–2000). A native of **Upper Austria** who served as **president** of the postwar Federal Republic of Austria with great distinction, Kirchschläger was a public prosecutor and magistrate before entering the Foreign Ministry. Between 1970 and 1974, he was foreign minister in the Socialist government of Chancellor **Bruno Kreisky**. A devout **Catholic** who had no declared party affiliation, he stood as the **Socialist Party of Austria**'s candidate for the federal presidency in 1974. Popularly acknowledged for probity and great modesty, he ran unopposed for the same office in 1980. *See also* CONSTITUTION; GOVERNMENT.

KLAGENFURT. Since 1518, it has been the capital of **Carinthia**. Archaeological excavations have uncovered Celtic and Roman artifacts in the neighborhood and on the outskirts of the modern city. The first medieval settlement in the immediate vicinity of Klagenfurt was to its north; this dated from the second half of the 12th century and was the creation of Duke Herman I of Carinthia. Around 1193, Klagenfurt was declared a market. Between 1246 and 1252, another local duke, Bernhard of Sponheim, laid the groundwork of the modern city. It was mentioned as a town by 1279.

Heavily fortified in the 16th century, Klagenfurt was a center of **Protestantism** during the Reformation. Lutheran nobles of Carinthia were responsible for the construction of what are today some of its most important municipal buildings. The modern cathedral is a rebuilt Protestant church from the 16th century; the current assembly hall of the Carinthian provincial legislature was built between 1574 and 1594 to house the Carinthian estates. The Counter-Reformation of the 17th century, which forced many middle-class as well as aristocratic residents of the territory into exile, began an economic decline in the region. Conditions grew bleaker as veins of precious metals once mined in the vicinity also ran out.

In 1719, Emperor Charles VI made the Habsburg port city of Trieste a center for his Oriental Trading Company. Although in itself this did not make the **Habsburg Empire** a major competitor in European mercantile enterprises, it markedly increased commercial activity in the southeast of the Habsburg lands. Lying conveniently to the north of Trieste, Klagenfurt revived as a transit point in north–south trade. A center of revolutionary activity in 1848–1849, Klagenfurt was made an autonomous city in 1850. With a population in 2006 of 92,404, Klagenfurt today has become especially important in the service sector of the Austrian **economy**. With its proximity to Lake

Wörth, it also benefits from the intense summer vacation business of the region. *See also* CATHOLICISM; RELIGION.

KLESTIL, THOMAS (1932–2004). When **Kurt Waldheim** decided not to seek a second term as **president** of the Austrian Republic in 1992, the **Austrian People's Party** called upon Thomas Klestil, the secretary-general of the Foreign Office, to run for the office. A graduate of the University for Economic Studies in Vienna and a diplomat with 18 years of service in the United States, he also had a great deal of experience with the **United Nations**, where he was Austria's ambassador from 1978 to 1986.

However, Klestil was virtually unknown in Austrian domestic politics. His campaign downplayed his connection with any of Austria's parliamentary parties. Instead, he construed the Austrian president as the ambassador-at-large for the country as a whole. The idea struck a resonant note with the public, which was given unprecedented media exposure to all four candidates for the office. In a run-off ballot between him and the **Socialist Party of Austria** (SPÖ) candidate, Rudolph Streicher (1939–), Klestil received the largest percentage of votes ever given to someone running for the Austrian presidency, almost 57 percent. He even won a majority in **Vienna**, long acknowledged as an SPÖ stronghold.

Klestil's first term in office was dogged by marital scandal and serious illness. He did, however, pursue an active policy of representing Austria abroad, where he supported, among other policies, the rapid integration of the former Soviet bloc states into Europe as a whole. In 1998, Klestil was reelected for a second term that he did not live to complete. *See also* CONSTITUTION; GOVERNMENT.

KLIMA, VICTOR (1947–). Becoming chairman of the **Socialist Party of Austria** (SPÖ) of Austria in 1997, Klima succeeded **Franz Vranitzky** as federal **chancellor** as well. Born in **Vienna**, he specialized in business information technology at Vienna's Technical University and at the **University of Vienna**. His subsequent career was both in business and Socialist politics. Klima worked from 1969 to 1992 for the Austrian petroleum **industry** in a variety of positions, particularly in its financial offices. Raised in a family in which SPÖ traditions were very strong, he began his party activities in 1966.

From 1992 to 1996, Klima was minister for **Nationalized Industry** and **Transportation**. He was federal minister of finance at the time that he was called to higher office. *See also* ECONOMY.

KLIMT, GUSTAV (1862–1918). Like several important Viennese **architects**, artists, and designers of his time, Klimt received his initial training from his father, who was an engraver. His formal schooling (1876–1883) was in applied **art** and handicraft at the Vienna School of Arts and Crafts (*Kunstgewerbe*), founded in 1868 to prepare students for work in traditional design and manufacture. From 1879, together with his brother Ernst (1864–1892) and a partner, Franz Matsch (1861–1942), Klimt completed several major commissions throughout the **Habsburg Empire** and abroad. During the period 1886–1888, he and Ernst did the decorative ceiling of the grand stairway of the new Vienna **Burgtheater**. Klimt's canvas of the old edifice just prior to its demotion won him the Emperor's Prize in 1890 and transformed him into one of the preeminent painters of Central Europe. In 1891, he did the main lobby of the **Museum** of Art (*Kunsthistorisches Museum*). Klimt also did paintings in theaters in Bucharest, Rijeka (Fiume), and Karlsbad.

In 1894, Klimt accepted the charge to do the ceiling painting for the auditorium of the newly built **University of Vienna** on the **Ringstrasse**. It was during this time that he became a leading advocate of the Austrian **Secession** movement, which called for a radical departure from the historically oriented classicism then prevalent in Viennese artistic circles. Klimt's own style and the content of his work changed dramatically, becoming far more symbolic than representational, more subjective in the use of color and surface, more psychological than pictorial.

The Secession itself, and Klimt along with it, did not lack for wealthy patrons. Nevertheless, not all of the artist's patrons and not all his clients were taken with the changes in his work, especially the explicitly sensual side of it that expressed Klimt's own erotic compulsions. Though he never married, he fathered a string of illegitimate children.

In 1905, Klimt had to abandon the university commission under heavy criticism from its faculty, whose vision of the triumph of reason over obscurantism—the general subject of the work—was a good deal more sober than the painter's rendering, which probed deeply into the subconscious for its imagery. Klimt also worked closely with the **Wiener Werkstätte** in its early years, designing the marble frieze of **Josef Hoffmann**'s Palais Stoclet in Brussels.

KOKOSCHKA, OSKAR. (1886–1980). One of the 20th century's most original painters, Kokoschka also drew and wrote poetry. Born to an artisan family in **Lower Austria**, he studied at the Vienna Academy of Applied Arts (*Kunstgewerbeschule*); in 1907 he joined the **Wiener Werkstätte**. A great deal of his productive career developed abroad; his most continuous residence was in Switzerland.

By 1910 Kokoschka was working in Berlin, having already dabbled in experimental **theater** with *Murderer, Hope of Women* (1909). However it was in the German capital that he became fully at home with the visual Expressionism that was so congenial to the grotesque psychological realism that informs much of his **art**. From 1919 until 1923, Kokoschka taught at the Dresden Academy and made even more use of the striking colors that had begun appearing in his early work in Austria (*Self-Portrait*, 1922–1923). He spent 1934–1938 in Prague and **World War II** in London. In 1953, he returned to Switzerland and to Austria as well, where he founded a School of Visual Art (*Schule des Sehens*) in **Salzburg** for summer students.

KÖNIG, FRANZ (1905–2004). Archbishop of Vienna from 1956 to 1985, König had served in a number of positions in the Austrian **Catholic** hierarchy. First a priest (1933), then a professor of moral theology (1949) in **Salzburg**, he was coadjutant bishop of St. Pölten (1956–1985) in **Lower Austria** before going to **Vienna**. He became a cardinal in 1958. During **World War II**, he was especially active in youth missions.

Of working class background himself, König believed that his church should encourage pluralistic unity rather than ideological discord in contemporary Austria. A committed ecumenist, he was a moving force behind the calling of the Second Vatican Council (1962–1965). In 1964, König established the Pro Oriente foundation, through which he developed significant cooperative relationships with Catholic churches behind the Iron Curtain and in Asia. He was chairperson of the organization until 1985. From 1965 to 1980, he also functioned as president of the Vatican office that reached out to unbelievers. His generally flexible approach to other faiths and willingness to engage in dialogue with them did much to repair the reputation for collaboration with authoritarian regimes that the church had acquired during the interwar period.

König's policies were especially helpful in smoothing relations between the Catholic establishment and the **Socialist Party of Austria** (SPÖ), though serious disagreements between the two sides continued to arise. The church vehemently opposed SPÖ-sponsored legislation in 1973 permitting abortion, at a mother's request, through the third month of pregnancy. To counter the measure, the church and its allies circulated a petition asking for reconsideration of the policy. Though almost 900,000 people signed it, the National Assembly let the rule stand when the matter came before it in 1976. *See also* EDUCATION; RELIGION; SCHÖNBORN, CARDINAL CHRISTOPH.

KÖNIGGRÄTZ/HRADEC KRÁLOVÉ, BATTLE OF. *See* SEVEN WEEKS' WAR.

KÖRNER, THEODOR. (1873–1957). A Socialist politician who was **Vienna**'s first mayor (1945–1957) after **World War II**, Körner had a background in military affairs. He was chief of staff for the **Habsburg** monarchy's Isonzo Army, which fought in Italy during **World War I**. Following that conflict, he served in the Office of Military Affairs in the First Austrian Republic, from which he was pensioned as a general in 1924 because of his critical position toward the regime. Formally joining the **Social Democratic Workers' Party** (SDAP) in 1924, he was a member of the Central Directory of the **Republican Guard**, the paramilitary arm of the party. Though Körner advised against armed SDAP resistance to the government of **Engelbert Dollfuss** in February 1934, he was arrested both by that regime and by the Austrian **Nazis**, in 1944.

Körner was among those who first began discussing the **government** of a new Austria in 1944. Following his years as mayor of Vienna, he was **president** of the Second Austrian Republic from 1951 to 1957. Though he played a generally conciliatory role in his country's politics, he opposed the participation of the Nazi-tainted

League of Independents into the governing coalition in 1953. *See also* POLITICAL PARTIES; SOCIALIST PARTY OF AUSTRIA.

KRAFFT-EBING, RICHARD VON (1840–1902). A devout German **Catholic** born in Mannheim, Krafft-Ebing took his medical degree at Heidelberg and practiced in Baden-Baden before leaving for the **Styrian** capital of **Graz** in 1873. There he headed a public insane asylum until 1889. He then went to **Vienna**, where he treated, among others, Archduke Rudolf (1858–1889), the son of Emperor **Franz Joseph**. His research was heavily focused on the paralysis associated with syphilis.

In 1886, he published his most influential work, *Psychopathia sexualis: Eine klinishe-forensische Studie* (*Sexual Psychopathy: A Clinical-Forensic Study*), a small book that stressed the close association of sexuality with psychoanalytic theory. Drawn largely from courtroom cases, it went through 17 editions by 1924, growing greatly in size during the process. Pointing out the relationship of sexuality to all forms of human activity, Krafft-Ebing declared that both art and religion offered satisfactions and experiences that were linked with, and similar to, sexual activity. It was Krafft-Ebing who coined the term *masochism*, from the writings of Leopold von Sacher-Masoch (1836–1895), who was living in Graz at the time the German psychiatrist arrived there. Krafft-Ebing's compilation of sexual disorders was of great use to **Sigmund Freud** in his research; however, he rejected Freud's notion of infant sexuality. *See also* MAYERLING.

KRAUS, KARL (1874–1936). Like so many leading intellectuals in fin de siècle **Vienna**, Kraus was not a native of the city, but he was raised there. Born in Bohemia of **Jewish** extraction, he was baptized a **Catholic** and remained in the church until 1923. Though he fell short of his ambition to become an actor, he had a large following as a mesmerizing solo reader. After 1910, he gave over 700 such performances. His journal, *Die Fackel* (*The Spark*), published irregularly from 1911 until his death, served as a vehicle for numerous causes that he pursued with relentless critical verve.

Persuaded that the corruption of middle-class society around him was paralleled by corruption of the German **language**, he punctured hypocrisy and uncovered deceit wherever he found them.

Although he was an admirer of the Habsburg heir apparent, Archduke **Franz Ferdinand**, for his willingness to confront the cautious establishment of the **Habsburg** monarchy with his reform programs, he turned on the government and the middle-class **press**, which echoed the official line during **World War I**. A particular target of Kraus's venom was Moritz Benedikt (1849–1920), the editor of the leading Viennese daily *Neue Freie Presse*, whom he accused of being far more interested in profit than in reporting the news. Kraus's *The Last Days of Mankind* (*Die Letzten Tage der Menschheit*), an epic drama published in *Die Fackel* in 1918 and 1919 and in book form in 1922, was a searing indictment of the perversion of the press in the interests of the powerful.

Following the war, Kraus became increasingly critical of capitalism, though he never became a socialist. Marxists, he believed, were just as materialistic as the bourgeoisie for whom he had such a deep contempt. He eventually drifted into the camp of **Austro-Fascism** as a way of combating **Nazism**. *See also* LITERATURE.

KREISKY, BRUNO (1911–1990). Perhaps the preeminent political personality of Austria in the second half of the 20th century, Kreisky was born in **Vienna** to well-to-do parents of Moravian background. The family had **Jewish** roots, though Kreisky personally disavowed all confessional identification. Trained as a jurist, he also worked as a journalist. Membership in a **Social Democratic Workers' Party** youth organization sensitized him to the human misery brought about by the unemployment of the interwar era.

Kreisky spent the period between 1935 and June 1936 in confinement for continuing his political activities even after the party was outlawed for its role in the **February Uprising** of 1934. Indeed, in March 1936 he was found guilty of treason for his role in the upheaval. Arrested by the Gestapo in 1938, he fled Austria for Sweden. Returning to his native country, he entered its diplomatic service in 1946. Ten years later, Kreisky also entered electoral politics, winning a seat in the National Assembly as a representative from **Lower Austria**. As foreign minister from 1959 to 1966, he shepherded Austria's entry into the **European Free Trade Association** (EFTA) and carried on negotiations with **Italy** concerning the thorny problem of German minority rights in the **South Tyrol**.

Becoming head of the **Socialist Party of Austria** (SPÖ) in 1967, Kreisky held that position until 1983. During this period, he was responsible for major ideological shifts in the organization in response to generational and occupational shifts in the Austrian electorate. Once the party of the urban proletariat, the SPÖ had now to win elections in which service-sector wage earners were rapidly gaining on **industrial** workers in numbers. Their concerns were driven far more by the desire to improve their personal standard of living and economic security than any need to limit the right to private property or to challenge middle-class values generally. With the examples of Soviet suppression of political dissent in Hungary in 1956 and Czechoslovakia in 1968 very much on the minds of many Austrians, Kreisky became a vocal critic of antidemocratic regimes, including communist examples. He strongly argued for the individualism that had always played a central role in **Austro-Marxist** doctrine. In 1978, he would say that while Marx had made central contributions to socialist thought, many of his teachings no longer applied in the modern world.

Kreisky won the powerful Austrian **trade unions** over to his more moderate point of view. He also gained the support of regional socialist parties as he traveled extensively throughout the country to win these organizations to his side. He thereby reduced the influence of Vienna's SPÖ, always among the most radical voices and not always the most popular ones, of the movement. In 1971, the SPÖ received the majority of votes in the national election, inaugurating a period of SPÖ governments that lasted until 2000. Domestically, they followed Kreisky's guidelines, which called for increasingly comprehensive social and **educational** benefits for the entire population, a program that the postwar prosperity of Austria made possible. Greater democratization was encouraged, as well, by such measures as lowering the voting age from 21 to 19, formal declaration of gender equality, and reorganizing the hierarchical structure of authority in universities

Kreisky was particularly eager that Austria play an active a role in **foreign policy**, in keeping with its neutral status. He promoted the construction of the **United Nations** (UN) City, which houses some of the international organization's agencies. Vienna thus became the third leg in the UN triad, the other two being New York and Geneva. Austria's neutral status and Kreisky's ongoing activities in the Socialist International encouraged him to become active in Arab–Israeli affairs. Although concerned about maintaining the security of the Jewish state, he also believed that Israel would have to come to a territorial accommodation with the Arab states on its borders and with the Palestinians, positions heavily criticized in Israel. In 1973 Kreisky, along with other European socialist leaders, recommended that the Palestine Liberation Organization (PLO) be allowed to speak officially for the Palestinian people as a whole.

Kreisky's domination of Austrian politics ended in 1983, as his party came under heavy attack for its role in major financial scandals. Chief among these were questionable practices of his finance minister, Hannes Androsch (1938–), who was for a time seen as Kreisky's successor as **chancellor**, and the building of the new, and supposedly hyper-modern, Vienna General Hospital, which absorbed vast sums of money, some of which was never accounted for. In 1983, Kreisky refused to enter any kind of coalition government; he gave up both the chancellorship and his role as party leader. He continued to play an active role as an elder statesman of the party and in international socialist affairs. When an SPÖ coalition with the **Austrian People's Party** assigned the position of foreign minister to a leading figure of the latter party, **Alois Mock**, a supporter of Austrian entry into the **European Economic Community**, Kreisky resigned his position as honorary president of the SPÖ. He feared that such policies would undermine Austrian **neutrality**. *See also* POLITICAL PARTIES.

– L –

LANGUAGE. Although there are small communities in Austria that claim Croatian, Hungarian, and especially Slovenian as their mother tongue, the preeminent language of the country is German. Behind that simple statement, however, lurks a very complex history that continues to stir up scholarly and public debate. Until the **Austro-Prussian War** (1866), which nullified political ties of **Habsburg** rulers to German lands beyond its dynastic territories, most of the people living in what today is the Austrian national state regarded themselves as "German," not only linguistically but ethnically and culturally. They recognized that they did not speak like residents of

Hamburg, Cologne, or Berlin, but they accepted these differences as part of what it meant to be a German, regardless of the political boundaries that separated them.

The reconfiguration of Austria as a national state after **World War I** made the issue of national language genuinely problematic; the question of whether "Austrian" and "German" are truly separate tongues is still raised, both on political and cultural grounds. The cause of treating "Austrian" as a language in its own right made considerable headway after the country's **Nazi** interlude (1938–1945), when many people, some for moral reasons, some for quite sinister ones, tried to disassociate themselves from all German connections, linguistic ones included.

Scholars today generally reject these arguments outright or qualify them to the point of meaninglessness. Specific Austrianisms exist, but not enough of them to constitute an independent language. Austrians, therefore, speak "German," though a variant of the language heavily colored by two widely acknowledged dialectical variants: Alemannic in the **Vorarlberg** and in parts of the **Tyrol** and Bavarian, found throughout the entire country, but dominant in **Styria**, **Carinthia**, **Salzburg**, **Upper Austria**, **Lower Austria**, and the **Burgenland**.

These dialectal strains have nevertheless influenced the pronunciation, vocabulary, word formation patterns, and even grammar of Austrian speech, making it difficult for many North Germans to understand, at least on first hearing. Intonations do not fall on the same elements in words—for example, Austrians accent the last syllable in the word for coffee, Germans the first; Austrians form diminutives quite differently than their linguistic relatives to the north; and the *Blumenkohl* (cauliflower) that Germans put on their plates is *Karfiol* when Austrians eat it. The articles of nouns are not identical either, particularly in foreign borrowings.

These differences are hardly fixed in stone, as standard North German patterns intrude more and more on local Austrian ones. The onetime Austrian salutation "Servus"("your servant"), either in greeting or farewell, has all but surrendered to the German "tschüss" ("so long"). German will probably never be a unitary language, but its speakers have enough in common to recognize that they truly share a tongue. Regionalisms continue, however, to be a problem, especially for non-native speakers of German.. In 1994, three Austrian federal ministries inaugurated a program (OSD) that would train students and certify them as competent in everyday usage and comprehension of Austrian dialect forms. These courses are available at specific locations in several European countries and in Argentina, Brazil, Mexico, and the United States. *See also* **WIENERISCH**.

LAW OF RESIDENCE. The Law of Residence (1 July 1993) considerably limited the rights of refugees and other foreign residents in Austria. Residence permits, good for six months, had to be completed in a country outside of Austria. Conditions under which marriage to an Austrian citizen conferred citizenship on a spouse of foreign origin were significantly tightened, as were the circumstances under which residency could be extended. The state of the Austrian labor market and housing opportunities are also considered in evaluating applications. *See also* **ASYLUM; IMMIGRATION**.

LEHÁR, FRANZ (1870–1948). Born in Komárom, at that time in Hungary and now largely in Slovakia, where it is named Komárno, the future master of the 20th-century Viennese **operetta** was the son of a military bandmaster. The elder Lehár's postings took him and his family all over the Habsburg lands. In the process his son became broadly acquainted with the many indigenous forms of **music** found throughout the dynasty's lands; his own work was quite consciously embellished with Slavic tonal coloration.

The composer himself trained as a military musician, an experience that may account for the acute sense of rhythm and orchestral sonority with which he wrote for the musical **theater**. But he was something of an innovator in his own right, especially in the merger of song and dance sequences that made his productions all the more captivating. *The Merry Widow* (1905), a worldwide success, and *The Count of Luxembourg* (1909), epitomized his style.

Lehár aspired to writing **opera** as well. Deeply impressed by the voice and talents of the famous contemporary tenor Richard Tauber, he dreamed of writing a major role for the singer. He also hoped to be a musical successor to Giacomo Puccini, the preeminent Italian opera composer of the early 20th century. Lehár's most notable attempt at opera was *Giuditta*, a classic conflict of duty and desire, which premiered at the Vienna State Opera in 1934. Though it was frequently performed for some time after that and contained a couple of arias that became popular songs—"My Lips Kiss Passionately" was one—it has never been established in the repertory.

LIBERAL FORUM/LIBERALES FORUM (LiF). The ascendancy of **Jörg Haider** in the **Freedom Party of Austria** (FPÖ) sharpened differences between the traditionally liberal and national factions of the movement. Haider's opposition to Austrian membership in the **European Union** and his open hostility to the increased foreign presence in Austrian society led Heide Schmidt, the Freedom Party presidential candidate in 1992, to establish a new party, the Liberal Forum, on 4 February 1993. Schmidt and other dissidents within the FPÖ supported the integration of Austria into the **economy** of Western Europe and the general concerns for human rights that liberalism had historically defended. Both the **Austrian People's Party** and the **Socialist Party of Austria** backed the creation of the LiF and its request for recognition as a parliamentary faction, a status that entitled it to government financial subsidies. The FPÖ opposed all these steps.

The Liberal Forum failed to gain much traction with Austrian voters. Like Haider's FPÖ, the Forum has often appeared to be exploiting opportunistic advantage rather than advancing a coherent program in its electoral campaigns. Though elections in 1994 and 1995 gave the Forum a smattering of seats in the parliament, it won none in 1999. Efforts to make a political comeback in the federal elections of 2008 did nothing to improve the movement's position. *See also* POLITICAL PARTIES.

LIENZ. The chief city of the East **Tyrol**, Lienz, is called Luenzina in documents from the early 11th century. The local counts of Görz founded it as a town in 1240 and governed it until 1500. Lienz was then incorporated into the Tyrol, which brought it under **Habsburg** control. Isolated from the central regions of the Tyrol, Lienz was, from medieval times to the 19th century, a center for mining and processing iron. Its medieval walls are still largely preserved. Following the **Nazi Anschluss** of 1938, it was placed in the administrative district or Gau of **Carinthia**. It was returned to the Tyrol in 1947.

LINZ. The capital city of **Upper Austria**, Linz has been settled since the Old Stone Age. Continuous habitation of the area dates from the New Stone Age; the Romans erected a castle there in the second half of the first century BCE. The city lies at a strategic point on the east–west and north–south axes of the **Danube River**, which runs between southeastern and northeastern Europe. Nevertheless, even in its years of Roman occupation, it never acquired imperial municipal status. Its name, however, is of Roman–Celtic origin, *Lentia* in Latin from the Celtic root *älentos*, meaning bent.

As elsewhere in the Austrian lands, Bavarians came to the region of Linz by the seventh century; the settlement served as a customs station during the Carolingian era. The **Babenbergs** acquired it in 1205–1206, after which Linz took on an increasingly important regional character. When it passed to the **Habsburgs** in the latter decades of the 13th century, it became a territorial administrative seat. At least one of the Habsburg dukes, Albrecht VI (1418–1463), a brother and bitter rival of Emperor **Frederick III**, resided in Linz between 1485 and 1486. Frederick himself made the city a territorial capital.

Linz, along with **Upper Austria** as a whole, was an important center of Austrian **Protestantism** during the Reformation. The recatholicization of the population was especially brutal. From the 17th and 18th to the early 19th centuries, the city was the scene of much destructive warfare. Napoleon alone occupied it three times (1800–1801, 1805–1806, 1809).

Though its **economy** suffered considerably under such upheavals, Linz began preparing the way in the 17th century for its leading role in the **industrialization** of modern Austria. The first factory of the Habsburg monarchy, a wool-making establishment, opened in the city in 1672. Its purpose was to encourage sheep husbandry for raw wool to be processed locally as well as to provide employment for the numerous beggars who haunted the roadways and towns of the area. The first **railroad** on the continent in the 19th century was drawn by horses on a track that ran from Linz to České Budějovice (Germ.: *Budweis*) after 1832 and carried salt from local mines eastward. There was some passenger traffic as well. The second half of the 19th century saw the expansion not only of the textile industry, but also of the manufacturing of heavy machinery such as locomotives, and commercial food processing. The city incorporated several outlying areas into its boundaries as well.

With a substantial industrial working class, Linz was a center of Austrian Social Democracy and the opposition to **Austro-Fascism** and **Nazism**. The **February Uprising** against the right-wing **Dollfuss** government and its supporters in the *Heimwehr* began there. Following the **Anschluss**, the Nazi government of Austria developed the industrial sector of the city's economy even more. Allied bombing during **World War II**, especially in 1944 and 1945, destroyed much of this infrastructure. However, after 1945 the city's industry was substantially rebuilt, especially its textile and steel mills, to make it the center of a complex array of industries, as well as an important Danube port. Air pollution, once a hallmark of the city, has been substantially reduced, and Linz is now the home of some of Austria's most important public and private companies. Its location has also made it a desirable place for foreign enterprises to locate, an increasingly important consideration for Austria as a member of the **European Union**. *See also* TRANSPORTATION.

LINZ PROGRAM (1882). Designed to heighten a sense of national solidarity among the German-speaking peoples of the Austrian half of the **Dual Monarchy**, the Linz declaration was the product of the German national movement in the **Habsburg Empire** led by Georg von Schönerer (1842–1921). It called for, among other things, turning the western half of the monarchy into a German state, a customs union with the new German Empire, and scaling back all political connections with Hungary except for a common monarch. Slavic-speaking regions such as Galicia and the Bukovina were to be joined to Hungary or granted some vague autonomy within the eastern half of the Habsburg Empire. The program also called for a broadening of the franchise and social reforms.

Though the party behind the Linz declaration had little electoral support, the document itself was the product of several young intellectuals who were to have important careers in the waning years of the **Dual Monarchy**. These included the social reformer **Engelbert Pernerstorfer**; the eventual leader of the Austrian **Social Democratic Party**, **Victor Adler**; and the German nationalist historian Heinrich Friedjung (1851–1920). All three became disenchanted with the anti-Semitism that was a prominent feature of Schönerer's movement.

LITERATURE. Where German literature ends and Austrian literature begins has long been contested by academics and ideologues. Poets in the Austrian lands were part of the general German literary scene of the Middle Ages; in the 12th and 13th centuries both the **Babenberg** court in **Vienna** and ecclesiastical institutions in the Austrian lands were cultural centers that drew such figures as the great poet Walther von der Vogelweide (ca. 1170–ca. 1230). Walther was not, however, born in the Babenberg territories, but probably around Würzburg. During the Renaissance, Emperor **Maximilian I** was a generous patron of the arts, literary, and otherwise, but his most important literary protégés, such as the humanist Conrad Celtis (1459–1508), were not native to the Austrian lands either. An argument has been made that **Protestantism** and **Catholicism** produced different intellectual and literary traditions following the 16th-century Reformation. But even if this distinction was unassailable, which it is not, it applies not to a specifically "Austrian" literature of the early modern era but to south **Germany** generally, where Catholicism retained its hold.

Austrians themselves began making distinctions between "Austrian" and "non-Austrian," meaning German, literature in the late 18th century. It is only in the 19th and 20th centuries, however, that an arguably Austrian literary tradition developed. The first genre to express it was the **theater**, particularly the popular comedy, which combines elements of local performance with often-vulgarized elements of school dramas put on at **Jesuit** and, to a somewhat lesser extent, **Benedictine** foundations. The theme of self-recognition combined with virtuosic use of language representing all classes of society extends from 19th-century masters such as **Johann Nestroy** and **Ferdinand Raimund** to their more abrasive 20th-century heirs, **Ödön von Horvath** and more recently, Wolfgang Bauer (1941–2005). The serious novel did not have a place in Austrian literature until the latter decades of the 19th century, but **Adalbert Stifter** used such introspective and self-regarding themes, as well as a microscopic focus on the details of the external world.

Intense concern with the uses and limitations of language to describe the inner and outer conditions of life has characterized

Austrian literature from the latter decades of the 19th century until today. Much of the work of **Hugo von Hofmannsthal, Arthur Schnitzler, Karl Kraus, Robert Musil,** and **Heimito von Doderer** turns on these issues. For Doderer, literature is virtually a literary experiment. The tradition was continued after **World War II** by the **Vienna Group** and the **Graz Group**, internationally represented by **Peter Handke** and somewhat less consistently by **Thomas Bernhard**. Handke and Bernhard, along with a younger cohort of writers such as Gerhard Roth (1942–) and Michael Köhlmeier (1949–), have far more autobiographical referents in their work than did their predecessors. The cool recounting of these details, however, places all of these authors squarely in the historical mainstream of their country's analytic literary tradition. *See also* BACHMANN, INGEBORG; JELINEK, ELFRIEDE; MAGRIS, CLAUDIO; MAYRÖCKER, FRIEDERIKE; NESTROY, JOHANN; RAIMUND, FERDINAND; STIFTER, ADALBERT; WEIGEL, HANS.

LUEGER, KARL (1844–1910). One of Europe's most successful municipal politicians, Lueger used his humble origins to great career advantage. The son of a caretaker at **Vienna**'s Technical University, he had a particular appeal to the city's lower middle classes, which counted him as one of their own. They faithfully supported Lueger as mayor between 1897 and his death, along with the **Christian Social Party** (CP), which he represented. In return, he gave them an array of municipal services—public transportation, a municipal gas supply, famously pure drinking water—that much of the world could only envy.

Trained as a lawyer, Lueger entered politics early in his professional life. He identified himself with democratic opposition to the liberal bourgeois oligarchy that had governed the city since the **Revolutions of 1848**. He was particularly critical of the vast corruption that had come to mark the regime. He entered the Austrian parliament in 1885, where he was increasingly drawn to the Catholic-Conservative element he found there, including the anti-Semitism that was a routine, and very troubling, part of its rhetoric. Just how much he believed all of this is unclear, but these views were certainly part of his public persona.

The Vienna City Council chose him as mayor in 1893, but Emperor **Franz Joseph**, concerned that Lueger's anti-Jewish and anti-Hungarian rhetoric would further envenom ethnic relations among the peoples of the **Habsburg Empire**, disallowed the election. It was only in 1897, after three more elections, that the monarch permitted the politician to take the office. By this time, advisors had convinced the Habsburg that the CP could serve as a bulwark against the rising appeal of Marxist Social Democracy.

LUTHERANISM. *See* PROTESTANTISM; RELIGION.

– M –

MACH, ERNST (1838–1916). A physicist and philosopher, Mach had a profound influence on Austrian science and culture generally. His teaching career at the **University of Vienna** was relatively brief, beginning in 1895 but severely curtailed by a serious stroke that he suffered three years later. Nevertheless, his work as a professor in both **Graz**, where he had lectured in mathematics, and Prague, where he had taught physics, had established him as an authority in both fields. Mach's experiments in ballistics, for which he used photographs of projectile bullets, demonstrated that these objects created not one but two shock waves when they exceeded the speed of sound. The ratio between the speed of sound and airflow velocity, the so-called Mach number, is now used to determine the speed of supersonic airplanes.

Mach deeply respected the scientific revolution of the 17th and 18th centuries for having purged study of the physical world science of what he believed to be misapplied notions of God, nature, and the soul. Nevertheless, he thought that these early experiments had not gone far enough. All true science, he argued, had to be reduced to formulae of measurement. Mach had little patience with what he called "pictorializations" such as *atoms* and *ether*, terms common in 19th-century scientific discourse. He took considerable pleasure in exposing false hypotheses in mechanics, optics, and acoustics held by his predecessors. Indeed, his research in this vein led him to be a pioneer in the history of science.

Mach discounted theory of any kind, be it in physics or psychology. There is no more basis for accepting the ego as part of human psychic makeup than there is for accepting the a priori existence of number. The only knowledge of the world comes from our sensations and the stimuli they provoke. Man is therefore awash in an ocean of appearances that intellect can certainly analyze, order, and even remember, but cannot establish their irreducible reality.

MAGRIS, CLAUDIO (1939–). An Italian essayist, poet, translator, and scholar of modern German **literature**, Magris has significantly influenced the outlook of Austrian intellectuals on their past. First published in Italian in 1963, *The Habsburg Myth in Austrian Literature* (*Der habsburgische Mythos in der österreichischen Literatur*) appeared in German translation in 1966. Magris criticized what he saw to be the idealized version of the pre–**World War I** empire held by such writers as **Hugo von Hofmannsthal**. He took a negative view of Austrian cultural tradition in general, holding it responsible for the entrapment of its representatives in, at best, a societal status quo, and, at worst, a moral vacuum. Magris has had a very strong influence on two major Austrian literary movements since 1945, the **Graz Group** and the **Vienna Group**.

MAHLER, GUSTAV (1860–1911). Of **Jewish** extraction and born in the kingdom of Bohemia, part of today's Czech Republic, Mahler excelled as a director and a composer. During his conservatory studies in **Vienna**, where he studied privately with **Anton Bruckner**, Mahler was part of a circle of young intellectuals that included social reformers such as **Engelbert Pernerstorfer** and **Viktor Adler**. Though their future careers followed somewhat different paths, all were much under the intellectual and aesthetic spell of the composer Richard Wagner and the philosopher Friedrich Wilhelm Nietzsche. Mahler occasionally turned to the latter for texts, which he incorporated into his music, such as the Third Symphony.

After holding a number of musical positions in cities throughout the Austro–Hungarian Empire and in Germany, in 1897 Mahler became director of what is today the **Vienna State Opera**. For the next 10 years, the house flourished as he devoted himself to bringing the finest singers to the Habsburg capital. He expanded the repertory as well. Mahler also conducted the **Vienna Philharmonic Orchestra** between 1898 and 1901. Impatience with Viennese artistic politics took him to New York in 1908, where he conducted the orchestra of the Metropolitan Opera; in 1909 he became conductor of the New York Philharmonic Orchestra as well. Ill health brought him back to Vienna in 1911.

Mahler's musical corpus was neither as large nor as varied as that of many of his contemporaries, not to mention his predecessors in the German tradition. He did some of his most significant composing during summer holidays from his other musical duties. Nevertheless, his work was original, was sometimes gargantuan in proportion, and can be deeply moving. Along with some important vocal composition, Mahler finished nine symphonies during his lifetime. He left a substantial draft of a 10th, which has now been realized. Much of the writing is hyper-personal, often reflecting the joys and the many strains of his tempestuous marriage in 1902 to Alma Maria Schindler (1879–1964), the daughter of a noted Viennese painter. She would later become the wife of the German *Bauhaus* architect Walter Gropius and finally of the novelist Franz Werfel (1890–1945). *See also* MUSIC.

MAKART, HANS (1840–1884). From 1869, the year he went to **Vienna** with an invitation and subsidies from the government of Emperor **Franz Joseph**, until his death, Makart dominated painting and the decorative **arts** in the imperial capital. Indeed, he may have been the most lionized man in the city. Trained in the school of historical realism under Karl von Piloty in Munich and in the Academy of Fine Arts in Vienna, Makart also studied during travels to London, Paris, and **Italy**.

Specializing in mammoth historical tapestries and canvases, Makart attracted huge audiences. He became a professor of historical painting at the Academy of Fine Arts in Vienna in 1878. That same year, 34,000 visitors viewed his painting *Charles V's Entry into Antwerp*. Some people came to look for likenesses of themselves or their contemporaries, which the artist often incorporated into his pictorial displays.

Makart also produced and designed historical pageants. The most famous, and certainly grandiose, of these was his public staging of the festivities for the 25th wedding anniversary of Emperor Franz Joseph and Empress Elisabeth (1837–1898) on 27 April 1879. The event took over five hours and featured parades of people in 17th-century costume, which Makart had seen at the Reubens tercentenary in Antwerp two years before. In 1881, he began decorative work for the staircase of the Vienna **Museum** of Art and on a bedroom for the empress.

The furnishings of Makart's own atelier, dense with richly colored floral detail, reflected his personal aesthetic leanings, particularly his admiration of Rubens, and those of his patrons and clients. A Makart-hat, a Makart-bouquet, and a Makart-salon belonged in the homes and closets of all among the Viennese bourgeoisie of his day who aspired to social position. Some of his designs were carried over into the work of **Gustav Klimt**. *See also* ARCHITECTURE.

MARIA THERESA, EMPRESS, QUEEN OF BOHEMIA AND HUNGARY (1717–1780). If ever there was a ruler who grew into the position, it was Maria Theresa. The daughter of Emperor Charles VI (1685–1740), the last **Habsburg** male ruler to claim direct descent from Rudolph I (1218–1291), her education was socially correct—dancing, languages, history as a series of moral lessons—but had little bearing on the tasks she would face. In 1736, she married Duke Francis Stephen of Lorraine (1708–1765), who was nine years her senior and her earliest important mentor in political and administrative affairs.

As it became increasingly apparent to Charles VI that the archduchess would be his legitimate heir, he attempted through a series of bilateral agreements, collectively known as the Pragmatic Sanction, to ensure that both the estates of the Habsburg lands and foreign powers would recognize her succession. Charles more or less accomplished this mission, but when he died in 1740, Frederick II of Prussia launched an offensive against the Habsburg lands with the aim of capturing the duchy of Silesia, part of the Bohemian crown and an important center of commerce and **industry**.

The episodic conflict with Prussia, which did not come to an end until 1763, left Silesia in Frederick's hands. It prompted a major reorientation of Habsburg government, which Maria Theresa and her ministers steered with uncommon skill and resolve. Generally intending to strengthen the position of the territorial ruler throughout the Habsburg lands, they established procedures for long-term financing of the dynasty's armies. They brought middle-class officials into the lower levels of their administration to curb the power of the aristocrats, who traditionally held high office. The Theresan regime also encouraged manufacture and **trade**, in part to compensate for the loss of Silesia, and worked to break down internal barriers to commerce. This was a particular issue in the case of Hungary, which had long been treated as a separate kingdom in fiscal affairs.

Interested in making her overwhelmingly **agricultural** population more productive as well, Maria Theresa supported measures to lighten the burdens of serfdom. She also took steps to modernize elementary **education** and widen access to it. Though herself very devout, she and her government took steps to reduce the hold that **Catholicism** had on the intellectual life and **economy** of the Habsburg lands. Steps were taken to regulate the number of people in clerical vocations, as well as to scale back religious holidays. *See also* BURGTHEATER; HABSBURG EMPIRE; JOSEPH II, HOLY ROMAN EMPEROR; PIARISTS; RELIGION; UNIVERSITY OF VIENNA; VIENNA SCHOOL OF MEDICINE.

MARIAZELL. A center of **tourism** and winter sports in **Styria**, Mariazell is also a much-visited pilgrimage site. It draws not only Austrians, but large numbers of Hungarians, Czechs, Slovaks, Slovenians, and Croatians.

Mariazell began as a small **Benedictine** cloister around the middle of the 12th century. By 1330, its church had begun to draw pilgrims and to acquire influential patrons such as the ambitious King Louis I (The Great) of Hungary (1326–1382), who was pursuing an active expansionary policy to his southwest. It was he who endowed the church with its eastern choir, main aisle, and Grace Chapel. The structure was heavily remodeled in the **Baroque** style in the 17th century.

Mariazell, with its Altar of the Virgin, was associated with miracles by the end of the 15th century. Pilgrimages increased in both size and number over the next hundred years. Beginning in 1632, the imperial family often participated in these processions. A so-called Sacred Road (Lat.: *Via sacra*) wound through **Lower Austria** to the site. Its 600-year jubilee in 1757 brought 373,000 people. Since 1893, a yearly pilgrimage of men from **Vienna** has traveled to the location. From 1975 to 1991, the basilica of Marizell was the temporary burial place of the Hungarian cardinal and opponent of Soviet communism, Joseph Mindszenty. *See also* CATHOLICISM.

MARSHALL PLAN. Although political stability came on the whole easily to post–**World War II** Austria, the country's **economy** recovered more slowly. It was not until 1948 that food rationing came to an end. The division of Austria into zones of **occupation** made the process all the more sluggish. The Soviet Union disapproved strongly of the Marshall Plan. Nevertheless, the Soviet representative joined in a unanimous resolution of the Austrian council of ministers in 1948, allowing American aid (through the Marshall Plan) to come into Austria that same year.

The first installment of $280 million went largely to feed the precariously nourished population; what was left, combined with later grants, helped to rebuild the manufacturing and industrial base of the country. Between 1948 and 1952, when the Marshall Plan came to an end, Austria received about $1 billion in cash donations from the program. Foodstuffs and raw goods were either shipped free of charge from the **United States** (U.S.) or from third countries, which the U.S. then reimbursed. Austrian payments for these supplies were deposited in an Austrian account that was then drawn upon for further investment in the country's economy. Freed from dependency on foreign credit markets—which had been the case after **World War I**—the Austrian economy improved. A great need for both capital construction and consumer goods both at home and abroad encouraged high **industrial** output.

Historians generally acknowledge that the Marshall Plan was crucial in getting Austrian business and industry moving once again. Other sides of the program were, from the American standpoint, somewhat less successful. Concerned to keep the appeal of communism to a minimum, the Americans encouraged Austrians to adopt corporate and competitive practices that maintain high rates of economic growth, thereby making work abundant. But the very principle upon which the political stability of the country was based—participation of both the **Austrian People's Party** and the **Socialist Party** of **Austria** in the postwar coalition government—forced the U.S. State Department to modify its other goals considerably. Austrian labor retained far more influence in the decisions on industrial policy than was the rule in the U.S. Both industry and labor were more comfortable with the cartel-like organization of heavy industry than was common in America. For their part, the Americans grew increasingly reluctant to interfere with a labor–management structure that grew and prospered rather quickly. That this development took place both in the private and nationalized sectors further weakened the appeal of the Soviet alternative. *See also* FOREIGN POLICY.

MAXIMILIAN I (1459–1519). Holy Roman emperor from 1493 until his death, Maximilian was one of the more dynamic and imaginative figures of his dynasty. Known even in his own lifetime as the Last of the Knights, he was skilled at self-dramatization, as can be seen in his two autobiographical epics, *Theuerdank* and *Weisskunig*. The first is a fanciful depiction of his journey to Brussels and his marriage to Duchess Mary of Burgundy (1457–1482); the second recounts his life as a whole, including numerous wars fought throughout much of Europe. His massive tomb complex in **Innsbruck** glorifies both his dynasty and himself. Dominated by oversized sculptures of ancestors both real and imagined, it was ordered by the emperor himself, though it was not until almost a century after his death that it was completed. Maximilian himself is not buried there.

Maximilian was one of Renaissance Europe's great patrons of **arts**, learning, and **music**. His efforts in all these directions laid the groundwork for the cultural infrastructure that would distinguish the **Habsburg** court in the centuries to come.

Maximilian's imagination extended to the practical side of princely rule as well. Much interested in military affairs, both as a matter of taste as well as need, he worked hard to make the imperial soldier, the Landsknecht, a more reliable fighting man. Maximilian was eager to reform the fiscal structure of the **Holy Roman Empire**, if only to provide himself with more predictable funding for the numerous conflicts in which he was engaged. These were often more focused on Habsburg, rather than German, concerns. One of his most sought-after changes was levying a so-called Common Penny to support a prototype of a standing imperial army. This he never got, though the idea would come up repeatedly in the empire's business throughout the next century and even beyond.

To manage his affairs in the Austrian lands, Maximilian tried to set up provincial administrations to function in his place during many absences that took him to Italy, Burgundy, and German lands other than his own. These arrangements encountered local resistance as well. Indeed, they all but foundered, as Austrian provincial estates denied him extraordinary aid unless they retained their traditional deliberative practices. These included direct personal contact with their ruler when his fiscal requests were on their agenda. Nevertheless, close variants of Maximilian's administrative schemes took hold under the regime of his grandson, **Ferdinand I**.

MAY CONSTITUTION/MAI VERFASSUNG. Promulgated on 1 May 1934 by the coalition **government** led by **Engelbert Dollfuss** of the **Christian Social Party** (CP), the May Constitution provided for an Austrian federal state based on principles of Roman **Catholicism**, occupational corporatism, and German ethnic identity. Its chief author was Otto Ender (1875–1960), who had served briefly as **chancellor** in 1931. It had been approved a month earlier by a vote of 74 to 2 by a rump of the Austrian parliament. It embodied many ideas put forth in a 1931 anti-Marxist encyclical of Pope Pius XI, *Quadragesimo Anno*, which urged more cooperation between labor and management.

Seven occupational groupings, or corporations, were to have advisory powers in the formulation of legislation. These seven were agriculture and forestry, industry, public service, manufacture, commerce and transportation, the financial industries, and the professions. The scheme was to promote a sense of mutual interest rather than hostility within obviously related economic endeavors.

The May Constitution called for bewilderingly complex legislative machinery. A five-chamber legislature embodying corporate principles was central to the entire structure. Its competence was largely consultative. It could review acts of the government but could not vote on them. These councils chose from their membership a federal diet of 59 members, who could vote yes or no on laws put before them, but could not propose any measures. Chancellor Dollfuss and his government were given dictatorial power; **political parties** were displaced by his generally conservative and right-wing **Fatherland Front**. Fundamental civil rights had little place in the document. Despite the support it received from CP members, the authoritarian branch of the *Heimwehr*, and the Italian dictator Benito Mussolini, who had been interested in having Austria take such a turn, the May Constitution was never fully operative. The only corporations to be formed were those representing agriculture and forestry and civil servants. *See also* CHAMBER, AGRICULTURAL; CHAMBER, ECONOMIC; CHAMBER, WORKERS AND SALARIED EMPLOYEES.

MAYERLING. A village in the province of **Lower Austria**, Mayerling was the site of a noble estate owned by the monastery of **Heiligenkreuz**, which was purchased and turned into a hunting lodge in 1886 by Archduke Rudolph (1858–1889), the only son and heir of Emperor **Franz Joseph**. The archduke was a mentally fragile and troubled young man, conditions further aggravated by gonorrhea, drug and alcohol abuse, and episodes of depression. His marriage to a Belgian princess, Stephanie (1864–1945), was unhappy as well. In 1888, he had toyed with ideas of taking his life and suggested the idea of mutual suicide to his mistress, Mizzy Caspar, who was sufficiently alarmed to have reported the proposal to the police.

Under circumstances not altogether clear, Rudolph met with the 17-year-old Baroness Mary Vetsera at Mayerling on 29 January 1889. Physically somewhat precocious and easily aroused—she had been smitten by the sight of the archduke at a racetrack—she probably allowed him to kill her around six o'clock the next morning, after which he shot himself. Details of the case are still uncertain. The court did its best to cover up the affair, particularly any evidence that the heir apparent had pulled the trigger on the girl. Until the end of the monarchy in 1918, it was officially forbidden to discuss the affair publicly. Indeed, Vetsera's position as a victim was not even mentioned. Fanciful rumors about Mary having been murdered, by **Jews**, by Hungarians, by **Freemasons**, even by the German chancellor, Otto von Bismarck, or by French Prime Minister Georges Clemenceau, continued to circulate.

In 1992, a furniture dealer in **Linz**, Helmut Flatzelsteiner, surreptitiously removed Mary's coffin from its resting place in the cemetery of Heiligenkreuz. A forensic analysis of the contents removed any doubts that the girl had been shot. There is still a box in the hands of the family of **Habsburg**–Lorraine that may shed some light on the episode—it is presumed to contain the murder/suicide weapon and some letters. Emperor Franz Joseph had the lodge at Mayerling itself converted into a Carmelite nunnery and church. *See also* KRAFFT-EBING, RICHARD VON.

MAYRÖCKER, FRIEDERIKE (1924–). One of the leading lyric poets in German **literature** in the second half of the 20th century, Mayröcker supported herself between 1946 and 1969 teaching English in various middle schools in **Vienna**. Her work is often interspersed with snippets of English. The poetry itself, though highly pictorial and often autobiographical, has an objective referent, based on documented events or on her interpersonal relations with known people, especially with her longtime lover and companion, the experimentalist poet, writer, and translator Ernst Jandl (1925–2000). Beneath the surface, however, lies an idiosyncratic psychological subtext, made more opaque still by the absence of poetry's conventional punctuation; periods, commas, and semicolons are rare. Multiple images drawn from superficially unrelated settings are crowded into short and longer poems. Even seasoned critics have decided to call her work "unique" and leave it at that.

For all of its demanding subjectivism, Mayröcker's work has won major prizes in Austria and Germany. Her countrymen awarded her the **Georg Trakl** Prize in 1977 and the **Anton Wildgans** Prize in 1981. In 2001, she received the German Georg Buechner Prize.

MEINL. One of the most famous names in the history of business in Austria, the Meinl grocery and supermarket chain was run by family members from its founding in 1862 by Julius Meinl Sr. (1824–1914) in **Vienna**. Meinl's origins were in Bohemia, where his immediate forebears were bakers.

At first specializing in processing and selling coffee, Meinl quickly expanded his offerings to other specialty items such as tea and imported fruit. Early success, the result in part of cleverly targeted advertising, encouraged Meinl to open other branches throughout the **Dual Monarchy**. By 1909, the Meinl name was on 48 such stores. The firm opened its own storage and production facilities in Vienna at about the same time; the Meinl enterprise took care of its own transportation as well.

During **World War I**, Julius Meinl Jr. (1869–1944) worked actively to withdraw the **Habsburg Empire** from the conflict. In 1915, he founded the Meinl Group, which was close to influential politicians, particularly those around the last Habsburg ruler, **Charles I**. Unlike many businesses in Austria, the Meinl chain survived the collapse of the Habsburg monarchy brilliantly. Julius Meinl Jr. expanded his operations in east central Europe to the successor states, particularly Czechoslovakia and Hungary. To supply these outlets, he built more factories locally. A man of decidedly progressive leanings, he introduced the five-day work week for his employees in 1931.

The communist regimes of east central Europe nationalized the Meinl holdings after **World War II**. The firm reacquired much of its former property in the region following the demise of these governments after 1989. By 1998, there were around 200 Meinl stores in Hungary, 100 in the Czech Republic, and 7 in Poland, all of which were initially successful. The Meinl firm also opened its own **bank** and brokerage service and invested heavily in real estate. The total worth of the family's capital in 1998 was estimated to be somewhere in the neighborhood of $1,200 million.

The firm, however, did not survive for long. It soon closed an unprofitable discount operation. The European retail grocery market was becoming increasingly competitive as large holding conglomerates such as Rewe (*Revisionsverband der Westkauf-Genossenschaften*) aggressively moved to acquire a large share of the Austrian grocery business. In 1998 the Meinl management, now in the hands of Julius Meinl V (1959–), sold most of the retailing branch to Rewe. By 2005, what remained of Meinl retail operations in east central Europe could no longer compete with such giant chains as Carrefour and Ahold. The firm got out of the grocery business altogether, concentrating on the investment operations of the Meinl bank and production of coffee, tea, and preserves under the Meinl label. *See also* ECONOMY.

MELK, CLOISTER. Situated in **Lower Austria** above the **Danube River**, the **Benedictine** cloister of Melk is one of Austria's most imposing structures. The town of the same name at the foot of the complex was the seat of the **Babenberg** margraves of Austria after 976. In 1089, a Benedictine monastery was installed in a renovated canonry monastery.

The cloister buildings have undergone several important **architectural** renewals throughout the centuries. In the 14th century, the complex doubled as a fortress, the remains of which are still to be seen. The present appearance of Melk dates from 1702–1736, when its central building was expanded into a monastery palace by the renowned Tyrolean architectural exponent of the **Baroque** style, **Jakob Prandtauer**. Stretching 362 meters along a promontory above the Danube and studded with 1,188 windows, it is the embodiment of triumphant **Catholicism**. The interiors of the monastery church and library contain works by important contemporary masters as well. The library ceiling (1731–1732) is especially notable. St. Koloman, a wandering Irish monk in the 11th century wrongly suspected of being a Hungarian and killed in the neighborhood, is buried at the monastery, as are the early Babenbergs.

METTERNICH, KLEMENS WENZEL NEPOMUK LOTHAR, PRINCE OF (1773–1859). Born in Koblenz, Metternich was the offspring of a Rhenish noble house that had worked its way up the rungs of titled distinction in the **Holy Roman Empire** during the 17th and 18th centuries. Like his father, he entered diplomatic service with the **Habsburg** emperors. He served as legate from **Vienna** in Dresden, Berlin, and after 1806 in Paris.

A marriage in 1795 to Countess Eleonor Kaunitz, the granddaughter of Empress **Maria Theresa's** state chancellor, gave Metternich access to the houses of the court nobility of Vienna. In 1809, he became the foreign minister of Emperor Francis I (1768–1835). In this position, he did his best to shield the Habsburg monarchy from the intense military and diplomatic pressure of Napoleon Bonaparte. In 1813, he joined with the pan-European coalition that eventually defeated the French emperor and permanently exiled him in 1815.

Metternich's political and diplomatic skills were conspicuously on display at the **Congress of Vienna,** which met from 1814 to June 1815. He had no desire to restore the Habsburgs to imperial status in a revived Holy Roman Empire. Nevertheless, he succeeded in creating a **German Confederation**, with the house of Austria serving in its presidency. He worked to reestablish Habsburg influence in Italy, where Napoleon had made major political changes. Metternich also brought a re-created Bourbon monarchy in France back into the mainstream of European state relations. Through his efforts, consultative procedures were developed from the 1820s through the 1840s by means of which the major powers of Europe together could maintain international peace and localize domestic unrest, particularly of nationalist leanings. As a reward for the prince's efforts, Emperor Francis I made Metternich his chancellor of state in 1821, a rare distinction in the **Habsburg Empire**.

Metternich had little sympathy with the nationalist and democratic impulses of his age. Although he was not a knee-jerk reactionary—he encouraged the study of ethnic cultures and national **languages** in the Habsburg lands—he loathed the pretensions of middle-class revolutionaries who demanded greater control over their government. Out of such movements would come, in his opinion, partisan factionalism, which would lead to political catastrophe. Nor did he sympathize with political nationalism, which he thought would destroy the multiethnic Habsburg state. In this, he was one with Emperor Francis I. Nevertheless, Metternich had his enemies in the Habsburg government, most notably the influential minister of state, Count Franz Anton Kolowrat (1778–1861). When liberal revolution broke out in Vienna in 1848, the mobs demanded Metternich's removal; a frightened Habsburg regime complied. Metternich fled to England, then in 1849 to Brussels. In 1851 he returned to Vienna, where he led an elegant, if politically marginalized, existence until his death. *See also* FOREIGN POLICY; GERMANY, RELATIONS WITH; ITALY, RELATION WITH; REVOLUTIONS OF 1848; RUSSIA, RELATIONS WITH.

MIKLAS, WILHELM (1872–1956). A secondary school teacher and educational administrator, Miklas was a member of the **Christian Social Party**. His legislative career spanned the **Habsburg Empire**, where he sat in the Austrian imperial assembly from 1907 to 1918 and in the national assembly of the First Republic until 1928. He was president of the latter body from 1923 to 1928. He also acted as the deputy secretary for religious affairs from 1919 to 1920.

In December 1928, Miklas was elected **president** of the First Austrian Republic and served in that office until the **Anschluss** with Germany in March 1938. It was in this office that he achieved a certain amount of notoriety. In 1933, the Austrian parliament dissolved itself through a series of procedural mishaps. Miklas could have called new elections to reconstitute the body but did not, preferring to have Austria governed under an enabling law established to meet emergency situations in wartime.

In March 1938, with Nazi invasion of Austria imminent, Hermann Göring asked for the resignation of Chancellor **Kurt Schuschnigg**, to be replaced by the Austrian **Nazi** leader Arthur Seyss-Inquart (1892–1946). Miklas refused to comply. Nor would he sign the measure recognizing the Anschluss, preferring to resign. *See also* GOVERNMENT.

MILITARY. With the collapse of Austria–Hungary at the end of **World War I**, the provisional government in **Vienna** released all officers and soldiers of the imperial army from their oaths of loyalty on 12 November 1918. A popular militia (*Volkswehr*) was quickly established. Assuming, however, that **Anschluss** with **Germany** was coming, officials modeled Austrian uniforms on German designs.

The victorious powers negotiating the final peace treaties in Paris in 1919 quashed all such schemes; the **Treaty of St. Germain** permitted the much-reduced Austrian state a militia of 30,000 troops for internal duty only.

In 1936, challenged domestically by political paramilitary groups such as the *Heimwehr* and *Schutzbund* and by potential Nazi takeover as well, the Austrian **government** of **Kurt Schuschnigg** reimposed the universal military service that the former **Habsburg** regime had required of all males after 1868. As Nazi invasion became imminent in 1938, Schuschnigg, who was also minister of defense, believed that his troops had no hope of winning. Repelled by the prospect of Germans killing fellow Germans, he ordered his army not to resist. The incorporation of the Austrian army into the German military structure followed immediately upon enactment of the so-called Law of Reunification, which amalgamated the First Republic and the Third Reich on 13 March 1938.

All Austrian anti-fascist groups joined on 27 April 1945 to declare Austria, including its armed forces, independent of German control. But the occupying powers—France, Great Britain, the Soviet Union, and the **United States** (U.S.)—discouraged the development of a serious military infrastructure. The new Austrian provisional government had no portfolio for defense.

Though the Soviets deeply opposed the move, the French, the British, and the Americans allowed Austrian emergency battalions of 500 men in their respective zones in 1949. By 1952, these forces together numbered 5,000; their commanders were Austrian officers with previous service in Hitler's armies. To hide this from the Soviets, one of the pension offices of the Austrian finance ministry managed these contingents.

The end of the Allied **occupation** in 1955 created the need for a state army. By May 1955, however, only 6,500 men had volunteered. After a section for territorial defense within the office of federal chancellor was set up in July 1955, a law passed on 7 September reinstated conscription for virtually for all males. First-time active duty lasted nine months; once deactivated, trainees could be recalled twice. Their specified purpose was to defend Austria's **neutrality** and constitutional arrangements—an obligation fixed in the **constitution** itself—to maintain internal order and assist in domestic emergencies such as landslides, floods, and other catastrophes. The first draft of 19-year-olds was in 1956; eight brigades were quickly deployed among all provinces of the country. By 1966, laws had established border patrols throughout all of Austria.

The **president** of the republic is the highest commander of the army; the power to deploy and to administer these forces rests with the ministry of defense. The National Defense Council (*Landesverteidigungsrat*), made up of military officers and representatives of the sitting government and the federal parliament, has a key advisory role in defense questions.

Austrian forces have served frequently under the auspices of the **United Nations**. Fully mobilized in 1993, the army stood at 200,000. It was considerably reduced after that; in 2006, its top strength was 55,000, including noncombatant personnel. Electing alternative civil service has been possible since 1974.

MOCK, ALOIS (1934–). Born in **Lower Austria**, Mock entered government service and national politics in the camp of the **Austrian People's Party** (ÖVP) as a young man. A strong advocate of European integration throughout his entire career, he served from 1962 to1966 in Austria's delegation to the Organization for European Cooperation and Development, the grouping of West European states with which Austria would be carrying on around 70 percent of its foreign **trade** after 1970. During the same period, Mock was the secretary and chief of staff of Josef Klaus (1910–2001), the federal **chancellor**, who was himself an active proponent of close Austrian economic cooperation with the west. Mock also worked in the foreign office of the Federal Republic.

Between 1971 and 1978, Mock was chairman of the **Chamber for Workers and Salaried Employees**; from 1979 to 1989 he was the national leader of the ÖVP. During that time, he was also president of the anti-Marxist European and International Democratic Union and did a stint in the ministry of education. In a coalition government with the **Socialist Party of Austria** led by Chancellor **Franz Vrantizky**, Mock was vice-chancellor and minister of foreign affairs from 1987 to 1995. He also has served in the Austrian national assembly.

It was as foreign minister that Mock handled the Austrian application for admission to the European Community to his French counterpart, Roland Dumas, in Brussels in 1989. An unwavering supporter of this step, Mock declared in 1990 that Austria backed both the economic and political integration of Europe, positions not altogether compatible with his country's official neutrality. He led the delegation that negotiated his country's entry into the **European Union** in 1995. *See also* FOREIGN POLICY.

MOSCOW DECLARATION. The outcome of a conference among Cordell Hull, the American secretary of state; British Foreign Minister Anthony Eden; and V. N. Molotov, the Soviet foreign minister for the Soviet Union, the Moscow Declaration of 1 November 1943 called for liberation of Austria from **Nazi** rule and its reestablishment as a sovereign country. It was the first clear indication of Allied intentions toward Austria. Although the statement acknowledged that Austria had been a genuine victim of Nazi aggression, it also reminded Austrians that they were cooperating with Adolf Hitler and would have to actively fight for their national independence. *See also* FOREIGN POLICY; RESISTANCE; WORLD WAR II.

MOSER, HANS (1880–1964). One of the most beloved of all Viennese popular comics, Moser was born Jean Julier to immigrant French parents who had come to **Vienna** from France. His father was an academic painter. The son took the stage name Moser after studying diction with an actor of the same name. He acquired a wide variety of theatrical experience after 1907 as he traveled throughout the lands of the **Habsburg Empire** as an itinerant player. Working in Vienna by 1910, he appeared in plays, cabaret performances, and vaudeville. He also played at the **Theater in the Josefstadt** and the **Salzburg Festivals**.

Both his local popularity and renown abroad, however, came largely from the enormous number of **films** he made from the 1920s until just before he died. In them, he generally played benevolent, though often wily, characters, always ready to deflate the pretentious and to help the deserving realize their hopes. The latter were often young people whom societal convention or financial problems kept from marrying. His mastery of local Viennese dialect (**Wienerisch**) gave his characters their remarkable authenticity and enduring appeal. *See also* THEATER.

MOZART, WOLFGANG AMADEUS (1756–1791). Christened Joannes Chrysostomus Wolfgangus Theophilus, the composer had an excellent **musical** lineage. His father Leopold (1719–1787) was a violinist, composer, and eventually assistant director of the choir at the court of the prince-bishop of **Salzburg**. He was also the first teacher of his prodigiously gifted son.

At the age of six the younger Mozart, his sister Maria Anna ("Nannerl," 1751–1829), and their father began a series of concert tours that took them to the major capitals of Europe. W. A. Mozart's first symphonies date from this time as well. In 1769, he became the concertmaster at the court in Salzburg, a position he continued to hold until 1777. During this period, however, he also paid several visits to Italy, where he won considerable musical acclaim. Mozart's work was not as well received during trips to Paris and **Germany**, so he found himself back in Salzburg and at the archbishop's court, until he finally left it for good in 1781. He settled in **Vienna**, where he married Constanze Weber (1762–1842), whom he had met in Germany. Composing independently for the next 10 years, he had great success in the imperial capital (*The Abduction from the Seraglio*, 1782) and deep disappointment as well. The comic opera *The Marriage of Figaro* (1786) was tepidly received in Vienna, though audiences in Prague were wildly enthusiastic.

At first Mozart had tried to work both as a composer and an impresario for his own music; a circle of nobles provided him with auditoriums for his concerts in their residences. He gave private lessons as well. However, the appeal of his music did not last, and from 1788 until his death, Mozart was in constant financial need, in part because of his profligate ways. He was buried in a common grave, which to this day remains unidentified.

If Mozart was not the greatest composer in the Western tradition, he is among the very few who have an arguable claim to that distinction. Though his 41 symphonies, especially the last three, and his five major operas are perhaps the high moments of his total oeuvre, he wrote brilliantly in all the musical genres of his day. These included concert arias; works for single instruments, among them 23 piano sonatas and fantasies; 41 sonatas and variations for violin and piano; a vast number of occasional pieces for small ensembles; and an impressive body of church music, particularly 18 masses. Gifted with an unsurpassed instinct for the psychology of musical sound, he could evoke a vast range of emotions, yet write economically. Mozart's music is a celebration of harmony and balance, in which close relationships are established among normally conflicting styles and feelings. Courtly grace is not far removed from the homely dignity of Austrian folk music; aching melancholy and longing are almost always resolved into joy.

MUSEUMS. Perhaps the clearest testimony to Austria's **Habsburg** past is the country's museums. Their number alone is strikingly disproportionate to the size of the population. Even more noteworthy is the quality of their holdings, which bear the stamp of continued patronage that began seriously under Emperor **Maximilian I**. **Artworks**, manuscripts, and incunabula in **Vienna** have often been scattered throughout Europe because of political changes, military defeats, or both. Monarchs were peripatetic, at least until the end of the 17th century. Emperor Rudolph II (1552–1612) ruled the Habsburg Empire from Prague, where he relocated many important paintings and sculptures, a number of which were seized by the Swedes and others during the **Thirty Years' War**. These were largely repatriated to Vienna, often by outright purchase, as was the case of many artworks carried off by the French who occupied the city during the Napoleonic Wars in 1809. The earliest watercolors, drawings, and prints by such luminaries as Albrecht Dürer and Michelangelo in the **Albertina**, one of the world's preeminent repositories of art on paper, were purchased in the 16th century by members of the ruling house. Nor was the practical side of **art** neglected. The Imperial and Royal Austrian Museum of Art and Industry was established by Emperor **Franz Joseph** in 1863.

Provincial museums also still serve as mementos to Habsburg rule. The Joanneum, founded in **Graz** in 1811, housed the library and natural history collection of Archduke Johann (1782–1859), who spent much time in **Styria** and dedicated himself to the improvement of the province's economy. The institute developed the first locomotive for use in mountain terrain.

But the most powerful examples of Habsburg patronage of art and, less consistently, science are the Art History Museum (*Kunsthistorisches Museum*) and Natural History Museum (*Naturhistorisches Museum*), which make up a grandiose site in central Vienna. Begun in 1872 to bring together imperial collections dispersed around Vienna, **Graz, Innsbruck**, Brussels, and Prague, the entire complex was finished in 1891. The neo-Romanesque exteriors were done by one of central Europe's leading architects of the day, Gottfried Semper, and Karl von Hasenauer (1833–1894), a professor and spokesman for the historicist school of design at the Vienna Academy of Art. Leading painters such as **Hans Makart**, **Gustav Klimt** and his brother Ernst (1864–1892), and the Hungarian Mihály Munkácsy (1844–1900) executed the interiors. The main building houses an immense collection of painting; divisions for old musical instruments, weapons, and ethnography are located nearby in the Homburg complex (1861–1913).

The extinction of Habsburg rule in 20th-century Austria did not bring an end to the creation of important museums, particularly in

Vienna. Austrian interest in modern art has been keen, especially after **World War II**. The Museum of the 20th Century opened in 1962. Dedicated to contemporary art, the building was partly made up of the Austrian pavilion for the Brussels World Fair of 1958. Austria's most elaborate statement of its commitment to modern and contemporary art, however, is its Museum Quarter (MQ), opened in 1991 after 15 years of planning and discussion. A former imperial stable, the complex is a celebration of modern and contemporary art and **architecture**. Though Austrian materials dominate much of its permanent installation, the MQ is always on the watch globally, particularly when programming temporary exhibitions. The MQ also reserves space for contemporary performing arts, including dance and technology that houses information systems on art production and criticism. It sponsors artists-in-residence and supports them with both living and working quarters.

The MQ is anchored by two buildings devoted to the holdings of two private connoisseurs of modern art. One, the Ludwig Foundation, is part of a huge collection that belonged to German chocolate manufacturer Peter Ludwig (1925–1996) and first came to Vienna in 1979. The other was in the hands of an Austrian ophthalmologist, Dr. Rudolf Leopold (1925–). A stunning assemblage of 19th- and 20th-century Austrian arts and crafts was purchased with funds from the state and the Austrian National Library in 1994.

The drawing power of many Austrian museums, however, is not always aesthetic. Of particular recent interest is a **Jewish** museum, opened in 1993 in a former city residence of Bernhard von Eskeles (1753–1839), a wealthy banker and financial advisor to the dynasty. It replaced another Jewish museum that had been in Vienna from 1897 to 1938.

For all of the richness of its museum culture, however, Austria has no national museum, a lack that has been the subject of public debate. Authorities have recently also tried to further the quality of exhibitions and overall management of major museums by giving them increased administrative autonomy. The step has been controversial: houses such as the Kunsthistorisches Museum and the Albertina have increasingly focused on attendance records and public relations and also mergers with smaller museums. By 2007, for example, the Kunsthistorisches had incorporated the Austrian Theater Museum and the

Ethnographic Museum into its programs. *See also* RESTITUTION, LAW OF.

MUSIC. Home to some of the world's premier musical institutions, such as the **Vienna Philharmonic Orchestra** and **Vienna State Opera**, Austria has a unique musical culture. Austrian composers and composers who worked in Austria, especially **Vienna**, have excelled in all of music's genres, from the most serious to the very lightest, from the iconically classical to the most modern and experimental.

The Habsburg rulers of the Austrian lands, particularly from **Maximilian I** through the 18th century, were both active patrons of music and, in some cases, talented composers. The first operatic performances north of the Alps took place at an episcopal court theater in **Salzburg**, and they soon began in Vienna. The great operatic composer Christoph Willibald Gluck (1714–1787) realized his most important musical reforms during his tenure as court composer in Vienna. By the 18th century, many nobles of the **Habsburg Empire** were subsidizing major composers as well, often because the master of the house himself, or someone in his family, was a dedicated musical amateur. The three great representatives of the Viennese classical school of music of the 18th and early 19th centuries, **Joseph Haydn**, **Wolfgang Amadeus Mozart**, and **Ludwig van Beethoven**, owed at least part of their existence to such people.

The advancement of serious music in Vienna shifted to more middle-class audiences following the end of the Napoleonic Wars in 1815. The work of **Franz Schubert** first gained a hearing in these circles. The **Society of the Friends of Music** played an important role in the careers of 19th-century composers such as Johannes Brahms (1833–1897), **Anton Bruckner**, and **Gustav Mahler**. Its subscriptions paid for the **Vienna Philharmonic**, which often played the works of these men. Mahler even conducted the orchestra.

Austrian audiences themselves were not always receptive to new developments in music. The work of Richard Wagner (1813–1883) was heavily criticized by the influential music critic **Eduard Hanslick**. Though Wagner had hoped to hold the premiere of *Tristan und Isolde* in the Habsburg capital, the opera was not given there until the year of the composer's death. Major Austrian composers such as **Arnold Schoenberg** and **Alban Berg** were pivotal in the development of the atonal musical style of the 20th century. They did not, however, enjoy wide popular acclaim. Moreover, their position, and that of the Second Vienna School of composition, to which they gave rise, was seriously hampered by the aesthetic dictatorship of the **Nazi** Party, which seized control of Austria following the **Anschluss** of 1938.

Post–World War II Austrian composers such as Friedrich Cerha (1926–) have continued to exploit this kind of tonal experimentalism, as does György Ligeti (1923–). The latter, though born in Hungary, has done much of his most controversial work in Austria, some of it at the **Salzburg Festival**.

Traditionally, however, the Austrian appetite for music has stretched from the most exalted to the humblest of genres. Some of Christendom's loveliest anthems are heard in Austria on religious holidays such as the Ascension of the Virgin Mary (*Maria Himmelfahrt*, 15 August). **Coffeehouses** and wine gardens or *Heuriger* have often offered decidedly popular musical entertainment, which is enjoyed by all elements of society. The Austrian **operetta**, epitomized in some of the works of **Johann Strauss Jr.** and **Franz Lehár**, have also played a central role in Austrian musical culture. The classic comic plays of **Johann Nestroy** and **Ferdinand Raimund** were interspersed with musical interludes, some of which have achieved folk song status.

Austrian **theaters** and concert halls have also been home to popular music and music theater from abroad. Major Broadway hits such as *The Man of La Mancha*, *My Fair Lady*, and especially *Cats* have had very long runs in Vienna. The fine classical pianist, Friedrich Gulda (1931–2000), had a lengthy career as a jazz performer, teacher, and entrepreneur in Austria and Europe generally. In the world of very new sound, a group of musicians dubbed the Neue Wiener Elektronik have developed international reputations with their highly imaginative combinatory and recombinatory techniques produced on electronic instruments.

MUSIL, ROBERT (1880–1942). Educated in military academies and as an engineer who wrote a dissertation on the physicist **Ernst Mach**, Musil was one of Austria's most important novelists and essayists in the first half of the 20th century. His first success, the novella *Die Verwirrungen des Zöglings Törless* (*Young Törless*, 1906), deals with adolescent encounters with sexuality and violence and the inadequacy of language for expressing the emotional and instinctive side of human existence.

Musil's sprawling masterpiece, *Der Man ohne Eigenschaften* (*The Man without Qualities*), was published posthumously in 1952, after appearing as fragments in 1930, 1933, and 1943. Only gradually incorporated into the German literary canon, it is a pitiless analysis of the weaknesses and delusions of cultural and social life in the last years of the **Habsburg Empire** and of modern societal conventions generally. The tension between reason and emotion, particularly its erotic side, plays a crucial role in the work as well. Though by 1930 he had won several literary awards in German literature, including the prestigious Kleist (1923) and Gerhart Hauptmann (1930) prizes, Musil died in poverty in Switzerland, to which he had immigrated in 1938. *See also* LITERATURE.

– N –

NADLER, JOSEF (1884–1963). An influential historian of German **literature** and essayist, Nadler was born in the kingdom of Bohemia when it was part of the **Habsburg Empire**. He taught at the universities of Freiburg in Switzerland and Königsberg in Germany before taking up a professorship at the **University of Vienna** in 1931. He held that position until 1945.

In multivolume works such as *Literaturgeschichte der deutschen Stämme und Landschaften* (*The Literary History of the German Tribes and Provinces*, 1923) and *Literaturgeschichte des deutschen Volkes* (*The Literary History of the German Peoples*, 1938), Nadler developed the idea that the history of German literature took place not as a series of literary movements represented by individual writers, but as the translation of the spiritual essence of the Germanic peoples from one "stem" to another. Thus 19th-century Romanticism was the result of the Germanization of groups whom he called the "new stems"—the Silesians and East Franks of the German east—by increased contact with the "old stems." The latter were the Alemanic and Frankish peoples. The cultural high point of the latter had been reached in the 18th-century Weimar of Goethe and Schiller. The

Bavarians, Nadler believed, played a unique role in mediating between the cultures of east and west.

NATIONALIZED INDUSTRY. The nationalization law of 26 July 1946 made the Republic of Austria the sole shareholder in 70 privately owned mining and manufacturing concerns throughout the country. These included all of the country's coal, iron, lead, and copper mines; oil fields and refineries; electrical power plants; and the chemical **industry**. In terms of overall employment, the nationalization measure made the **government** the controlling force in about one-fifth of the nation's industry. The three major investment banks—the **Creditanstalt**, the Länderbank (Provincial Bank), and the Mortgage and Credit Institute—were also affected.

The purpose of the legislation was to give Austria control over economic resources that had become German assets after the **Anschluss** and that were not governed by Austrian legislation immediately after **World War II**. Industries in the Soviet zone were under the direct supervision of the **occupier** and were therefore not subject to the nationalization measure until the **Austrian State Treaty** of 1955. A second law—of 26 March 1947—covered electrical power plants owned by the various provinces and other power-producing installations.

Until around 1965, the state played an active role in the management of these industries. Inefficient though they sometimes were, their productivity did rise, spurred on by profits from an expansive export market in which global competition was weak. The relatively quick pace of economic recovery in Austria, along with philosophical differences over the role of central planning in the **economy** between the dominant **political parties** in Austrian coalition governments, led to a restructuring of the arrangement in 1970. The government became the largest shareholder in the **Austrian Industrial Management Corporation**. The management of the firms within this organization was largely in the hands of their individual directors, though these people were often closely tied to the major parties, the **Socialist Party of Austria** and the **Austrian People's Party**.

The function of the nationalized undertakings was not only to show a profit, but to keep Austria employed and socially harmonious. By 1972, the state industries accounted for 20 percent of Austria's

Gross Domestic Product and employed 29 percent of its labor force. No country in Western Europe had a higher percentage of its productive capacity under state control. In terms of absolute size, the nationalized segment of the Austrian **economy** in non-Soviet Europe was second only to that of France.

Until the middle of the 1970s, social goals and economic realities ran on parallel courses. However, the worldwide energy crisis of that decade, along with shrinking markets for the output of heavy industry, upset this relationship. Austria's nationalized industries received much criticism from those who thought that state control was an open invitation to bureaucratic inefficiency, political favoritism, and outright corruption. A mounting national debt contributed to the persuasiveness of their arguments.

From 1975 to 1985, intensive consolidation and reorganization of the state industries took place, though employment remained at acceptable levels. In December 1993, a new law was passed opening the way for a **privatization** process that is still going on. Many industries have been downsized, disbanded, or sold off to private owners. Although some state-held businesses still remain and do well, others continue to underperform.

NAZI PARTY, AUSTRIAN. Known as the German National Socialist Workers' Party (DNSAP), the organization won a serious following in the urban centers of the First Republic. Outlawed for its role in the **July Putsch** of 1934, the party came to be known as the Illegal Movement (*Illegale Bewegung*).

Between 1923 and 1930, the Austrian Nazis were the beneficiaries of strained economic circumstances. Significant numbers of **trade union** members shifted their allegiance to the party. So did students troubled by bleak prospects for employment. By 1936, after two years of reorganization with clandestine financial support from Germany and Austrian sympathizers, the Nazis had approximately as many supporters as did the governing **Fatherland Front**. Nazi leadership, however, was badly divided, though it paid lip service to the *Führerprinzip*, according to which the party chief was not elected but simply emerged. One large faction was located in the eastern part of Austria and one in the alpine regions to the south and west.

Kurt Schuschnigg, the federal **chancellor**, negotiated sporadically with the more moderate wing of the party to bring it into the Fatherland Front and met with some success. However, after the July 1936 agreement between the German Nazis and Schuschnigg, which called for granting amnesty to imprisoned Nazis and incorporation of the party into the Austrian government at some time, the movement grew ever bolder. Its leadership, however, remained fragmented, a situation further complicated by German Nazi efforts to control the activities of their Austrian counterparts. In the final days before the **Anschluss** of 1938, the Austrian Nazis had become the de facto governing party in several provinces of the First Republic.

NESTROY, JOHANN NEPOMUK EDUARD AMBROSIUS (1801–1862). Like many of his fellow playwrights of the **Biedermeier** popular comedy in Austria, including the equally important **Ferdinand Raimund**, Nestroy was a master of many trades that the stage demands. Beginning his career as an opera singer, he not only wrote for the **theater**, but was an immensely gifted actor as well. His plays, which make heavy use of the local Viennese dialect (**Wienerisch**), are tests of a performer's lingual agility and quick-wittedness. They were an ideal showcase for his own talents as a mimic, a punster, and a social critic.

All of Nestroy's major works stem from his central productive period (1833–1844), beginning with *The Evil Spirit Lumpazzivagibundus*, the adventures of three unemployed journeymen making their way through the world. These pieces characteristically leave ample room for the *quodlibet*, an interval during the action in which characters on stage directly address the audience on topics of their choosing. Though generally intended to amuse, these episodes can also be a vehicle for calling attention to political skullduggery, social injustice, or cultural pretension. Nestroy the actor was famous for these sallies in his own plays.

Though he used French and English as well as German comic models, Nestroy drew his most memorable characters from familiar types in Austrian society: from Knieriem, the down-on-his-luck cobbler in *Lumpazzi*, to whom a comet reveals the winning numbers in the lottery, to Weinberl, the clerk in *Einen Jux will er sich Machen* (in British playwright Tom Stoppard's adaptation, *On the Razzle*,

1981), who allows himself and a younger apprentice a final night of freedom before he assumes the responsibilities of an associate in a grocery store.

These plays are so bound to their linguistic and social context that they have never found much of a public beyond the German world. An important exception is *Jux*, a work that inspired not only Stoppard, but the American Thornton Wilder's *The Merchant of Yonkers*.

Following the **Revolution of 1848**, Nestroy became an increasingly bitter critic of contemporary society. His work took on a harsh edge not associated with popular comedy. His last play, *Frühere Verhältnisse* (*Previous Relationships*, 1862), with a minimal cast, is a dissection of a marriage in which the prior love affairs of the partners intrude disastrously. Its general theme is that one can never outlive one's past. *See also* LITERATURE.

NEUE FREIE PRESSE/NEW FREE PRESS. The leading daily of the Viennese upper middle classes of liberal persuasion, the *Neue Freie Presse* was published between 1864 and 1939. Before **World War I**, it generally took pro-**government** editorial positions and defended the integrity of the **Habsburg Empire**. It was opposed to pan-Germanism. By 1920, its circulation had reached its high point of 90,000. It succeeded a newspaper called simply *Die Presse*, which got its start during the **Revolutions of 1848**.

The *Neue Freie Presse* was widely read and respected among the culturally conscious members of the city's middle-class Jewish community, some of whom wrote for the journal on either a regular or occasional basis. Among them were the music critic **Eduard Hanslick** and **Theodore Herzl**, whose work as a correspondent for the paper landed him in Paris during the Dreyfus affair. The experience sensitized him to the dangers of late 19th-century anti-Semitism.

From 1908 to 1920, the *Neue Freie Presse* was edited by Moritz Benedikt (1835–1920), a Jew who during World War I became a particular target of the journalist and monologuist **Karl Kraus**. The latter accused Benedikt and the **press** generally of collusion with government authorities who wished to conceal from the public the horrors of the conflict and the sufferings of Austro–Hungarian troops on the front. A successor to *Neue Freie Presse*, once again *Die Presse*, appeared after **World War II** and is still published today.

NEUES ÖSTERREICH/NEW AUSTRIA. The first newspaper to be established in Austria after **World War II**, *Neues Österreich* appeared for the first time on 23 April 1945, even as the Soviet armies were rounding up suspected **Nazis** in **Vienna** and **Lower Austria**. Envisioned as a voice for democratic unity, its editorial board, was made up of conservatives, socialists, and communists. The editor was Ernst Fischer (1899–1972), a leading figure in the **Communist Party of Austria**. The communists formally left the editorial board of the paper in 1947, when they resigned from the coalition regime then governing the country. They retained their financial stake in *Neues Österreich*, however, until much later.

Speaking for a large bloc of Austrians who supported the idea of an independent Austria, and who disliked both Germans and exploitative capitalism, *Neues Österreich* was at first very successful. It was editorially nonpartisan, a position that was especially popular during the **occupation**, when high ideological profiles were undesirable. With the return of more divided political debate following the conclusion of the **Austrian State Treaty** in 1955, its readership declined. *Neues Österreich* ceased publication in 1967. *See also* PRESS.

NEUTRALITY. The recognition of Austria as a neutral state in perpetuity took place as part of the general negotiations for the **Austrian State Treaty** in 1955. The policy was then especially favored by the foreign minister, **Bruno Kreisky**, and had been demanded unconditionally by the Soviet secretary of state, V. N. Molotov, before the Soviet Union would give up the **occupation** of the country.

The **Moscow Declaration**, agreed to by a delegation of the Austrian government on 15 April, one month before the conclusion of the general treaty, obligated Austria to remain neutral in perpetuity and to fight with arms to retain that status should it be threatened. The North Atlantic Treaty Organization (NATO) had serious reservations about the arrangement. Italy, a member of the alliance, was troubled by the loss of a direct overland connection to West Germany, and many feared that Soviet influence on Austria would remain heavy. Nevertheless, the prospect of any Soviet pullback from central Europe offset these caveats.

The conditions of neutrality for Austria were formally drawn up as a matter of constitutional principle and accepted by the National

Assembly (*Nationalrat*) on 26 October 1955. Austria was to enter no **military** alliances and to allow no foreign power to establish military installations on its territory. Its military forces were to be used for self-defense only. Well into the 1980s, both **foreign policy** experts and the **Constitutional** Court agreed that Austria's sovereignty hung upon strict construction of the provision.

Neutrality did pose some problems for the development of post–World War II Austria. Membership in the European Community, desirable because of the close commercial relations Austria had with **Germany** and **Italy**, was virtually closed, at least until the collapse of the Soviet Union in 1990, in part because participation carried with it certain military responsibilities.

Austria used its position as a neutral state to advance peacekeeping both in Europe and throughout the world. As a member of the **United Nations** (UN) since 1955, it quickly took an active role in such UN bodies as the Committee on the Peaceful Uses of Outer Space and the Human Rights Commission. Austrian forces have participated in many UN peacekeeping forces throughout the world. The neutrality of Austria played a significant role in easing the tensions between the NATO states and the Soviet bloc from 1955 on. Revolutionary groups in Hungary sought the same status in 1956 when they attempted to rid their country of Soviet control.

During the 1990s, however, Austrian neutrality was noticeably compromised. The **government** granted NATO the right to fly through Austrian air space during the Persian Gulf War of 1990–1991. The Austrian admission to the **European Union** in 1995 and the current discussions of a European security system have made Austrian neutrality an ongoing subject of reevaluation. In 1995, **Russia** declared that Austrians could determine the meaning of neutrality for themselves. *See also* FOREIGN POLICY; TRADE.

NEW AUSTRIAN FILM. The New Austrian Cinema of the 1980s arose out of complex cultural cross-currents. One branch, associated with the director Peter K Kubelka (1934–) and his "metric films," in which he calculates, then closely integrates, every linear and coloristic element into his final product, was strongly influenced by experimental cinematography throughout postwar Europe generally.

The second wing was far more explicitly political. It had strong affinities to **Viennese Actionism** and its program for shaking modern Austrian society loose from its attachments to private comfort, hypocritical morality, and refusal to confront the **Nazi** elements of its 20th-century past. With the realities of human suffering, both psychological and bodily, at the center of its plotlines, the New Austrian cinema also has distant roots in the art of the Austrian **Baroque**, which used extreme physical trials to make theological points.

The linguistic extremes of such directors as Franz Novotny (1949–) also have close affinities with Baroque rhetorical strategies. His casual and frequent use of common vulgarity shocks audiences into awareness of how fragile the base of human civility really is. Novotny's *Exit—but Don't Panic* (*Exit—aber keine Panik*, 1980) was emblematic not only of his work but of the Austrian New Film as a whole. His adaptations of some of **Elfriede Jelinek**'s fiction was yet another way of unmasking the underside of one of Austria's sacrosanct pillars of society, the home. Indeed, the theme of deadly family relations has been taken up by others in the movement, such as the Munich born Michael Haneke (1942–), in his *The Seventh Continent* (*Der Siebte Kontinent*, 1989).

Radical feminism has made its own contribution to the shock value of the New Austrian Film. Especially original has been the work of Valié Export (Waltraut Höllinger, 1940–). In her 1968 *Tapp und Tastfilm* (*Groping and Touching Film*), she strapped a camera-like box to her chest, then urged viewers to feel her breasts, a tactic, she said that cleared away the distance between audience and performer along with the male delusions found in the film business and society generally. *See also* FILM.

NORICUM. A short-lived kingdom strung together after 113 BCE by the Celts, Noricum covered terrain that today includes much of modern Austria along with modern western Hungary. The location of the capital, Noreia, is not precisely known; it was probably in either **Styria** or **Carinthia**.

The artifacts from Noricum indicate that inhabitants were quite sophisticated technologically. They appear to have devised a method for extracting salt by infusing it with water, then evaporating the fluid rather than just chipping the mineral out. They also developed a way of using bellows to harden iron, which was then sold in the markets of the Roman empire. Noricum became a Roman province around 45 CE, with a Roman governor whose administrative seat was in Carinthia. *See also* HALLSTATT CULTURE.

– O –

OCCUPATION. From 1945 to 1955, the four victorious powers of World War II—France, Great Britain, the Soviet Union, and the United States—occupied Austria. In July 1945, they agreed that the French would hold **Vorarlberg** and the **Tyrol**; the United States, **Salzburg** and **Upper Austria** south of the **Danube River**; the British, **Carinthia** and **Styria**; and the Soviet Union, **Upper Austria** north of the Danube, **Lower Austria**, and the **Burgenland**. The Soviet zone was the largest of the four. **Vienna** itself was divided in four, with the exception of the First District, which was an international area under the control of all four powers. In all, around 350,000 Allied troops were present in the country.

Thus, until the **Austrian State Treaty** of 1955, the final authority of the country was an Allied Commission, headed by a council of four commissioners, one for each of the victorious powers. This body technically regulated the constitutional life of Austria, because all laws passed by the re-created National Assembly could not go into effect until the commission approved them unanimously. Moreover, after 1946, no single Allied power had a unilateral veto over proposals that came out of the Austrian legislature.

Each of the zones experienced the occupation differently. Although none escaped problematic encounters with foreign military personnel and their policies, the Soviet administration of eastern Austria was frequently punitive. Private land of all kinds, industrial infrastructure, even personal property down to home furnishings, were summarily confiscated. Such behavior did much to convince the overwhelming majority of Austrians, regardless of party affiliation, that their only hope for material recovery lay in cultivating the closest possible relationship with the West. The Soviet domination of east central Europe's economies during the **Cold War** further confirmed these views.

Cold War tensions and other rivalries made it difficult for the Allies to agree on anything that came before them. Austrian **political parties** were used by the victors as surrogates for their own ideological and strategic purposes, with the fate of the Austrian **Communist Party** being particularly crucial. Nevertheless, although the Soviet Union took exception to over 550 statutes that came out of the Austrian National Assembly between 1946 and 1955, it was powerless to overturn them single-handedly. Therefore, the legislative agenda of the Austrian coalition government, drawn after 1947 from the **Austrian People's Party** and the **Socialist Party of Austria**, went forward almost unhindered throughout the entire occupation. Its work was further aided by a provision that made legislative measures operative 31 days after they were passed if the Allied commission raised no objections.

Strong Allied pressure was responsible for whatever de-Nazification measures the regime took. Former **Nazi Party** members were excluded from political office and, until 1949, from voting. In all, around 524,000 Austrians were covered by these regulations. But those who belonged to the only somewhat less authoritarian **Fatherland Front** were exempt from these restrictions. By 1949 a new **political party**, the League of Independents, had emerged to represent far right-wing views in the Austrian political debate.

The allies found the occupation so expensive that they soon began trying to arrange a withdrawal from Austria. Once again, however, political and strategic considerations slowed the pace of negotiations, to the point where the Austrian political establishment feared that the country might be formally divided, as had happened in Germany. But the State Treaty was indeed signed in May 1955. The last Allied troops evacuated the country the following October. *See also* FOREIGN POLICY.

OIL. From the final decades of the 19th century to the end of **World War I**, the petroleum needs of the **Habsburg Empire** were supplied by oil fields that had been opened during the 1850s in Austrian Galicia, today in Poland. Cut-rate imports, largely from the United States, were a further important source. The first systematic exploration for specifically Austrian reserves began in the neighborhood of **Vienna** in 1913. The development of these and other resources discovered in

Upper Austria got underway in 1925 under the aegis of an Austrian subsidiary of the American Standard Oil Company. Serious production began in 1934.

The **Nazis** heavily exploited Austria's oil reserves between 1938 and 1945, and a great deal of the petroleum industry's capital came from **Germany**. Treated as German property by the Allies, all but a very small fraction of Austria's oil fields came under the control of the Soviet Union after **World War II**. Austria reacquired them only after the **State Treaty** was signed in 1955. A **nationalized** administrative body, the Austrian Oil Management Company (*Österreichische Mineralverwaltung,* ÖMV) directed production, refinement, and marketing.

Austria pumped 3.66 million barrels of oil in 1955, the highest annual output the country would ever record. In 1956, reserves were estimated to be about 58 million barrels. By the 1990s, production had dropped below one million barrels, and it continues to fall. The ÖMV, however, continues to be one of Austria's most successful business operations, as it acquires new resources in Eastern Europe, especially Romania, and initiates cooperative ventures in the Middle East. *See also* FOREIGN POLICY; TRADE.

OPERA. Of Italian origins, the genre made its first appearance in **Vienna** in 1626. A year later, this new form of **music theater** arrived in Prague; by 1628, opera performances were taking place in the then-autonomous archbishopric of **Salzburg**. By the middle of the 17th century, Italian opera had come to **Innsbruck** as well. Habsburg courts, particularly that of Emperor Leopold I (1640–1705), who was himself a passable composer, drew some of the leading Italian composers of music drama.

Operas in these early years were characteristically put on as part of lavish court festivals. Among the more staggering was Pietro Antonio Cesti's *Il Pomo d'oro,* the most famous of **Baroque** grand operatic entertainments, written for Leopold's wedding to his niece, Infanta Margherita of Spain, in 1667. Five acts with 66 scenes and 24 sets required complex backstage machinery, custom built for the occasion. Several dance sequences interspersed each act; a triple ballet brought the mammoth spectacle to an end.

Though Viennese opera remained notable for its relatively formal style, grandiose productions, staging, and liberal use of chorus and dance, the classicizing simplicity of 18th-century aesthetics gradually curbed such extravaganzas. An increasingly stingy Habsburg court cut back its budgets, too. Though **Joseph II** tried through the use of German in the so-called *Singspiel* to introduce the public to morally uplifting theatrical experiences, Italian opera in Italian continued to be a major presence on the Viennese musical scene, as well as in the Austrian provinces. Favored composers were Antonio Salieri, the court composer, and Gioacchino Rossini. Though the latter never wrote an opera specifically for performance in Vienna, the public adored his work. All of his operas were put on in the city or just outside of it between 1816 and around 1836. Performances took place not only at the imperial court theater, renovated by Empress **Maria Theresa** for opera and comedy in 1741, but also in public auditoriums such as the Theater on the Wien. A large number of Italian composers continued to work in the city in both the serious and comic veins. Most notable was Salieri, known less for the quality of his music, which was by no means bad, than for his alleged hostility to the prodigiously gifted **Wolfgang Amadeus Mozart**.

Neither Vienna nor the Austrian provinces characteristically produced great opera composers. Mozart stands apart from this generalization, but even he used Italian-language libretti for most of his important operatic works, except for the comic *Abduction from the Seraglio* and his paean to **Freemasonry** and high seriousness, *The Magic Flute*. The Habsburg capital preferred to look to Europe generally for its operatic entertainment. Christoph Willibald Gluck (1714–1787), who worked in Paris and Vienna to simplify operatic vocal and orchestral lines in the name of classical beauty and emotional depth, was born in Germany of Czech parents and trained as a young man in Italy. **Ludwig van Beethoven**, whose highly politicized *Fidelio* was revised twice after its initial performance in Vienna in 1805, was from the German Rhineland.

The pattern continued even after the current house on the Vienna **Ringstrasse** opened on 25 May 1869. The preeminent foreign composers of the time did not find a welcome there. The reigning Austrian critic of the last decades of the 19th century, **Eduard Hanslick,** was intensely hostile to new musical currents of the day, especially the chromatic progressions and cultural agenda found in the New German style of Richard Wagner and his followers.

The Vienna opera remained unfriendly to Wagner's successors as well. **Alban Berg's** pathbreaking *Wozzeck* premiered in Berlin in 1925. Richard Strauss's *Elektra*, with a libretto by the great Austrian poet, dramatist, and man of letters, **Hugo von Hofmannsthal**, was first performed in Dresden in Germany in 1909, the site also for the opening night of the Strauss-Hofmannsthal *Der Rosenkavalier* (1911), a comic but tender look back at rococo Vienna as the composer and his poet imagined it to be. Ernst Křenek's (1900–1991) jazz opera, *Jonny spielt auf*—in which the protagonist is a black saxophonist who, to critical contemporaries, represented an attack of American barbarity on the European musical tradition—was first performed in Leipzig in 1927.

Important contemporary opera composers have not had much better luck in Austria since 1945. Gottfried von Einem's (1918–1996) *Dantons Tod* (*Danton's Death*) had its premier at the **Salzburg Festival** in 1947, but others have seen initial performances of their work in Switzerland, Germany, and elsewhere. Perhaps the most radically experimental composer to work in Austria in the second half of the 20th century, the Hungarian György Ligeti (1923–), saw the first performances of his operatic works (*Adventures and New Adventures*, 1966; *The Macabre One*, 1978) in Stuttgart and Stockholm, respectively. *See also* MUSIC; THEATER.

OPERETTA. A diverting form of **musical** entertainment still closely associated with **Vienna**, operettas are frequently performed in quarters such as the "People's Opera" (*Volksoper*). Their composers were some of the most famous names in the history of popular music, the transplanted Hungarians **Franz Lehár** and Emmerich Kálmán (1882–1953), Oskar Strauss (1870–1954), and **Johann Strauss**, the "Waltz King." Based on models from France, where the genre had a large following, the latter Strauss's effervescent *Die Fledermaus* captures the spirit of the entire genre.

Operetta came to Vienna only around 1870. It quickly attracted a large segment of a general public that was turning away from musical forms and settings, (e.g., churches), and even the popular comedy of the 18th and 19th centuries. Operettas abound in tuneful melodies;

plots focus on the joys, complications, and disappointments of love. Couples quarrel bitterly for one reason or another in the second act, and reconcile blissfully in the third. What they sing can be sexually very suggestive. Productions almost always include much spoken dialogue, a feature that once distinguished them from grand opera and proscribed them from stages where high musical culture ruled. Elaborate, even exotic costuming and scenery added to their audience appeal. That operettas were intended to amuse helped a lot, too. Frivolous though operetta characters may often be, their scores call for rich-voiced singers and plausible actors. Not every opera star can successfully negotiate the crossover to operetta.

The operetta played a crucial role in the development of the 20th-century musical **theater**, especially in the United States. Operetta has found its way to grand opera stages today in the United States, even as the style falls out of favor in Europe. *Die Fledermaus*, along with Lehár's *The Merry Widow*, have near classical status in such American houses as the Metropolitan Opera and the City Opera in New York. *See also* FILM; THEATER.

OSTEND COMPANY. This mercantile undertaking, founded in 1723 by the Emperor Charles VI (1685–1740) in the Austrian Netherlands, was intended to promote foreign **trade**, particularly overseas. By the end of the 17th century, a great deal of the capital resources of the **Habsburg Empire** had been consumed in religious warfare and the effort to repulse the Ottoman Empire from central Europe. With these pressures abating, the emperor and his advisors wanted to position the Habsburg state in the worldwide mercantile **economy** through which England, Holland, and to a lesser extent France, were prospering. Charles and the traders of Ostend specifically hoped to challenge English and Dutch interests in East Asia. Stockholders in the undertaking had already recovered their initial investment by 1730. However, the firm had lost its imperial charter as Charles found himself forced to make concessions to England and the Dutch, who were unhappy with an alliance he had concluded with Spain. The company continued to operate profitably for a while longer, but in private hands.

ÖTZI. The name given to the mummified corpse found in the Ötz Valley range of the **Alps** on 19 September 1991. Preserved in glacial ice since approximately 3000 BCE, it was sent to the University of Innsbruck for radiocarbon analysis. Careful study revealed that the body was of a male, probably a shepherd or a peasant, who was approximately 30 years old when he died. Wearing skin garments, he was carrying tools made of wood, stone, and bone and a six-foot-long bowstave along with arrows. Because the body lay just within the borders of modern **Italy**, it is now housed and displayed in the archaeological museum of Bolzano, once part of Austria's **South Tyrol**.

– P –

PARITY COMMISSION FOR PRICES AND WAGES/PARITÄTISCHE KOMMISSION. Together with Proportionality or *Proporz*, the Parity Commission was a major instrument of social stability in Austria after **World War II**. Established in March 1957, during a period of inflation, it consisted of two representatives from organizations that spoke for the concerns of employers, labor, agriculture, and the **trade unions**, respectively. The **chancellor** and the ministers of trade and industry, social affairs, and the interior were also members, but after 1966 they could not vote. The main charge of the commission was to set wages and prices at levels that were socially equitable without choking off the development of a free market, a duty that made the body the virtual arbiter of Austria's economic development. For policy to move forward, the commission had to make its recommendations unanimously, an arrangement that encouraged the art of compromise among its members.

The commission's cooperation proposals encountered little political opposition. Because the leaders of the four great economic corporations were usually part of the commission, they were positioned to exact compliance from their constituencies. Although such an arrangement marginalized the legislative mandate of the Austrian parliament, members of the commission were close to the major political parties. The commercial and agricultural chambers had ties to the **Austrian People**'s **Party**, the trade union organization to the **Socialist Party of Austria**. Austria's membership in the **European Union** and the globalization of many economic concerns such as environmental pollution have somewhat marginalized the significance of the commission, though it continues to function. *See also* AUSTRIAN FEDERATION OF TRADE UNIONS; CHAMBER, AGRICULTURAL; CHAMBER, ECONOMIC; CHAMBER, LABOR AND SALARIED EMPLOYEES.

PERNERSTORFER, ENGELBERT (1850–1918). Pernerstorfer's career trajectory—from teacher to politician— exemplifies the fluid quality of political life in late 19th-century **Vienna**. Born to an impoverished family that had participated in the proletarian insurrections during the **Revolutions of 1848**, Pernerstorfer was first drawn to socialist ideas. Strong official opposition to these positions led him and other young radicals to support the German national movement of Georg von Schönerer (1842–1921). An advocate of joining the German population of the Habsburg Empire with the newly unified Germany, Schönerer also supported social and economic reforms with decidedly populist overtones. The high point of Pernerstorfer's commitment to these views was the **Linz Program** of 1882, which he coauthored with the later **Social Democratic Workers' Party** (SDAP) leader **Viktor Adler**.

The anti-Semitic side of Schönerer's platform led Pernerstorfer to withdraw from the circle. In 1896, he joined the now-legal **SDAP**; he served as one of its parliamentary delegates from 1901 to 1918. In 1907, Pernerstorfer became the first SDAP vice president of the lower chamber of the imperial parliament in Vienna. As a rule, however, he spoke for German national interests within the workers' movement.

PIARISTS. A small **Catholic** teaching order, the Piarists have played an important role in the development of **education** in Austria. The order was founded in Rome during the 16th century and in 1597 used a rectory there for the first free public school in Europe. The papacy recognized the order in 1617.

As part of her reform of teaching and school curricula in the 18th century, Empress **Maria Theresa** and her advisers adopted much of a program suggested by Gratian Marx (1720–1810), the director of a Piarist academy in Savoy. Although his ideas included clerical control of schools, they also called for giving more weight to subjects such as history, geography, arithmetic, and German. Classical languages began to lose their centrality in the curriculum, though Latin remained a required examination subject for admission to a gymnasium or high school. The schools were theoretically open to all, though the academic qualifications of young nobles and sons of civil servants were far less rigorously scrutinized than those from humbler classes. The Piarists operated 24 high schools in Austria during the 18th century and sponsored dramatic offerings of high literary quality. In the 19th century, they were at the center of a Catholic social movement that addressed the needs of the urban industrial classes. *See also* CHRISTIAN SOCIAL PARTY.

POLITICAL PARTIES. A centralized parliament of sorts existed in the Habsburg Empire after 1861. Delegates, however, came from the provincial estates, which chose them. These people were not representatives of organized political parties but rather of four prescribed voting blocs or *curia*, in which membership was determined by the amount of direct taxes individuals paid. The sum was set high enough to exclude the overwhelming majority of Habsburg subjects.

Direct election of parliamentary representatives in the Austrian half of the **Dual Monarchy** began only in 1873, and still only for those who could meet an expensive property qualification. Only some 6 percent of adult males could vote. Nevertheless, all of the major political parties in Austria in the 21st century have roots, however modified, in factions and programs that evolved in the Austrian Imperial Council (*Reichsrat*) between approximately 1870 and 1914.

For all that representatives to the Imperial Council had formal agendas, their parliamentary clubs were often indistinguishable from opportunistic factions and tactical coalitions. Name changes were routine. In all, probably around 40 parties, bundled into some 20 political clubs for public deliberative purposes, were operating in the Council at one time or other by the outbreak of **World War I**.

A number of these organizations were closely tied to the ethnic interest groups of the Habsburg Empire, including the German-speaking Austrians. Most significant among the latter were the German Liberals, initially led by Prince Karl von Auersperg (1814–1890). Reconfigured as the United Left in 1871, they, along with the much smaller Progressive Club, dominated the Reichsrat until 1879. Many Liberals were inspired by the Josephinian tradition in Habsburg history, which promoted centralized administration, economic modernization, and secularly oriented education. Others in their camp were more closely attached to the reformist ideals of the **Revolutions of 1848**: a written **constitution**, civil liberties, and representative **government**. A German Clerical Party, which spoke for both the **Catholic** church and large rural landholders, was much more conservative, particularly in its critique of freethinking intellectuals.

By 1880, the German Liberals were at odds among themselves over economic, ethnic, and national issues. The more doctrinaire among them increasingly sided with big business at the expense of the small bourgeoisie and artisans and the agricultural classes generally. One highly exclusionary wing of United Left opposed increasing the number of non-Germans among the Habsburg peoples. The most radical members of the faction, spearheaded by Georg von Schönerer (1842–1921), urged German-speaking provinces to secede from Austria–Hungary and become part of the newly united German Reich.

Two major alternatives to traditional liberal and conservative factions emerged in the last decades of the Habsburg monarchy. One came from the Marxist-inspired **Social Democratic Workers' Party** (SDAP), who first appeared in **Vienna** during the revolutions of 1848. Brought together in 1888 by **Viktor Adler** from local socialist splinter groups, the party dedicated itself to improving the material lives of Austria's laboring poor. Though Austrian social democracy never foreswore its collective solutions for the economic and social problems of the Habsburg lands, it vowed to work for them through parliamentary deliberation rather than violent revolution.

The other significant new party, the Christian Social Workers' Union or **Christian Social Party** (CP) after 1895, grew out of concern within the Catholic church about people adversely affected by the consequences of **industrialization** and urbanization. Its first leaders, Karl von Vogelsang (1818–1890) and Prince Alois von Liechtenstein (1846–1920), had a social program for artisans, shopkeepers, and even workers that liberals had never consistently offered and socialists only partly endorsed. **Vienna**'s multiterm mayor **Karl Lueger** (1844–1910) and the CP of Vienna used their dominant position in the city at the turn of the 20th century to initiate major public works programs that improved the health and welfare of all residents of the city.

The CP, soon to be led by **Ignaz Seipel**, and the SDAP, under the stewardship of **Karl Renner**, were the only major parties in post-1918 Austria to retain their prewar character after the collapse of the Habsburg monarchy in 1918. A German National Party, an amalgamation of 17 smaller parties and provincial groupings, appeared in 1919. Like Renner's Social Democrats, it advocated **Anschluss** with Germany. Though a National Socialist Party then present in Austria did not join with them, the German Nationals quickly declared **Jews** to be a "foreign" element that was best removed from the Austrian body politic.

The CP and SDAP dominated political life in Austria until 1933; the strength of the latter was in Vienna, and of the former in the provinces. Relations between the two parties became irreparably antagonistic and sometimes openly violent. In 1933, Chancellor **Engelbert Dollfuss**, a member of the CP, organized the **Fatherland Front**, which promised to be nonpartisan and to act for Austrians "true to the regime." Multiparty deliberation ground to a halt; Dollfuss disbanded the SDAP in 1934. He had also declared the National Socialist Party illegal a year earlier, though this did not end its clandestine activities. An attempted putsch failed in 1934, but the Nazis maintained close contact with their German counterparts. One-party rule prevailed in Austria following the **Nazi**-led Anschluss of 1938.

Austria's major political organizations reconstituted themselves quickly after **World War II**, but on a less adversarial basis. The CP and some remnants of the Fatherland Front became the **Austrian People's Party** (ÖVP); the party's new agenda affirmed a commitment to not only Austrian culture and Austrian independence, but democracy as well. Religion was less central to its core program than before 1938. The reconstituted party's leaders—Leopold Kunschak (1871–1953), **Leopold Figl**, **Julius Raab**, and Felix Hurdes

(1901–1974)—played key roles in the reestablishment of the Austrian republic. Social Democrats and a much smaller group, the Revolutionary Socialists, came together as the **Socialist Party of Austria** (SPÖ). This party, too, tempered its ideological rhetoric, especially on religious matters. Its Party Program of October 1947, presented by **Adolf Schärf**, reiterated socialist concerns for the proletariat and a more egalitarian society and economy. Like the ÖVP, however, the SPÖ supported Austria's freedom, independence, and **neutrality**. By 1958, class hostility was toned down even more in a new SPÖ program. Along with the ÖVP, the Socialists promised to maximize human freedom, though through material changes rather than defense of traditional family values and religious institutions, as the ÖVP prescribed. All Austrians were welcome in the party, including those of faith, which was reserved to a private sphere for all. Socialists supported neither capitalism nor dictatorship of any kind, the communist variety included. Nevertheless, the Austrian **Communist Party**, outlawed in 1933, reappeared under Ernst Fischer (1899–1972), who returned from the Soviet Union in 1945 to chair it. Communists participated in the newly formed Austrian government in 1945. Even they, however, accorded private enterprise a role in rebuilding the country.

In February 1949, some of the National Socialists who remained in Austria, along with others not affiliated with any party, came together in the League of Independents (*Verein der Unabhängigen* = VdU). This group joined forces in 1955 with the Freedom Party (*Freiheitliche Partei*) to form the **Freedom Party of Austria** (FPÖ), led from 1958 to 1978 by Friedrich Peter (1921–2005). Though Peter's career in the Nazi SS during **World War II** troubled many of Austria's politicians and voters, he was willing to bend doctrine at will to form coalitions with mainstream parties, particularly the SPÖ. Its program was far more procapitalist and antistatist than that of either of the two major parties. Advocating a tighter rein on government spending, the FPÖ consistently attacked politicized administrative appointments that kept loyalists of the SPÖ and the ÖVP paid and pensioned, but were, according to FPÖ doctrine, irrelevant to the common good.

In the 20 years after 1945, the ÖVP and SPÖ dominated the coalitions that governed Austria. In 1966, however, having won an absolute majority of seats in the parliamentary elections, the ÖVP became the first party to lead post–World War II Austria alone. Joseph Klaus (1910–2001) remained federal **chancellor** until 1970. One-party government continued until 1983, but under the SPÖ led by Chancellor **Bruno Kreisky**. When the Socialists lost their majority in 1983, Kreisky refused to cooperate in forming a coalition, leaving his successor as **chancellor**, Fred Sinowatz (1929–2008), to arrange a controversial coalition with the FPÖ. The ascendancy of the major parties weakened as new groupings emerged. A **Green Party** had been established in 1981. By 1983, the Greens (*Grünen*), along with another leftist faction, the Austrian Alternative List (ALÖ), were siphoning off votes from both major parties. The Socialists were very hard hit. Several other splinter parties added to the general political realignment in national elections between 1983 and 1999.

The rise of the mercurial **Jörg Haider** in the FPÖ in the 1980s made formation of coalition governments even more difficult. Combining a strong nationalist bent with bold antistatist economic proposals, Haider capitalized on fears about unrestricted **immigration** and restlessness, particularly among younger voters, with an increasingly ingrown party system. When Haider became FPÖ chairperson in 1986, alarms went off around the world about a resurgence of political and ethnic xenophobia in Austria, which was displacing old-fashioned neo-Nazism but continued to have a racist subtext. The country's mainstream parties were wary of working with Haider, although the ÖVP under the leadership of **Wolfgang Schüssel** would take the plunge after a tight election in 2000. Nor were all members of Haider's own party enthusiastic about his leadership. Heide Schmidt (1948–), the vice-chairperson of the FPÖ, broke away to found the **Liberal Forum** (LiF) in February 1993, in protest against Haider's agenda. Its appeal to the electorate stalled, however, and internal wrangling quickly marginalized the movement. Though elections in 1994 and 1995 gave the LiF a smattering of seats in the parliament, it won none in 1999. Haider himself established his own splinter party, the Alliance for the Future of Austria (BZÖ), in 2005. Though the movement drew a surprising 11 percent of the vote in the national elections of 2008, Haider's death in that same year left the future of the party in serious doubt. *See also* AUSGLEICH; JOSEPH II.

POPPER, KARL RAIMUND (1902–1994). Knighted in England in 1965, Popper spent most of his life there or in the English-speaking world. He lived in New Zealand, where he taught at the University of Canterbury from 1937 to 1945. He was professor of logic and theory of knowledge at the London School of Economics after 1960. He received his doctorate, however, at the **University of Vienna** in 1928, having studied mathematics and physics. He frequented the discussions of the **Vienna Circle** and shared the group's general skepticism about metaphysics.

Popper is generally recognized as the founder of critical rationalism. Unlike the Vienna Circle, he did not believe that knowledge was limited to the contents of verifiable statements. For Popper, all general propositions of knowledge were tentative and unprovable, either empirically or rationally. However, through the process of falsification, an observer can at least establish what is not true. Popper was also a bitter opponent of political authoritarianism.

PRANDTAUER, JAKOB (1660–1726). One of the masters of **architecture** in the Austrian **Baroque**, Prandtauer was baptized at Stanz bei Landeck in the **Tyrol**. He received his formal training, closely associated with the construction handicrafts, in his native province, but his career unfolded throughout the Austrian **Danube** Valley. Charging lower fees than many of his illustrious contemporaries, he was much in demand. With the canny financial support of Berthold Dietmar, the abbot of **Melk**, Prandtauer redesigned the **Benedictine** cloister in **Lower Austria** and had a hand in the early phase of the work on the building itself. Other major religious edifices in the region that he designed and constructed were the cloister of Herzogenburg (1714–1726) and several sections of the monastery of St. Florian in **Upper Austria**. He was highly imaginative at incorporating older structures into his plans.

PRATER. Today a vast amusement park (Lat.: *pratum* = meadow) in **Vienna**'s Second District, the Prater was sequestered as a hunting preserve by Emperor **Ferdinand I** in 1560. The chief thoroughfare through the complex, the Hauptallee, had been laid out in 1537. It was much prized by the **Habsburgs**, both for sport and for court festivals, though the terrain, originally very close to the **Danube** River, was prone to serious flooding. In 1766, **Joseph II** opened the area for public use. However, the Hauptallee long remained a passageway for the nobility and their retainers. Just north of this lay what is popularly called the Würstelprater (Sausage Prater), which Joseph also turned over to the more plebeian among his subjects as the Volksprater (People's Prater) in 1786. By 1800, large numbers of people were making use of the park.

Near one of Vienna's main railway stations, the Würstelprater was completely destroyed at the end of **World War II**. Though rebuilt, it is considerably smaller than the original. The Prater's emblematic landmark is the huge Ferris wheel. However, mechanical amusements are a comparatively small part of the park's attractions. Much of it is reserved for walking, cycling, bathing, and the other pleasures of a warm summer day.

PRESIDENT, FEDERAL REPUBLIC. The presidential office in Austria's federal **government** was an innovation of the First Republic. As in many other European parliamentary regimes between the two world wars, the position was at first ceremonial. Changes in the Austrian **constitution** after 1929 gave presidents more authority to intervene in federal and local politics, and their actions, or failure to act in the crisis-ridden 1930s, hastened the First Republic's descent into right-wing dictatorship even before the **Anschluss** with Nazi Germany in 1938. Federal President **Wilhelm Miklas** accepted the legally questionable suppression of parliamentary rule by Chancellor **Engelbert Dollfuss** after legislative deliberations ground to a standstill in March 1933 because no one would serve as presiding officer in the lower house. In March 1938, Miklas did, however, refuse to sign the announcement of Austria's unification with Germany.

As federal president from 1945 to 1950, **Karl Renner** played an important role in restoring parliamentary democracy to Austria. He was, however, given his office by the provisional parliament and not by general popular mandate.

Direct election of presidents of the Austrian Republic was restored in 1951. Their term of office is six years. Though they are not prohibited from running at some future date, they may have no more than two consecutive terms. They are not altogether powerless. Although they cannot intervene directly in administrative and legislative affairs, they can reject high ministerial nominations without reason and dismiss the **chancellor** and the entire **government**. Presidents may also declare a state of emergency, though only after the government requests it. They can bestow honors, grant pardons, and the like, but only after consulting with the appropriate ministers. In the case of state honors, the president's wishes are normally respected.

Though candidates for the Austrian presidency normally carry some kind of party identification, they do not have to in order to run for election. Perhaps the most successful and cherished president of the Second Republic, **Rudolf Kirchschläger**, ran with no party label. Austrians seem to prefer such an outlook in their chief executives. People holding the office do engage in public philosophical discourse, particularly when opening conferences, festivals, and other special occasions. **Thomas Klestil** (1932–2004), federal president 1992–2004, made speaking for Austria in world affairs a central mission of his career. Nevertheless, Austrian presidents can be very controversial. Most problematic, by far, was the presidency from 1986 to 1992 of **Kurt Waldheim**. Dogged by accusations of covering up his complicity in Nazi military atrocities, he was elected only in a second round of voting. Although Klestil, his successor, also went through the same process to win his first term in office, his majority in the runoff far exceeded Waldheim's. When Klestil ran for reelection in 1998, he received 63.5 percent of the first-round vote, second only to the vote the exemplary Rudolf Kirchschläger had received for a second term in 1980: 80 percent of the electorate. *See also* FISCHER, HEINZ; RENNER, KARL; SCHÄRF, ADOLF.

PRESS. Today's *Wiener Zeitung (Vienna Journal)*, the country's official newspaper of record, is among the oldest dailies in the world. Founded in 1703 as a court journal called the *Wiener Diarium (Vienna Daily)*, it changed its title following a merger with another paper in 1724.

The content of 18th-century newspapers in the **Habsburg** seat, particularly the *Wiener Zeitung*, could be quite wide ranging. Several articles from the 1770s, for example, covered the crumbling Ottoman Empire and the rebellion of Great Britain's North American colonies. What these publications lacked was a place for editorial opinion, a concession to government and church censorship that only intermittently relaxed. Emperor **Joseph II** encouraged free circulation of opinion at the outset of his reign in 1780, but as dissidence with some of his other policies flared up in some of his lands, he became as restrictive as his predecessors.

The end of the Napoleonic Wars reinstalled intellectual conservatism throughout the Austrian lands, but serious periodical literature did survive. The *Wiener Jahrbücher der Literatur* (*Vienna Literary Yearbooks*) and the *Archiv für Geschichte, Statistik, Literatur und Kunst* (*Archive for History, State Affairs, Literature and Art*) were both informative and open to a diverse group of writers and intellectuals. It was only after the **Revolutions of 1848**, however, that newspapers became genuine organs of public opinion and criticism.

A golden age of Austrian journalism unfolded after 1867, when the **constitution** for the Austrian half of the **Dual Monarchy** made freedom of the press a protected civil right. Censorship still took place: the press bureau of the Austrian Ministry of the Interior watched newspapers and magazines regularly, though not always with equal intensity. Some papers were ideologically better positioned to influence **government** thinking than others. By the beginning of the 20th century, Friedrich Funder (1872–1959), editor of the *Reichspost* (*Imperial Post*), the voice of the **Christian Social Party**, belonged to the circle of men who advised Archduke **Franz Ferdinand**. But even the *Reichspost* carried articles read throughout Europe, as were stories and *reportage* in other partisan dailies such as the **Social Democratic Arbeiter Zeitung** (*Workers' Journal*), which began publishing in July 1889. The generally liberal *Neue Freie Presse* (*New Free Press*) was even more widely respected, both domestically and abroad.

Austrian reporters and editors from several political camps were co-opted into government propaganda efforts during **World War I**, sacrificing both their independence and their credibility in the process. Nevertheless, journalism in **Vienna** revived quickly after 1918; what the city lacked in material well-being, it made up for, to a certain extent, with the lively array of local publications. The first tabloid in the city, *Die Stunde* (*The Hour*), appeared in 1923. Combining readability with a smattering of hard content, the format remained an enduring part of the Austrian newspaper scene.

Any independent press had vanished by 1940 in **Nazi**-run Austria. Not until 21 September 1945 did the *Wiener Zeitung* resume operation, as the paper of record for the Austrian provisional government. The **occupation** powers restored the guarantee to publish freely in the country later that year. By 1954, the American-influenced *Wiener Kurier (Vienna Courier)* had become the *Neuer Kurier (New Courier)*. Combining *boulevard* irreverence with often probing investigative reporting, it would be postwar Austria's first journalistic success story.

Competition for readership, however, was keen. The thoughtful *Neues Österreich (New Austria)* closed. Audiences deserted papers published by **political parties**, such as the communist *Volksstimme (People's Voice)* and the *Arbeiterzeitung*. Some readers shifted to the serious national dailies that emerged, *Die Presse*, for one, then in 1988 *Der Standard*, along with the *Salzburger Nachrichten (Salzburg News)*. Despite the regional ring to its title, the **Salzburg** daily has covered world events and the arts consistently and independently. National news weeklies also appeared; among the first was *profil*, a venture of *Standard* publisher Oskar Bronner (1943–). The largest readership, however, was, and is, of tabloids, such as the Vienna *Neue Kronen Zeitung (One-Crown Journal)*, whose origins go back to 2 January 1900, the day after the crown became the basic unit of **currency** in the Habsburg Empire, where one crown bought a monthly subscription to the paper. Its combination of celebrity-watching and soft porn with little-guy conservative indignation and folksiness have made it enduringly popular. The most widely read of these papers nationally has, for many years, been *Die Kleine Zeitung (The Little Journal)*, based in **Graz**, but sold throughout much of the country, with special sections devoted to local provincial news. A new entry into the Austrian tabloid scene since 2006 is *Österreich*. Produced by one of Austria's most powerful media companies, the **Fellner** group, its tone and layout was designed, like all of the organization's publications, for specific audiences, generally the young, more affluent, and lifestyle conscious, without wholly abandoning significant investigative reporting. *Österreich* has forced many of Austria's leading dailies to rethink their format, content, and pricing policies.

The Austrian press is characterized by considerable concentration of ownership. The *Kurier* and the *Kronen Zeitung* are holdings of the Mediaprint organization. The Fellner group now controls the country's three major news magazines, *News*, *Format*, and *profil*.

The publication and editing of *Österreich*, however, no longer has any connection with the three weeklies. The **government** itself has often subsidized papers in the interest of keeping the public informed and maintaining some diversity of opinion in the print media.

PRESSE, DIE/THE PRESS. Today, with a daily readership of approximately 103,000, *Die Presse* is not Austria's most widely read newspaper. Nevertheless, with intensive coverage of local events and a network of foreign correspondents, *Die Presse* is the only Austrian newspaper that comes close to playing the role of such dailies as the *New York Times*, the *Frankfurter Allegemeine* of Germany, or the French *Le Monde*. Editorially, it supports free market economies and liberal democracy, though it has been highly critical of leftist politics and the countercultural philosophies of the 1960s.

Die Presse was founded in the wake of the **Revolutions of 1848**. Modeled after an eponymous periodical in Paris (*La Presse*), it supported liberal positions. It was equally progressive in its production technology. A group of editors split from the journal in 1864 to establish the ***Neue Freie Presse***, which became the premier daily of the Habsburg Empire.

In 1946, the new *Die Presse* appeared. Initially published as a weekly by the Austrian press magnate Ernst Molden (1888–1953), it became a daily in 1949. Longtime editor Otto Schulmeister (1916–2001) generally endorsed liberal positions and pragmatic approaches to political, economic, and social problems of the Second Austrian Republic. A sharp critic of the Austrian left in the 1960s and 1970s, Schulmeister became identified with what were increasingly called conservative views. His successor, Thomas Chorherr (1932–), continued to orient the paper along centrist liberal-conservative lines. Under considerable competitive pressure from new dailies, most notably *Der Standard* (1988), tabloids, and electronic news sources, and beset by editorial infighting, *Die Presse*'s circulation failed badly from 2000 to 2006. Now more topically focused, it has recovered considerably. *See also* PRESS.

PRIVATIZATION. Austria came away from its **occupation** after **World War II** with one of the most heavily nationalized and in-bred economies of noncommunist Europe. Not until the 1980s did the

Vienna stock exchange become a useful provider of investment capital. State-owned **banks** lent to state-owned or state-dominated companies. In the 1980s, however, balance sheets of state-run industries grew alarmingly passive because of fiscal mismanagement, outright corruption, a redundant workforce, and competition abroad. Serious recession added to the dismal economic atmosphere, and privatization became an attractive alternative.

Though recovery was underway by 1984 and 1985, the finances of nationalized Austrian heavy **industries** remained catastrophic. By the beginning of 1986, Austria's major **political parties** had agreed on a partial privatization of nationalized industries. The Second Republic gradually began selling off its equities in these enterprises, at first as a way of raising revenue to keep them afloat.

In the mid-1990s, the **Austrian Industrial Management Corporation** (ÖIAG), initially created to manage the country's **nationalized industries**, transformed itself into a management agency to market government holdings in various enterprises. By 2000, the last state-owned bank was privatized. The venerable government **tobacco** monopoly went private in 2001; private television stations were allowed to enter the **communications** market in the same year.

An especially emblematic case was the traditional postal service. In 1996, it was renamed the Austrian Postal and Telecommunications Corporation (*Post & Telekom Austria AG*), with its governance now conducted under private law. For the next 10 years, its many subsidiary enterprises were sold off, often in the face of protesting workers. In 2000, Austria Telekom shares were listed on the New York Stock Exchange. In 2006, the state divested itself of 49 percent of its equity in the postal service.

PRIVILEGIUM MINUS. See BABENBERG, HOUSE OF.

*PROPORZ/***PROPORTIONALITY.** Closely observed from the signing of the **Austrian State Treaty** in 1955 until 1966, the proportionality system guaranteed that each of the major postwar Austrian **political parties**, the **Socialist Party of Austria** (SPÖ) and the **Austrian People's Party** (ÖVP), received a certain number of political offices and government jobs filled through patronage. These positions were in **nationalized industries**, **railroads**, **banks**, and postal facilities, as well as in federal and local **governments** and administrations. The policy, although it undercut the legislative powers of the new parliament, helped to curb the party antagonisms that had split Austria into implacably hostile camps between 1918 and 1938. It contributed materially to the political stabilization of Austria and to the economic recovery of the country after **World War II**.

Following general elections, each party named delegates to a Coalition Committee that allocated the positions after voting to set the number each fraction received. Nevertheless, the ÖVP usually received the ministries of **education**, **trade**, **agriculture**, and defense. The SPÖ consistently controlled interior, justice, **welfare**, and **transportation**. Should an ÖVP member be minister of education, the undersecretary would be a Socialist, and the other way around. Upon unanimous consent among its members, the committee also sent legislative proposals to the parliament, which normally approved what was put before it. *See also* PARITY COMMISSION FOR PRICES AND WAGES.

PROTESTANTISM. The Reformation of the 16th century brought Lutheranism, and somewhat later Calvinism, to the Habsburg Austrian lands and the **Habsburg Empire** generally. As part of the German-speaking community, Austrians were open to all of the confessional innovations that originated in Switzerland and the **Holy Roman Empire**. Aside from the **Tyrol**, where **Catholicism** was not seriously challenged, all of the Austrian lands were heavily Protestant by the latter third of the 16th century. In **Styria**, **Carinthia**, and **Lower Austria**, Protestant noblemen who played central roles in the provincial estates wrested permission to conduct Lutheran religious services from the Catholic Habsburgs who ruled them. Archduke, later Emperor, **Ferdinand I** was himself a devout Catholic and had little use for what he saw as Protestant sectarianism. His son, Emperor Maximilian II (1527–1576), was more flexible in his confessional outlook but did not like religiously divided subjects either. Both, however, were willing to make concessions to the new faith to get financial aid from the deliberative bodies with which they were forced to bargain. However, they never permitted the formal establishment of any Protestant church.

At the turn of the 17th century, the status of Protestantism in the Austrian lands grew more precarious. In Styria, Archduke, later Emperor, **Ferdinand II** restricted Lutheran freedoms systematically. By 1600, all of his middle-class subjects were forced to attend Catholic services. Although the nobility still carried on private devotions in their castles, full Lutheran religious services were forbidden. A key figure in the central European Counter-Reformation, Ferdinand took the opportunities that victories in the **Thirty Years' War** gave him to effectively drive Protestantism from the Austrian lands. In 1627, Protestant preachers and schoolmasters were banished from Lower Austria. Although the nobility of that province retained somewhat greater religious freedom than their counterparts elsewhere in the Habsburg lands, they were vigorously encouraged to convert to Catholicism.

From roughly 1630 to 1700, around 100,000 Protestants emigrated from the Austrian territories, among them some of the most productive elements in the population. Only in eastern Hungary, where Calvinism had found a home among the nobility, did the Reformed church survive openly in the Habsburg Empire. For the most part, the evangelical confessions, if they survived at all, did so only clandestinely. In the 18th century, bands of Protestants were driven from the Austrian lands or areas closely associated with them, such as the prince-bishopric of **Salzburg**. Some of these people found their way to the New World.

Moved by the Enlightenment and pressures to foster a more productive citizenry, the Habsburg rulers of Austria began to change their attitude about Protestantism in the 18th century. Emperor **Joseph II** issued a Patent of Toleration in 1781 allowing both Calvinists and Lutherans freedom of worship and the right to churches of their own. However, the location and design of these facilities was closely regulated. Catholic practice continued to intrude into Protestant ecclesiastical affairs. Regulation of interfaith marriages and the confessional training of the children born in such unions were especially thorny issues. It was not until 1861 that Protestants throughout the Habsburg Empire, officially designated as non-Catholics (*Akatholiker*), received a governing council of their own, with separate subsidiary offices for Calvinist and Lutheran affairs.

The **Treaty of St. Germain** required religious liberty for all confessions in the First Republic, and in 1922, faculties of Protestant theology were incorporated into the university system. Nevertheless, the territorial settlements that came out of **World War I** put Austrian Protestantism in a vulnerable position once again. Reformed churches once in the Habsburg Empire were now in Hungary and Czechoslovakia; their Austrian coreligionists were often dependent on foreign donations to keep their houses of worship solvent.

The number of Austrian Lutherans and Calvinists now is about 376,000, with the former predominating. All faiths are equally protected under the current Austrian **constitution**. *See also* RELIGION.

– Q –

QUALTINGER, HELMUT (1928–1986). Cabaretist, actor, and satirical essayist, Qualtinger was best known as the creator of the characters Herr Travnicek and especially Herr Karl, the Austrian Mister Everybody. Herr Karl, created in collaboration with Carl B. Merz (1906–1979), was a man much given to the pleasures of the table and the boudoir, in that order. His chief aim in life was to get along without unduly bestirring himself. He commented on much that was serious—the **July Putsch** of 1927, political party life in his own Austria—but committed himself to nothing other than avoiding responsibility. His cynicism could sometimes be cruel—his view of women was grossly instrumental—but was never far from humorous. The production began as a television show in 1961.

Qualtinger was also a staple of the cabaret **theater** that plays a major role on **Vienna**'s intimate stages, such as the Lieber Augustin and the *Volkstheater*. His performances were widely recorded. He was also known for his readings from the *Last Days of Mankind* by **Karl Kraus** and from Adolf Hitler's *Mein Kampf*.

– R –

RAAB, JULIUS (1891–1964). Trained as a building engineer, Raab began his political career as a representative to the National Assembly of the First Austrian Republic from 1927 to 1934. He was also a leader of the ***Heimwehr*** in **Lower Austria**. In 1938, he served as minister of trade and transport in the government of **Kurt Schuschnigg**.

Following **World War II**, Raab was one of the founders of the modern **Austrian People's Party** (ÖVP), which he served, both directly and indirectly, in several important capacities. Between 1945 and 1964, he was a delegate to the reconstituted National Assembly; from 1952 to 1960 he was party chairman (*Bundesparteiobmann*). As president of the federal **Economic Chambers**, he argued for a careful balance between economic and social policy.

Austrian **chancellor** during the years 1953–1961, Raab cooperated closely with the **Socialist Party of Austria** in the Grand Coalition that governed the country. Together, the major parties pursued policies of **currency** stabilization, full employment, and wide-ranging social benefits, which have characterized Austria through much of its recent history. To integrate the Austrian **economy** with other European countries, Raab supported his country's membership in the **European Free Trade Association**. He was also a major player in the events leading to the conclusion of the **Austrian State Treaty** in 1955. Raab was the ÖVP **presidential** candidate in 1963. Intraparty quarreling weakened his position, and he went down in defeat. *See also* POLITICAL PARTIES.

RADETZKY, COUNT JOHANN JOSEF WENZEL (1766–1858). The most distinguished of the **Habsburg** generals in the first half of the 19th century, Marshall Radetzky entered the dynasty's service as a cadet during the reign of Emperor **Joseph II**. He received his marshal's title in 1836. He distinguished himself as the head of the quartermaster's office in the battle of Leipzig (1813), in which the European Grand Coalition defeated Napoleon.

Radetzky's renown, however, came from his accomplishments in Italy during the **Revolutions of 1848**. Under his command, Habsburg forces recaptured control of Lombardy–Venetia from Italian nationalist opposition under the leadership of King Charles Albert of Sardinia–Piedmont. Radetzky is memorialized in one of the poet-dramatist **Franz Grillparzer**'s most famous poems, "An Radetzky" ("To Radetzky") and in Austria's widely played *Radetzky March*, by Johann Strauss the Elder (1804–1849).

RAILROADS. The first steam engine on Austrian rail lines began operation in 1837; it replaced the horses that had up until then been drawing carriages along the tracks. Until the **Seven Weeks' War** between Austria and Prussia, small private companies ran most of the **Habsburg Empire**'s trains. Austria's defeat led both government ministers and legislators to worry about the military and commercial drawbacks of a fragmented and inefficient rail network. Initial routes went between major cities in the Austrian lands—**Vienna–Linz**, Vienna–**Graz**, for example—but not to secondary centers such as **Innsbruck**. Non-Austrian Habsburg holdings were better served. The first steam locomotive line in the empire ran from Vienna to Olomouc in Moravia. Only after 1873 did construction of secondary lines within the Austrian lands themselves pick up.

The empire had started nationalizing its rail lines in 1841, but fiscal pressures forced the government to restore them to private companies in 1854. Systematic nationalization remained a priority of the monarchy, especially because **Germany** was already far along in the process. The cost of these changes, however, was great and slowed down their implementation. The regime in Vienna not only had to buy out these firms, but often had to take responsibility for company benefits promised to workers. Yet another asset to be purchased was property connected with rail **transportation**, such as mines. The southern stretch of the Austrian railroad lines remained private until 1923.

For all these difficulties, the Austrian railroads were technologically progressive. Electrified rails operated locally in the Habsburg Empire after 1883. By 1887, they functioned dependably enough to withdraw steam engines. Some of the latter were, however, kept in reserve on the line in case the electric conveyance failed. The Habsburg Empire went to great lengths to maintain the system. In 1910, the state spent more for railroads than any other single budgetary item.

Rail transport was adapted to intraurban use as well. City trams started using electric power in 1895. Construction of the Vienna City Rail Line *(Stadtbahn),* which encircled an inner perimeter of the city, began in 1893. Following existing tracks, its stations and station facilities were planned and designed by the architect **Otto Wagner**. The service was available to the public in 1898, though construction was not finished until 1902. It was fully electrified between 1923 and 1925. The national rail system also stepped up its conversion to electric power after **World War I** to take the place of coal now lying in other successor states to the Habsburg Empire.

The allied **occupation** ended its control of Austrian railroads in 1946. A major first step in their rehabilitation was restarting the electrification program, which eventually took steam power out of the system altogether. The Second Republic also sponsored a major expansion of mass rail transportation, especially in the Vienna metropolitan area. A rapid transit line *(Schnellbahn)* that runs circumferentially in the city was extended to Lower Austria in 1962. It has expanded considerably since then. Construction of the Vienna subway began in 1969; in 2007 it was still ongoing. Incorporating some of the routes of the former Stadtbahn, the network carried passengers over 46 kilometers of track by 1993.

RAIMUND, FERDINAND (1790–1836). Born in **Vienna** with the family name Raimann, Raimund, along with **Johann Nestroy**, was a master of the Viennese popular **theater**. Like many who plied their talents in the genre from the 17th to the 19th centuries, Raimund worked as actor, director, author, and less frequently, composer.

Raimund made his first contacts with the Vienna **Burgtheater** while still fending for himself as a bakery salesman. From 1814 to 1817, he was associated with the **Theater in the Josefstadt**, but his most important pieces were produced at the Theater in the Leopoldstadt, where he worked from 1817 to his death. In 1821, he became stage manager of this establishment; from 1828 to 1830 he served as its director.

Raimund's most important play, *Der Alpenkönig und der Menschenfeind* (*The King of the Alps and the Misanthrope*), was first performed in 1828. It featured the author himself in the leading role of Mr. von Rappelkopf—he has no given name—a well-to-do burgher, whose choleric suspicions of all who come in contact with him is the despair of his family and servants. Through a series of magical interventions, a staple of Viennese popular comedy that owes much to the theater of the **Baroque**, Rappelkopf is spirited away from his home. Removed altogether from his environment, he is forced to reevaluate his character as he watches a miraculously created double replicate his nasty behavior with his fellow man. Appalled by the spectacle, Rappelkopf comes to see his fellow man more positively. The change allows him to rejoin his household. The members of the latter are at first nonplused by his altered demeanor, but soon adjust to it happily. The piece, which modern psychiatrists have noted employs techniques used in behavior modification, ends with Rappelkopf declaring that his new self is his true self, a theme echoed in many of Raimund's other works.

For all that his plays argue for the basic goodness of humankind and the quiet accommodation to one's station in life, Raimund was himself a tortured soul. His relations with the women he loved were bumpy. He aspired to write tragedy rather than comedies, even when the latter were spectacularly successful. He was prone to melancholia and hypochondria, yet feared that whatever cures were available to him would destroy his theatrical gifts. He committed suicide in 1836, after having been bitten by a dog he believed to be rabid. *See also* LITERATURE.

REFUGEES. *See* ASYLUM.

REINHARDT, MAX (1873–1943). Born Max Goldmann in the Austrian resort town of Baden, just south of **Vienna**, Reinhardt was a true man of the **theater**. An actor, director, theater manager, and author, he was also the husband of Helene Thimig (1889–1974), a member of one of the German stage's theatrical dynasties. Reinhardt made his theatrical debut in the Austrian capital in 1890, but then moved on to Berlin, where he established both his career and much of his reputation. The director of one of that city's most significant houses, the Deutsches Theater, Reinhardt was also active in smaller settings, founding the Berlin Kammerspiele (Chamber Players) in 1906, as well as in cabaret productions.

Reinhardt was a cofounder and director of the **Salzburg Festival**; from 1920 to 1938, when he left Austria, he directed the annual performances of *Jedermann*. In 1924, he became director of the Vienna **Theater in the Josefstadt**, and in 1929 he founded the Reinhardt Seminar, a school for theatrical performers that is still part of the Austrian University for Music and Theater.

Both practically and theoretically, Reinhardt was an influential force in the development of modern theater and film. His actors were trained to speak and move naturally. Reinhardt believed that audiences should be made part of the production, to lower the barriers between themselves and performers. He was attracted to the Salzburg Festival because he thought that the environment of the city and the surrounding landscape would strengthen the impact of the material he was staging.

Mass scenes became standard features of Reinhardt's offerings, and he was especially successful at directing mob sequences. He was also a technical innovator, making use of the revolving stage and dramatic lighting effects. All of this served him well in his numerous films, the most successful of which was *A Midsummer Night's Dream* (1935). In 1938, Reinhardt immigrated to New York, where he tried to continue his career, though with indifferent results. He died in the United States. *See also* HOFMANNSTHAL, HUGO VON.

RELIGION. The Christianization of the Austrian lands took place as part of the general Christianization of southern **Germany**, which began in the sixth and seventh centuries. Major Catholic monastic orders, particularly the **Benedictines** and Cistercians, played key roles in the cultural, educational, and economic life of the medieval Austrian lands. The most important Austrian bishopric was in **Salzburg**, though Passau, today in modern Germany, was very influential as well. Both establishments had extensive territorial holdings throughout the Austrian lands, which often frustrated the efforts of secular rulers to consolidate their domains. Gurk in **Carinthia** played a similar role to the southeast.

As was true in Germany as a whole, the **Protestantism** of the Reformation made deep inroads into Austrian **Catholicism**. With the exception of the **Tyrol**, the Austrian provinces were either predominantly, or close to predominantly, Lutheran by the end of the 16th century. Led by the **Habsburg** dynasty itself, the Counter-Reformation made the Austrian lands almost totally Catholic once again by the end of the 17th century. The **Jesuit** order played a crucial role in this process. Its educational programs were especially influential, and the brotherhood would have heavy input into instructional activities until well into the 18th century.

Guided in part by the notions of the European Enlightenment, 18th-century Habsburg rulers, particularly **Maria Theresa** and her son, **Joseph II**, had several reasons to revise religious life and practice in their lands. Monasteries routed potentially productive members of society into contemplative pursuits, and restrictions on Protestants and **Jews** also limited their contributions to the **economy** of the empire. By the latter third of the 18th century, the state was taking a far greater role in the **education** of the young, and both Protestants and Jews had been given a carefully spelled out degree of toleration.

Some reversal of these changes took place in the 19th century, as a concordat signed with the papacy in 1855 reasserted Catholic control over education, particularly in the primary grades. However, the rights of Jews and non-Catholics, as Protestants were called, to religious freedom were increasingly accepted. The **Fatherland Front** of the 1930s under chancellors **Engelbert Dollfuss** and **Kurt Schuschnigg** steered Catholicism along an exceedingly right-wing course, from which its leaders strained to extricate it after **World War II**. But the guarantee of freedom of religion and conscience made to the Austrian half of the **Dual Monarchy** after 1867 is part of the Austrian **constitution** today.

With the several branches of Eastern Orthodox Catholicism counted separately, there were 18 officially recognized religious communities in Austria in 2004. Nevertheless, Austria has remained overwhelmingly Roman Catholic, with religious affairs administered by two archbishoprics, in **Vienna** and **Salzburg**. The numbers of parishioners are dropping dramatically, as are figures for those studying for the priesthood. Recent controversies in the church over abortion; sexually abusive clergy, some of whom stood high in the hierarchy; and the general secularism of the modern age are thinning the ranks of Austria's once dominant faith. In 1995 alone, 40,000 Austrians broke their ties with the Roman confession. There are currently around 6 million declared Catholics, of whom roughly 18 percent attend church services regularly. From 90 percent of the Austrian population in 1950, they are now around 75 to 76 percent. Protestants are less numerous too, though their decline has not been so dramatic. There are around 8,000 Jews, most of whom are in Vienna, but they are very secularized.

The number of Muslims grew rapidly in the second half of the 20th century. *See also* AUSGLEICH; ISLAM.

RENNER, KARL (1870–1950). Born in Moravia, Renner was a leading socialist politician and political theorist whose activities spanned the latter years of the **Habsburg Empire**, the **First Austrian Republic**, and the Allied **occupation** of Austria after **World War II**.

As a delegate of the **Social Democratic Worker's Party**, Renner became a member of the Reichsrat, the legislature of the Austrian half of Austria–Hungary, in 1907. There, he was a prominent advocate of a federal solution to the national unrest within the Habsburg Empire, a position he continued to argue throughout **World War I**. His economic program followed the mainstream of **Austro-Marxist** thinking. It called for an ongoing state takeover of property and capital and an elaborate network of state-financed social services. Renner was also eager to expand educational opportunities for the socially and economically disadvantaged, a concern that became a hallmark of Austrian socialism.

From the collapse of the Habsburg monarchy toward the end of October 1918 to June 1920, Renner was the chancellor of what was at first called the Provisional Republic of German Austria, then the First Austrian Republic. In 1919 and 1920, he also served as Austrian foreign minister; it was in this position that he led the Austrian delegation to the Paris Peace Conference and signed the **Treaty of St. Germain**. With a succession of conservative governments dominating Austria after 1922, Renner devoted himself to party affairs. From 1931 to 1933, he was president of the parliament; in 1934 he was briefly imprisoned by the authoritarian regime of **Engelbert Dollfuss** during the civil unrest that accompanied the collapse of Austrian parliamentary government. In 1938, he supported the **Anschluss** with Nazi **Germany**.

It was in good part through Renner's initiative that a provisional **government** was formed in Austria as World War II drew to a close. Although the Soviets, whose army participated in the occupation of the country, had never liked his reformist outlook and his support of the Anschluss, Renner was a known quantity for them, and they believed that they could work with him. He served as the head of the three-party coalition that would govern the country provisionally until elections could be held. These took place in November 1945. A month later, Renner was elected Austrian **president**. *See also* ECONOMY; EDUCATION.

REPUBLICAN GUARD/REPUBLIKANISCHER SCHUTZBUND. The paramilitary arm of the Austrian **Social Democratic Workers' Party** (SDAP), the Schutzbund was organized throughout the First Republic in 1923–1924 under the leadership of Julius Deutsch (1884–1968). The growing conservatism of regular army leadership, and the formation of rightist military bands throughout the provinces of the republic, prompted the move. Commanded centrally from headquarters in **Vienna**, the Schutzbund acquired a substantial arsenal. By 1928, its membership was believed to be around 80,000. Uniforms and conventional army labels for its divisions—companies, battalions, and regiments–made plausible its assertions that it was ready to defend the interests of the proletariat with force.

As part of his effort to cripple the influence of the SDAP, **Engelbert Dollfuss**, the **chancellor** in 1933, banned the Schutzbund. Its leadership and materiel largely untouched, it went underground. Repeated police searches to uncover illegal caches of weaponry followed, particularly in the provinces. Some Schutzbund leaders in the countryside were also arrested. The final confrontation between the government and the Schutzbund took place in 1934. Rejecting advice he received from his leadership in Vienna, Richard Bernaschek (1888–1945), a socialist militia leader in **Linz**, the capital of **Upper Austria**, decided to strike back after a police raid for weapons. The authorities faced machine-gun fire when they arrived at the suspect locality. The action provoked other Schutzbund bands to begin skirmishing in Vienna, **Graz**, and elsewhere. Their action got them little; 196 of their number throughout the country were killed, and 10 of their leaders were executed. A ban on all socialist organizations followed. *See also* FEBRUARY UPRISING.

RESISTANCE. The **Anschluss** of 1938 had great support in Austria from circles that normally had strong ideological differences with one another, such as elements of the **Catholic** church and the **Social Democratic Workers' Party**. Some members of the former *Heimwehr* and monarchists were also troubled by the new regime.

Nevertheless, groups of workers, especially in the industrial centers of Austria and among the Catholic laity, began to take shape as early as the summer of 1938 to oppose the new **Nazi** regime. A broad spectrum of political, ideological, moral, social, patriotic, and religious motives prompted these actions. There was, however, no Austrian government-in-exile to be the external voice for these sentiments abroad, unlike Poland or what was then Czechoslovakia. Monarchists, whose spokesmen were **Otto von Habsburg** and two of his brothers, Robert (1915–1996) and Felix (1916–), were more engaged in Western Europe and the **United States**. **Communists** and radical socialists attached themselves to the Soviet Union. From 1942, the socialists were largely responsible for establishing pockets of armed resistance, particularly among Slovenians in the southeast of the country and among **Styrian** communists in the mountains around Leoben.

From 1943 until 1945, Austria experienced the full force of Allied bombing; the threat of widespread loss of life and property became a reality. Toward the end of the war, serious cells of resistance gathered together. Ideological preference was not a requirement of membership, nor was connection to any social or economic class. Their sole purpose was to save the country from senseless destruction. Many hoped to avoid Soviet **occupation**. There were Austrian participants in the failed plot to assassinate Adolf Hitler in July 1944; it was they who were to take over the **government** of their country once the dictator was dead.

The best known of these resistance organizations was the so-called Group 05, which had contacts with the Allies in Switzerland. It also cooperated with a military command post (XVII) in **Vienna**, under the leadership of Major Carl Szokoll (1915–2004), who plotted to negotiate a cease-fire with the advancing Soviet armies on 3 April 1945. Discovered by the yet-functioning Nazi government, some of the leading conspirators were executed in that same month, before the war came to an end.

A resistance movement in the **Tyrol** actually freed the city of **Innsbruck** before the arrival of American troops, who would occupy the city. Around 27,000 Austrians were executed for their participation in resistance movements. Another 32,000 died in concentration camps and other forms of confinement. Approximately 15,000 fought in Allied armies against the Nazis, as partisans, or in other European resistance groups. *See also* RUSSIA, RELATIONS WITH.

RESTITUTION, LAW OF. The **Nazi** regime that governed Austria from 1938 to 1945 ruthlessly confiscated and often sold artworks owned by political émigrés, Jewish and non-Jewish alike. Formal restitution began after 1945, but only to claimants who clearly identified these materials as theirs. The objects in question also had to have been found in repositories officially set up to hold looted and deaccessioned art during **World War II**. Even if possession was confirmed, the Austrian government had to wave an export prohibition for people who wanted to take their property out of the country or to sell it abroad. Originally put in place on 1 December 1918 during the fiscal crisis that followed the collapse of the **Habsburg Empire**, these restrictions were to keep financially pressed Austrians from liquidating the cultural heritage of their country in exchange for hard foreign currency. The provisions served as the prototype for a general Historical Monuments Preservation Law issued in 1923, which was most recently revised in 2000. Modified several times throughout the 20th century, the Austrian Office of Monument Preservation (*Bundesdenkmalamt*), a federal office housed in the Ministry of Education, has administered export permissions since 1945.

The application of this law by successive Austrian **governments** and general bureaucratic evasiveness aroused worldwide criticism of Austria's commitment to restitution. In 1946, the Austrian branch of the Rothschild banking family asked to have their artworks returned; although they got back a large number of their possessions, it was only on condition that they "donate" some major items to the state as part of Austria's "cultural heritage." By 1997, the debate on restitution policy swirled around claims of two Jewish families whose plaintiffs were both U.S. citizens for return of two paintings by **Egon Schiele** then on exhibition in the Museum of Modern Art in New York as part of the Rudolf Leopold Collection, purchased by the Austrian state in 1994. In January 1998, New York district attorney Robert Morgenthau impounded the two pieces. One of them, the *Portrait of Wally*, remains the subject of continuing litigation. The other, *Dead City II*, went back to Austria after the testamentary claims of the plaintiff were deemed groundless. *See also* UNITED STATES, RELATIONS WITH.

The uproar in the international **art** world that surrounded the case, along with pressure from the American Department of State, persuaded the Austrian government and its minister of education and cultural affairs, Elisabeth Gehrer (1942–), to take action. On 13 January 1998, she ordered Austrian museums to inventory all materials relating to acquisitions during World War II and in the period following. The provenance of all artworks in state hands had to be clarified.

A restitution law for artworks was announced on 5 November 1998. The export ban can be waived for all properties that were in state possession and in Austrian museums through forced "donations." Laws that had cleared Austrian governments from any responsibility for artworks that came under arrangements made before 1945 were reversed. All unclaimed works were to be managed by an Austrian National Fund, which would turn proceeds from auctions over to victims of National Socialism. The Rothschild family had the rest of their property restored to them in 1999. Thousands of works claimed by no heirs, that had been stored in a monastery near Vienna, had been turned over in 1946 to the city's Jewish Community, to be sold at auction for its benefit.

Another case, the ownership of several paintings by **Gustav Klimt**, was complicated less by export prohibitions than by stipulations in the wills made by the Bauer-Bloch family, Viennese **Jews** whose wealth had come from sugar manufacturing. In 2006, an arbitration panel in Austria ruled that the works belonged to Maria Altmann, a citizen of the United States, and a niece of the man who had given Klimt the commission.

By 2007, the $201 million fund set aside to compensate Austrians who had been robbed of their artworks was running out. There was, however, a website (www.kunstrestitution.at) listing 8,715 items of suspicious provenance in Austrian museums through which people could identify and claim property once theirs.

REVOLUTIONS OF 1848. On 13 March 1848, mass demonstrations broke out in **Vienna**. Instigated by students, more radical elements of the city's middle class, and some factory workers, the dissidents called upon Austrian Emperor Ferdinand I (1793–1875) to grant a **constitution** to ensure greater popular representation. Parallel outbursts, though with a pronounced national slant, followed in northern **Italy**, Hungary, and the Kingdom of Bohemia. Among the first major changes in the **government** of the **Habsburg Empire** was the dismissal of Imperial Chancellor **Metternich**, whose name the crowds associated with the antiliberal policies of the ruling regime.

For the first weeks of the upheavals, the Habsburgs and their advisors worked to pacify the mobs. Two constitutional proposals were offered; the second, accepted by the revolutionaries, called for a unicameral legislature. This body began its deliberations by July 1848 and produced some important and lasting measures. Among them was the abolition of serfdom, though the process by which this was realized took several years.

But even as such major changes were being adopted, the Habsburg government had begun to recover its nerve. Vigorous military intervention in Italy and Prague quelled nationalist dissidence there, though not permanently. Hungarian resistance was far more stubborn, enduring until 1849, when combined Austrian and Russian forces suppressed it—though not before an outright declaration of independence, inspired by the radical revolutionary Louis Kossuth. Fleeing abroad, Kossuth continued to serve as an eloquent spokesman for the Hungarian anti-Habsburg cause. The revolution in the Austrian lands also ebbed, as middle-class supporters grew increasingly wary of student and proletarian radicalism. Peasant commitment weakened too, once it became clear that serfdom would end. In December 1848, after considerable discussion among members of the **Habsburg** dynasty, Ferdinand I abdicated. Replacing him was the very youthful **Franz Joseph**, who would rule the Habsburg lands until his death in 1916. *See also* RADETZKY, COUNT JOHANN JOSEF WENZEL.

RINGSTRASSE. In 1857, Emperor **Franz Joseph** ordered that the fortifications that had long enclosed the three sides of **Vienna**'s Inner City, or First District, be razed. His chief purpose was to remove what had become a major obstacle to the growth of the city, although populations in the immediately adjacent outer districts had been growing for well over a century. In the place of the walls was to be an internal boulevard, for which designs were solicited in an international competition held in 1858.

As an urban thoroughfare, the Ring, as it is colloquially known in Vienna, opened in 1865. The various building projects lining either side of it took until 1888 to complete and were designed by some of Europe's leading **architects**, among them August Sicard von Siccardsberg (1813–1891), Gottfried Semper (1803–1879), and Heinrich Ferstel (1828–1883). All three were strongly influenced by the historicizing styles of their day, particularly neo-Renaissance designs. These features can still be seen on the new university building by Ferstel, the new **Burgtheater** by Semper, and the **Vienna State Opera** by Siccardsberg and Eduard van der Nüll (1815–1868).

Though most of these structures remain and are still in use, the character of the Ring has changed considerably over the past century. Its residential buildings, both aristocratic and upper middle class, were converted in the late 20th century into commercial quarters or luxury hotels. The **coffeehouses** that were once a feature of the Ring landscape have also largely disappeared.

RINTELEN, ANTON (1876–1946). Trained as a jurist, Rintelen was a professor at several universities before **World War I**, including the German University of Prague between 1903 and 1911. In the latter year, he took a position at the University of **Graz**, where he taught civil procedure. Active in **Christian Social** politics, he was elected deputy governor of the province of **Styria** in 1918. He served as governor of the region between 1919 and 1926 and 1928 and 1933. In that position, he played an instrumental role in equipping the paramilitary regional *Heimwehr* with heavy weapons. During part of that period, he was also the education minister of the First Austrian Republic. In 1933, Rintelen was Austrian ambassador to **Italy**.

Rintelen was a crucial figure in the Austrian **Nazi July Putsch** of 1934, which ended in the murder of the **chancellor**, **Engelbert Dollfuss**. The Styrian was the choice of his coconspirators to assume the now-vacant office. Though radio broadcasts announced that he had assumed the office, they were false. Rintelen was arrested and jailed. In 1935, he was condemned to life imprisonment for treason. Released in 1938, he withdrew from serious political life.

ROTH, JOSEPH (1894–1939). Writing under his own name as well as under pseudonyms such as Hamilkar or Christine v. Kandl, Roth was born a **Jew** in the Bukovina, one of the easternmost reaches of the **Habsburg Empire**. He studied Germanic philology and philosophy at both the local university in Lemberg (Ukr.: Lv'iv) and in **Vienna**. He served as an officer in the Habsburg army during **World War I**.

Roth's literary career, which began in journalism in Vienna after the war, was extraordinarily varied; he was equally accomplished as an essayist, short story writer, and novelist. Nor did he work in Austria alone; from 1923 to 1932 he was also a correspondent of the prestigious German daily, the *Frankfurter Zeitung*. After 1933, he went into exile in Paris, where he died from the effects of his long-term alcoholism in 1939.

Roth never came to grips with the Europe that emerged out of World War I. His depression only increased as Fascism and Nazism began to dominate the political scene of the late 1920s and 1930s. His most famous novel, *Radetzky March* (1932), was an elegiac look at three generations of a South Slavic family of Trotta who had served the **Habsburgs**, and the ideals they read into that empire. *The Crypt of the Capuchins*, published posthumously in 1938, treats a similar theme. *See also* LITERATURE; MAGRIS, CLAUDIO.

RUDOLPH, ARCHDUKE (1858–1889). *See* MAYERLING.

RUSSIA, RELATIONS WITH. Only after the beginning of the 18th century was Tsarist Russia a problematic element in the **foreign policy** of the **Habsburg** monarchy. The ongoing expansion of the Romanov dynasty's holdings to the west and southwest at the expense of two crumbling megastates, the kingdom of Poland and the Ottoman Empire, posed a potential threat to the house of Austria's eastern borders. The thrust of Vienna's foreign policy toward Russia was to avoid warfare but curb its territorial ambitions. Habsburg rulers participated with Russia in 1772 and again in 1795 in the partitions of Poland. Where possible, the Habsburgs used mutual advantage to make Russia an ally. Russia fought for a time on the Austrian side against Prussia in the Seven Years' War (1756–1763) and joined **Joseph II** in a fruitless Balkan War between 1788 and 1791. Russia and Austria were part of the Grand Coalition that beat back Napoleon Bonaparte and cooperated with Imperial Chancellor **Klemens von Metternich** and Emperor Francis I in keeping Europe monarchical between 1815 and 1848. The armed intervention of Tsar Nicholas I (1796–1855) brought nationalist separatism in Hungary to a halt in 1849.

The **Habsburg Empire**, however, did not always reciprocate. Russia expected the help of Emperor **Franz Joseph** during the Crimean War (1853–1856), but none was forthcoming. In the second half of the 19th century, relations between St. Petersburg and Vienna grew markedly more tense. Russia continued to press for military and naval advantage south to the Black Sea, where the Ottoman regime was often unable to resist. Nationalist movements in Greece, Serbia, Bulgaria, and to a lesser extent, today's Romania, where populations were primarily Eastern Orthodox, also opened the way for the Romanovs to serve as protector of peoples whose faith the Russian dynasty shared.

Franz Joseph and his foreign ministers managed to embarrass Russia twice in this role: once at the Congress of Berlin (1878), where participants trimmed back a newly advantaged position following a Bulgarian uprising against Ottoman rule, and again in 1908, when the Habsburgs annexed Bosnia, to the great distress of the kingdom of Serbia and its Russian advocate.

It was Russia's support of Serbia that brought it into **World War I** in 1914. Losses for both sides on the eastern front were enormous. Perhaps the high point of the entire conflict for the Habsburg Empire was the Treaty of Brest-Litovsk (March 1918), which yielded a great swath of territory to be divided among the Central Powers at Russian expense. These arrangements, however, were of purely academic interest following the conflict that brought an end to both empires.

The **Communist Party** of Austria, founded in 1918, drew much of its inspiration from the Bolshevik Revolution of 1917. Austrian foreign policy initiatives toward the new Soviet Union were negligible, however, partly on ideological grounds, partly because of more pressing tasks. **World War II**, however, put the Soviet Union squarely in Austrian territory as part of the **occupation**. In the 10 years before the signing of the **Austrian State Treaty**, Vienna's treatment of the Moscow regime was exquisitely circumspect. Popular experience of Soviet occupation, particularly in its zone, convinced Austrians that they did not want to be part of the Soviet bloc. But even after the State Treaty was in place, Austria's eastern boundary abutted on

Soviet satellites, and Vienna treated the Communists of Moscow cautiously and often deferentially. The Soviet Union was quick to block any serious signs of Austrian cooperation with the European Community (EEC/EC) and North Atlantic Treaty Organization (NATO). In 1967, the Soviets would not allow Austria to join the European Common Market.

Austria had other reasons to preserve good relations with the Soviet Union. It needed to reactivate **trade** with Eastern Europe generally. In 1956, Austria negotiated free passage down the **Danube** to the Black Sea with the Soviet Union. In 1960, Austria joined the Danube River Commission, a body completely dominated by the Communist Bloc. The only Western government represented in the group was the German Federal Republic, and only with observer status. Austria was also eager to have the Soviet Union as a market. In 1958, Vienna signed a set of protocols that expanded economic exchanges with Moscow. In 1979, Austria would be the first Western country to have free trade relations with the Soviet Union on the basis of completely convertible **currencies**. Austria also wanted to regain sovereignty over assets that the Soviets had commandeered during the occupation. After intense discussion, the Moscow government agreed in 1958 to reduce by 50 percent oil deliveries guaranteed to it in the State Treaty.

The implosion of the Soviet Union in 1989 changed the tenor of Austrian–Russian relations dramatically. As it had done with Hungarian refugees in 1956 and their Czech counterparts in 1968, Austria opened its borders to East Germans fleeing to the West in 1989. This time, however, Moscow kept its armies at home. Indeed, as subsequent events showed that the Soviet government could not retain its territorial buffer in east central and southeastern Europe, Austria intensified its efforts to join the **European Union** (EU), a step that the Soviets would have once quickly challenged as a violation of Austria's pledge of **neutrality**. Not until 1995, with Austria a member of the EU, did the Russian vice-minister of foreign affairs, Sergei Krylow, declare that Austria alone could determine the meaning of its neutrality in interstate relations. For its part, the Austrian foreign ministry recognized the new Russia as the legitimate successor of the Soviet Union, a measure that other members of the EU had taken one year earlier. Austria also promised to support Russian admission to the Council of Europe and relief from restrictions on trade many European countries had adopted on trade during the **Cold War**.

Austrian and Russian foreign policies have since then differed sharply at crucial moments. Austria supported the military intervention of the **United States** in Kosovo in 1999; Russia, along with China, did not. Vitally interested in seeing a natural gas supply line run directly from the Caspian to central Europe without touching Russian territory, Austria, along with Great Britain, Sweden, and some of the former Soviet bloc countries, deplored Russian military incursions into Georgia in 2008. They made known their reservations about further integration of Russia into the EU. Some of the small states, most notably Lithuania, continued to oppose extensive EU cultivation of Russia. However, Benita-Ferrero Waldner (1948–), a one-time minister of foreign affairs for Austria who had become EU commissioner of external affairs in 2004, agreed in November 2008 that discussions with the Russians about economic, security, and energy matters should resume. *See also* FOREIGN POLICY.

– S –

SALZBURG, CITY. One of Austria's most durable tourist attractions, Salzburg is both a city and a province of the modern Federal Republic. The first human habitation of the region dates from Paleolithic times. Mammoth salt deposits around Hallein brought people to extract it as early as the sixth century BCE. Celtic settlers were especially active in this work around 450 BCE in the area in and near Hallein. Copper was mined in the Salzburg region during the Bronze Age.

Roman troops displaced the Celts in Salzburg in 15 BCE. Roman Juvavum, as it was known, included both the modern city of Salzburg, which was an administrative center, and an extended territory around it. The Roman road through the Tauern Pass was one of the empire's most important north–south links. As the Germanic tribal migrations began crossing the region at the end of the fourth century CE, the sessile population diminished. Nevertheless, when the Romans withdrew in 488, they left a substantial number of Celto–Romanic peoples behind, particularly around what would become the city of Salzburg. The Bavarians appeared in the region during the sixth century and put down roots. Slavic peoples moved into some valleys as well.

The Christianizing of the region took place under Bavarian auspices. Duke Theodo sent a Rhenish clergyman, Bishop Ruprecht (ca. 650–716?), to begin the task in 696. Later canonized, Ruprecht was generously rewarded for his labors in this life, too, with extractive rights to the salt deposits around Reichenhall and other lucrative possessions. It was at this time that the territory and its most important city became known as Salzburg. Strategically located for eastern missions, Salzburg served as the center for the evangelization of both the Slavs and the Magyars in the eighth and ninth centuries. During this period, German kings granted additional land throughout **Lower Austria**, **Carinthia**, and **Styria** to the bishopric.

The see thus established proprietary beachheads in those provinces that often frustrated the ambitions of local secular authorities until the dissolution of the **Holy Roman Empire**. Indeed, the bishops of Salzburg became ecclesiastical princes. Closer to their base, they consolidated their hold on such economically valuable areas as the forests of the Pongau, which they cleared and settled. In 1342, Bishop Heinrich referred to Salzburg as "his land." By the end of the 14th century, the bishopric had acquired most of the territories radiating from Salzburg. The dukes of Bavaria had formally withdrawn their claims to the area as well.

The **economy** of the prince-bishopric of Salzburg reached its high point in the late 15th and 16th centuries. Not only did the salt mines turn a profit; gold and silver came out of the region as well. However, not all of the territory's peoples prospered. Between 1525 and 1526, a particularly nasty uprising of peasants and miners against their ruler, Cardinal Matthäus Lang (1468–1540), took place. The cleric had to call upon the **Habsburg** archduke in **Vienna**, **Ferdinand I**, for military aid.

Such wealth did not last. Five-sixths of Salzburg's terrain is mountainous, a serious limitation on economic growth in early modern times. Indeed, the 17th-century archbishops who built the **Baroque** city that lures so many admirers today—Wolf Dietrich von Raitenau (1559–1617), Marcus Sitticus (1574–1619), and Paris Lodron (1586–1653)—were drawing upon dwindling resources that they supplemented with higher and higher taxes. The **Catholic** Counter-Reformation, to which they owed their positions, had significant and unpleasant religious consequences for a sizable segment of Salzburg's population. By the 1680s, the **Protestant** community of the land was coming under pressure to leave. In 1731–1732, more than 20,000 peasants of evangelical faith emigrated. Many of them went to the kingdom of Prussia, and a significant number came to the British North American colonies, particularly in the south. A few landed in the Netherlands.

The prince-bishopric disappeared as a territorial principality in 1803 with the reconfiguration of Germany during the Napoleonic Wars. It passed in 1816 to the new Austrian Empire of the Habsburgs as part of the territorial settlement reached at the **Congress of Vienna**. The change brought neither riches nor prestige to the province. It was not until the second half of the 19th century, with the construction of transit **railroads** and the beginning of **tourism**, that economic growth returned to Salzburg. This accelerated considerably after **World War I** under the energetic leadership of the territorial governor, Franz Rehrl (1890–1947), of the **Christian Social Party**. The newly created **Salzburg Festival** proved to be an international attraction.

The **Anschluss** with **Germany** in 1938 had much popular support in Salzburg. The Great Depression had increased the already large numbers of unemployed, who bitterly resented the economic privileges accorded to functionaries of the major **political parties**. The Allies bombed the region heavily during **World War II**; in one industrial center, Hallein, around 15,000 people were killed as a result of such attacks. The Americans **occupied** Salzburg after the war until 1955 and did much to encourage its revival, especially its summer festival. Today, with a reestablished university (1962) and the elevation of the Mozarteum to a **music** academy (1971), it is among Austria's most economically dynamic and sophisticated regions. *See also* ALPS; HALLSTAT CULTURE; RELIGION.

SALZBURG, PROVINCE. *See* SALZBURG, CITY.

SALZBURG FESTIVAL. A year before **World War I** ended, a society was founded to support the construction of a festival building in **Salzburg**. Its general purpose would be to celebrate and perform the work of the city's most renowned native son, the composer **Wolfgang Amadeus Mozart**.

Proposals to use Salzburg for such purposes had long been in the air. The local **music** academy, the Mozarteum, had first suggested the idea at the end of the 19th century, but growing doubts about the viability of the **Habsburg Empire** and its eventual collapse in November 1918 gave the notion far grander dimensions. With the new Austrian First Republic, a fragment of the old empire, straining to develop a plausible national identity, the poet, essayist, opera librettist, and general man of letters **Hugo von Hofmannsthal** suggested that the Salzburg enterprise dedicate itself to presenting what he believed to be the best and universal elements of Austrian culture, the Catholic **Baroque** and the music of Mozart being chief among them. These, he thought, ultimately stemmed from popular rather than elite traditions and did not depend on transitory political structures. Rather, they were the basis of the **religion, literature**, and music of all the Austrian lands and of southern and Catholic **Germany**. The German classical dramatists, such as Johann Wilhelm Goethe, were to be part of the program as well, because they belonged to the larger German cultural patrimony. Experiencing these works collectively in **theaters** would increase audience awareness of national and human commonality, which would counteract social fragmentation and rootlessness.

In 1920, Hofmannsthal's reworking of the medieval morality play *Jedermann* (*Everyone*), a paradigmatic drama of sin, death, and redemption, was performed before the entrance to the Cathedral of St. Peter in Salzburg. The director was the extravagantly imaginative young impresario **Max Reinhardt**, who used the opportunity to realize his ideas for open-air productions. Despite shaky finances, the Salzburg festival soon became a noteworthy event in the European cultural calendar, though the musical side of its offerings quickly eclipsed the dramatic ones. Both classical and more contemporary works, most notably the operas of the Bavarian Richard Strauss, were staged.

The Festival became something of a cultural battleground following Adolf Hitler's appointment as German chancellor in 1933. Artists who could no longer work in Germany, such as the conductor Bruno

Walter (1876–1962), found summer employment in Salzburg. Following the **Anschluss** of 1938, however, Austria was no longer so hospitable to these people, especially if they were **Jewish**. Both Walter and Reinhardt immigrated to the United States, and many other figures who played significant roles at the festival went into exile as well. Still others, such as the Italian conductor Arturo Toscanini, refused to participate. Performances continued, however, most notably those of the **Vienna Philharmonic Orchestra** under the direction of Clemens Krauss (1893–1954) and Wilhlem Furtwängler.

Following the end of **World War II**, the province of Salzburg was **occupied** by the Americans, who supported the continuation of the festival. The program took on a far more international and contemporary character, even though such staples as *Jedermann* were, and are, put on annually. Almost every summer between 1947 and 1961 saw the performance of a 20th-century opera, often for the first time. The conductor **Herbert von Karajan**, who was first charged with the artistic direction of the festival between 1956 and 1960 and was general director from 1964 until he died in 1989, sought far and wide throughout the world for musicians, actors, directors, and stage designers who could meet his exacting performance standards. During these years, the Salzburg Festival became a social as well as a cultural event. Even matinees were black-tie affairs. Gone, as critics sourly noted, were the audiences of the 1920s, who, in the spirit of the occasion, attended performances in provincial Austrian loden cloth and dirndls. Although the atmosphere of the festival has become less formal than in von Karajan's day, it is still a comparatively elegant event. Some theatrical and musical performances, particularly experimental offerings, are now performed in locations beyond the city itself.

SCHÄRF, ADOLF (1890–1965). President of the Second Austrian Republic from 1957 until his death, Schärf had worked with the **Social Democratic Workers' Party** (SDAP) from his adolescence. After service in **World War I**, he represented the party in the National Assembly and taught in the SDAP workers' academy. He continued to school himself in agrarian matters, becoming one of the few Social Democrats with serious expertise in that area.

During the crisis in Austria of the late 1920s and 1930s, Schärf spoke for the more moderate membership of his party. When the SDAP was outlawed in 1934, he opened a law practice to support himself and his family rather than going into exile or underground, as did many of his colleagues. In July 1944, Schärf was arrested by the Gestapo along with several other Austrians suspected of links to the conspirators who tried to assassinate Adolf Hitler. In the newly liberated Austria, he was elected chairman of the reconstituted **Socialist Party of Austria**. As president, Schärf characteristically tried to avoid the ideological conflicts that had been the bane of the First Austrian Republic.

SCHIELE, EGON (1890–1918). The most eloquent representative of Expressionism in Austrian painting, Schiele achieved not only fame but also notoriety for his graphic and often grotesque depictions of nudes, sometimes in full sexual acts. Some critics still see him as little more than an extraordinarily visionary pornographer. In 1912, Schiele was punished with a 24-day jail term for his anatomically explicit drawings of schoolgirls. Schiele enjoyed the protection of **Gustav Klimt**, but while the latter hid the physical longings of his subjects behind densely textured decorative veneers, his protege scorned all hints of innuendo. Toward the end of his career, Schiele was also studying the work of Edvard Munch, Henri Toulouse-Lautrec, and Vincent Van Gogh.

Schiele did not look away from his subjects as he initially drew them, a technique that he took over from the French sculptor Auguste Rodin. The result was the long, intertwining lines that are the hallmark of his **art**, designed to render emotion, particularly of the erotic sort, more compellingly than the interplay of light and darkness. Schiele's work, however, was not improvisatory; he often did multiple sketches of a model, adding color only when his basic outlines satisfied him. And his work did rise above the pornographic; sexuality for him could also be a surrogate for feelings of aloneness and the desire for connectedness. Schiele died, along with his wife, in the great influenza pandemic that came toward the end of **World War I.**

SCHNITZLER, ARTHUR (1862–1931). Born in **Vienna**, Arthur Schnitzler was the son of a prosperous **Jewish** laryngologist. The future novelist and playwright was himself a physician, who, as a student, had an early interest in neurology and psychiatry. He did clinical work, as did **Sigmund Freud**, in the laboratory of Theodore Meynert (1833–1892), who was interested in classifying mental disorders through the study of the brain. Schnitzler himself used hypnotism in his early medical practice and would, as a mature man, confess that many of his plots had come to him in dreams.

Schnitzler's plays and fiction, marked by detached and transparent language, the absence of authorial intrusion, withering psychological realism, and a subtle understanding of interpersonal dynamics, were almost always set in Vienna and its environs. His characters—ambitious Jewish professionals, bored but erotically driven members of the high middle classes and aristocracy, self-righteous clergymen, the often helpless poor of the city's teeming outer districts—were all familiar on the local scene. Duplicity was everywhere, but especially in marital relationships. Self-revelation and self-discovery, whether therapeutic or painful, were consistent themes throughout his work.

Schnitzler's first major success on the stage, *Liebelei*, which premiered at the **Burgtheater** in 1895, was the story of the daughter of a coachman, driven to suicide by the apparent faithlessness of a young man of good family who takes their relationship all too casually. Much of his work however, was far more controversial and brought him much trouble. The play *Leutnant Gustl* (1900), which centered around the problem created by a duel over a woman's attentions, showed the military code of honor in an unfavorable light and cost the writer his officer's rank. *Das grüne Kakadu (The Green Bird)*, set during the French Revolution, offended circles around Emperor **Franz Joseph**. *Reigen*, better known as *La Ronde* to French and English audiences, reduced romantic bonds to the drive for self-gratification; it circulated at first only in manuscript form and provoked scandal even in 1920, when it was finally staged. Schnitzler himself refused to allow further performance of it.

After **World War I**, Schnitzler lost much of his audience in his native land, which deemed his work too frivolous and cynical to be worthy of attention. Before his death, he tried writing scripts for American films, without great success. *See also* JUNG WIEN; LITERATURE.

SCHOENBERG, ARNOLD (1874–1951). Among the 20th century's major musical innovators, Schoenberg was largely self-taught. His first compositions, heavily influenced by Alexander Zemlinsky (1871–1942), who eventually married Schoenberg's sister, were lushly tonal in the style of late19th-century Romanticism (*Verklärte Nacht*, 1899). However, in his Symphony Op. 9 of 1907 and the 1908 song cycle, *The Book of the Hanging Gardens*, Schoenberg set off in a radically new direction. Proclaiming "the emancipation of dissonance," he rejected classical patterns of tonality, thus setting a norm for the First Vienna School, as he and his followers would later categorize their **music**. He grew equally dismissive of the lush ornamental excesses of Viennese *Jugendstil* (Young Vienna), and its musical equivalent in the music of **Gustav Mahler** and **Anton Bruckner**. He continued, however, to admire the work of Brahms for its use of brief snatches of rhythm and melody in larger harmonic structures.

Schoenberg perfected the 12-tone style of musical composition, with which he was deeply associated after **World War I**. In it, the eight steps of the conventional major and minor musical scales are abandoned. It requires the use of each of the halftones of that scale in the series of rows that make up a musical work. By making all halftones equal, Schoenberg believed he was expanding the harmonic possibilities of music.

Though they did influence the work of such Austrian composers as **Alban Berg**, these ideas found little favor among audiences in **Vienna**. From 1925 to 1933, Schoenberg conducted a master class at the Prussian Academy of the Arts in Berlin, where he had already spent extended periods of time. He then immigrated to the United States, where he taught, first in Boston, then in Los Angeles, until 1944. Schoenberg was also a talented painter with affinities to both late 19th-century Impressionism and Central European Expressionism. He left around 70 canvases.

SCHÖNBORN, CARDINAL CHRISTOPH (1945–). Born in what is now the Czech Republic, Schönborn was taken by his parents to the **Vorarlberg**, where he grew up. His first clerical training was at a Dominican seminary in Bonn, then the capital of the Federal

Republic of **Germany**. He took more advanced academic and theological studies in France, receiving his doctorate in theology from the **Catholic** Institute in Paris in 1975. Schönborn became archbishop of **Vienna** in 1995; a year later Pope John Paul II named him to the College of Cardinals.

Widely traveled and deeply involved in ecumenical activities both with fellow Christians as well as **Jews** and Muslims, Schönborn has been much concerned about the relationship between religion and science. In 2005, both professional scientists and general intellectuals heavily criticized an Op-ed letter Schönborn published in the *New York Times* in which he tried to address the secular and spiritual dimensions of biological evolution. While he granted that the Christian faith made room for common ancestry as the beginning of an evolutionary process, he firmly ruled out the notion that subsequent species development was unplanned, a proposition that lies at the root of neo-Darwinism. In Schönborn's homeland, liberals read the essay as one more sign of an unwelcome conservatism that John Paul II had restored to Austrian Catholicism. *See also* KÖNIG, FRANZ; ISLAM; RELIGION.

SCHUBERT, FRANZ PETER (1797–1828). The greatest of all composers to work in the genre of the art song, Schubert was born and spent his first years in Lichtental, then one of the outlying districts of **Vienna**. His father was a schoolteacher and gave him his first instructions in **music** theory and violin. A brother, Ignaz, taught him piano. Schubert sang as a choirboy in the University Church in the center of the city. We know relatively little about his childhood and his family relations; frustrated biographers have speculated much about Schubert's psyche and his feelings, but have relied heavily upon the memoirs of the composer's friends and acquaintances for their information.

Franz Schubert assisted his father at the latter's school for a time. Between 1814 and his death, however, gifted with seemingly inexhaustible melodic resources and an uncanny feel for sometimes subtle, sometimes startling, modulation, the youthful composer turned out a staggering amount of music that probed a wide range of emotions. Taking his texts from the famous, such as Johann Wilhelm Goethe, as well as from the modest and all but unknown poets of his day, Schubert wrote more than 600 songs with piano accompaniment. They often had their first performances at so-called Schubertiades, held initially in Schubert's family home, then in the quarters of musically inclined friends who represented the spectrum of cultivated Viennese society. These occasions finally became full rehearsals and orchestral concerts. Though Schubert was financially more astute than some of his biographers have believed, his intimates occasionally published his works at their own expense.

Beyond his songs, his 18 string quartets and quartet movements, his piano quintet *The Trout* (1819), two piano trios, and several of his 23 sonatas for piano, along with many smaller works for the instrument, such as the eight impromptus and six *Moments musicaux*, are classics of their type. His eight symphonies were more problematic, suffering from awkward orchestration and fitful inspiration. The best known, the B minor, has gone down in posterity as the "Unfinished" because it ends after the second movement. It has long been believed that Schubert suffered from pangs of inadequacy brought on by comparing his own symphonic resources to those of **Ludwig van Beethoven**, who was working in Vienna at the same time. But the relationship of the two men is still a matter of debate. If their careers were parallel at all, it was in their mutual failure to write successfully for the theater. Nevertheless, Schubert's music toward the end of his life suggests that the author very much wished to follow structural patterns that his great contemporary had perfected for the piano and symphonic works. Schubert gave a eulogy at Beethoven's funeral in 1827. *See also* BIEDERMEIER.

SCHUSCHNIGG, KURT (1897–1977). Born in the **South Tyrol**, Schuschnigg was trained as a lawyer. Active in **Christian Social Party** politics as a young man, he served in the parliament of the Austrian First Republic from 1927 to 1934. Schuschnigg was a devout **Catholic** and sympathetic to some form of **Habsburg** restoration in Austria. In 1930, he founded the Stormtroopers of the Eastern March (*Ostmärkische Sturmscharen*), in part as a counterweight to the German national and far more secular orientation of the powerful Starhemberg faction within the *Heimwehr*. The rivalry between Count **Ernst Rüdiger Starhemberg** and Schuschnigg would be intense and color their political relationships throughout the decade.

In 1932, Schuschnigg was appointed minister of justice; in 1933–1934 he served as minister of education in the government of **Engelbert Dollfuss**. Following the assassination of the latter, Schuschnigg became federal **chancellor** and held that position until the **Anschluss** in 1938. As chancellor he held the portfolios of defense, education, and foreign affairs. He was the head of the **Fatherland Front** after the *Heimwehr* was disbanded in 1936.

Schuschnigg continued to govern in the authoritarian style established by his immediate predecessor. Sympathetic to the idea of a Habsburg restoration—he repealed the **Habsburg Exclusion Law** in 1935—Schuschnigg offended many in German nationalist circles among his countrymen. This split in conservative and right-wing circles seriously compromised his position, both domestically and abroad. He did not denounce Nazism and tightened the Austrian connection with Benito Mussolini.

This tie, however, grew increasingly problematic. A close ally of Italy, Austria could not renounce Mussolini's invasion of Ethiopia in 1935. European powers who deplored Mussolini's strike grew much less sympathetic to Austria's perpetual financial problems. Schuschnigg was nevertheless firmly committed to maintaining the sovereignty of his country. While agreeing in July 1936 to call his Austria the "second German state," to loosen restrictions on local **Nazi Party** activity, and to take some Nazis into his **government**, Schuschnigg did get Adolf Hitler to recognize Austria's independence at a meeting of the two in Berchtesgaden, Hitler's Bavarian hideaway, in February 1938.

Nevertheless, rumors of German invasion and a Nazi takeover of Austria continued to circulate, often with documentary evidence. Facing an imminent crisis, Schuschnigg called on 3 March 1938 for an Austrian plebiscite on independence. This was to be held four days later but was preempted when the German army crossed the Austrian border. On 11 March, under intense Nazi pressure, Schuschnigg resigned the chancellorship; he was imprisoned until 1945. After the end of **World War II**, Schuschnigg went to the United States, where from 1948 until 1967 he taught international law at the University of St. Louis, a Catholic institution. He then returned to the **Tyrol**. *See also* GERMANY, RELATIONS WITH; ITALY, RELATIONS WITH.

SCHÜSSEL, WOLFGANG (1945–). Schüssel began his service to the **Austrian People's Party** in 1968, the same year he received his law degree from the **University of Vienna**, the city of his birth. A career politician, he held positions in coalition governments of Chancellor **Franz Vranitzky** between 1989 and 1994. In 1995, Schüssel became both foreign minister and national leader of his party.

As **chancellor** between 2000 and 2006, he was often caught up in controversy. His willingness to bring the nationalist **Freedom Party of Austria** (FPÖ) under **Jörg Haider** into his coalition led to an informal boycott of Austria's **government** by the **European Union** between February and September 2002. Schüssel's most closely held goal, however, was to bring balanced state budgets to Austria. This he was never able to do, in part because the intermediate steps to this end were fiscally painful to many. His regime, with the aid of the FPÖ, did win approval of several cost-cutting measures, such as increasing fees for university students and reduction of future pension benefits. Ordinary taxes were raised in a system in which the highest marginal rate was 50 percent. Corporate taxes, on the other hand, went down, and the pace of **privatization** accelerated.

Schüssel was not altogether hostile to the Austrian **welfare** system. In 2002, his government extended postnatal leave by three years. But the disclosure in 2006 that a member of his family had used an illegal home care worker from Slovakia, at a time when Austrians were finding indigenous providers very expensive, was a political disaster for him.

SECESSION, AUSTRIAN. Under the leadership of the well-known painter **Gustav Klimt**, the Society of Plastic Artists of the Austrian Secession (*Vereinigung bildender Künstler österreichischer Secession*) was founded in 1897. Klimt was joined in the movement by 19 painters and **architects** who were members of an older artistic organization, the Artists' Society (*Künstlergenossenschaft*), connected with the eponymous *Künstlerhaus* (House of Artists).

Their program, inspired by contemporary **art** movements elsewhere in Europe—the British pre-Raphaelites, French Impressionists, Belgian Naturalists, and German *Jugendstil*—rejected the historicizing classicism of academic painting as mediocre. Improvement could come only by greater openness to artistic experimentation, both formally and thematically. "To the Age Its Art, to Art Its Freedom" (*"Der Zeit ihre Kunst. Der Kunst ihre Freiheit"*) was the motto emblazoned on a building constructed in 1898 for the Secession's exhibitions. From 1898 to 1903, their journal, *Ver Sacrum* (*Sacred Spring*), sought to create an international audience for their efforts to save art from the sclerotic grip of its Viennese elder statesmen.

The subject of the Secession's artistic endeavors was to be the true nature of modern man. Their finished paintings, graphic designs, and decorative inventions featured thick floral ornamentation, a heavy use of simple geometric forms often rendered two dimensionally, and what for the time was startlingly frank eroticism. Their agenda had a popular side as well—the common man was just as much in need of aesthetic repair as the rich one—and good art had to be brought into the household. The result of such thinking was the founding of the **Wiener Werkstätte** (Vienna Atelier) to design furniture, kitchen implements, home accessories, and architectural projects that met this ideal.

In 1905, a split in the Secession took place, with some of its most important associates such as Klimt, the architect **Otto Wagner**, and the painter Koloman Moser (1868–1918) deciding to exhibit their works in a show called *"Kunstschau Wien"* ("Vienna Art Show"), the first of which took place in 1908.

During the interwar period, other provincial artistic societies in Austria took up the Secession's challenge to innovation. The Artists' Guild of the Innviertel and the interdisciplinary MAERZ Group founded in 1913 in **Upper Austria** and **Salzburg** kept the ideas of the Secession alive after 1920. The **Graz** Artists' Union (*Künstlerverband Graz*), founded in 1923, promoted Expressionism in Austrian painting. In 1939, the Vienna Secession was merged with the older Künstlerhaus; after 1945, it was reestablished as an independent organization to promote modern art of all kinds.

SEIPEL, IGNAZ (1876–1932). The son of a coachman, Seipel became a priest in 1899 and subsequently a professor of moral theology in **Salzburg** and at the **University of Vienna**. From 1917 until November 1918, he was the minister for social affairs in the last government of the Austrian half of the **Habsburg Empire**.

Becoming active in the **Christian Social Party** (CP) of the First Austrian Republic, Seipel rose quickly in its ranks, serving as party chairperson from 1921 to 1929. He became federal **chancellor** in May 1922, at a particularly bad moment. Inflation was rising rapidly, and government expenses were far outrunning revenues, in part because of the generous social benefits enacted by the **Social Democratic Workers' Party** (SDAP) in the early years of the First Republic.

Believing that his country needed financial assistance from abroad to establish fiscal stability at home, Seipel embarked upon a series of visits to European capitals to present the case for supporting an independent Austria. He was rewarded in October 1922 with loan guarantees in the sum of 650 million Austrian crowns from Great Britain, France, **Italy**, and the new Czechoslovakia (Geneva Protocol). In return, Austria was expected to trim its generous budgets. Seipel and his finance minister, Victor Kienböck (1873–1956), thereupon embarked upon a program of domestic fiscal austerity, sharply cutting entitlements, reducing the ranks of government employees, and raising taxes. The policy brought the desired results. Inflation ebbed, and a new, and sounder **currency**, the schilling, was introduced in December 1924.

All of this came at a cost. Seipel, who was never able to form a parliamentary majority, and governed in coalition with the Agrarian League and the Greater German Party, was vulnerable to criticism from many sides. The Greater Germans, whose membership was heavily middle class, suffered from the reduction in civil service employment. They also objected to another promise the chancellor made in the Geneva Protocol—that Austria would not bring up the question of **Anschluss** with Germany for 20 years. The SDAP, which had a large constituency, especially in **Vienna**, was outraged at the cuts in social spending and at Seipel's apparent willingness to put Austria at the mercy of foreign capitalists.

In January 1924, Seipel was seriously wounded in an attempted assassination, which he attributed to a never proven socialist plot. That year, Seipel withdrew from the chancellorship; he returned to the office in 1926. In 1929, suffering from bad health and depression over his inability to persuade his country to return a CP majority to parliament, he stepped down from the position permanently. In 1930, he served as foreign minister. Called upon to form a national government during the financial crisis that followed the collapse of the Vienna **Creditanstalt Bankverein** in 1931, he was unable to persuade the SDAP to cooperate.

Seipel accepted the collapse of the Habsburg monarchy, democratic rule, and the establishment of the First Austrian Republic. But he grew increasingly hostile to the Marxism and secularism that had entrenched themselves in the new state. His political views became increasingly authoritarian; he wished to strengthen substantially the powers of the Austrian **presidency**, a largely ceremonial office. He also found the right-wing nationalist *Heimwehr* increasingly useful in maintaining civil order, particularly after the burning of the Ministry of Justice building in Vienna during a socialist political demonstration in 1927. Seipel, the onetime democrat, endorsed the corporate state toward the end of his career. *See also* AUSTRO-FASCISM; FOREIGN POLICY; SPANN, OTHMAR.

SEITZ, KARL (1869–1950). A teacher, socialist political leader, and mayor of **Vienna** from 1923 to 1934, Seitz began his legislative career in the regional parliament of **Lower Austria** in 1897. He was a member of the Imperial Assembly from 1901 to 1918. Here, he argued toward the end of **World War I** for granting extensive autonomy to the many nations within the **Habsburg Empire** as a way of saving it in some form. From 1918 to 1920, Seitz was one of the three presidents of the Provisional National Assembly in the new Austria. Until December 1920, he served as the first president of the Constituent Assembly. From 1923 to 1934, he was the head of the Austrian **Social Democratic Workers' Party**.

It was as Vienna's mayor, however, that Seitz had his greatest impact on the country. He oversaw the massive public works program for which the city acquired a worldwide reputation in the interwar years. Along with **Otto Glöckel**, Seitz had been a member of the Free School (*Freie Schule*) movement before World War I. This program called for the complete secularization of public **education** and for extending the opportunity for schooling to all Austrians, regardless of social class or economic background. Seitz continued to support these ideas and gave Glöckel the opportunity to implement them. During the armed conflicts with the ruling **Christian Social Party** in 1927 and the brief **February Uprising** of 1934, Seitz generally argued within the Socialist leadership for caution and continued negotiation with the opposition. He was arrested in 1934, then detained in a concentration camp between 1944 and 1945. Following the end of **World War II**, he served in the parliament of the Second Austrian Republic until his death.

SEVEN WEEKS' WAR (1866). Provoked by Prussian Minister of State Otto von Bismarck, the conflict was designed to end the influence of the **Habsburg** monarchy in the **German Confederation**. It was, indeed, a humiliating defeat for Emperor **Franz Joseph**. Heat, fog, and logistic snarls plagued both sides, but the new Prussian needle gun, which allowed troops to load and fire while lying down, so intimidated some Habsburg units that they refused to attack. On the other hand, Habsburg forces performed well against **Italy**, which had allied itself with Prussia to acquire some north Italian territories still under Habsburg control.

Beginning in June, the war effectively ended with the battle of Königgrätz (Czech.: Hradec Králové) in the kingdom of Bohemia on 3 July. Bismarck, however, was not eager to punish Austria excessively. The Treaty of Prague, signed in August, required the **Habsburg Empire** to hand over Venetia to Italy and to pay a modest amount of reparations to Prussia. The German Confederation was dissolved, with a North German Confederation under Prussian leadership taking its place. *See also* DUAL ALLIANCE; GERMANY, RELATIONS WITH.

SOCIAL DEMOCRATIC WORKERS' PARTY OF AUSTRIA/ SOZIALDEMOKRATISCHE ARBEITER PARTEI (SDAP). The long-standing voice of Marxism in Austrian politics, the party returned to its original name in 1991, though with a different acronym. Founded in 1888–1889, the SDAP lost its legal standing in the First Austrian Republic under the regime of Chancellor **Engelbert Dollfuss** in 1934. Under the leadership of such figures as **Karl Renner**, **Adolf Schärf**, and **Theodor Körner**, it reconstituted itself in 1945 as the **Socialist Party of Austria** (SPÖ).

Though its first congress took place in 1874, the early years of the socialist movement in the **Habsburg Empire** were internally contentious. These differences were largely tactical, but they were significant, as supporters were divided between a more moderate faction, which took its inspiration from the German socialist leader Ferdinand Lassalle, and those who wished to adopt the more violent methods of contemporary anarchists. The Hainfeld Program of 1888–1889, largely the work of **Viktor Adler**, brought these factions together.

By setting an agenda of broad social and economic reform, the SDAP hoped to represent the entire proletariat in the Habsburg Empire, even though its leadership was largely German speaking. This they never quite managed to do. Though the party never dissolved completely into national units before 1918, antagonism between German and Czech workers was especially deep. Furthermore, its electoral appeal was largely concentrated in the region around Vienna and in growing industrial areas in **Lower Austria**, **Styria**, Bohemia, and Moravia. The franchise reform of 1907 in the western half of Austria–Hungary gave the socialists an increasingly strong voice in the Imperial Assembly. With 87 delegates, they made up the second strongest fraction in that body.

A good part of the party's success was the result of its organization, particularly the complex network of cultural, political, and social organizations associated with it: workers' educational clubs, **trade unions, women**'s and young workers' groups, not to mention cyclists and conservationists. The party newspaper, the *Arbeiterzeitung*, played a leading role in the lively journalistic life of late 19th-century Vienna. The result of this work soon became clear. The year following the death of Vienna's popular **Christian Social** mayor **Karl Lueger** in 1910, the SDAP became the governing party of the city, a position it has yet to yield, with the exception of the period 1934–1945.

Though the party initially supported the **Habsburg** monarchy at the outbreak of **World War I**, it came to oppose Austrian participation in the conflict. Indeed, in 1916 Friedrich Adler (1879–1960), the son of the party leader, assassinated the Austrian minister-president, Count Karl Stürgkh (1859–1916), because of the latter's antidemocratic policies. The SDAP did endorse the creation of German Austria, the initial step in the establishment of the First Republic.

However, it was ambivalent about Austrian independence. Among the party's most important leaders at the time was the ideologue **Otto Bauer**, who urged that Austria become part of **Germany** to reinforce proletarian solidarity. Another important figure was the more conciliatory Karl Renner. The head of the provisional state was a close ally of Renner's, **Karl Seitz**.

In the provisional National Assembly, the SDAP had 71 of the 170 seats. From the middle of 1920 until the suppression of democratic government in Austria in 1933, the Socialists were forced into the opposition. Nevertheless, they continued to dominate the city of Vienna itself. With countless organizational ties and through its paramilitary **Republican Guard**, the SDAP remained prominent in the public life of the First Republic. In 1930, the party still had the single largest delegation in the Austrian parliament. In proportion to the population of Austria, it constituted the largest social democratic movement in the world. Unlike its counterpart party in Germany, the SDAP also managed to maintain a united front, though there were persistent regional tensions within the membership.

Proscribed and driven underground in 1934, many leading figures in the party simply emigrated. Some prominent members such as Karl Renner continued to call for incorporation into Germany and supported the **Anschluss** of 1938. Other Austrian Socialists spent part or all of **World War II** in Nazi concentration camps.

SOCIALIST PARTY OF AUSTRIA/SOZIALISTISCHE PARTEI ÖSTERREICHS (SPÖ). With the collapse of the **Nazi** regime in 1945, the **Social Democratic Workers' Party**, or what was left of it, resumed an active life in Austria. Tarnished by the support that many of its leading members had given to the **Anschluss**, at least in its initial stages, it tried to distance itself from its immediate past with a new name, the Socialist Party of Austria. Though the party is once again known as the Social Democratic Party of Austria, it still uses the SPÖ acronym. It remains a highly centralized operation, governed from a central committee. From the outset, however, the new organization was far more inclined toward political compromise than it had been during the interwar years. It also took a relatively relaxed position on the restoration of former Austrian **Nazis** to the postwar body politic and dropped its earlier antagonism to the Austrian

Catholic church. Particularly influential in driving this change were **Adolf Schärf**, who acted as party chairman from 1945 to 1957, and Bruno Pittermann (1905–1983), the head of the SPÖ from 1957 to 1967. The Nazis had persecuted both men before and during **World War II**. Coalition **governments** of the SPÖ and the more conservative **Austrian People's Party** (ÖVP) ruled Austria until 1966. Under the system of *Proporz*, which both groups endorsed, it regularly held the vice-chancellorship and the ministries of the interior, social affairs, transportation, and state enterprises. Both parties committed themselves to a social partnership in which both state and private enterprises competed and which provided an elaborate social safety net for all.

By 1970, facing an ever younger electorate, the SPÖ had succeeded in broadening its constituency far beyond the industrial workers who were once its core support. Much credit for this development went to **Bruno Kreisky**, who was convinced that the party had to refashion its image to appeal to a more prosperous people. The following year, the SPÖ won an absolute majority in the national elections and began to govern in its own name. It continued to do so until 1983, when, plagued by allegations of corruption at the highest levels and general mismanagement of important responsibilities, it began working in coalitions once again.

The SPÖ's ideological profile has continued to soften, to the distress of those who support the party's radical traditions. After long years of internal discussion, the party announced in 1998 that it was dropping all references to the class struggle in a proposed platform for upcoming national elections. Commitment to the parliamentary system has inevitably brought with it the need for compromise. With members of the SPÖ often concerned about maintaining their offices in provincial and communal governments, the programs and positions of the national party sometimes run up against purely local interests. Neoliberal economic policies of the final two decades of the 20th century and the **privatization** of the economy that went with them flew in the face of socialist egalitarianism. Yet these programs prevailed throughout the chancellorships of **Franz Vranitzky** and **Viktor Klima**, both from the SPÖ. Nor, by the 1990s, was the SPÖ the sole "radical" alternative in Austrian politics. The environmentalist **Green Party** challenged the full-employment policies of both

Kreisky and Vranitzky, and the economic nationalism of right-wing parties such as the **Freedom Party of Austria** and the Alliance for the Future of Austria, led by **Jörg Haider**, drew off SPÖ votes as well.

In the opposition from 2000 to 2007, the SPÖ hammered out an updated party platform that supported market economic principles, but not to the exclusion of state investment or social justice. Under the leadership of **Alfred Gusenbauer**, the chairperson of the party from 2000 to 2008, it also succeeded in eliminating the considerable debt it had piled up over the years. In elections held in 2006 and 2008, the SPÖ won a dominant, though small, plurality of votes in Austrian national elections. A new SPÖ chancellor, Werner Faymann (1960–), was sworn in in December 2008. Nevertheless, the party no longer commands the reliable constituency that it once enjoyed, even in the city of **Vienna** itself. *See also* AUSTRO-MARXISM; POLITICAL PARTIES.

SOCIETY OF THE FRIENDS OF MUSIC/GESELLSCHAFT DER MUSIKFREUNDE. Founded in 1812 by **music** lovers from both aristocratic and bourgeois circles, the Society was to revive Viennese music life, which had declined badly during the Napoleonic Wars and the French occupation. Conceived as a private organization, members were entitled to professionally prepared concerts of serious music as part of their subscription price.

The number of subscribers expanded rapidly in the first decades of the 19th century, making the "private" nature of the society something of an affectation. Tickets were not, however, available at the door. Connected to the society was a conservatory open to its members. From the outset, the society made it clear that it would promote serious, rather than popular, music. Even in its first years, it programmed whole symphonies by eminent composers such as **Wolfgang Amadeus Mozart**, **Ludwig van Beethoven**, and Luigi Cherubini, along with the selections from Italian operas and other vocal pieces that were the conventional concert fare of the day.

The present home of the society, the Musikverein building, was designed by **Theophile Hansen**, the architect of many prominent buildings on the **Ringstrasse**. It was opened in 1870. In the same year, the **Vienna Philharmonic Orchestra**, which shares some of its personnel with the orchestra of the **Vienna State Opera**, began holding its subscription concerts there.

With some of Europe's most notable composers and performers on past membership lists, the society has one of the most important musical archives in the world. Its conservatory has been incorporated into Austria's University for Music and the Performing Arts.

SOUTH TYROL. Situated south of the Brenner Pass with its capital in Bolzano (Bozen), the South Tyrol is a region of mixed population and language. At the end of **World War I**, with the Italian army occupying the area, it contained roughly 220,000 Germans and about half that number of Italians, a large percentage of whom were very recent arrivals. A small minority spoke Ladin, a Latin derivative found in some regions of the **Alps**.

Though the situation called for the plebiscitary procedures mandated by the Paris Peace Conference, political concerns led the Allies to recognize the cession of the area to **Italy**. American President Woodrow Wilson wanted to compensate the Italians for territories on the Adriatic coast that they had aspired to but that were turned over instead to the new kingdom of the Serbs, Croats, and Slovenes, soon to be known as Yugoslavia.

The embittered German population of both the north and East **Tyrol**, which remained within Austria, voiced their resentment clearly and vigorously in the earliest years of the interwar period. In an effort to avoid any partition at all, the Tyrol voted in 1919 (unsuccessfully) to become an independent state. Though sentiment remained strong there to secede from the First Austrian Republic and to join **Germany**, the **Nazis** did not pursue the issue out of consideration for the interests of their alliance with Benito Mussolini and Fascist Italy. The German-speaking inhabitants of the region hoped at the end of **World War II** that, with Austria officially recognized as a Nazi-occupied country, they would be incorporated into that newly freed state, as part of a territorial settlement with a now-vanquished Italy. Should that prove impossible, they hoped to win wide concessions of autonomy.

Once again, however, politics interfered. The Soviet Union, now a victorious power, did not wish to offend the powerful Italian Communist party by supporting such territorial excisions. With the anticommunist parties of Italy and Italian voters at home in mind, the

United States was equally loath to be provocative. It was left to the Austrian foreign minister, Karl Gruber (1909–1995), and his Italian counterpart, Alcide de Gasperi, to arrange some compromise, which they did in September 1946. They agreed that, although the South Tyrol would remain a part of Italy, the province of Bolzano would enjoy extensive autonomy. The compact was incorporated into the general peace treaty with Italy in 1947. In 1948, however, the government in Rome joined the South Tyrol administratively with the province of Trentino to the south. Known as Trentino–Alto Adige, the new district now became primarily Italian.

After the signing of the **Austrian State Treaty** in 1955, the German-speaking elements in the South Tyrol asked Vienna to support their case for genuine autonomy. In 1961, representatives from the government in Rome, meeting with more moderate leaders from the South Tyrol, began discussing ways to resolve their differences. These talks were seriously compromised, however, by periodic waves of terrorism carried on by local nationalist cells. These groups looked to both Austria and Germany for material support and sanctuary and often received it.

Nevertheless, with the aid of the **United Nations**, a 137-point settlement was in place by 1969. Austria agreed not to intervene in the area, which was to be granted substantial autonomy in incremental steps laid out in a timetable. As each stage was completed, Austria and Italy were to acknowledge the step. At the end of the process, Austria was to declare its fulfillment. A South Tyrolean assembly endorsed the agreement in November 1969, followed by similar actions on the part of the Austrian and Italian parliaments a month later. *See also* ST. GERMAIN, TREATY OF; RUSSIA, RELATIONS WITH.

SPANN, OTHMAR (1878–1950). Although often unmentioned even in studies of European right-wing thought, Spann profoundly influenced the conservative and fascist ideology of the interwar period. An economist and sociologist equally at home with close statistical analysis and theory, he took up a professorship at the **University of Vienna** in 1919, holding the position until 1938. There he set forth his vision of state and society before a large and enthusiastic student audience. These lectures were the basis of his best-known book, *Der* *wahre Staat: Vorlesungen über Abbruch und Neubau der Gesellschaft* (*The True State: Lectures on the Destruction and Reconstruction of Society*), published in 1921.

An implacable foe of egalitarianism, in whatever philosophical packaging it came, and of capitalism, Spann advocated what he called Universalism. This he described unapologetically as an elitist form of social and political organization in which the interests of the whole rather than those of single members were paramount. The state was conceived as a hierarchy of estates or corporations, with the highest among these teachers and educators. These members passed on their wisdom to the next highest segment in the pyramid—political, military, ecclesiastical, and public leaders—who modified and handed down these ideas to the next group in the structure. The whole process came to an end with the bottom corporation, manual workers, and those responsible for turning out goods.

Political parties would be largely debating societies, limited to discussing fundamental ideas and concerns of the various corporations. **Trade unions** would be superfluous. To forge greater harmony between labor and owners of industrial capital, employees and employers would iron out their problems within subsections of their corporations or guilds.

Just how all this was to work out in practice was not altogether clear, even to sympathetic contemporaries. Spann himself seems to have felt the need to answer this question; in the third edition of *The True State* (1931), he introduced the notion of a "state-bearing segment" in his pyramid, in which political power would be concentrated.

Spann endorsed both Italian Fascism and **Nazism**; his thinking played a significant role in the Austrian *Heimwehr* and **Austro-Fascism**. However, the universalist approach to state organization did allow the corporations a certain degree of autonomy. Such ideas were fundamentally incompatible with dictatorship; following the **Anschluss** of 1938, Spann was removed from his teaching position in **Vienna**, then arrested, and for a short time, imprisoned.

SPORT. Systematic gymnastics and organized sport in Austria were developments of the 19th and 20th centuries. Physical education became a requirement in Austrian schools after 1869, though it was optional for girls after 1882.

Europe's most popular sport, football (soccer), came to the **Habsburg Empire** well before **World War I**. Though efforts to create an all-empire league failed, the game was widely played locally. Its popularity soared, however, after 1918, when Vienna became the seat of sociologically contested matches between squads from the more sophisticated and affluent districts of the central city and more proletarian teams from outlying areas. Commercialization, the sponsorship of big businesses and banks, and the public media turned football from a Vienna-centered spectator attraction into a national one after **World War II**. Austrian teams have qualified for the World Cup, for example in 1998, but have never been serious contenders for the final rounds. Though it cohosted with Switzerland the 2008 European Cup games, Austria was quickly eliminated from competition.

Other Austrian athletes, however, have been much more successful in a variety of international settings. In 1923, Vienna was dubbed "the city of strong men," after winning four titles in world championship weight lifting. Throughout the 1920s and early 1930s, Austrian prizefighters excelled at all weight levels in a variety of competitions. Though nationalist politicians disapproved of Olympic Games because of their cosmopolitan goals, Austrian boxers, equestrians, and rowers won four gold, six silver, and three bronze medals at the Berlin games in 1936. Gymnastic associations were, however, intractably politicized. Austria's German Nationalist Party, **Christian Social Party**, and **Social Democratic Workers' Party** all had their own clubs. The right-wing regime of **Engelbert Dollfuss** suppressed the Social Democratic Turnverein in 1934.

Individual Austrians have had impressive careers in international sport since 1945. Stock car racer Niki Lauda (1949–) has been a three-time Formula 1 champion (1975, 1977, 1984). Thomas Muster (1967–) performed powerfully in tennis on European clay courts; he took one Grand Slam title at the French Open in 1995. Austrian tennis players continue to play at Grand Slam events, but largely fail to move beyond the quarterfinals. Though Austria, along with Switzerland, cohosted the European Cup soccer matches in 2008, the Austrian team performed poorly. Austria's most attractive, and most promising, competitive athlete at the beginning of the 21st century has been swimmer Markus Rogan (1982–). Trained largely in the **United States**, where he attended high school and Stanford University, he won a series of gold medals for the backstroke in world and European competition. Although he took two silver medals in the 2004 Athens Olympics, he disappointed Austrian fans, who were hoping for gold once more. Rogan was, however, named Austrian Sportsman of the Year. His performance in Beijing in 2008 was mediocre, as was the Austrian effort as a whole, which ended with three medals, none gold.

It has in winter events that Austria became an enduring front-runner internationally. Austrians won gold medals in individual and paired figure skating in 1923. The female champion, Herma Szábo (1902–1986), won seven world titles in all. At the 1932 Winter Olympics, Austrians took two gold medals in men's figure skating. Following **World War II**, Austria established a reputation for exceptional athletic accomplishment on the ski slopes. Indeed, although soccer has a huge and enthusiastic following, skiing is the authentic national sport. It is widely taught, even to schoolchildren; ski champions are consistently the sport heroes of the country. The first and perhaps the most accomplished of these was Toni (Anton) Sailer (1935–), who won three gold medals in downhill, slalom, and the giant slalom in the 1956 Olympics. Austrians dominated the 1964 Innsbruck Olympics in skiing, along with tobogganing, bobsledding, and figure skating, capturing four gold medals, five silvers, and three bronzes. Austrian skiers, male and female, took 14 medals at the Alpine Ski World Championship in 1999 in Vail, Colorado. More recently, Hermann Maier (1972–) has been a very impressive performer.

SRBIK, HEINRICH VON (1878–1951). A historian, Srbik began his teaching career at the University of **Graz**, then moved to the **University of Vienna**, where he taught from 1922 to 1945. He was federal minister of education from 1929 to 1930. Born in **Vienna**, he died in the **Tyrol**.

Srbik's three-volume biography (1925–1954) of **Metternich** remains an authoritative treatment of its subject. During the interwar period, however, he was best known for his efforts to create a German-oriented version of history that would justify Austria's incorporation into a Greater German Empire, which he and many of his colleagues believed to be inevitable. The cultivation of a sense of common history would end in the creation of a common German people. Srbik's thinking in this vein is encapsulated in his *Deutsche Einheit* (*German Unity*, 4 vols., 1935–1942). Though he would come to change his mind, Srbik regarded the 1938 **Anschluss** as a realization of his ideas.

ST. GERMAIN, TREATY OF. Named after the Parisian suburban palace where it was signed on 10 September 1919, the treaty set the territorial and military conditions for the First Austrian Republic that emerged from the wreckage of the **Habsburg Empire** at the end of **World War I**. Like the companion settlements of Versailles and Trianon, which dealt with Germany and Hungary, respectively, the provisions of St. Germain were part of the general European order established by the victorious Allies during that year. Austria acknowledged the independence of Czechoslovakia, Yugoslavia, Poland, and a Hungary stripped of almost all of its historic principalities and crown lands such as Transylvania and Croatia. To the south, the Trentino, the **South Tyrol**, and Trieste were ceded to Italy. To the southeast, a part of **Styria** with its chief city of Maribor (Germ.: Marburg) went to the new Slavic kingdom that was to become Yugoslavia. Eastern Galicia was turned over to Poland, though the final disposition of that question did not come until 1923. The new Austrian army was limited to 30,000. Austria was forbidden to relinquish its independence by joining **Germany** or any other central European state. Like Germany, Austria had to pay reparations over 30 years for damage allegedly done during the conflict.

The treaty was not wholly unfavorable to Austrian interests. The plebiscitary procedure set up by the Paris Peace Conference to adjudicate territorial disputes helped Austria to beat back Yugoslav efforts to incorporate parts of **Carinthia** into its new kingdom in 1920. The accord also paved the way for the Austrian acquisition of the largely German-speaking region of western Hungary, the **Burgenland**, in 1921. This area was largely agricultural and crucial in keeping the city of **Vienna** fed. Austria was enjoined to protect the rights of the minorities living within its new borders, the Slovenians of Carinthia being the most notable; the new states of Czechoslovakia, Yugoslavia, and a much-expanded Romania were obligated to do the same for the German-speaking peoples within their borders.

Among the 381 articles of the treaty were many **economic** provisions, some of which bound not only Austria but also new states such as Czechoslovakia and Poland to continue the exchange of goods and services with one another. Nevertheless, the arrangement as a whole was regarded in Austria as punitive, since at the outset of the negotiations the Austrian delegation had asked that the country be treated as a successor state like Czechoslovakia—a new political entity that was not responsible for the policies of the Habsburg Empire. Although arguable, the Austrian position lacked something in sincerity because the fledgling republic's representatives took it upon themselves to speak for the German-speaking minorities of the former Habsburg lands throughout central eastern, southern, and southeastern Europe. The victorious Allies in Paris—Great Britain, France, the **United States**, and **Italy**—dismissed this contention. France, in particular, was especially concerned to maintain the independence of the new Czechoslovakia and Yugoslavia as buffers against any future German-speaking bloc in central Europe. *See also* FOREIGN POLICY.

STARHEMBERG, ERNST RÜDIGER, COUNT (1899–1956).

From one of the most distinguished and oldest of **Upper Austria**'s noble houses, Starhemberg, while a university student, fought with the German Freikorps Oberland, a volunteer private militia, after **World War I** . On 9 November 1923, he participated in Adolf Hitler's abortive Munich putsch. He remained in **Germany** for some time after that, serving as a volunteer in the army.

These experiences, along with the renown of his family, striking good looks, and genuine oratorical gifts, served Starhemberg well in his career as a politician and leader of the paramilitary *Heimwehr* in the First Austrian Republic. From 1930 to 1936 he was head of the organization, in which he represented the German-national position. He was deeply under the spell of Benito Mussolini and supported the **Austro-Fascism** of Chancellor **Engelbert Dollfuss**, which drew much inspiration from Italian corporatism.

Following the assassination of Dollfuss, the *Heimwehr* and Starhemberg reached the height of their direct political leverage with the government. Starhemberg became vice-chancellor and the head of the **Fatherland Front**. He held these positions until May 1936, when his vigorous advocacy of very close ties to Italy and his ambition to head the Austrian army led Chancellor **Kurt Schuschnigg** to dismiss him.

Starhemberg emigrated in 1937; from 1942 to 1945 he lived in South America. Over strong protests from the Austrian **Socialists**, he returned to the country in 1952.

STIFTER, ADALBERT (1805–1868). Primarily known as a masterful poetic realist, Stifter was also a painter and pedagogue. Born in the wooded area that reaches from **Upper Austria** into the Czech Republic, his family was in the flax and linen trade. The household fell into economic difficulties following the death of Stifter's father in 1817. His young son grew very close to his grandfather, who made it possible for him to attend a Latin school in Kremsmünster that introduced him to **literature** and science. Stifter went on to the **University of Vienna** in 1826, where he studied law and natural science—though he took no degrees. Leaving the university in 1830, he worked as a private tutor in the household of Imperial Chancellor **Metternich**, among others. In 1837, he married.

By 1840, Stifter had gained some recognition for his poetry and was about to write some of his most important fiction but could hardly support himself and his wife with such earnings. The **Revolutions of 1848** left Stifter a vigorous advocate of public **education** as the basis of a morally unified and free civic society. In that year he moved to **Linz**, where, in 1850, he became the provincial supervisor of primary schools. His idealism brought him into conflict with the authorities, who denied him a higher position. His last years were spent in growing unhappiness over his childless marriage, financial difficulties, and finally, the onset of liver cancer. Deeply depressed, he tried to commit suicide before he succumbed to the disease.

Stifter saw both his literary and pictorial work as exemplars of what he called the gentle law (*Sanfte Gesetz*). As defined in the preface to *Many-Colored Stones* (*Bunte Steine*, 1853), a collection of the author's writings, this principle stressed the harmony between nature and man, the enduring over the temporary, and change through quiet inward evolution rather than explosive interaction with the environment. His prose is characterized by its measured pace and painstaking descriptive language. Although Stifter did not enjoy great critical acclaim in his own time, modern scholars have assigned him a prominent place in the Austrian literary canon.

STRACHE, HEINZ-CHRISTIAN (1969–) Formally trained as a dental technician, Strache became national leader of the **Freedom Party of Austria** (FPÖ) in 2005. His earlier political career had been in local politics in **Vienna**. Though initially close to onetime FPÖ chairman **Jörg Haider**, Strache had fallen out with him by hinting that he might run against Haider's sister for the office. The possibility that Strache might win was one reason that Haider broke with the FPÖ to form the Alliance for the Future of Austria (BZÖ) in 2005.

Strache's national campaigns in 2006 and 2008 combined appeals to populist resentment of major party elites and fears that new immigrants from eastern Europe, Africa, and the **Islamic** regions of the world will cut into the social services and jobs available to Austrian citizens. His sloganeering in 2006 was especially offensive to the large Turkish community in Vienna. Like the late Jörg Haider, he has also been accused of neo-Nazi sympathies, charges that he has vigorously denied. Under his leadership, the FPÖ has seen a considerable revival of its fortunes at the polls, winning over 20 percent of the vote in the national elections of 2008. *See also* POLITICAL PARTIES.

STRANITZKY, JOSEF ANTON (1676–1726). Generally acknowledged as the father of Viennese popular **theater**, Stranitzky was an actor, a writer, a theatrical entrepreneur, and, until the end of his life, a practicing dentist. The leader of a group of itinerant players around **Salzburg**, he drifted to **Vienna** in 1705. There, despite the opposition of municipal authorities and the **Habsburg** court, which favored the numerous Italian theatrical companies in the city, he presented comic plays in German. These became very popular with the local middle classes.

By 1712, Stranitzky was director of his Theater at the Kärntnertor (Carinthian Gate), where he and his players offered broad, often downright vulgar, spoofs and parodies of the static and pompous **Baroque** drama of the day. Much of the action was improvised, not scripted, and owed a great deal to the Italian *commedia dell' arte*. Hanswurst, or Johnny Sausage, a German-language Harlequin, often played by Stranitzky himself, had a central role in the action. Dressed in Salzburg peasant garb and speaking the dialect of the area as well, he derided the manners and mannerisms of the high and mighty and made his way through life by nimble wit and amoral self-interest. Audiences were overwhelmingly enthusiastic. As the years went by, Hanswurst gradually became a Viennese stereotype, now using the patois of the capital city, **Wienerisch**. The plays themselves added many other visible Viennese figures—confectioners, bakers, recently arrived servants from the countryside, and the like.

STRAUSS, JOHANN, JR. (1825–1899). The son of a very talented composer and orchestra leader, Strauss was forbidden by his father to follow in his footsteps. It was his mother who encouraged his career. In 1844, following his study of **music** theory and composition with the choirmaster of St. Stephen's Cathedral, Strauss made his debut conducting his own orchestra at a casino in one of **Vienna**'s outer districts. When his father died in 1849, the son combined the two ensembles.

Popularity came to Strauss quickly; only his association with dissidents during the **Revolutions of 1848** kept him, until 1863, from the directorship of the Court Ball, one of the highlights of the Vienna **Fasching** or Carnival season. He never lost his unconventional streak, renouncing his Catholicism to marry his third wife, who was Jewish, in the Lutheran church. His lengthy tours through Europe with his orchestra were enormous successes, as was his visit to the United States in 1872.

Strauss Jr. is known for his many graceful and melodic waltzes ("Blue Danube," "Emperor Waltz," "Tales from the Vienna Woods") and a wide variety of other dance compositions. Some of these are really concert pieces, so musically elaborate that they defy execution in normal ballroom settings. The great popularity of **operettas** by the French composer Jacques Offenbach, especially *Orpheus in the Underworld*, which premiered in Vienna in 1860, moved Strauss to explore the genre. He wrote two classics, *Die Fledermaus* (1874) and *The Gypsy Baron* (1885). The appeal of both comes in large part from the composer's fluent interweaving of harmonic and rhythmic structures found in common dance forms. Nevertheless, both works—Strauss called them light operas—show the composer's familiarity with Richard Wagner's technique of musical leading motifs. They are still performed today.

STYRIA/STEIERMARK. Styria is known to Austrians as the Green Mark (Eng.: march) because of the lush hues of that color that are seen there in the spring. Although today it is one of Austria's most industrialized provinces, it has retained the spectacular rural scenery that has long drawn much local **tourism** and large numbers of retirees to the region. The capital city of **Graz** has traditionally been second only to **Vienna** in its cultural and intellectual life. Its university, founded in 1585 as a center of **Jesuit** scholarship during the **Catholic** Counter-Reformation of the late 16th and 17th centuries, has attracted many illustrious scholars from the German-speaking areas.

Styria has an extensive prehistory. In the fourth century BCE, Celts settled the region and founded a kingdom called **Noricum**, which the Romans turned into a province of the same name when they conquered it in 15 BCE. The eastern reaches of today's Styria were in yet another province, Pannonia. Christianity appeared in the area in the fourth century CE. By the beginning of the ninth century, it was under the ecclesiastical supervision of the bishop of **Salzburg**.

Both the Avars and alpine Slavs penetrated the area in the last quarter of the sixth century and established their control over a territory called Karantania. Combining with the Slavs to drive the Avars from Karantania around the middle of the eighth century, the Bavarian Duke Odilo became its ruler. In 803, now part of the Frankish Carolingian Empire, Styria was made a Mark, though it was still technically part of Bavaria. For the following century and a half, Styria was divided into three separate administrative districts.

Around 1050 a new dynasty, the Otakars, who called themselves the counts of Steyer after their family castle, became counts of Styria. They would give the region its present name. Throughout the 12th century, they gradually reunited the province. Count Otakar III (1129–1164) is generally acknowledged as the father of the Styrian principality. In 1180, Emperor Frederick Barbarossa raised Styria to the status of an independent duchy, thus breaking the tie with Bavaria for good. When the Otakar line died out in 1192, Styria passed to the **Babenbergs** of Austria. In 1276, Styria came under **Habsburg** control.

Throughout these many changes, Styria retained its juridical independence and a strong sense of provincial identity. A well-developed structure of estates, dominated by the local nobility and prelates, added to the duchy's sense of territorial distinctiveness. These developments became particularly important in the 16th century, as Styria became a center of Austrian **Protestantism** during the Reformation. The great astronomer and mathematician Johannes Kepler (1571–1630) taught in a Protestant high school in Graz.

The Habsburg family custom of dividing their lands among their sons furthered the separateness of Styria. The last of these, in 1564, was especially important. Graz became the capital of Inner Austria, which included modern **Carinthia**. It was a front-line border between Christendom and the Ottoman Empire. The territorial arrangement lasted until 1619; the court in Graz of Archduke Charles (1540–1590), Emperor **Ferdinand I**'s youngest son, and his wife, Archduchess Maria (1551–1608) of Bavaria, became a cultural and religious center. Both devout Catholics, Charles and his wife inaugurated measures to roll back the tide of the Lutheran reform in the area. Their son, Emperor **Ferdinand II**, acted as the political spearhead of the Counter-Reformation throughout central Europe during the first decades of the 17th century. He would reunite the Austrian Habsburg lands once again.

Following **World War I**, Styria lost a significant amount of territory to Slovenia, then part of what would become the new kingdom of Yugoslavia. Among the excisions was the province's second largest city, Marburg, today's Maribor. During the interwar period, Styria was a hotbed of right-wing activity with an especially large and well-armed *Heimwehr*. A center of heavy **industry** because of its rich iron and coal deposits, Styria, including the city of Graz, was heavily bombed after 1943 by the Allies. At the very end of the war, the Nazi armies and the Soviet forces fought pitched battles in parts of the province. During the Allied **occupation**, it was under the control of Great Britain.

The deindustrialization of the latter decades of the 20th century has much reduced the Styrian industrial infrastructure. However, the service sector of the provincial **economy** has shown considerable vitality.

SUTTNER, BERTHA VON (1843–1914). Born in Prague to the Bohemian noble house of Kinsky, Suttner first hoped to be a singer. Realizing that her talents did not match her ambitions, she taught **music** for a time. She became a governess and social secretary in the **Vienna** home of Baron von Suttner in 1873. Following a short stint as a secretary to the Swedish industrial magnate Alfred Nobel, she returned to Vienna. There she married her employer's son, Arthur (1850–1902), much against the wishes of his family.

The couple fled to Tiflis in Georgia, a part of the Russian Empire. Suttner was horrified by the suffering she witnessed among Russian soldiers during the Russo–Turkish War of 1877–1878, turned her home into a hospital for the wounded, and resolved at that point to devote herself to the cause of world peace. Upon returning once again to Vienna in 1885, she started to write pacifist fiction. Her *Die Waffen Nieder! Eine Lebensgeschichte (Throw Down Your Arms! A Story of a Life*, 1889) was a one of the 19th century's most influential best sellers. The great Russian novelist Leo Tolstoy said that the work had the same effect on contemporary thinking as Harriet Beecher Stowe's *Uncle Tom's Cabin* had in the United States. Its central theme was the despair and grief felt by **women** whose husbands and sons either died or suffered life-altering wounds in battle.

Suttner had also opened contacts with the International Arbitration and Peace Association in London and studied pacifist doctrines. In 1890, she founded the Austrian Peace Society, known since 1964 as the Suttner Society. From 1892 until 1899, she edited a monthly, *Die Waffen Nieder (Lay Down the Weapons)*, with a Jewish bookdealer, Alfred Fried, whom she met in Berlin. In 1891, her husband helped found the Vienna branch of the Union for Defense against Anti-Semitism.

Also active in feminist causes, after 1902 Suttner was chairperson of the Peace Committee of the Federation of Austrian Women's Clubs. Deeply troubled by the world armaments race of the late 19th and early 20th centuries, she represented Austria–Hungary in world peace conferences and was the president of the Office for World Peace in Bern. It was she who prompted Nobel to establish the eponymous Peace Prize, which she herself won in 1905. Suttner intended to call a world peace conference in Vienna during August 1914. In the midst of preparations for this gathering, she suddenly died, one week before Archduke **Franz Ferdinand** was assassinated in Sarajevo.

– T –

TANDLER, JULIUS (1869–1936). A physician, Tandler was among the practical activists of the Austrian **Social Democratic Worker's Party**. He became a professor at the **University of Vienna** in 1910. In 1919–1920, Tandler served as federal undersecretary for public health. He achieved prominence, however, as the **Vienna** councilor for health and public welfare from 1919 to 1934.

Tandler believed that material improvement led to human improvement. Good housing conditions, for example, would create changes in one's germ plasm, which could be passed on to succeeding generations. He devoted himself to creating an elaborate network of government programs in Vienna that would realize his theories. Children were a particular concern. Tandler sponsored the establishment of kindergartens, pre- and postnatal clinics, school dental clinics, day care centers, and the like. Social workers were dispatched throughout the city to safeguard the welfare of the young. As early as 1922, marriage counselors met with prospective brides and grooms to certify their physical health.

In discussions of abortion, Tandler took the position that society, represented by the government, not individuals, had the sole right to order the termination of pregnancy. Though this view brought him closer to the **Catholic** conservative view of this matter, Tandler was heavily criticized in right-wing circles for the intrusive impact of his program on the family. He died in Moscow, to which he had been invited as a consultant on hospitals.

THEATER. Religious spectacle had a central place at the **Habsburg** courts of the early modern era and in **educational** programs of monastic foundations, especially the **Jesuits** and **Benedictines**, throughout the monarchy's lands. The central theme in all of these settings was the struggle between the sacred and the secular for control of the human spirit. By the end of the 17th century, two stage genres, each devoted to entertainment, had intruded upon this lofty theme. Italian and, occasionally, English improvisatory theater was immensely popular among all social classes, and **opera** whetted local appetites for musical interludes on stage and eye-catching visual effects. When combined, they created a distinctive theatrical tradition in the Austrian lands.

A central step was the installation of the theatrical company of **Josef Anton Stranitzky** in Vienna's Theater at the Carinthian Gate around 1711. Highly popular, his productions frequently featured stock peasant figures speaking the **language** of stereotypical rural Austrians. These performances were derusticated to a certain extent by the middle of the 18th century, as stage bumpkins became more urbane and magical interventions took the place of religious mystery in scenarios. Playwright Philipp Hafner's (1735–1764) *Megära the Terrible Witch* (1755) fixed the genre in Viennese theaters. The government, however, particularly under Emperor **Joseph II**, for a time discouraged conventional popular comedy as a way of promoting a standard oral German and the habit of empirical reasoning. In support of both programs, Joseph converted the court theater (***Burgtheater***) into a German National Theater in 1776.

Though the *Burg* quickly lost that exclusively German focus, graceful elocution, naturalness of presentation, and seamless ensemble work made it the premier theater of the German-speaking world in the 19th century. Crucial in this development were two directors, Joseph Schreyvogel (1788–1832) and Heinrich Laube (1806–1884), who incorporated plays from several European traditions into the repertory and encouraged the acting style for which the company was famous. The classical drama at the heart of its program, represented by **Franz Grillparzer**, one of the great dramatic poets of the German language, however, had to make some room for the popular comedy. This was especially the case in the second half of the 19th century, when Eduard von Bauernfeld (1802–1890), a general man of letters who cleaned these materials up a bit to suit middle-class and noble audiences. But it was in the hands of the masters of Viennese comedy, **Ferdinand Raimund** and **Johann Nestroy**, that the genre flourished, critical interpolations, music, and all. The work of both frequently appeared on other Vienna stages, such as the **Theater in the Josefstadt**.

At the beginning of the 20th century, writers like **Arthur Schnitzler** and Hermann Bahr (1863–1934) had introduced Viennese audiences to European realism and naturalism in houses such as the German People's Theater (*Deutsches Volkstheater*, 1889). Such changes came at the expense of popular comedy. Indeed, Vienna was beginning to yield to Berlin as the premier city of theater in German central Europe. Expressionist or highly abstract modernist drama never took hold in the Viennese theater.

One of the city's most successful stage styles, cabaret theater or "cellar theater" (*Kellertheater*), was a borrowing from the new German capital. In 1901, Felix Salten (Siegmund Salzmann, 1869–1945), the author of *Bambi*, opened his Theater zum lieben Augustin (Theater at Friend Augustine's) for a few performances. At first specializing in light entertainment and small ensemble revues, even magic shows, it flourished after 1906. The Simplicissimus theater, which opened in 1912 in the Café Simpl, has performed since then, except when the **Nazis** closed it from 1944 until the end of **World War II**. Although the regime tolerated light entertainment, it was implacably hostile to the political and social criticism that was among the staples of cellar theater entertainment in the interwar period. The genre also took hold in **Graz**, **Innsbruck**, and **Linz**. But it was once again in Vienna that notable cabarettists appeared, especially in the 1960s: Gerhard Bronner (1922–2007), Carl Merz (Carl Czell, 1906–1979), and **Helmut Qualtinger**.

Although serious Austrian theater continued to program work with traditional themes between 1919 and 1938, it was heavily politicized by every major movement along the ideological spectrum. The right wing was especially critical of foreign plays, especially explicitly modernist ones. It took the Theater am Fleischmarkt (Theater at the Meat Market, 1958) to introduce Austrian audiences at large to French avant gardists such as Eugene Ionesco, Jean Cocteau, Jean Genet, and Samuel Beckett. From the perspective of the 21st century, however, the most influential Austrian voice in its postwar theater may have been **Ödön von Horvath**. His merciless stripping of cliché from everyday Viennese life in *Tales from the Vienna Woods* (*Geschichten aus dem Wiener Wald*, 1931) and focus on human degradation, particularly the female variety, in *Faith, Hope, and Charity* (*Glaube, Liebe, Hoffnung*, 1936), were not well received in his lifetime. They did, however, inspire the modern, and socially very negative, folk play (*Volksstück*) as conceived by Wolfgang Bauer (1941–2005) and Peter Turrini (1944–). Another significant body of work, more linguistically surrealistic but with a similar social thrust, has come from the **Vienna Circle**. Austrian dramatists with worldwide audiences, such as **Peter Handke** and **Thomas Bernhard**, have often replicated its local themes and settings.

THEATER IN THE JOSEFSTADT. Next to the *Burgtheater*, the Theater in the Josefstadt is the oldest dramatic stage in **Vienna**. Founded in 1788 by an actor, Karl Mayer (1753–1830), it was the first of three playhouses in the adjacent outlying districts of the city, the other two being the Theater an der Wien and the Theater in der Leopoldstadt. It is also the smallest, but nevertheless it is central to the rich theatrical history of the **Habsburg Empire** and the modern Austrian capital. Its repertory, both popular and classical, is known for its variety, which over the centuries has ranged from **opera** to boulevard comedy. Its company and guest players have been known for their high performance standards. Many of the major figures of the Austrian stage, and more recently, screen, have worked here, often early in their careers. **Ferdinand Raimund** made his debut at the Theater in the Josefstadt in 1814 as Franz Moor in the German dramatist Friedrich Schiller's *The Robbers* (*Die Räuber*). When a new theater was completed in 1822, it opened with the "Consecration of the House" overture by **Ludwig van Beethoven**.

In 1924, the theater was once again substantially rebuilt. For the next two years, it functioned under the direction of **Max Reinhardt**, who wanted to turn the house into a showcase for fine acting. The reputations of several major names of the German-speaking theater—notably the members of the **Thimig family**—spread through central Europe and beyond, in part because of their participation in Reinhardt's theater. Though Reinhardt's presence was short-lived, his program survived. As late as 1972, one of Reinhardt's successors, Ernst Haeusserman (1916–1984), announced that the Theater in the Josefstadt was to be an actor's house, open to the dramatic work of both Austrian authors and those of the rest of the world.

THIMIG, FAMILY. Among the several theatrical dynasties of Austria, the Thimigs have been the most important. Their presence in **Vienna** was established by Hugo Thimig (1854–1944), who was from Dresden but emigrated to the imperial capital, where he was an honorary member of the *Burgtheater* ensemble from 1904 to 1923. He served as its director between 1912 and 1917. Especially noted for character and comic roles, he continued to act almost until the end of his very long life. The theatrical memorabilia that he assembled have become the basis of the current collection of the **Austrian National Library**.

Hugo Thimig was the father of three leading figures of the 20th-century Austrian theater. Helene Thimig (1889–1974) was a notable actress in the German- and English-speaking worlds. After a career in Vienna, Berlin, and other German theaters, she emigrated with her husband, the director and impresario **Max Reinhardt**, to the United States in 1937. There she worked in Hollywood until her return to Vienna after World War II. She was in the companies of both the *Burgtheater* and the **Theater in the Josefstadt** from 1946 to 1968 and of the revived **Salzburg Festival**, where she was especially known for her performances in the *Jedermann* of **Hugo von Hofmannsthal**.

While in the United States, Helene Thimig had served as director of the Max Reinhardt Workshop, experience she put to good use in directing the Reinhardt Seminar of the Vienna Academy of Music and Theater, where she also taught.

Helene Thimig's two brothers also had distinguished careers in the German-speaking, particularly the Viennese, theater. Hermann Thimig (1890–1982) and Hans Thimig (1900–1991) were, like their sister, closely associated with Max Reinhardt both in Berlin and in Vienna, at the Theater in the Josefstadt. Hermann was especially well known for his comic character roles, which gave him a chance to display the verbal athleticism that was his hallmark. He starred in the comedies of the 18th-century Venetian playwright Carlo Goldoni and in leading roles of the classic Viennese popular theater created by **Ferdinand Raimund** and **Johann Nestroy**. Hans Thimig also specialized in comic characters, though of the less spectacular sort. He was a great favorite in the Vienna Volkstheater (People's Theater), where he made his debut in 1916. He played roles at the *Burgtheater*, both as a member of the company and as a guest. He also worked as a stage and film director and on the radio. In 1946, and then again from 1959 to 1960, he was the head of the Reinhardt Seminars.

THIRTY YEARS' WAR (1618–1648). Though a conflict of vast scale throughout the European continent, the focus of the Thirty Years' War was on issues peculiar to the Habsburg lands and **Germany**, where the **Habsburgs** acted as emperors. The Reformation had brought **Protestantism** to much of central Europe; the kingdom of Bohemia, under Habsburg control since 1526, was, confessionally speaking, a very special case. Here, since the first third of the 15th century, a local variant of Christianity, Utraquism, had flourished among a broad segment of the population. Both laity and clergy partook of communion in both kinds. The ascent of the devoutly Catholic **Ferdinand II** as king of Bohemia (1617) and German emperor (1619) alarmed Protestants of all persuasions. In 1619, the Bohemian estates refused to accept Ferdinand as their king, calling instead upon Elector Frederick V of the Palatinate to rule them. The latter's acceptance of the position set off a general constitutional crisis in the **Holy Roman Empire**, which, together with Ferdinand's decision to fight for his position in Bohemia, led to warfare throughout central Europe.

The Habsburg armies crushed the Bohemian rebels at the Battle of the White Mountain, just outside of Prague, in 1620. The Renewed Land Ordinances, which Ferdinand issued in 1627, firmly established hereditary rule of his dynasty in the kingdom. A program of systematic recatholicization, which forced many Protestants to flee abroad or to go underground, brought the realm back under the control of the Church of Rome. Although Ferdinand's forces in Germany won some significant victories against Protestant armies, the emperor's attempts to restore **Catholicism** ultimately failed. Denmark, Sweden, and finally France entered the war against the Habsburgs and frustrated Ferdinand's ambition. The Peace of Westphalia (1648) confirmed the status of both Calvinism and Lutheranism, along with Catholicism, as territorial churches within the German lands of the Holy Roman Empire. The German principalities won the official right to conduct foreign policy free of imperial oversight. *See also* RELIGION.

THUN-HOHENSTEIN, LEO, COUNT (1811–1888). Serving as Austrian minister of **education** from 1849 to 1860, Count Thun was the **Habsburg Empire**'s most important academic reformer in the 19th century. An enlightened conservative aristocrat from Bohemia, Thun had served as the governor of the kingdom in 1848. It was this experience that underlay his strong support for bilingual education in Czech and German in territories of the empire where both populations were heavily represented. He also thought that if the empire were to survive in an increasingly modern Europe, it would have to encourage multinational political parties. This idea, however, remained little more than a suggestion.

Following the ideas of thoughtful collaborators such as Franz Exner (1802–1853), Thun undertook the modernization of Austrian secondary and university education. He promoted the revision of the curriculum in the classical Gymnasium and the creation of the Realschule, a secondary school emphasizing the study of modern languages and technical and scientific subjects. On the university level, Thun introduced a greater number of fields leading to terminal degrees. He supported and won for faculty greater academic freedom than had been the custom in the empire and a policy of appointing professors on the basis of their scholarly credentials, not on their political or **religious** preferences. Though a devout **Catholic**, Thun allowed **Jews** and **Protestants** to hold university teaching positions. Protestants could have their own theological faculties as well. The law curriculum was also updated under Thun's aegis.

TOBACCO. As early as the 16th century, the Imperial Library of the **Habsburg** government in **Vienna** held volumes written by Dutch pharmacists who accompanied Spanish and Portuguese voyages to South America. They were quick to note that local aboriginal peoples smoked, either ceremonially or therapeutically, an aromatic plant that reputedly had an analgesic effect upon headaches.

First planted in **Upper Austria** in 1648 and in **Lower Austria** in 1649, its use spread throughout the 17th century. By 1723, the Habsburg government, eager to capitalize on the popularity of tobacco use, established a state-run factory in the Lower Austrian town of Hainburg to process snuff and cigars. The region would become the center of Austrian tobacco manufacture, which Emperor **Joseph II** made a state monopoly in 1784.

Production and consumption of tobacco grew sharply throughout the entire **Habsburg Empire** in the 19th century. Cigarettes appeared in 1865; by 1907–1908 their consumption matched, then outdistanced, that of cigars.

The Austrian Tobacco Monopoly (*Österreichische Tabakregie* or *Austria Tabak*) continued to be a profitable state enterprise for both the First and Second Republics. By 1995, the company had become a corporate conglomerate, with holdings and managerial responsibilities in areas far from tobacco production, such as sporting goods. In 2003, the Austrian State Holding Company relinquished its control over tobacco production by selling its 41 percent share in the company's equity to a British firm for 769 million euros. *See also* AGRICULTURE; ECONOMY.

TOURISM. Austria is unusually well positioned to develop a broad tourist clientele. Though the largest segment of foreign visitors comes from the Federal Republic of Germany, who can reach their southern neighbor easily by car and have no language problems when they arrive, Austria has many attractions for people throughout the world. For the culturally minded, it has rich musical and artistic traditions, epitomized by such institutions as the **Salzburg Festival**, the **Vienna State Opera**, and the **Vienna Philharmonic Orchestra**. For winter athletes, it has the **Alps**. For European travelers in general, it is a transit area where many must stay, if only overnight. Austrians themselves are some of their country's best customers, favoring both Alpine skiing resorts and, in the summer, the lakes of **Carinthia**.

Few states have turned themselves so single-mindedly to developing a tourist infrastructure as has Austria. Its hotels and restaurants, considerably behind Western standards even in the 1960s, now offer comforts and conveniences that meet the expectations of the most discriminating guests. Many such enterprises are still in family hands, particularly outside of the city of **Vienna**. Although efficiency experts deplore such arrangements, they often bring with them memorably pleasant personal service and return trips.

These efforts have made tourism a cornerstone of the Austrian **economy**. Austria leads the **European Union** in terms of per capita income from tourist enterprise. Since the end of **World War I**, Austria has depended very heavily on tourism from abroad to maintain a favorable balance of **trade**. Only with the beginning of the 21st century did this situation consistently appear to have reversed itself. Nevertheless, with 32 million visitors from abroad in 2007, Austria continues to cultivate itself as a tourist target. The state underwrites 32 Austrian tourist offices throughout the world and actively markets itself in 61 countries. *See also* GERMANY, RELATIONS WITH.

TRADE. Though centrally placed in Europe, Austria was historically a side road in European and worldwide trading patterns. **Vienna** and **Linz**, both on the **Danube** River, had lively mercantile communities in the Middle Ages, but their turnover did not generate the revenues spun off by cross-border commerce in northern Italy, northern France, and the Netherlands, and along the basins of the North, Baltic, and Mediterranean seas. Prague, on the other hand, one of the urban hubs in the **Habsburg Empire** after 1526, was a prime business and manufacturing center of medieval east central Europe.

The reorientation of European trade toward the Atlantic coast shunted commerce even farther from central Europe in the 16th and 17th centuries. At the same time, the repeated assaults of the Ottoman Empire on the region made towns and markets of eastern and southeastern Austria risky places to do business. The burdens of defense forced **Habsburg** governments to steer capital into military equipment and manpower rather than into commercial infrastructure and investment.

By the latter third of the 17th century, Habsburg emperors and their advisors were concluding that other European rulers had enriched themselves considerably by revenues from foreign trade. In 1665, the regime in Vienna created a separate office to encourage commerce (*Kommerzkollegium*), the first such body in the Western world. Merchants from Constantinople—**Jews**, Turks, and especially Armenians—had been selling Levantine wares in Vienna and elsewhere in the Habsburg lands for some time. Contemporary Habsburg rulers, beginning with Emperor Leopold I (1640–1705), began to see the Ottoman Balkans and even the Levant as options for trading opportunities and partners.

The first government-sponsored Oriental Company, founded in 1667, dealt in luxury goods from the east and cattle from Ottoman Hungary. It fell apart, however, in 1683 in the wake of the second, but final, Ottoman siege of Vienna. Another one was established in 1719, again to exploit trading possibilities with Constantinople and elsewhere in the Middle East. Undercapitalization led to its collapse in 1734. Though individual merchants from the Austrian lands often did well in Constantinople, their collective profits were modest compared to the earnings of their French and British competitors. A Habsburg effort to enter the colonial trade in Africa and the Far East on the Atlantic with the Ostend Company, set up in 1722, prospered briefly, but political concerns persuaded the government to disband it in 1731.

More characteristically, the Habsburg Empire preferred to protect its own **industry** and **agriculture**. In 1775, the government of Empress **Maria Theresa** divided the dynasty's holdings into two separate toll and tariff zones, one dominated by the Austrian lands and Bohemia, which were somewhat more industrialized; the other by Hungary and its crown lands, which were overwhelmingly agricultural. These areas were expected to trade between themselves rather than abroad. Although the Hungarians were very good at evading these regulations, the plan did nothing to encourage foreign trade, either. Her son and successor, Emperor **Joseph II**, understood the importance of exports in state finance—he promoted the sale of dairy cattle abroad for slaughter. Nevertheless, he was reluctant to work through overseas trading companies because the Habsburg Empire had no navy to defend them. They were also unwelcome competition for other mercantile states, especially Great Britain, which the Habsburgs occasionally cultivated as a military and diplomatic ally. Though the Habsburg government largely abandoned internal customs charges between 1817 and 1827, it was not until 1881 and the removal of tariffs charged on trade with Hungary that the dynasty's empire was an internal economic unit.

The liberal views that sparked the abolition of internal restrictions on trade also persuaded the Habsburg government to adopt the international free trade model followed by other European countries in the 1850s and 1860s. Free trade agreements were signed by Vienna with England in 1865, France in 1866, **Italy** in 1867, and **Germany** in 1868. Austria–Hungary became a heavy importer of manufactured goods. Competition from a rapidly industrializing Germany after 1871 and a savage economic crash in 1873 once again led the

Habsburg Empire to shelter its own manufactures with protective tariffs. Hungary, poorer and much more agricultural than industrial, had an economic stake in preserving open competition between domestic manufactured products and their imported equivalents and much resented the program. Disagreement over toll and tariff policy would vex relations between the Austrian and Hungarian halves of the Dual Monarchy until its end in 1918. Governments in Vienna did not abandon foreign trade altogether; Germany and the newly emerging states in the Balkans such as Serbia and Romania remained significant trading partners. But the bulk of the exports from the Habsburg lands were agricultural, not industrial.

The collapse of Habsburg rule in 1918 virtually wiped out foreign trade for the new Austrian republic. Seventy percent of the industrial infrastructure of the former Habsburg Empire stayed in Bohemia. Near-total devaluation of the **currency** in 1919 all but excluded the new Austrian republic from the operations of the world economy, thereby severely crippling what was left of Austrian industry as well. Fiscal pressures even forced the new government to abandon sovereignty over its borders for a time. In 1922, foreign creditors loaned Austria the money to reestablish its currency on the condition that the government in Vienna turn over revenues from customs duties and excise taxes on **tobacco** as collateral.

With the success of the new and soon-solid schilling, adopted in 1923, Austrian industry began to recover. The First Republic's neighbors, however, raised their own trade barriers and other fees, which discouraged Austrian exports directly and indirectly. In March 1930, Swiss and German **railroads** increased their charges for freight transit over their respective countries. Austrian shipments of wood to France fell accordingly. The gathering world economic crisis in the early 1930s pushed the Austrian balance of trade even further into the red. The only serious offset to this otherwise dismal scene was a temporary spurt in **tourism**, especially from Germany. On 12 April 1930, eight years before the **Anschluss**, Germany and Austria completed the preliminaries for a tariff union between them. From March 1938 to 1945, the Austrian and German economies were formally the same.

Independent Austrian export activity started up quickly after **World War II**, although on a rudimentary level. The government begged citizens to cut down wood that could be converted to paper, which could then be bartered abroad for heating coal. Goods for goods exchanges did not end—in 1948 Austria exchanged Styrian-made Puch motorbikes with Brazil in return for coffee. Each zone of Allied **occupation** was encouraged to begin trading with neighboring foreign states. Western zones sent their goods to Switzerland, Germany, and Italy; Upper Austria restored economic relations with Czechoslovakia. By 1948, having signed trade pacts with Poland, Czechoslovakia, Hungary, and Yugoslavia, Austrian trade was strongly directed at first toward Eastern Europe. It dropped off markedly in the 1960s, as the Austrian economy improved and its manufactures became more attractive in the West. The very first Austrian trade agreement with France was signed on 29 October 1946.

Austrian exports in 1947 were showing a substantial uptick. Especially active were textiles, manufactured in the Vorarlberg on the Swiss border, where factories established after 1938 were allowed to begin producing for export. By 1951, Austria was trading actively not only with European nations but also with South American and African countries. In that same year, Austria joined the General Agreement on Trade and Tariffs (GATT), a world organization that promotes nondiscriminatory tariffs and tolls. As long as the occupation lasted, some forced exporting went on of manufactured wares and commodities, oil for example. Even after the victorious Allies withdrew in 1955, Austrians had to be careful not to violate their official **neutrality** by exporting strategic goods to participants in the **Cold War**.

Austria's trade balances have often shifted between surplus and deficit, but the overall development of foreign trade has been positive. An intense period of economic growth in Austria in 1967 led to an upswing in exports, which by two years later were covering 86 percent of the cost of the country's imports. Indeed, in 1969, Austria's export growth exceeded that of both the **European Free Trade Association**, in which Austria participated, and the European Economic Community (EEC). All of this also depended on the recovery of Austrian **industry**.

Trading within the single market of the **European Union** (EU) since 1995, Austria has profited considerably from the relationship. In 2005, the **Austrian National Bank** estimated that every

Austrian had gained between 700 to 5,000 euros in profits on the basis of the country's EU membership. Austria has also benefited from the globalization of world markets; the industrializing countries of Asia have been good customers for highly specialized Austrian tools and machinery. The obvious financial gateway to post-Soviet east central and eastern Europe, Austria has become a major exporter of Western goods, including its own apparel brands and supermarkets, to the Czech Republic, Croatia, and Hungary, among other countries. Austrian **banks** have also played a major role in bringing investment capital to these lands. In 2005, around two-thirds of the companies listed on the Vienna Stock Exchange were active in eastern Europe.

In 2002, Austria began to run a favorable balance of trade that has not reversed its course. In 2007, the surplus was 8.8 billion euros, which amounted to 3.2 percent of the Gross Domestic Product (GDP). The **alp**ine republic's most important trading partner was **Germany**, which received a little over 31 percent of Austria's exports. Germany also accounted for 41.5 percent of all Austrian imports. Austria's second most significant customer abroad was **Italy**, which took 8.9 percent of its imports from its near neighbor to the north. Of Austria's imports, 6.9 percent also came from Italy. The third best customer for Austrian exports—5.1 percent of them—was the **United States**. China, however, had risen to be Austria's third most important source of imports.

TRADE UNIONS. Initially organized as economic self-help groups to tide people over in periods of unemployment, physical disability, and the like, trade unions were a by-product of Austrian **industrialization** in the 19th century. A workers' committee established during the **Revolutions of 1848** was the first to make formal demands for laws governing conditions of labor. Laws regulating freedom of assembly and freedom of association progressively relaxed after 1867. The founding of the **Social Democratic Workers' Party** in 1888–1889 turned the labor movement into a serious and lasting political force, not only in the Austrian lands but throughout the **Habsburg Empire**, particularly in Bohemia. During the First Austrian Republic, all of the **political parties** or factions sponsored some form of ideologically compatible trade union organization.

Following **World War II**, a central **Austrian Federation of Trade Unions** (*Österreichische Gewerkschaftsbund*) was formed with social democratic, conservative, and communist factions. Charged with speaking for the economic, social, and cultural interests of all wage labor in Austria, it was one of several stratagems developed to promote the social harmony that the Second Republic required to get back on its economic and political feet. Over the years, however, the Federation has become heavily associated with the **Socialist Party of Austria** and its financial resources. *See also* BAWAG; WELFARE.

TRAKL, GEORG (1887–1914). Born and raised in **Salzburg**, Trakl had a troubled childhood and an even more problematic adolescence. His relationship with his mother was particularly strained. Though he was intensely close to a younger sister, her claim that they had an incestuous relationship has not been corroborated. His death from heart failure was triggered by alcohol and drug abuse, habits he picked up as a teenager. A trained pharmacist, he had easy access to these substances.

Trakl lived to see the publication of only one volume of his verse, *Gedichte* (1913). Nevertheless, his dreamlike, sometimes nightmarish lyrics have qualified him as one of the master expressionist poets in German **literature** generally. A relentless autumnal melancholy haunts both his prose and his poetry; awareness of temporality and death itself intrude on even the most innocent settings. Quick juxtaposition of seemingly disassociated images intensifies the all-over sense that his writing has been processed through his subconscious. His visions of death do have a kind of **Baroque** tactility to them, absent, however, conventional hopes for salvation. His repetition of images from poem to poem—lonely landscapes, metallic sounds, or the feel of metal on the body, shepherds and/or hunters trudging across solitary fields—was a standard Baroque technique as well.

TRANSPORTATION. Commercial and **military** needs triggered the development of modern transportation networks in the Austrian lands of the **Habsburg Empire**. By the beginning of the 18th century, the dynasty's ministers knew well that overseas **trade** had enriched royal treasuries in Great Britain and France and wished to encourage such activity where they could. Among the first measures they took was to extend overland roads. Construction of a route between **Trieste** and **Salzburg** was underway by 1717. Another over the Brenner Pass was begun in 1728.

The historic avenues of Austrian trade were along and on rivers, chiefly the **Danube**. Following the Ottoman Empire's evacuation of Hungary in 1699, commerce increased greatly along this route as well. Though **railroads** changed the face of the transportation infrastructure of the 19th-century Habsburg monarchy, the Danube trade was still central to its **economy**. In 1829, an English consortium founded the Danubian Steamship Transportation Company. By 1830, its vessels were running to Budapest and, after 1834, to the mouth of the river itself.

Supported in 1836 by Imperial Chancellor **Metternich** and **bank** capital from Rothschild financiers, a consortium of insurance companies founded the Austrian Lloyd Company in Trieste. The city, part of Habsburg dynastic land since the end of the 14th century, would become the hub of the empire's overseas trade, with lanes to the Middle and Far East and the Americas. By 1854, Austrian Lloyd had a fleet of 60 ships.

The Habsburg Empire's densest transportation network, however, was its railroads. Built in fits and starts after the 1830s, their first mission was to bring together the empire as a whole, and only later the Austrian lands alone. By 1896, a minister for railroads had a portfolio in the Habsburg government. With mountain tracks put down after 1900, the Austrian territory of the Habsburg Empire was well linked by rail by 1912.

A network of postal buses that helped to link rural and less-populated areas of Austria to larger transportation facilities began operation in 1907. Initially financed by both the postal system and local communes, it was largely taken over by the former during the interwar era. After **World War II**, it was systematically coordinated with railroad schedules.

Drawn by horses, the first **Vienna** streetcars began service in 1865; the Vienna Tramway Company built and ran streetcars in the immediate suburbs of the capital. Other major Austrian cities also introduced similar systems and converted them to electric power, as did Vienna, from 1895 through the first decades of the 20th century.

Under Mayor **Karl Lueger**, all of Vienna's municipal transportation lines were electrified. There were also a few steam-powered tramway lines.

By the 1990s, streetcar ridership in Austria had begun to decline in favor of bus and subway transportation. The groundbreaking for the latter, financed in part by a special tax on Vienna's businesses, was in November 1969; the network has grown incrementally since that time. But the most vigorous part of the Austrian transportation sector since World Was II has been automotive traffic, both freight and personal. Planned between 1938 and 1940, the Austrian Autobahn (super highway) has become a major thoroughfare for domestic traffic and international truckers and tourists, particularly on the system's north–south axis. With its first route, **Salzburg–Linz**–Vienna, completed in 1968, the Autobahn now covers roughly 1,700 kilometers.

Civil air service under full Austrian control got underway in June 1955. Air Austria, the first Austrian airline, opened in 1956; a year later it merged with Austrian Airways to form Austrian Airlines (AUA). It began transatlantic travel in 1969. When it began weekly service to Moscow in 1959, AUA was one of the first airlines in the Western world to fly there. Under competitive pressure that has never let up, AUA discontinued its domestic service in 1970, turning it over to smaller lines. Now part of the Star Alliance that includes the **German** airline Lufthansa, it has experienced continued financial difficulties. Repeated bids from airlines such as Lufthansa to buy Austrian state shares in AUA have been rebuffed by both major **political parties**, the **Austrian People's Party** and the **Socialist Party of Austria**, on the grounds that such a move would cost Austrians many jobs.

TYROL. Lying between the Germanic and Italianate regions of Europe, the Tyrol has been a crossroads of the two cultures for 2,000 years or more. It has thus played a significant role in the history of both regions. The site of some of the most daunting mountain ranges in the world, it was thinly settled in prehistoric times. After Roman conquest in 15 BCE, the administration of the Tyrol was split among several provincial authorities of the empire. These areas now lie either in modern Italy or in Austria.

Following the collapse of imperial authority in the west in the fourth and fifth centuries CE, the Germanic Lombards established a kingdom in the southern reaches of the area. During the sixth and seventh centuries, Slavs, and then Bavarians, penetrated the north. The legal practices differed substantially as a result. So-called Alpine Romans, who spoke a dialect of Latin, lingered in some valleys. By the end of the eighth century, the Tyrol was a county within the Frankish Empire of Charlemagne.

Christian missions to the Tyrol came in the fifth century, from Trent to the south. Others appeared somewhat later, from Bavaria. Under the patronage of the Bavarian duke Tassilo III, the monastery of Innichen was founded in 769 to promote Christianity among the Slavs. The bishoprics of the Tyrol played an important role in the defensive thinking of German emperors who, until the end of the 11th century, were able to determine who held these offices. In 1004 and 1027, countships over Trent, Bolzano, and the Vintschgau were conferred upon the bishop of Trent; the bishop of Brixen came to enjoy the same authority over important passes through the **Alps** by the end of the 11th century.

As clergymen, however, they could not engage directly in military activity. They therefore appointed guardians (*Vogt*) to defend their holdings and administer their legal affairs. Members of the local high nobility acted in these positions, which brought them into conflict with the secular counts of Tyrol—who came to carry that title after around 1140. Serving as guardians over Brixen and later the cloister of Trent, they held some of the lands attached to these institutions as well. By the end of the 13th century, the counts of Tyrol, in this case Meinhard II, had reunited much of the medieval province and had even begun to expand it.

The counts of Tyrol continued to practice partible inheritance until the extinction of the Meinhard line in a female succession. In January 1363, the heirless Countess Margaret of the Tyrol (1316–1369) passed the land to her **Habsburg** cousins, Rudolph IV (1339–1365), Albrecht III (1350–1395), and Leopold III (1351–1386). Representatives of the territorial clergy, bourgeoisie, and 12 noblemen were cosignatories to the document, a sign of the growing power of the estates in the province, which would peak in the 16th century with an unusual provision for free peasant representation. The Tyrolean Territorial Libel of 1511 gave the estates the privilege of setting conditions for their participation in Habsburg military undertakings. This arrangement lasted through **World War I** and the collapse of the Austro–Hungarian empire.

Around 1420, the Habsburg count Frederick IV (Freddy Empty-Pockets, 1382–1439) made **Innsbruck** his residence. His heirs continued the practice, and the city became the administrative center of the province in a short time. Meran, to the south, remained its official capital until 1848. Emperor **Maximilian I** was especially fond of the area, in part because he was an avid hunter, in part for its productive silver mines around Schwaz and Hall. Through purchase and war, he added important territories to the Tyrol, such as Kitzbühl and Kufstein, acquired from Bavaria in 1504.

The Tyrol lost its economic importance as its veins of precious metals substantially ran out by the 17th century. Its mountainous terrain was unsuited to any **agriculture** of scale; famine visited the region frequently. The Tyrol played an unexpectedly prominent role during the 19th-century Napoleonic Wars, when it was divided by the French and partially occupied by the Bavarians allied with Bonaparte. A species of guerrilla warfare led by a native son, **Andreas Hofer**, broke out, though it was later discouraged by authorities in Vienna, who were not eager to promote regional consciousness among any of the Habsburg Empire's subjects.

Territorial controversy erupted once again after World War I, when **Italy** acquired the **South Tyrol** as part of the **Treaty of St. Germain**. From the end of that conflict to the **Anschluss** in 1938, the Tyrol remained a bastion of the Catholic **Christian Social Party**. After Austria became part of Adolf Hitler's Third Reich, the **Nazi** government fused Tyrol and **Vorarlberg**. Tyrolean Catholics, however, sometimes openly resisted such official efforts to curb the influence of the church as closing religious schools. There was also considerable local resentment over Italy's continued control of the South Tyrol. The presence of industrial centers in Innsbruck and its environs and the area's centrality to transcontinental communication links made it the target of heavy Allied bombing. The Tyrol was part of the U.S. zone of occupation from 1945 to 1955.

Today, numerous hydroelectric installations and a wide range of industries, both large and small, make the Tyrol one of Austria's most economically dynamic regions. Extensive **tourism**, furthered by the completion of an elaborate network of mountain tunnels and highways, still contributes heavily to local income.

The several regions of the Tyrol have produced many artists and writers significant not only in the Austrian lands, but within the larger German-speaking world. The **Baroque** painter Paul Troger (1698–1762) worked in Salzburg and Lower Austria. His ceiling in the library of the cloister of **Melk** is a masterpiece of the genre. Oswald von Wolkenstein (1377–1445), who died in Meran in the South Tyrol, was among the most accomplished of medieval German lyric poets; his writing had an exceptionally expressive and often erotic content. Characterized by gripping linguistic and visual expressiveness, the work of the contemporary Tyrolean playwright Felix Mitterer (1948–) is widely played in German-speaking theaters today. *See also* ECONOMY.

– U –

UNITED NATIONS (UN). The United Nations played a significant role in restoring Austria to the international state system after **World War II**. In November 1947, Austria was admitted to the United Nations Educational, Scientific, and Cultural Organization (UNESCO), a special subsidiary of the UN charged with advancing education, research, and human and civil rights for all peoples.

In July 1952, Dean Acheson became the first American secretary of state to visit Austria. There he vowed to work for full Austrian membership in the United Nations. The secretary general of the international organization, Trygve Lie, also supported the idea. One condition of membership was sovereignty; on 20 December 1952, the UN General Assembly, with the Soviet Union and its eastern bloc states absent, formally urged the Allied powers that made up the Austrian **occupation** to reach agreement on the **Austrian State Treaty**.

Once independence was achieved in 1955, Austria became a sitting member of the UN. The position gave **governments** in **Vienna** a way of participating in activities abroad without compromising the state's official **neutrality**. In 1956, the UN made Vienna the center for the International Atomic Energy Organization (IAEO), a special body of the international organization that advances the peaceful uses of nuclear technologies. Vienna hosted its first UN conference in 1957 and has filled that role many times since. Among the most noteworthy gatherings was the 1993 UN Congress on Human Rights, only the second of its kind since the actual Declaration of Human Rights was issued in 1948. UN City in Vienna, a complex of administrative buildings financed by the municipal government and the Austrian state, opened in April 1987. Austrian troops have also provided support services for UN peacekeeping activities in places as diverse as the Congo (1960) and Cyprus (1964–2001).

On 22 December 1971, the UN chose **Kurt Waldheim**, the resident Austrian ambassador to the body, as its secretary general. Waldheim, who had held several ministerial positions in Austria, would continue in the position until 1981. His further career in Austria would be haunted by his evasive replies to questions about his army service during World War II and his possible violations of human rights. *See also* FOREIGN POLICY.

UNITED STATES OF AMERICA (U.S.), RELATIONS WITH.
The Second Continental Congress in Great Britain's rebellious North American colonies sent an ambassador to Vienna in 1778 to enlist aid from the **Habsburgs** in the War of Independence. Neither Empress **Maria Theresa** nor her heir apparent, the future **Joseph II**, were interested. Nor did their successors have much in the way of a **foreign policy** with the new United States of America throughout most of the 19th century. The first Habsburg consulate in the United States was opened in 1820 to deal with commercial questions. **Trade** was also the chief preoccupation of all the monarchy's other consular operations throughout the country until the end of the American Civil War in 1865. After that, consuls from the **Habsburg Empire** devoted ever more time to servicing the needs of immigrants from the Dual Monarchy to the United States.

Relations with the United States became far more complex for the Habsburg monarchy at the outbreak of **World War I**. The press office in the common Ministry for Foreign Affairs and the press bureaus of both the Austrian and Hungarian parts of the monarchy tracked the behavior of American ethnic communities with roots in the Habsburg lands that might be reinforcing sedition back home. By 1915, both Austria–Hungary and its German ally were known to be mobilizing East European industrial workers in the United States for strikes that would cripple America's support of Great Britain and France.

Once the United States entered the war on the Allied side in 1917, Habsburg foreign policy took even more account of attitudes in Washington. By the end of February 1918, Emperor **Charles I**, who had been trying to come to some kind of separate peace with the allies, informed the administration of Woodrow Wilson that he could accept Wilson's Fourteen Points, with some reservations.

After the Central Powers extracted the very harsh highly punitive treaty of Brest-Litovsk from the fledgling Soviet Union on 3 March 1918, Wilson's patience with Austria–Hungary ran out. When Emperor Charles proposed full federalization of the dynasty's empire on 16 October, the American president refused to listen. At the Paris Peace Conference in 1919, Wilson vigorously pursued the dismemberment of the Habsburg Empire; he also opposed any form of **Anschluss** with Germany.

The American banking house of Morgan and Company was among the participating institutions in a crucial loan to the Austrian First Republic arranged in 1922 by the League of Nations. Austro–American relations were, however, not a high priority in the foreign policy of either country. But even before **World War II** ended, Austrian spokesmen in Washington, among them **Otto von Habsburg**, the claimant to the long-gone thrones of his ancestors, were trying to negotiate favorable treatment for Austria. Formal diplomatic relations between Vienna and Washington got underway again in 1947. The United States was enormously helpful with emergency aid to Austria after the war. Indeed, such deliveries continued even after the **Austrian State Treaty** was in place in 1955.

Austria's acceptance of **neutrality** as stipulated by that agreement made the country somewhat less significant as a player in the **Cold War**. John Foster Dulles, the American secretary of state, agreed with Konrad Adenauer, the German chancellor, that the policy was "immoral." President John F. Kennedy found the arrangement more useful, both as a model for state-building in other states of eastern

Europe and as an alternate avenue to information about **the Soviet Union** that Austrians such as Foreign Minister **Bruno Kreisky** were willing to offer after 1959.

Austrian neutrality could, however, frustrate American policy in both Europe and other parts of the world. In 1958, Austria objected to American violation of its airspace to supply troops in Lebanon. The United States both expressed its apologies and discontinued the practice. As federal chancellor, Kreisky supported a serious American military commitment in Europe, though he differed sharply on several important questions with the United States, its efforts to curb socialist movements in Central America among them. With war in Iraq under discussion in Washington in 2002, Austrians made it clear when polled that they would not participate in any joint European Union (EU) military force to support the venture, as some member states were considering. Within the **EU**, Austria joined Finland, Sweden, and Ireland in deploring the American invasion of Iraq in 2003, though Foreign Minister Benito Ferrero-Waldner (1948–) rescinded her initial declaration of Austrian **neutrality**, having decided that the regimes in Baghdad and Washington were not morally equivalent. In 2005, the decision of the U.S. under the presidency of George W. Bush to send only a relatively low-level representative, Senator Rudy Boschwitz from Minnesota, to the 50-year commemoration of the signing of the Austrian State Treaty was taken as an affront in Austria and a sign generally in Europe of the loss of Europe's centrality in American foreign affairs.

The United States has, however, moved even more aggressively with Austria on more sensitive issues of Austrian treatment of Jews and others who cooperated with the **Nazi** regime from 1938 to 1945. Washington prodded governments in Vienna to compensate victims of the Austrian National Socialist regime. Deputy Finance Secretary Stuart Eizenstat completed negotiations in 2000 for Austrian compensation for an estimated 150,000 people who did forced labor under Nazi rule.

Payments out of a 3.7-billion-schillings (440 million euros) fund allocated for that purpose began at the end of the year. By 2002, about 50 percent of the money had been spent, with about 68,000 applications having been received. Eizenstat also won a similar pledge in 2001 for Austrian **Jews** specifically who suffered property losses at **Nazi** hands and who were still alive. In both cases, Austrian negotiators made clear that while these arrangements legally closed these issues, they did not terminate them morally.

UNIVERSITY OF VIENNA. Following the model of the medieval University of Paris, Archduke Rudolph IV (1339–1365), known as "the Founder" (*der Stifter*), established the Austrian university in 1365 along with his brothers, Archdukes Albrecht III (1349 or 1350–1395) and Leopold III (1351–1386). Named after the eldest archduke, *Alma Mater Rudolphina*, it was the second university to be established in central Europe, after Prague. It is today the oldest of its kind in the German-speaking world.

At first consisting of three faculties—arts, law, and medicine—it acquired a theological wing in 1384. The university enjoyed considerable renown throughout the Renaissance of the 15th century, both for the work of its scholars—such as Georg von Peuerbach (1423–1461) in mathematics, astronomy, and the development of instruments of measurement—and for the study of history and classical languages. Especially significant in the latter disciplines was the German humanist, Conrad Celtis (1459–1508), who enjoyed the patronage of Emperor **Maximilian I**. Between 1451 and 1518, the university had around 30,000 enrollees.

The **Protestant** Reformation and the threat of the Ottoman Empire, which laid siege to the city of **Vienna** in 1529, contributed to a precipitous fall in student enrollment during the 16th century. Repeated outbreaks of the plague kept young scholars away, too. As part of the Counter-Reformation, the theological and philosophical faculties were put in the hands of the **Jesuits** in 1623, and the size of the student body began to grow again. During the reigns of **Maria Theresa** and **Joseph II**, the university came under the complete control of the state; the study of medicine was particularly encouraged.

Following the **Revolutions of 1848**, the University of Vienna underwent another period of change, under the direction of Minister of Education **Count Leo Thun-Hohenstein**. Professors were called to positions based on their academic prominence alone, new disciplines were added to the curriculum, and new institutes such as the Institute for Austrian History were added to promote research. In 1884, it moved to its present neo-Renaissance headquarters on Vienna's

Ringstrasse after centuries in the inner city near Jesuit and Dominican establishments.

The collapse of the **Habsburg Empire** in 1918 brought more difficult years to the University of Vienna, although in some fields, such as philosophy and economics, it retained considerable eminence. Today it has eight faculties; about one-third of all Austrian university students study there. The physical plant of the university has expanded considerably to the north and west of the main building, as well as into outlying districts, since the last decades of the 20th century. *See also* AUSTRIAN SCHOOL OF ECONOMICS; CATHOLICISM; EDUCATION; RELIGION; VIENNA CIRCLE; VIENNA SCHOOL OF MEDICINE.

– V –

VIENNA, CITY. *Wien*, or Vienna in English, is in all likelihood a derivative of **Vindobona**, a name traced to the Celts who inhabited the area in pre-Christian times. Lying in a geographic basin that provides the only break in the Alpine–Carpathian mountain chain running from the Gulf of Liguria in the west to the Black Sea, it was well situated both strategically and commercially.

The region around today's Vienna was inhabited from the Stone Age; the origins of the city itself date from a Bronze Age settlement around 800 BCE. During the first and second centuries CE, Vienna was occupied and fortified by the Romans. Their artifacts still remain in the First District of the city. As the imperial legions withdrew in the fourth and fifth centuries from their many positions in the region, they were replaced, though often transitorily, by Slavic, Germanic, and even Asiatic tribes. The Carolingian Empire of the eighth and ninth centuries touched down here as well, leaving some traces on what is the site of the 11th-century church of St. Ruprecht, the oldest extant religious edifice in the city.

The first references to Vienna as a municipality date from 1137. In 1156, the **Babenberg** rulers of the Austrian lands made it the seat of their court; in the following century they substantially expanded the peripheral fortification of the town. Their successors, the **Habsburgs**, continued the process through the 16th and 17th centuries. The constraints of the extensive city walls left the First District of Vienna with a cramped and convoluted street pattern. The city became a major Danubian hub for medieval commerce; by the 14th century it was an intellectual center as well, with a number of important ecclesiastical foundations within its limits. The **University of Vienna** was established in 1365.

Political instability in the **Danube River** valley and the shift of European commerce westward with the opening of the Americas made Vienna far less attractive as a political and mercantile center during the 15th and 16th centuries. From 1485 to 1490, the city was controlled by the aggressive and ambitious king of Hungary, Matthias Corvinus. Vulnerability to the expanding Ottoman Empire also frightened many. The sultan's army reached the walls of the city in 1529 and threatened to do so again in 1532. Emperor **Maximilian I** preferred **Innsbruck** as a residence; Emperor **Ferdinand I** often quartered his large family in the Tyrolean capital for security reasons. Emperor Rudolph II (1552–1612) chose Prague as a capital.

Only in the 17th century did Vienna become the seat of Habsburg government. It remained so until the dissolution of the dynasty's empire in 1918, though after 1867 and the **Ausgleich**, Budapest was the domestic administrative center of Hungary. Under Emperor Leopold I (1640–1705), the **Hofburg** palace complex was substantially enlarged beyond its medieval outlines for the first time. With the victory over the Turks in 1683 and the rollback of Ottoman presence in east central Europe that followed, the immediate area beyond the fortified Inner City opened up for residential and commercial use. Land speculation spurred some of this process; today's Josefstadt, or the Eighth District of the city, was a conspicuous example. Religious considerations also dictated settlement policy. The Second District, the Leopoldstadt, was established to house the city's **Jews**.

However, it was only after 1858 and the dismantling of the city walls that Vienna grew to its present size. The now-obsolete fortifications were replaced by a circumferential boulevard, the *Ringstrasse*. This was further embellished by new, and often grandiose, construction, which became the city's hallmark. The **Vienna State Opera** was finished in 1869; between 1871 and 1890 the **Museum** of Natural History, the Museum of Fine Arts, the Parliament, the New City Hall, the *Burgtheater*, and the new university building were all completed. Largely through the incorporation of outlying villages, whose names were often retained for administrative convenience, the city reached its present configuration of 23 districts.

In these outlying areas housing, often in sizeable tracts and often appallingly inadequate, was put up in the 19th and 20th centuries for a swelling population. In 1800, Vienna had around 232,000 residents. Encouraged by the development of the city as an industrial and financial center, domestic migration within the empire helped to increase that figure to 842,951 in 1869, 1,341,900 in 1890, and 2,031,498 by 1910. At first from countryside areas that were largely German speaking, the newcomers and their ethnic backgrounds rapidly came to reflect the multinationality of the **Habsburg Empire** as a whole. Czechs were especially numerous by the end of the 19th century, but there were Hungarians, Italians, Jews from the easternmost lands of the empire, and many others as well.

During the first decades of the 16th century, Emperor Ferdinand I had acquired substantial control over the political life of the city after he had forcibly suppressed demands for greater municipal freedoms from the mayor and city council. By 1861, much of the municipality's former communal autonomy had been restored; substantial numbers among the middle classes of the Habsburg metropolis were enfranchised. They and the Liberal Party, which usually spoke for them, ran the city in their interests for a good part of the century.

Massive administrative corruption and the progress of democratization in the Austrian half of the monarchy after 1867 put heavy pressure on municipal politicians to broaden the appeal of their programs. It was in this atmosphere that **Karl Lueger**, the leader of the new **Christian Social** movement, came to be mayor of the city. From 1894 to 1897, he was elected to the office by the city council three times, but Emperor **Franz Joseph** refused to allow him to take office on the grounds that his inflammatory rhetoric, often harshly anti-Semitic, would create even more ethnic tension than then existed. In 1897, the monarch finally relented, persuaded that a Christian Social mayor might counter the rising attractiveness of the Marxist Austrian **Social Democratic Workers' Party** (SDAP).

For all his unsavory qualities, Lueger is generally acknowledged as having been one of Europe's great municipal leaders in the 19th century. Many of the public services and amenities that still distinguish

Vienna are the outcome of his programs. Under his administrations, the city developed a first-class public **transportation** system and a city water supply that is still among the best on the Continent. He also left future governments with a substantial deficit, which came due only after **World War I** and the collapse of the Habsburg Empire.

In 1922, the city became an autonomous province within the new Austria; it held approximately one-third of the population of the entire country. Because of substantial **immigration** of peoples from the so-called successor states (countries carved out of the erstwhile Austria–Hungary) and refugees from eastern Europe, especially from Bolshevism, Vienna lost only between 1 and 2 percent of its population after 1919. Nevertheless, its preeminence in central and east central Europe faded considerably. Viennese **banks** never recaptured their leading role among financial institutions in the newly sovereign nations of the region, which were eager to be as independent as possible from the one-time Habsburg capital.

The new Austria was at first inflation ridden and without the opportunities for foreign **trade** or capital resources available to the old monarchy. Nevertheless, Vienna undertook an ambitious and generous social agenda, paid for in large part at first by luxury duties and heavy taxes on rents from residential property. After 1923, a general tax to underwrite housing construction was introduced. Leadership for these programs came from the SDAP. Though the party lost control of Austria's national government after 1920, it commanded huge electoral majorities in the city until 1934, when the authoritarian regime of **Engelbert Dollfuss** installed an administration more to its liking. Particularly outstanding were its public housing projects, which drew the attention and respect of urban planners and social reformers throughout the world. New hospitals, parks, schools, and **sport** facilities were established as well.

The city, however, was neither socially nor politically harmonious. Tensions between the local Social Democrats and the more conservative national government, which had its seat in Vienna, were continually high. In 1927, a workers' protest led to the burning of the Ministry of Justice building. In 1934, the two parties and their supporters took up arms against one another in the streets and in housing projects. A massive demonstration welcomed Adolf Hitler in 1938, when he came to the city to announce the **Anschluss** of Austria and Germany.

Once under **Nazi** control, Vienna was officially known as The Imperial District of Greater Vienna (*Reichsgau Gross-Wien*); 97 neighboring areas were incorporated into the municipality, giving it 26 administrative units. During **World War II**, Allied bombing and ground troops heavily damaged the city. In 1944 and 1945, some of its most notable buildings and landmarks, such as St. Stephen's cathedral and the State Opera building, suffered the most damage.

Under the Allied **occupation** of Austria, Vienna, like the country as a whole, was divided into four zones. Great Britain, France, the Soviet Union, and the **United States** governed the Inner City jointly. A substantial portion of the **Lower Austrian** territory, which the Nazis had folded into the city, was returned to the province to which it had once belonged. This left the city with 23 districts, its current number despite major population shifts to the municipal periphery.

Once again in power, the Socialists, now called the **Socialist Party of Austria**, embarked upon a massive rebuilding program. New transportation facilities, most notably a rapid transit railroad, linked Vienna with outlying suburbs and a subway that is undergoing continued extension. Years of prosperity and an easing of social tension since World War II have led to a massive refurbishing of the city's building stock, which, along with its cultural attractions and rich history, has made it a major center of **tourism**. The imperial **Hofburg** is now the setting for international conferences and meetings, and the **United Nations** has several important offices in the city. Its proximity to the former Soviet satellite states has also restored Vienna's position as an international banking and investment center. *See also* SEITZ, KARL.

VIENNA CHOIRBOYS/WIENER SÄNGERKNABEN. Known throughout the world today for the purity of their voices and precision of their singing, the Vienna ensemble also exemplifies the institutional impact of the collapse of the **Habsburg Empire** in 1918. The dynasty's rulers had sought out young voices for their liturgical choirs and occasional secular entertainments since the Renaissance; the choir was singing in the chapel of the imperial **Hofburg** in 1498.

With no emperor to support them at the close of **World War I**, however, the group faced dissolution.

Josef Schnitt, the singers' spiritual mentor, was a man of some private means. He personally underwrote the group, which reappeared in the Hofburg in 1924; local concerts followed. A year later the ensemble became the "Vienna Choirboys." By 1926, Schnitt's funds were running low; to make up the difference the boys sang on the Austrian radio and in small-scale **Mozart** and **Haydn** operas. Trips abroad followed and continue to this day. The ensemble has a permanent home in the Augarten Palace in **Vienna**'s Second District, the Leopoldstadt. The total number of choristers is now roughly 100, with four companies ready to travel. Their repertory now includes both spiritual and secular works. *See also* COMMUNICATIONS; MUSIC.

VIENNA CIRCLE/WIENER KREIS. The Vienna Circle dominated this discipline at the **University of Vienna** in the interwar period. Its members and their students had a great influence throughout Europe and the United States even after **World War II**, because so many of them emigrated during the years when **Austro-Fascism** and the **Nazi Party** dominated the Austrian political scene. In the United States, the doctrines of the Circle came to be known as logical positivism. Among its most famous representatives were the Berlin-born Moritz Schlick (1882–1936), Otto Neurath (1882–1945), Rudolph Carnap (1891–1970), and Kurt Gödel (1906–1978). All had studied logic as well as either mathematics or physics, and their outlook reflected this training.

The program of the Circle first appeared in a 1929 pamphlet, *Wissenschaftliche Weltanschauung: Der Wiener Kreis* (*Knowledge and an Understanding of the World: The Vienna Circle*), which abandoned all metaphysics. Henceforth, the goal of philosophy was to unify logic and empiricism. Such principles had already been advanced by the Viennese physicist **Ernst Mach**; indeed, the first name of the Vienna Circle was the Ernst Mach Society. Crucial to the Circle's undertaking was the creation of a formal language, with the properties of mathematics or physics, for all the concepts of philosophy.

The extent to which this goal defined the totality of philosophy soon created factions in the circle. Neurath and Carnap represented a wing that argued that the sole standard of truth was the logical consistency of statements. Schlick himself, who was assassinated in 1936 by a disgruntled student, maintained that truth was also to be found in empirical observation. *See also* POPPER, KARL RAIMUND.

VIENNA GROUP/WIENER GRUPPE. To several young writers in **Vienna** after **World War II**, Austrian society had taken a wrong direction even before it had fully recovered from the conflict. In 1946, Friedrich Achleitner (1930–), H. C. Artmann (1921– 2000), Konrad Bayer (1932–1964), Gerhard Rühm (1930–), and Oswald Wiener (1935–) joined together in an **art** club. By 1952, they were known and recognized as the Vienna Group. Short-lived though it was—it began to fall apart in the late 1950s and had lost all its collective character by the middle of the next decade—the Vienna Group epitomized the cultural unrest in Austria's younger generation, which would make itself felt in the 1960s and 1970s. It also exercised a strong influence over the much more widely known **Graz Group**, which began to take shape in 1960. Contemporary Austrian poets such as Ernst Jandl (1925–2000) and **Friederike Mayröcker** (1924–) also drew much from their contact with the Group.

The political and cultural views of the Vienna Group were closely tied to their aesthetic agenda. The cautious ways of Austrian governments, in which partisanship was actively discouraged, and the materialism of Austrians in general drew members' scorn and anger. They bitterly opposed the Austrian rearmament that began in 1955. The Group was especially critical of public reluctance to discuss its **Nazi** past. They identified with artistic and literary movements such as Dada, Expressionism, and surrealism, officially labeled "degenerate" by Nazi ideologues. The linguistic nihilism of **Ludwig Wittgenstein** and those associated with his epistemology also figured prominently in the outlook of the Group. Oswald Wiener was especially in debt to the Italian Futurist Filippo Marinetti, who had argued even before **World War I** for freeing **language**—and therefore the discourse that uses it—from the constraints of linearity and syntactic convention. Words, to the Vienna Group, were just that; what they signified or designated was immaterial. The most unconventional themes could also be incorporated into **literature**. In 1956, Wiener's *Coole Manifest* found artistic qualities in business signs, advertisements, even the texts of crossword puzzles.

The work of the Group generally targeted what these writers saw as bourgeois convention in all forms of literature. In 1953, H. C. Artmann's *Eight-point Proclamation of the Poetic Act* (*Acht-Punkte-Proklamation des poetischen Actes*) called upon artists to abandon middle-class values of individual inspiration, permanence, and marketability. Nor should they respect the critical standards of such audiences. An expression of human spontaneity and subconscious processes, their work was an impromptu event rather than a painstaking creative enterprise. Such views led the Vienna Group to offer its work as readings in stripped-down cellar **theaters** and even on the city streets. Their emphasis on nontraditional language led some members, most notably Artmann, to experiment with plays and poetry in Austrian dialect, a direction still followed by contemporary Austrian dramatists such as Felix Mitterer (1948–).

However, the Group's oeuvre often seemed little more than a series of bizarre images realized in an idiosyncratic language that bordered on glossolalia. Much of the work of the Vienna Group went unpublished. Nevertheless, it met its goal: to offend large numbers of people.

VIENNA PHILHARMONIC ORCHESTRA. Today one of the world's most celebrated **music** ensembles, the Philharmonic was drawn together for the first time in 1842 by the composer and conductor Carl Otto Nicolai (1810–1849), who was then choir director for the Imperial Chapel. His purpose was to give "philharmonic concerts," with his musicians coming largely from the orchestra of the Imperial Court Opera. Even today, many of the Vienna Philharmonic's instrumentalists play in the pit of the **Vienna State Opera**. Their first performance took place on 28 March. Subscriptions to the concerts have been sold since 1860.

Since 1870 the Philharmonic, when in **Vienna**, has performed in its present location, the **Society of the Friends of Music** hall. It has had a long line of distinguished conductors, among them **Gustav Mahler** (1898 to 1901), Felix Weingartner (1908–1927), Wilhelm Furtwängler, Clemens Krauss (1930–33), Claudio Abbado, and, on occasion, **Herbert von Karajan**. Only guest conductors, invited by the orchestra, now direct it in the 10 or so subscription concerts it presents, along with performances for special occasions, such as on New Year's Day.

The repertory of the orchestra is heavily weighted toward the central European classical tradition, with Austrian masters dominating. The uniquely mellow and effortless sound that characterizes the ensemble stems in part from the rigorous selection procedure that determines membership and also from the unity of the group's schooling. Training takes place in Austrian musical academies, found in Vienna (1817), **Salzburg** (Mozarteum, 1870), and **Graz** (1815), and even in musicians' families. Instrumentalists are sometimes the offspring of fathers who were, or are, members of the orchestra. The Philharmonic engaged its first female member in 1997.

VIENNA SCHOOL OF MEDICINE. At the beginning of the 18th century, Western medical science still accepted the doctrine of the four humors present in human body fluids. Disease was present when one or more of the humors were out of balance; the common cures for restoring them to equilibrium were bleeding or purging.

With the arrival of the Dutch physician and scholar Gerard van Swieten (1700–1772) at the court of Empress **Maria Theresa** in 1745, the medical faculty at the **University of Vienna** struck out in an altogether different direction. Van Swieten was a disciple of the great Dutch physician Hermann Boerhave, who taught in Leiden that sound medicine was based on the close observation of disease and trauma. The duty of the physician was to encourage the vast healing powers of nature rather than to prescribe treatments that he half understood. Van Swieten was also very concerned with public health.

Progress was remarkably swift. In 1754, Vienna opened its first medical clinic; local physicians developed both techniques and instrumentation to improve their diagnostic capabilities. Emperor **Joseph II** established the Vienna General Hospital (*Allgemeines Krankenhaus*) in 1784, which became a center for van Swieten's program. The Dutch obstetrician Johann Lukas Boer practiced there following the principle that parturition was a natural process, which the good physician simply allowed to take its course. His contemporary Vinzenz von Kern (1760–1829), who taught at the university from 1805 until his death, developed a revolutionary treatment for wounds. Rejecting the use of traditional ointments and pressure bandaging, he dressed traumas in loose, water-saturated cloth to maximize the healing process. This practice was widely followed in the first half of the 19th century; it was said that by 1850, the only medication prescribed in the General Hospital was brandy for those in desperate pain.

Great diagnostic advances certainly took place. Central to the detailed understanding of the human organism so necessary for medicine was the work of Karl von Rokitansky (1804–1878). Reportedly performing more than 85,000 autopsies during his long career, he turned anatomical pathology into an effective clinical tool. Though he himself did not make much use of his findings, a successor, Josef Skoda (1805–1881), certainly did. It was Skoda who refined the technique of chest percussion, first advanced by a **Graz** physician, Leopold von Auenbrugger a century earlier, in the examination of patients. Surgery, the only accepted therapeutic intervention, was developed to a highly sophisticated art, culminating in the work of Theodore Billroth (1829–1894). Joining the medical faculty of the University of Vienna in 1867, he pioneered in such procedures as the resectioning of the stomach (1881) and the removal of the larynx (1874). His students joined the staffs of hospitals throughout Europe.

Substantial though these achievements were—Vienna continued to be a medical center even after the collapse of the monarchy—its therapeutic philosophy, particularly its disdain for pharmacological or chemical intervention, had its critics even in the 19th century. The Hungarian physician Ignaz Semmelweis (1818–1865) was never able to persuade the chief of his clinic to support good sanitary practices in obstetrical clinics. An insistent man, he was dismissed for his pains. The indifference to suffering patients became legendary, as diagnosis often seemed to be favored over cure.

VIENNA STATE OPERA. Usually under the sponsorship of the **Habsburg** court, **opera** performances began in **Vienna** in the 17th century. Some were the gala extravaganzas so dear to **Baroque** tastes, such as *The Golden Apple* (*Il pomo d'oro*, 1667) by Marco Antonio Cesti. Taking five and one-half hours and dauntingly elaborate stage technology to perform, it allowed the current, and very musical, Emperor Leopold I (1640–1705) to write several arias for the piece.

Less grandiose operatic works amused the Habsburg establishment as well. During the reign of Emperor **Joseph II**, opera took on a more didactic character. Hoping to put **music** drama in German on a par with the Italian imports that had been traditionally played at the court, Joseph opened the *Burgtheater* for both spoken and musical performances. One of the most successful outcomes of the emperor's program was **Wolfgang Amadeus Mozart**'s *The Abduction from the Seraglio*, which had its premier at the relatively new house in 1782.

Opera continued to be given in the old *Burgtheater* as well as in other theaters, such as the Theater an der Wien, where **Ludwig van Beethoven**'s *Fidelio* was premiered in 1805. The opening of the present building on Vienna's **Ringstrasse** in 1869 made this the headquarters of grand opera in the city. Its heyday was from the latter part of the 19th century through the beginning of **World War I**, when it was under the directorship of the composer **Gustav Mahler**. He not only brought major singers into the company, but promoted new techniques of stage lighting adapted from a style that originated in Bayreuth, the German musical center devoted to the operas of Richard Wagner.

The interior of the Vienna State Opera was badly damaged in **World War II**. The reconstruction, however, began as early as 1948 and was finished in 1955. It reopened on 5 November of that year with a performance of *Fidelio*, under the direction of Wilhelm Furtwängler.

VIENNESE ACTIONISM/WIENER AKTIONISMUS. A highly provocative form of painting and drawing, Viennese Actionism came to public attention in the 1960s. Its characteristic themes were the irrational and ignoble qualities of human thought and behavior and the conversion of all **art**, **music**, and **literature** into visual images. Advocates, such as the painters Günter Brus (1938–) and Otto Mühl (1925–), often ran afoul of public authorities with their antics. On 31 July 1968, they were sentenced for putting on a program called "The Art of Presenting Humanity," in which Brus, who pled guilty, had stripped himself naked, then relieved himself publicly. In 1997, however, Brus received the Great Austrian State Prize and in 2000 the Oskar Kokoschka Prize. *See also* ART; FILM.

VINDOBONA. A name of Celtic origin and a reminder of the tribes who once inhabited the region, Vindobona was a Roman settlement situated at the heart of today's Inner City of **Vienna**. The Romans themselves, attracted by the gold deposits in the region, fortified Vindobona in 100 BCE. It became the headquarters of the 10th Roman legion, while the outlying areas, today's Third District (*Landstrasse*) and Tenth District (*Favoriten*), were the civilian settlement associated with the army and the navy headquarters, respectively. Emperor Marcus Aurelius died in Vindobona in 180 CE.

By 250 CE, Vindobona had a population of around 20,000; 30 years later, Emperor Probus authorized the cultivation of vineyards in the **Danube** River region around the city, thus setting the groundwork for one of Austria's most enduring agricultural occupations. By 395, the first barbarian tribes to challenge Roman rule began to infiltrate the area. Only 10 years later, the imperial forces withdrew from their garrison. In 433, Vindobona was laid waste by the Huns. *See also* WINE.

VORARLBERG. With the exception of **Vienna**, Vorarlberg is the smallest in territory of the nine Austrian federal provinces. Local **language** usage is also exceptional. Its inhabitants largely speak an Alemanic form of German, more akin to the idiom of Swiss German and Swabian than the Bavarian-based dialect found throughout the rest of Austria.

Only modestly endowed with natural resources and arable land, the area has made manufacturing its chief livelihood since the 19th century. Taking advantage of the power supply offered by abundant streams and rivers, it developed a varied textile industry after long experience in domestic production of linen. At first concentrating on cotton, the factories of the Vorarlberg today turn out a number of products made of synthetic fabrics. The Vorarlberg also has a significant dairy industry. The capital is **Bregenz**, the Brigantium Municipium of the Romans.

Some form of settlement of the Vorarlberg took place in the Old Stone Age. Its copper deposits were exploited during the Early Bronze Age as well. The Celts appeared around 400 BCE; the Romans occupied the area after 15 BCE, about when they moved into many other regions of the Austrian lands. Vorarlberg was part of the

Roman province of Raetia. Indeed, some elements of the population became so romanized that it was not until the 17th century that the language of the area acquired its overwhelmingly Alemanic character. Christianity came to the Vorarlberg at the beginning of the seventh century. St. Columban and St. Gallus both reached the area around Lake Constance.

From the eighth century until the 14th, local dynasties and new settlers ruled the various lands that made up the Vorarlberg. Perhaps the most significant of these were the Alemanic Walser, or Free Walser, who came from what is today the Swiss Canton of Wallis in the 14th century and gradually settled around a quarter of the Vorarlberg. Around 1160, Hugo of Tübingen, the son-in-law of the last count of Bregenz, assumed that title. His younger son, also Hugo, called himself Count of Montfort in 1260. The coat of arms of modern Vorarlberg is that of the house of Tübingen-Montfort. Through aggressive promotion of new settlements and opening up new roads through the alpine valleys, the dynasty did much to consolidate the territory.

The **Habsburgs** began to acquire territory in the area in the first decades of the 14th century. Though they had taken over a great deal of the area by the 16th century, it took them 300 more years to complete the process. Until 1752 Vorarlberg was governed from offices in **Innsbruck**. For the next 30 years, its affairs were administered from Freiburg im Breisgau, which was ruled directly from Vienna until 1782. After that, the Habsburg government in the **Tyrol** resumed its former responsibilities.

With a tradition of peasant and middle-class representation in the estates reaching back to the 14th century, Vorarlberg had more experience in democratic deliberative settings than did most of the other regions of the Habsburg Austrian patrimony. In 1861, Vorarlberg was granted its own provincial parliament. In 1918, it separated its government from the Tyrol and became a province of Austria in its own right. Economic considerations led a substantial portion of the population to advocate secession from Austria altogether and incorporation into Switzerland. More than 80 percent of those who voted in a plebiscite held in May 1919 endorsed such a proposition. Only vehement opposition from the government in Vienna and the refusal of the victorious allies blocked the move. There was substantial support for unification with Germany in the region as well. *See also* HABSBURG EMPIRE.

VRANITZKY, FRANZ (1937–). Serving as chairperson of the executive committees of both the **Creditanstalt Bankverein** (1976–1981) and the Austrian Provincial Bank (*Länderbank*) (1981–1984), Franz Vranitzky was minister of finance in the cabinet of Chancellor Fred Sinowatz (1929–2008) from 1984 to 1986. Overwhelmed by scandal and charges of ineptitude, Sinowatz withdrew from the government in 1986, to be replaced as **chancellor** by Vranitzky.

In choosing Vranitzky as their ministerial leader, the **Socialist Party of Austria** (SPÖ) hoped to field a person who would appeal to the increasingly middle-of-the-road Austrian electorate and who could work in a coalition government with the **Austrian People's Party** (ÖVP) should this prove necessary—as it indeed did. Vranitzky pulled the Socialists out of their Small Coalition with **Jörg Haider**'s increasingly right-wing **Freedom Party**. From 1987 to 1997, Vranitzky served as chancellor in a Great Coalition with the opposition ÖVP. The Socialists held the ministries of finance, interior, social affairs, and transport and state industries; the ÖVP received the portfolios for defense, agriculture, science, trade, and foreign affairs. **Alois Mock**, the vice-chancellor, was the head of the Foreign Office. From 1988 to 1997, Vranitzky was also the head of the SPÖ itself.

Although recognizing that Austria had to bring its mounting budget deficits under control and rationalize its increasingly unproductive state industries, Vranitzky moved very cautiously on these fronts. Both parties in the coalition were, in fact, reluctant to anger voters with the austerity program that would inevitably accompany such reforms. However, Vranitzky did not push to enlarge the **nationalized** sector of the Austrian **economy**, nor to equalize incomes any further. Vranitzky did, however, support Austrian entry into the **European Union**, a position that Mock endorsed vigorously.

Highly popular, Vranitzky was chiefly interested in domestic politics. Many members of the international community, however, refused to have anything to do with Kurt Waldheim, whose time in office as Austrian **president** coincided with several years of

Vranitzy's chancellorship. Therefore, both Vranitzky and Mock found themselves performing representational functions normally reserved to the president. Following his withdrawal from active political life early in 1997, Vranitzky has served, among other things, as a special envoy of the **United Nations** to deal with the Albanian–Serbian crisis.

– W –

WAGNER, OTTO (1841–1918). Equally accomplished in **art**, **architecture**, and city planning, Wagner was also a significant polemicist and theoretician. Trained at the Vienna Technical University, the highly selective and traditionalist Academy of the Fine Arts, and briefly in Berlin, he plunged into the speculative development of the city's *Ringstrasse* in the 1860s. There he worked for the most important architects in the capital in the monumental neo-Renaissance building style that dominated much of the new construction along the thoroughfare. He also had important commissions in **Germany** and Budapest. In 1894, he was made a professor at the Academy of Fine Arts in **Vienna**, an influential position he held until 1912.

During the 1890s, Wagner immersed himself in municipal development projects. These led him to a thoroughgoing reassessment of his creative principles. Like members of the contemporary **Secession**, with whom he was in close contact, he renounced the eclectic classicism from which he himself had profited. Wagner argued (*Modern Architecture*, 1895) for the renewal of art and urban design by harmonizing aesthetic considerations with actual purpose. The useful could be beautiful, he contended, if its form was kept simple. Equally important, the useless could never be beautiful. The symbolic and the functional carried equal weight in his thinking and that of his many students. His most important buildings reflect this philosophy. These are the grounds and station buildings of the Vienna urban railway (*Stadtbahn*, 1895–1902), the church Am Steinhof (1902–1907), and the Postal Savings' Bank office (1904–1906). *See also* WIENER WERKSTÄTTE.

WALDHEIM, KURT (1918–2007). Trained as a jurist, Waldheim served as Austrian foreign minister from 1968 to 1971. In 1971, he was the **Austrian People's Party** (ÖVP) candidate for **president** of the republic, but lost the election. He then served two terms from 1971 to 1981 as secretary general of the **United Nations**.

During a second campaign for the presidency of the Austrian Republic in 1986, charges were brought against Waldheim by the World Jewish Congress and by the Office of Special Investigation of the United States Department of Justice that he had not been fully candid about his record and role as an army officer during **World War II**. He was thought to be covering up his complicity in **Nazi** war atrocities in Greece and in what was then Yugoslavia. Alleged inconsistencies in dates when he was finishing his legal studies while on furlough in 1943 and differences in detail between the English and German editions of his memoirs fueled these suspicions.

Waldheim's election to a five-year term as president in Austria in 1986 set off a firestorm of criticism throughout much of the world. During his term in office, Waldheim was effectively isolated from formal diplomatic channels. An international tribunal of historians found no evidence that Waldheim had participated in Nazi war crimes. Nevertheless, doubts about the former president's veracity still linger. In 1991, lacking support in his own ÖVP, Waldheim announced that he would not run for the office again. His decision made him the first president of the post–World War II Austrian Republic not to seek a second term of office.

WEIGEL, HANS (1908–1991). Critic, translator, essayist, novelist, and editor, Weigel was among the founders of the cabaret Theater am Naschmarkt in 1934. For a few years thereafter he wrote several librettos for their productions. His parents were **Jews**; they fled to the United States in the 1930s and never set foot in Austria again. Weigel himself immigrated to Switzerland in 1938. Unlike his father and mother, however, he remained strongly attached to his native city. He returned to **Vienna** in 1945, bringing with him two senses—presence in a place and absence from it—that helped him to toggle between acceptance and criticism of an environment that he had left out of necessity, not choice.

By 1947, Weigel was the center of a group of intellectuals who gathered at the Café Raimund directly across from the Vienna People's Theater (*Volkstheater*). Almost without exception they were burdened with the experience of having lived through **World War II** either as young adults or as children.

Among them was the young Austrian poet **Ingeborg Bachmann,** with whom Weigel had an exceedingly complex erotic and professional relationship. His most important novel, *Unfinished Symphony* (*Unvollendete Symphonie*, 1992), is a frankly autobiographical account of an exiled Jew's return to Austria and his efforts to reconnect with, yet retain, his sense of Jewish particularity. The specific conceit in which he centers this personal drama is a relationship with a youthful Austrian female artist, whom Weigel later admitted was Bachmann. Written chiefly from the perspective of a female protagonist who expresses herself through inner monologues, which Bachmann used heavily, the narrative also reveals the emotional bonds between Weigel and Vienna's distinctive features: its differentiated neighborhoods, its psychologically resonant **architecture**, and its still-powerful commitment to a **musical** and **theatrical** heritage that had survived the military and moral catastrophe of the Nazi regime and World War II.

For all of his self-involvement, Weigel was sincerely supportive, intellectually and materially, of fresh literary talent in Austria. He also labored to keep alive the work of great Austrian writers of the past. His commentaries on the work of the great comic playwright **Johann Nestroy** were notably sensitive. In his last years, Weigel became an ardent anticommunist. He led the movement to deny Bertolt Brecht Austrian citizenship when the stateless German poet and playwright left the United States in 1947 under pressure from the House of Representatives Committee on Un-American Activities. *See also* LITERATURE.

WELFARE AND SOCIAL SERVICES. Even in a Europe friendly to state-financed welfare systems, Austria stands out for the depth and extent of such support and its exceptionally high level of income redistribution through taxation. In part, these arrangements are a legacy of the country's history of **government** intervention to meet social needs. The obligation to care for one's own was traditionally met by individual householders, rural landlords, and communes that financed hospices. None of these arrangements applied to the homeless unemployed, who by the end of the 15th century were begging their way through central Europe in disturbingly larger numbers. In 1552, **Ferdinand I** ordered towns and markets to care for their poor. The more modest the commune, the more it struggled with this obligation; a common solution was to point supplicants toward richer municipalities, **Vienna** chief among them. By the 18th century, beggars and other homeless people were officially divided into two groups: the deserving worthy of support and the undeserving, whose mendicancy was criminalized.

Emperor Leopold I (1640–1705) established the first workhouse in the city in 1671. His son, Charles VI (1685–1740), tried to create a network of these institutions, along with orphanages, throughout the **Habsburg Empire**. People sent to workhouses actually drew small salaries, but their fellow inmates often included the insane and outright criminals, who made the general environment very inhospitable.

The classical economic liberalism that prevailed in Habsburg Empire from around 1850 to 1880 discouraged government-sponsored welfare. To support themselves through sickness, accidents, old age, and burial, Austria's middle classes joined and paid into self-help clubs and benevolent societies. By 1880, around 2,800 of such organizations existed in the Austrian half of the Dual Monarchy, and the model was working its way into peasant communities as well.

Many Austrian industrial workers had local factory cash funds (*Fabrikskassen*), often created by laborers themselves. By 1872 there were 172 of them, spread through various types of enterprises. Nevertheless, the sharp gyrations of 19th-century business cycles, the social rootlessness of these men and women, and the new militancy of the Austrian **Social Democratic Workers' Party** (SDAP) forced the government to develop more comprehensive welfare arrangements. The first workers' protection legislation was put in place on 11 March 1885. Setting the maximum daily hours of labor at 11 (without any break), it also forbade heavy and night work for young people. **Women** were not allowed to work at night either, and child labor was completely proscribed. The regime itself took over all pension and health insurance obligations for employees of once-private

railroads, which were largely taken over by the state in the final decades of the 19th century.

Among the several crises to challenge the First Austrian Republic from 1918 to 1919 was a general collapse of public welfare. Health care, particularly for children and the elderly, was in deep disarray; malnutrition and tuberculosis took a disproportionately heavy toll on those populations. Food from abroad, especially Switzerland, then the **United States**, helped significantly. To forestall the spread of Bolshevism, the SDAP national government of **Karl Renner** quickly promised sweeping social reforms, which became law in 1919–1920. Among the most important were the continuation of wartime rent control, the eight-hour working day, unemployment insurance, and forcing businesses of a certain size to hire jobless workers. Initial steps were also taken to introduce paid holidays for workers. In 1921, accident and illness insurance was extended to agricultural laborers and state employees.

Inflation and other economic upheavals in the 1920s and early 1930s heavily compromised these measures. Part of the **Nazi** appeal to Austrians was welfare programs that raised the pensions of the elderly and restored unemployment insurance.

The Austrian government after 1945 recommitted itself wholeheartedly to the comprehensive social policies begun under the First Republic, though on a firmer economic footing. In 1947, the 40-hour workweek and four-week paid vacations were put in place. The *Allgemeines Sozialversicherungsgesetz* (General Social Insurance Law, 1955) has brought all elements of Austrian society into the social network, even rural populations, which had been especially hard to reach. Amendments in 1957 and 1971 have brought pensions for farmers and farm workers up to standard levels of the country.

It is now possible for Austrians to live quite alone, in part because of earnings, but in part because of payments from a welfare system unavailable to previous generations. Austrians in the 1990s were not only retiring in flocks, but also finding ways to do it at comparatively young ages. With women able to leave the workforce for good when they turned 60, the average age of both sexes starting to collect pensions in 1994 was 58. The National Assembly voted in 2004 to make 65 the retirement age for almost everyone by 2033, though early retirement will still exist. The Austrian health care system is also under continued fiscal pressures, and more and more restrictions are being built into it. An especially sensitive issue that exploded in 2006 was payment for home care, for which costs of domestic, rather than illegal immigrant, labor have dramatically outpaced incomes and the level of state reimbursement. A large number of Austrians, particularly younger ones, have also been buying private pension insurance on the assumption that their national system will not cover their needs. *See also* FREEMASONS; IMMIGRATION; INDUSTRIALIZATION; SCHÜSSEL, WOLFGANG; TRADE UNIONS.

WIENER KREIS/VIENNA CIRCLE THEATER. A group of late 20th-century playwrights, associated with the Hungarian-born writer and director George Tábori (1914–2007), that was unsparingly critical of official and public Austria's reluctance to examine the nation's **Nazi** past and persistent anti-Semitism. **Elfriede Jelinek** and **Thomas Bernhard** had ties to the movement, though the work of both authors reaches beyond the polemical. Tábori's career excited one controversy after another: Typical was his allegedly "tasteless" production at the **Salzburg Festival** in 1987 of the *Book with Seven Seals,* an oratorio by the Austrian composer Franz Schmidt (1874–1939). *See also* THEATER.

WIENER LIEDER/VIENNA SONGS. Usually performed by singers accompanying themselves on the accordion, these are staples of musical entertainment at many **wine** locales in and around the city. They are also performed in hotels and restaurants, especially those frequented by **tourists**.

After a dip in popularity in the post–**World War II** period, when celebrations of local culture had yet to be uncoupled from Nazi racism, the genre revived in the 1970s. In 2006, there were an estimated 10,000 such songs in existence. The lyrics are normally in a semistandardized form of the local dialect (***Wienerisch***). They express a broad range of joyous emotions as well as less attractive ones—aching melancholy and occasionally plain meanness. The hero of the text is often alcohol, especially wine. The narrative line is generally linked to Viennese society of the past.

The earliest of the songs date from the beginning of the 18th century. At first sung largely at student gatherings, they were often downright obscene. The heyday of the Wiener Lied, however, was the 19th century, when vocalists used such **music** to criticize social and political arrangements in an environment of state censorship. As public amusement facilities, such as the **Prater**, expanded in the latter decades of the era, opportunities for popular singers grew, too; the Wiener Lied was a major item in their repertoires, and the numbers of these songs grew accordingly. *See also HEURIGER.*

WIENER WERKSTÄTTE. The **art** exhibitions of the Austrian **Secession** had often featured new directions in handicraft design and production; the show of 1897 announced as its program a global aesthetic renewal of all things created and developed by man. No object was too humble for it to be well made and attractive, quite unlike the mediocre design and workmanship found in the mass-produced furniture and household utensils most people could afford. Modest means should be no reason for absence of beauty in any human life. These ideas had already been circulating in Europe, in England with William Morris and John Ruskin, and particularly in the circle of Charles Rennie Mackintosh in Glasgow. Mackintosh's contrasting patterns of black and white, the still elegance of his interiors, and his rectangular ornamental inlays, on view at the **Secession** exhibition of 1900, were especially influential among his Austrian counterparts.

Under the leadership of the architect and designer **Josef Hoffmann** and the artist and designer Koloman Moser (1868–1918), the Wiener Werkstätte Corporation opened its first atelier in 1903. The studio was also a training place for others who could continue the program. A bright, well-lit, and quiet atmosphere was provided to encourage careful and pleasing work. Artists and craftspeople combined forces to produce tableware, furniture, and textiles that were both useful and beautiful. The shape of their products followed simple geometric forms: spheres, rectangles, cylinders, and cubes. Decorative interest was added through the use of high-quality materials, which were then finished, often by intensive polishing alone, to highlight their natural beauty.

In their classic simplicity and use of the very best woods, metals, and stones, the Werkstätte artists had much in common with the best of their earlier **Biedermeier** counterparts. For a time, their work enjoyed worldwide sale in franchises, even after **World War**

I. Their commissions came not only from the lands of the erstwhile **Habsburg Empire**, but from New York (1922) and Berlin (1929). The most grandiose of the Werkstätte's designs, the Palais Stoclet (1905–1911), planned by Hoffmann, was a Brussels villa for a Baron Stoclet, whose resources were apparently limitless.

Though the household goods of the Wiener Werkstätte were allegedly functional, many were obviously not. Only the well to do had the discretionary income to afford them, so the studio's hope that its handiwork would touch the lives of the most humble was at best partially fulfilled. In 1932, the Wiener Werkstätte closed its doors, a victim to changing tastes and, ultimately, bankruptcy.

WIENERISCH. The urban patois of **Vienna**, Wienerisch has many affinities with the dialects of eastern and southeastern Austria. Nevertheless, it is also quite distinctive. Like all of these regional idioms, it is grounded in the Bavarian dialect of German, which in turn retains strong connections with the changes in the pronunciation of the German **language** that began in the eighth century (second sound shift) and ended in the Middle High German of medieval times. Technically, Wienerisch is a variant of east Middle Bavarian. It is characterized by such pronunciation features as the blurring of differences in the articulation of "b" and "p," and "d" and "t," distinctive renderings of the sounds for "e," "o," "ö," "au," and "ei," and frequent diphthongization of the vowels "a," "i," and "u."

The vocabulary of Wienerisch can be quite idiosyncratic, laced as it is with often unrecognizable borrowings from the tongues of all the peoples of east central and southeastern Europe who once belonged to the **Habsburg Empire**. To this have also been added elements from French, Italian, and Spanish, all of which were court languages at various periods from the 16th through the 18th centuries. The city's position as the traditional capital of Austria has spread certain linguistic usages throughout the country that were once associated with Vienna alone. The term for a late-day sandwich, *Brotzeit* (Bread Time), is increasingly the Viennese usage, *Jause*, a word that has come down from the Middle High German of medieval times.

WILDGANS, ANTON (1881–1932). A versatile intellectual, Wildgans was both a poet and dramatist. He was also trained as a jurist and from 1909–1911 served in the Austrian **judiciary** as an investigating magistrate. Two of his plays, *Armut* (*Poverty*, 1914) and *Dies irae* (1918), sharply criticized the social and economic conditions of his time. From 1921 to 1922 and again in 1930–1931, Wildgans was the director of the Vienna ***Burgtheater***. A prize for Austrian **literature** is given today in his name.

Wildgans was a convinced partisan of an independent Austria after **World War I**; it is for these views that he is most often remembered. In the fall of 1929, he wrote a paper, "Der österreichische Mensch" ("The Austrian"), which he was supposed to deliver before the king of Sweden and other local notables in Stockholm. Becoming ill en route to the north, Wildgans turned back.

He read his text instead as a radio address in **Vienna** on New Year's Day in 1930. His countrymen, he said, were defined by several qualities—their ability to understand others, to empathize with them, and to reconcile differences; by their dedication to international political pluralism; and by their patience with deprivation (clearly a reference to the Austrian experience immediately after World War I). In addition to these qualities, said Wildgans, they were more inclined to improvise than to follow mechanical formulas and basically skeptical of all radical change.

The address deeply impressed a broad spectrum of his intellectual contemporaries. Following **World War II**, many public readings of the speech took place in Austria under the Allied **occupation**. *See also* THEATER.

WINE. Vineyards have been encouraged in the eastern **Danubian** regions of Austria since the Roman occupation of the third century and probably before. Their vintages, however, have had an up and down history in foreign **trade**, particularly because under the **Habsburg Empire** Austrian wines faced stiff competition from Hungarian growers, whose vines were usually much more productive. A very serious scandal over adulterated wine in 1985 put a virtual stop to Austrian exports for a few years. Even today, Austrians consume close to 70 percent of their domestic crop.

Wine has long been closely associated with Austrians' daily life, celebrations, and entertainment. Favored varietals are the traditional Grüner Veltliner, a white wine with a faintly green-yellow tinge, and the Riesling. Quality red wines have been more difficult to achieve; Austrians looked to the southern **Tyrol** and the Hungarian-style wines grown in the **Burgenland** for them—but the rich-colored Zweigelt has begun to fill this gap. Several regions of **Lower Austria** now lay claim to outstanding white wine production, and fine growths now produce excellent vintages in **Styria**.

Vineyards cover around 127,000 acres of land in the country, chiefly in Lower Austria and the Burgenland. Approximately 70 percent of this crop goes into 22 varieties of white wine. Thirteen varieties of red wine account for the remaining 30 percent of production. There are approximately 6,000 estates, many of which are very small and will sell directly from their cellars. Roughly 700 hectares in the city of **Vienna** itself are turned over to cultivating both red and white wine; appropriate soils for both lie within the city limits. Traditionally Vienna wine was very unpretentious, of no high quality, but younger vintners are working to change that. This same cohort has begun serious experimentation with organic varietals. *See also* AGRICULTURE; *HEURIGER*; VINDOBONA; WIENER LIEDER.

WITTGENSTEIN, CARL (1847–1913). One of the leading **industrialists** to appear during the great surge in the **economy** of the **Habsburg Empire** in the second half of the 19th century, Wittgenstein was born outside of Leipzig in Germany. He was of **Jewish** extraction. Musically talented, he spent the year 1865–1866 in the United States, where he supported himself playing in theater pit orchestras. He also acquired a lifetime taste for the American style of competitive capitalism and its practitioners, including the steel magnate Andrew Carnegie, whom Wittgenstein greatly admired.

Returning to Austria, Wittgenstein, who had some training as an engineer, embarked in 1877 upon an ambitious program of acquiring iron, steel, and related industries throughout the Habsburg Empire. Some of his tactics were legally and ethically questionable. Nevertheless, they brought him huge industrial holdings throughout Bohemia and **Styria**. His greatest triumph was becoming the majority stockholder in the Austrian Alpine Mine Works in 1897 (*Oesterreichische-Alpinen Montangesellschaft*), which he then proceeded to rationalize and consolidate.

After the turn of the 20th century, Wittgenstein withdrew from daily business activity. He wrote widely about what he believed to be the problems of commerce and manufacture within the Habsburg Empire, among them politicians who had no understanding of economic matters and the financial concessions to Hungarian nationalism embedded in the **Ausgleich**. The father of the philosopher **Ludwig Wittgenstein**, Carl Wittgenstein was a generous patron of the arts.

WITTGENSTEIN, LUDWIG (1889–1951). Though he spent much of his career in England, Wittgenstein had important ties to **Vienna** and Austria generally. The son of an aesthetically and intellectually gifted industrialist, he volunteered for service in the Austro–Hungarian army in **World War I**. It was during this time that he completed his most influential philosophical work, the *Tractatus Logico-Philosophicus*, though it was not published until 1921.

Spared by inherited wealth from any financial pressures, Wittgenstein taught school in **Lower Austria** between 1920 and 1926 out of a sense of social duty. He also worked as a gardener, including stints at the monastery of Klosterneuburg and with a group of monks in Hütteldorf, a suburb of Vienna. A man of many talents, he helped to design the modernistic Wittgenstein house in Vienna's Third District for his sister, Margarethe Wittgenstein-Stonborough.

As a student before World War I at Cambridge University in England, Wittgenstein was close to the mathematician and logician Bertrand Russell. The *Tractatus* betrayed those influences, though its general thrust went well beyond Russell's work. An analysis of the conditions that Russell claimed were needed for a logically perfect language, the book sought to establish what could be meaningfully said. If something could not be said with perfect clarity, it could not be said in philosophical discourse at all. The epistemological reliability of language was narrowed considerably; the work was enthusiastically received by the **Vienna Circle** of philosophers, whose queries paralleled Wittgenstein's own. His work would also have a significant influence on the American school of logical positivism.

Wittgenstein returned to Cambridge on a fellowship in 1929 at the invitation of Russell and another philosopher, G. E. Moore. Here he continued his critical speculation about language, which appeared posthumously in 1953 as *Philosophical Investigations*. In 1939 he was appointed to Moore's chair, which he held until 1947.

WOMEN. As elsewhere in the Western world, the attack on gender as the basis of social, political, economic, and intellectual discrimination began in the **Habsburg Empire** during the 18th century. Educational reforms in 1774 made **education** obligatory for children of both sexes between the ages of 6 and 12. The higher education of women, however, was limited to daughters of the nobility, army officers, and civil servants, for whom special institutes were available.

Compliance with mandatory schooling was less than perfect; the Imperial Education Law of 1869, which lengthened the years of mandatory education from six to eight, reaffirmed the requirement that girls attend school. Teaching as a licensed profession was opened to women for the first time as well. **Marianne Hainisch** founded the Organization of Female Teachers and Educators in 1869. The Society for the Higher Education of Women, established in 1888, opened the first secondary school (*Gymnasium*) classes for girls four years later. By 1900, there were only 11 academic high schools for females throughout all of the Habsburg lands. However, women could enroll in the university faculties of philosophy (arts and sciences) in 1897; by 1900 medicine and pharmacy were open to them as well. Law, however, remained closed to women until 1919.

Women had long engaged in menial labor and cottage enterprises. They entered factories from the outset of Austrian **industrialization**, though they were not welcomed by many of their male coworkers. Though vocational schools were opened for women in the 1860s, a conference of Lower Austrian Trade Unions demanded in 1895 that females be excluded from salaried employment generally. At the same time, however, specific professional niches were being turned over to women, such as kindergarten teaching and nursing.

Legally forbidden to engage in political activity, indeed even to join parties, Austrian feminist movements in the late 19th century developed a strongly idealistic strain. Although these groups happily took help from men who supported them, they actively avoided working with male-run organizations. Ideally speaking, women were supposed to think for themselves if they were to counter the corrupting impact of male power wherever it was expressed, including in **political parties**. Getting the franchise was merely the beginning of a great reorientation of social behavior and ethical norms.

More pragmatic heads, however, prevailed. Some Austrian women began to form women's clubs that were tied to the political agendas of the empire's parliamentary fractions. The Federation of Austrian Women's Clubs, a union of 13 middle-class liberal groups, was founded by Hainisch in 1902. It joined the International Council of Women in 1904. The **Social Democratic Workers' Party** (SDAP) had parallel associations, such as the Organization for the Education of Working Women (1890) and a reading and discussion club, Libertas (1893). In that same year, the Social Democratic daily, the *Arbeiterzeitung*, carried a supplement for women. By the beginning of the 20th century, there were several **Catholic** women's organizations as well. At first dominated by the aristocracy, they gradually extended their reach to the middle class and the working women of the Habsburg Empire. The International Council of Women convened in **Innsbruck** in 1910.

With the exception of female owners of agricultural properties, Austrian women did not receive the right to vote until 1919. But the depletion of Austria's adult male population in **World War I** gave them a role in the **economy** that was readily convertible into electoral power. Large numbers of women entered public employment, such as the post office and **railroads**. They worked in armaments factories as well, where law forbade the use of foreign labor. University positions were more readily available as well. However, relatively few women held elected office, either locally or in the federal parliament of the First Republic. Though women represented around a third of the membership in the SDAP, none reached the ranks of its leadership. There were even fewer women in the other parties. However, educational opportunities for women continued to increase. After 1918, they were able to attend most Austrian high schools, if they chose not to avail themselves of institutions specifically reserved for instructing girls.

World War II and its aftermath brought even more dramatic changes for Austrian women. Coeducation became a general rule during the conflict; the number of female teachers grew in secondary schools and opportunities for employment in all segments of public and private life grew substantially. The number of women receiving university-level training increased greatly as well. Nevertheless, while organizations representing women's interests and advancement appeared once again, their actual numbers in political life grew only slowly. In 1971, 11 out of 183 members of the National Assembly (*Nationalrat*) were women; in 1994 there were 43. The presence of Austrian women in leading political positions became the rule only with the cabinets of **Bruno Kreisky**, who, as **chancellor**, never appointed fewer than two female ministers, and, from 1979 to 1983, had six. These numbers continue to increase. In the national elections of 1994, both the new **Liberal Forum** and the **Green** parties chose women to lead them in the contest. Susanne Riess-Passer (1961–), from the **Freedom Party of Austria** (FPÖ), served as vice-chancellor in the government of **Wolfgang Schüssel** of the **Austrian People's Party** (ÖVP) between 2000 and 2003, the first woman to hold such high office in Austria. In the same government, Benita Ferrero-Waldner (1948–), who became the Commissioner of Foreign Affairs of the European Union after a failed run for the Austrian presidency in 2004, was the foreign minister. And on the provincial level, where a great deal of Austrian political activity takes place and where pensions for government employees can exceed those of their federal counterparts, the incorporation of women into local legislatures and party positions has been striking. Between 1996 and 2005, all of the provincial deliberative bodies registered increases in the percentage of female delegates. The most striking gains, however, came in the traditionally conservative **Tyrol**, where the local legislature went from 8 percent female in 1996 to 17 percent in 2005, and in the **Burgenland**, which raised the percentage of females in its parliament from 8 to 19 percent between 1996 and 2005.

Though the institutionalization of gender equality in Austria made a solid beginning in the 1970s, the realization of the ideal for women has raised some thorny issues that are yet to be resolved. The public media in 2004, particularly the mainstream news reports, continued to report the activities of male politicians far more frequently than the work of their female counterparts. Just how affirmatively the government should support women's interests has been under debate since the first Kreisky government, which throughout the 1970s created a series of state secretaryships for women's affairs; by 1983, these offices were being disbanded or folded into other portfolios. The coalition governments of the ÖVP–FPÖ from 2000 to 2003 abolished a ministerial position for women's issues in favor of Minister for Health and Women. In 2001, the FPÖ was able to push through a subdivision for women's affairs in the Ministry for Social Welfare.

The century-old tradition of state intervention in the economy to protect women specifically from exploitation in industry has also given rise to accusations of reverse discrimination against men. Early **welfare** measures reduced hours of work for women specifically. In the Second Republic, women were allowed to begin drawing their pensions at age 60, five years earlier than men, on the ground that females, who even as jobholders were often responsible for child care and household management, worked harder than the average man. Financial shortfalls and a very generous disability retirement program that allowed women to leave the workforce even sooner, at age 58, led to a pension reform in 2004 that set 65 as the age of retirement for both sexes by 2033.

For all of the rancor that gender equality has provoked in political circles, however, women in Austria have a very high public profile. Austrian theater, film, and musical stage have long produced female performers who have received public acclaim from members of both sexes. Film star Paula Wessely (1907–2000), the comedienne Elfriede Ott (1925–), and opera soprano Leonie Rysanek (1926–1998) are only three among a legion of examples. From prize-winning poets such as **Ingeborg Bachmann**, **Elfriede Jelinkek**, and **Friederike Mayröcker**, to journalists such as Annaliese Röhrer, whose career has stretched across two Austrian major newspapers, *Die Presse* and *Der Kurier*, and Ulrike (Ushi) **Fellner**, who has focused on women's issues, sometimes irreverently, it is clear that Austrian women have a wide number of career options. *See also* MARIA THERESA; SUTTNER, BERTHA VON.

WORLD WAR I. On 28 June 1914, Archduke **Franz Ferdinand**, the heir apparent to the crowns of Austria–Hungary, and his wife were killed on a visit to Sarajevo. The Balkan city was the capital of Bosnia, a province technically still part of the Ottoman Empire, but annexed by the Dual Monarchy in 1908.

From the beginning of the 20th century, **Habsburg** governments in both **Vienna** and Budapest had been intensely worried by a growing movement among the south Slavs of the Balkans to create some sort of a South Slavic state. The crucible of these sentiments was the kingdom of Serbia, fully independent of Ottoman overlordship after 1878. From then until the beginning of the 20th century, relations between Austria–Hungary and the new state were comparatively cordial. However, in 1903 the ruling Obrenović dynasty had been overthrown and replaced by the house of Karageorgević, which was heavily under the influence of several nationalist politicians. Their hopes for South Slavic unity were spreading to Serbian and Croatian ethnic communities living within the confines of the **Habsburg Empire** itself, including Bosnia.

Austria–Hungary's political and **military** leaders feared that such an innovation would inevitably undermine the monarchy as a whole. With Belgrade now becoming a center of anti-Habsburg propaganda, particularly after Austria's takeover of Bosnia, some of Emperor **Franz Joseph**'s officials had begun to argue that Serbia would have to be curbed by force. The archduke's assassination created the pretext for such a move. Several of the men who advised the aged monarch continued to regard war as a last resort. However, those who called for a quick strike against Serbia prevailed. Most insistent among them was the chief Habsburg commander, Field Marshal Franz Conrad von Hötzendorf (1852–1925), who had urged preemptive war with Belgrade since 1907.

An ultimatum, so insulting that Serbia was bound to reject it, was sent to the government in Belgrade on 23 July. When Serbian Prime Minister Nicholas Pasić, under great pressure from the nationalist Serbian military establishment, did indeed refuse to allow officials from Austria–Hungary to investigate the evidence for a murder conspiracy in Serbia itself, Franz Joseph declared war on the kingdom on 28 July 1914. He was assured of help from **Germany**, with whom the Habsburgs had concluded the **Dual Alliance** of 1879. To forestall **Russian** intervention, a likely prospect because the tsarist government had grown increasingly close to its coreligionists in the Balkans, the Habsburg ruler declared that he had no intention of annexing further territory in the southeast. He, like even the most hawkish of his advisors, hoped that the war would be brief and confined to Serbia.

These illusions vanished when Russia indeed entered the war. Now the entire eastern boundary of Austria–Hungary was open to invasion. Furthermore, the Russian move prompted the Germans to attack France, which was allied to the tsarist regime and had moved ever nearer to the British since their Entente Cordiale of 1904. By the first week of August, the continent was deep in war.

Combat went badly for the Habsburg forces almost from the outset. Military plans for eastern campaigning had been betrayed to the Russians even before the conflict began, giving the tsar's armies an advantage that they exploited very effectively. The Serbs fought doggedly in their own defense as well, leaving it up to the German armies to rescue their allies in **Vienna**. The Serbs were defeated in 1915, but that same year **Italy**, despite an alliance with Germany and Austria–Hungary concluded in 1882, entered the conflict on the side of the Western allies. Rome's reward, specified in the secret Treaty of London of that same year, would be the **South Tyrol** and Trieste, among other Habsburg-held lands. The most immediate impact of the move on Austria–Hungary was that its armies had to open yet another front.

The beginning of active combat turned the Austrian half of the Habsburg Empire into a police state, governed under the emergency provision in Article 14 of its **constitution**. This was resented by many political leaders of more liberal persuasions, who continued prewar discussions about reform of the monarchy despite the repressive environment. Numerous public clashes between dissidents and the police ended in arrests and imprisonment. Those called to the armed forces, however, fought with a loyalty that surprised many commentators. Somewhere around two million Austro–Hungarian troops ended up as prisoners of war in Russia and Italy. Despite blandishments from their captors, especially strong in Russia, where the Bolshevik Revolution had taken place in November 1917, most of the empire's soldiers remained true to their original cause. Clashes among various ethnic groups of the Habsburg monarchy in the prison camps were, however, legion.

Mounting casualty lists, growing economic deprivation, and the death of Franz Joseph in November 1916 all eroded resolve on the domestic front. Desertions from the armies increased, particularly among Czech troops. The new emperor, **Charles I** (Charles IV of

Hungary), was eager to gain the goodwill of his people. One reason for his position was the assassination in October of the dictatorial Austrian minister-president, Count Karl Stürgkh (1859–1916), by Friedrich Adler (1879–1960), the son of a leading socialist, **Viktor Adler**. He therefore, against the advice of his ministers, resolved to call the parliament back into session. It met in May 1917 for the first time since March 1914, and immediately became a platform for those promoting demands for greater national autonomy. The Slavic peoples of the empire were especially insistent.

Encouraged by his strong-willed wife, Empress Zita of Bourbon-Parma (1892–1989), Charles began exploring ways to pull Austria–Hungary out of the war. Though his German partners were not above such tactics either, the new emperor's schemes came to light through the French in a particularly embarrassing way in 1918. Charles was forced to visit German Emperor William II in the latter's wartime camp in Spa and to offer an abject apology. The gesture, plus Austria–Hungary's evident military dependence on Germany, confirmed the opinion among many of Charles's subjects that the Habsburgs would be no more than puppets manipulated from Berlin in the future. The pretense that the dynasty could protect their national identities within the monarchy was ebbing fast. A very bad winter in 1917–1918, during which rations were reduced and a wave of strikes hit key industries, made things even worse.

In October 1918, facing certain defeat, Charles offered to turn the monarchy into a federation of peoples. His minister-president, Heinrich Lammasch (1853–1920), had long argued for this arrangement and for ending the war with a pact of mutual understanding among the belligerents. However, the proposal was largely taken as an invitation to throw off Habsburg government altogether. The empire broke apart during the last weeks of October. Charles himself withdrew from any role in governing Austria in November. The **Treaty of St. Germain** of September 1919 and the Treaty of Trianon of June 1920, which applied to Hungary, effectively completed the collapse of Austria–Hungary.

WORLD WAR II. Effectively incorporated into Adolf Hitler's **Germany** following the **Anschluss** of 1938, Austria in fact did not exist as a state when the German dictator set off a pan-European conflict with the invasion of Poland on 1 September 1939. For the second time in the 20th century, Austrians found themselves involved in a world war, though the narrow question of responsibility for the conflict did not dog them as it did in **World War I**.

The general public reaction to the new hostilities was as guarded as in Germany itself. Any real enthusiasm for the war broke out only with the collapse of France in 1940. However, this mood rapidly disappeared in Austria, to be replaced by increasingly open local resentment of the German officials who were largely responsible for the government of the region. The feeling was especially evident in **Vienna**, though the **Catholic Tyrol** did not take kindly to National Socialism either. The **Nazi** campaign in Russia in 1941–1942 cost Austria dearly. Large numbers of men from major population centers such as Vienna and **Lower Austria** were killed or made prisoners at the Battle of Stalingrad, which began in August 1942.

Heavy Allied bombing, which began in earnest in 1943 and continued to the end of the war, weakened the will of the population as well, especially when it did extensive damage to such population centers as Vienna, **Graz**, Villach (a rail transit center near the Italian border), and Wiener Neustadt (an industrial center to the south of Vienna). Though areas such as **Styria** profited from Nazi investment in heavy metal industries, by September 1944 police reports from Vienna and Lower Austria indicated that many Austrians had lost whatever enthusiasm they had for National Socialist rule. News of the brutalities of German armies in southeastern Europe, often brought back by furloughed troops, and a growing knowledge of what was happening to Europe's **Jewish** population in Nazi concentration camps, also repelled many. Mauthausen, in **Upper Austria**, was among the largest of these establishments, and was used for non-Jewish dissidents as well.

Pockets of **resistance** to the virtually complete Nazi takeover of Austria had existed almost from the day of the Anschluss. Young people, especially in Vienna, had sometimes given voice to a romantic Austrian patriotism. By 1940, more realistic people, often men who had returned from service or concentration camps, were beginning to come together and discuss ways of throwing off the regime. By the winter of 1944–1945, their agenda had acquired more profile and supporters, though it was not enough to spare Austria Allied conquest and serious destruction. Early in 1945, Soviet armies crossed the eastern boundary of the country. British troops moved into **Carinthia** from **Italy**; the Americans pushed into the Tyrol, **Salzburg**, and Upper Austria; and the French invaded the **Vorarlberg**. Anti-Nazi resistance, which had strengthened markedly in the Tyrol and the region around Salzburg, helped to save these areas from further damage. Efforts to spare Vienna from this fate were only partially successful. The Gestapo, along with Austrian supporters, decided to make a stand there; the last days of the war, which ended for Austria during the last week of April 1945, brought bitter and destructive fighting to the capital. *See also* OCCUPATION.

Appendix: Heads of State

BABENBERG MARGRAVES, DUKES (AFTER 1156)

Leopold I (r. 976–994)
Heinrich I (994–1018
Adalbert (1018–1055)
Ernst (1055–1075)
Leopold II (1075–1095)
Leopold III (1095–1136)
Leopold IV (1136–1141)
Heinrich II (1141–1177)
Leopold V (1177–1194)
Friedrich I (1194–1198)
Leopold VI (1198–1230)
Friedrich II (1230–1246)

Other

Margrave Hermann of Baden (1247–1250)
Ottokar II of Bohemia (1251–1276)

HABSBURG DUKES, ARCHDUKES (AFTER 1543), EMPERORS OF AUSTRIA (AFTER 1804), EMPERORS OF AUSTRIA AND KINGS OF HUNGARY (AFTER 1867)

Rudolf I (1276–1291)
Albrecht I (1282–1308)
Friedrich III (1308–1330)
Albrecht II (1330–1358)
Rudolf IV (1358–1365)
Albrecht III/Leopold III (jointly 1365–1379)

HABSBURG TERRITORIAL DIVISION, 1379

Albertine Line (Austrian)

Albrecht III (1379–1395)
Albrecht IV (1395–1404)
Albrecht V (1404–1439)
Ladislas (1440–1457)

Leopoldine Line (Styrian)

Leopold III (1379–1386)
Wilhelm (/1386–1406)
Leopold IV (1386–1411)

STYRIAN/TYROLEAN DIVISIONS OF 1406 AND 1411

Styrian Line

Ernst (1406–1424)
Friedrich V (1424–1493)
Maximilian I (1493–1519)
Charles V (1519–1521/1522)
Ferdinand I (1521/1522–1564)

Tyrolean Line

Friedrich IV (1406–1439)
Sigismund (1439–1490)

DIVISION OF 1564

Austrian Line

Maximilian II (1564–1576)
Rudolf II (1576–1612)
Matthias (1612–1619)

Tyrolean Line

Ferdinand II (1564–1595)

Styrian Line

Charles II (1564–1590)
Ferdinand II (1590–1637)
Ferdinand III (1637–1657)
Leopold I (1657–1705)
Joseph I (1705–1711)
Charles VI (1711–1740)
Maria Theresa (1740–1780)

HOUSE OF HABSBURG–LORRAINE

Joseph II (1780–1790)
Leopold I (1790–1792)
Francis I (1792–1835)
Ferdinand I (1835–1848)
Franz Joseph (1848–1916)
Charles I (1916–1918)

FIRST AUSTRIAN REPUBLIC

Presidents

Michael Hainisch (1920–1928)
Wilhelm Miklas (1928–1938)

Chancellors

Karl Renner (30 October 1918–7 July 1920)
Michael Mayr (7 July 1920–21 June 1921)
Johann Schober (21 June 1921–26 January 1922)
Walter Breisky (26 January 1922–27 January 1922)
Johann Schober (27 January 1922–31 May 1922)

Ignaz Seipel (31 May 1922–20 November 1924)
Rudolf Ramek (20 November 1924–20 October 1926)
Ignaz Seipel (20 Ocotber 1926–4 May 1929)
Ernst Steeruwitz (4 May 1929–26 September 1929)
Johann Schober (26 September 1929–30 September 1930)
Carl Vaugoin (30 September 1930–4 December 1930)
Otto Ender (4 December 1930–20 June 1931)
Karl Buresch (20 June 1931–20 May 1932)
Engelbert Dollfuss (20 May 1932–25 July 1934)
Kurt Schuschnigg (25 July 1934–11 March 1938)

SECOND AUSTRIAN REPUBLIC

Presidents

Karl Renner (1945–1950)
Theodor Körner (1951–1957)
Adolf Schärf (1957–1965)
Franz Jonas (1965–1974)
Rudolf Kirchschläger (1974–1986)
Kurt Waldheim (1986–1992)
Thomas Klestil (1992–2004)
Heinz Fischer (2004–)

Chancellors

Leopold Figl (1945–1953)
Julius Raab (1953–1961)
Alfons Gorbach (1961–1964)
Joseph Klaus (1964–1970)
Bruno Kreisky (1970–1983)
Fred Sinowatz (1983–1986)
Franz Vranitzky (1986–1997)
Viktor Klima (1997–2000)
Wolfgang Schüssel (2000–2006)
Alfred Gusenbauer (2007–2008)

Bibliography

This bibliography is divided into the following categories, with subheadings relevant to the thematic concentration of the material.

I. Bibliographies, Bibliographical Studies, and Reference Works
II. Scholarly Periodicals
III. Newspapers and General Periodicals
IV. General Studies of the History of Austria and the History of the Habsburg Empire
V. The History of Austria from Antiquity to 1273
VI. The History of Austria from 1273 to 1519
VII. The History of Austria from 1519 to 1789
VIII. The History of Austria from 1789 to 1867
IX. The History of Austria from 1867 to 1918
X. The History of Austria from 1918 to 1945
XI. The History of Austria from 1945 to the Present

The literature here, as in the dictionary as a whole, is for readers and speakers of English who want a basic guide to the history of Austria. The selection represents only a fraction of the material available in a variety of other European languages, especially German, which has increased vastly since the first edition of this work appeared in 1999.

For systematic guidance to further reading, consult the relevant bibliographical suggestions in section I. The *Österreichische Historische Bibliographie/Austrian Historical Bibliography*, which covers historical literature published in Austria only and is primarily of interest to scholars, can be found at www.uniklu.ac.at/groups/oehb/oehbquery. The HABSBURG website, although far from exhaustive, offers a quick picture of the current literature that it receives and very thorough reviews. It is most easily accessed through the links provided by the Center for Austrian Studies at the University of Minnesota at www.cas.umn.edu. The center also publishes a lively series, Working Papers in Austrian Studies. Titles appear on the center's website.

The *Mitteilungen des Instituts für österreichische Geschichtsforschung* also tracks work done in the field very closely, but appears irregularly. The 10-volume *Österreichische Geschichte*, a collaborative effort that has been appearing since 1995, includes excellent scholarly bibliographies at the end of all chapters. The *Geschichte der Habsburger Monarchie 1848–1918*, a topically organized multivolume work, presents essential literature for this crucial phase of Austrian history and the history of Central Europe generally. There is an exhaustive list of reading and sources for the history of Vienna in Felix Czeike's five-volume *Historisches Lexikon Wiens*. Readers should also consult Peter Csendes's *Historical Dictionary of Vienna* (1999) in the Scarecrow Press series of historical dictionaries on the world's cities. The Center for Austrian Culture and Commerce at the University of New Orleans (www.centeraustria.org) publishes *Studies in Austrian and Central European Studies* and *Contemporary Austrian Studies*, both of which focus on the history and affairs of modern Austria. Major American research libraries such as the New York Public Library and the libraries of the University of Chicago, Columbia University, Harvard University, the University of California at Berkeley, and the University of Minnesota also have extensive collections in Austrian history.

Austria's history also crosses the path of many other countries. Highly relevant are Wayne C. Thompson, Susan L. Thompson, and Juliet S. Thompson, *Historical Dictionary of Germany* (1994) in the European Historical Dictionary series of Scarecrow Press, along with Angel Smith, *Historical Dictionary of Spain* (1996) (2nd ed. forthcoming 2008) and Arend H. Huussen Jr., *Historical Dictionary of the Netherlands* 2nd ed. (2007).

Bibliographical references to books about the non-Austrian lands of the former Habsburg Empire have been limited to topics crucial to the history of the empire or that critically affected developments in the Austrian territories. Those wishing to pursue research on the several non-German peoples of the erstwhile multinational monarchy should also consult the relevant volumes in the Scarecrow European series: Ante Cuvalo, *Historical Dictionary of Bosnia and Herzegovina* 2nd ed. (2007); Jiři Hochmann, *Historical Dictionary of the Czech State* (1998); Zeljan Suster, *Historical Dictionary of the Federal Republic of Yugoslavia* (1998); George Sanford and Adriana Gozdecka-Sanford, *Historical Dictionary of Poland* 2nd ed.(2003); Robert Staellerts and Jeannine Laurens, *Historical Dictionary of the Republic of Croatia* (1995); Stanislaw J. Kirschbaum, *Historical Dic-*

tionary of Slovakia (1989); and Leopoldina Plut-Pregelj and Carole Rogel, *Historical Dictionary of Slovenia* 2nd ed. (2007). Hungary, the joint partner of the Austro–Hungarian monarchy after 1867, has been covered by Steven Belá Vardy in the *Historical Dictionary of Hungary* (1997).

Research in the history and culture of Austria is greatly facilitated by the availability of a wide variety of archives, documentary collections, and libraries within the country itself. Vienna alone has more than 700 libraries, special collections, and archives; there are many more scattered throughout the provinces that can be very useful, depending upon one's scholarly interests. This essay deals with Vienna alone, and that only selectively. Readers are urged to consult a comprehensive online guide published by the Union of Austrian Libraries (*Österreichische Bibliotheken Verband*), with links to important archives at www.obvsg.at. Most frequented by professional historians are the various sites of the Austrian State Archives, which have four major divisions: the Court and State Archives (Haus-, Hof-, und Staatsarchiv), the Finance and Exchequer Archives (Finanz- und Hofkammerarchiv), the Administrative and Police Archives (Verwaltungsarchiv), and the Military Archives (Kriegsarchiv). All but the Court and State Archives are housed in the central state archives located in the Nottendorferstraße, which can be reached on the metro line 3.

The subdivisions of the Austrian State Library (Österreichische Nationalbibliothek) are other major resources. Aside from its printed holdings and an enormous manuscript collection, drawn from all over the world, the library is the repository for important musical collections, including manuscripts; a papyrus collection; and a documentation center for Austrian history, politics, and general culture.

For those concerned with the history of Vienna, the Museum of the City of Vienna (Wien Museum) documents the history of the city in all its aspects. The Archives of the City and Province of Vienna (Wiener Stadt- und Landesarchiv) has key holdings, along with a library and documentation center. It is particularly useful for those interested in the history of political parties in the city or in its social history. The Jewish Historical Museum of Vienna (Jüdisches Museum der Stadt Wien) is central to the study of the Jewish community in Vienna and in Austria as a whole.

A number of other museums and centers have materials that bear on Austrian history. Military historians should certainly consult the holdings of the Military Museum (Herresgeschichtliches Museum). The "Adler" Heraldic and Genealogical Society (Heraldisch-Genealogische Gesellschaft "Adler") is crucial for those who are pursuing family histories. The

Socialist Party of Austria (SPÖ) and its predecessor, the Social Democratic Workers' Party (SDAP) has a number of archives that contain materials important not only to the history of socialism in Austria but to related topics such as the women's movement and environmental questions. Essential materials on the Catholic Christian Social movement are kept in the Karl von Vogelsang Institute for Research in the History of the Christian Democratic Movement (Karl von Vogelsang Institut zur Erforschung der Geschichte der christlichen Demokratie). The Vogelsang Institute holds the archives of the current Austrian People's Party. For those interested in significant phases of Austrian history from during World War II to the present, the Documentary Archive of the Austrian Resistance (Dokumentationsarchiv der österreichischen Widerstandes) and the library of the Austrian Society for Contemporary History (Österreichische Gesellschaft für Zeitgeschichte) are essential. The latter is especially important for current affairs. The Vienna Museum Quarter has a wide variety of electronic resources available for the study of contemporary and modern art both in Austria and the world.

Musicologists will find the archives of the Society of the Friends of Music (Gesellschaft der Musikfreunde in Wien) to be the richest collection of its kind in the world. Also useful, especially on 20th-century Austrian music, are the holdings of the Documentary Institute for Austrian Music (Institut für österreichische Musikdokumentation). Twentieth-century Austrian writing, as well as the work of modern authors from east central Europe, can be studied in the Documentary Center for Austrian Literature (Dokumentationsstelle für österreichische Literatur im Literaturhaus). The center also has significant holdings on the work of Austrian writers who went into exile before and during World War II. For those interested in Austrian handicrafts, including the development of the Wiener Werkstätte, the Austrian Museum for Applied Art (Österreichische Museum für angewandte Kunst) is essential.

The following websites are particularly informative for people who plan to visit Austria or need up-to-date details about the country's affairs: www.austria.org/content/view/53/77/ Austrian Embassy, Washington, D.C., and www.acfdc.org, Austrian Cultural Forum, New York City. Scholars should turn to www.cas.umn.edu/links/academic.html at the University of Minnesota Center for Austrian Studies. Researchers with a special interest in literature should also look at www.MALCA.org, the home page of the Modern Austrian Literature and Culture Association.

Ten years have passed since the bibliography for the first edition of this dictionary was compiled, but in the world of English-language scholarship on the history of Austria, both as a constituent element of the Habsburg Empire and as a sovereign republic, massive gaps still remain. The history of the Austrian lands in the early, high, and late Middle Ages is all but terra incognita to Anglophonic historians. Although a couple of general accounts listed below do take a stab at an overview of the Austrian Middle Ages, they lack both the detail and the depth that are available to those who can handle the rich and often illuminating studies now available in German. The situation is only slightly better for the history of the Austrian lands in the early modern era from the 15th through the 17th centuries. Although there are now several able monographs on religious, social, and political history written in English on these regions, the literature is heavily focused on the history of the Habsburg monarchy, which took place all over continental Europe, rather than the dynasty's Austrian holdings alone. Scholarly biographies of Habsburg rulers in English are now available, but they are no substitute for a synthesis of the history of the Austrian lands from the Renaissance to the Enlightenment. They are also often written for informed scholarly audiences and not the interested, but uninitiated, layperson. The volumes by Winkelbauer and Vocelka in the *Österreichische Geschichte* are an excellent place to begin one's study of the period, and are written in a clear and straightforward German, but one must be prepared to read the works in that language. Two recent publications that will be especially helpful to an English-only reader are Elisabeth Lichtenberger, *Austria: Society and Regions*, a wide-ranging physical and demographic geography of Austria that brings into play the findings of several disciplines to explore the subject dynamically rather than from the more conventional perspective of static fact, and Steven Beller's *A Concise History of Austria*. The latter is a rare and good faith effort in English to tie the imperial and postimperial experiences of the country together.

The focus of Anglophonic historians, particularly in the United States, has shifted since the first edition of the *Historical Dictionary of Austria* appeared, from the troubled interaction of government and national communities to questions of factors that kept the monarchy together as long as it did and closer analysis of informal political, social, and especially economic relations that created a functional interdependency of the Habsburg peoples. The literature in this vein has been revealing, but has largely concentrated on traditional hot spots of ethnic relations in the monarchy,

German–Czech interactions in the kingdom of Bohemia particularly. The interactions of the Austrian lands with non-Austrian provinces have received far less attention, though a notable and very important exception is Pieter Judson's *Guardians of the Nation: Activists on the Language Frontiers of Imperial Austria*.

Other historians who write in English have done serious, and often provocative, histories of the Habsburg Empire. Robin Okey's *The Habsburg Monarchy: From Enlightenment to Eclipse* is more chronologically constrained but is thoughtful and interesting. Its annotated bibliography covers books and articles in several languages, but captures the important materials in English down to the time of publication. Andrew Wheatcroft's *The Habsburgs: Embodying Empire* starts slowly, but is an informed and engaging, quasi-biographical introduction to the Habsburg dynasty, from the Middle Ages to the present. It is also beautifully illustrated.

Older studies of the Habsburg monarchy that still remain useful are Robert Kann, *A History of the Habsburg Empire 1526–1918*; A. J. P. Taylor's lively and readable *The Habsburg Monarchy 1809–1918: A History of the Austrian Empire and Austria Hungary*; and C. A. Macartney, *The Habsburg Empire, 1790–1918*. Alan Sked's provocative *The Decline and Fall of the Habsburg Empire, 1815–1918* has reappeared in a second edition and does a good job of introducing readers to historiographic questions about the monarchy.

All of these works are, however, devoted to the last century and a half of the Habsburg Empire's existence. For the preceding period, one can usefully consult Charles Ingrao, *The Habsburg Monarchy 1618–1815*, a very reliable presentation that is now in a second edition, and the less detailed Paula Sutter Fichtner, *The Habsburg Empire, 1490–1848: Attributes of Empire*. There is a comprehensive study of the Habsburg monarchy available in English in two volumes, Jean Bérenger's *A History of the Habsburg Empire, 1273–1700* and *A History of the Habsburg Empire 1700–1918*. Translated from a one-volume French original, it has the great virtue of containing far more material on the monarchy before the 18th century than do the previously mentioned works. The extensive bibliographical sections of each book are compiled with the English-speaking reader in mind. The second volume, however, is rather superficial, compared to the first, and both parts are unreliably translated.

Barbara Jelavich's *Modern Austria. Empire and Republic 1815–1986* is still useful for the decades from 1918 to around 1980. It is both fair and accessible. For contemporary history, an English-language reader should consult Peter Thaler, *The Ambivalence of Identity: The Austrian Experience of Nation-Building in a Modern Society,* and Anton Pelinka, *Austria: Out of the Shadow*, both of which are written from an institutional and socioeconomic viewpoint and make for exceptionally interesting reading. Ernst Bruckmüller's discursive *The Austrian Nation* is topically organized and presumes some prior general knowledge of Austrian history, but is very informative on social questions particularly.

The English-only scholar will have the greatest trouble finding materials on Austria from the Middle Ages through the Renaissance (see sections V and VI). There is only one general survey, Alexander W.A. Leeper's *A History of Medieval Austria*, a basic political narrative. Otto Brunner's *Land and Lordship: Structure of Governance in Medieval Austria* comes far closer to meeting the modern standards taste for social history but is relatively limited in its reach. For the later Middle Ages through the Renaissance, Gerhard Benecke, *Maximilian I 1459–1519*; Thomas Brady, *Turning Swiss: Cities and Empire, 1450–1550*; Louise Cuyler, *The Emperor Maximilian I and Music*; Marie Tanner, *The Last Descendant of Aeneas: The Habsburgs and the Mythic Image of the Emperor*; and R. Po-chia Hsia, *Trent 1475. Stories of a Ritual Murder* give important social, political, and cultural insights. Nevertheless, none of these has the vast scope of the five-volume work of Hermann Wiesflecker, *Kaiser Maximilian I: Das Reich, Österreich und Europa an der Wende zur Neuzeit,* nicely abridged to one volume as *Maximilian I: Die Fundamente des habsburgischen Weltreiches.* Even more fundamental are Alois Niederstätter's *Das Jahrhundert der Mitte: An der Wende vom Mittelalter zur Neuzeit* and *Die Herrschaft Österreich: Fürst und Land im Spätmittelalter.*

The period from the Protestant Reformation through the French Revolution offers more for those who read comfortably only in English. Charles Ingrao's *The Habsburg Monarchy 1618–1815* touches all important bases—cultural, political, economic, and social—and makes intelligent use of most of the important recent literature. Its coverage of the French Revolutionary era is somewhat brief. Ernst Wangerman's *The Austrian Achievement, 1700–1800* is equally sketchy here, but is still a very interesting and informative picture of the Austria of Maria Theresa and Joseph II. The illustrations will give a student a wonderful introduction to the Austrian Baroque. Of a different order is R. J. W. Evans, *The Making of the Habsburg Monarchy, 1550–1700*. Although the title promises a general treatment of the subject, the book is a highly detailed study of the political and religious foundations of the empire. It argues that culture, particularly Counter-Reformation Catholic culture, became the unifying element of the empire, a thesis to which all scholars pay close attention. The work is, however, heavy lifting for the novice. The same can be said of his earlier *Rudolph II and His World: A Study in Intellectual History, 1576–1612*. Although it is an original and stimulating picture of late Renaissance thought in central Europe, it is not for beginners. Those looking into Habsburg court culture for the first time are wiser to begin with Hugh Trevor-Roper, *Princes and Artists: Patronage and Ideology at Four Habsburg Courts, 1517–1633*. A practical and eminently readable view of the impact of the Habsburg court on Austrian, and especially Viennese, society is John P. Spielman's *The City and the Crown*.

Scholars from the Anglo-Saxon world have made important contributions to the political history of this period. Very important is Derek Beales's comprehensive *Joseph II* in two volumes. Two shorter but valuable biographies of Joseph and his mother, Empress Maria Theresa, are William McGill, *Maria Theresa*, and T. C. W. Blanning, *Joseph II*. Habsburg Enlightened absolutism was a product of the dynasty's ministers. A significant study of one of the most important is Franz A .J. Szábo, *Kaunitz and Enlightened Absolutism, 1733–1780*. A major contribution in German, particularly for scholars, is Petr Mat'a and Thomas Winkelbauer, eds., *Die Habsburgermonarchie 1620 bis 1740: Leistungen und Grenzen des Absolutismusparadigmas*.

The 18th century ushered in an extended period of achievement in Austrian musical culture, and the modern literature in English on the topic is very rich. Modern critics still turn to Charles Rosen's *The Classical Style: Haydn, Mozart and Beethoven*. More recently, however, musicologists have been working to situate composers in the cultural and social context of their times, and the results can be impressive. Robert Gutman's *Mozart: A Cultural Biography* is a magisterial contribution to the genre. It is also fascinating to read. H. C. Robbins Landon's *Beethoven: His Life, Work, and World* and his *Mozart and Vienna* should still be consulted. For the contemporary theater there is Bruce Alan Brown, *Gluck and the French Theatre in Vienna*. The plastic arts are less well covered in English, but Thomas daCosta Kaufmann, *The Eloquent Artist: Essays on Art, Art Theory and Architecture, Sixteenth to Nineteenth Centuries* provides authoritative background to the Habsburg patronage of art and architecture, which was crucial to Austria's built environment and the holdings of today's state museums. It is very well illustrated. Eric Garberson's *Eighteenth-Century*

Monastic Libraries in Southern Germany and Austria: Architecture and Decorations is unfortunately illustrated in black and white, but is a plainly written and most informative look at one of Austrian Catholicism's most important visual art forms at its zenith.

There are no satisfactory general studies in English for the period 1789–1867 in Austrian history. A welcome exception is Herman Freudenberger's *Lost Momentum: Austrian Economic Development, 1750s–1830s*. Although it tells a familiar tale of the zigzag nature of Austrian economic development, it conveys the individual, institutional, and social texture of early industrialization in the region without abandoning scholarly seriousness. More generally, readers are advised to consult the above-mentioned work by Alan Sked, who is especially good on the Revolutions of 1848 and their aftermath. The relevant sections of Robert Kann's survey of the Habsburg monarchy, also discussed earlier, are also useful here. A valuable set of introductory essays, edited by Kinley Brauer and William Wright, is *Austria in the Age of the French Revolution*.

The dominant figure of the age, at least according to conventional wisdom, was Prince Klemens Wenzel von Metternich, foreign minister, then chancellor, of Emperor Francis I. He has been the subject of two sound introductory biographies in English, Alan Milne's *Metternich* and Alan Palmer's *Metternich*. Francis himself, who played a central role in the policy making of his government, has had no English-language biographer since Walter C. Langsam, *Francis the Good: The Education of an Emperor, 1768–1792*. The book still merits attention, however. Those wishing to study the 1848 revolutions in greater detail should see R. John Rath, *The Viennese Revolution of 1848*, a detailed and extended narrative that has no peer in English.

The culture of the era has been much better served in English. Once again, some of the most fruitful scholarship turns on placing major Austrian writers and composers in their sociocultural, political, and even economic milieus. *Schubert's Vienna*, edited by Raymond Erickson, is a good place to start. Some of the essays are a trifle specialized for a beginner, but the more general ones are not, and all chapters end with useful suggestions for further reading. Alice M. Hanson, *Musical Life in Biedermeier Vienna* remains essential. Ernst Hilmar separates fact from legend in his *Franz Schubert in His Time*, and Elizabeth Norman McKay does a close reading of the psychosexual life of the composer in *Franz Schubert: A Biography*. The above-mentioned work by Landon on Beethoven also tells us much about music in the Biedermeier era. Two works that give the English-only reader a very good introduction to Austrian theatrical culture of the era are Simon Williams, *German Comic Actors of the Eighteenth and Nineteenth Centuries* and W. Edgar Yates, *Theatre in Vienna: A Critical History, 1776–1995*. The latter has relatively little to say about the theatrical literature itself, but it is very good on the social and political environment in which the works were written. Michael Cherlin, Halina Filipowicz, and Richard L Rudolph, eds., *The Great Tradition and Its Legacy: The Evolution of Dramatic and Musical Theater in Austria and Central Europe* is no substitute for the general history of the Austrian theater still to be written in English. Nevertheless, it has very useful essays on the classical comic playwrights of the period. Dorothy Prohaska, *Raimund and Vienna*, is a rare and very fine treatment in English of one of the genre's iconic figures. Donald Daviau, ed., *Major Figures of Nineteenth-Century Austrian Literature* covers some essential territory in solid and accessible essays.

For the period from 1867 through to 1938, the English language scholarship on Austrian history and the history of the Habsburg monarchy is both extensive and accomplished. Once Great Britain and the United States found themselves involved in continental wars that began in 20th-century central and east central Europe, their academic interest in the region grew proportionately. An understandable concern in both countries with contemporary affairs produced especially impressive work on the background and outbreak of World War I and the history of National Socialism and its various branches.

For a general introduction to the political history of the Habsburg Empire from 1867 to 1918, see John W. Mason, *The Dissolution of the Austro–Hungarian Empire, 1867–1918*, which also has a useful documentary appendix. Paula Sutter Fichtner, *The Habsburg Empire: From Dynasticism to Multinationalism* covers much of the same ground in less detail, but with several documents that are translated for the first time into English and are useful in the classroom. The history of the monarchy in its final decades is closely tied to the reign of Emperor Franz Joseph, who has been the subject of several recent biographical treatments, all of which are readable introductions to larger problems. Among these are Jean Paul Bled, *Franz Joseph*; Stephen Beller, *Francis Joseph*, which is organized around subheadings; and Alan W. Palmer, *Twilight of the Habsburgs: The Life and Times of Emperor Francis Joseph*, which ranges significantly beyond the biographical.

The nationality question has been a central concern of students of the Habsburg monarchy since its collapse in 1918. Current historiography now questions the importance of this issue to the exclusion of social and economic concerns, but it is still the focus of much scholarly attention. The writing in the field is largely monographic; Robert Kann's *The Multi-National Empire* was unquestionably the most important effort in English to synthesize the issue. The East European Monographs series, published by Social Science Monographs, continues to bring out an extraordinarily large number of such studies, many of which are listed in section X. Volumes III.1 and III.2 of *Die Habsburger Monarchie 1848–1918*, edited by Adam Wandruszka and Peter Urbanitsch, are essential for a comprehensive treatment of the nationality question through World War I. A very thoughtful compilation of essays is *The Habsburg Legacy: National Identity in Historical Perspective*, volume 5 of the series Austrian Studies, edited by Ritchie Robertson and Edward Timms, which has contributed significantly to both the history of the Habsburg monarchy and of Austria generally.

The new focus on the economic, social, and cultural history of the Austro–Hungarian Empire has produced much important work. The debate over the economic development of the Habsburg state was opened by Alexander Gerschenkron in *An Economic Spurt that Failed*. He saw the process as essentially incomplete. David Good in *The Economic Rise of the Habsburg Empire, 1750–1914* argues that the Austrian economy performed far more impressively. A related and very significant long-term issue is treated in John Komlos, *The Habsburg Monarchy as a Customs Union: Economic Development in Austria–Hungary in the Nineteenth Century*.

Closely attending upon the industrialization of the empire were social and political changes, both rural and urban. The appearance of mass political parties in Austria after 1867 has been studied widely but at different levels of intensity. John Boyer's *Political Radicalism in Late Imperial Vienna: Origins of the Christian Social Movement, 1848–1897* and *Culture and Political Crisis in Vienna: Christian Socialism in Power, 1897–1918* cover the Christian Social movement and its impact exhaustively. Richard Geehr, *Karl Lueger: Mayor of Fin de Siècle Vienna* is a good introduction to a controversial, and very successful, Christian Social mayor. *Hitler's Vienna: A Dictator's Apprenticeship*, by Brigitte Hamann is also illuminating. The Austrian Social Democrats have yet to be studied comprehensively in English, nor are there good biographies of leading figures. A useful introduction to their thought is Tom Bottomore's *Austro-Marxism*.

Individual social issues are being examined ever more closely in English. Peter Pulzer's *The Rise of Political Anti-Semitism in Germany and Austria* is still useful in a revised edition. Marcia Rosenblitt, *The Jews of Vienna,*

1867–1914: Assimilation and Identity and Robert S. Wistrich, *The Jews of Vienna in the Age of Franz Joseph* also have remained valuable. The very important question of education has received excellent quantitative analysis in Gary B. Cohen, *Education and Middle Class Society in Imperial Austria, 1848–1918*. Robert Wegs, *Growing Up Working Class: Continuity and Change among Viennese Youth, 1890–1938* treats a neglected but important topic closely and sympathetically.

But it is high thought and culture generally in late 19th-century Austria, particularly Vienna, that has commanded the most attention among scholars who write in English. For an encyclopedic treatment of Austrian thought there is William Johnston, *The Austrian Mind: An Intellectual and Social History*. Although written from a specific point of view—Johnston stresses the analytic rather than activist side of the Austrian intellectual tradition—the book is very informative and amply equipped with useful biographical details such as birth and death dates. Also helpful is Donald Daviau's workmanlike anthology *Major Figures of Turn-of-the Century Austrian Literature*.

The book that brought the fin de siècle Habsburg Empire to world attention was Carl Schorske's *Fin-de-Siècle Vienna: Politics and Culture*. Structurally a collection of essays that Schorske had already published in various scholarly journals, the work explored what the author saw as the decline of political liberalism and the growing centrality of the irrational, expressed both in mass movements and aesthetic programs of the day. The book gave new stature to figures such as the painters Gustav Klimt and Egon Schiele, who had long been marginal to the European artistic canon, and to the applied arts, represented by such movements as the *Wiener Werkstätte*, which were all but forgotten by the 1950s. Schorske's study also reawakened interest in the Jewish contribution to Austrian culture, the topic of such books as Denis Klein's *Jewish Origins of the Psychoanalytic Movement* and Steven Beller's *Vienna and the Jews, 1867-1938: A Cultural History*. All this scholarship was reinforced by a series of exhibitions at major museums in Paris, New York, and Vienna.

Architectural historians examined the Vienna style of the late 19th century throughout all corners of the former Habsburg Monarchy, Eve Blau's and Monika Platzer's edited volume *Planning the Great City: Modern Architecture in Central Europe 1890–1937* being both typical and among the first. Efforts to use the built environment of turn-of-the century Vienna as a mirror of social and political as well as aesthetic values continue to appear. Leslie Topp, *Architecture and Truth in Fin-de-siècle Vienna* is an exceptionally well-integrated example.

Nevertheless, the critique and revision of the Schorske thesis, neatly encapsulated in Steven Beller, ed., *Rethinking Vienna 1900*, began fairly soon after his book was published and has become something of a cottage industry among academics. Historians have raised questions about Schorske's analysis—his understanding of the term *middle class* and his evaluation of Jewish contributions to the culture of the era, along with the centrality of Sigmund Freud to his overall approach, have come in for some searching criticism. Beller has objected very sharply to Schorske's weighting of Jewish influences. But the greatest reservations have been about the author's approach to Austrian liberalism, which he regards as virtually aborted by the beginning of the 20th century. Peter Judson, *Exclusive Revolutionaries: Liberal Politics, Social Experience, and National Identity in the Austrian Empire, 1848–1914*; Deborah A. Coen, *Vienna in the Age of Uncertainty: Science, Liberalism, and Private Life*; and Malachi Haim Hacohen, *Karl Popper, the Formative Years, 1902–1945: Politics and Philosophy in Interwar Vienna* see a great deal of creative continuity in the Austrian liberal experience through the end of the Habsburg monarchy.

The outbreak of World War I, which brought all of this to an end, is thoroughly but readably analyzed in Samuel R. Williamson Jr., *Austria–Hungary and the Origins of the First World War*. The collapse of the monarchy in Vienna itself as a social and economic experience is well analyzed in *Vienna and the Fall of the Habsburg Monarchy: Total War and Everyday Life in World War I*, by Maureen Healy, who makes good use of personal testimonials in letters and memoirs.

Francis L. Carsten's *The First Austrian Republic, 1918–1938* is a useful introduction to the history of the Austrian First Republic. Nevertheless, this story has until now interested historians in the Anglo-Saxon world largely for two reasons: first and foremost, its connection with the rise of Fascism and Nazism, and secondarily the programs of Austria's Socialists, who used Vienna as something of a laboratory model for egalitarian communitarianism in the 1920s. The two issues intersected significantly, as we see in Anson Rabinbach's *The Crisis of Austrian Socialism: From Red Vienna to Civil War 1927–1934* and Helmut Gruber's *Red Vienna: Experiment in Working Class Culture 1919–1934*. Charlie Jeffery's *Social Democracy in the Austrian Provinces: Beyond Red Vienna* breaks a long tradition of viewing Austrian Socialism only from the Vienna standpoint. There are now two significant monographs on the intersection of aesthetics and politics: Eve Blau's *The Architecture of Red Vienna 1919–1934* and Robert Pyrah's *The Burgtheater and Austrian Identity: Theater and Cultural Politics in Vienna, 1918–1938*.

On the rise and effect of Fascism and authoritarianism generally, Carsten has published a very thorough monograph, *Fascist Movements in Austria from Schönerer to Hitler*. Bruce Pauley has written two key works on Austrian Nazism and anti-Semitism: *Hitler and the Forgotten Nazis* and *From Prejudice to Persecution: A History of Austrian Anti-Semitism*. Evan Bukey, *Hitler's Austria: Popular Sentiment in the Nazi Era, 1938–1945* stresses the wide support that the Hitler regime received in Austria. C. Earl Edmondson, *The Heimwehr and Austrian Politics, 1918–1936* covers essential material. On the Christian Social Party, Alfred Diamant, *Austrian Catholics and the First Republic, 1918–1934* remains useful, as does *Ignaz Seipel: Christian Statesman in a Time of Crisis*, by Klemens von Klemperer.

The failure of the Viennese Creditanstalt Bank in 1931 contributed significantly to the worldwide economic crisis of the 1930s. This has been well covered in Aurel Schubert, *The Credit-Anstalt Crisis of 1931*. Essential background is in Edward März, *Austrian Banking and Financial Policy: Creditanstalt at a Turning Point, 1912–1923*. The problems of Austria's literary intellectuals is thoughtfully covered in C. E. Williams, *The Broken Eagle: The Politics of Austrian Literature from Empire to Anschluss*. David Luft's *Eros and Inwardness in Vienna: Weininger, Musil, Doderer* offers a stimulating discussion of literary life in interwar Austria. One way of resolving the perceived cultural dislocations of World War I is explored by Michael Steinberg in *The Meaning of the Salzburg Festival: Austria as Theater and Ideology 1890–1938*.

Austria has decidedly not occupied center stage for historians in the Anglo–Saxon world since 1945. Nevertheless, the country's connection with Nazism and continued pockets of sympathy for its racial positions always generate interest, as shown in the controversy over former president Kurt Waldheim's career during World War II. This is perhaps best addressed in English in Robert E. Herzstein's *Waldheim: The Missing Years* and Richard Mitten's *The Politics of Antisemitic Prejudice: The Waldheim Phenomenon in Austria*. The rise of a populist right wing in the country is provocatively analyzed by Lothar Höbelt, *Defiant Populist: Jörg Haider and the Politics of Austria*.

Austria, which was one of the few areas in the world from which the Soviet Union withdrew, has been more closely studied for its Cold War connections. The conclusion of the Austrian State Treaty of 1955 and the Austrian policy of neutrality that accompanied it merited close attention. Donald R. Witnah and Edgar I. Erickson, *The American Occupation of Austria: Planning and Early Years* deals not only with its announced topic but with the Allied occupation generally. Audrey Kurth Cronin, *Great Power Politics and the Struggle Over Austria, 1945–1955* provides essential coverage. Günter Bischof, *Austria in the First Cold War, 1945–1955: The Leverage of the Weak* stresses Austria's active role in dealing with the occupying powers. Very useful for the study of Austria's relationship with the European Community, which it joined in 1995, are various volumes listed in the Contemporary Austrian Studies series found in section IX.

Still helpful on internal politics are two studies by Melanie Sully, *A Contemporary History of Austria*, which remains informative on the transformation of the social democratic movement, and *Political Parties and Elections in Austria: The Search for Stability*, which covers its topic solidly up to the time of publication. On cultural developments see Willy Riemer, ed., *After Postmodernism: Austrian Literature and Film in Transition*, which offers very broad coverage of these matters and has interviews with key players. One should also consult Katrin Kohl and Ritchie Robertson, eds., *A History of Austrian Literature, 1918–2000*. An interesting insight into questions of gender and Austrian society is *Jews and Queers: Symptoms of Modernity in Late-Twentieth Century Vienna*, by Matti Bunzl.

I. BIBLIOGRAPHIES, BIBLIOGRAPHICAL STUDIES, AND REFERENCE WORKS

Aigner, Wolfram. *Austrian Law: A Survey*. Linz: Trauner, 2006.
The Austrian Financial Markets. Vienna: Austrian National Bank, 1994– . Annual.
Austrian Foreign Policy Yearbook. Vienna: Federal Ministry for Foreign Affairs, 1988–. Annual.
Austrian Foreign Trade. Annual supplement to *Österreichs Außenwirtschaft*. Vienna: Forschungsschwerpunkt Internationale Wirtschaft, 1998–2004, 2007–. Annual.
Austrian Literature Online. Graz: Universitätsverlag, 2000.
"The Austrian State Archives." *Austrian History Yearbook* nos. 6/7 (1970–1971): 3–74.

Buchhart, Helmut. *Österreich in Bibliographie und Dokumentation.* Vienna: Vereinigungösterreichischer Bibliothekare, 1986.
Czeike, Felix. *Das grosse Groner Wien Lexikon.*Vienna: Molden, 1974.
——. *Historisches Lexikon Wien.* 5 vols. Vienna: Kremayer & Scheriau, 1992–2004.
Dachs, Herbert, and Peter Gerlich, eds. *Handbuch des politischen Systems Österreichs.* Vienna: Manz, 1991.
Eckman, Charles. *Vienna's Municipal Building Program, 1918–1934: A Bibliography.* Monticello, Ill.: Vance Bibliographies, 1988.
Endler, Franz. *Vienna: A Guide to Its Music and Musicians.* Translated by Leo Jecny. Portland, Ore.: Amadeus Press, 1989.
Filler, Susan M. *Gustav and Alma Mahler: A Guide to Research.* 2nd ed. New York: Routledge, 2008.
Gesamtverzeichnis österreichischer Dissertationen. Vienna: Verband der wissenschaftlichen Gesellschaften Österreichs, 1966–1984.
Hardin, James N., and Donald C. Daviau, eds. *Austrian Fiction Writers, 1875–1913.* Detroit: Gale Research, 1989.
Hamann, Brigitte, ed. *Die Habsburger. Ein biographisches Lexikon.* Munich: Piper, 1988.
Hausmaninger, Herbert. *The Austrian Legal System.* 3rd ed. Vienna: Manz, 2003.
Jessup, John J. *Balkan Military History: A Bibliography.* New York: Garland, 1986.
Kaufmann, Thomas da Costa. *Art and Architecture in Central Europe, 1550–1620: An Annotated Bibliography.* Boston: G. K. Hall, 1988.
Kleindel, Walter. *Das grosse Buch der Österreicher: 4500 Personendarstellungen in Wort und Bild. Namen. Daten. Fakten.* Vienna: Kremayer & Scheriau, 1987.
——. *Österreich. Zahlen. Fakten. Daten.* 5th ed. Salzburg: Andreas and Müller, 2004.
Koller, Fritz. *Das Salzburger Landesarchiv.* Salzburg: Pustet, 1987.
Krauss, Gottfried, ed. *Musik in Österreich. Eine Chronik in Daten, Dokumenten, Essays und Bildern: Klassische Musik, Oper, Operette, Volksmusik, Unterhaltungsmusik,Avantgardemusik, Komponisten, Dirigenten, Virtuosen, Sänger, Musikstätten, Festspiele Instrumentenbau.* Vienna: Brandstätter, 1989.
Lukan, Walter, and Max Demeter Peyfuss. *Ost-und Südost Sammlungen in Österreich: Verzeichnis der Bibliotheken, Institute, Archive und Museen.* 2nd enlarged ed. Vienna: Verlag für schichte und Politik, 1990.

Magocsi, Paul Robert. *Historical Atlas of East Central Europe*. 2nd ed. Seattle: University of Washington Press, 2002.

Malina, Peter, and Gustav Spann. *Bibliographie zur österreichischen Zeitgeschichte, 1918–1985. Eine Auswahl*. Vienna: Verlag für Geschichte und Politik, 1985.

Österreich Lexikon. Edited by Richard Bamberger et al. 2 vols. Vienna: Verlagsgesellschaft Österreich-Lexikon. 1995. Available at www. aeiou.at.

Österreichische Historische Bibliographie/Austrian Historical Bibliography. Santa Barbara, Calif.: Clio, 1967– . Available at www.onb.ac.at/katalogue/oesterreichische_bibliographie.htm.

Österreichisches biographisches Lexikon. Vienna: Akademie der Wissenschaften. 1815–1950.

Österreichisches Jahrbuch für Politik. Vienna: Federal Press Service. 1977–. Annual.

Österreichisches Personenlexikon der ersten und zweiten Republik. Edited by Isabella Ackerl and Friedrich Weissensteiner. Vienna: Ueberreuter, 1992.

Neue österreichische Biographie ab 1815. Vienna/Munich: Almathea. 1923–. Running series.

Politisches Handbuch Österreichs. Vienna: Federal Ministry for Education, Science, and Art. 1945–, Annual.

Presse-Handbuch. Vienna: Verband österreichischer Zeitungsherausgeber und Zeitungsverleger. 1985–. Annual.

Roman, Eric. *Austria–Hungary and the Successor States: A Reference Guide from the Renaissance to the Present*. New York: Facts on File, 2003.

Salt, Denys. *Austria*. Oxford: Ariadne, 1986.

Stock, Karl Franz, et al. *Bibliographie osterreichischer Bibliographien, Sammelbiographien und Nachschlagwerke*. Graz: K.F. Stock, 1977–.

Uhlirz, Karl/Mathilde Uhlirz. *Handbuch der Geschichte Österreich-Ungarns*. Graz: Böhlau, 1963–.

Zophy, Jonathan W. *An Annotated Bibliography of the Holy Roman Empire*. Westport, Conn.: Greenwood, 1986.

II. SCHOLARLY PERIODICALS

Many of the following publications have current book reviews and bibliographical sections.

Austrian History Yearbook. Minneapolis, Minn. 1965–, Annual.
Austrian Studies. London. 1990–. Annual.
Central European History. New York. 1968–. Quarterly.
Der Donauraum. Vienna. 1960–. Quarterly.
East European Quarterly. Boulder, Colo. 1967/1968–. Quarterly.
Études danubiennes. Strasbourg. 1985–. Biannual.
Historisches Jahrbuch der Stadt Linz. Linz. 1949–. Annual.
Jahrbuch des Vereins für die Geschichte der Stadt Wien. Vienna. 1939–. Annual.
Jahrbuch für die Geschichte des Protestantismus in Österreich. Vienna. 1884–. Annual.
Jahrbuch für Landeskunde von Niederösterreich. Vienna. 1929–. Annual.
Jahrbuch für österreichische Kulturgeschichte. Eisenstadt. 1973/1974–. Annual.
Mitteilungen der Gesellschaft für Salzburger Landeskunde. Salzburg. 1861. Irregular.
Mitteilungen des Instituts für österreichische Geschichtsforschung. Vienna. 1880–. Annual.
Mitteilungen des oberösterreichischen Landesarchivs. Linz. 1950–. Irregular.
Mitteilungen des österreichischen Staatsarchivs. Horn. 1948–. Annual.
Modern Austrian Literature. Binghamton, N.Y. 1968–. Annual.
Oberösterreichische Heimatblätter. Linz. 1947–. Biannual.
Österreich in Geschichte und Literatur. Vienna. 1957–. Bimonthly.
Österreichische Zeitschrift für Geschichtswissenschaften. Vienna. 1990–. Quarterly.
Österreichische Zeitschrift für Kunst und Denkmalpflege. Vienna. 1947–, Quarterly.
Österreichische Zeitschrift für Politikwissenschaft. Vienna. 1971–. Quarterly.
Österreichische Zeitschrift für Volkskunde. Vienna. 1895–. Quarterly.
Südtirol in Wort und Bild. Innsbruck. 1957–. Quarterly.
Tiroler Heimat. Innsbruck. 1936–. Annual.
Tiroler Heimatblätter. Innsbruck. 1923–. Quarterly.
Unsere Heimat. Zeitschrift für Landeskunde von Niederösterreich. Vienna. 1929–. Quarterly.
Wiener Geschichtsblätter. Vienna. 1946–. Quarterly.
Wiener Jahrbuch für Kunstgeschichte. Vienna. 1921–. Annual.

Zeitschrift des historischen Vereines für Steiermark. Graz. 1850–. Annual.

III. NEWSPAPERS AND GENERAL PERIODICALS

Format. 1998–.
Die Kleine Zeitung. 1904–.
Der Kurier. 1954–.
Die Neue Kronen Zeitung. 1959–.
News. 1992–.
Österreich. 2006–.
Die Presse. 1946–.
Profil. 1970–.
Salzburger Nachrichten. 1945–.
Der Standard. 1998–.
Wiener Zeitung. 1703–.
Woman. 2001–.

IV. GENERAL STUDIES

Ableitinger, Alfred, ed. *Steiermark.* Vienna: Böhlau, 2002.
Beller, Steven. *A Concise History of Austria.* Cambridge: Cambridge University Press, 2006.
Bérenger, Jean. *A History of the Habsburg Empire, 1273–1700.* Translated by C. A. Simpson. London: Longman, 1994.
———. *A History of the Habsburg Empire, 1700–1918.* Translated by C. M. Simpson. White Plains, N.Y.: Longman, 1997.
Bruckmüller, Ernst. *The Austrian Nation.* Translated by Lowell A. Bangerter. Riverside, Calif.: Ariadne, 2003.
———. *Sozialgeschichte Österreichs.* 2nd ed. Vienna: Verlag für Geschichte und Politik, 2001.
Burmeister, Karl. *Geschichte Vorarlbergs.* Vienna: Verlag für Geschichte und Politik, 1998.
Csendes, Peter. *Geschichte Wiens.* Vienna: Verlag für Geschichte und Politik, 1981.
Czeike, Felix. *Geschichte der Stadt Wien.* Vienna: Molden, 1981.
Davies, Norman. *God's Playground: A History of Poland.* 2 vols. New York: Columbia University Press, 1982.

Ernst, August. *Geschichte des Burgenlandes.* Vienna: Verlag für Geschichte und Politik, 1987.
Fichtner, Paula Sutter. *The Habsburg Empire: From Dynasticism to Multinationalism.* Malabar, Fla.: Krieger, 1997.
——. *The Habsburg Empire, 1490–1848. Attributes of Empire.* Houndsmills, UK: Palgrave, 2004.
Fräss-Ehrenfeld, Claudia. *Geschichte Kärntens.* Klagenfurt: Heyn, 1984–. 3 vols. to date.
Gutkas, Karl. *Geschichte Niederösterreichs.* Vienna: Verlag für Geschichte und Politik, 1983.
Haider, Siegfried. *Geschichte Oberösterreichs.* Vienna: Verlag für Geschichte und Politik, 1987.
Jászi, Oscar. *The Dissolution of the Habsburg Monarchy.* Chicago: University of Chicago Press, 1929.
Jelavich, Barbara. *Modern Austria: Empire and Republic 1815–1986.* Cambridge: Cambridge University Press, 1987.
Kann, Robert A. *The Habsburg Empire: A Study in Integration and Disintegration.* New York: Praeger, 1957.
——. *A History of the Habsburg Empire 1526–1918.* Berkeley: University of California Press, 1974.
Macartney, C. A. *The Habsburg Empire, 1790–1918.* London: Weidenfeld and Nicolson, 1969.
Osterreichische Geschichte. Ed. Herwig Wolfram. 10 vols. Vienna: Uebereuter, 1995–2004. Individual volumes are listed by title in appropriate chronological subdivisions of this bibliography.
Riedmann, Josef. *Geschichte Tirols.* Vienna: Verlag für Geschichte und Politik, 2001.
Sayer, Derek. *The Coasts of Bohemia: A Czech History.* Translated by Alina. Sayer. Princeton, N.J.: Princeton University Press, 1998.
Sked, Alan. *The Decline and Fall of the Habsburg Empire, 1815–1918.* 2nd ed. Harlow, UK: Pearson, 2001.
Stadler, Karl. *Austria.* New York: Praeger, 1971.
Sugar, Peter F., and Peter Hanak, eds. *A History of Hungary.* Bloomington: Indiana University Press, 1990.
Taylor, A. J. P. *The Habsburg Monarchy 1809–1918: A History of the Austrian Empire and Austria–Hungary.* Reprint of 2nd rev. ed. Chicago: University of Chicago Press, 1976.
Teich, M. *Bohemia in History.* Cambridge: Cambridge University Press, 1998.

Wandruszka, Adam. *The House of Habsburg.* Garden City, N.Y.: Doubleday Anchor, 1965.
Wandruszka, Adam, and Peter Urbanitsch, eds. *Die Habsburger Monarchie 1848–1918.* Vienna: Österreichische Akademie der Wissenschaften, 1973– . 7 vols. to date.
Wandycz, Piotr S. *The Lands of Partitioned Poland, 1795–1918.* Seattle: University of Washington Press, 1974.
Widder, Roland, ed. *Burgenland.* Vienna: Böhlau, 2000.
Zaisberger, Friederike. *Geschichte Salzburgs.* Vienna: Verlag für Geschichte und Politik, 1998.
Zöllner, Erich. *Geschichte Österreichs: Von den Anfängen bis zur Gegenwart.* 7th ed. Vienna: Verlag für Geschichte und Politik, 1984.

V. THE HISTORY OF AUSTRIA FROM ANTIQUITY TO 1273

1. General

Alföldy, Géza. *Noricum.* Translated by Anthony Birley. London: Routledge & Kegan Paul, 1974.
Bowlus, Charles R. *Franks, Moravians, and Magyars: The Struggle for the Middle Danube.* Philadelphia: University of Pennsylvania Press, 1995.
Brunner, Karl. *Herzogtümer und Marken: Von Ungarnsturm bis ins 12. Jahrhundert.* Vienna: Ueberreuter, 1994.
Brunner, Otto. *Land and Lordship: Structure of Governance in Medieval Austria.* Translated by Howard Kaminsky and James Van Horn Melton. Philadelphia: University of Pennsylvania Press, 1992.
Dopsch, Heinz, Karl Brunner, and Maximilian Weltin. *Die Länder und das Reich: Der Ostalpenraum im Hochmittelalter.* Vienna: Ueberreuter, 1999.
Leeper, Alexander W. A. *A History of Medieval Austria.* New York: AMS, 1978. Reprint.
Lhotsky, Alphons. *Europäisches Mittelalter: Das Land Österreich.* Vol. 1, *Aufsätze und Vorträge,* edited by Hans Wagner and Heinrich Koller. 5 vols. Vienna: Verlag für Geschichte und Politik, 1970.
Urban, Otto. *Der Lange Weg zur Geschichte: Die Urgeschichte Österreichs.* Vienna: Ueberreuter, 2000.
Wolfram, Herwig. *Grenzen und Räume. Geschichte Österreichs vor seiner Entstehung.* Vienna: Ueberreuter, 1995.

Zibermayr, Ignaz. *Noricum Baiern und Österreich.* Horn, Austria: Berger, 1956.

2. Cultural

Lengyel, A., and G. T. B. Radan, eds. *The Archaeology of Roman Pannonia.* Lexington: University of Kentucky Press, 1980.
Wagner-Rieger, Renate. *Mittelalterliche Architektur in Österreich.* Edited by Artur Rosenauer. St. Pölten: Niederösterreichisches Pressehaus, 1988.
Zeman, Herbert, ed. *Die osterreichische Literatur: Ihr Profil von den Anfängen im Mittelalter bis ins 18. Jahrhundert (1050–1750).* Graz: Akademische Druck-und Verlagsanstalt, 1986.

3. Legal and Political

Fichtenau, Heinrich. *Von der Mark bis zum Herzogtum: Grundlagen und Sinn des "Privilegium Minus" für Österreich.* Vienna: Verlag für Geschichte und Politik, 1958.
Hageneder, Othmar. *Die geistliche Gerichtsbarket in Ober- und Niederösterreich: Von den Anfängen bis zum Beginn des 15. Jahrhunderts.* Graz: Böhlau, 1967.

4. Social and Economic

Herrschaftsstruktur und Ständebildung: Beiträge zur Typologie der österreichischen Länder aus ihren mittelalterlichen Grundlagen. 3 vols. Vienna: Verlag für Geschichte und Politik, 1971–1973.

VI. THE HISTORY OF AUSTRIA FROM 1273 TO 1519

General

Hern, Gerhard. *Der Aufsteig des Hauses Habsburg.* 2nd ed. Düsseldorf: ECON, 1988.
Hödl, Günter. *Habsburg und Österreich 1273–1493: Gestalten und Gestalt des österreichischen Spätmittelalters.* Vienna: Böhlau, 1988.

Macartney, C. A. *The House of Austria.* Edinburgh: Edinburgh University Press, 1978.
Niederstätter, Alois. *Die Herrschaft Österreich: Fürst und Land im Spätmittelalter.* Vienna: Ueberreuter, 2001.
———. *Das Jahrhundert der Mitte: An der Wende vom Mittelalter zur Neuzeit.* Vienna:Ueberreuter, 1996.

Cultural

Cuyler, Louise. *The Emperor Maximilian I and Music.* New York: Oxford University Press, 1973.
Feuchtmüller, Rupert. *Kunst in Österreich: Vom frühen Mittelalter bis zum Gegenwart.* Vol 1. Vienna: Forum Verlag, 1972.
Feuchtmüller, Rupert, ed. *Renaissance in Österreich: Geschichte, Wissenschaft, Kunst.* Vienna: Berger, 1974.
Shank, Michael H. *Unless You Believe, You Shall Not Understand: Logic, University and Society in Late Medieval Vienna.* Princeton, N.J.: Princeton University Press, 1988.
Spitz, Lewis W. *Conrad Celtis the German Arch-Humanist.* Cambridge, Mass.: Harvard University Press, 1957.
———. *The Religious Renaissance of the German Humanists.* Cambridge, Mass.: Harvard University Press, 1963.
Tanner, Marie. *The Last Descendant of Aeneas: The Habsburgs and the Mythic Image of the Emperor.* New Haven, Conn.: Yale University Press, 1993.

Political

Baum, Wilhelm. *Sigmund der Münzreiche: Zur Geschichte Tirols und der habsburgischen Länder im Spätmittelalter.* Bolzano: Athesia, 1987.
Benecke, Gerhard. *Maximilian I, 1459–1519: An Analytical Biography.* London: Routledge & Kegan Paul, 1982.
Brady, Thomas A. *Turning Swiss: Cities and Empire, 1450–1550.* Cambridge: Cambridge University Press, 1985.
Forcher, Michael. *Um Freiheit und Gerechtigkeit: Michael Gaismair. Leben und Program des Tiroler Bauernführers und Sozialrevolutionärs (1490–1532).* Innsbruck: Haymon, 1986.
Franzl, Johann. *Rudolf I: Der erste Habsburger auf dem deutschen Thron.* Graz: Styria, 1986.

Klaasen, Walter. *Michael Gaismair, Revolutionary and Reformer.* Leiden: E.J. Brill, 1978.
Rill, Bernd. *Friedrich III: Habsburgs Europäischer Durchbruch.* Graz: Styria, 1987.
Wiesflecker, Hermann. *Kaiser Maximilian I: Das Reich, Österreich und Europa an der Wende zur Neuzeit.* 5 vols. Munich: Oldenbourg, 1971–1986.

Social/Economic

Eidelberg, Schlomo. *Jewish Life in Austria in the XVth Century as Reflected in the Legal Writings of Rabbi Israel Isserlein and His Contemporaries.* Philadelphia, Pa.: Dropsie College for Hebrew and Cognate Learning, 1962.
Hsia, R. Po-chia. *Trent 1475: Stories of a Ritual Murder Trial.* New Haven, Conn.: Yale University Press, 1992.

VII. THE HISTORY OF AUSTRIA FROM 1519 TO 1789

General

Evans, R. J. W. *The Making of the Habsburg Monarchy, 1550–1700.* Oxford: Oxford University Press, 1979.
Ingrao, Charles. *The Habsburg Monarchy 1618–1815.* 2nd ed. Cambridge: Cambridge University Press, 2000.
———, ed. *State and Society in Early Modern Austria.* West Lafayette, Ind.: Purdue University Press, 1994.
Koenigsberger, Helmut G. *The Habsburgs and Europe, 1516–1660.* Ithaca, N.Y.: Cornell University Press, 1971.
Vocelka, Karl. *Glanz und Untergang der Höfischen Welt: Repräsentation, Reform und Reaktion im Habsburgischen Vielvölkerstaat.* Vienna: Ueberreuter, 2001.
Wangerman, Ernst. *The Austrian Achievement, 1700–1800.* New York: Harcourt, Brace, Jovanovich, 1973.
Winkelbauer, Thomas. *Ständefreiheit und Fürstenmacht.* 2 parts. Vienna: Ueberreuter, 2004.

Cultural

Braunbehrens, Volkmar. *Mozart in Vienna, 1781–1791.* Translated by Timothy Bell. New York: Grove Weidenfeld, 1990.

Brewer, Charles. *The Fantastic Style: Instrumental Music in the Habsburg Lands during the Later Seventeenth Century.* Aldershot, UK: Ashgate, 2002.

Brown, Bruce Alan. *Gluck and the French Theatre in Vienna.* Oxford: Clarendon Press, 1991.

Coreth, Anna. *Pietas Austriaca.* Translated by William D. Bowman and Anna Maria Leitgeb. West Lafayette, Ind.: Purdue University Press, 2004.

Duindam, Jeroen. *Vienna and Versailles: The Courts of Europe's Dynastic Rivals, 1550–1780.* Cambridge: Cambridge University Press, 2003.

Evans, R. J. W. *Rudolph II and His World: A Study in Intellectual History 1576–1612.* Oxford: Clarendon Press, 1973.

Garberson, Eric. *Eighteenth-Century Monastic Libraries in Southern Germany and Austria: Architecture and Decorations.* Baden-Baden: Koerner, 1998.

Gay, Peter. *Mozart.* New York: Viking, 1999.

Geiringer, Karl, and Irene Geiringer. *Haydn: A Creative Life in Music.* 3rd ed. Berkeley: University of California Press, 1982.

Gutman, Robert. *Mozart: A Cultural Biography.* New York: Harcourt Brace, 1999.

Hildesheimer, Wolfgang. *Mozart.* Translated by Marion Faber. New York: Farrar, Straus & Giroux, 1982.

Kann, Robert A. *A Study in Austrian Intellectual History: From Late Baroque to Romanticism.* New York: Praeger, 1960.

Kaufmann, Thomas daCosta. *The Eloquent Artist: Essays on Art, Art Theory and Architecture, Sixteenth to Nineteenth Centuries.* London: Pindar, 2004.

———. *The Mastery of Nature.* Princeton, N.J.: Princeton University Press, 1993.

———. *Painterly Enlightenment: The Art of Franz Anton Maulbertsch, 1724–1796.* Chapel Hill: University of North Carolina Press, 2005.

———. *The School of Prague: Painting at the Court of Rudolf II.* Chicago: University of Chicago Press, 1988.

———. *Variations on the Imperial Theme: Studies in Ceremonial, Art and Collecting in the Age of Maximilian II and Rudolph II*. New York: Garland, 1978.

Landon, H. C. Robbins. *Mozart and Vienna*. New York: Schirmer Books, 1991.

Landon, H. C. Robbins., and David Wyn Jones. *Haydn: His Life and Music*. Bloomington: Indiana University Press, 1988.

Larsen, Jens Peter. *The New Grove Haydn*. New York: Norton, 1983.

Louthan, Howard. *The Quest for Compromise: Peacemakers in Counter-Reformation Vienna*. Cambridge: Cambridge University Press, 1997.

MacHardy, Karin J. *War, Religion and Court Patronage: The Social and Cultural Dimensions of Political Interaction, 1521–1622*. Houndsmills, UK: Palgrave, 2003.

MacIntyre, Bruce C. *The Viennese Concerted Mass of the Early Classic Period*. Ann Arbor: University of Michigan Research Press, 1986.

Melton, James Van Horn. *Absolutism and the Eighteenth-century Origins of Compulsory Schooling in Prussia and Austria*. Cambridge: Cambridge University Press, 1988.

Morrow, Mary Sue. *Concert Life in Haydn's Vienna: Aspects of a Developing Musical and Social Institution*. Stuyvesant, N.Y.: Pendragon Press, 1989.

O'Brien, Charles H. *Ideas of Religious Toleration of Joseph II: A Study of the Enlightenment and Catholics in Austria*. Philadelphia, Pa.: American Philosophical Society, 1969.

Packull, Werner O. *Mysticism and the Early South German–Austrian Anabaptist Movement. 1525–1531*. Studies in Anabaptist History, 19. Scottsdale, Pa.: Herald Press, 1977.

Pörtner, Regina. *The Counter-Reformation in Central Europe: Styria 1580–1630*. Oxford: Clarendon Press, 2001.

Rosen, Charles. *The Classical Style: Haydn, Mozart and Beethoven*. New York: Norton, 1971.

Rushton, Julian. *Mozart*. Oxford: Oxford University Press, 1999.

Sadie, Stanley. *The New Grove Mozart*. New York: Norton, 1983.

Saunders, Steven. *Cross, Sword, and Lyre: Sacred Music at the Imperial Court of Ferdinand II of Habsburg (1619–1637)*. Oxford: Clarendon, 1995.

Trevor-Roper, Hugh. *Princes and Artists: Patronage and Ideology at Four Habsburg Courts 1517–1633*. New York: Harper & Row, 1976.

Diplomatic/Military

Anderson, M. S. *The War of the Austria Succession, 1740–1748.* London/ New York: Longman, 1995.
Barker, Thomas M. *Army, Aristocracy, Monarchy: Essays on War, Society and Government in Austria 1618–1780.* New York: Columbia University Press, 1982.
———. *Double Eagle and Crescent.* Albany: State University of New York Press, 1967.
———. *Raimondo Montecuccoli and the Thirty Years' War: A Military Intellectual and His Battles.* Albany: State University of New York Press, 1975.
Browning, Reed. *The War of the Austrian Succession.* New York: St. Martin's Press, 1995.
Frey, Linda, and Marsha Frey. *A Question of Empire: Leopold I and the War of the Spanish Succession.* Boulder, Colo.: East European Monographs, 1983.
Haskins, Janina W. *Victory at Vienna: The Ottoman Siege of 1683, a Historical Essay and a Selective List of Reading Materials.* Washington, D.C.: Library of Congress, European Division, 1983.
Henderson, Nicholas. *Prince Eugene of Savoy.* New York: Praeger, 1965.
Hochedlinger, Michael. *Austria's Wars of Emergence 1683–1797.* London: Pearson, 2003.
Kaplan, Herbert H. *The First Partition of Poland.* New York: Columbia University Press, 1962.
Roider, Karl. *Austria's Eastern Question, 1700–1790.* Princeton, N.J.: Princeton University Press, 1982.
Rothenberg, Gunther E. *The Austrian Military Border in Croatia, 1522–1747.* Illinois Studies in the Social Sciences, 48. Urbana: University of Illinois Press, 1960.
Stoye, John. *The Siege of Vienna.* London: Collins, 1964.

Political

Asch, Ronald G., and Adolf M. Birke, eds. *Princes, Patronage, and the Nobility: The Court at the Beginning of the Early Modern Era, c. 1450–1560.* London: Oxford, 1991.
Banac, Ivo, and Frank E. Sysyn, eds. *Concepts of Nationhood in Early Modern Eastern Europe.* Cambridge, Mass.: Harvard Ukrainian Studies, 1986.

Beales, Derek. *Joseph II.* 2 vols. Cambridge: Cambridge University Press, 1987–.
Bernard, Paul. *From the Enlightenment to the Police State: The Public Life of Johann Anton Pergen.* Urbana: University of Illinois Press, 1991.
———. *Jesuits and Jacobins: Enlightenment and Enlightened Despotism in Austria.* Urbana: University of Illinois Press, 1971.
———. *The Limits of Enlightenment: Joseph II and the Law.* Urbana: University of Illinois Press, 1979.
Bireley, Robert S. J. *Religion and Politics in the Age of the Counterreformation: Emperor Ferdinand II, William Lamormaini, S.J. and the Formation of Imperial Policy.* Chapel Hill: University of North Carolina Press, 1981.
Blanning, T. C. W. *Joseph II.* London: Longman, 1994.
Davis, Walter W. *Joseph II: An Imperial Reformer for the Austrian Netherlands.* The Hague: Martinus Nijhoff, 1974.
Dickson, Peter G. *Finance and Government under Maria Theresia, 1740–1780.* 2 vols. Oxford: Oxford University Press, 1987.
Dillon, Kenneth J. *King and Estates in the Bohemian Lands, 1526–1564.* Studies Presented to the International Commission for the History of Representative and Parliamentary Institutions, 57. Brussels: Les Éditions de la Librairie Encyclopédique, 1976.
Evans, R. J. W., and T. V. Thomas, eds. *Crown, Church, and Estates: Central European Politics in the Sixteenth and Seventeenth Centuries.* New York: St. Martin's, 1991.
Fichtner, Paula Sutter. *Emperor Maximilian II.* New Haven, Conn.: Yale University Press, 2001.
———. *Ferdinand I of Austria: The Politics of Dynasticism in the Age of the Reformation.* Boulder, Colo.: East European Monographs, 1982.
Hughes, Michael. *Law and Politics in Eighteenth Century Germany: The Imperial Aulic Council in the Reign of Charles VI.* Royal Historical Society Studies in History, 55. Wolfboro, N.H.: Boydell and Brewer, 1988.
Ingrao, Charles. *In Quest and Crisis: Emperor Joseph I and the Habsburg Monarchy.* West Lafayette, Ind.: Purdue University Press, 1979.
Karafiol, Emile. *Unenlightened Absolutism and Reform: Maria Theresa and the Reform of the Lower Austrian Government, 1740–1764.* Philadelphia, Pa.: American Philosophical Society, 1970.
Király, Belá K. *Hungary in the Late Eighteenth Century: The Decline of Enlightened Despotism.* New York: Columbia University Press, 1969.

Levy, Miriam J. *Governance and Grievance: Habsburg Policy and Italian Tyrol in the Eighteenth Century*. West Lafayette, Ind.: Purdue University Press, 1988.

Mat'a, Petr, and Thomas Winkelbauer, eds. *Die Habsburger Monarchie 1620 bis 1740, Leistungen und Grenzen des Absolutismusparadigmas*. Stuttgart: Franz Steiner, 2006.

McGill, William J., Jr. *Maria Theresa*. New York: Twayne, 1972.

McKay, Derek. *Prince Eugene of Savoy*. London: Thames and Hudson, 1977.

Perjés, Géza. *The Fall of the Medieval Kingdom of Hungary*. Translated by Mario D. Fenyo. Boulder, Colo.: Social Science Monographs, 1989.

Polasky, Janet L. *Revolution in Brussels 1787–1793*. Brussels: Académie royale de Belgique: 1987.

Spielman, John. *Leopold I of Austria*. London: Thames and Hudson, 1977.

Strakosch, Henry E. *State Absolutism and the Rule of Law: The Struggle for the Codification of Civil Law in Austria, 1753–1811*. Sydney: University of Sydney Press, 1967.

Subtelny, Orest. *Domination of Eastern Europe: Native Nobilities and Foreign Absolutism*. Montreal: McGill-Queens University Press, 1986.

Szabo, Franz A. J. *Kaunitz and Enlightened Absolutism 1753–1780*. Cambridge: Cambridge University Press, 1994.

Walker, Mack. *The Salzburg Transaction: Expulsion and Redemption in Eighteenth-Century Germany*. Ithaca, N.Y.: Cornell University Press, 1992.

Zacek, Joseph. *The Enlightenment and the National Revivals in Eastern Europe*. Special Issue of *Canadian Review of Studies in Nationalism* 10, no.1. Charlottetown: University of Prince Edward Island, 1983.

Social/Economic

Freudenberger, Hermann. *Lost Momentum: Austrian Economic Development, 1750s–1830s*. Vienna: Böhlau, 2003.

——. *The Waldstein Woolen Mill: Noble Entrepreneurship in Eighteenth-Century Bohemia*. Kress Library of Business and Economics, 18. Boston: Baker Library Harvard Graduate School of Business, 1963.

Komlos, John. *Nutrition and Economic Development in the Eighteenth-Century Habsburg Monarchy*. Princeton, N.J.: Princeton University Press, 1990.

Link, Edith Murr. *The Emancipation of the Austrian Peasant, 1740–1798.* New York: Columbia University Press, 1949.
Rebel, Hermann. *Peasant Classes: The Bureaucratization of Property and Family Relations under Early Habsburg Absolutism, 1511–1636.* Princeton, N.J.: Princeton University Press, 1983.
Spiel, Hilde. *Fanny von Arnstein: A Daughter of the Enlightenment.* Translated by Christine Shuttleworth. New York: Berg, 1991.
Spielman, John P. *The City and the Crown.* West Lafayette, Ind.: Purdue University Press, 1993.
Wright, William E. *Serf, Seigneur and Sovereign: Agrarian Reform in Eighteenth-Century Bohemia.* Minneapolis: University of Minnesota Press, 1966.

VIII. THE HISTORY OF AUSTRIA FROM 1789 TO 1867

1. Cultural

Agnew, Hugh L. *Origins of the Czech National Renasence.* Pittsburgh, Pa.: University of Pittsburgh Press, 1993.
Basa, Eniko. *Sándor Petofi.* Boston: Twayne, 1980.
Brown, Maurice J. F. *The New Grove Schubert.* New York: Norton, 1983.
Bunnell, Adam. *Before Infallibility: Liberal Catholicism in Biedermeier Vienna.* Rutherford, N.J.: Fairleigh Dickinson University Press, 1990.
Chase, Linda, and Karl Kung. *The World of Biedermeier.* London: Thames and Hudson, 2001.
Cherlin, Michael, Halina Filipowicz, and Richard L. Rudolph, eds. *The Great Tradition and Its Legacy: The Evolution of Dramatic and Musical Theater in Austria and Central Europe.* New York: Berghahn, 2003.
DeNora, Tia. *Beethoven and the Construction of Genius: Musical Politics in Vienna, 1792–1803.* Berkeley.: University of California Press, 1997.
Erickson, Raymond, ed. *Schubert's Vienna.* New Haven, Conn.: Yale University Press, 1997.
Hanson, Alice M. *Musical Life in Biedermeier Vienna.* Cambridge: Cambridge University Press, 1985.
Hilmar, Ernst. *Franz Schubert in His Time.* Translated by Reinhard G. Pauly. Portland, Ore.: Amadeus, 1985.
Kagan, Susan. *Archduke Rudolph, Beethoven's Patron, Pupil, and Friend: His Life and Music.* Stuyvesant, N.Y.: Pendragon Press, 1988.

Landon, H. C. Robbins. *Beethoven: His Life, Work, and World.* London: Thames and Hudson, 1993.
Lockwood, Louis. *Beethoven: The Music and the Life.* New York: Norton, 2002.
McKay, Elizabeth Norman. *Franz Schubert: A Biography.* New York: Oxford, 1996.
Nemoianu, Virgil. *The Taming of Romanticism: European Literature and the Age of Biedermeier.* Cambridge, Mass.: Harvard University Press, 1984.
Osborne, Charles. *Schubert and His Vienna.* New York: Knopf, 1985.
Prohaska, Dorothy. *Raimund and Vienna: A Critical Study of Raimund's Plays in the Viennese Setting.* Cambridge: Cambridge University Press, 1970.
Ward, Mark G., ed. *From Vormärz to Fin-de-Siècle: Essays in Nineteenth Century Austrian Literature.* Blairgowrie, Scotland: Lochee Publications, 1986.
Wilkie, Angus. *Biedermeier.* 2nd ed. New York: Abbeville, 2006.
Williams, Simon. *German Comic Actors of the Eighteenth and Nineteenth Centuries.* Westport, Conn.: Greenwood, 1985.
Yates, W. E. *Nestroy: Satire and Parody in Viennese Popular Comedy.* Cambridge: Cambridge University Press, 1972.
———. *Theatre in Vienna: A Critical History, 1776–1995.* Cambridge: Cambridge University Press, 1996.

2. Diplomatic/Military

Billinger, Robert D. *Metternich and the German Question: States' Rights and Federal Duties, 1820–1834.* Newark: University of Delaware Press, 1991.
Blumberg, Arnold. *A Carefully Planned Accident: The Italian War of 1859.* Cranbury, N.J.: Susquehanna University Press, 1990.
Kraehe, Enno. *Metternich's German Policy.* 2 vols. Princeton, N.J.: Princeton University Press, 1963–1983.
Reinerman, Alan J. *Austria and the Papacy in the Age of Metternich.* 2 vols. Washington, D.C.: Catholic University of America Press, 1990.
Rothenberg, Günther E. *Napoleon's Great Adversaries: The Archduke Charles and the Austrian Army, 1792–1814.* London.: Batsford, 1982.
Schroeder, Paul. *Austria, Great Britain and the Crimean War: The Destruction of the European Concert.* Ithaca, N.Y.: Cornell University Press, 1972.

———. *Metternich's Diplomacy at Its Zenith, 1820–1823*. Austin: University of Texas Press, 1962.
Sondhaus, Lawrence. *In the Service of the Emperor: Italians in the Austrian Armed Forces 1814–1918*. Boulder, Colo.: East European Monographs, 1990.

3. Political

Bödy, Paul. *Joseph Eötvös and the Modernization of Hungary, 1840–1870: A Study of Ideas of Individuality and Social Pluralism in Modern Politics*. Philadelphia, Pa.: American Philosophical Society, 1972.
Brauer, Kinley, and William Wright, eds. *Austria in the Age of the French Revolution*. Minneapolis, Minn.: Center for Austrian Studies, 1991.
Deme, László. *The Radical Left in the Hungarian Revolution of 1848*. Boulder, Colo.: East European Quarterly, 1976.
Eyck, F. Gunther. *Andreas Hofer and the Tyrolean Uprising of 1809*. Lanham, Md.: University Press of America, 1986.
Emerson, Donald E. *Metternich and the Political Police: Security and Subversion in the Habsburg Monarchy, 1815–1830*. The Hague: Nijhoff, 1968.
Haas, Arthur G. *Metternich: Reorganization and Nationality, 1813–1818*. Wiesbaden: Steiner, 1963.
Hitchins, Keith. *The Rumanian National Movement in Transylvania, 1780–1849*. Cambridge, Mass.: Harvard University Press, 1969.
Kimball, Stanley B. *The Austro–Slav Revival: A Study of Nineteenth-Century Literary Foundations*. Philadelphia, Pa.: American Philosophical Society, 1973.
Kozik, Jan. *The Ukrainian National Movement in Galicia: 1815–1849*. Translated by Andrew Gorsky and Lawrence Orton. Edmonton: Canadian Institute of Ukrainian Studies, 1986.
Langsam, Walter C. *Francis the Good: The Education of an Emperor, 1768–1792*. New York: Macmillan, 1949.
Magocsi, Paul Robert. *The Shaping of a National Identity: Subcarpathian Rus', 1848–1948*. Cambridge, Mass.: Harvard University Press, 1978.
Milne, Alan. *Metternich*. Totowa, N.J.: Rowman and Littlefield, 1975.
Niederhauser, Emil. *The Rise of Nationality in Eastern Europe*. Budapest: Corvina Kiado, 1981.
Orton, Lawrence. *The Prague Slav Congress of 1848*. Boulder, Colo.: East European Monographs, 1978.

Palmer, Alan. *Metternich*. London: Weidenfeld and Nicolson, 1972.
Pech, Stanley A. *The Czech Revolution of 1848*. Chapel Hill: University of North Carolina Press, 1969.
Radványi, Egon. *Metternich's Projects for Reform in Austria*. The Hague: Martinus Nijhoff, 1971.
Rath, R. John. *The Provisional Austrian Government in Lombardy–Venetia, 1813–1815*. Austin: University of Texas Press, 1969.
——. *The Viennese Revolution of 1848*. Austin: University of Texas Press, 1957.
Roider, Karl. *Baron Thugut and Austria's Response to the French Revolution*. Princeton, N.J.: Princeton University Press, 1987.
Spira, György. *A Hungarian Count in the Revolution of 1848*. Budapest: Akadémiai Kiado, 1974.
Stroup, Edsel Walter. *Hungary in Early 1848: The Constitutional Struggle against Absolutism in Contemporary Eyes*. Buffalo, N.Y.: Hungarian Cultural Foundation, 1976.

4. Social/Economic

Halleiner, Karl F. *The Imperial Loans: A Study in Financial and Diplomatic History*. Oxford: Clarendon, 1965.

IX. THE HISTORY OF AUSTRIA FROM 1867 TO 1918

1. General

Bled, Jean Paul. *Franz Joseph*. Translated by Teresa Bridgeman. Oxford: Blackwell, 1993.
Cornwall, Mark, ed. *The Last Years of Austria–Hungary: A Multi-National Experiment in Early Twentieth-century Europe*. 2nd ed. Exeter: University of Exeter Press, 2002.
——. *The Undermining of Austria–Hungary: The Battle for Hearts and Minds*. Basingstoke, UK: Palgrave, 2000.
Hanisch, Ernst. *Österreichische Geschichte 1890–1990: Der Lange Schatten des Staates. Österreichische Gesellschaftsgeschichte im 20. Jahrhundert*. Vienna: Ueberreuther, 1994.
Jelavich, Barbara. *History of the Balkans*. 2 vols. Cambridge: Cambridge University Press, 1983.

Jelavich, Barbara, and Charles Jelavich. *The Establishment of the Balkan National States*. Seattle: University of Washington Press, 1977.

Kann, Robert A. *The Multi-National Empire*. 2 vols. New York: Octagon, 1964. Reprint.

Kann, Robert A., Belá K. Király, and Paula Sutter Fichtner, eds. *The Habsburg Empire in World War I: Essays on the Intellectual Military, Political and Economic Aspects of the Habsburg War Effort*. Boulder, Colo.: East European Quarterly, 1977.

Rumpler, Helmut. *Eine Chance für Mitteleuropa: Bürgerliche Emanzipation und Staatsverfall in der Habsburger Monarchie*. Vienna: Donauland, 2005.

Sked, Alan. *The Decline and Fall of the Habsburg Empire, 1815–1918*. 2nd ed. Harlow, UK: Pearson, 2001.

2. Cultural

Alofsin, Anthony. *When Buildings Speak: Architecture as Language in the Habsburg Empire and Its Aftermath, 1867–1933*. Chicago: University of Chicago Press, 2006.

Alter, Max. *Carl Menger and the Origins of Austrian Economics*. Boulder, Colo.: Westview, 1990.

Anderson, Mark M. *Kafka's Clothes: Ornament and Aestheticism in the Habsburg Fin de Siècle*. Oxford: Clarendon Press, 1992.

Beller, Steven. *Vienna and the Jews, 1867–1938: A Cultural History*. Cambridge: Cambridge University Press, 1989.

———, ed. *Rethinking Vienna 1900*. New York: Berghahn Books, 2001.

Eve Blau, and Monica Platzer, eds. *Shaping the Great City: Modern Architecture in Central Europe, 1890–1937*. Munich: Prestel, 1999.

Borsi, Franco. *Vienna 1900: Architecture and Design*. Translated by Marie-Helene Aqueros. New York Chelsea House, 1986.

Bottomore, Tom B., and Patrick Goode. *Austro-Marxism*. Oxford: Oxford University Press, 1978.

Broch, Hermann. *Hugo von Hofmannsthal and His Time: The European Imagination, 1860–1920*. Translated by Michael Steinberg. Chicago: University of Chicago Press, 1984.

Cacciari, Massimo. *Posthumous People: Vienna at the Turning Point*. Translated by Rodger Friedman. Stanford, Calif.: Stanford University Press, 1997.

Carr, Jonathan. *Mahler*. Woodstock, N.Y.: Overlook Press, 1998.

Cherlin, Michael. *Schoenberg's Musical Imagination*. Cambridge: Cambridge University Press, 2007.
Clegg, Elizabeth. *Art, Design and Architecture in Central Europe 1890–1920*. New Haven, Conn: Yale University Press, 2006.
Coen, Deborah R. *Vienna in the Age of Uncertainty: Science, Liberalism, and Private Life*. Chicago: University of Chicago Press, 2007.
Cohen, Gary B. *Education and Middle Class Society in Imperial Austria, 1848–1918*. West Lafayette, Ind.: Purdue University Press, 1996.
Crittenden, Camille. *Johann Strauss and Vienna: Operetta and the Politics of Popular Culture*. Cambridge: Cambridge University Press, 2001.
Daviau, Donald G. *Hermann Bahr*. Boston: Twayne, 1985.
———, ed. *Major Figures of Nineteenth-Century Austrian Literature*. Riverside, Calif.: Ariadne, 1998.
———, ed. *Major Figures of Turn-of-the Century Austrian Literature*. Riverside, Calif: Ariadne, 1991.
De La Grange, Henri-Louis. *Gustav Mahler: Vienna: The Years of Challenge (1897–1904)*. 2 vols. Oxford: Oxford University Press, 1973–1994.
Donn, Lucinda. *Freud and Jung: Years of Friendship, Years of Loss*. New York: Scribner, 1988. New York: Collier Books, 1990. Reissue.
Field, Frank. *The Last Days of Mankind: Karl Kraus and His Vienna*. London: Macmillan, 1967.
Francis, Mark, ed. *The Viennese Enlightenment*. New York: St. Martin's Press, 1985.
Gatt-Rutter, John. *Italo Svevo: A Double Life*. New York: Oxford University Press, 1988.
Gay, Peter. *Freud: A Life for Our Time*. New York: Norton, 1988.
———. *Freud for Historians*. New York: Oxford University Press, 1985.
———. *Freud, Jews, and Other Germans: Masters and Victims in Modernist Culture*. New York: Oxford University Press, 1978.
Grassl, Wolfgang, and Barry Smith, eds. *Austrian Economics: Historical and Philosophical Background*. New York: New York University Press, 1986.
Hacohen, Malachi Haim. *Karl Popper, the Formative Years, 1902–1945: Politics and Philosophy in Interwar Vienna*. Cambridge: Cambridge University Press, 2000.
Hanslick, Eduard. *Hanslick's Music Criticisms*. Translated and edited by Henry Pleasants. Baltimore: Penguin Books, 1963. Reissue: New York: Dover Publications, 1988.

Hayman, Ronald. *Kafka: A Biography.* New York: Oxford University Press, 1982.

Hirschmüller, Albrecht. *The Life and Work of Joseph Breuer: Physiology and Psychoanalysis.* New York: New York University Press, 1989.

Janik, Allan, and Stephen Toulmin. *Wittgenstein's Vienna.* New York: Simon & Schuster, 1973.

Johnston, William M. *The Austrian Mind: An Intellectual and Social History.* Berkeley: University of California Press, 1972.

———. *Vienna: The Golden Age, 1815–1914.* New York: Crown Publishers, 1981.

Kallir, Jane. *Viennese Design and the Wiener Werkstätte.* New York: Braziller, 1986.

Klein, Dennis B. *Jewish Origins of the Psychoanalytic Movement.* New York: Praeger, 1981.

Le Rider, Jacques. *Modernity and Crises of Identity: Culture and Society in Fin-de-Siècle Vienna.* Translated by Rosemary Morris. New York: Polity, 1993.

Lesky, Erna. *The Vienna Medical School of the 19th Century.* Translated by L. Williams and I. S. Levij. Baltimore: Johns Hopkins University Press, 1976.

Luft, David. *Eros and Inwardness in Vienna: Weininger, Musil, Doderer.* Chicago: University of Chicago Press, 2003.

McColl, Sandra. *Music Criticism in Vienna, 1896–1897.* Oxford: Clarendon, 1996.

McGrath, William. *Dionysian Art and Politics in Austria.* New Haven, Conn.: Yale UniversityPress, 1974.

———. *Freud's Discovery of Psychoanalysis: The Politics of Hysteria.* Ithaca, N.Y.: Cornell University Press, 1986.

Mitsch, Erwin. *The Art of Egon Schiele.* Translated by W. Keith Haughan. 2nd ed. New York: Hudson Hills Press, 1988.

Monk, Ray. *Ludwig Wittgenstein: The Duty of Genius.* New York: Penguin, 1990.

Monson, Karen. *Alma Mahler, Muse to Genius: From Fin-de-Siècle Vienna to Hollywood.* Boston: Houghton Mifflin, 1983.

Nyiri, J. C., ed. *Austrian Philosophy: Studies and Texts.* Munich: Philosophia Verlag, 1981.

Olin, Margaret. *Forms of Representation in Alois Riegl's Theory of Art.* University Park, Pa.: Penn State Press, 1992.

Olsen, Donald J. *The City as a Work of Art: London. Paris. Vienna.* New Haven, Conn.: Yale University Press, 1986.
Oxaal, Ivar, Michael Pollak, and Gerhard Botz, eds. *Jews, Antisemitism, and Culture in Vienna.* London: Routledge and Kegan Paul, 1987.
Powell, Nicolas. *The Sacred Spring: The Arts in Vienna, 1898–1918.* Greenwich, Conn.: New York Graphic Society, 1974.
Ritvo, Lucille B. *Darwin's Influence on Freud: A Tale of Two Sciences.* New Haven, Conn.: Yale University Press, 1990.
Salinger, Herman, and Herbert W. Reichert, eds. *Studies in Arthur Schnitzler.* Chapel Hill: University of North Carolina Press, 1963.
Smith, Kimberly A. *Between Ruin and Renewal: Egon Schiele's Landscapes.* New Haven, Conn: Yale University Press, 2004.
Schorske, Carl E. *Fin-de-siècle Vienna: Politics and Culture.* New York: Alfred Knopf, 1980.
Schweiger, Werner J. *Wiener Werkstätte: Design in Vienna, 1903–1932.* Translated by Alexander Lieven. New York: Abbeville Press, 1984.
Seckerson, Edward. *Mahler: His Life and Times.* New York: Hippocrene Books, 1983.
Segel, Harold B., ed. and trans. *The Vienna Coffeehouse Wits, 1890–1938.* West Lafayette, Ind.: Purdue University Press, 1995.
Sekler, Eduard. *Josef Hoffmann: The Architectural Work.* Princeton, N.J.: Princeton University Press, 1985.
Shedel, James. *Art and Society: The New Art Movement in Vienna, 1897–1914.* Palo Alto, Calif: SPOSS, 1981.
Smith, Joan Allen. *Schoenberg and His Circle. A Viennese Portrait.* New York: Schirmer, 1986.
Stepansky, Paul E. *In Freud's Shadow: Adler in Context.* New York: Analytic Press, 1983.
Timms, Edward. *Karl Kraus. Apocalyptic Satirist.* 2 vols. New Haven, Conn.: Yale University Press, 1986–2005.
Topp, Leslie. *Architecture and Truth in Fin-de-siècle Vienna.* Cambridge: Cambridge University Press, 2004.
Vegesack, Alexander von, et al. *Thonet: Classic Furniture in Bent Wood and Tubular Steel.* London: Hazar, 1996.
Vergo, Peter. *Art in Vienna, 1898–1918: Klimt, Kokoschka, Schiele and Their Contemporaries.* London: Phaidon Press, 1975.
Waissenberger, Robert. *Vienna Secession.* New York: Rizzoli, 1977.
———, ed. *Vienna, 1890–1920.* New York: Rizzoli, 1984.

Werkner, Patrick, ed. *Egon Schiele: Art, Sexuality, and Viennese Modernism*. Palo Alto, Calif.: SPOSS, 1994.
Whitford, Frank. *Oskar Kokoschka: A Life*. New York: Atheneum, 1986.
Yates, W. E. *Schnitzler, Hofmannsthal, and the Austrian Theatre*. New Haven, Conn.: Yale University Press, 1992.
Zanuso, Billa. *The Young Freud: The Origins of Psychoanalysis in Late Nineteenth-Century Viennese Culture*. Oxford: Basil Blackwell, 1986.

3. Diplomatic/Military

Bagdasarian, Nicholas der. *The Austro–German Rapprochement, 1870–1879: From the Battle of the Sedan to the Dual Alliance*. Cranbury, N.J.: Fairleigh Dickinson University Press, 1976.
Breuilly, John. *Austria, Prussia and Germany, 1806–1871*. Edinburgh: Pearson, 2002.
Bridge, F. R. *Great Britain and Austria–Hungary, 1906–1914*. London: Routledge and Kegan Paul, 1972.
———. *The Habsburg Monarchy among the Great Powers, 1815–1918*. Oxford: Berg Publishers, 1991.
Deák, István. *Beyond Nationalism: A Social and Political History of the Habsburg Officer Corps 1848–1918*. New York: Oxford University Press, 1990.
Decsy, János. *Prime Minister Gyula Andrássy's Influence on Habsburg Foreign Policy during the Franco–German War of 1870–1871*. Boulder, Colo.: East European Quarterly, 1978.
Dioszegi, István. *Hungarians in the Ballhausplatz: Studies in the Austro–Hungarian Common Foreign Policy*. Budapest: Corvina, 1983.
Evans, R. J. W., and Hartmut Pogge von Strandman, eds. *The Coming of the First World War*. Oxford: Clarendon, 1988.
Fest, Wilfried. *Peace or Partition: The Habsburg Monarchy and British Policy, 1914–1918*. New York: St. Martin's Press, 1978.
Godsey, William. *Aristocratic Redoubt: The Austro–Hungarian Foreign Office on the Eve of the First World War*. West Lafayette, Ind.: Purdue, 1999.
Jenks, William A. *Francis Joseph and the Italians, 1849–1859*. Charlottesville: University of Virginia Press, 1978.
Rothenberg, Gunther. *The Army of Francis Joseph*. West Lafayette, Ind.: Purdue University Press, 1972.

Silberstein, Gerard E. *The Troubled Alliance: German–Austrian Relations 1914–1917*. Lexington: University of Kentucky Press, 1970.

Sked, Alan. *The Survival of the Habsburg Empire: Radetzky, the Imperial Army, and the Class War*. London: Longman, 1979.

Sokol, Anthony. *The Imperial and Royal Austro–Hungarian Navy*. Annapolis, Md.: United States Naval Institute, 1968.

Sondhaus, Lawrence. *Franz Conrad von Hötzendorf: Architect of the Apocalypse*. Boston: Humanities Press, 2000.

——. *The Naval Policy of Austria–Hungary, 1867–1918: Navalism, Industrial Development, and the Politics of Dualism*. West Lafayette, Ind.: Purdue University Press, 1994.

Treadway, John D. *The Falcon and the Eagle: Montenegro and Austria–Hungary, 1908–1914*. West Lafayette, Ind.: Purdue University Press, 1983.

Tunstall, Graydon A., Jr. *Planning for War against Russia and Serbia: Austro–Hungarian and German Military Strategies, 1871–1914*. Boulder, Colo.: Social Science Monographs, 1993.

Wawro, Geoffrey. *The Austro–Prussian War. Austria's War with Prussia and Italy in 1866*. New York: Cambridge University Press, 1996.

Weber, Frank G. *Eagles on the Crescent: Germany, Austria, and the Diplomacy of the Turkish Alliance, 1914–1918*. Ithaca, N.Y.: Cornell University Press, 1970.

Williamson, Samuel R., Jr. *Austria–Hungary and the Origins of World War I*. Houndsmills, UK: Macmillan, 1991.

4. Political

Banac, Ivo. *The National Question in Yugoslavia, Origins, History and Politics*. Ithaca, N.Y.: Cornell University Press, 1984.

Bárány, George. *Stephen Széchenyi and the Awakening of Hungarian Nationalism, 1791–1841*. Princeton, N.J.: Princeton University Press, 1968.

Beller, Stephen. *Francis Joseph*. London: Longman, 1994.

Boyer, John W. *Culture and Political Crisis in Vienna: Christian Socialism in Power, 1897–1918*. Chicago: University of Chicago Press, 1995.

——. *Political Radicalism in Late Imperial Vienna: Origins of the Christian Social Movement, 1848–1897*. Chicago: University of Chicago Press, 1981.

Bradley, John F. *Czech Nationalism in the Nineteenth Century.* Boulder, Colo.: East European Monographs, 1984.
Brock, Peter. *The Slovak National Awakening: An Essay in the Intellectual History of East Central Europe.* Toronto: University of Toronto Press, 1976.
Brook-Shepherd, Gordon. *Archduke of Sarajevo: The Romance and Tragedy of Franz Ferdinand of Austria.* Boston: Little, Brown, 1984.
Cassels, Lavender. *The Archduke and the Assassin: Sarajevo, June 28th 1914.* New York: Stein and Day, 1985.
Cohen, Gary B. *The Politics of Ethnic Survival: Germans in Prague, 1861–1914.* Princeton, N.J.: Princeton University Press, 1981.
Deák, István. *The Lawful Revolution: Louis Kossuth and the Hungarians, 1848–1849.* New York: Columbia University Press, 1979.
Despalatovic, Elinor Murray. *Ljudevit Gaj and the Illyrian Movement.* Boulder, Colo.: East European Monographs, 1975.
Donia, Robert J. *Islam under the Double Eagle: The Muslims of Bosnia and Hercegovina, 1878–1914.* Boulder, Colo.: East European Quarterly, 1981.
———. *Sarajevo: A Biography.* Ann Arbor: University of Michigan Press, 2006.
Elon, Amos. *Herzl.* London: Weidenfeld and Nicolson, 1975.
Garver, Bruce M. *The Young Czech Party 1874–1900 and the Emergence of a Multi-Party System.* New Haven, Conn.: Yale University Press, 1978.
Geehr, Richard S. *Karl Lueger: Mayor of Fin de Siècle Vienna.* Detroit, Mich.: Wayne State University Press, 1990.
Glassheim, Eagle. *Noble Nationalists: The Transformation of the Bohemian Aristocracy.* Cambridge, Mass.: Harvard University Press, 2005.
Hamann, Brigitte. *Bertha von Suttner: A Life for Peace.* Translated by Ann Dubsky. Syracuse, N.Y.: Syracuse University Press, 1996.
———. *The Reluctant Empress. A Biography of Empress Elizabeth of Austria.* Translated by Ruth Hein. New York: Knopf, 1986.
Healy, Maureen. *Vienna and the Fall of the Habsburg Monarchy: Total War and Everyday Life in World War I.* Cambridge: Cambridge University Press, 2004.
Himka, John-Paul. *Galician Villagers and the Ukrainian National Movement in the Nineteenth Century.* New York: St. Martin's Press, 1988.
———. *Socialism in Galicia: The Emergence of Polish Social Democracy and Ukrainian Radicalism, 1860–1890.* Cambridge, Mass.: Harvard University Press, 1983.

Hitchins, Keith. *Rumania 1866–1947*. Oxford: Oxford University Press, 1996.
Jenks, William A. *Austria under the Iron Ring, 1879–1893*. Charlottesville: University of Virginia Press, 1965.
———. *The Austrian Electoral Reform of 1907*. New York: Columbia University Press, 1950.
Judson, Pieter M. *Exclusive Revolutionaries: Liberal Politics, Social Experience, and National Identity in the Austrian Empire, 1848–1914*. Ann Arbor: University of Michigan Press, 1966.
———. *Guardians of the Nation: Activists on the Language Frontiers of Imperial Austria*. Cambridge, Mass: Harvard University Press, 2007.
Kelly, T. Mills. *Without Remorse: Czech National Socialism in Late Habsburg Austria*. Boulder, Colo.: East European Monographs, 2006.
King, Jeremy. *Budweisers into Czechs and Germans: Local History of Bohemian Politics 1848– 1948*. Princeton, N. J.: Princeton University Press, 2005.
Király, Belá K. *Ferenc Deák*. New York: Twayne, 1975.
Knapp, Vincent J. *Austrian Social Democracy, 1889–1914*. Washington, D.C.: University Press of America, 1980.
Mackenzie, David. *Apis, the Congenial Conspirator: The Life of Colonel Dragutin T. Dimitrijevic*. Boulder, Colo.: East European Monographs, 1989.
Malcolm, Noel. *Bosnia: A Short History*. London: Macmillan, 1994.
Markovits, Andrei S., and Frank E. Sysyn, eds. *Nationbuilding and the Politics of Nationalism: Essays on Austrian Galicia*. Cambridge, Mass.: Harvard University Press, 1982.
Markus, Georg. *Crime at Mayerling: The Life and Death of Mary Vetsera*. Translated by Carvel de Bussy. Riverside, Calif.: Ariadne, 1995.
Mason, John W. *The Dissolution of the Austro–Hungarian Empire, 1867–1918*. 2nd ed. New York: Longman, 1996.
May, Arthur. *The Passing of the Habsburg Monarchy, 1914–1918*. 2 vols. Philadelphia: University of Pennsylvania Press, 1966.
McCagg, William. *A History of the Habsburg Jews, 1670–1918*. Bloomington: Indiana University Press, 1989.
Okey, Robin. *Taming Balkan Nationalism: The Habsburg "Civilizing Mission" in Bosnia 1878– 1914*. Oxford: Oxford University Press, 2007.
Palmer, Alan W. *Twilight of the Habsburgs: The Life and Times of Emperor Francis Joseph*. London: Weidenfeld and Nicolson, 1995.
Pawel, Ernst. *The Labyrinth of Exile: A Life of Theodor Herzl*. New York: Farrar, Straus & Giroux, 1989.

Pulzer, Peter. *The Rise of Political Anti-Semitism in Germany and Austria.* Rev. ed. London: Halban, 1988.

Redlich, Joseph. *The Emperor Francis Joseph of Austria.* Hamden, Conn.: Archon, 1969. Reprint.

Rees, H. Louis. *The Czechs during World War I: The Path to Independence.* Boulder, Colo.: East European Monographs, 1992.

Robertson, Ritchie, and Edward Timms, eds. *The Habsburg Legacy: National Identity in Historical Perspective.* Edinburgh: Edinburgh Press, 1994.

Rogel, Carole. *The Slovenes and Yugoslavism, 1890–1914.* Boulder, Colo.: East European Quarterly, 1977.

Salvendy, John T. *Royal Rebel: A Psychological Portrait of Crown Prince Rudolf of Austria–Hungary.* Lanham, Md.: University Press of America, 1988.

Seton-Watson, Hugh, and Christopher Seton-Watson. *The Making of a New Europe: R.W. Seton Watson and the Last Years of Austria–Hungary.* Seattle: University of Washington Press, 1981.

Stokes, Gale. *Politics as Development: The Emergence of Political Parties in Nineteenth-Century Serbia.* Durham, N.C.: Duke University Press, 1990.

Szporluk, Roman. *The Political Thought of Thomas G. Masaryk.* Boulder, Colo.: East European Quarterly, 1981.

Unowsky, Daniel L. *The Pomp and Politics of Patriotism: Imperial Celebrations in Habsburg Austria 1848–1916.* West Lafayette, Ind.: Purdue University Press, 2005.

Vermes, Gabor. *István Tisza: The Liberal Vision and Conservative Statecraft of a Magyar Nationalist.* Boulder, Colo.: East European Monographs, 1985.

Whiteside, Andrew G. *Austrian National Socialism before 1918.* The Hague: Nijhoff, 1962.

———. *The Socialism of Fools: Georg Ritter von Schönerer and Austrian Pan-Germanism.* Berkeley: University of California Press, 1975.

Winters, Stanley B., Robert B. Pynsent, and Harry Hanak. *T.G. Masaryk.* 3 vols. New York: St. Martin's Press, 1989–1990.

Zaçek, Joseph Frederick. *Palacky: The Historian as Scholar and Nationalist.* The Hague: Mouton, 1970.

Zeman, Z. A. B. *The Break-Up of the Habsburg Empire, 1914–1918.* London: Oxford University Press, 1961.

5. Social/Economic

Anderson, Harriet. *Utopian Feminism: Women's Movements in Fin-de-Siècle Vienna.* New Haven, Conn.: Yale University Press, 1992.

Blum, Mark. *The Austro-Marxists 1890–1918: A Psychological Study.* Lexington: University of Kentucky Press, 1985.

Bottomore, Tom B., and Patrick Goode. *Austro-Marxism.* Oxford: Oxford University Press, 1978.

Bukey, Evan. *Hitler's Hometown: Linz, Austria, 1908–1945.* Bloomington: Indiana University Press, 1986.

Cohen, Gary B. *Education and Middle Class Society in Imperial Austria, 1848–1918.* West Lafayette, Ind.: Purdue University Press, 1995.

Frank, Alison. *Oil Empire. Visions of Prosperity in Austrian Galicia.* Cambridge, Mass.: Harvard University Press, 2005.

Gerschenkron, Alexander. *An Economic Spurt That Failed.* Princeton, N.J.: Princeton University Press, 1977.

Good, David. *The Economic Rise of the Habsburg Empire, 1750–1914.* Berkeley: University of California Press, 1984.

Good, David, Margarete Grandner, and Mary Jo Maynes, eds. *Austrian Women in the Nineteenth and Twentieth Centuries: Cross-disciplinary Perspectives.* New York: Berghahn, 1996.

Hamann, Brigitte. *Hitler's Vienna: A Dictator's Apprenticeship.* New York: Oxford, 1999.

Helleiner, Karl F. *Free Trade and Frustration: Anglo–Austrian Negotiations 1860–1870.* Toronto: University of Toronto Press, 1973.

Jenks, William. *Vienna and the Young Hitler.* New York: Columbia University Press, 1960.

Komlos, John. *The Habsburg Monarchy as a Customs Union: Economic Development in Austria– Hungary in the Nineteenth Century.* Princeton, N.J.: Princeton University Press, 1983.

———, ed. *Economic Development in the Habsburg Monarchy in the Nineteenth Century.* Boulder, Colo.: East European Monographs, 1983.

Kornberg, Jacques. *Theodor Herzl: From Assimilation to Zionism.* Bloomington: Indiana University Press, 1993.

Pauley, Bruce. *From Prejudice to Persecution: A History of Austrian Anti-Semitism.* Chapel Hill: University of North Carolina Press, 1992.

Rotenberg, Robert. *Landscape and Power in Vienna.* Baltimore: Johns Hopkins University Press, 1995.

Rozenblit, Marsha. *The Jews of Vienna, 1867–1914: Assimilation and Identity.* Albany.: State University of New York Press, 1983.

Rudolph, Richard L. *Banking and Industrialization in Austria–Hungary: The Role of Banks in the Industrialization of the Czech Crownlands, 1873–1914.* Cambridge: Cambridge University Press, 1976.

Sugar, Peter F. *Industrialization of Bosnia–Hercegovina, 1878–1918.* Seattle: University of Washington Press, 1963.

Vyleta, Daniel. *Crime, Jews and News: Vienna 1895–1914.* New York: Berghahn, 2007.

Wegs, J. Robert. *Growing Up Working Class: Continuity and Change among Viennese Youth, 1890–1938.* University Park: Pennsylvania State University Press, 1989.

Wistrich, Robert S. *The Jews of Vienna in the Age of Franz Joseph.* New York: Oxford University Press, 1989.

———, ed. *Austrians and Jews in the Twentieth Century: From Franz Joseph to Waldheim.* New York: St. Martin's Press, 1992.

X. THE HISTORY OF AUSTRIA FROM 1918 TO 1945

1. General

Bruckmüller, Ernst. *The Austrian Nation.* Translated by Lowell A. Bangerter. Riverside, Calif.: Ariadne, 2003.

Carsten, Francis L. *The First Austrian Republic 1918–1938.* Aldershot, UK: Gower, 1986.

Gulick, Charles A. *Austria: From Habsburg to Hitler.* 2 vols. Berkeley: University of California Press, 1981. Reprint.

Stadler, Karl R. *The Birth of the Austrian Republic.* Leyden: A.W. Sijthoff, 1966.

Weinzierl, Erica, and Kurt Skalnik, eds. *Österreich 1918–1938: Geschichte der Ersten Republik.* 2 vols. Graz: Styria, 1983.

2. Cultural

Baker, Gordon. *Wittgenstein, Frege and the Vienna Circle.* Oxford: Blackwell, 1988.

Dassanowsky, Robert von. *Austrian Cinema: A History.* Jefferson, N.C.: McFarland, 2004.

Daviau, Donald, ed. *Austrian Writers and the Anschluss: Understanding the Past—Overcoming the Past*. Riverside, Calif: Ariadne, 1991.
Kohl, Katrin, and Ritchie Robertson, eds. *A History of Austrian Literature 1918–2000*. Rochester, N.Y.: Camden House, 2006.
Luft, David S. *Eros and Inwardness in Vienna: Weininger, Musil, Doderer*. Chicago: University of Chicago Press, 2003.
———. *Robert Musil and the Crisis of European Culture, 1880–1942*. Berkeley: University of California Press, 1980.
Papanek, Ernst. *The Austrian School Reform: Its Bases, Principles and Development—The Twenty Years between the World Wars*. New York: Frederick Fell, 1962.
Perle, George. *The Operas of Alban Berg*. 2 vols. Berkeley: University of California Press, 1980–1985.
Pyrah, Robert. *The Burgtheater and Austrian Identity: Theater and Cultural Politics in Vienna, 1918–1938*. London: Legenda, 2007.
Runngaldier, Edmund. *Carnap's Early Conventionalism: An Inquiry into the Historical Background of the Vienna Circle*. Amsterdam: Rodpoi, 1984.
Segar, Kenneth, and John Warren, eds. *Austria in the Thirties: Culture and Politics*. Riverside, Calif: Ariadne, 1991.
Steinberg, Michael. *The Meaning of the Salzburg Festival: Austria as Theater and Ideology 1890– 1938*. Ithaca, N.Y.: Cornell University Press, 1990.
Textor, Mark., ed. *The Austrian Contribution to Analytic Philosophy*. London: Routledge, 2006.
Williams, C. E. *The Broken Eagle: The Politics of Austrian Literature from Empire to Anschluss*. New York: Barnes & Noble, 1974.
Zeps, Michael. *Education and the Crisis of the First Republic*. Boulder, Colo: East European Monographs, 1987.

3. Diplomatic/Military

Dixon, Joe C. *Defeat and Disarmament: Allied Diplomacy and the Politics of Military Affairs in Austria, 1918–1922*. Newark: University of Delaware Press, 1986.
Eisterer, Klaus, and Günter Bischof, eds. *Austria and Latin America in the 19th and 20th Centuries*. Innsbruck: Studien Verlag, 2006.
Gehl, Jürgen. *Austria, Germany, and the Anschluss, 1931–1938*. London: Oxford University Press, 1963.

Katzenstein, Peter. *Disjoined Partners: Austria and Germany since 1815.* Berkeley: University of California Press, 1976.
Keyserlingk, Robert H. *Austria in World War II: An Anglo–American Dilemma.* Kingston, ON: Queens University Press, 1988.
Low, Alfred D. *The Anschluss Movement, 1918–1919, and the Paris Peace Conference.* Philadelphia, Pa.: American Philosophical Society, 1974.
Luza, Radomir. *Austro–German Relations in the Anschluss Era.* Princeton, N.J.: Princeton University Press, 1975.
Rusinow, Dennison I. *Italy's Austrian Heritage, 1919–1946.* Oxford: Oxford University Press, 1969.
Sully, Melanie A. *Continuity and Change in Austrian Socialism: The Eternal Quest for the Third Way.* Boulder, Colo: East European Monographs, 1982.
Suval, Stanley. *The Anschluss Question in the Weimar Era: A Study of Nationalism in Germany and Austria, 1918–1932.* Baltimore: Johns Hopkins University Press, 1974.

4. Political

Black, Peter. *Ernst Kaltenbrunner: Ideological Soldier of the Third Reich.* Princeton, N.J: Princeton University Press, 1984.
Brook-Sheperd, Gordon. *Dollfuss.* London: Macmillan, 1961.
Carsten, F. L. *Fascist Movements in Austria from Schönerer to Hitler.* London: Sage, 1977.
Diamant, Alfred. *Austrian Catholics and the First Republic, 1918–1934.* Princeton, N.J.: Princeton University Press, 1960.
Edmondson, C. Earl. *The Heimwehr and Austrian Politics, 1918–1936.* Athens: University of Georgia Press, 1978.
Friedenreich, Harriet Pass. *Jewish Politics in Vienna, 1918–1938.* Bloomington: Indiana University Press, 1991.
Ganglmair, Siegwald. *Resistance and Persecution in Austria, 1938–1945.* Vienna: Federal Press Service, 1988.
Goldner, Franz. *Die österreichische Emigration 1938–1945.* Vienna: Herold, 1945.
Jeffery, Charlie. *Social Democracy in the Austrian Provinces: Beyond Red Vienna.* New York: St. Martin's Press, 1995.
Kindermann, Gottfried-Karl. *Hitler's Defeat in Austria, 1933–1934: Europe's First Containment of Nazi Expansionism.* Translated by Sonia Brough and David Tayler. Boulder, Colo.: Westview, 1988.

Kitchen, Martin. *The Coming of Austrian Fascism*. Toronto: McGill University Press, 1980.
Klemperer, Klemens von. *Ignaz Seipel: Christian Statesman in a Time of Crisis*. Princeton, N.J.: Princeton University Press, 1972.
Lewis, Jill. *Fascism and the Working Class in Austria, 1918–1934: The Failure of Labour in the First Republic*. New York: Berg, 1991.
Luza, Radomir. *The Resistance in Austria, 1938–1945*. Minneapolis: University of Minnesota Press, 1984.
Maass, Walter B. *Assassination in Vienna*. New York: Scribner's, 1972.
——. *Country without a Name: Austria under Nazi Rule, 1938–1945*. New York: Ungar, 1979.
MacDonald, Mary. *The Republic of Austria, 1918–1934: A Study in the Failure of Democratic Government*. London: Oxford University Press, 1946.
Maimann, Helene. *Politik im Wartesaal: Österreichische Exilpolitik in Großbritannien 1938 bis 1945*. Vienna: Böhlau, 1975.
Molden, Fritz. *Fires in the Night: The Sacrifices and Significance of the Austrian Resistance, 1938–1945*. Translated by Harry Zohn. Boulder, Colo.: Westview, 1989.
Parkinson, Fred, ed. *Conquering the Past: Austrian Nazism Yesterday and Today*. Detroit, Mich.: Wayne State University Press, 1989.
Pauley, Bruce F. *Hitler and the Forgotten Nazis*. Chapel Hill: University of North Carolina Press, 1981.
Snyder, Timothy. *The Red Prince: The Secret Lives of a Habsburg Archduke*. New York: Basic Books, 2008.
Swanson, John. *Remnants of the Habsburg Monarchy: The Shaping of Modern Austria and Hungary, 1918–1922*. Boulder, Colo.: East European Monographs, 2001.
Valiani, Leo. *The End of Austria–Hungary*. London: Secker and Warburg, 1973.
Wagner, Dieter, and Gerhard Tomkowitz. *Anschluss: The Week That Hitler Seized Vienna*. Translated by Geoffrey Strachan. New York: St. Martin's Press, 1971.

5. Social/Economic

Gruber, Helmut. *Red Vienna: Experiment in Working Class Culture 1919–1934*. Oxford: Oxford University Press, 1991.

Kirk, Tim. *Nazism and the Working Class in Austria: Industrial Unrest and Political Dissent in the "National Community"*. Cambridge: Cambridge University Press, 1996.

März, Eduard. *Austrian Banking and Financial Policy: Creditanstalt at a Turning Point, 1912–1923*. Translated by Charles Kessler. New York: St. Martin's Press, 1985.

Rabinbach, Anson. *The Crisis of Austrian Socialism. From Red Vienna to Civil War 1927–1934*. Chicago: University of Chicago Press, 1983.

———, ed. *The Austrian Socialist Experiment*. Boulder, Colo.: Westview, 1985.

Ránki, György. *Economy and Foreign Policy: The Struggle of the Great Powers for Hegemony in the Danube Valley, 1919–1939*. Boulder, Colo.: East European Monographs, 1983.

Rozenblit, Marsha L. *Reconstructing a National Identity: The Jews of Habsburg Austria during World War I*. New York: Oxford University Press, 2001.

Rothschild, K. W. *Austria's Economic Development between the Two Wars*. London: Frederick Muller, 1947.

Schubert, Aurel. *The Credit-Anstalt Crisis of 1931*. Cambridge: Cambridge University Press, 1991.

Teichova, Alice, and P. L. Cottrell, eds. *International Business and Central Europe, 1918–1939*. New York: St. Martin's Press, 1984.

Vaughn, Karin. *Austrian Economics in America: The Migration of a Tradition*. Cambridge: Cambridge University Press, 1994.

XI. THE HISTORY OF AUSTRIA FROM 1945 TO THE PRESENT

1. General

Bauer, Robert A., ed. *The Austrian Solution*. Charlottesville: University of Virginia Press, 1982.

Bischof, Günter, and Anton Pelinka, eds. *Austria in the New Europe*. Contemporary Austrian Studies, 1. New Brunswick, N.J.: Transaction Publishers, 1993.

———. *The Kreisky Era in Austria*. Contemporary Austrian Studies, 2. New Brunswick, N.J.: Transaction Publishers, 1994.

———, with Rolf Steininger, eds. *Austria in the Nineteen Fifties*. Contemporary Austrian Studies, 3. New Brunswick, N.J.:Transaction Publishers, 1995.

———. *Austro-corporatism. Past, Present, Future.* Contemporary Austrian Studies, 4. New Brunswick, N.J.: Transaction, 1996.
———. *Austrian Historical Memory and National Identity.* Contemporary Austrian Studies. 5. New Brunswick, N.J.: Transaction, 1997.
———. *Women in Austria.* Contemporary Austrian Studies, 6. New Brunswick, N.J.: Transaction, 1998.
Kurt, Luther, and Peter Pulzer, eds. *Austria 1945–1955.* Aldershot, UK: Ashgate, 1998.
Sully, Melanie A. *A Contemporary History of Austria.* London: Routledge, 1990.
Steiner, Kurt, ed. *Modern Austria.* Palo Alto, Calif.: SPOSS, 1981.
———, ed. *Tradition and Innovation in Contemporary Austria.* Palo Alto, Calif.: SPOSS, 1983.
Wright, William E., ed. *Austria 1938–1988: Anschluss and Fifty* Years. Riverside, Calif.: Ariadne, 1995.
———, ed. *Austria since 1945.* Minneapolis: University of Minnesota Press, 1982.

2. Cultural

Bachem, Michael. *Heimito von Doderer.* Boston: Twayne, 1981.
Best, Alan, and Hans Wolfschütz, eds. *Modern Austrian Writing: Literature and Society after 1945.* London: Wolff, 1980.
Demetz, Peter. *After the Fires: Recent Writing in the Germanies, Austria, and Switzerland.* San Diego: Harcourt Brace Jovanovic, 1986.
Grabovszki, Ernst, and James Hardin, eds. *Literature in Vienna at the Turn of the Centuries: Continuities and Discontinuities around 1900 and 2000.* Rochester, N.Y.: Camden House, 2003.
Wagnleitner, Reinhold. *Coca-Colonization and the Cold War: The Cultural Mission of the United States in Austria after the Second World War.* Translated by Diana M. Wolf. Chapel Hill: University of North Carolina Press, 1994.
Lamb-Faffelberger, Margarete, ed. *Literature, Film, and the Culture Industry in Contemporary Austria.* New York: Peter Lang, 2002.
Riemer, Willy, ed. *After Postmodernism: Austrian Literature and Film in Transition.* Riverside, Calif.: Ariadne, 2000.

3. Diplomatic/Military

Allard, Sven. *Russia and the Austrian State Treaty.* University Park: Pennsylvania State University Press, 1970.
Bader, William. *Austria between East and West, 1945–1955.* Stanford, Calif.: Stanford University Press, 1966.
Barker, Thomas. *Social Revolutionaries and Secret Agents: The Carinthian Slovene Partisans and Britain's Special Operations Executive.* Boulder, Colo.: East European Monographs, 1990.
Bischof, Günter. *Austria in the First Cold War, 1945–1955: The Leverage of the Weak.* New York: St. Martin's Press, 1999.
Clute, Robert E. *The International Legal Status of Austria.* The Hague: Nijhoff, 1962.
Cronin, Audrey Kurth. *Great Power Politics and the Struggle over Austria, 1945–1955.* Ithaca, N.Y.: Cornell University Press, 1986.
Grayson, Cary Travers, Jr. *Austria's International Position 1938–1953.* Geneva: Droz, 1953.
Hagelin, Bjorn. *Neutrality and Foreign Military Sales: Military Production and Sales Restrictions in Austria, Finland, Sweden, and Switzerland.* Boulder, Colo.: Westview, 1990.
Höll, Otmar, ed. *Small States in Europe and Dependence.* Vienna: Braumüller, 1983.
Neuhold, Hanspeter, and Hans Thalberg, eds. *The European Neutrals in International Affairs.* Vienna: Braumüller, 1984.
———, ed. *The European Neutrals in the 1990s: New Challenges and Opportunities.* Boulder, Colo.: Westview, 1992.
Pelinka, Anton. *Austria: Out of the Shadow.* Boulder, Colo: Westview 1998.
Riekhoff, Harald von, and Hanspeter Neuhold, eds. *Unequal Partners: A Comparative Analysis of the Relations Between Austria and the Federal Republic of Germany and Between Canada and the United States.* Boulder, Colo.: Westview, 1993.
Schlesinger, Thomas O. *Austrian Neutrality in Postwar Europe: The Domestic Roots of a Foreign Policy.* Vienna: Braumüller, 1972.
Stearman, William Lloyd. *The Soviet Union and the Occupation of Austria.* Bonn: Verlag für Zeitgeschichte, 1961.
Toscano, Mario. *Alto Adige-South Tyrol: Italy's Frontier with the German World.* Baltimore: Johns Hopkins University Press, 1976.
Verdross, Alfred. *The Permanent Neutrality of Austria.* Vienna: Verlag für Geschichte und Politik, 1978.

Wagnleitner, Reinhold, ed. *Understanding Austria: The Political Reports and Analyses of Martin F. Herz, Political Officer of the US Legation in Vienna 1945–1948*. Quellen zur Geschichte des 19. und 20. Jahrhundert, 4. Salzburg: Neugebauer Verlag, 1984.
Witnah, Donald R., and Edgar L. Erickson. *The American Occupation of Austria: Planning and Early Years*. Westport, Conn.: Greenwood Press, 1985.
Witnah, Donald R., Edgar L. Erickson, and Florentine E. Witnah. *Salzburg under Siege: U.S. Occupation, 1945–1955*. New York: Greenwood, 1991.

4. Political

Alcock, Antony E. *The History of the South Tyrol Question*. Geneva: Michael Joseph, 1970.
Bassett, Richard. *Waldheim and Austria*. New York: Penguin, 1989.
Bluhm, William T. *Building an Austrian Nation: The Political Integration of a Western State*. New Haven, Conn.: Yale University Press, 1973.
Fitzmaurice, John. *Austrian Politics and Society Today: In Defence of Austria*. New York: St. Martin's Press, 1991.
Herzstein, Robert E. *Waldheim: The Missing Years*. New York: Arbor House, 1988. Reissued, New York: Paragon House, 1989.
Höbelt, Lothar. *Defiant Populist: Jörg Haider and the Politics of Austria*. West Lafayette, Ind.: Purdue University Press, 2003
Lauber, Volkmar. *Contemporary Austrian Politics*. Boulder, Colo.: Westview, 1996.
Mitten, Richard. *The Politics of Antisemitic Prejudice: The Waldheim Phenomenon in Austria* Boulder, Colo.: Westview Press, 1992.
Pelinka, Anton, and Fritz Plesser, eds. *The Austrian Party System*. Boulder, Colo: Westview, 1989.
Riedlsperger, Max Ernst. *The Lingering Shadow of Nazism: The Austrian Independent Party Movement since 1945*. Boulder, Colo.: East European Quarterly, 1978.
Shell, Kurt L. *The Transformation of Austrian Socialism*. New York: State University of New York Publishers, 1962.
Steiner, Kurt. *Politics in Austria*. Boston: Little, Brown, 1972.
Stourzh, Gerald. *Geschichte des Staatsvertrages 1945–1955: Österreichs Weg zur Neutralität*. 3rd ed. Graz: Styria, 1985.

Sully, Melanie A. *Political Parties and Elections in Austria: The Search for Stability.* New York: St. Martin's Press, 1981.

Peter Thaler. *The Ambivalence of Identity: The Austrian Experience of Nation-Building in a Modern Society.* West Lafayette, Ind.: Purdue University Press, 2000.

5. Social/Economic

Arndt, Sven W., ed. *The Political Economy of Austria.* Washington, D.C.: American Enterprise Institute for Public Policy Research, 1982.

Bunzl, Matti. *Jews and Queers: Symptoms of Modernity in Late-Twentieth Century Vienna.* Berkeley: University of California Press, 2004

Gross, Inge. *Disparities of Living Conditions among Women and Men in Austria: Statistical Analysis.* Vienna: Austrian Federal Ministry of Labour and Social Affairs, 1989.

Katzenstein, Peter J. *Corporatism and Change: Austria, Switzerland, and the Politics of Industry.* Ithaca, N.Y.: Cornell University Press, 1984.

Keizer, Willem, Bert Tieben, and Rudy van Zijp, eds. *Austrian Economics in Debate.* London: Routledge, 1997.

Laursen, Finn, ed. *EFTA and the EC: Implications of 1992.* Maastricht: European Institute of Public Administration, 1990.

Powell, G. Bingham, Jr. *Social Fragmentation and Political Hostility: An Austrian Case Study.* Stanford, Calif.: Stanford University Press, 1970.

Richter, Sándor. *The Economic Relations of Austria, Finland, Yugoslavia, and Hungary with the Soviet Union: A Comparative Analysis.* Vienna: Vienna Institute for Comparative Economic Studies, 1989.

About the Author

Paula Sutter Fichtner received her B.A. from Bryn Mawr College, her M.A. from Indiana University, and her Ph.D. from the University of Pennsylvania. She studied in Vienna on a Fulbright Fellowship. She has also held grants and fellowships from the Ford Foundation, the American Association of University Women, the City University of New York, and the National Endowment for the Humanities.

A member of the history faculty of Brooklyn College of the City University of New York for 36 years, Fichtner chaired the department from 1983 to 1986 and from 1989 to 1995. She also was on the executive committees of the Conference Group for Central European History, the Society for the Study of Austrian and Habsburg History, and the Sixteenth Century Studies Association. She also served on the editorial panel of the *Austrian History Yearbook.*

Dr. Fichtner has written extensively on several aspects of Austrian history, the history of the Habsburg Empire, and the history of early modern Germany. *Protestantism and Primogeniture in Early Modern Germany*, published by Yale University Press in 1989, won the American Academy of Religion Prize for the Study of Religion in the Historical Category. Fichtner has written two biographies of Habsburg rulers, Emperor Ferdinand I and his son, Emperor Maximilian II. Her study of the latter, *Emperor Maximilian II*, also published by Yale, received the prize of the Austrian Cultural Forum for the best book published on the history of the Habsburg Empire and Austria in North America in 2002. Her most recent books are *The Habsburg Monarchy 1490–1848: Attributes of Empire* and *Terror to Toleration: The Habsburg Empire Confronts Islam, 1526–1850*. She is currently at work on a full study of the dynasty.